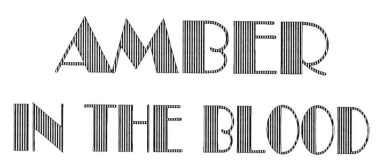

# AMBER IN THE BLOOD

## A History of
## NEWPORT COUNTY

*By Tony Ambrosen*

Published by:

## YORE PUBLICATIONS

12 The Furrows,
Harefield, Middx.
UB9 6AT.

Printed by:
**THE BATH PRESS**

ISBN 1 874427 40 2

Published by:
Yore Publications
12 The Furrows, Harefield,
Middx.  UB9 6AT.

© Tony Ambrosen 1993

...............................

British Library Cataloguing–in–Publication  Data.
A catalogue record for this book
is available  from the British Library.

ISBN 1 874427 40 2

YORE PUBLICATIONS specialise in football books, generally of an historic theme, relating to both League and non–League football.

Current and past titles include Club histories (Cardiff City, Peterborough United and Southend United), Who's Who books (Newport County and Coventry City)  histories of ex–league Clubs (Rejected F.C. Volumes 1 and 2 plus Rejected F.C. of Scotland), general football interest (Through The Turnstiles and Grounds For A Change), and non–League (More Defunct F.C. and Gone But Not Forgotten).

Please see page 176, or send a S.A.E. to the above address for full details of these and other books (plus relevant football videos).

Free Newsletters are circulated three times per year

(The photograph on the jacket was taken at Somerton Park on the occasion of Newport AFC's return to their 'home' on Wednesday the 22nd of August 1993, for the first competitive match, versus Redditch United)

# Foreword by Richard Shepherd

I can't remember the first time I saw Newport County, but I do recall that I was taken by my father, a well-known Newport medical practitioner, and I was only interested in the trains which ran past the ground, before gradually becoming aware of the amber-and-black figures on the pitch.

That would have been in the early 1950's and I can recall seeing the numerous buses lining up in Rodney Road near the Rugby ground to take the fans from the town to Oakley Street near the ground.

There was a greyhound track around the pitch, a huge tote-board at one end, and to this moment whenever I hear Doris Day singing "The Deadwood Stage", I can still hear it being played over the tinny public-address system before each home game.

County always seemed to win at home in the old Third Division (South), an away victory was something to celebrate. For several days afterwards, the South Wales Argus billboards would still carry the message *"Away Win For County"*, as if it were something to be savoured for as long as possible.

Promotion was always a possibility up to Christmas as well as F.A. Cup glory. Then came the usual cup exit, and an invariable decline into the undistinguished mid-table position. And with nothing to play for in the closing few weeks, a new young hopeful from the reserves would be given a chance by Manager Bill Lucas who usually had to sell one of his stars to cover summer wages.

Bill was player/manager when I first went to Somerton, and throughout my connection with the Club – as spectator, programme-editor and radio-commentator, he was always there in some capacity as was long-serving administrator Keith Saunders who somehow kept the wolf from the door in the face of constant financial adversity.

I once called into the ground in midweek to record an interview, and Bill Lucas, then in retirement, was visiting to see how things were going. I found him in the gym with his jacket off, playing head-tennis with some of the Club's apprentices. He was in his mid-60's and could still outplay them!

Later on came the glory days of the late 1970's and early 80's with Colin Addison, Len Ashurst and Colin again. Whenever I see Colin Addison now, we talk of the days of Aldridge, Tynan and Co., and of what might have been if County had gone up from Division Three in 1983.

How was it that a club which was on the verge of a bright future, never recovered, and slid into oblivion? With respect to teams like Rochdale, Halifax and Doncaster who are still going, were Newport County worse off than them?

In my professional capacity as broadcaster and journalist, I once tried to get to the truth of what certain Directors had been up to. They were prepared to go to any lengths to keep things quiet, but one day it will all come out. Until then, I'll remember the good and not-so-good times on the pitch, the players who delighted, the ones who frustrated. I still see the Argus placards one sunny afternoon in February 1956... *"Johnson To Leave County!"* Goalscoring hero Tommy Johnston was going to Leyton Orient. As a young boy I thought the end of the world had come.

Old Mr. Cashmore, a neighbour of ours and member of the family firm of Newport shipbreakers, used to come to matches with us in the 1950's.... *"That man McSeveney"* he would say with an air of resignation when we discussed the afternoon's prospects in the huge Saturday afternoon traffic queues trying to get across the town bridge, the only way over the River Usk in those days, apart from the Transporter Bridge.

Yes I remember Johnny McSeveney, and many more like him. They're all there, in Tony Ambrosen's well-researched history of the Club. Enjoy reading it – there'll never be another County.

Richard Shepherd

# ACKNOWLEDGEMENTS

In my previous volume, the *"Ironsides"*, I expressed my gratitude to many people – old players of Newport County and their relatives, members of the Association of Football Statisticians, librarians, the staff of various Leagues and Associations and others – who had helped in its preparation. Since this book concerns the same subject, clearly my thanks goes out to them again. There are a few people in particular whom I should like to thank, however. Richard Shepherd has taken the time to write the introduction and has lent freely of his extensive photograph collection. The programmes he edited and the booklets he wrote in the past gave a vivid picture of County's history. Brian Tabner has provided the official attendance figures for League matches between 1925 and 1951 and has filled in numerous holes in later seasons. Obviously, thanks also goes out to the Football League for permission to use these details. The *"South Wales Argus"* has also been a major source of photographic material, and thanks go to John Francis in particular, for his ability to unravel the *"Argus"* filing system. Martin Bartley has permitted the use of his photograph taken at County's final League match, and I should also like to thank Wallace Brown, the *"Voice of AFC"*, and Ray Taylor for their help and encouragement. Finally, I should like to give a word of credit to those unsung heroes, the reporters of local newspapers, who have stood out in all weathers to chart the course of Newport football.

Every effort has been made to acknowledge above, where applicable, the source of specific items and to ensure that copyright has not been infringed.

This book is Dedicated

To Stanley Saunders,

A Distant Observer

Of Newport Football.

# - CONTENTS -

# CHAPTER 1

## The Birth of Newport Soccer

A green and cream double decker trundles its way along the motorway, pursuing an old amber and black coach which has seen better days. What is this?.... A new motor sport?.... No. These are football fans, leaving one ground to play at another that is half the size and 50 miles away. Confused? Well, it's a long story, so let's start at the very beginning, before we return to the delights of modern motorway travel....

To discover precise details of the birth of soccer in South Wales – long dominated by rugby football – is difficult due to the lack of newspaper coverage. One of the first teams in old Monmouthshire was Rogerstone. The club was formed by Ironworkers, who moved South to work at the newly opened Nettlefolds Works, some time prior to 1889. A founder member (in 1893) of the South Wales and Monmouth. League, Rogerstone lost 0–1 to Aberystwyth in the 1900 Cup Competition; two thousand watched the match, at Aberdare. In the 1899/1900 season, a Newport Garrison side appeared, a worthy forerunner of 'County', that went all season without a win!

1902 was something of a turning point for the Newport & District League was established with half a dozen members. In May, a visiting Aston Villa side played an exhibition game against a Newport X1, winning 2–1. Although no 'big names' played for Villa, a large crowd turned up and the match created an appetite for organised soccer. The Newport side consisted of:–

> G.F.Simmons, C.Perry, Joe Waites,
> A.Taylor, C.Clapp, Jim Jones, Martin
> Braddon, Albert Groves, F.Forrest,
> R.Burns and G.Wheeler.

The game developed locally, especially with the inauguration of the Woodcock Cup, and in the 1906/07 season, a Newport F.C. club was set up. Its ground, on Corporation Road, was easily reached by tramcar, and the side played in Division Two of the Western League. Sadly the side, which performed well in its League and finished second – as well as winning the South Wales League – closed down at the end of the season for economic reasons. The team at least created history, with the playing of the first F.A.Cup tie in Newport, on the 6th of October 1906, when Frome were beaten by 5–0. The line–up consisted of:–

> G.F. Simmons, L.Nash, W.Pritchard,
> E.Goldsmith, J.Yarr, J.Waites, 'Yank'
> Powell, Albert Groves, Willie 'Ike' Fyfe,
> W.Ward and A.Talbot.

The game was one–way traffic, with Fyfe scoring within two minutes of the start. But for a splendid display by Frome goalkeeper Clarke, the score could have reached double figures. No newspaper reports have been found for the next round, which suggests that the team must have 'scratched'. The club's closure was unfortunate after such a promising start.

Local football still flourished, with the Woodcock Cup Final as the sporting highlight of the season, and this entailed an annual pilgrimage to Caerleon. In 1912, Newport County's prospectus mentioned that: 'A few years ago there were only four (Newport) sides, whereas there are now over 50, and the gates from the local Cup Final have increased 400% in six years'

The set–up at the various local clubs was, naturally, basic. 'Pivot' (reporters of the day had such quaint pseudonyms) recalled in a 1939 article the position with regard to Barbarians. This team played down Malpas Road, a large tump making a natural bank on one side of the ground. Pressmen, who stood out in all weathers, had to cycle back to town with their first half reports, there being no phones at the ground. A rapid cycle ride back had to be made, and a local committeeman would have to be interrogated about any missed action!

Clubs initially struggled through lack of support, but around 1910, the Woodcock Cup Final drew crowds of three or four thousand. The Cup, donated by A.J.Woodcock of 'The Globe', on Chepstow Road, was played for on Easter Monday at Caerleon's pretty little ground.

The Southern League attempted to recruit clubs in South Wales – Cardiff City, formed from the old Riverside F.C., was set up in 1910 – and the first Monmouthshire side to enter Division Two was Cwm Albion. It was a hopeless proposition, for Albion had a team made up mainly of local semi–professionals who were simply not good enough. With poor gates, made even worse by a miners' strike, the club continued for three–quarters of a season before collapsing.

The idea of a Newport side began to germinate, but any soccer club would clearly face enormous competition from the world famous 'Invincibles' of Newport rugby union. But this was not the only source of opposition, since, although few realise it today, Northern Union (i.e. rugby league) was played in such places as Merthyr and Swansea. In 1912, a syndicate was ready to begin a Newport club, and an option was secured on a ground behind East Usk Road, where a pitch was even marked out. By then, Ebbw Vale were the only such side left in South Wales, but on the 4th of September, they instructed Huddersfield not to travel down and informed the Northern Union they were disbanding. This scuppered the plans for rugby league in Newport.

In 1911, Harry Bradshaw, the Secretary of the Southern League, visited Newport to try and induce local supporters to form a side and in April 1912 there followed a letter to Bert Moss, a well known local builder and referee. Moss approached a number of members from the old Committee of the Newport & District League, which by now was well established, and the team was formed in a quite casual manner. The night before the Southern League A.G.M., a band of stalwarts met around a table in the "Tredegar Arms", High Street. There with Moss were the previously mentioned "Pivot", Harry Cockroft (an accountant with the Brecon & Merthyr railway), plus Dick Gordon, a G.W.R. representative and later Stationmaster of Newport. No doubt emboldened by a few of the hostelry's refreshments, they decided to form a team. To broaden the appeal, it was decided that the team would be called "Newport & Monmouth County", but being such a mouthful, the side was only ever known as "Newport County".

Following the meeting, Dick Gordon was despatched to London to seek membership of the Southern League. Although no company existed and no player had been approached, the Southern League was persuaded to take on the new team, and the news published that Newport was to have a soccer side. Enquiries were made, in the hope that Somerton Park could be obtained on a seven year lease. The ground lay close to W.R. Lysaght's steelworks, and to the newly migrated Midlands workers, who were by nature soccer supporters.

The "Magnificent Seven" of Newport's first Board were:–
**Harry Cockcroft** – a Chartered Accountant of Summerhill Avenue, **Albert Edward Moss** – a Builder of Hawthorne Avenue (the County's original registered Office), **Percy Williams** (licensee of the "Vulcan" Hotel, Dock Street), **Albert Cox** – an ironworker of Collingwood Street, **Horace Leonard Vincent Fellows** (a commercial traveller of Blenheim Road), **David Love** – licensee of the "King of Prussia", Lliswerry, and **Richard Ernest Gordon** – of Beda Road, Cardiff – who became the Honorary Secretary.

In July, items began appearing in the local press. On the 16th, it was announced that work would begin on "stands and offices", a fancy way of saying that hundreds of loads of rubbish would be tipped and banked around the pitch, with a corner hut as the office. At the start, players would change in the "King of Prussia" and walk down Somerton Road, but later dressing rooms and a bath appeared, along with a wooden contraption for pressmen; this took three reporters with ease, four with a squeeze, but was doubtless preferable to the old bike ride down Malpas Road!

Newport & Monmouth County A.F.C. was actually registered on July 12th, and a public meeting was later held at the Town Hall, where 4,000 shares were offered at 10 shillings (50p) each. The response from local tradesmen was poor, and most support came from Lysaght's work force, with many of the first shareholders being described as shearers, furnacemen and the like.

Time was short – for the season began in early September. Moss, with his little army of carpenters and labourers, began fencing in 6½ acres of land. The pitch was surrounded by railings and the ground's exterior by an 8½ foot fence – although in places it was 21 feet high to prevent the free view from Somerton Bridge! From a long list of applicants, Davy McDougall was chosen as player–manager, having filled the same post at Cardiff, and as was the custom the County advertised in the sporting press for players.

At such a late stage, the club, hard up anyway, had to settle for old hands, supported by local youngsters. As interest grew, features began appearing in the national papers, with one Sunday newspaper stirring things up by claiming that some of the famous Newport rugby side were turning to soccer.

The team strip colours of black and amber quarters was decided upon, the same as both both the Newport rugby and Wolverhampton Wanderers clubs; many of the Lysaght's workers followed the Wolves. Trainer Fred Good had a fortnight to get the recent recruits into trim. By various means, including pony and trap, supporters headed for a friendly at Risca. All the hard work that had been put in was rewarded for the team triumphed by 1–0, then at Somerton Park, the Club took on a side of local amateurs and won 4–0. A move to form a Supporters' Club was made at this time, with the final decision being deferred until the first League game, on the next Saturday.

The big day arrived, but in truth, the Division was little more than a motley collection of mainly Welsh teams, who kept going more by hope than by their gate receipts. Still, 5,000, including various celebrities, turned up for the inaugural game. Davy McDougall, already player–manager, was persuaded by the players to also become the Captain. The pitch was rough, but had been converted in no more than six weeks from a hayfield.

The first match opposition was Mid–Rhondda, a Tonypandy side, which had struggled to start the season, and the County side for that historic match was composed of:–

A 1912 cartoon, published after County's first game, versus Mid-Rhondda

*Husbands, Lean, Taylor, Cox, Thornton, McDougall, Holt, Hall, Vowles, Fyfe and Westwood.*

Following the playing of a military band before the kick–off, McDougall lost the toss to Mason. The first half was tame, but interest increased after the break, and from a beautiful Holt centre, Fyfe scored the first Newport goal. After McDougall netted from the penalty spot, Fyfe laid on a goal for Vowles. Thomas of the visitors was sent off towards the end. The match had been successful, although Vowles was reported as lacking in speed at centre–forward.

The following Saturday, 1,000 fans travelled to Ninian Park, a quite different venue from today. There was a wooden stand, a hut in the corner of the ground, and the players had to make their way through the crowd on to the pitch. An unchanged Newport side lost 0–1, although early on Thornton injured his ankle, which kept him out of the team until November. With only thirteen professionals such problems were inevitable, and, as so often occurs, are compounded by hard luck. A 0–1 home defeat by Swansea, due to the display of the giant goalkeeper Whittaker,

was followed by a 1–2 defeat at Llanelli, where Lean inadvertently handled the ball, and gave away a penalty.

Clearly in for a bad season, the club's gates began to slump and the finances suffered, especially due to postponements in the exceptionally cold Winter. Somerton Park became a lake, and then a quagmire. Supporters were out every day in all weathers to drain the pitch, and with Bert Moss amongst them they dug a hole at the Cromwell Road end that was big enough to take two Corporation buses. For the fans, spectating was unpleasant with no cover on the terraces. One match produced just 17 shillings (85p), although the average gate amounted to £20, but even then with a £27 wage bill plus other expenses, it was one long struggle. The Directors paid the travelling expenses, aided by the staunch Supporters' Club. Friday night's scramble for fares was followed by Monday's problems in finding the wages!

October and November produced a string of bad results, including a 4–0 defeat at Aberdare in the Welsh Cup and 0–5 to Mardy in the League, but due to their late formation (in July), Newport were unable to compete in the F A.Cup.

However, the signing of "Ike" Fyfe and Ernie Hammett in December gave the team more heart. Christmas Day saw a bumper 11,000 crowd at rain-sodden Southend, although the game - which included a broken collar-bone for one player - almost developed into a free for all. Then began the best spell of the season when Llanelli were beaten 3-1 followed by victory over Luton (5-1) and a 4-1 win over Ton Pentre - with Somerton Park the normal quagmire. Before the Southend return game, volunteers attempted to mop up heavy rain by spreading ashes on the pitch, and with the referee upholding Southend's objection, arriving supporters found the visitors going in the opposite direction!

Following this postponement things looked black financially, but then - fortunately - came the match of the season, with Cardiff. An 8,000 crowd produced takings of £156, but Cardiff, with only one defeat behind them, were three up at half-time. Later, Holt scored the best goal of the match, and was soon to be on his way to Ninian Park for £100 - the first of many talented Newport players to be sold over the years. After his departure the side seemed to lose heart and only one of the last nine games was won. Pitches home and away did little to help; Somerton Park was described by one visiting reporter as *"nothing short of a cinder tip and a refuse tip...except at the four corners there was not a vestige of grass on the playing area and the surface was made up of screened ashes."* There were many quaint grounds, and at Treharris the pitch was reached by steep stone steps - without a safety rail. On one side only a loose rope prevented a 50 foot drop on to the street and roofs below. At Pontypridd, the ball had to be frequently fished out of the River Taff with a net on a long pole.

It had been a rough first year, financially and playing-wise, and at the first A.G.M. the club reported an operating loss of £583-44 and a bank overdraft of £154.50. The season's receipt's of £1520 had included £60 from the Supporters' Club and £60 from the sale of hay! The wage bill for the first season was £912 and travelling costs amounted to £169. To say there was a clear out is something of an understatement. Not only did Davy McDougall leave - to become club steward of the "Excelsior" - but all of the players departed, with the exception of Ernie Hammett and Ted Husbands, the latter becoming the reserve goalie. The struggling club could clearly not afford Summer wages.

As the new Manager the County appointed ex-Bristol City boss, Sam Hollis. An experienced Manager with definite ideas, he insisted on the erection of adequate stands before he would take over. Work started prior to the season on the building of a Stand which cost £600, offered seating accommodation for 1,500, and held within it dressing rooms and press seats. New director Vincent Evans, from the timber trade, helped to obtain the materials, while the bank at the bottom of the ground was covered and the pitch reseeded and given new drains. The latter proved to be inadequate and another wet Winter presented further problems. At this time the Southern League became concerned over the number of teams that were closing down.

The Welsh Inn-keeper: " Hi! Stop Thief!"
The Croydon Robin: " Two bottles of the best 'New Port' for our promotion dinner next April. Ta! Ta!"
(Croydon Common beat Newport County last Saturday

A cartoon from 1913. The Cocky Robins of Croydon were crowing after beating Newport, but County had the last laugh - they outlasted Croydon by 70 years!

However, after a visit to Newport, Harry Bradshaw commented: *"Newport County are to be congratulated on the transformation of Somerton Park".*

With his contacts Hollis signed some useful players for little outlay, the first four being Flanders - a promising full-back from Derby - Spittle, Green and Lindley. Experienced Billy Matthews was made Captain. On August the 18th, County made their best capture in goalkeeper Bob McLeod, who had recently played in the Scottish Cup Final. McLeod was the only one on anything approaching the maximum wage, of £4 per week.

The local "Football Post" ran a competition to find a nickname for the side. There were many suggestions of "Wasps" and a number of "Cromwellians", but the name which won the 7/6d. prize (37½p) was "Ironsides", which combined the nearby Cromwell Road with the influence of Lysaght's.

Once again the club struggled with insufficient playing staff, and after local player Stan Griffiths was used - although registered with Caerleon - County were censured, after Hollis had apologised and reimbursed Caerleon. More trouble ensued when the Reserves were withdrawn from the Welsh League without due notice and entered the newly formed midweek Southern Alliance. County were fined a hefty £50, but this figure was halved on appeal.

When County played Cardiff in September, despite the Southern Alliance status of the match, 2,000 travelled down, with the train arriving at 5.15p.m. for a 6.00 kick-off. The players, who had to run to the ground, carried their own kit and arrived just a quarter of an hour before the kick-off. County won a memorable game 1-0, with Hammett setting up the goal for Tomlinson. On the Saturday, the County – who this season had changed to what became the familiar black and amber stripes – won their first Southern League match. Tomlinson scored both goals in a 2-1 victory over Pontypridd, which produced a pleasing £123 in gate receipts.

At the beginning of October, the club made its first major signing, when the Irish international forward Joe Enright was bought from Leeds City for £50, £5 more than the previous season's total team cost. Enright made his debut at the cramped Mardy ground and by scoring two minutes from the end saved a point. An encouraging start produced 6-1 wins in the F.A.Cup - versus Mond Nickel Works and Cardiff Corries - followed by a 6-0 Welsh Cup defeat of Mid-Rhondda. Matthews scored a hat-trick against Corries and Enright netted three against Mid-Rhondda.

However, Enright failed to make the expected impact, playing his best game for the Club against Stoke on December 6th, when appalling weather reduced the anticipated large crowd. The County's patron, W.R. Lysaght kicked off, to great applause from the spectators. Two down early on, County hit back with two in a minute before half-time, the first an 18 yard shot from Enright. The teams took no half-time break because of the weather, and Billy Matthews won the game with a great goal.

December the 13th was not County's luckiest day, for apart from a 2-3 defeat at muddy Mid-Rhondda there came the news that Tomlinson had been suspended for *"absenting himself without leave"*. After apologising, he returned to the side on January the 31st, and never missed another match. The next two home games saw a 4-0 demolition of Mardy and a welcome 2-0 Christmas present win against Luton, with Hammett – home for his holiday from college – playing in the latter match. In the Boxing Day return at Luton, County lost 0-1, despite McLeod saving two penalties.

The remodelled County side now won five games on the trot, but this success was not mirrored off the pitch, for financial disaster loomed again in January. On the evening following a 2-6 defeat at Barry (February 14th), a meeting was held in the Town Hall. The English League Board had ordered the club the option to pay off £100 in respect of transfer fees by March 31st, with a further £65 to follow by

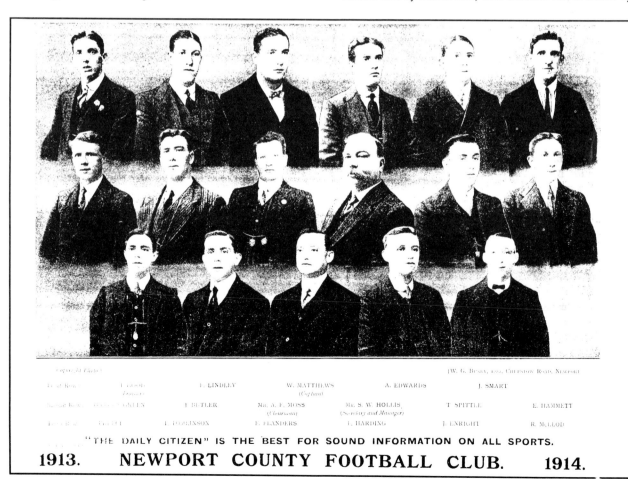

"THE DAILY CITIZEN" IS THE BEST FOR SOUND INFORMATION ON ALL SPORTS.

1913.    NEWPORT COUNTY FOOTBALL CLUB.    1914.

April 11th, leaving the directors to find £750 to cover the current liabilities. At a surprisingly optimistic meeting, offers of £400 were made, with Mr. Lysaght giving a cheque for £50, and Lord Tredegar and Mr. Gale of the "Cross Hands" taking 50 shares each. Speakers, convinced that football would not be allowed to die pointed out that gates had doubled since the first season, none of the players had been allowed to go without pay, and the £60 arrears of wages from the previous season had been paid off. Amongst other things, it was decided to charge a minimum 1/- (5p) entrance fee for the forthcoming Brentford match.

The season continued satisfactorily, but without County threatening to take any honours. In the away game at Croydon, McLeod had to be escorted from the pitch after ankle tapping one of the ballboys! A fortnight later, the team gave Cardiff Corries another six goal thrashing, this time in the South Wales Senior Cup, with Matthews again scoring a hat-trick.

At the end of a much better season County were unbeaten in their last five games. The side beat Brentford 3-2 in outstanding fashion, but the crowd numbers were badly affected by Newport R.F.C. who played the Harlequins the same day, although the worst attendance (around 2,000) came when bottom side Treharris were smashed 6-0. Hammett scored four goals, with County easing off after a 5-0 interval lead. Barry made the trip to Somerton their annual outing, and their well-known band was to accompany them through the streets. There was no sign of the band at the start, but it duly arrived during the first half and played at half-time.

The season wound up with a 1-0 home win over Llanelli. Promising centre-forward Bob Hammett had his debut in this match, but never played again, for he enlisted in the Royal Warwickshire Regiment, and died of his war wounds, on the 25th of September 1916.

County could have finished higher than their quite satisfactory position if it had not been for the inadequate playing staff numbers, which resulted in half-fit players having to turn out. To make matters worse this highly promising team had to be disbanded, only Flanders being retained. The offer was made that any player still unattached at the start of the season could return, but apart from the locals, only Spittle, Albert Edwards and Tomlinson were back in September.

Events were underway, which would make the new season an irrelevance, for The Great War began and early expectations that it would be *"all over by Christmas"* soon evaporated. The battle of Mons heralded ever increasing carnage, as the infantry became cannon fodder. Despite the opposition to the continuance of football in the midst of this wholesale slaughter, the Southern League carried on that season to its conclusion.

County began with a 5-1 win at Leyton, followed by defeats at Stalybridge and Mardy. The Leyton and Mardy

results were later deleted, when those teams packed in. Because of the opposition to football continuing there was little press coverage of matches. The side which did battle with Merthyr on September the 19th included goalkeeper Harold Sedgeley from Barry and full-back Arthur Cleverly from Brentford, as well as such stalwarts as Flanders, Ernie Hammett and the promising George Groves, the father of Billy Lucas; Hammett scored the winner.

Despite the War, County maintained a fairly settled side. Two newcomers were inside-forward Crad Evans, brother of Welsh international goalie R.O. Evans, and the Lysaght's forward Ivor Williams. The club had an exceptional F.A.Cup run, beating Rhiwderin 8-0, Milford 6-0 (Hammett claiming a hat-trick), Rhymney 3-1 and Barry 4-2. The side went out 0-1 at Swansea, where Town missed two penalties and Sedgeley played an outstanding game. Abertillery were beaten 3-0 in the Welsh Cup, but County appear to have scratched after that.

County, doing reasonably well in the Southern League, were suddenly hit by the biggest defeat they had ever suffered – 1-10 at Coventry – and to rub salt into the wound, the previously discarded Joe Enright scored four. On December the 19th, the side lost its fourth successive League game, but then came a remarkable holiday turnaround. After a 4-2 win at Abertillery on Christmas Day, the return was played on a sticky Somerton pitch on Boxing Day. 5-0 up at half-time, County went on to win 13-0, with Hammett scoring four and eight different players finding the net. Unfortunately, Abertillery later withdrew and the two results against this team were deleted.

With newspapers containing ever more details of battles and local deaths, the County side came to contain names of more unknown amateurs, as established players left to make their contribution to the War. On March the 15th, Ernie Hammett left for Llandudno to join the Royal Welch Fusiliers, and by the final match most of the professionals had departed. On April the 24th, County were hammered 0-6 by Ton Pentre, with the team containing half a dozen amateurs.

Unlike some, County had seen the season through, but it had been a hard struggle, and was hindered by low gates plus unsympathetic landlords. In April, Mr. Lysaght gave a generous donation of £75 to keep the club going, and the Lysaght's staff met a County X1 to raise funds. The County side, which lost 2-3, included not just players – such as Groves and Preece – but directors Bert Moss and Dick Williams.

In 1915, normal football closed down, being replaced by war-time leagues. County continued, but the side comprised men on munitions work and soldiers on leave or stationed nearby, with the majority of the names meaning nothing to us today. The results, likewise, tell a story; 1-9 at Barry, 0-8 at Bristol City, 1-7 at Southampton, and with only two matches won by the year's end.

What a different world now! A modest attendance saw the first match, in Southampton, and; *"the spectators included convalescents from a number of local military hospitals"*. The convalescents might have given the Saints a tougher match, for County conceded six in the second half! At six foot plus, County's regular goalie, A.E. Hall must have developed backache from picking the ball out of the net. The trip to Bristol City was delayed through a troop train on the line, with County arriving 15 minutes late.

For the Bristol Rovers' match, the Directors decided to donate the proceeds to the French Flag Day Fund, but no more than 500 turned up.

On January the 1st, the South Western Combination began, a competition which had been set up after a conference in Bristol. Although County won 2 and lost 10, Bert Moss had the chance to spread favourable propaganda, for the side were now playing the likes of Portsmouth and Southampton, and this was to lead eventually to Southern League Division 1 membership.

On January the 22nd, Newport lost 1–8 at Southampton, scarcely surprising, as Saints turned out as advertised, whilst County made drastic changes, arriving with 10 men and having to borrow one player, B.A.Youtman. Supporters must have thought it was a joke on April Fool's Day, when the Saints turned up at Somerton and only drew 0–0. Ted Husbands played excellently between the sticks, and at outside–right was old favourite, Andy Holt.

The following season, County played five friendlies in the Autumn of 1916. A few familiar faces were in evidence, such as Groves, Holt and "Ginger" Davies, along with the well–known international forward Evan Jones – a singer who was good enough to appear in Concert. On November the 18th, the side lost 1–5 at Barry, and the following Saturday, the home match with them was drawn 0–0. But that was it, for due to the struggle and unsympathetic landlords, there was no practical measure other than closure. In November 1917, Sam Hollis – still acting as Manager in an honorary capacity – penned an official letter in his familiar copperplate writing, winding up the Company. Newport and Monmouth County were no more.

After the First World War, the County were able to embark on a Football League career.

The front cover of the (now very rare) County handbook of 1920.

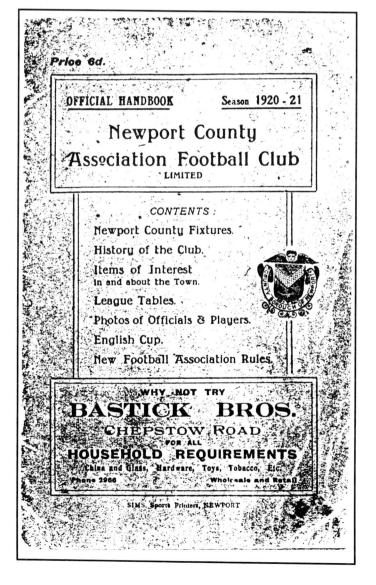

Price 6d.

OFFICIAL HANDBOOK          Season 1920 - 21

Newport County
Association Football Club
LIMITED

CONTENTS :

Newport County Fixtures.

History of the Club.

Items of Interest
in and about the Town.

League Tables.

Photos of Officials & Players.

English Cup.

New Football Association Rules.

WHY NOT TRY
BASTICK BROS.
CHEPSTOW ROAD
FOR ALL
HOUSEHOLD REQUIREMENTS
China and Glass, Hardware, Toys, Tobacco, Etc.
Phone 2966                  Wholesale and Retail

SIMS, Sports Printers, NEWPORT

# CHAPTER 2

## Rebirth and the League

Apart from one isolated match with Caerleon, in December 1917, Newport soccer recommenced on Christmas Day, 1918. With the signing of the Armistice there was now hope of normal life returning, and a regular series of friendlies was arranged, which led to the resumption of proper football the following season. The encounter with Cardiff provided an appropriate return, and a 3,000 home crowd saw Newport win 2-1, with goals from Evan Jones plus the dependable Groves. The return, on Boxing Day, was lost to three second half goals.

Despite fairly regular friendlies, team changes were necessary for every game. Beside the recognised names – such as Husbands, Groves and Flanders – a host of unfamiliar ones appeared, including Peplow, Sutton and Baker, who were generally obscure local amateurs. Despite a reasonable start, the team were to fall away later.

Gates varied greatly, for over 5,000 saw the away game at Swansea – where Newport let in five – but possibly fearing the worst, less than 1,000 turned up for the return the following week. County triumphed 1-0, with Evan Jones sending a first half shot into the corner of the net. The high spot came with an 11-3 thrashing of the Western Cavalry Depot, with Billy Richards scoring five, but County lost five of the remaining six matches. At Cardiff, City put out a weakened side – as they were also playing Mid-Rhondda the same day – but were still good enough to put seven past Newport. For their final game County fielded an experimental side at Barry, and duly lost, 5-0, but all this was to change with professional football resuming on May the 1st.

It was a strange close season, which started with West Ham and Coventry leaving the Southern League for the Football League in a blaze of publicity. The First Division of the Southern League was extended by four, where Newport and Swansea were the favourites to take two of the places. However, it was the Swans, Merthyr, Gillingham and Brentford who were elected, and County – who failed by four votes – were destined to struggle on in the sadly depleted Division 2. However, within a few weeks, Stalybridge Celtic (an anachronism in the Southern League), transferred to the Central League and Newport were chosen to take their place. The club had around six weeks to prepare for what was shortly to become Division 3 of the Football League.

New Manager Harry Parkes was an excellent choice for he had numerous Midlands contacts, and this was an important point since all the best players had been signed by other clubs. Parkes managed to obtain players such as the eccentric, but talented, goalie Jack Cooper, and Wolves' full-back "Pat" Collins, both of whom had played in the F.A.Cup Final.

A public meeting was called and it was decided to form a new Company, with capital of £4,000 to be divided into 16,000 shares of 5/- (25p). The first Board consisted of Bert Moss, George Thorneycroft, Albert Cox, Jack Carwardine, Dick Williams, J.S. Johnson and William "Fishy" White. Always a generous patron, W.R. Lysaght went to the lengths of purchasing Somerton Park for £2,200 and presenting it to his Workmen's Recreation Committee. They elected to lease it to County for a nominal rent, and to complete the repairs necessary after 4 years of war. A new Supporters' club was set up, initially with 400 paying members. On August the 8th, the new Company of Newport County was incorporated, with the aim of; *"promoting the game of Association Football"*.

Fred Good, who had trained the team in pre-war days, had a fortnight to get the team in trim, an unenviable task as many lived away from the area. Much needed renovation had to be done to bring Somerton Park up to scratch, with work to the baths, dressing rooms and Grandstand required.

With the talented Hammett having turned to rugby, at which he was later capped by England, the following side opposed Norwich in the opener:-

> *Cooper, Barnacle, Collins, Brookes, Jones, Harris, Lockley, Dobson, Mann, Savage & Gaughan.*

Most of that side played regularly, indeed one of the problems was the reserve eleven, which proved inadequate comprising mainly local youngsters.

The use of borrowed blue and chocolate kit from West Bromwich Albion didn't change County's luck for 5 of the first 6 matches were lost. The Norwich and Southend games (with County arriving late for the latter) ended in defeat, and a run of three successive home games brought just one point. Groves forced his way into the side, and was to miss only one more match. League leaders Watford arrived on Newport's traditional Thursday and won 1-0, after Harris had handled in the penalty area; the temperature that day was 82 degrees Fahrenheit.

Half-back, Jimmy Hindmarsh was signed in time for the Watford game, but fell asleep in the dressing-room after an 18 hour journey from the North-East! He later played, however, in a local derby at Merthyr which was watched by 8,000. After the side's first win, versus Plymouth on September 20th, the team had to wait until October 25th for the next – 3-1 at Gillingham. In an eventful season, the match with Bristol Rovers was affected by a rail strike, and County had to travel to Cardiff, take a paddle steamer over to Weston Super Mare, and then make a road journey to Stapleton Road. They must have wondered whether it was worthwhile for Rovers achieved their first win of the season. The strike was still on when Newport entertained Reading. Collins and Brookes made their way from Birmingham by a roundabout route and a car was sent to fetch Mann from West Bromwich. The 6,000 crowd, swollen by workers affected by the strike, saw a 0-0 draw.

County were firmly entrenched at the bottom, and after a 1-5 thrashing at Millwall, a home point from Luton provided a welcome boost to morale. The match saw the side turn out once more in black and amber, and overjoyed supporters greeted the sight by singing *"Here We Are Again"*. The F.A.Cup provided a further boost, as did the signing of Ernie Edwards, and Billy Devlin. A 5-2 defeat of Bath City in the first tie was followed by 1-0 victories over Merthyr and Exeter. On January the 10th, County played illustrious Leicester City. A 9,500 crowd saw a goalless draw, and five days later the team went down 0-2 before a replay crowd of 22,000 at Leicester. The side for both games consisted of:-

> Cooper, Collins, Griffin, Groves, Edwards, Kelson, Savage, Dobson, Devlin, Mann & Gaughan.

If County had beaten Leicester, they would have played Chelsea in the next round and would have been presented to King George V.

However, the League results were not always bad. On Christmas Day 5,671 fans – with no tram service – stood in pouring rain to watch their side beat Northampton, and on January the 3rd the side scored five against Norwich at Somerton Park. Average gates of 6,000 were good considering the terrible start and the competition from Newport rugby. By the end of February, the team had hoisted itself up to third from bottom. The main problems were in attack, for there was no consistent goalscorer among the lightweight forwards, who suffered barracking from the Somerton crowds at times.

Away form continued to be appalling, and the final four away games were lost, with three goals being conceded on each occasion. But the home performances were much brighter, with Gillingham being beaten 4-0, Exeter 4-1, followed by a 1-0 victory over Crystal Palace on Good Friday. In the latter match, before a record attendance of 10,084, Devlin broke his nose but pluckily stayed on the pitch.

The eventful season reached new extremes at Plymouth on April the 14th, as four players missed their connection because of the Cheltenham races, and were stuck on Snow Hill Station. 4,000 fans turned out in hail and driving rain, to see County beaten 3-0. Manager Parkes played in goal – where he had never played before – trainer Good turned out at outside-right, and Worden (a Plymouth amateur from the crowd) filled in at inside-right. Kelson sliced the first goal into his own net!

For once, the season did not end in an anti-climax, for on May the 1st, champions-elect Portsmouth visited Somerton, and a best ever home gate of 10,371 produced takings of

£616.89. Talented winger Gaughan scored the winner for County, and it was a great fillip for the club, which was about to embark on another major adventure. The Football League, at its A.G.M. on May the 31st, decided upon the long mooted move of converting the top Division of the Southern League into Division 3 of the Football League. In 8 short years (minus the duration of the Great War!), Newport County had moved from obscurity to the greatest League in the world. During this period much in Newport had altered. By 1920, David Love, Dick Gordon plus Percy Williams were dead, whilst Horace Fellows and Harry Cockcroft had left the town, though the latter still took a keen interest in the club's performances.

The useful squad built up by Parkes in the 1919/20 season formed the basis for the historic new season. Faced with an enforced move to Newport, Collins and Mann decided to leave the club, whilst Savage and Lockley also departed. Most of the regulars were signed up with uncharacteristic speed. Sammy Blott was bought for £225, and Chivers – from Merthyr – for £400, but the latter soon had a nervous breakdown and never appeared in the first team. Bert Moss made optimistic comments in the "Football Post": *"The dawn of a brighter day and happier times has dawned for Newport County and the dark clouds which have overshadowed the club in years past have now rolled away. If ever perseverance merited its reward, the promoters of first class Association Football on Uskside have earned a right to enjoy some".*

County could look forward with some hope to the new Season. Along with the players mentioned, there were new, experienced signings, such as Pullen, Wright, Thompson, Walker, Wolstenholme and Billy Edwards. Four days after the staff had been treated to an outing around the Wye Valley, the side entertained Reading, before a record 14,500 crowd. On a fine, sunny day, Newport lined up with:-

> Cooper, Davis, Pullen, Groves, Ernie Edwards, Blott, Thompson, Dobson, Walker, Wolstenholme and Gaughan.

County spent almost the whole of the game attacking, but succumbed to an 18th minute Bailey goal. On the following Wednesday, the short trip to Bristol Rovers brought a 2-3 defeat. Eccentric goalkeeper Jack Cooper, in attempting to clear, accidentally threw the ball into his own net. In those days, the same teams were played on consecutive Saturdays, and County gave a sorry performance when they went down 0-4 at Reading. An undeserved 0-2 defeat versus Bristol Rovers was followed by a 1-5 thrashing at Plymouth. After 5 games, no points and a goal difference of 3-15, earlier optimism seemed misplaced!

County then broke their duck with a home 0-0 draw against Plymouth, and then – although firmly entrenched at the bottom – they began a mini revival. Exeter, with the illustrious Dick Pym in goal, were beaten twice (by 1-0 and 2-0), and Millwall were overcome 3-1, with Davis playing fearlessly and Devlin scoring twice. The return at the Den, which the Lions won in the final minute, was memorable.

The spirited Cooper, forced to endure a shower of missiles and abuse, went over the wall to sort out the ringleaders in the Millwall crowd. Extricated by the referee, policemen and team, Cooper was reported to the Welsh F.A. and severely cautioned. County were exonerated, but the Den was closed for a fortnight. That season there was also trouble during the reserves' match at Mid-Rhondda. With County winning 2-0, there was a demonstration against the referee, resulting in the players and officials forming a bodyguard. The referee was penned in the dressing-room for some time, and the Tonypandy ground was closed for a week.

The double was achieved over Portsmouth, with a 25 yard Devlin drive finding the net at Fratton Park. Gillingham were then beaten twice, and 15 points had been obtained from 10 matches, as Newport hauled themselves up to mid-table.

In this topsy turvey season, the side now had another bad patch, although this was largely due to injuries. A scoreless F.A.Cup draw with Merthyr was watched by a record Somerton crowd of 15,000, which produced receipts of £1,067. In the replay, with Blott and Pullen out injured, the team was overrun 0-4. In the next six League matches only two points accrued. At Swindon the side included five reserves and went down 0-5, with Devlin taking a knock which was to keep him out of the team until March. The skilful and consistent Gaughan was also out for a couple of months. At Watford, a young amateur named Woodall – with just a few reserve games under his belt – played centre-forward, but in a snowstorm, County lost 1-5.

1921 began with two victories, but thereafter wins were scarce. The 3-1 defeat of Brentford was notable, as Andy Walker, after missing a penalty, scored with a 40 yard effort in the final minute of the match. After a 4-0 Welsh Cup win over Ebbw Vale came defeat by Merthyr. On March the 12th, County obtained a welcome win over Grimsby, Devlin scoring his first goal since his return. Cooper had earlier given away one of his silly goals when the ball was kicked against centre-forward Clark and rebounded straight into the net. Away to Merthyr, Cooper finally missed his first match, but the game was still won, with goals from Devlin and Gaughan.

County were unbeaten in their final six matches, and their best home performance of the season came in beating Luton 2-0, with both goals coming from Devlin. The season had turned out rather better than it had threatened to do so earlier, for the team had held its own in the new League, though up front only Devlin had reached double figures on the goal scoring chart. One notable event took place at the end of the season, when Cardiff City – who had reached the F.A.Cup semi-finals – were entertained in a Friendly. Their charabanc was met at Ebbw Bridge by the Lysaght's band, which preceded them through the town, playing *"See the Conquering Hero Comes"*. The hospitality ended there however, for a second half Dobson goal beat the visitors.

The financial situation had been serious at one stage, and the "Football Argus" had even reported rumours that the club had been taken over by Cardiff City. League Gates had held up reasonably well with total receipts of £12,788. The first – against Reading – was the best at £738, conversely the mid-week match with Norwich produced only £210. The competition of Newport rugby and Cardiff City adversely affected attendances, and the reserves – now playing in the Welsh League – attracted poor gates and were a drain on finances. There was little strength in reserve, and over 50 players were used during the season. Nevertheless the team secured the club's first trophy, when Ebbw Vale were beaten 1-0 in the Final of the Monmouthshire County Cup on April 16th.

At this time, there was an extremely strong Supporters' Club, which had already acquired 1,500 shares in Newport County. Arguments about Somerton Park now simmered at the surface again during the close season. It was an awkward situation, for apart from the fact that the Supporters' Club – which was largely based on the nearby Lysaght's works – made donations to, and held these shares in the Club. Mr. Lysaght had bought the ground himself (and given it to his workmen), when it was threatened with being given over to building work. The situation was bound to create friction, and although it was ultimately resolved in a satisfactory manner, the delay prevented Harry Parkes from signing various good class players who had been available earlier. The Board attempted to obtain a lease on the ground, and had been offered one for five years, but only on the condition that workmen dominated the Board. With the matter finally resolved, over £5,000 was spent on securing, preparing and equipping the ground. The workmen began a subscription scheme which brought in £1,000 for the club. After many years at the helm, Bert. Moss was replaced as Chairman by J.S. Johnson, but continued on the Board.

At least on the playing front there seemed to be stability with many of the old faces, such as Groves, Cooper and Dobson being retained. Andy Walker, who had appeared in the "Khaki" Cup Final at the outbreak of the War, had been considering an offer from an overseas club. However he signed at a late stage and was made Captain, while the injured Blott was signed on a temporary contract. Flanders returned, Lythgoe, Arch and Price were signed, and Jack Lewis was regarded as a highly promising youngster.

The season again commenced against Reading, with the only two newcomers being Flanders at left-back and the experienced Lythgoe at inside-left, but the team was defeated three minutes from time. In the first home game, the team went down to another 0-1 defeat, on a slippery pitch. Groves unluckily deflected a shot into his own net and chances were missed through poor marksmanship.

If the overall start was poor, it was at least better than the previous season. At home to Reading, County were on top throughout, with Devlin scoring the winner after ten minutes.

A cartoon from the 1920's. Contrary to the suggestion, County never signed on ace jockey Gordon Richards!

After a 1–2 defeat at Q.P.R., Walker and Gaughan were unfit for the visit to Luton, where County were one goal down ten minutes from the end, but then the defence cracked and the team finally lost 0–4. County bounced back with a 2–1 win over Southend, but the game saw some poor shooting, and Southend were later adjudged the worst side to visit Somerton all season.

After six games, the team had collected only four points, but at least it was three more than a year earlier. After two consecutive 2–2 draws, County gained an excellent 1–0 victory over Norwich. In a late rally, Dobson scored with a 20 yarder, his only goal of the season. In the away game at Swindon, County were two down, when Billy Edwards moved to inside–right and scored twice, but the team still lost 2–3. In the return at Somerton, County were irresistible, for they scored twice in each half, to produce a convincing 4–0 win. The side by now had risen to the top half of the table.

A home point against Plymouth, in atrocious weather, was the last of the good news, as County then hit a run of four consecutive defeats. It began, as so often was the case, with bad luck, for at Plymouth the defence played brilliantly, then Arch was adjudged to have brought down Richardson, and Plymouth scored a penalty on the stroke of time. At Merthyr, Dobson was out with flu, and with the injured Lythgoe unable to come out for the second half County were left with ten men. Dobson and Lythgoe were unavailable for the return match, when Billy Edwards scored after five minutes, but County went down to an undeserved 1–2 defeat. At Portsmouth, County were 0–3 down at half-time, but fought back to lose 3–4.

From the end of November until the turn of the year, Newport had their best spell of the season, with an undefeated run of nine League and F.A.Cup games, including six away from home. A home point from Portsmouth was followed by a 2–0 Cup defeat of non–League Bath City. On December the 10th, County secured a 1–0 win at Southend – their first away success. There had been a mad scramble to reach the Kursaal, because of a breakdown in the Severn Tunnel; Price scored with an 84th minute

header. In the F.A.Cup, a scoreless draw at Wrexham was followed by a great 3–0 win, Devlin scoring a hat–trick. This was, strangely, the only hat–trick ever achieved by a County player against League opponents in the F.A.Cup. This victory was followed by three away draws and a home win over Millwall, with Billy Edwards netting seconds from time in the latter. In sunny Exeter, County were twice behind, but equalised with a 35 yard left footer from Edwards and a late goal from Groves.

A home defeat by Swansea, caused by a bad mistake from Cooper, preceded Newport's biggest game to date, an F.A.Cup–tie against mighty Newcastle. Unfortunately, half the side was suffering from flu and Griffin became ill on the journey up North. A crowd of 28,507 saw Newport give a staunch first half display, and Newcastle were lucky to be one up, when a snap shot from Harris crept into the corner of the net. Afterwards, pressure told and County lost 0–6, but Newcastle were so impressed with the plucky Welshmen that they agreed to visit Somerton later.

Further woe saw Newport unceremoniously dumped out of the Welsh Cup 1–7 by Cardiff. Charlie Brittan played his first game in this match, then in a 4–3 victory scored twice on his League debut, at Bristol Rovers.

From then on, County's form was distinctly average, but there were plenty of incidents. Against Bristol, a Rovers' defender picked up the ball, mistakenly thinking the referee had blown for an injury. The "Football Post" claimed that Walker had deliberately missed the ensuing penalty, but was later forced to withdraw the allegation. In a 0–3 defeat at Brighton, Griffin had three stitches in his head and Price was knocked unconscious. In the return game, Ernie Edwards scored the only goal of the match – in his own net – and both McAllister and Gaughan were sent off.

On April the 10th, Newcastle honoured their promise, and their illustrious side triumphed 5–1 over Newport. Right to the end County were threatened with a re–election bid, but four points over the Easter holidays were a great boost. Although the final two matches, against Southampton (in the home game three amateurs turned out), were both lost,

Newport managed to avoid the dreaded application, on goal average. One of the main weaknesses over the season was the inability of the inside-forwards to finish, and winger Billy Edwards ended up as top scorer. Andy Walker also made his contribution notably from the penalty spot. The reserves were again of little help, over 50 players being used, and this team normally contained only two or three professionals.

Dobson had already been sold to Southend at the end of February, and many of the experienced players now left including Cooper, Flanders, Walker, Devlin, Lythgoe, Arch and Price. The popular Harry Parkes resigned, and was replaced by Jimmy Hindmarsh, who had been looking after the reserves. The new trainer was Bob Chatt, who had achieved the rare distinction of winning both F.A.Cup and Amateur Cup medals.

The club could afford to buy no big names, although in Anthony Carr it found an able replacement for the charismatic Cooper. On August 26th, the side made its customary losing start, against Southend, whom it had beaten twice the previous season. With two 1-3 defeats following, County had no points and Southend had already completed the double over them. In their fourth game, County created a mild sensation by beating Bristol Rovers 4-1, with four close range goals. The Bristol goodwill did not extend to City, who beat Newport 2-0 and 1-0. In the second encounter, the famous Harry Hampton, by now well in the veteran stage, made his debut.

Two tough games with League leaders Portsmouth did nothing to improve County's position. In the away game, Hampton and centre-half Martin both received their marching orders; Tom White made his debut, thereby becoming the 20th player to be used in 8 games. The home encounter saw County's best performance of the season, and Pompey were lucky to draw. After the Portsmouth games came three draws, then three defeats, including defeat at Luton from a goal in the last five minutes.

A home victory over Q.P.R. was only the second win of the season, and it saw yet more new blood, with the introduction of Conner and Wood, the latter scoring the only goal. By this time 24 different players had been used in League games. At least the centre-forward problem was solved, with the acquisition of Conner after previous experiments with Whitton, Venables, Patterson and Ogley. Jack Conner was in fact to earn nationwide fame, when on the way back from a match he daringly rescued a woman who had fallen on to the track of the London Underground Circle Line. He leapt from the platform and pulled the woman clear of an oncoming train.

Although things perked up after Conner's signing, County's progress in the F.A.Cup was ended by Aberdare, for after two 1-1 draws, the second replay was lost 1-2 at Ninian Park. Conner secured a 1-0 victory over Brighton, but then the side went eight matches without a win. A Christmas Day postponement, through heavy rain, was followed by a 1-5 reverse at the Vetch on Boxing Day. Carr had trouble dealing with the heavy, greasy ball, and Lowe replaced him in the return match with Swansea the following day, but the side suffered an unlucky 1-2 loss.

The New Year saw County gaining a point at Swindon with two goals from Harry Hampton, and Billy Charlton - who had arrived from West Ham in exchange for Billy Edwards - making his debut. The side ended the month dismally, losing 2-6 at Aberdare. By coincidence, the score was exactly reversed against Exeter, which created a new record Football League score for County. The bubble soon burst, for a 0-4 defeat at Exeter followed. At Northampton - with Jack Evans making his League debut - the side unluckily went down 1-2, Carr letting in a 30 yard effort from Lockett. Myers, who had earlier broken his nose, was sent off after a clash with Jimmy Griffin.

Strangely enough while the team was now in the middle of a nine match run without a victory, the reserves were banging in the goals, which included a 10-1 win over New Tredegar and 12-1 over Mardy. After hovering between 20th and 21st all season, County were now firmly bottom of the Third Division South, a position they would retain until the finish.

Bad play was often mixed with bad luck, and at Norwich, Conner missed an open goal after running right through the defence and City equalised with a penalty. A 0-1 defeat by Brentford was due to a defensive mix-up, and on Good Friday, White was badly injured and Carr's brilliance could not prevent a 0-2 defeat. The next day, Carr was less convincing at Watford, misjudging a swerving shot, and Ernie Edwards left the pitch with a head injury.

The season continued on its erratic way. The team was overrun at Charlton - going down 0-6 - but the return was won 4-0, Charlton's heaviest defeat of the season. In the final match, Newport beat Plymouth 1-0 with a first half Conner header, but with typical bad luck they were robbed of a good gate by incessant rain.

County, having collected only 27 points had to stand for re-election, having gained no victory and only five points away from Somerton. Twenty-nine players were used in total, with only four making over 30 appearances. Ironically, the reserves had played much better, doubling their tally of points and scoring 130 League and Cup goals. Patterson obtained five hat-tricks and Gittins scored six in one game. Roy McDonald became the first County player to gain an amateur cap, Charlie Brittan played for the Welsh League, and Patterson (from Scotland) was chosen for the match, but was not released.

J.S. Johnson resigned as Chairman, for business reasons, but stayed on to plead County's case, and the Club was duly re-elected. The new Chairman was Tom Crowther, and the Vice-Chairman - A.E. Cox - a refreshment contractor, ran the canteens on the ground. Despite the re-election application, the backbone of the side was retained.

Although some moved on, not just veterans such as Ernie Edwards and Harry Hampton, but also promising youngsters including Roy McDonald and Harry Graham. However, four extremely useful players were signed on; Fred Cook, a young winger from Aberdare (who was destined to play for Wales), Frank Knowles – an experienced centre–half formerly with both Manchester clubs – who was made Captain, Jonny Bell a goalscoring Scottish centre–forward, and Jimmy Carney an experienced wing–half, who was still involved with the club thirty years later.

There was a surprising degree of confidence in the club, and 10,000 saw the team beat Exeter 2–0, but the confidence was soon dispelled following two bad defeats. Erratic as usual, County then won three matches in succession. Portsmouth were beaten 2–1, Southend thrashed 5–0 (the half–time score of 4–0 being a club record since their entry into the Football League) and a 3–0 win came at Q.P.R. County then came down to earth with a two–nil defeat in the return at Southend. Although the side went six games without a win, there were few team changes – which was in stark contrast to the previous season – for after 11 matches, only 14 players had been used.

There was no great pattern to the season. Ogley missed a penalty at home to Charlton and Bell missed another, as County's F.A.Cup progress came to a 0–2 halt at Exeter. Jack Nicholls, destined to become Newport's first Welsh international, made his debut at Plymouth and scored twice, when County lost by 2–3. Conner scored a Christmas Day hat–trick against Merthyr and, remarkably, the teams followed this 3–3 result with a 4–4 draw. Home wins over Watford and Q.P.R. preceded a 2–8 reverse at Watford, where Mummery scored five. Promising Jack Lewis was sold to Cardiff, shortly before the Brentford game, and because of an imminent rail strike, the side left by charabanc on the Friday. At this stage, County were respectably placed in mid–table, while neighbouring Cardiff were top of Division 1.

Newport now had a good Welsh Cup run, which started with a Tommy Lowes hat–trick that contributed to a 5–2 defeat of Llanelli, and in the next round, they played out a remarkable succession of three draws with Cardiff. Because of a fixture pile–up, City left out some of their internationals in the fourth match and lost by 0–3. County eventually went out 0–1 at Wrexham, on April 16th.

Three consecutive wins late in the season helped maintain the side's mid–table position, but they were unable to score in their final two matches – against Aberdare – with Cup

1923/24 season programme cover (match versus Swindon)

Final referee Russell officiating at the Somerton game. In a satisfactory season, Conner and Lowes had easily beaten Newport's previous goals record in a season, with 16 and 15 respectively.

Experienced players Knowles, Bell, Groves and Gaughan moved on, the talented Jack Nicholls opted for Cardiff – where his father was Chairman – and because of financial necessity, Carr was transferred to Sheffield Wednesday for £1,200. Jimmy Maidment, who was Carr's replacement, was virtually the only new face, and he was to give the club years of solid service.

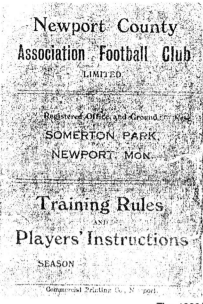

# Newport County Association Football Club

LIMITED

Registered Office and Ground

**SOMERTON PARK**

**NEWPORT MON**

# Training Rules

AND

# Players' Instructions

SEASON

Commercial Printing Co., Newport

### Training Rules and Players' Instructions.

1.—All players whose time is wholly engaged by the Club shall attend the Ground for training at 10.15 a.m. daily (match days excepted), and shall be under the orders of the Trainers for the rest of the day.

2.—Players engaged in business must attend training on Tuesday and Thursday evenings as early as possible, but not later than 6.30 p.m., unless excused by the Secretary.

3.—The Club Doctor is Dr. T. G. Lewis, of "Rosedale" Corporation Road, Newport, who can be seen at the above address. Any visit to the Doctor should be reported at once to the Secretary and Trainer.

4.—When a player is incapacitated by illness or injury from following his training, he must at once report the fact to the Secretary, and accompany the same with a doctor's certificate.

5.—Players must note any announcements upon the notice board in the dressing room, as they will not necessarily be advised through the post.

6.—A Training Book will be in charge of the Trainer to record any complaints which he may have to lay before the Directors when necessary.

7.—All players must clearly understand that their duties will be allotted to them by the Trainer, and the Directors inform the players his instructions MUST be carried out.

8.—It is the duty of the players to assist the Trainers in preserving cleanliness and order in the dressing rooms and upon the ground, and any player MISUSING ARTICLES used for training purposes, etc., will be liable to fines or suspension.

9.—All players are provided with outfit necessary for playing (which is the property of the Club).

10.—Match jerseys and knickers are not to be used for training purposes.

11.—Players will not be allowed to bring friends into the dressing room either during practice or on match days under any circumstances whatever, and the Trainer has strict injunctions and is held responsible for same.

12.—Players must be on the ground for home matches at least half an hour before the kick-off, and at the station for away matches at least a quarter of an hour before the departure of the train.

13.—Wages will be paid every Friday from 3 p.m. to 4 p.m. in the afternoon, and from 5 p.m. to 6 p.m. in the evening, unless otherwise notified.

14.—Any player desirous of not returning with the team from an out match, must give at least THREE DAYS' NOTICE to the Secretary in writing to get permission granted.

15.—Players are requested to note that no one is allowed in the saloon or on the brake except PLAYERS AND OFFICIALS.

16.—These Rules and instuctions are subject to any alterations the Directors may from time to time deem necessary, and due notice of any such alterations would be announced upon the players' notice board.

17.—As the Trainers are held responsible for the carrying out of these rules, they must report any breach of same.

By Order of the Directors.

The 1923/24 Players Regulations: The rules make interesting reading!

Bill Ogley and Jimmy Carney at the railway end, during training. (1923/24 season)

The terrace at the Cromwell Road end was covered at a cost of £1,200, and at this time the Club claimed a ground capacity of 30,000 – a figure that was never tested – with weather protection for a third of this number. The Supporter's Club, still as active as ever, were using the "New Bridge Inn" as their Headquarters and charged subs. of 1/– (5p) per fortnight.

The first five games of the 1924–25 season were strangely inconclusive, with neither County nor their opponents scoring more than one goal, but at least it proved that the defence, which had played well in the final few months of the previous season, was tight. In the 1–1 home draw with Reading, Fred Forward made his debut at inside–left, and together with Cook was destined to play for Portsmouth in their glory days. In the next match, versus Northampton,

came the debut of Fred McKenzie, later to play in the successful Plymouth side. At this time, incoming players, who often had to leave their families a great distance away, were issued with a list of lodgings, and since no cars were allowed they had to live within walking distance of the ground.

After an excellent win over Northampton and a 0–2 defeat at Brentford, the team proceeded to Watford, who were unbeaten in six matches. It was quite a game, for with Gittins out, Charlton played his first match at centre–forward, and on a rain–sodden pitch scored four times. Conner supplied the last goal of the match. After three poor results, two games on the trot were won. At Bristol, Rovers were outclassed, but Newport only won 1–0, due mainly to Whatley's performance.

Exeter were then beaten, when towards the end Lowes trapped the ball on the run and shot, giving goalkeeper Bailey no chance.

The F.A.Cup was approaching, and a 3-1 League win over Swindon must have put the team in good heart for the Cup match, which ended in a 0-0 draw at Aberdare. This and was followed by a 3-0 victory at Somerton five days later. A 3-0 League win over Norwich preceded two Cup draws with Exeter. The tie was ultimately decided at Ashton Gate, when County lost 0-1. On December the 16th, Conner left for Bristol City. Possibly the club felt able to let him go because of Charlton's performances at centre-forward, but he soon reverted to outside-right, with reserve Fred Taylor taking over the central berth.

The year's end saw County in a satisfactory seventh position, and 1925 started off in spectacular fashion with the side reeling off four successive victories. Taylor, who had scored twice in the last game of 1924, found the net in every match, making it five games in a row. Taylor, who missed the 4-1 defeat of Bristol Rovers, also scored in three of his next five matches, as well as in the 2-0 Welsh Cup win against Wellington. By now County had achieved a consistent fourth position in the table.

In the Welsh Cup, Newport disappointingly lost 0-1 at Wrexham. In the League the side dropped only one point in their final six home games, but unfortunately lost every one of the last four away matches. County bowed out with a pleasing 3-0 win over Merthyr and finished sixth in the table. The defence had played admirably with twelve clean sheets at home, and goalscorers Charlton and Taylor had reached double figures, the latter in virtually just half a season. No away wins after February the 28th had scuppered any chance of Championship honours, but 49 League points was still a record for the club at that time.

Mid-June saw the departure of Billy Charlton to Cardiff, and his replacement, Jack Davis, soon made his presence felt at the start of the new season, with a hat-trick against Brighton. He was the only Newport County player ever to score three goals on his debut. A fortnight later, Davis obtained another hat-trick, against Q.P.R., and after six games he had netted 10 times. Alas, the bubble burst, and he could only score ten more over the rest of the season.

The gates for the opening matches were around the 10,000 mark, but despite a reasonable start, by October they had fallen to half that figure. Goalscoring at this time noticeably increased, because of a change in the offside law, and the County's goals against column began to show a significant increase. Although beating Brighton, the defence conceded three, with four more coming at Luton. Contrary as ever, the side lost only one of its first four away games, but had a run of six home games without a win. At least, the team had a settled look, with only thirteen players used in the first nine matches. Hopes were raised by a 2-0 victory at Bournemouth, then were quickly dispelled by a 4-0 home defeat to Swindon, the first goal coming from a long wind-

assisted clearance, and the second from the sun getting in Maidment's eyes.

On October the 1st, the side began a terrible run, when they obtained only two points from seven matches. In the F.A.Cup, a 1-0 win at Weymouth was followed by a home defeat to Northampton. At least, County won the last two fixtures of the year, and in the Boxing Day match Carney was tried at centre-forward against Merthyr, and came good with a hat-trick. This sudden surge of success continued with County winning five games out of six. Carney had a run of seven games at centre-forward, and scored in six of them. Indeed, from the end of December he played 13 times in all in this position, scored in ten of the matches and accumulated fourteen goals.

Over the final three months County's form reverted to no more than moderate, and in the Welsh Cup the side overcame Barry, plus Merthyr (after replays), but succumbed to Ebbw Vale on April the 21st. The win at Barry, played under the rules of the day, was thought to be the longest match seen at Jenner Park, when two periods of extra time were necessary before Coates headed the winner.

After the previous season, 1925/26 had been somewhat disappointing. Matters had not been helped when County had been forced to sell the talented Fred McKenzie to Plymouth on February 20th for a record fee. The outstanding winger Fred Cook - capped against England and Scotland - was sold to Portsmouth at the end of the season. Jack Davis, who had scored a record 20 goals for the club, was allowed to depart, as were regulars Frank McKenzie and Walter Coates, along with Tommy Lowes plus Fred Taylor. At this time Newport's average takings were £320 per match, and this was to fall by £30 during the forthcoming season, with the General Strike taking its toll. County officials had to scamper around trying to find the players' wages. The married men would be paid with the half-crowns and florins from the turnstiles, and the single men, in digs, would receive their wages from the shillings and sixpences.

The County's side, at this time one of the least expensive in the League, understandably included some new faces for the start of the 1926/27 season. For the first two matches, Bobby Anderson played right-back, and he was to prove admirably consistent at Somerton Park. From the third game onwards, the position was filled by Ivor Hinton - who was for most of his career associated with Barry - and who was to die young. Three other players to make their debuts, in the first march versus Plymouth, were Sheffield-born winger George Johnson, the well travelled inside-right Jack Holland and Billy Price, a centre-forward from Ebbw Vale.

As often happened, the first match of the season provided the best gate, with £483 being paid at the turnstiles. County were losing until Nairn headed in, and a few minutes later, Forward laid on the winner for Holland. By their standards, County made a fantastic start to the season, for in the first nine games, six were won, two were drawn, and the team shared second place in the table. However, the side had failed to score more than two goals in any match, despite the defence playing well (especially Maidment and young Bowsher). But after half a dozen games, Price's one goal from the centre-forward position did not compare with Davis' ten the previous season.

Some of the side's early success came from scrappy matches, but team spirit was good, and the side was unbeatable at Somerton Park in the first half of the season. After victories over Gillingham and Charlton, Crystal Palace were then beaten 2-1 – after Price equalised with a header fifteen minutes from the end, before Gittins scored with a minute to go. Against Luton, Pugh, who had signed professional only the previous week following some impressive reserve performances, played at centre-forward. Around this time, new iron fencing arrived, which the club bought to replace the old wooden palings, which had surrounded the pitch.

County had gone seven matches without loss, but while they maintained their home form their away record went to pieces. Five successive away games were lost including the League encounters at Southend (by 5-0) and 1-4 at Millwall. But in many respects the most catastrophic defeat was the last of this series, for they travelled to lowly Poole Athletic in the F.A.Cup and were beaten 0-1; a fair comparison to this result was England's defeat to the U.S.A. some twenty five years later! County allowed themselves to be bustled out of the game, and dreams of Cup glory were over for another year. At the end of 1926, County had obtained 25 points from 26 League matches which was a satisfactory position, but it was a revealing fact that the leading scorer was right-half Billy Nairn, with six.

As in the previous season, County opened the New Year with a sudden surge of form, when in the first six matches, five were won. Johnson's opportunism beat Northampton, but it was a mediocre match with both sides suffering from absentees. Centre-half John Connor was outstanding, but he was to play only a few more games in the County first team. Gillingham were beaten 1-0 when Price beat Alex Ferguson eight minutes from time, and to say that County were lucky is an understatement, for the Gills missed two penalties – apart from the handicap of the second half injury to Hillier. A 1-4 reverse at Plymouth was followed by wins over Merthyr, Aberdare and Watford. However, two days before the Watford match, the club had been forced to sell both consistent left-back Ted Smith and outstanding left winger Fred Forward, to Portsmouth, where the pair joined Fred Cook. Although the side maintained its home form for a while, the transfers were bound to have a long term effect.

County soon succumbed to another Cup blow, when they were eliminated from the Welsh Cup by neighbouring Lovells Athletic. The little works side, set up just after the War, had already proved to be doughty Cup fighters, having previously won the Welsh Amateur Cup.

County had two more League home wins, 3-0 over Southend and 5-3 over Swindon, but from the end of March they were unable to register another victory. Indeed in their final nine home games they scored only one goal, that being obtained by right-half Frank Walker against Brentford. The way the Directors were forever changing the forward line did nothing to help matters. Brighton became the first team to lower County's colours at Somerton Park, on March 31st, and the side obtained only another three points in a disastrous run-in to the season.

The economic situation was having a calamitous effect, with dwindling gates and the enforced sale of players. County had opened the season with a near five figure attendance, but by the end of January even a local derby with Aberdare could pull in only 3,436. In the second half of the season, only the Good Friday game with Q.P.R. exceeded £300 at the gate, and most match receipts were around the £200-£260 mark. A succession of wet Saturdays did not help and over the season the club lost more than £1,000.

Until the disastrous end of season run, things had gone reasonably well. County were lucky that their great servant Jimmy Hindmarsh had decided to stick with them, for although he had been shortlisted for the Swansea job, he withdrew at the last minute. Home form had been good, with only seven points dropped, but the away record was poor, and the forwards had disappointed. With 57 goals, the team had scored less than Aberdare, who finished bottom of the table and failed to retain their Football League status. No player had reached double figures, the top scorer being the future international Wilf James, with nine. Towards the end of the season, promising youngsters Pritchard, Walker, Wardell and Weaver had been given their chance.

With a miserable end to the season, and scant financial resources, a large turnover of players took place. On their way out were such regulars as Price, Johnson and Drinnan, but Hindmarsh – who was offered the chance of the Crystal Palace post during the season – turned up trumps and signed on an excellent squad. The most noticeable signing proved to be the Scot Archie Waterston, who was to score regularly throughout the season. Others included Sammy Richardson – a West Bromwich stalwart – Peter Barratt who had recently played in the Scottish Cup final, young Billy Thomas from Lovells, and Peter Brittan who returned from Barry.

A visit to Q.P.R. began the season, with a reconstructed forward line which included Harper, Waterston, Barratt and Young. The half-backs performed well, especially Tommy Pritchard, but the side went down 2-4. The team opened their home campaign with a 3-1 victory over Brighton, but it was significant that while Q.P.R. received around £900 through the turnstiles for their match, Newport obtained little more than £300 at Somerton. Although this was only the second match, the side had been completely reshuffled, with Richardson, Weaver and Brittan replacing Nairn, Barratt and Harper; Gittins moving over to inside-left.

Waterston scored his first goal for the club, and the promising Reg Weaver netted twice.

In contrast to the previous season, there was a high scoring start, and, after six matches, County had obtained 17 goals and conceded 12. After appearing in the first four matches, Waterston missed the next nine, but his place was admirably filled by Weaver, whose goal tally included a hat-trick in a 4-1 victory at Brighton. Unfortunately his goal scoring for County was to come to an abrupt end, for just as they had been recently forced to allow their promising players to move to Portsmouth, they were now forced to sell their best to Wolves, when Tommy Pritchard was transferred to Molineux for £1,100 in the middle of September; Weaver followed on the 10th of November for a similar fee. Pritchard's pivotal role was filled, after a few performances from the veteran Sims, by the up and coming Stan Bowsher and Waterston resumed the centre-forward position.

From the beginning of October, the Newport side enjoyed an undefeated run of six games. Walsall were beaten 3-0, all the goals coming in the final twelve minutes. Against Luton, and in bad conditions, the side drew 1-1. Skipper Richardson asked Anderson to take a penalty, but with divided loyalties he refused, because he had played for Luton. Goalkeeper Maidment, who was having a brilliant game, ran up to take his first ever penalty. Approaching the ball, he called out, *"It's all right, this one's going in!"* Such confidence reaped its due reward. Not content with that, he also scored in the following match, when Brentford were beaten 3-0.

The side's unbeaten run came to an end on November 12th, the first game after Weaver's departure and County's first home defeat. It was also the game which set Millwall off on their promotion surge. In a 0-2 reverse at Crystal Palace, Blackmore and Taylor made their debuts, Pugh played his first game of the season, and Gittins had a penalty saved.

The tale of woe extended to the next game, with County once again out of the F.A.Cup at the first attempt. In the first two minutes, the normally reliable Maidment, restored in goal, stopped a shot, only to let it roll down his back and into the net. Despite this, and Bowsher's temporary absence with a knee injury, County should have won against Swindon. Terrible shooting prevented a victory, with Gittins and Waterston missing open goals.

The year had a miserable ending, with Swindon winning on December 26th and 27th, but the side again had a good start to the New Year, taking five points from three games. The adverse factor was the appalling weather which affected gates, and these had already been reduced by the widespread economic situation. The Cup match with Swindon had raised £510, with many fans travelling up from Wiltshire, but in fourteen subsequent home games, only three broke the £200 mark, despite £350 being the breakeven figure.

In the 4-3 home win over Charlton, Waterston, who was now hitting form, scored all the goals. An unlucky 1-2 reverse at Bristol Rovers and a 1-1 draw with Plymouth preceded a welcome 2-0 win at Merthyr, with Gittins scoring twice, from 25 and 30 yards. In the home match with Walsall, grand old battler Charlie Brittan nabbed a hat-trick, and a sobering 0-4 defeat at Gillingham was followed by County's highest League score up to then – 7-2 over Luton. Waterston was again on the mark with a hat-trick, but, worryingly, the gate was down by more than 1,500.

Over the second half of the season, the defence virtually selected itself (Maidment, Anderson, Hinton, Richardson, Bowsher and Pugh), strangely so, for the side let in one six, three fives and rarely kept a clean sheet. A 15,000 crowd at Millwall on a wet afternoon produced £1,000, a figure of five times the County's average. The game also produced five goals for the Lions, against one from Richardson. An unfortunate Welsh Cup reverse at Rhyl was followed by a spell of four matches in five days over Easter. After a 1-6 home drubbing by Q.P.R., County stayed overnight in London, as the team was making its longest trip of the season, to Norwich. A draw there was followed by two victories over Coventry. In the home match, Waterston notched another hat-trick, and the away game was particularly notable, with Wardell being taken off injured after half an hour.

The finale to the season was disappointing, with three defeats in four matches. A crowd of 2,554 saw an appalling 0-3 defeat by Crystal Palace. This ensured another low attendance for the last home match, with Northampton, but ironically the side gave one of its best displays of the season by winning 4-1. The final match was lost 1-5 at Southend. Around this time, neighbouring Lovells won the Welsh Amateur Cup for a record third consecutive time.

Despite disappointments, it had been a successful season on the goal scoring front, and although missing twelve matches, Waterston easily created a new Football League record for County with 27 goals, and old warhorse Jimmy Gittins was only just behind the previous best with his 18. The reserve sides had also shown excellent form, with the Southern League team having beaten Merthyr and Bristol Rovers each by 9-1, plus Weymouth 12-2; additionally the Welsh League title was won. Indeed, the Welsh League side had been undefeated until it met Cardiff City on March 7th. Despite hope on the playing side, there was, however, considerable room for gloom. Gates were crumbling in the economic recession and there was also strong competition to be faced. Cardiff City had won the F.A.Cup in 1927, even stopping by Somerton Park on the rail journey home. Where were County's Summer wages to come from? The club faced an uncertain future.

The 1928 close season, strangely, saw few changes of staff. Certainly, the club was in no position to sign any newcomers early in the Summer, and the "Argus" launched a "shilling fund" to help the club. The only close season signings to make any impact were George Richardson plus full-back Joe Reid, and for the first time ever, the line-up for the opening match did not include one new face.

The team made a truly average start, winning the first game, losing the sixth, and drawing the four in between. For some reason, Waterston fell out of favour, and was regarded as less successful than the previous season, even though he had scored nine goals in thirteen games by the time he departed, and had bagged a hat-trick against Gillingham. After their moderate start, County lost seven games out of ten, with even worse to follow in December. Gates continued on the same decreasing curve.

The downward spiral in the League really began with a home defeat by Northampton, the first time they had won in ten visits to Somerton. Waterston soon became a passenger in the game which the Cobblers won 3-0. For the following match, the "Argus" spoke of a "new Newport County side", and three players made their first appearances of the season, viz. Blakemore, Witton and Pick. County were 1-0 up at half-time on a rain-sodden pitch, but Coventry scored three in the second half.

A 1-2 home defeat by Luton was amazingly followed by the first away win, 3-1 at Brentford. Blakemore and Bowsher were excellent, and Gittins beat three men to score the first goal. A 0-2 home defeat by Bournemouth was followed by a miracle, a 7-0 F.A.Cup drubbing of Woking, which was the top score of the day, and Young obtained a hat-trick. Pugh, who scored twice, fractured a shinbone and was taken to hospital. The game was played on a heavy ground, and in a strong wind.

A home draw with Southend on the 1st was the only light in December. There were a few changes at this time, with Pick being exchanged for Ward, and Waterston joining Southport. With Ward ineligible, Gittins became a make-shift centre-forward in the next round of the F.A.Cup. Tommy Harper, recalled after playing in the first two matches of the season, became a passenger after ten minutes, and the side, which showed no heart for the fight, went down 0-6 at Norwich. Over the season the centre-forward berth caused major problems, and all of the following players were used: Waterston, George Richardson, Witton, Pugh, Ward, Gittins, Hill, Reid, Blakemore (the goalkeeper!) and the obscure amateur, Buckler.

On a slippery pitch, with Bowsher missing through tonsillitis, County lost 1-2 at home to struggling Brighton, and at this time they were still sixth from bottom, on goal average. The following Saturday, the side visited Norwich, and their line-up was incredible. They had played Norwich only a fortnight before in the F.A.Cup, and only Young retained his place, on the left wing. The only others to survive in the team were Anderson and Reid, who were both moved to different positions. At least, the score was a more respectable 1-3, with "Nippy" Wardell finding the net.

The Christmas holidays saw two defeats by Watford, and a 1-3 reverse at Walsall, County were now rock bottom and a thoroughly dispirited side. As previously, however, the New Year coincided with a sudden improvement in form, though the use of full-back Reid as centre-forward did little to help matters. As February arrived, a 4-1 home win over Torquay preceded two excellent away victories, at Gillingham and Fulham. The run of good fortune coincided with George Richardson's conversion from left-half to centre-forward, and in a 5-1 Welsh Cup thrashing of Swansea, he scored four times.

County's change of fortune was all the more remarkable, since they has been forced, on January 25th, to sell their budding star Bowsher to Burnley. He had already been selected to play for Wales and made his international debut two days after leaving the club. The transfer was now to catch up with the team, for in the space of 18 days the defence conceded seven, five and six goals. Eventually, the side began to take on a more settled look, and Riley added much needed class at left-half.

After a narrow 0-1 Welsh Cup defeat by First Division Cardiff came four successive League wins. The side completed the double over Bristol Rovers, and Merthyr were hit for six, with Pugh netting a hat-trick. Four points scraped from the final half dozen games avoided the ignominy of re-election. Clearly, the side had some ability, and it was ironic that two players who had been played at left-half – Pugh and Richardson – should end up as the top scorers, with 12 and 11 goals respectively.

It says much for the commitment of Hindmarsh, that he could turn down a third move in three years, for each time that a County player reached a certain standard, he needed to be sold. What a team the County could have had, if they had been able to keep together such players as Cook, Forward, Bowsher, McKenzie, Pritchard and Weaver. Pugh was now to join the exodus, leaving for Bury, and he later reached his peak with Nottingham Forest.

A rare action shot of record scorer Tudor Martin (1929/30)

There was little the club could do, with average gate takings of now less than £220. The reserves had threatened to win the Southern League but eventually finished second to Plymouth. Jack Hill scored twice as many goals as any other player.

At this time Somerton Park was used for other sports, such as motor bike soccer, and a fifteen round boxing contest between Ben Marshall and Roy Martin. In the past, flower shows were also held at the ground, and it was once used for a soup kitchen in a time of need.

Pugh and Wardell – who went on the Welsh F.A. tour of Canada – along with Young, were the principle departures, and new signings included Hector Lawson, Hugh Morris, Frank McKenna and Charlie Seymour. Two promising locals, Ron Hugh and Billy Bagley, made their debuts in the first team, also a young centre-forward by the name of Tudor Martin joined the club, and he would make his mark before the season was over.

Councillor Wardell, that pillar of Newport County, stated in plain fashion before the season opened, that it would be sink or swim for County. For much of the year, it seemed as though it would be sink, although it was not all despondency before the start, with promising form being shown in the trials, and a young amateur from Rogerstone, Ron Hugh, scoring a hat-trick.

On a scorching hot day, County travelled to Southend for their opening match. Despite being bolstered by the inclusion of Lawson, Morris and McKenna, the side lost 1-2. For the next few matches, Clifford and Seymour came in for Sammy Richardson and McKenna, and home wins were recorded over Swindon and Watford. Warning signs were there, however, for while at one time Newport would have had 10,000 present for their first home match, now they were down to half that figure. Unfortunately, the side then hit a disastrous run, which made the financial situation even worse. In a sequence of twelve matches, nine were lost, and after the team had beaten Watford 1-0 on September the 7th, no further win was recorded until December the 7th.

Tudor Martin appeared at inside-right versus Coventry in September, but his first couple of months were spent in the reserves. On November the 2nd, in the away game at Walsall, he began a run at centre-forward. Martin did not find the net in the 1-2 defeat, but made up for it in the next game, scoring a hat-trick at home to Q.P.R. However such was the County's form at that time that the match was lost 4-5! This was the first home defeat of the season, and did a great deal of damage to the club, financially. The next game was played before Fulham's lowest crowd of the season (a mere 28,111!), due to a downpour; Martin headed a goal in the second minute, but Fulham eventually won the match. At this stage County were hovering next to the bottom of the table, with neighbouring Merthyr Town below them.

In their next home game, against Norwich, County again scored four – and drew 4-4! At least, the "Football Argus" spoke of a "brilliant recovery", for the team had been 0-3 down at one time. Martin scored twice, and Riley almost sealed a victory, when he rattled the crossbar. Non-League Kettering were beaten 3-2 in the F.A.Cup, with Martin scoring the winner, and the following Saturday, he scored his second hat-trick, in a 5-1 drubbing of Gillingham. In the next round of the F.A.Cup, even Football League opponents in the form of Walsall could not attract more than 4,121 to Somerton, with takings which realised £222.80. The Saddlers won 3-2, with Walters netting three times, once when Maidment slipped on the greasy turf.

Against Exeter, Martin grabbed another two goals – now having scored in seven consecutive matches – and with thirteen to his credit. But the alarm bells were well and truly ringing, for the 4-1 win was seen by only 2,606, which produced receipts of just £130. The programme for the next game contained the remark; *"Still better support is needed. 2,500 is not a paying proposition for a Third Division side."* That match produced an extra thousand, but for a Christmas Day fixture, 3,337 was a poor crowd.

The financial crunch came on January the 4th, when Jimmy Hindmarsh had difficulty in obtaining the fares for the trip to Watford, and urgent action had to be taken. Fortunately, there was a good response to County's pleas, for the working men of Risca, Newport, Cross Keys and Cwmbran donated their humble sixpenses, and the tradesmen contributed to the plight as they had never done before. Martin was obviously now a star player and the Directors promised in mid-season that they would not in the future transfer their good players.

Having managed to reach Watford the side played as if their lives depended on it, and came away with both points, Martin netting two goals and McKenna one. County maintained their excellent form, beating Coventry 4-2 in the next game, and by now it was almost monotonous, for Martin scored another hat-trick, and, after the earlier appeals a larger crowd turned up. For the remainder of the season the gates hovered around the 4,000 mark, and clearly Martin's goal scoring ability had helped to attract more spectators.

The next home game with Southend attracted the best attendance so far, although Martin, shadowed everywhere by defenders, failed to score in a 0-0 draw. Scouts from four Football League clubs were present to watch his performance. He missed the next home game, versus Brentford, when Gittins deputised and scored, but the side lost 1-3.

Hundreds of fans travelled to Bristol Rovers, where the team was applauded on to the pitch. Balkemore, who had relegated the consistent Maidment to the reserves, kept the half-time score down to 1-1. If Martin had not headed wide in the second half, he would have obtained yet another hat-trick. The team still triumphed 3-2, but the defence had been leaking goals all season, and the side was still languishing in the bottom half of the table.

After the win at Rovers came three successive draws. Against Brighton, Martin put County two up, but the visitors were allowed to steal a point with two soft goals. The following game with Walsall took an opposite turn, for it was the visitors who were soon two up. For the first goal Blakemore dropped the ball and Walters shot home from 20 yards. Three minutes later, County were level through Gittins and Martin, and shortly after half-time Seymour scored the winner from 15 yards.

On February the 1st, County received a rare honour when both Hugh and Martin were selected to represent Wales, in Ireland. The outcome was less successful, for the Irish won 7-0 with Bambrick scoring six! One week later Hugh played for the Welsh amateur side versus Scotland, at Hampden Park.

A Martin goal failed to stave off a bad reverse at Q.P.R., with Goddard obtaining a hat-trick. County were by then eighth from the wrong end of the table, and Merthyr were five points adrift at the bottom. In a six match spell County's only victory was a 3-2 Welsh Cup win over Lovells that was played in heavy rain and wind. However, on April the 10th the County came good with a bang, and even the conservative "Western Mail" announced; *"Merthyr Town Annihilated"*, as County won 10-0 in their biggest ever Football League win. *"Play the game Tudor"*, chided the Newport fans, in mock reproof, as Martin scored after 25, 30, 40, 47 and 85 minutes. Gittins was also in brilliant form, with his mastery of ball control.

Any euphoria soon evaporated, for the team then went down 0-5 at Gillingham. As County's Welsh Cup match was scheduled for the same day, a reserve team was sent to Colwyn Bay and lost 0-4! The first team lost at Plymouth, but had the consolation of their largest away crowd for five years. Home to Northampton, on a gusting day, Martin scored two goals and secured two points. The return match against Plymouth brought the biggest gate for five years, with 10,766 fans and receipts of £583. Plymouth were confirmed as Champions, and were carried shoulder high from the pitch. Another Martin hat-trick helped County defeat Exeter 4-0, but alas there would be no more, for Newport were forced to sell their star man to Wolves just before the end of the season. In an amazing change of fortune, County now played Merthyr, in the Town's final Football League encounter. The Martyrs, who had so recently been demolished by County, won 5-1, with Parker hitting four. The "Football Argus" expressed the expectation that Merthyr would not be readmitted to the League, and the crowd of 1,189 did little to dispel that view.

It had been a great achievement for the club to complete the season at all, and the absence of a re-election plea was an added extra. It may seem strange that in such a dire season the club accumulated a profit of £1,034, but this had included a surplus of £2,300 that was received on transfers. Martin, who in just 29 matches had set a Newport record that was to never be equalled by anyone in 46 games, raised £1,500 by his transfer. By coincidence, Lovells had their own star goalscorer, Jimmy Gardner, who had scored 46 goals, and was soon to have a successful spell at Somerton Park.

New Chairman George Nixon had little to look forward to, for the sale of Martin had simply bought time, and the new season would take place before a background of vast unemployment and dwindling gates. There were many changes of playing staff, for apart from Martin, the wonderfully consistent Maidment and Anderson both left for Lincoln, and Reid, McKenna plus Morris also moved on. In came, amongst others, Cyril Pearce – in part exchange for Martin – the cricketer Victor Fox, Bill Hickie and Henry Brown. Outside-right Matson who scored in the opening match never appeared again, and centre-forward Billy Welsh had also left by the middle of November.

On August the 30th, the team kicked off against Torquay, before 3,905 – a gate that would soon seem enormous! The result would also later be seen as brilliant, for County triumphed 2-1. The next six matches were all lost, leaving County firmly anchored to the bottom of the table, with six goals for and twenty-one against.

The initial away game was at Clapton Orient, and this was the first match played at Lea Bridge. County lost this encounter 1-3, but were unlucky to go down to a 17th minute goal in the following match at Northampton. For the next game the side travelled to Gillingham, where the local Picture House was showing *"The Port of Lost Souls."* This proved to be an apt omen, for only Balkemore's brilliance kept the score down to 1-4.

The second home game, versus Brentford, attracted only 2,758. Seymour went off, the team played badly, and the Bees won with two easy goals. After Gillingham had completed the double, County travelled to Crystal Palace, where the flag was flying at half-mast for Palace's recently deceased Chairman. But by the end of the match this could have been for the County, as the side was thrashed 1-7. Boots deputised for Blakemore, who stood down as his brother had been killed during a match in Durham. By half-time Boots had seen four goals go past him, and the whole performance was a shambles. After seven games, Newport had used a total of 21 players.

Against Southend, Vince Davies scored straight from the kick-off, and County won 3-1, but the comment of the "Football Argus" that *"County prove they are not a bottom League team,"* was less than convincing. Yet another player was tried, amateur Len Apsey from Trethomas, but he was discarded after two matches. It was soon back to normal, with one point from four matches, and a superb Gittins goal brought no points reward at Luton, although Bristol Rovers were held 1-1 at Somerton. Runaway leaders Notts County were the next visitors, and the

Directors must have been overjoyed with the 5,245 gate. Within seconds, Keetley scored for Notts, and he later completed his hat-trick. Seymour, who was tried at centre-forward for the first time netted twice for Newport. On October the 25th, the side travelled to Watford, and still without an away point they went down 2-6. Pearce, in his first appearance at centre-forward, scored twice, whilst White obtained a hat-trick for Watford. On the same day, the *"Welsh Unknowns"* (robbed of their Football League players), travelled to Ibrox and meritoriously drew 1-1. Billy Thomas, a developing talent, played in the match.

The following game was something of a sensation, for County were 2-3 down to Bournemouth at half-time, decided to give up the short passing game, and ran out eventual 7-3 winners, with Seymour and Pearce scoring rare double hat-tricks. At Swindon, black and amber in the crowd indicated the presence of many Newport supporters, and they were no doubt delirious when the side was 4-2 up at half-time, with Pearce having scored twice. Alas, the final score was 4-4, but at least an away point had been secured. The next game was against Fulham, and the "Football Argus" carried the headline, *"Newport County Half-back Shot."* It was not the work of some irate supporter however, for Jack Clifford who had been out shooting with Len Blakemore, received pellets in various parts of his anatomy. Seymour was carried off within a minute of the start, and, despite another storming goal from Pearce, Newport lost 1-3.

After another high scoring game – 4-6 at Norwich – County were paired with Dulwich Hamlet in the F.A.Cup. In goal for Dulwich was Alf Solly, who later became a popular player with Newport. Pearce scored with a first minute header and a second goal after ten minutes. In the second half, Smith pulled one back, then Levy was fouled. Blakemore pushed out Hugo's spot kick, but the centre-half followed up to ram the ball home. The replay was won 4-1, but significantly the attendance was 3,000 less than the gate that the amateurs had achieved. County now suffered two more hammer blows. On a foggy day in Shepherd's Bush, County suffered their second 1-7 defeat of the season. The side was 0-3 down after half an hour, with Goddard obtaining a hat-trick. In the F.A.Cup, hundreds of supporters travelled to Walsall and saw their side demolished 0-4 on a pitch resembling a ploughed field.

After such poor performances, the attendance for Norwich's visit was a pitiful 1,116. As often happens on such occasions, the team played well but with barely anybody there to see it. Pearce, who had disappointed at Q.P.R. – after scoring in seven successive matches – was back to form with two goals, with County winning 3-0. Two days later, the side visited the short-lived Thames F.C., at the West Ham stadium. To talk of a *"crowd"* is overstating matters, for only 816 were present. A Pearce goal could not stave off a 1-3 defeat, but on Christmas Day a rare 4-0 victory was achieved, over Exeter City, with Pearce bagging another two. Because of the holiday, the attendance was up, to 3,264.

In the following two days the team went down 0-3 to both Exeter and Torquay, and at the year's end, County were firmly rooted to the bottom of the table, with just 12 points. Only one of these points had been obtained away from Somerton, and the defence had already conceded 67 goals.

On January the 3rd, Newport made their customary good start to the New Year. On a muddy pitch, the County forwards – particularly Bagley – showed outstanding second half form to beat Northampton 5-2. They were now 21st, the same position in the table as Cardiff City in Division 2. With no victory in the next two matches, the gate for the visit of Crystal Palace was down to 1,967. Tremendous grit secured two points, and with Pearce, Bagley and Seymour out, full-back Hickie played at centre-forward. Davies became a passenger, and Riley went to hospital with a fractured collar-bone. County were 0-1 down, but veteran Jimmy Gittins pulled the fat out of the fire, his first goal coming direct from a free kick.

On a freezing January day, Newport let in six goals at Southend, though Witton – deputising for Pearce – scored two. He also scored in the next game, and with Glidden netting twice, County beat Luton 3-1. Without four first-teamers, it was a good performance, but the encouraging run ended, for five successive games were then lost. Four League matches were lost by two goals or more, and in the Welsh Cup, Shrewsbury triumphed 5-2. Bogey side Notts County thumped Newport 5-0, when the County were forced to change their strip, but green jerseys brought no luck. With the Notts right-back carried off, the Ironsides conceded four goals against ten men in the second half. On a bright, frosty day, Bournemouth won 4-2, which left County six points behind third from bottom Thames and staring re-election in the face.

After two successive wins had brought renewed hope, it was downhill for the rest of the season. Somehow a Gittins goal secured a win at Fulham, but at the end the side had accumulated a pitiful total of three points away from Somerton. Brighton triumphed at Hove by 5-0, though County surprisingly won the return 2-0 on Easter Monday, this being the only win in the final eight matches. The home game with Q.P.R. was the last chance to finish outside the bottom two, but two Pearce goals could not save a final 2-3 reverse.

April the 17th, memories were revived of happier times, when Tudor Martin played for Wolves in a friendly at Somerton, and netted a hat-trick, in a 3-3 draw. County's final two matches were drawn 1-1, the latter of the pair against Clapton Orient.

Newport County were being sucked into a downward spiral, and around this time there were accumulated debts of over £6,000. The bright spot of the season had been the discovery of Pearce, but on June the 6th, he was on his way to Swansea. The record of the defence had been appalling, for on the team's visits, they had lost 19 games, and conceded 80 goals; only 4 clean sheets had been kept in 42 matches.

The situation was not helped, when County were taken to court for running an illegal lottery, something which would see them banned from the F.A.Cup the following season. Nevertheless, there was an expectation that County would be safely re-elected to the Football League, but such thoughts were to be rudely shattered, for, on June 1st, the "Argus" headline read:-

> "Newport County Rejected....Mansfield
> Town Win Place in Southern Section".

In the Southern Section, the club had won 19 votes, compared with 38 for Norwich, and 25 for Mansfield.

The County's expulsion was even more of a shock because the Third Division clubs had recommended the club's re-election, but it was the higher Division sides who commanded the votes. County had feared Aldershot as the danger team, but massive lobbying by Mansfield had won the day. The Mayor of Newport - County Director Tom Crowther - expressed his indignation, but to no avail. South Wales soccer had been well and truly blighted by the depression, with Football League representation down from five clubs to two, and with former highflying Cardiff now destined for Division Three (South).

The new Grandstand at Somerton Park - which was built in 1932.

# CHAPTER 3

## From Wilderness to Promised Land

Despite the shattering blow of rejection, the Directors of Newport County were determined to carry on and apply for Football League membership once again the following year. During the 1931–32 season, County's first team played in the Southern League and Welsh League, though more local youngsters played in the latter. The number of players departing was in double figures, and along with Pearce, out went veteran Billy Nairn, and such experienced performers as Sammy Richardson, Riley, Fox and Brown. The most colourful of the newcomers was Argentine born Frank Peed, who had been brought up in Lliswerry and had earlier joined the Army, being later bought out by Aston Villa. Charlie Brittan was back, and various youngsters were signed, including George Kitson, who was to be connected with the club for fifty years.

With the drop in status, support was naturally reduced to its hardcore fans. Apart from the reduction in staff numbers, players were forced to accept lower wages, but despite this a large debt still remained.

On August the 29th, County opened their campaign at home to Merthyr, and won 4–2 with no-nonsense centre-forward Frank Peed knocking in two headers. The side included some old hands – such as Blakemore and Gittins – and the forwards played well, as did George Wheeler, who was being watched by a Derby County scout. The team drew 1–1 at Cardiff Corries in the first Welsh League game, and 1–1 with a Yeovil side which included the famous Dick Pym in goal.

After the initial win over Merthyr, County created a remarkable record, for the next eight first team games were all score draws. This run included the local derby with Lovells Athletic, who were 2–0 up in the second half, before County equalised through Billy Clarke and Peed. County were also 0–2 down at Bath, but two goals from Peed and one from Brittan secured a point. One of the advantages of a reduced squad was that the side more or less picked itself. The team was very settled, and when Davies and Clifford were transferred, Kitson and Bill Jones replaced them.

For most of the season Southern and Welsh League games were interspersed, with Boots appearing in the Welsh League matches with Swansea and Aberaman, the only two occasions when Blakemore was missing in goal. After Aberaman had been beaten 3–2, County drew 1–1 with visiting Exeter, making it nine score draws from ten matches. Newport were the only unbeaten side in the Southern League, but had unfortunately taken only one point from most of their matches. Gittins won the points at Eastville with a ten yard shot, but the bubble burst at home to Llanelli with a 1–2 defeat. In the latter match, County

were by far the better side, hitting the bar four times in a matter of minutes, but their only reward was a fine solo goal by Peed. After a similar defeat at Taunton, the side hit back with four consecutive victories.

On Guy Fawkes' Night, County gained a 2–1 win at Swansea, thanks to Billy Thomas, but more fireworks were to follow with 19 goals scored in the three ensuing matches at Somerton Park. On November 7th, the "Football Argus" was ecstatic, claiming that Ebbw Vale had been *"caught in a flood"* and *"pounded to dust"* – a rare combination! 5–1 up at half-time, County ran out 7–2 winners with both Gittins and Peed achieving hat-tricks. A fortnight later, Bristol Rovers' reserves appeared, but the gates were suffering with this low grade of football, and barely 200 were present at kick-off. In two minutes Gittins had scored the first of two penalties, after ex-County full-back Smith had fisted the ball away. County eventually won 6–2 with centre-half Billy Clarke netting a pile-driver from outside the penalty area. The goal rush continued against Swindon Town reserves, when the Directors were hoping for a bumper gate, but streaming rain put paid to this. But at least County had the consolation of a 6–1 result. All the forwards scored, and Sam Jones – deputising for the unfit Peed – hit two early in the game.

It was frustrating that just when the Newport side was hitting its peak, it was robbed of the chance of F.A.Cup success. The club's fine for the illegal sweep resulted in the F.A. – in its wisdom – deciding to ban the team from the Cup for one season, even though the club had already been punished in the Courts. Apparently there was a change of heart, even at the time – by the officials involved – and there were hopes that either Clapton Orient or Thames would fold, with Newport as a replacement, but it was not to be and County were robbed of some much needed revenue.

Over the Christmas holidays, Newport had local derbys with Barry. The match on Christmas Day was lost 2–4 at Jenner Park, but there was no need for despondency, for on the following day County won 11–1, with Gittins knocking in four, and Peed three. Gittins, a general on the pitch, was an excellent Captain looking after the local young players.

At the start of 1932 Newport drew 3–3 at Merthyr, with Peed running from the half-way line to score. After a 4–0 Welsh League win over Cardiff City, it was back to double figures with a 10–2 drubbing of Taunton. There was a howling Winter wind as the teams took the pitch, but it made no difference to County who scored five in each half. It was certainly Peed's match, for he scored six goals, including four in the first half.

In early 1932, with the club on the point of bankruptcy, the Lysaght's Works Committee – the trustees of Somerton Park – agreed to sell the ground to local bookmaker Jimmy Jones. £7,500 was received, and Mr. Lysaght's original £2,200 was repaid. Jones immediately resold the stadium to the Cardiff Arms Park Greyhound Company, although he had agreed to allow Newport County to remain. However, the Greyhound Company wanted to throw them out, although they later relented, as the 1932/33 season was fast approaching.

In the Welsh League, County were beaten 1-3 at home by Cardiff Corries, but the same fixture produced a 2-0 victory in the Welsh Cup. For the home encounter with Llanelli both sides had three players missing, due to the Welsh League playing the Irish Free State League. Hugh, Peed and Bagley played in the match, as did three Lovells Athletic players, including ex-Ironside, Billy Hiles. Lliswerry lad Lloyd scored on his only appearance for the club, before leaving for the delights of Trethomas Bluebirds.

A 1-3 reverse at Exeter thwarted County's attempts to overhaul Yeovil at the top of the Southern League table, and after a 3-0 win over Torquay the team's title challenge sadly fell apart. From the 20th of February, County's fixtures followed a strange pattern, since eight of the ten first team matches were in the Southern League. This campaign ended at Yeovil on March 29th, and thereafter the team played eight Welsh League games and one Welsh Cup replay. The bubble burst on March 5th, when for the first time all season, the side failed to score; the team played eight games in March and failed to find the net in five of them. The defence, which had only once let in more than three goals, suddenly conceded six, with five coming in the second half, Parkin completing a hat-trick.

Peed scored three in a 6-1 Welsh League win over Penrhiwceiber, and the side fought out a respectable 0-0 Welsh Cup draw with Swansea, but in the next Southern League game, at Swindon, the team collapsed to a 0-5 defeat. The only Southern League win was over Ebbw Vale, which was hardly surprising, as Vale were bottom of both Leagues. Even then it was a narrow 3-2 victory over a weakened team, on a rain-soaked pitch.

After the Southern League fixtures had ended with a 0-3 defeat at Yeovil, the side clearly relished completing their campaign against weaker opposition, and the next five Welsh League games were won. Peed scored five in a 9-2 defeat of Merthyr, and so one-sided was the match, that even before the interval the Somerton Park crowd were shouting, *"Play up, Merthyr"*, to try and stir up the opposition! Wins over Ebbw Vale and Merthyr, were followed by a 1-0 victory at Llanelli followed, where only goalkeeper Owen kept the score down. On April 23rd, only a few spectators turned up for the home game with Aberaman, since it was the day of the F.A.Cup Final and many supporters had journeyed up to London.

The "Football Argus" reported that *"hundreds more were literally tied to their wireless sets"*, a comment which conjures up the strangest images! Peed netted twice in a 4-1 win, and on the same day, the Football League Management Committee announced that election to Division Three (South) would be sought by Aldershot, Guildford and Newport County.

After a 0-1 defeat at Lovells, Barry were entertained. Barry were trounced 5-1, and the Saturday night report spoke of *"Newport County's Star Forward"*, a young Scotsman, who had scored two goals in minute. Gittins, who netted a mere hat-trick was overlooked in favour of Wilson, a young amateur from Cowdenbeath. The lad, who was staying with friends in Newport, was given a game, with topscorer Peed dropping back to right-back. After his splendid match, Wilson the Wonder Man headed back to the Scottish mists and was never heard of again!

The final match was lost 2-5 at Barry, by which time both Merthyr and Llanelly had also applied for Football League membership. Thames announced they would not be seeking re-election, with one home gate of 469 it was hardly a surprise, and Luton (the opposition that day) decided to frame their cheque for 1/8d. (9p)! The Southern Section clubs had nominated Gillingham for re-election, along with Newport and Aldershot as other alternatives. Would County get back in? Although they had performed quite well, they had won neither championship, finishing second to unbeaten Lovells in the Welsh League. Peed had made an excellent contribution, with 24 goals in the Southern League, and 21 in the Welsh.

An attractive brochure was prepared for the A.G.M., which was signed by George Nixon who had been involved in football since 1909. On Monday, June 6th, the "Argus" broke the wonderful news, *"Newport County Re-elected to the Third Division."* Gillingham had attracted 41 votes, Newport 36, and Aldershot 35.

Apart from the obvious benefits, including increased gates and local derbys with Cardiff City, there were problems, particularly for Jimmy Hindmarsh who had from June 6th to build up an adequate squad. The Mayor, carried away on a tide of euphoria, spoke of Newport County in the future entering the First Division and winning the F.A.Cup. This was unlikely with free transfers only now available to Hindmarsh!

There was a vast amount of work for Hindmarsh and newly appointed Trainer Tommy Gibbon, and despite the lack of money available for transfers, the club still ended up with a wagebill of £120 per week. The playing staff was transformed, for out went Blakemore, Brittan and some of the local youngsters, and in came a host of new players from Internationals to former amateurs. With the likely increased support, the Greyhound Company set about transforming the Ground, noticeably with the construction of a new Grandstand opposite the old one.

Changes were also needed to accommodate the greyhound track, and the terrace at the Railway End was demolished in order to provide an oval central area.

Because of a variety of difficulties training had been carried out at cramped Rexville (Lovell's home ground), leaving the players unprepared for the broad acres of Somerton, and only one trial match was played. On August the 27th, County took the field on a sunny afternoon against Clapton Orient, by coincidence the last team they had previously faced in the Football League. The atmosphere was different this time, for the previous morbid occasion had been witnessed by 1,873, but this later match attracted 7,805 elated supporters, no doubt curious to see the newcomers in the reconstructed side. The band played, a new club flag fluttered in the soft Summer breeze, as the men stood around in their flannels. Unfortunately, there the dream ended, for lowly, distressed Orient ran out 2-0 winners.

Fans who thought that things could only get better were in for a shock. The next game, at Swindon, saw no less than five new faces, but County went down by the same scoreline. However, that was the good news, for the side then went to Northampton and let in eight, with Dawes bagging four. After three matches, County had no points and a goal difference of 0-12. For their second home match the crowd had more than halved, and ten-man Swindon scored the winner in the final minute. At least, Weale had obtained County's first goal!

On September the 10th, the crowd was back up to 6,025 for the visit of Bristol City, and a Gittins goal brought the first point of the season. It was then back to normal with four successive defeats. After seven games, 22 different players had been used, and even the inclusion of talented goalie Alf Solly and the Scottish international Bill Summers could not prevent defeats by Southend (0-3), Coventry (1-3), Brentford (1-6) and Torquay (0-4). Brentford were top, County bottom and Holiday scored a hat-trick, in the match when County suffered their record home defeat. After eleven matches, Newport had accumulated three points, scored 7 goals, and conceded 34, yet strangely enough they had seven full or amateur internationals on their books.

When Newport journeyed to Ninian Park, such was the interest that 2,450 cheap day G.W.R. tickets were issued. But such is life that before a crowd of 10,163, County ran out 3-1 winners, with Bagley, Thomas and Peed scoring. Unfortunately Peed, now back permanently from Norwich, was unable to rediscover his form against better opposition. The next match, against Reading, was significant since it saw the opening of the new Grandstand by the Mayor. Capable of holding 1,000, it held dressing-rooms and a Directors' room, whilst the old stand had been partly demolished. On a dreadful day with teeming rain and wind, the sides drew 3-3, Solly stopping a penalty.

A spectacular 5-2 win over Brighton was the exception rather than the rule, and the team was not to rise above bottom place until February, but at least it began to have a more settled look about it, with the likes of Hugh, Bagley, Thomas, Solly and John as regulars. For the first round of the F.A.Cup, 4,900 turned up to see Ilford defeated 4-2, with inside-right "Tucker" Green scoring a hat-trick. This was followed by two bad reverses. At the White City, County were thumped 1-6 by Q.P.R., and in the F.A.Cup the side was unceremoniously despatched 1-2 by non-League Folkestone, on the coldest day of the year. After this County could win only one of their next seven matches, a 2-0 defeat of Watford on Boxing Day.

By the year's end the side had gathered 12 points from 22 matches, and by the third home match of the New Year the attendance was down to 1,902, about the level when the club had gone out of the League. At times like this Newport County depended on its Supporters' Club, which was always its backbone. With the re-entry into the League, membership had swollen from the "gallant nine" of non-League days to 800. It was always looking for new methods of fundraising, and was now selling "stopwatch" tickets. With neighbouring Cardiff also struggling, a recruiting drive was made in the Valleys, and interest was renewed in such places as Rogerstone, Cwmbran and Pontnewydd. Among the leading lights of the Supporters' Club at this time were Fred Snook - a well-known local personality who wrote as "Ironside" in the "Western Mail" - and William Chapman, who left school at ten, and spent 40 years with the G.W.R. - including ten as Head of the Goods Department at Alexandra Dock.

The second half of January saw two 2-1 home wins, and a narrow 2-3 defeat at Ashton Gate. On February 1st, the team returned to Ashton Gate, this time securing a 4-3 Welsh Cup win, and Lumley - back at centre-forward - scored a hat-trick. Only 800 bothered to turn up for the game. Brentford had now slipped down to second in the table, but were still good enough to wallop six goals into the County net where a healthy attendance of 10,060 attended at Griffin Park.

County now made their best transfer move of the season, for after the Brentford debacle (and a 1-3 home defeat by Southend), Jimmy Gardner was signed on loan from neighbouring Lovells, the Supporters' Club paying part of his wages. He was not the same Jimmy Gardner who had started the season, although erroneously the two players' appearances were added together in the "Athletic News". Always a good goalscorer, he began with two goals in a 3-1 win over Torquay, and by the end of the season had accumulated twelve goals in thirteen matches, finishing top scorer together with Billy Thomas.

Although the club's playing position seemed hopeless, the off the field situation seemed stabilised. The Directors agreed to a meeting with the Supporters' Club at the low point of the season, and George Nixon's oratory and optimism helped to sway most of those present to his point of view. Gates began to increase, and the advent of Gardner brought a new spirit to the Football Club.

The goalscoring ability of the newcomer could do little to fill the gaps in the defence, and four more 4's were conceded, including one in a Welsh Cup replay at Southport. The forwards started scoring goals however, and Cardiff were beaten 4–2, before an excellent crowd of 7,933. The rest of March brought three defeats, but April turned out to be the best month of the season, with four wins. Against Q.P.R., County recorded their best victory of the season, 5–1, and their final game, against Crystal Palace was witnessed by 5,168.

After such an appalling start, it proved virtually impossible to avoid having to seek re-election, but with two games to go County briefly hauled themselves up to the dizzy heights of 19th. However, defeats in their final two matches dragged them back to 21st. It was not difficult to detect the cause of their predicament, for in 42 games the defence had conceded 105 goals. With Newport County having been back in the League for only one season, they were given another chance at the re-election meeting, though Mr.McKenna dropped a broad hint that any further bid for re-election would not be successful.

The long suffering Hindmarsh wielded the axe in no uncertain manner. Of the 26 who had played for the club in the 1932/33 season, 21 did not reappear during the next. Out, along with veteran Gittins, went such experienced performers as Solly, Charlton, Summers, Peed and Lennox. Gardner, together with George Wheeler, went back to Rexville – the latter having become fed up with persistent attempts to transfer him. Bagley, in the long line of County assets, was sold to Portsmouth. The only players to remain were Emlyn John, Billy Thomas, "Tucker" Green and locals Ron Hugh and Billy Clarke.

Hindmarsh must have been somewhat busy in the close season, and the local newspaper kept tally. By the time County had signed Burgess, it was up to ten, and with the arrival of McLachlan the total was sixteen. No wonder the first edition of the "Football Argus" contained the photographs of fifteen Newport players, for the fans would have been hard pressed to pick out who were the opposition, but such was the club's position, that few would remain for more than a season or so!

For some reason there was a certain muted optimism around Somerton Park, and season ticket sales were up. The Ground had been improved, with the bank on the Grandstand side heightened and broadened to give a better view.

On August the 26th, the team met Swindon in the first match. The previous year there had been six debutants, but on this occasion, if Bowsher and Clifford were included (back from Rochdale and Crystal Palace respectively), there were nine. The only old hands were Emlyn John and Billy Thomas. Bowsher was appointed team Captain, but he played only five League games and Andy Higgins took over. Despite a goal from inside-right Burgess the team lost 1–2, but the attendance was an encouraging 8,871. The side went down 0–3 in its first away game, against Orient,

who were struggling against closure, and changes in the County line-up were quickly made. Of the players who appeared in the first three encounters, Smith, Clifford, Bowsher, Millar, Griffiths and Barklam failed to make double figures in appearances during the season.

This was to be the year of the draw, and three of the next four matches finished 1–1, but matters eventually began to stabilise on the playing front with a more settled side. Except on a few occasions, noticeably when Jordan was injured in a 1–6 thrashing at Charlton, the defence did not give away more than two goals, but there was nobody in the attack knocking in the goals, apart from George Taylor, who netted four in his first five games.

In the F.A.Cup, County were paired with old opponents Dulwich Hamlet, and on November the 25th, County travelled to Champion Hill and were lucky to draw 2–2. The attendance of 11,500 – with receipts of £700 – put County's gates into the shade. The replay was a much more comfortable affair for County won 6–2, with Burgess and Taylor both scoring twice, however, the midweek attendance was only a third of the gate produced at Dulwich. In the second round, Newport lost away at distant Workington – a non-League side – who included Billy Charlton in their team. The better news was that County had just begun a run of seven League games without defeat, though six of the matches were draws.

The first game of 1934 was a Welsh Cup-tie at Lovells. Such was the status of the competition at the time that the only player who had appeared in the last County match was Millar, and he was played out of position on the left wing. The side gave a good performance to win 3–1 and record their first win at Rexville. Haycox scored on his County debut, and Bowsher's final goal came from 25 yards.

Despite their mediocre time in the League, Newport were doing rather better in Cup competitions. In the recently inaugurated Division 3 Cup they hammered Swindon 7–2 at Somerton, with Thomas netting three times. At this time the club were arranging the re-erection of a large canvas screen at the Somerton Bridge end to prevent spectators – especially the unemployed – crowding on to vantage spots and viewing matches for free. In the Welsh Cup the side drew 2–2 with Crewe, then won the replay in Cheshire 5–4 after extra time. The luck ran out however, with defeat by Brighton in the Division 3 Cup, and then by Tranmere – again in a replay – in the Welsh Cup.

From March the 3rd, the League form produced one win (5–3 at Southend, with newcomer Reed scoring four) and four draws. Reed, a saxophone wizard, only made his debut on February 10th, but still contributed 10 goals from his 16 games played. County's last share of the points came versus Norwich on March 30th, and by that stage they had a remarkable record, having drawn 17 matches out of 35. Although not one of their final seven games ended up all square, countrywide, only Southport could equal their record by the end of the season. Because of this quirk the team also ended up with the fewest wins throughout the Football League.

Easter was fairly disastrous with just one point from three games, and to cap it all the ultra consistent Thomas was injured on Easter Monday and forced to miss the end of the season. Two of the last five matches were won, including Southend who were beaten 3–0, with two memorable goals from Green. It was touch and go until the end, but it was Bournemouth and Cardiff – the latter with their lowest gates since entering the League – who had to seek re-election.

The close season followed the pattern of the previous two, but at least this time the side retained a nucleus of experienced players, including Thomas, Emery, Robinson, Burgess and Green. Among those leaving were Reed, Jordan, John and Taylor. Newcomers included Odell, Bird, Russell, White and two 'old boys' – Weaver from Chesterfield and McKenzie from Plymouth. Hindmarsh was still at the helm and now with Charlie Bates as his Trainer.

Things could scarcely have started better, with Bird scoring a debut goal to beat Exeter 1–0 away from home. The picture became even brighter, for in the first home game a crowd of 7,651 saw Bournemouth soundly thrashed 6–1. County were at this point top of Division 3, but could this good run continue? 10,978 supporters turned up to see Bristol City beaten 2–0, with goals from Higgins and Bird, but the excited County fans must have felt severely deflated after the next match, when Bournemouth beat them 3–1. At least Bird had scored in all four matches, but he failed to find the net two days later when Newport went down 0–2, before a 16,142 crowd at Millwall.

The side bounced back to form with a 2–0 home win over Coventry, when Bird scored again, and Weaver netted his first goal since his return to Newport. The match was viewed by another five figure attendance, and by this time the side was comfortably placed fifth in the table. The rot then began to set in when the side was hammered 0–4 at Orient. The normally consistent Billy Thomas was dropped, and Higgins – after a great deal of barracking at Somerton – secured a transfer to Exeter. Such is the fickleness of football crowds that for the next home match, with Gilingham, the attendance was less than half of that for the earlier Bristol City game. Bird, something of a one–man band in attack, scored twice against Gillingham to secure a County point. Of the Club's first 16 goals Bird had obtained 10. At this point of time Hindmarsh became unwell, and this factor had a detrimental effect upon the team.

On October the 6th, the team suffered its worst setback (to that time), losing 1–6 at Reading, and for the Brighton game, a fortnight later, the Somerton crowd had dropped to 3,696. There was something of a respite at the end of October, with three League games out of four won. The side was victorious by 4–3 in a well attended match at Ninian Park, and on November the 10th, Bird netted another

goal which secured both points at Brighton. That was the end of the good news, for to say the rest of the season was a disappointment is something of an understatement. After a 2–0 victory over Aldershot, on December the 19th, only two more games were won all season, and the defence was such that it kept only one clean sheet in all that time.

The first game of this miserable spell was a 1–4 home defeat to Torquay, with Walters netting all four for the visitors. After the match, supporters gathered behind the Grandstand calling for the Directors. Bert Moss appeared – ringed by policemen – and reinforcements were then called, with the crowd taking a quarter of an hour to disperse. In the F.A.Cup, the team succumbed 0–4 to Swindon. After defeat at Crystal Palace, the team was annihilated 0–6 at Charlton, which was not the most auspicious debut for goalkeeper Williamson. After the 2–0 win over Aldershot, and an away point at Swindon, it was downhill all the way, with seven successive defeats.

Christmas 1934 was not the happiest time for self–respecting County supporters, for it started with a 0–1 defeat to Watford. Whether the side had too much turkey is not recorded for posterity, but Boxing Day saw the team stuffed 0–7 in the return at Vicarage Road. A 1–3 home defeat was then inflicted by Exeter – Bird scored but must have felt by now that he was knocking his head against a brick wall.

The first ten matches of 1935 – which included a 2–3 Welsh Cup defeat at Cardiff – comprised two draws and eight losses, and by the time the side had crashed 0–5 at Coventry, seven successive games had been lost. A rare point came when Orient were held 3–3, with diminutive Alfie Clarke scoring twice on his Football League debut. Over the season County had dropped from first to nineteenth, and things were looking grim. In order to offset ever increasing financial problems, the President (Mr. W.R. Lysaght) plus the Directors increased their bank guarantees, and additionally the officials and players offered to take a 25% cut in wages.

Injuries to Odell and Green affected the team, Bird lost his form, and Haycox, Weaver plus Paget were all tried at centre–forward. The habitual barracking by some supporters did nothing to help matters.

A 4–0 victory over Cardiff – with Weaver and Clarke both scoring twice – was the only bright spot in the closing weeks, for nine of the final ten matches were lost, including the final six. The defence conceded six goals at Crystal Palace, five at Bristol Rovers and at home to Southend, plus four each in the two games with Luton. It was not the County's greatest end to a season!

At this time the unthinkable happened, for Jimmy Hindmarsh, the Newport County Manager for thirteen years, had had enough and in April he announced that he would be leaving the club. It was the end of an era. The side was firmly at the bottom by the end of the season, with the defence having conceded no less than 112 goals. George Nixon was left to make a tour of Lancashire in order to canvass votes, and it must have been a successful trip for County were duly voted back into the fold.

The greatly missed Hindmarsh was replaced by the famous ex-Burnley and England forward Louis Page, one of four footballing brothers. This boosted interest and a full-time Secretary was appointed, in order that the new manager could concentrate more on the football side. There was a certain air of optimism and season tickets sold well. An increased Board, with by now over a dozen members, gave greater stability, and there were also Ground improvements, with terracing which was added to the Cromwell Road end.

Considerable changes were naturally made on the playing side. More than a dozen players departed, including experienced performers, such as Emery, Robinson and Weaver. Apart from Burgess, Green and the durable Thomas, it was mainly locals who were retained. Because of the delay caused by the re-election meeting, the best available free transfers had been snapped up, but County still managed to obtain Scottish international Bobby McKay, Jimmy Smith – holder of the Scottish League goal-scoring record – and Jimmy Kelso, who was destined to become a popular figure at Somerton. Other signings were solid lower Division players, such as Briggs, Craven, Helsby and Jenkins.

The first game of the 1935/36 season, at home to Swindon, was watched by a healthy 11,408 crowd, due to the renewed interest in the Club. There were no less than eight new players in the side which drew 2-2. The first away game, at Ashton Gate, was won 2-1, when the brains behind the team belonged to the quick thinking and tricky McKay. He was one of the old-fashioned inside-forwards who seemed to run around with the ball glued to his boots. The first worrying cracks appeared a few days later when County crashed 1-7 at Coventry, with City's Bourton scoring a hat-trick. Inconsistent as ever, County then went four games without defeat, before again losing 1-7, this time at Brighton.

The following week the side lost 3-4 at home to Q.P.R., but of more significance than the result was the fact that reserve outside-right Albert Derrick made his debut at centre-forward. Derrick had turned professional the previous season, along with local Tommy Appleby, and both played in the game because of an ever increasing injury list which now included Haycox, Hugh, Green and White.

A week after the Q.P.R. game, came the County's best performance of the season. Smith obtained a hat-trick as the side won 5-2 at Watford. Newport were in a quite respectable seventh position, but in the next five games only one goal was scored, and after that run the side found themselves struggling in 20th position. On October the 26th, County drew 0-0 with Bournemouth, a significant event for the defence did not keep another clean sheet until

the Bristol Rovers match on March the 21st. There were also injuries amongst the forwards, with Haycox, Smith and Green out. The veteran Luton goalscorer Andy Rennie was signed, but lasted only three matches.

At Luton, there was another debacle as the side went down 0-7. In a four match spell the team scored three goals and conceded 18, but still continued to attract reasonable gates. In the F.A.Cup, Newport went down to a hotly disputed Southend goal, with Williamson claiming that he had stopped the ball crossing the goal line. Drafting Burgess into the attack against Northampton worked wonders, with a 5-1 win, but then it was back to normal. The following week, the side was trounced 0-6 at Crystal Palace, and the next Saturday (Christmas Day) by the same score at home to Torquay. At this time it was felt that anything was worth trying to change the team's luck, and the playing strip was changed to red and white stripes, whilst in order to mark this alteration the programme cover was changed from amber to red.

Things perked up at the start of 1936, for two of the first three games in the New Year were won 2-1, including the away game at Southend, but after a 3-3 draw at Exeter the revival petered out. Seven of the next eight matches were lost, including the Welsh Cup-tie at Swansea. Five goals were conceded at home to both Watford and Crystal Palace, and the gate for the Notts County match was under 3,000.

Three successive home wins gave renewed hope, but the away form was still terrible with five of the last six games being lost, and from then on the team never rose above 21st place. The introduction of Trevor Jones, Matt O'Mahoney and young Alfie Clarke stabilised matters, with ten points gained from the last eleven games, but by then it was too late to avoid seeking re-election again. The attack had scored 60 goals with the emerging Albert Derrick ending up as top marksman, but the sieve-like defence had let in 111, with the opposition scoring in every away match.

Newport County paid their £100 fee, and were duly re-elected to the Football League in June 1936. Even the Directors were not immune to the changes at Somerton Park and initially half the Board left. During the season, there had been challenges and counter-challenges, and after further resignations – including that of founder Bert Moss – the Board was down to five Directors. Those left comprised Nixon, Wood, A.A. Wright, Dr. Wade and H.J. Petty – the latter was to become the Newport Coroner.

Louis Page was still Manager, but old hand Stan Bowsher followed Charlie Bates and Harry Martin as Trainer. During the close season a record amount was spent to try and attract a better standard of player. Once again there were an amazing number of changes, and although half a dozen players remained – including Kelso, Thomas, Derrick and Appleby – many regulars, such as Briggs, Burgess and Green departed. Among those to arrive were the Everton and Wales full-back Ben Williams, Arthur Hickman, Billy 'W.M.' Owen and Ray Lawrance.

Harry Duggan and Jimmy Kelso in training.
(1936/37 season)

On August the 29th, the team ran out to oppose Watford, and amongst all the other changes, the banking at the Ground had been improved, with over 1,000 tons of soil taken from the Newport Castle precincts. Once again the side that lined up before a healthy five figure crowd was unrecognisable from a few months earlier, with nine players making their debuts for Newport. Despite a goal from Hickman, County lost 1–3. With goalkeeper Joe Hillier injured, his place was subsequently taken by Jack Bowles, then by the hastily signed Fred Marsh. The second game was lost 0–2 at Brighton, and three days later, at Southend, Bowles had to retrieve the ball nine times from the back of the net, with United's Lane and Goddard scoring hat–tricks. The first five games were all lost – with County scoring six and conceding 21. As something of a consolation, the gate for the home game with Cardiff was a record 16,732, producing takings of £877. Billy Thomas was recalled for the fourth match, at home to Brighton, and scored County's only goal in a 1–4 defeat. After the match, 100 or so supporters congregated at their usual pitch, behind the Grandstand, giving vent to their disapproval.

County's best performance of the season, up to then, came when they travelled to unbeaten Bristol Rovers and drew 1–1. In the next three games, County scored only one goal, but secured two points, from home draws with Gillingham and Swindon. Then trips to London brought a 2–7 defeat at Millwall – where Williams suffered from pulled muscles in the first five minutes – and a 1–6 reverse at Crystal Palace, when Lawrance was injured.

Around this time, County made a few significant signings which were to form the springboard for their future promotion. First to arrive was the veteran right winger Harry

Duggan, for £1,500. After him came South–African left winger Lance Carr, the incomparable centre–half Norman Low, – for £1,750 – and utility player Tommy Wood from Aston Villa, although they did not really make their presence felt until the New Year.

At the end of November the side gave an excellent display beating Bristol City 3–0 in the F.A.Cup, but in the second round came disaster at Reading. Les Edwards' illness meant a last minute reshuffle, and Duggan's two goals were not enough to stave off a 2–7 reverse. Home gates were holding up remarkably well after County's efforts to improve their side, for hundreds of new supporters had been found in Newport and the nearby Valleys. In those days, there was none of the modern commercial aspect to football, and everything depended upon gates and transfers. At Newport, the bank manager would arrive at home games by taxi and take away the receipts!

On January 2nd, the lowest crowd of the season turned up, but there were still 4,574 present, and that would have seemed an excellent gate a few years earlier. The missing fans must have been kicking themselves afterwards, for the Ironsides gave their best display of the season, beating Southend 6–2, with Chadwick netting a hat–trick. The following Saturday, the side came away 1–0 winners from Ninian Park, thanks to Duggan, who was rapidly making himself a favourite.

Derrick, recalled to the first team, scored three in a 4–4 draw at Gillingham, and followed up with two in a comprehensive 4–0 home defeat of Aldershot. After a splendid 2–1 win at Swindon, it was a blow when the team were unable to beat Millwall or Crystal Palace at home. But at least there was some consolation, when Porth were hammered 5–0 in the Welsh Cup, with Derrick scoring another hat–trick. After a 1–3 reverse at Exeter, Reading visited County. This was Ben Williams' first match since October 10th, and his experience helped County to a 3–0 victory, with Chadwick obtaining another hat–trick.

The county defence was proving as inconsistent as ever, for in a five match spell, County kept four clean sheets, and in the other match at Q.P.R. let in six! The attack was proving much livelier than early in the season, and in the next round of the Welsh Cup, Swansea went down 0–7, with Derrick scoring four. The reserves were also showing good form, beating Caerphilly 10–1 and Aberdare 12–1.

Despite a 0–5 aberration at Bournemouth, four of the next five League matches were won, and this clearly stood the side in good stead for their re–election battle. A stubborn fight against the threat of relegation can often bring in the crowds, and the games with Bournemouth and Notts County attracted gates of 10,007 and 12,324.

In the semi–final of the Welsh Cup, County went down 2–3 to Rhyl at Gay Meadow. In the League, only one of the final four games was won, but enough points had been scraped up to ward off re–election. The team may have got back into the Football League, but Ipswich were waiting in the wings, and the following year were admitted, at Gillingham's expense.

The County team had suffered because of the absence of Captain, Ben Williams, and their avoidance of re-election owed much to his leadership at a critical stage of the season. There were considerable bright spots over the season. Support had been good, indeed, it was only marginally worse than that of promoted Luton, and the reserves, splendidly skippered by Ray Lawrance, won the Welsh League with a goal tally of 114. Only the brilliance of Low had kept Lawrance out of the first team.

At last, stability seemed to be returning to Newport County. The club retained more experienced players than normal during the close season, and the nucleus of a promotion side was being built. Although it is Billy McCandless, who is normally associated with the promotion side, it was Louis Page who signed many of the players and set the ball in motion. Some players – such as Thomas, Vickers and Alfie Clarke – were now given free transfers, and others, including Lance Carr, Hillier and John, were made available for transfer. Although Derrick was transfer-listed, he was subsequently retained. Six of those retained were destined to play in the promotion side – Hickman, "W.M." Owen, Low, Duggan, Wood and Lawrance. Among the new arrivals was another Billy Owen; he was designated "W.E." (Exeter), to distinguish him from "W.M." (Manchester). Other arrivals were the Brinton brothers, Pearson and Webb. On May the 12th, came a signing that was to contribute greatly to the post-war side, that of Ray Wilcox. For once, the first County side had a familiar ring about it, with old favourites such as Kelso, Low and Duggan.

The start was also familiar, with a 2-2 home draw versus Exeter being followed by away defeats at Gillingham and Swindon. Home form soon picked up, with wins over Gillingham and Aldershot. The away form was disastrous however, with the first five games being lost.

By the County's standards, a great deal of money had been ploughed into the team, with the signing of players such as Duggan and Low. The mediocre start to the season had clearly disgruntled the Board, for when the team for the Gillingham match on September 9th was announced, there were six changes. Eventually three changes were made, and Louis Page, who had been ill at the end of the previous season, was sacked. The move was not without acrimony, for Page took Newport County to Court for wrongful dismissal. He subsequently won his case, but by that time McCandless had been appointed Manager, and Page was unable to regain his post. As part of the new set-up, Bill Poyntz took over from Stan Bowsher as Trainer.

Despite everything, there seemed to be more interest in Newport County than for many years. At the start of the season, the "Football Argus" had spoken of " *A going concern with a bright future....a healthy body of support, immense optimism and an enthusiasm nothing can quench.* " 11,574 turned up as Newport gave a magnificent performance in defeating Notts County 3-0. Even better was to follow a week later, for a crowd of 24,268 was present to see the side take on local rivals, Cardiff City. This was the highest ever attendance at Somerton Park. The gates opened up at mid-day, an unheard of event, and the staff took until the next day counting the coins. A cracking game finished 1-1, County's goal coming from Duggan. Remarkably, only Kelso remained of the side which had entertained Cardiff the previous season, and he was destined to be transferred to City at the end of the season.

(Left) Early September 1937. Tommy Appleby and Jimmy Kelso, after a 0-2 defeat at Brighton. The team stayed on, and lost 2-9 at Southend!
(Above) Ray Lawrance and Norman Low in pre-season training - 1937.

County's squad meet Willy Pantzers midgets from a local circus. Usually the team's forwards were the midgets!

After the Notts County match the side went eight League games without defeat, conceding only three goals. The team now playing regularly, showed only two changes from the one that Page had started with, Lawrance and Derrick replacing Webb and Edwards.

At the end of November, Newport were paired with Kidderminster in the F.A.Cup. County scored in the last seconds, to draw 2-2 away, and won 4-1 at Somerton. Jack Brinton, who had played only a handful of first team matches, scored a hat-trick. A day later, the team gained a useful League point at Mansfield, in snow and driving wind. In the Second Round of the F.A.Cup, Bournemouth were beaten 2-1. County were through to the third round for the first time since 1922, when they had played Newcastle. Unfortunately, they had just hit a patch of bad form, and from four League matches the team had secured just one point, failing to find the net once.

In the Third Round, Newport made their first ever visit to Bradford Park Avenue. Nobody could have forecast the result, for the previously goalshy attack scored four times, but disasters at the other end meant a 4-7 defeat! The run of bad results adversely affected attendances, and for the next home match, with Torquay, only 3,713 were present. Despite the odd bad result, including a 0-5 thrashing at Aldershot, performances were a great improvement on earlier years. The defence was no longer leaking goals at the rate of 100 a season, and there was the great benefit of having a settled side. By the end of the season, seven players had made 34 League appearances or more, and Duggan was only prevented from doing so by injury.

In the Welsh Cup, the County enjoyed a good 6-2 win over Bristol City. Six days later, the scoreline was exactly reversed, when the team made its first visit to the Continent, meeting a Combined Dutch XI, in Rotterdam. It was a sign of the times that the gate at Ninian Park, 25,608, was considerably less than expected because of rain.

The game was lost 1-3 to Cardiff, but thereafter the defence did not concede more than two goals in any match, and indeed in a nine game spell the side let in only four goals. The Welsh Cup competition was at something of a low ebb at this time, being dominated by English clubs. Having beaten Bristol City and Cheltenham, County were drawn away to Shrewsbury in the semi-final. W.M. Owen reverted to his original centre-forward role, and scored twice, but it was insufficient to ward off a 2-3 defeat after extra time. County agreed to play on because of their backlog of outstanding matches.

Overall, 1937-38 had been a good season, with an unfamiliar consistency beginning to develop. Neighbouring Lovells had also done well, winning the Welsh League for the second time; their highest goalscorer was ex-Ironside, Alfie Clarke, with 25.

At the end of the season, A.A. Wright, an autocratic Chairman, resigned. There were also some changes on the playing side. Kelso joined Cardiff, for £1,050, Pearson left, and Chadwick joined newly elected Ipswich. Promising Maurice Sullivan was transferred to Derby, where he shared digs with Jack Brinton who had moved there earlier. For the forthcoming season County had a nucleus of experienced players who could hold their own with any Third Division team. The club was fortunate to sign a few players who would enhance the squad even more. To replace the consistent Pearson in goal, County obtained Alex Ferguson, a Scot with an especially long kick of the old leather ball. Two contrasting new full-backs arrived, Bill Roberts who would tackle first and ask questions afterwards, and the cultured Len Richards. The other two pieces that completed the jigsaw, were Arthur Hydes – a red-haired goalscorer from Leeds – and Lance Carr, who had seen the error of his ways and returned to Somerton Park.

The fixture list could scarcely have been less kind to County, for after two away games, they were due to meet Cardiff in their first home encounter. The team, in fact, did itself a power of good by winning 3-1 at Orient, courtesy of Duggan, Carr and Hearty (own goal). A strange phenomenon was now to descend upon Newport County. The club, which normally liked to change the side like nobody's business, put out the same team for the first seven matches of the season. The situation became even stranger as the year progressed, for, by the penultimate game of 1938, only 13 different players had been used for League matches, the only newcomers being Jack Webb and W.M. Owen.

For the first home match, with Cardiff, the club programme reverted to an amber cover, which was meant to mirror a reversion to the club's traditional black and amber kit. All did not go according to plan however, for when the shirts arrived, instead of being amber shirts with black hoops, they were black shirts with amber hoops! These had to be used for the early matches until the matter could be rectified. There was a tremendous interest in the Cardiff match, and when the teams took the field, there were 18,387 spectators present, the receipts amounting to £1,103. The County had a welcome 3–0 victory, with goals from Hydes (two) and Carr.

There was now real optimism at Somerton Park, with gates ten times what they had been in the dark days. Efforts had been made to improve the Ground with better banking and a new buffet bar, and on the playing side the introduction of an "A" team was a constructive move.

The second home game, versus Watford, was won, and two 1–1 draws followed. After six matches, Newport were in joint second place, with eight points. After a 0–2 reverse at struggling Notts County, Newport began a winning run. They first defeated top of the table Aldershot, then, after a grand 2–0 win at Bristol City, they returned to Somerton Park to beat second placed Crystal Palace 2–0. On October the 8th, County were top of the table and they never lost that position. The following Saturday the team won 4–1 at Ipswich, and County were showing impressive form, especially in defence. During the first seven home matches only one goal was conceded, against Northampton – a far cry from the days when nine goals would be conceded in one game. The team then had a run of nine games with only one goal against, including a 1–0 victory of Bristol Rovers in the Division 3 Cup. This was a disastrously unpopular competition, for the match attracted only 709 spectators and receipts of £34.

Newport were now in the middle of a promotion winning run, for in a spell of twelve matches, only two points were dropped, from successive 0–0 draws with Exeter and Bristol Rovers. From September 24th until Boxing Day the side was undefeated. The Annual Report in mid October painted an optimistic picture. Average gates had risen from 8,650 to 9,364, the best ever. From November the 5th to Christmas Eve, the nine League and Cup games resulted in eight wins and a draw. The only draw came at Reading in the F.A.Cup, but County triumphed 3–1 in the replay, and lowly Horden Colliery were overcome 3–2 in the Second Round. The 2–1 win over Orient, in quagmire conditions on Christmas Eve marked County's sixth successive League win.

The long–suffering Newport fans must have wondered whether they were watching the right side, but memories of the past came flooding back on Boxing Day with the most incredible result in the club's history. Before the match, the team's record read: played 19, won 13, goals for 30, goals against 10. Those numerous fans who travelled to Swindon can scarcely have believed their eyes, as the team was slaughtered 0–8. At six goals down, Bill Roberts rolled up his sleeves and shouted, " *Come on, lads, we're still in with a chance !* " Even stranger things were to follow the next day, for County won the return match by 6–4. Throughout the season the attack was overshadowed by the defence, and the Swindon game saw the side's only hat–trick, performed by winger Lance Carr.

31st December 1938. County beat Cardiff 2-1 at Ninian Park, before almost 40,000 fans.

This game was watched by the highest home attendance of the season, 20,586, and an even bigger crowd saw the next fixture. 40,187 turned out at Ninian Park, to see County win 2–1.

The New Year marked the only really disappointing point of the season. Walsall were entertained in the Third Round of the F.A.Cup and went away 2–0 winners. This was one season, when the old cliche about concentrating on the League had a truthful ring about it, for, barring accidents, County were heading for Division Two for the first time in their existence. By some fluke, the next five games after the Swindon matches were all played away. Three of these were won, with only three goals conceded, to maintain the club's top of the table position.

February was not the most thrilling month, with five points gained from five matches, but with no outstanding side in the Division, County remained top. It suited Newport that, in the promotion tussle, Crystal Palace were held 1–1 before a crowd of 29,155, Derrick equalising with two minutes left. A thousand Newport fans travelled up, and the *"Excursion de Luxe"* cost 17/9d (89p) – including dinner and supper!

Despite their League excellence, County had a disappointing year, cup-wise. A 1–3 home defeat by Torquay in the Third Division Cup was followed by a 1–5 Welsh Cup hammering at Ninian Park, with City's Egan grabbing a hat-trick. Many of those fans who read the disappointing news the next day would have been more interested in the other news. Newport County and their former Chairman A.A. Wright, the well-known local fruiterer, had fallen out, and the club was desperate for money. *"Town Fund for Newport County"*, announced the "Western Mail" on March the 9th, after an extraordinary shareholders' meeting the previous night. Wright had obtained judgement against the club for £4,621–75 plus costs. He had resigned at the end of the 1937–38 season, and claimed money during the close season. The club had offered £250 down and the rest as soon at it could be raised. Wright had turned this down, and instead claimed 10% of all match receipts plus a share of transfer fees. Having made a loss of £2,000 the previous season, the Directors felt unable to accept this method. The unhappy situation could have led to liquidation or the sale of leading players. At the meeting, it was resolved to discharge the debt in full, with the Supporters' Club donating the first £100.

In March, the local heroes were awarded a rare accolade. They were filmed, by the Newport and District Amateur Film Society, the film being shown at the Little Theatre, Dock Street on March 27th and 28th. Could it still exist, in some dark vault?

From the beginning of March, the County had an unbeaten run of nine games, although six of these were draws. It kept the team out in front, and the defence was still playing excellently, keeping six clean sheets. The final game of the run was a 3–0 home victory over Southend, the last goal

being a Wood 35 yarder. A wildly excited crowd invaded the pitch and carried Low and Duggan to the dressing rooms, for Newport County had won a well merited first promotion.

After all the euphoria, the final two games became an anti-climax. Only 7,260 saw the last home match, with Port Vale, when the Potteries team became the only side to do the double over County. The final match, at Southend, was used to blood local youngsters Turner and Newall, and resulted in a humiliating 0–5 defeat. County obtained 55 points, an exceedingly low total to achieve promotion, but were, undoubtedly, the best side in the Division. The defence, superbly marshalled by Low, conceded only 45 goals, with 12 coming in the Swindon matches. For the first time ever County made a profit, excluding outgoing transfers. Gate receipts had amounted to more than £13,500. The same season, Lovells were also Champions, of the Western League Division 1.

The County side will long be etched in the minds of those supporters who saw them, but the Board also deserve great credit, for in tremendously difficult circumstances they held firm. They kept the best players, and the result was promotion. The Chairman at that time was Capt. H.J. Petty, a well-known solicitor and the local Coroner. Other directors were the Mayor – J.R. Wardell – George Nixon, now resident in Bognor Regis, businessman C.V. Wood and Dr. W.E. Wade, brother of a Cardiff City director.

1939. The Division 3 (South) Championship Shield on display.

On April the 21st, the "Echo" stated that J.R. Wardell had promised Mr. Wright the full amount outstanding by May 15th. The League had indeed insisted that the liability must be discharged by its meeting in the last week in May. With the local pride aroused by the team's performances, New-portonians rallied round, and the problem was overcome.

The season's end had a gala air about it. Derby, as part of Jack Brinton's transfer, had promised to play a friendly, and their star-studded side arrived at Somerton. On May 5th, a celebratory Dinner was held at the King's Head, when an ornate souvenir menu was produced, which contained various photographs.

**RICHARDS.**
Newport County's left-back, at Home Park on Saturday.

**ERNIE BRINTON.**
Newport County's left half-back, if the team to play at Home Park on Saturday.

(Left and right) 2 caricatures of the 1939 promotion side.   (Centre) Promotion manager Billy McCandless in usual unsmiling pose!

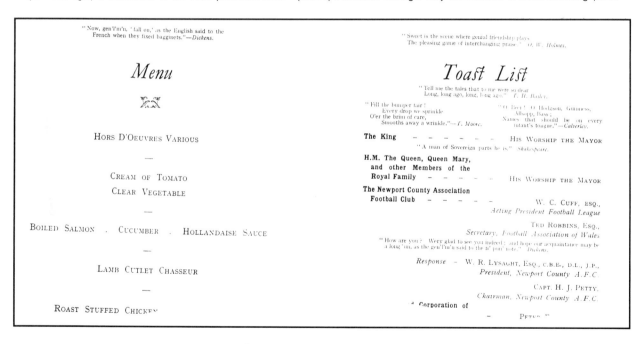

County's Promotion menue - 1939.

Doubtless, amid the banter over the Ice Pudding Tutti Frutti and Pineapple Charlotte, there was little thought given to the dark clouds rolling in from Europe. Even before the season's end, the club programme had carried an advertisement: *"Join the T.A. and protect your home. Enlist at the Corn Exchange."* The civic banquet was aimed at the 'bigwigs', with the likes of Stanley Rous of the F.A. and William Cuff of the Football League attending, but for the ordinary supporters a meeting was held at the Little Theatre,

Dock Street. The place was packed out with every comment receiving thunderous applause. J.R. Wardell was there with the Championship shield. Many Old Boys, including Billy Gaughan, were also in attendance.

Always a Cinderella club, County's success was well received, and many telegrams of congratulation were received. One came from E.J. Morgan, of Caerphilly, who had refereed County's first ever match:

"I can remember the days when the club's matches did not draw enough support to pay the officials, and their position today is due largely to the generosity and pioneer enthusiasm of my friend, Mr. Bert Moss".

Thoughts now turned to 1939–40. " Our task has only started", announced Billy McCandless. All the promotion squad was retained, with the exception of reserves, Reid, Morris and Harvey. Only one signing of note was made. As the side had been somewhat lacking in firepower, goalscorer Walter Robbins was bought from West Bromwich for a substantial sum. In view of the side's previous performances, there was no reason to suppose it would not do well in Division Two.

Various ground improvements were made for the new season. The pitch appeared larger, because the greyhound syndicate had altered the bends, and moveable fencing had been installed, which would be taken down for football matches.

There were new goalposts, for the League had now ruled that they should be elliptical instead of square. A new scoreboard had been erected, next to the Tote, replacing one which a gale had blown down. A new drainage system had been installed too, to prevent the build-up of mud, for which Somerton Park was famous.

The (rare) handbook that was issued following promotion, and the County's Promotion Board together with their Patron and the Mayor.

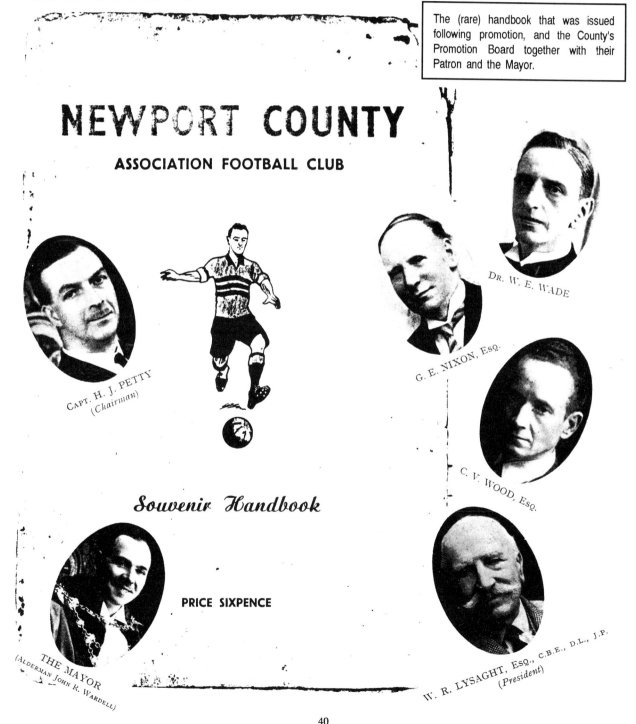

# NEWPORT COUNTY
## ASSOCIATION FOOTBALL CLUB

CAPT. H. J. PETTY
(Chairman)

DR. W. E. WADE

G. E. NIXON, ESQ.

C. V. WOOD, ESQ.

*Souvenir Handbook*

**PRICE SIXPENCE**

THE MAYOR
(ALDERMAN JOHN R. WARDELL)

W. R. LYSAGHT, ESQ., C.B.E., D.L., J.P.
(President)

With what pride must the 13,000 supporters have watched their side turn out to play Southampton? J.R. Wardell led the sides out on to the pitch, and County proceeded to give a fine display, beating the Saints 3–1, with goals from Hydes (two) and Hickman. On August the 31st, 19,700 fans assembled to see the team play Tottenham Hotspur. What illustrious company County were now keeping! On that day, the Government called up all Armed Forces recruits. Wardell, with his Wolverhampton twang, warned over the loudspeakers that it could be the last match. At half-time, came a request over the loudspeaker for all Monmouthshire Territorial Volunteers to report to their depots, as soon as possible. The game itself was hard fought, with Hickman securing a 1–1 draw. On September the 2nd, County arrived in Nottingham 40 minutes late because of a rail delay, and lost 1–2. But of greater moment was the fact that on that morning Germany had invaded Poland. On the following day, war was declared.

Initially clubs arranged a series of friendlies. The handbook, which had been produced to celebrate promotion, had been intended for release at the Coventry game, but that and the away game with Burnley were cancelled. From now on, with men called up for the war, or given other duties, it would be difficult to put out a proper side. For the County's first friendly, at Cardiff on September the 16th, young Wilcox came in, and County lost 0–2. In the makeshift programme appeared the words: *"Every man and woman is carrying on calmly, steadfastly. That is the spirit that will smash the Nazis and free their victims from slavery."* The Armed Forces were now being admitted into matches at half price.

For the next friendly, a 0–5 defeat at Reading, Derrick, Mogford, Robbins and the veteran Higgins came in. The first home match, versus Birmingham, took place on September 30th and a respectable crowd of 3,066 turned up. A guest player, Donald of Airdrie, played at centre-forward. Hickman scored twice, in a 2–2 draw, but missed a penalty. The Chief Constable of Birmingham had banned all matches in the city, and the £156 gate receipts, less expenses, all went to the victors. By this time, Ferguson, Webb, the two Owens, Lawrance and Higgins were firemen, Richards was working at Newport Docks, Robbins at Cardiff; Low, Brinton and Carr were at Bristol Aerodrome and almost all the others were in the A.R.P. Roberts and the former soldier Derrick had already been called up.

The home game with Swansea attracted only 1,677, and after the return game at the Vetch, the ban on competitive football was lifted. A network of war-time Leagues was set up. County were in the League (West), along with a small number of Football League teams, which would play each other twice.

A 0–2 home defeat by Swindon was followed by a 3–2 victory at Bristol Rovers, and a 2–1 win at Swansea. The next home game, versus Torquay, which was won by a Robbins goal, was seen by 802. From the after-tax takings of £30, County derived £10. Because of the financial situation, McCandless and his staff were now acting in an honorary capacity.

After a 3–1 win over Cardiff, came a 0–2 reverse at Plymouth, before a 3,500 crowd. County were guilty of less than gentlemanly behaviour, for the match was held up for several minutes following a punch-up, during which Gorman was hit. The next match, at Swindon, was lost by a doubtful last minute penalty.

December 16th marked a memorable event, for Newport County played its first match at Rodney Parade. The military had already taken over the buffet premises at Somerton, and now a move to the rugby ground was necessitated by the imposition of the blackout. The Company which owned Somerton desired to stage greyhound meetings on Saturday afternoons. It was decided that both sets of fans could use their season tickets to watch soccer and rugby. The match, against Bristol Rovers who were similarly homeless, was lost 0–1 on a bitterly cold day, but the gate was up – to 1,752. Hickman and Wood returned to Birmingham. Hydes made a brief return, but by this time Roberts and Derrick were serving in France. In the last game of 1939, County lost 2–6 at Torquay. A 2–0 Welsh Cup replay win over Lovells opened 1940.

It was a strange season, and, after the Christmas morning match with Bristol City, the side played ten consecutive League and Cup matches away from home. Newport demolished Cardiff 5–0 in a Welsh Cup replay, but only 800 turned up. After a 5–3 midweek victory over Bristol Rovers, a 4,179 crowd saw the return, three days later, but Newport lost 0–2.

Because of the great difficulties, the season was considerably extended, and this meant that Rodney Parade had to be vacated due to the onset of the cricket season. Fortunately, Lovells were prepared to let the club use their little Rexville ground, enabling County to fulfil their fixtures. Things turned out remarkably well on the pitch, for five games were played at the ground, and every one was won, and by at least a three goal margin! Interest had by now waned however, and only around 500 were turning up for each game. Players were now receiving very little, and McCandless suggested that a team of amateurs should be used, but the players would not hear of it, and insisted on carrying on.

After Swindon were beaten 5–2, for the next match, Richards, Low and Brinton were absent on war work, and Robbins was out injured. All four, who had played regularly, missed the rest of the season. County still won the game, and did even better on June the 1st, beating Torquay 11–0. Tommy Appleby scored four, and W.E. Owen three. On June 7th and 8th, County played the same fixture twice, at home to Plymouth. Just the one programme was produced, and the suggestion was made that one game should be played and four points awarded, but Argyle decided on an overnight stay, with County agreeing to contribute towards their expenses. County won 6–3 and 5–2, with Appleby scoring a hat-trick in the second game. County's Rexville stay produced the remarkable record of played five, won five, 31 goals for and 8 against. Appleby scored in every match and contributed twelve goals.

A panorama of pre-war Somerton Park, with County's promotion side in action.

The match on June 8th was Newport's last competitive encounter for five years. Things had been going downhill, without even a ground to play on, and the death of Capt. Petty was a further blow. During these five years, the only match played was a friendly with Lovells on Christmas Day, 1940, to pay for expenses the club had promised Plymouth. The single sheet programme carried *"A Denial."* *"Rumour had been current in parts of Newport that "the County" has closed down indefinitely. The Board of Directors of Newport County A.F.C. which to deny these statements, and to assure supporters that on resumption of League football, Newport County's team will be ready to take its place amongst the clubs of the Second Division of the English League. Newport County has thrived on its difficulties, and it still lives"*.

With County's closure, the normally neglected Lovells Athletic was suddenly thrust into the limelight. Lovells now became the main team of the town and began to mix with the elite of the football world. In 1941-42, the side missed its claim to invincibility only by an end of season charity defeat, but it was the following season that it hit the headlines. Bolstered by various County players, Lovells appeared in the Football League West, facing various Football League teams. The side got off to a great start, winning nine games out of ten. Cardiff City were hammered 8-4, with Billy Lucas scoring four.

On November the 14th came some amazing scenes at Ninian Park. City were awarded an obscure penalty, and eventually, Ferguson saved Wright's shot. A Cardiff player was kicked, and pandemonium broke out. Part of the crowd invaded the pitch, and the referee was surrounded by spectators and players. The players went off for a while, and Herbert Merrett insisted on both sides lining up and shaking hands. With Lovells doing so well, a record 4,000 saw thew beat Bath 2-1. A former "Argus" employee sent home a cutting from the *"Vancouver Sun"*. Headed *"Candy Club"*, the article read: *"The greatest surprise of Britain's*

*football season is the mighty challenge of a business house team – Lovells Athletic – which is making war-time sports history".* Because of the peculiar structure of war-time football, the League West finished on Christmas Day, when Lovells beat Aberaman 5-0. Lovells had won the League, with 30 points from 18 games. In the North Championship, from Boxing Day to May 1st, Lovells finished second to Liverpool, and above the dozens of Football League sides participating.

1943-44 saw Lovells again topping the League West, one point clear of Cardiff. Capable of beating Swansea 9-0 and Bristol City 6-0, the side began to build up a large following. A cup match with Cardiff attracted 7,000 and the second round game with Bath 7,200. In the latter match, Ferguson argued against a penalty decision, and was sent off. At the end, supporters invaded the pitch and booed off the referee, who was escorted away by the police.

The following season, Lovells finished third in the League West, and this time were an impressive third in the League North Cup, behind Liverpool and Stoke (52 clubs competed.) When Lovells played Cardiff in the Cup, 12,000 were present at Ninian Park, and an incredible 10,000 at the little Rexville ground. Things were changing however, for the War was drawing to a close, as were the club's glory years. On May 19th, the side played its last home game as a "League" club, beating Swansea 3-0, the return game taking place the following week.

Throughout the War years, Lovells had represented Newport with pride. Now the club was to revert to its former position as a Works side, and with the European War ending in April – and the Far East in August – despite all the doubts and rumours, Newport County was back in business. It took great faith from all concerned, for County had not played a competitive match for five years. Somerton Park resembled a disaster area and the players on the club's books were by now in the veteran stage.

# CHAPTER 4

# Back To Normality

**With the Compliments of**

## LOVELL'S ATH. A. F. C:

PRESIDENT.             G. F. LOVELL ESQ. J. P.
VICE PRESIDENTS:  RT. HON. WM. BRACE P.C.
                              R. J. LANGMAID ESQ
                              LT. COL.
                              R. C. L. THOMAS J.P. D.L.
CHAIRMAN            H. LOVELL ESQ.
HON. TREASURER:  J. M. PARRY:
SECY. MANAGER: R. W. MACDONALD.

THE FOOTBALL LEAGUE WEST
&
THE FOOTBALL LEAGUE (WAR) CUP
QUALIFYING COMPETITION

FIXTURES
SEASON 1944-45

Lovell's Athletic successfully flew
the flag for Newport during the War

## Newport County A.F.C.

●

FIXTURES
SEASON 1945/6

●

Price : One Penny.

In 1945 the County came back upon the scene

In April 1945, a new Board was formed. Negotiations were concluded with the Arms Park Company, but the final go-ahead was not received until early July. County had almost ceased to exist, and Harold John and his fellow Directors took on the liabilities, of £15,890-78. Such was the enthusiasm of Board and supporters, that within four years the debt was cleared.

On July the 1st, McCandless was re-appointed Manager. Around that time, he made his famous comment, that he was not starting at rock bottom, but 100 yards below it! The Ground, which the club had only just received permission to use, was available only on matchdays, with players meeting just a few hours before kick-off. The Ground, in a dreadful state, had been used to store equipment during the War, with obvious results. McCandless had no office until July 14th, and no phone until a month later. With only veterans and local youngsters to call on, nobody could expect a flying start.

On the playing front things looked black for County. The football authorities had decided to institute two regional Leagues, made up of First and Second Division clubs, for the forthcoming season. This meant that County, with a makeshift team, would have to take on the likes of Arsenal and Aston Villa. The Football League agreed that teams could make use of up to six "guest" players in their matches, but in the F.A.Cup only registered players and amateurs could be used.

On August the 18th, the Final Trial took place, and one week later County walked out at Brentford to play their first competitive match for five years. The team included eight of the earlier promotion side – six years later! The line-up was:- *Ferguson, Webb, Warhurst, Owen, Low, Brinton, Derrick, Mogford, Appleby, Wood and Carr.*

County put up a gallant fight but lost, although a minute from the end Derrick scored the club's first goal for five years. Things went downhill five days later, when on a rain-soaked Somerton pitch, Fulham won 5-1. The *"Echo"* summed thing up the following day: *" Manager Billy McCandless, sitting on his old seat on the touch-line, like the sphinx of Somerton, was the least demonstrative, as he watched Newport County swamped by Fulham last evening, but no doubt he did a lot of hard thinking".* A last minute penalty enabled rugged Ronnie Rooke to complete his hat-trick in the match. After defeats by Brentford (0-5) and Chelsea (1-3), County created a shock by beating Charlton (with four wins behind them) 2-1. County soon reverted to form, with five of the next seven games lost. The post-war boom meant gates of over 10,000. Despite heavy defeats, the defence remained much the same, with Owen–Low–Brinton almost always forming the half-back line. The veteran Derrick was a regular, scoring frequently, but the rest of the forward line came and went.

A 1-7 defeat by Coventry was not an ideal preparation for the F.A.Cup. County were drawn against lowly Torquay, the competition being staged on a home and away basis that season. As a Second Division club, Newport should not have been playing them, but their exemption forms had been submitted too late. Such was County's luck, that on the day before the away leg, there was a break-in at Somerton Park, and the team's kit was stolen from the dressing-rooms. In those days of rationing, clothing was almost impossible to come by and the reserves' kit was used, leaving the reserves to find what outfits they could, for their match with Barry. The stolen kit was found the next day, strewn along Chepstow Road. Goals from Derrick allowed the side to win the first cup match, and draw the second.

Lovells were now playing at a level far below their ability, and lost only five of 36 Welsh League games. In the F.A.Cup, they went through against Bournemouth, winning the first leg 4–1.

County beat Luton 4–0 in the League, with Derrick hitting a hat-trick, before the Second Round of the F.A.Cup, when Exeter were beaten twice, with recently demobbed Hydes scoring twice. Such was life at the time, that the club was even unable to give away fixture lists. There were also long delays in obtaining a licence from the Food Controller to re-open the buffet, leaving visiting fans famished.

The next five games were lost, not surprisingly, as these included star-studded Villa and Arsenal, who were each played twice. What holiday fixtures! Christmas Day, home to Arsenal, Boxing Day, away to the Gunners at White Hart Lane – Highbury being a Civil Defence Depot. In the home game, Newport gave a fine performance. In the first half, full-back Avery lobbed the ball over Griggs, but later goals by Cumner and Henley gave Arsenal an undeserved win. The next day however, an Arsenal side which included such names as Hapgood, Joy and Bastin, triumphed 7–0. Batty, just signed full-time from Villa, played in the match.

A bad start to the New Year, with two Third Round defeats by Southampton, was followed by County's best spell. Five of the next six matches were won. Recently signed Channel Islander Fred Leamon scored in his first six matches. After their 3–0 victory over Plymouth on January the 12th, County were five points above bottom-placed Argyle. Two wins over Plymouth were followed by a more unexpected double over Portsmouth.

When County left the F.A.Cup, Lovells were also knocked out, but it was a great achievement for the town to have two sides in the Third Round. After beating Bath twice, Athletic were drawn against mighty Wolves. Nearly 10,000 packed into the little ground, with the local side facing three internationals. Lovells went in front, but ultimately fell to four late goals. The away leg was lost 0–4.

There were numerous changes in the County team, and departures included Derrick and Hydes. At Molineux, Wolves won 5–2, with Westcott scoring a hat-trick. The home game with West Ham was broadcast on radio. The famous Newportonian commentator, Raymond Glendenning, announced that Bill Roberts would be leaving to go into

business. In the match itself, County obtained an honourable draw, with Leamon netting twice.

That was the end of the good news however, for the team, which had struggled, went to pieces and lost its final nine games. To be fair, County began to put out a completely different side, with various loan players, such as the West Brom. trio of Harris, Southam and McNab.

13,410 turned up to witness the final home match, versus Birmingham, which was a disappointing affair. On the same day the retained list was published. There were ten names on it, but after the first few months of the following season, only four of them were left. The final four games were all away from home, and provided little confidence for the forthcoming Football League season.

On April the 9th, the old stalwart, McCandless departed, in somewhat acrimonious circumstances. He was replaced by Liverpool personality Tom Bromilow, and in July Jimmy Marshall was appointed Trainer. They had an uphill task before them to put up even a respectable performance. The club still possessed no training ground, and the players were forced to train in a public park, and to gather together on a Saturday before the match.

To prepare for the new season, a dozen signings were made. The programme notes for the opening match read: *"So now another season opens, this time one which gives us the opportunity to make a mark in a sphere which war prevented us from doing seven years ago".* It was, indeed, a strange situation – promoted seven years before, and yet to kick a ball.

The season was to follow the same pattern as the abandoned one of 1939–40. The intended first match, versus Southampton on August 31st, was abandoned due to a waterlogged pitch. On September 7th, the side travelled to Nottingham, to face a Forest team which had lost its first two games. Of the County team that lined up for that first League match, only three players were destined to make more than 13 appearances. To Leamon went the honour of scoring County's first post-war League goal, but the side went down 1–6. Poor Charlie Turner had no chance with any of the goals. A more unfortunate defeat at Burnley followed, but even so 14,104 turned up for the first home match, and saw County beat Coventry 4–2. The revival was short-lived, for the side lost 10 of the next 12 games, with the defence conceding 46 goals!

After a home defeat by Spurs, and a fair away draw at Birmingham, the side went to pieces, when West Brom. beat them 7–2 at Somerton. Doug. Witcomb, who had guested for Newport, masterminded the side, and the veteran Low was no match for "Nobby" Clarke, who scored four goals in a row. Albion could have scored 14, and in the next match Newcastle almost did! Charlie Wayman missed an early penalty, but another 13 went in, with newly signed Shackleton bagging six. It still stands as a record Football League defeat. The Newcastle forwards were all international class, while County's side consisted of veterans and untried youngsters.

The crowd of 52,137 was the biggest ever to watch County play. It was Low's last match, for he moved on to Norwich, where he later became Manager. Turner, at least, must have been relieved, for he returned to find that the reserves had lost 1–11 to Cardiff, and he retained his place for the next match at Spurs!

There was no point in making excuses, and an appeal was launched at the old Central Hall, on October the 17th, for money to buy players. By the turn of the year £3,000 had been raised. The staunch Supporters' Club had over 1,000 members, and apart from its usual functions, it was at this time raising money by selling off old A.R.P. rattles, and appealing for clothing coupons to obtain kit. Its Chairman won his own moment of glory, when his song won second prize in the radio programme, *"Saturday Night at the Palais"*. It earned him £125, a small fortune in those days.

12th of October 1946. County in action with Swansea.

18,715 turned up for the home game with Swansea, to see five new County faces. Three stayed only briefly, but Wilcox – back from the War – played until the 1960's, and the other was to become a folk hero – the rotund Eddie Carr, who soon won the hearts of Newport supporters. Newport lost 2–4, and a 1–0 win at Bury, thanks to Batty, was followed by five consecutive losses. On November the 23rd, only the attendance of the Fire Service enabled the game with Millwall to go ahead, but on a sea of mud County won 3–1, with Rawcliffe scoring twice.

The home game against Frank Swift and illustrious Manchester City was understandably lost, but the next two games were won. Sheffield Wednesday were beaten 4–3, with Carr obtaining a hat–trick, and Fulham 4–2, on Christmas Day. The side then went down 1–4 at Craven Cottage on Boxing Day, and 1–5 at Southampton, two days later. By then County had used 35 players, and many had never been introduced! Only a few of the newcomers made any impact. Hayward was to become a long–serving member of the team, Harper was to play in the F.A.Cup run, two years later, and Harold Williams was destined to

play for Wales. Williams was first given a trial with the reserves at Llanelli, and following a good report from George Kitson, Bromilow took a taxi down to Neath. Williams was on the move with his horse and milk–cart, when signed.

With a sieve–like defence, and thick snow, the New Year was a far from happy time for County. The first game of the year was lost 2–5 at Forest, and was followed by a similar defeat at Coventry in the F.A.Cup, a game played in terrible conditions. The defence let in three at Barry, in the Welsh Cup, then six at Coventry, in the League. By mid–March, despite numerous postponements, the defence had achieved its century of goals against, and the first victory of the year did not arrive until March 22nd, when Chesterfield were beaten 3–0.

Postponements helped to disrupt whatever rhythm the side possessed, with the season being ultimately extended until the middle of June. It was a supremely disappointing campaign for County, and in March rumours began circulating that they would be leaving Newport.

On May 3rd, which should have been the end of the season, Cup finalists Burnley were entertained on a sunny evening. 18,000 tickets were sold, and 14,751 fans had passed through the turnstiles, when the gates were partly opened to admit some season ticket holders. The crowd rushed through, so that the final attendance was never known. Hap scored direct from a corner in the 3rd minute, and further goals were scored by Morris and Potts. Two days later, Midland League Shrewsbury were defeated 1–0 in the Welsh Cup. This was at the fifth time of asking, after a draw and postponements. In the next round, County went down to a 2–3 defeat at Chester.

After a 3–6 loss at Luton, County played their last ever home game in Division Two, in the middle of a heatwave. Their opponents were the dreaded Newcastle. Rawcliffe opened the scoring after 15 minutes, and in the next six minutes the side had added two more, with a 35 yard Haddon rocket, and a Carr header. A further Carr goal eventually secured a 4–2 win. How great are the changes in human fortune! After losing 0–13, County – with an almost completely different side – had won, and Newcastle failed to go up. A week later, County played their final match, against Champions Manchester City. The result was a 1–5 reverse, which just about summed up the season.

Newport were scarcely the Welsh success story of the year. Cardiff, under the discarded McCandless, had stormed away with the Third Division title, and Lovells had won the Welsh League. Attractive opposition and lack of alternative entertainment had, however, brought in gate receipts of £18,960, and some players had begun to come through, notably Carr. An irrepressible character, he was once left out of the side by Harold John. Soon after, he scored seven in a reserve match, and was heard to comment, on leaving the pitch: *"How's that for holding back the forwards"!*

On August the 23rd, the side now back in Division Three (South), drew 0–0 at Reading. Not one of the eleven had played in the opening match of the previous season. The first home game, watched by 16,565 fans, was won by a Batty goal. A Carr hat-trick saw County to a 4-2 victory over Walsall, and despite a 0-1 reverse at Ashton Gate, County were fourth after four matches. Despite a string of respectable results, the team was unable to maintain its promotion challenge; the forwards lacked penetration and the defence rarely kept a clean sheet.

The game at Orient saw the introduction of little terrier, Billy Shergold, long to be a County stalwart, and Billy Lewis made his debut versus Notts County. Four games later, Bryn Allen played his first match in a 1-1 draw at Northampton. A 0-1 defeat by Torquay saw the side's unbeaten home record go, but gates were still good. Life was still governed by rationing, much to the chagrin of the buffet staff. The Swindon programme stated: *"Unrationed only can be purchased – it is not possible to get milk, tea, sugar and other rationed commodities, but minerals, black coffee, hot cordials and such like will be available"*.

Two late fight-backs augured well for the Cup, and Southend were duly despatched 3-2, but after a 0-0 League draw with Champions-to-be Q.P.R., the team went out 0-3 at Reading in the Second Round. Approaching the year's end, the side had an unbeaten run of eight games, but five were draws, and after 22 matches County were eighth.

1948 began with the side playing good football, despite a 1-3 Welsh Cup reverse at Merthyr, but, at the end of January, County started a disastrous run which saw the side conceding 21 goals in five matches. The bad patch ended only when Scottish goalie Bobby Loveman was drafted into the team, and he played superbly against Crystal Palace (3-1) and Aldershot (2-1). From March the 29th, the team took four points from three home games. The final match, with Port Vale, saw the debut of the promising John Aston, whose progress – like that of many – was marred by National Service.

After the previous traumatic season, 1947-48 had been relatively pleasant, and home receipts had amounted to £19,322. There was more local good news. For the only time Lovells Athletic won the Welsh Senior Cup, beating Shrewsbury 3-0 at Wrexham. Lovells became the first pure works side to be admitted to the Southern League, and even applied for Football League membership. They received one vote!

Bromilow was still in charge, and Ray Lawrance became the new Trainer, after a spell in Holland. Despite numerous changes, the side was beginning to get a more settled look about it, with a nucleus of long-term servants such as Hayward, Wilcox, Parker and Shergold. An opening 1-2 home defeat by Bournemouth did nothing to boost confidence, and, after a 2-2 draw at Watford, came a 1-5 defeat at Ipswich. After ten games, County's record showed four draws and six defeats. What a start! Nevertheless, 11,657 turned up to see the side take on Swindon, at the start of October, and they were rewarded with a 4-1 win. A 2-5 defeat at Orient quickly put matters back into perspective, and despite a Carr hat-trick against Norwich, County were

still struggling with Crystal Palace at the foot of the table. By the time the F.A.Cup came around, the side had lost nine successive away games. Fortunately, Newport were drawn at home to Brighton, and the side won 3-1, with goals from Comley (two) and Parker.

The team lost 2-5 at Swindon, to put their unsuccessful away run into double figures, and for their next F.A.Cup match, they were on their fourth goalkeeper of the season. After Matthews, Roberts and Loveman, in came the experienced Alec Grant. County goalies were always a little bit different, and schoolmaster Grant would read poetry on away trips, while the lesser mortals in the side would indulge in cards and similar activities! The Second Round was away, but at non-League Leytonstone, and in a wonderful game, County came through 4-3, after extra time. As if to prove this was no fluke, the side then won an away game at Bournemouth.

County now went mad. The two holiday games with Crystal Palace were won (5-0 on Christmas Day), as was the New Year's Day encounter with Ipswich. A third round cup encounter at Leeds attracted 31,500. County met with a serious blow, when ace goalscorer Parker went down with bronchitis two days before the game, which meant that utility man Morrall had to deputise. The team left for Yorkshire on the Friday, the players being visited in their hotel by Duggan and Hydes. There was a panic, when Grant was found to be missing, his bed unslept in. It transpired that he had gone to the wrong hotel room and slept there all night! In an epic struggle, the side was a goal down after nine minutes, but fought back to overcome their illustrious opponents, with goals from Roffi, Carr and Comley.

In the League, the side scored one goal at Notts County, but unfortunately, Notts scored eleven! In poor conditions, both Lawton and Sewell scored four. The game followed a 0-2 defeat at Milford in the Welsh Cup. These results did not augur well for the Fourth Round of the F.A.Cup, in which the side had been drawn at home to First Division Huddersfield. It was a big day for the town, and 22,500 turned up. Unfortunately, thick fog enveloped the little ground, and the match should never have been played. Whenever the action became visible, the crammed crowd pushed forward down the terracing. Newport scored after eleven minutes, but were twice behind. After 90 minutes, the score was level. Because of the post-war regulations, extra time was played, and Newport were unlucky not to win.

A week later, County trooped off to Yorkshire for the replay. Both sides were unchanged, and 2,000 fans made the long trek, the total attendance being 34,183. Midway through the first half, County hit their stride with goals from Carr and Parker. Metcalfe pulled one back just after, but in the 76th minute Carr set the ball up for Parker to net from 18 yards. At the finish, Carr and Parker were carried from the field, to the singing of the Welsh National Anthem. In those days, it was possible to walk to Newport Station from High Street, and 5,000 massed to greet their heroes.

The Mayor was there to give a civic welcome, but the crowd went out of control, and the idea had to be abandoned. Bromilow and Wilcox were trapped up against the barrier, and Carr had his coat torn off. The players beat a hasty retreat leaving through a rear entrance, all apart from Newall. He was carried over Newport Bridge and down Corporation Road, before he could manage to explain that he had moved house some time before!

A week later, County were drawn away to Portsmouth. Pompey were top of Division One, Newport third from bottom of Division Three. Moreover, Portsmouth were unbeaten at home since Boxing Day, 1947. Eight special trains went there from Wales. The gates were closed half an hour before the start, and the gate of 45,581 was a Portsmouth record. On a rainy day, fans sang "Cwm Rhondda" and "Sospan Fach", to the accompaniment of rattles, whistles, trumpets and beaten saucepans. The County ran on to the pitch to thunderous applause, the opposition to the "Pompey Chimes".

Within three minutes of the kick-off, Wilcox had slipped up, and Phillips was in for the first. County hearts sank. After 15 minutes, Newport forced a corner, and there was Harper to round Scoular and Hindmarsh and crash the ball into the net. Grant made a great save, Williams almost scored and then, just after half an hour, County switched the ball from defence to attack, and there was Carr to net calmly, from a few yards out.

12th February - the Portsmouth cup-tie.
Alec Grant saves from Len Phillips.

A half-time 2-1 lead was lost when Phillips equalised, resulting in extra time; a perfectly good Carr goal after 75 minutes had been ruled offside. In extra time, Comley missed an open goal, then Wilcox stopped Clarke's rocket with his hands. Grant made a wonder save, smothering Barlow's penalty shot, then heartbreak. After 115 minutes of football, Scoular made an opening for Froggatt to barge through and score. Nobody could criticise County, who had given one of the best performances in their history.

The rest of the season was bound to be something of an anti-climax, but the next four matches were all won, and the local derby with Bristol Rovers attracted over 20,000 to Somerton. The run came to an end, when County lost 0-4 to Torquay. It was a significant result, for it came on March 23rd, and was the first League game of the season in which Newport had failed to score.

In the final ten games, the side suffered six defeats, but there was still plenty of excitement. Swansea, now managed by McCandless, were going for promotion. On Good Friday, an all ticket crowd of over 21,000 turned up at Somerton and saw McCrindle break his leg, as County went down 2-5. The crowd at Swansea, on the following Monday, was 7,000 more, and the gates were locked. In a closer match, a Parker goal was insufficient to avert a 1-2 defeat.

County had been buoyed up by that season. The Cup run had meant a record profit, and the club's overall deficit was reduced to less than £5,000. However, players were now the targets of other clubs. In March, tricky Harold Williams had played against Ireland, the first County player since Billy Thomas to be capped, and he also represented Wales in Switzerland. With indecent haste he left for Leeds, Newport receiving £4,000 plus Depear. This reduced the club's deficit still further, but, as with Cardiff's sale of Toshack many years later, stuck in the gullets of supporters, and showed the lack of ambition of the Directors.

As Newport prepared for the new season, the famous F.A. Cup side had already begun to break up. Apart from Williams, Grant had departed, after being turned down for a Newport teaching appointment, and Lew Bradford had left for pastures new.

On August the 20th, the team entertained Norwich, who included five Welshmen. In goal County now had Harry Fearnley, and the defence included three more newcomers, in Amphlett, Depear and Glen Williams. Over 16,000 were present to see Newport go two up within ten minutes, through Comley and a Hayward penalty. A Parker goal overcame two from Kinsey, and despite the absence of Roffi and Wilcox, County had won their first match. That was the end of the good news, and the next six matches were all lost, with 26 goals conceded.

In the side's second match, Depear was injured, and at the time of the third game, the club was struck by food poisoning. Fearnley collapsed and was taken to hospital, a telling comment on the six goals he let in at Southend. For the next three games, Hodge, who had impressed in the pre-season trials, took over and newcomer Staples from Leicester also played. Northampton won 4–1 at Somerton, and before the next game, at Ashton Gate, there were rumours that Bromilow's selections had been changed, when Comley and Carr were replaced by Roffi and Newall, at inside-forward. It made no difference, as Newport went down to another 0–6 defeat, to be followed by a 3–5 reverse, at Torquay. It was against Torquay eight days later, however, that the losing trend was reversed, when Harper scored the winner after 37 minutes.

Bad form and injuries meant a prolonged spell of team changes. Hayward suffered a facial injury against Brighton and missed the next eight games. An even worse blow was struck two games later, when Wilcox fractured an ankle at Walsall and missed the next thirteen matches. Fred Stansfield, who had lost his own place at Cardiff through injury, was signed on loan. Fred Gardner made his debut, much delayed by the cricket season, and scored two against Millwall. "Joe" Payne was signed for a record Newport fee of £5,000.

On October the 8th, came a game still remembered by older fans. Notts County, along with Tommy Lawton, came to Somerton, and a crowd of 21,543 arrived for the match. Depear, a former Commando, made use of all his training, as he tried any method, legal or otherwise, to stop Lawton. The tactics worked as Notts were held to a 1–1 draw, Newall's goal being equalised by one from Sewell. Two weeks later, Carr played his last game. Out of the blue, and much to the dismay of supporters, he was suddenly transferred to Bradford City.

By the time the side beat Orient 3–2, on November 5th, three full-backs were out of action, and Fearnley had broken a finger. In the next match, with Reading, Hodge was injured and Parker was a passenger for most of the game. This unfortunate preparation could not prevent the side from winning a brilliant 3–0 victory over Crystal Palace in the F.A.Cup. On the same day, Eddie Carr scored four for Bradford City versus Fleetwood.

Entertainment was never short for County fans, as illustrated by events in December. Newport began with a 5–0 demolition of Bournemouth, then overcame Gateshead, in a Cup replay. A 0–4 defeat at Norwich was followed by an abandoned match with Southend, which 11,720 "saw". With County leading through a Comley penalty, the fogbound match was called off after 70 minutes. Then came a 6–0 drubbing of Aldershot, the biggest win since the War. After a 1–4 reverse in the return at the Rec., County bounced back to beat Bristol City 6–4, with recalled Bowen scoring a hat-trick.

Things suddenly looked black. A 1–2 home defeat by Port Vale in the F.A.Cup was followed by a 0–3 reverse at Merthyr in the Welsh Cup, and a 0–5 League drubbing at Brighton. Bromilow departed with Lawrence acting as the stand-in. Stansfield, on extended loan from Cardiff, was later appointed acting-Manager. Matters did not noticeably improve, for in the first eleven League and Cup games of 1950, nine were lost, and two drawn. The return with Notts County was a 0–7 rout. Apart from injuries to Parker and Newall, Fearnley had to move to the wing, with Hayward going into goal.

In mid-March, the "re-election derby" with Exeter was lost 1–2, and there were few bright spots over the rest of the season, apart from a 4–1 victory over Nottingham Forest.

 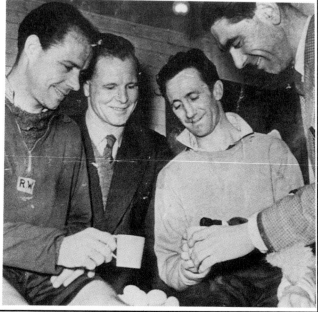

(Above) January 1950. The Annual Dinner Dance at the 'Westgate'. The group includes Ray Wilcox, Ray Lawrance – and their wives – and Chairman Lt.Col. W. Harold John. (Right) The County train on sherry and eggs in mid-January 1950, before the 4th round cup-tie with Norwich.

Such was County's luck, that in the return with Forest, Hayward again had to go in goal with Ashton spending the last few minutes on the wing. The only good thing was that the Football League was being extended by four clubs, so that there was no threat to the club's status.

At the end of the season, Stansfield retired, to become full-time Manager. His comment that; *"I feel we shall enjoy a fairly successful season"*, seemed more hopeful than confident. Many of the previous season's players departed, including Les Orphan, who had appeared with Bert Williams in the Welsh amateur team. Luton offered £2,000, but he wanted to stay amateur and joined Lovells. Eight newcomers were first signed, soon being joined by another three. When new man George Morgan discovered that he had to give up football immediately, Norwich offered Birch instead, and he began a successful spell at Somerton. Roffi, for whom Cardiff had offered £12,000, soon suffered a sad mental breakdown, and was forced to retire. It was not all new faces at the club, for long-serving Wilcox and Newall were due for their benefits.

After two opening defeats, the side won four successive matches, to boost their fans' morale. On September 2nd, Roffi, not even down in the programme, scored four as the team pulverised Aldershot 7-0. By the end of the month, Guido Tomazo Roffi had kicked his last football. His last game was a 0-1 defeat at Bristol Rovers, and the next three matches were also lost. After a 1-0 home win over Gillingham another three matches were lost. County had taken a nosedive down the table.

To offset the bad luck of injuries and the loss of Roffi, Newport signed two players who would make a significant contribution to the club – Birch and Beattie, the latter costing a four figure sum from Gloucester. In bad conditions, the team then scored five against Reading, without reply, and with the speedy Birch netting two. It was a good omen for the F.A.Cup, and Walsall were beaten 4-2.

In the Second Round, County were drawn at non-League Hereford, with 3,000 fans travelling up to the all-ticket match. Hereford started off in storming fashion, but County eventually triumphed through Shergold (35 minutes), Moore (85 minutes) and Parker, in the final seconds. Newport were now showing slightly improved League form, and in the Third Round, were drawn against Reading whom they had earlier demolished in the League. This was a much harder encounter, and at one point County were 0-2 down, but they made a magnificent 2nd half recovery, to win 3-2.

Everything was now geared up to the Fourth Round match with Norwich, who were managed by Norman Low. Such was the interest in football at the time, that the "Argus" produced a special four page supplement. Because of a 'flu epidemic, the players arrived for training on the Tuesday, to find sherry and eggs waiting for them in the dressing room. Because of a colour clash, Newport turned out in white, Norwich in green. Local Terry Pope, who had made his debut only the previous week, was a surprise choice in goal, whilst Norwich had been unchanged for over 20 matches. A crowd of over 20,000 saw County go down to a 0-2

defeat, which could have been worse, as Newall kicked two shots off the line.

Newport then began a run in the Welsh Cup, beating Ebbw Vale 2-1. League form was now much better, and by the time the side beat Millwall 4-2, they were unbeaten in their six matches of the New Year. The Swansea side, which now faced Newport in the Welsh Cup, included only four men who had played in the previous League match. The Swans paid the price, County winning 2-1.

The rest of the season, with many games played on heavy pitches, saw some remarkable results. Southend were beaten 6-1, with Moore scoring after 28 and 48 seconds, and a midweek 4-1 win at Northampton was followed by a 0-5 walloping at Reading. After two good wins, County travelled to Brighton, and lost 1-9!

On Good Friday, came a notorious match with Norwich. In a superb display, amid mud and wind, County had stretched a 2-1 half-time lead to 5-1 six minutes after the interval. In the 73rd minute, Norwich centre-half Foulkes was knocked out heading the heavy ball, and referee Blythe called off the match. 2,000 fans surrounded the club offices, the referee eventually leaving disguised as an ambulance man. Another referee was chosen for the replay!

Harry Fearnley in control against Millwall (May 1950)

On March the 23rd, County faced Merthyr at Ninian Park in the semi-final of the Welsh Cup, a match which attracted a remarkable 23,401 crowd. The game ended 1-1, through Moore and Wilcox (own goal). After a 1-1 draw in the replayed Norwich match, came the replayed Welsh Cup semi-final the very next day. It was Newport's fifth game in eight days, and Birch and Stroud were out injured. 18 year old Albert Davies came in, along with Lunn, who had been out of the team since September. Moore's opener was cancelled out a minute later, and Merthyr ran out 4-1 winners, going on to beat Cardiff in the Final. Another four matches were crammed into the end of the season, followed by a Festival of Britain game, with Dutch side Eindhoven. Lovells attracted a crowd of 7,000 for their match with the Africans from the Gold Coast, which they won 5-3.

At Lovell's, July 1951. County's cricket line-up. (Back) Staples, Lucas, Fearnley, Stansfield (Manager), James, Newall, Hill (Umpire). (Front) Stroud, Evans, Lawrance (Trainer), Hayward, Wilcox.

The County team had stabilised, after a bad patch, and newcomer Birch had been impressive enough to be picked for the Welsh League. Parker, unhappy with the terms offered to him, had a few days on the transfer list but soon rejoined the fold. Around this time, Newport had a squad of 17, one of the smallest in the League.

The club, now out of debt, received a house from the Supporter's Club and, by December, the Directors were able to purchase another. There were only three years left on the Somerton Park tenancy however, and the Board wanted to embark on improvements to terracing, and covered accommodation.

The opening match of the 1951/52 season was lost 1–3 at Ashton Gate. Rodgers scored after 40 seconds, and Atyeo netted on his debut. County's side was unchanged for the first six matches, and three successive victories were registered. The first big reverse came due to the team's success. Four members of the side represented the Welsh League in Belfast, Parker scoring a hat-trick in a 7–3 win. Having made the long return journey, their form was less good the next day, as the side went down 0–5 in Northampton. But following a 1–1 draw with Gillingham, the team was back on a winning streak.

On September the 12th, the side was a joy to behold, as Reading were overcome 2–1 away, the win putting County eighth in the table. A brilliant 2–1 victory at Brighton lifted the side to fifth. A 3–1 victory, at home to Reading, and County were second. On the Saturday, the team scraped a 2–1 win over Millwall, to keep the run going. The luck did not hold in the next three matches, which were lost; 1–5 at Bournemouth, 0–4 at Aldershot, and 2–5 at home to Watford. For the latter match, Poyner was rushed from his National Service unit at Oswestry, when Wilcox was injured. He was no match for Cyril Thompson, who scored three.

Despite excellent draws, with Bristol Rovers and Plymouth, there were signs of cracks appearing. James and Fearnley asked for transfers, as Molloy, Birch and Stroud had already done. The team had drifted down from second to tenth place, despite still playing well at times. A 2–1 win over Norwich was excellent, as was a 4–0 home victory over Exeter, whose amateur goalie, Lear, saved them from a worse beating. In the First Round of the F.A.Cup, Barry were defeated, with Beriah Moore netting a hat-trick. In the Second Round, amateurs Leytonstone fought back to draw 2–2, but five days later County won 3–0 at Somerton. Leytonstone goalkeeper, John Hughes, was serving in the Royal Navy and should have met up with the team at Bath. He missed the train, and Leytonstone began with ten men, and centre-forward Vic Groves in goal. Hughes turned up 20 minutes later, in a police car.

Two good wins over newcomers Shrewsbury at Christmas, were followed by a disappointing home defeat to Torquay in the last game of the year. 1952 began on a brighter note however, with an 8–2 Welsh Cup victory over Connah's Quay. This match marked the debut of Tony Nelson, son of the famous old Cardiff full-back, Jimmy. Nelson found the net twice, and Beriah Moore scored a hat-trick in the game. The first League game of 1952 was at Gillingham. With nine minutes left, County were 1–2 down, but Nelson equalised, and Moore scored five minutes from the finish.

The team was only just in the top half of the table however, and interest in the F.A.Cup was curtailed, when the side put up a good show, but lost 0–2 at Sheffield United. The season continued, with the attack usually scoring, and the defence usually giving away goals. The Welsh Cup match with Rhyl was lost 2–3, but the League form was reasonable. The home game with Southend was won 3–0, in atrocious conditions, with Fearnley playing almost the whole match with a broken finger.

A goalkeeping crisis forced County to call up amateur Wyn Griffiths, a local vet, for three games, and Mitchell made his only first team appearance in the Rhyl match.

Five unbeaten games ended with a 0–5 defeat at Plymouth. Some good results were still achieved, including a 4–3 home victory over Exeter, in the midst of a blizzard, and a 4–2 win against Walsall, with Moore netting a hat–trick, and Fearnley saving a penalty. As the season ended, the side had achieved a highly respectable sixth position, without ever really challenging for promotion. Away form had been excellent, with eight wins and five draws, but at home the team had failed to win ten of its matches. The future looked reasonably promising however, and, off the field, the Directors had decided to terrace the Somerton Road side with railway sleepers – and the help of volunteers!

There were no significant transfers inwards or outwards during the close season, and a crowd of 11,111 saw a familiar side take on Gillingham in the first match. Moore's 8th minute goal only flattered to deceive, and, in the end, only Beattie impressed in the defeat. A 3–1 victory at Walsall was more encouraging, and after a 1–2 reverse at Crystal Palace, three successive home games were all won. The side stretched the run to seven matches without defeat. An excellent 4–1 win over Northampton, which produced an ovation from the crowd, took the team to second place. The next, remarkable, match is still remembered by older supporters. Full–back Staples, who twisted an ankle, swapped places with Moore and proceeded to score two goals from the wing, as County drew 4–4 with Coventry.

With injury problems accumulating, the side went down to three successive defeats. The rot came to a temporary halt with a 4–2 win over Shrewsbury, and after a 2–4 loss at newly relegated Q.P.R., came a significant match with Swindon. Parker scored twice, once from a penalty, to notch his hundredth League and Cup goal for Newport. Only the abandoned Norwich match prevented him reaching his 100th League goal, and no player ever approached his total.

Three League matches without a win gave little encouragement for the F.A.Cup, although Fearnley dislocated a finger early in the Aldershot game, and Moore had to perform in goal. Fortunately, humble Walsall were County's opponents in Round One, and Newport won a game of missed chances 2–1. In the next round, non–League Gainsborough were beaten by the same score.

By the end of the year, the team had failed to win its last eight matches. A 0–3 Christmas morning defeat by Brighton was typical. In the first few minutes, young John Rees received a blow in the face and walked around dazed

Vol. III. No. 1. v. Gillingham, Saturday, 23rd August, 1952.

By courtesy of South Wales Argus.

DIRECTORS:
Chairman: Lt.-Col. W. Harold John, O.B.E.
Vice-Chairman: Alderman J. Wardell, O.B.E., J.P.
Councillor Percy Jones, Messrs. E. W. T. King, H. J. Brewer,
A. Chaston, W. Ivor Lewis, W. Adams, C. C. Lewis.

Hon. Secretary: F. Lionel Watkins.
Trainer: R. Lawrance.

Manager: Fred Stansfield.
Assistant Trainer: G. Kitson.

Registered Office: SOMERTON PARK

'Phone: 71543.

OFFICIAL PROGRAMME 3d

The Author (can just be seen in School cap!) – watches Danny Newall lead out the side (versus Northampton in 1951) – as Grandad looks on.

for a long time. Hayward scored an own goal and later twisted an ankle, becoming a passenger on the left wing. The team, which had started so brightly, was now firmly in the bottom half of the table. Around this time, Bert Moss, who had built up the County from nothing, died.

The side had a good 8–1 victory over Haverfordwest in the Welsh Cup. After a 3–2 League win at Crystal Palace, Sheffield United were entertained in the F.A.Cup, and over 20,000 were present, when Hawksworth crossed for Browning to net. United were one up after 30 seconds. Fifteen minutes later, Bottom headed in, from a Ringstead corner. County went on to lose 1–4.

Emrys Evans played his first home League match against Torquay, and scored a hat–trick. The game was full of incident, as two penalties were missed, and Pope was carried off. Unfortunately, that match was the only bright spot, for in a run of seven League matches, the other six were all lost, without a goal being scored by Newport.

51

The side was also beaten 2-3 at Swansea in the Welsh Cup. Parker, who had not scored since the Gainsborough match, had lost form.

3rd of April 1953 versus Watford.
George Beattie beats a defender.

Despite Harold John's warnings of low gates and mounting losses, enough cash was found, in February, to sign Graham and Wharton from Blackburn Rovers, in an effort to stem the flood of defeats. Parker, Pope and Nelson were out for the season, and with a string of bad results re-election was looming.

There was an inauspicious start for the newcomers, in a 0-3 reverse at Ipswich, but the team was soon on a more even keel, and only one of the next dozen matches was lost. Graham opened his goalscoring account against Q.P.R., and by the season's end had collected eight. Wharton, an old-fashioned winger, contributed much without scoring A 2-1 home win over Aldershot was the turning point of a deteriorating season, with Graham and Beattie scoring. On April the 13th, 5,000 fans came over from Bristol, for the local derby, and traffic jams built up in the evening rush hour. It was a great game, with Graham outstanding. Stroud scored after four minutes, but Lambden and Bradford put Rovers ahead before half-time. In the 57th minute, Waite was fouled and Graham, who fractured an arm in the match, equalised from the ensuing penalty. The return game was quite an occasion. Almost 30,000 turned up to watch Rovers, who were heading for promotion. County, with their usual luck, saw Fearnley break his collarbone and Birch took over in goal. Bradford scored a hat-trick, breaking his club's seasonal goalscoring record, with a total of 34. At the end, the Rovers – led by the Captain, Ray Warren – received the acclaim of their supporters, to the singing of their theme song, *"Goodnight, Irene"*. For the final match, Pugsley took over in goal and suffered from another hat-trick, this one coming from Stobbart.

The season, after a good start, had gone downhill, and only the shrewd capture of Graham and Wharton had saved the day. The reserves had performed well in the Welsh League however, winning the title. A further football honour befell the town, when local Headmaster, B.M. Griffiths was chosen to referee probably the best known post-war Cup Final, the *"Matthews Final"*. As far as the forthcoming season was concerned, County were to encounter big changes.

20th July 1953. Pre-season training at Somerton Park.

# CHAPTER 5

## The Lucas Years

During the close season three regulars departed, Beattie, Moore and Fearnley. The only newcomer of note was international goalie Iorrie Hughes. It was impossible to foretell what kind of season County would have; as J.R. Wardell wrote, in the opening club programme, *"The 34 years as a Director of Newport County have taught me that it is futile to make any forecast...."*. Events would soon endorse his words.

Newly appointed player/manager Billy Lucas meets the Somerton Park staff

The Reading match, watched by a five figure crowd was won 4–1, with Graham rattling the crossbar twice, but the euphoria was shortlived. At Swindon, two days later, Ray Wilcox was injured and the team lost 1–7. At home to Southampton, with Crad Wilcox deputising for his brother, the side lost 0–4 with Graham missing a penalty. The home match with Walsall was won 4–2, but bad weather cut the crowd down to 3,770, and already alarm bells were ringing. Then County lost 0–4 at Southampton, with Flood scoring a hat–trick. Defeat at Northampton meant a losing run of six matches, and that factor, together with a deteriorating financial situation meant that things were also happening off the pitch.

On September 2nd, an Extraordinary General Meeting of the Supporters' Club was held at the "Kings Head". Subsequently, all seven members of the Board resigned. A special shareholders' meeting of the club, at the "Westgate" on October 26th (attended by more than 400), saw stormy scenes and a new Caretaker Board set up. The Mayor launched an appeal, to which Cardiff City subscribed £1,000. The entrance fee to the terraces was cut from 2/- (10p) to 1/9 (9p), to try and attract bigger gates.

From the beginning of September until the end of November, only two matches were won. Bad weather cut the crowd for the Aldershot match down to 2,836, and to cap it all in the F.A. Cup, County went out to unknown Cambridge United in a replay. Only the previous year Newport had set a club record, by reaching the Third Round for the fifth year in succession, and they had by now grown used to this source of income. Cardiff stalwart Ken Hollyman was signed before the Cambridge replay, but had been forced to watch from the stands, through ineligibility.

More momentous events were taking place. Billy Lucas, whose father had played for the County in its very first season, was licensee of the "Black Horse", a stone's throw from Somerton Park. Still a Swansea player, he returned from Doncaster to find most of the County Directors in the bar. He was offered the Manager's job, and accepted. One of his first tasks was to sign experienced Doug Witcomb, who added class to the County half–back line.

As in the previous year, new blood brought a revival, and in December four successive games were won. A 1–0 victory over Gillingham marked the first clean sheet of the season. On the same day, Colin Hudson made his debut for the reserves. It was as well that other players were coming through, for by December, Parker was out injured, and was destined to hang up his boots at the season's end.

On December the 19th, Lucas was in charge of his first match, and his former club Swindon, were beaten 2–0 on a heavy pitch. Shergold fractured a rib in the game. On Christmas Day, County entertained Bristol City, and although there was no public transport, almost 15,000 attended, and saw an exciting end to end game. Lucas was outstanding, as Newport triumphed 3–2.

On January the 1st, Saward – who had scored a Cup goal against County – was signed. Technically still registered with Crystal Palace, his signing meant that Newport ended up paying fees to both Palace and Cambridge! Saward had a run in the first team, but did not prove an adequate successor to Parker. At the start of 1954, the side was very different from the one which had started the campaign, with the inclusion of Saward, Hollyman, Witcomb, Lucas and the improving George Thomas.

53

Old faithfuls Parker and Newall did not appear in the second half of the season, and Staples made only one first team appearance.

County showed decent form in January, and at the end of the month hammered Swansea 6-2 in the Welsh Cup. Graham, a regular goalscorer, netted twice, as did Lucas against his old side. League displays still generally went well – despite a 1-5 reverse at Q.P.R. With the country in the grip of Winter weather, the Colchester match was postponed, and before Northampton's visit there were tractors on the pitch and men clearing the terraces. The result was an excellent 2-0 win, and it was followed a week later by Newport's best performance of the season. Norwich, who had just defeated Arsenal in the F.A. Cup, were beaten 4-1, with Graham netting a hat-trick.

County won 5-1 at Bangor to reach the semi-finals of the Welsh Cup. After this came a 1-0 victory over League leaders Brighton, despite the loss of Hayward, who went off injured for ten minutes. In the Welsh Cup semi-final with Chester, which was held at Ninian Park, County were two up, but were put off by bustling tactics and could only draw. In the replay, at Wrexham, Chester triumphed 2-0. Of the side's final seven matches, four were won. The final game, against promotion seeking Ipswich, saw the team's first home loss since October 10th. Lucas' arrival had clearly improved the club's fortunes.

Lovells were still very much of a going concern, and on April the 24th, three of their players were capped against England Amateurs, the match taking place at Rexville. The club also won the Welsh Amateur Cup, for the first time since 1928.

Despite County's improvement, there was still much to be done, with Parker and Witcomb now leaving and Newall now nearing the end of the road. Up front the team had been a one-man band, relying on Graham. Saward had scored just four goals in 16 matches. The only new signing of any real significance was full-back "Buller" Lever. It was for his youth policy that Lucas came to be known, and it was just as well for Newport had the smallest number of staff in the League. Youngsters such as Hudson and Harris were now beginning to come through.

12,710 hopeful supporters turned up for the opening match with Northampton. The forwards were unable to find the net on a pitch saturated by a pre-match thunderstorm, but English scored for Northampton. Optimism was such however, that the Supporter's club ran out of membership cards, and even more turned up for the next game with Norwich. Disappointingly it was drawn 1-1, after which there came two away defeats. In the first ten games, the only success was a 3-2 victory over Southend. The side threw away a two goal lead in the match, but with the crowd streaming away, Graham scored an 86th minute penalty. It was ironic that while the first team could not score, Kemp was scoring a record six goals for the reserves, at Barry.

McGhee, signed from Barry, found the net only once, and Saward did not even break his duck. Graham was only a third as prolific as the previous season, and County were struggling. Something had to be done, and in October Lucas made probably his best signing. Tom Johnston, who had enabled Norwich to beat Arsenal in the Cup, arrived for a paltry £1,800 fee. He was to become Newport's hottest property in the period between Tudor Martin and John Aldridge, possessing not just goalscoring ability, but skill. He failed to score in his first two outings, but by the turn of the year had notched up eight goals.

There was no overnight transformation, for the side was still encountering more defeats than victories, and went out of the F.A. Cup 0-2 at Gillingham. With the team affected by injuries, the end of the year saw some poor performances.

In January, Newport signed a young goalkeeper, Len Weare. At this time, County were third from bottom, and support was becoming apathetic. Later that month, the unsuccessful Saward was released. Pope, after numerous lapses, was dropped for Hughes. After a 0-2 defeat by Watford, during which match Pope let in a 40 yard free kick and Johnston ballooned over from two yards, County were involved in three high scoring matches. In the Welsh Cup, Abergavenny were hammered 6-0. After a 3-3 draw at Bournemouth, Newport game one of their best displays of the season, to wallop Q.P.R. 4-0. On a thawing pitch, Johnston and Harris both netted twice.

In the Welsh up, County lost 1-3 at home to Cardiff, before a crowd of over 10,000. It was an excellent game, but marred by poor County finishing; even Johnston contrived to miss a penalty. By the beginning of March, Newport were next to bottom, although they were not having the greatest of luck.

Things began to look up, and after drawing their first three away games of the New Year, County won 2-1 at promotion seeking Orient. Lucas' move back from inside-forward to right half helped matters, and re-election fears were gradually dispelled. Johnston finished up scoring 26 goals, in three quarters of a season. The reserves, under Sam Prangley, won the Welsh League title for the third time.

On May the 5th, County played an All Star XI for the Players' Benefit Fund in a match which attracted 15,636. In goal for County was young Len Weare, while the international Iorrie Hughes turned out for the All Stars, who boasted the 40-year-old Stanley Matthews, Alf Sherwood, Trevor Ford and the Allchurch brothers. Every time that Matthews touched the ball, a crowd of boys ran up and down the dog track. After 40 minutes, County were 0-5 down, but Johnson pulled two back before half-time. By 47 minutes, the score was 4-5, and 12 minutes later it was 5-8. When Johnston scored again, the crowd invaded the pitch thinking it was all over, but the score reached 8-8 before Mervyn Griffiths blew the final whistle. Johnston netted six in the match, and Ford and Ivor Allchurch obtained hat-tricks.

The close season, during which time Billy McCandless died, was a period of great activity. Players such as Pope, Newall and McGhee departed, and Graham was sold to Watford. Quite a number were signed on, including Cyril Beech, Tom Docherty and Gordon Brown.

Unfortunately, the opening two matches were away from home, and a 0–5 beating at Shrewsbury, followed by a 0–1 reverse at Aldershot shattered any early optimism. The side, with Weare making his League debut, did well against newly relegated Ipswich, who were then managed by Alf Ramsey. Little Billy Shergold scored twice, and despite Hayward being crocked, County won 2–1. After a narrow home defeat by Aldershot, the County managed a 3–3 draw at Walsall, with Weare giving an excellent display.

County were showing reasonable form, but a scheming inside-forward was badly needed and attempts to attract Billy Rees proved unsuccessful. Johnston was still proving a big asset. Against Leyton Orient, on October the 8th, he obtained a hat-trick, and this was ultimately to lead to his departure from Somerton Park. Young Harry Harris, from Magor was also knocking in a few goals.

On November the 19th, came a rare event in Newport football with both the County and Lovells appearing in the First Round of the F.A. Cup. At Orient, Lovells were 0–3 down after 20 minutes, and went on to lose 1–7. County, who had warmed up with a 4–2 win at the Den, thanks to a Harris hat-trick, went one better. At Brighton, they lost 1–8, Johnston scoring the consolation goal. It was a hammer blow for the club. With their average gate already down by more than 2,000, the possibility of a profitable Cup run had now been snatched away. Results were not running for the side, and from the start of December five successive League games were lost, but at least the final two matches of the year brought some relief. Brighton and Walsall were both beaten, the matches being played in atrocious conditions.

1956 did not start well in the League, the first win not being registered until March. Only the Welsh Cup brought some comfort, for Barry were thrashed 8–1, with Johnston and Hudson scoring hat-tricks, and Llanelli were despatched 5–1. At Orient, on February the 18th, Johnston made his 31st League appearance, and scored his 20th goal. It was to be his last for Newport County. On the following Friday, he signed for Orient in the buffet bar of Newport Station. The deal involved £4,000, and the transfer of Mike Burgess. To the fans, the loss of their great hero came as a shattering blow, and the deal seemed a poor one. Apathetic supporters now became ex-supporters, so that by the time of the Swindon game in April, only just over 2,000 were present.

Johnston, later to emigrate to Australia, became a folk hero with Orient and went on to score goals for Blackburn Rovers in Division One. Burgess, suffering the same kind of backlash as Depear, was never to settle at Somerton Park.

The Welsh Cup victory over Llanelli was followed by two League wins, but the next six League matches were all lost. Without Johnston, the side forced 16 corners against Watford, but failed to score!

In the Welsh Cup semi-final at Ninian Park, nerves got the better of the side, which went down 2–5 to the star-studded Swansea team. At Griffin Park, County scored their fourth goal in seven games, while on the same day Johnston netted Orient's 100th goal of the season! The final home game was a memorable 4–2 win over Coventry. Well-known goalie Reg. Matthews was injured in the sixth minute, and eventually had to go off. After numerous fouls by the upset players, two were sent off early in the second half, on top of which Lever missed a penalty. After two away defeats, Newport finished 19th having lost nine home games during the season.

On May the 3rd, another high scoring All Star match was played, which ended 4–6. The County side included three players with whom Lucas was negotiating, but none of them joined. Two old stalwarts departed in the close season – Hayward and Shergold. On July the 9th, came one of Lucas' best signings. Welsh international left-back Alf. Sherwood was secured from Cardiff, for around £2,000. Other signings were inside-forward Howard Sheppeard and Charlton's reserve centre-forward Pat Terry, an accomplished header of the ball.

On August the 11th, the new Social Club was opened. It soon proved so popular that it needed to be extended. There was an all round air of optimism at Somerton Park, and an attendance of over 11,000 saw the side – skippered by Sherwood – defeat Northampton 3–0. Terry netted twice in the second half, and the improving Harris also scored. After two away draws, County entertained Southend. With Newport two up, the game was almost abandoned by Dennis Howell 20 minutes from time, during a tremendous thunderstorm. A 2–1 win saw County go fourth, and after a 4–1 victory over Plymouth, County met their first defeat, at Exeter. The last Welsh team to have lost its unbeaten tag, the County side was unchanged for its first eight matches.

A 3–0 win over Watford in September, took County to second place. This was followed, at Crystal Palace, by the first League match the club had played under floodlights. The team was a good blend of experience and youth, and at Bournemouth, schoolboy Graham Reynolds made his debut and scored. On October the 27th, top side Torquay came to Somerton, and Lucas inspired County to a 3–0 win.

Sherwood, despite his Division Three status, became the first Newport player to captain Wales. He was having such a good season, that 82-year-old legend Billy Meredith gave him one of his caps. Alf played in a 2–2 draw with Scotland, watched by 60,000 at Ninian Park. On November the 14th, Kelsey was carried off after 7 minutes at Wembley, and Sherwood took over in goal.

| Alf Sherwood | Pat Terry |

In the F.A. Cup, Weare made wonder saves to put the side through to a Second Round tie at Gillingham, where Brown tapped in a last minute winner. The following week, the team achieved its only away win, a factor which cost County dear over the season.

Another negative factor was a spate of postponed matches due to both the weather and Cup engagements. Neither holiday match with Coventry was completed. The home match was abandoned near the end, with the pitch invisible, and the Boxing Day match was called off. The fruitless journey North brought a collision with a car near Warwick.

A scheduled League encounter with Southampton became an F.A. Cup match. In driving rain, County were two up after 11 minutes, 2–3 down in the second half, then Harris scored a lucky equaliser. On a gloomy Wednesday, 1,200 fans travelled to the Dell for the replay. Sherwood was injured early on, and moved to the wing. After 76 minutes, a Harris shot went in off the post for the only goal, and he was carried in triumph from the pitch. The winners were due to play Arsenal, and Southampton had received thousands of requests from confident fans for match tickets!

The next four games were disastrous. Against Reading, before a large crowd seeking Cup vouchers, County lost their first home match, a bad Hollyman back pass contributing. After a 0–5 disaster at Watford, came the Arsenal match. A crowd of over 20,000 saw County equal the Gunners in midfield, but go down 0–2, Herd scoring the second two minutes from time. The League match at Colchester was lost 0–1 and County were down to 13th.

Newport could score at home but not away. On a Thursday afternoon, Hudson netted four times against Bournemouth. The re-signing of Harold Williams for £750 achieved little. Scot George McMillan, who managed five first half goals against Swansea reserves, was never tried in the first team. Newport reached the Welsh Cup semi-finals, and drew 1–1 with Swansea before losing the replay 0–3.

County won only one of their final five matches, to finish a disappointing 12th. The players' merits were not always recognised. Weare was overlooked by Wales, even when Kelsey fractured a finger, and Sherwood was dropped – after 33 consecutive matches – for Charlton's Trevor Edwards, who had played few Football League matches.

In the close season, "Rocky" Hudson, the hard running hard shooting winger left for Ninian Park. In the opposite direction came Neil O'Halloran, Cecil Dixon and John McSeveney. There were other types of changes, for Newport County became the first Welsh club to install floodlights. The lights, at a cost of £8,000, would allow Valleys supporters to attend midweek matches in Winter. It was going to be a vital season, for the Football League had decided to convert the two regional Leagues into a Third and Fourth Division.

The opening day was a disaster, the team being stuffed 0–4 at Swindon, and the first two home matches were not won. Fortunately, the next three games all ended in victory, including two away from home. Lucas was an inspiration at right half, despite his advanced years, and there was no shortage of humour with Lucas around.

On one occasion, he was participating in a practice match, when suddenly a young lady appeared jumping up and down on the touchline. The players were nonplussed. Was this the first football groupie, powerless to resist the charms of Third Division stars? She was there from the "Black Horse", it transpired, to point out that the Draught Guinness had run out, and Lucas had to leave the match!

After half a dozen games, with County eighth, Graham was re-signed for £1,250, and he replaced Lucas at right half. Against Exeter, Weare went off, and was replaced in goal by Sherwood. He kept a clean sheet, and received a tremendous ovation at the end. The Mayor switched on the floodlights on October the 21st, when an All Star XI was played. Despite less than 10,000 attending it was a great success. Because of atrocious weather, the following match, with Reading, attracted only 5,000.

County went out of the F.A. Cup to a Northampton side, who were later to beat Arsenal. The real priority was the new Third Division, and just before Christmas, leaders Swindon were beaten 4-1, with Terry scoring two superb goals. The year ended with Newport just in the top half of the table.

An excellent 1-1 draw with Southampton was followed by a 5-0 hammering of Gillingham, in which Harris scored his 50th goal after 20 seconds. County lost to Swansea in the Welsh Cup, and St. David's Day saw the start of a terrible run, with five out of seven matches being lost. The side slipped from fourth, at the start of February, to tenth. At this time, some variety was added by floodlit friendlies played against European sides Red Star of Paris and Spandau.

All was set for a nail-biting finish, with four of County's final five fixtures away. Sherwood missed his only League penalty for Newport, as Crystal Palace drew 0-0. Two days later, the team beat Aldershot 3-2, with young Singer scoring twice. There were two defeats in the last five games, but a 1-0 victory over 4th placed Norwich saw Newport scrape into the new Third Division, with a final 11th place. How much easier it would have been with Johnston, now the League's leading scorer.

The Summer of 1958 was one of excitement, with the Commonwealth Games in Cardiff, and the new Third Division to look forward to. Harris was sold to Portsmouth for a record fee, and goalscorer Terry also left, along with Docherty. Lucas hung up his boots at forty years of age. In late June, Ken McPherson was bought for £2,000. An awkward looking goalscorer, he first came to the attention of the Somerton crowd when sent off for Coventry. The boos from that occasion turned to cheers, as he became a favourite of the crowd. Four useful half-backs were signed, long-throw expert Les Riggs, Cliff Jones' brother Bryn, Dudley Peake, and the influential John Rowland. The team went back to the pre-war style of amber shirts with three black hoops, the theory being that they would lose one hoop with each promotion!

With new faces and new opponents, the team took time to settle. Eight of the first eleven matches were against Northern sides. Numerous injuries, including a fractured shoulder for McPherson, marred the early season, and veteran Wilcox won a recall. After 13 games, the side had scored only 13 goals, but the long term future looked good with such young talent around as Bird, Burton, Hill, Fry and the two Herritys.

On October the 27th, an All Star match was played for Wilcox, who had been 20 years with the club. On November the 5th, he made his 500th appearance with County versus Doncaster. Weare, for whom Leicester had offered £15,000, was outstanding in the game. In the F.A. Cup, Wisbech were encountered, and only a last minute goal from McPherson saved County. In the replay, Newport again seemed to be heading for disaster, with Pye scoring after four minutes. Many had left the ground, when McPherson levelled the score 20 seconds from the end, causing chaos at the exits. Fitness told in extra time, with County winning 4-1. 3,000 travelled to Hereford for the Second Round. Hereford's goalie was injured, and his deputy was carried off shoulder high by the crowd, as County were restricted to victory from two late goals. The side was unbeaten in its last five League matches of the year, and had scored 30 goals in the last 11 League and Cup matches. Disappointingly, County drew 0-0 with Torquay in the Third Round, but a journey through snow was rewarded with a 1-0 replay win, McPherson netting after 82 minutes. Round Four, and mighty Spurs!

Meyer, Dixon, McSeveney and Hollyman prepare for the 'Spurs game.

5,000 Newportonians were among the White Hart Lane crowd of 50,561. At the game's start, Weare was charged by burly Bobby Smith, and he collapsed and needed treatment. After eight minutes, Dunmore scored. A superb Hollowbread save from Graham was followed by a second Dunmore goal five minutes before half-time. After 64 minutes, a 30 yard Hollyman shot found the corner of the net.

Right back Ken Hollyman (out of picture), scores a 30 yarder at mighty 'Spurs - as McSeveney looks on.

Sixteen minutes later came a hammer blow. Smith collided with Wilcox, who dislocated his elbow and went off. Two late Smith goals did not reflect the performance put up by the Third Division Club.

Of the next eight matches, six were lost, including the Welsh Cup match with Swansea. Burly Barrie Meyer was bought in February, and he went on to net half a dozen goals. In March, there was a brief revival, with three consecutive home victories, but then came four odd goal defeats on the trot. Around this period Jimmy Hindmarsh died.

Seven points from the final six matches meant safety for the club. In the last game, the promising Burton made his debut at left half. Gates were now diving alarmingly, as Northern sides proved no attraction to fans reared on the Southern Section. The Stockport match attracted only 2,447 and Summer wages of £6,000 had to be found. Things were even worse for Lovells. Despite their excellent performance in the Welsh Cup Final, losing only 0-2 to Cardiff, gates of 200 meant resignation from the Southern League and a future in the Welsh League.

During the close season, a few familiar faces, such as Brown and Graham departed, but the only new signing was winger Wendell Morgan. Thus, it was a familiar team which did battle at Wrexham, on August the 22nd. The Lucas youth policy was now in full swing, for the opening day's line-up included locals Weare, Bird, Rowland and Singer, and later to make the side were Fry, Burton, Clarke and the Herrity brothers.

A 0-0 draw at Wrexham was followed by a 3-2 home win over Reading, thanks to a Bryn Jones hat-trick. By now there had been alterations to Somerton Park. Nearly 1,000 tons of soil had been tipped on the pitch, and there was a new asbestos roof on the Stand.

There were also plans to improve the Enclosure, to re-roof the Cromwell Road end, and to cover the Railway end.

Newspaper reports suggested that Trainer Kitson had got the side its fittest for years, and of the first dozen games six were won and only three lost. It was 80 degrees in the shade when fourth placed Bradford City arrived. They went away beaten thanks to McSeveney and Riggs. Against Bournemouth, County were losing, but hit back to score five second half goals. Sherwood scored his third penalty in five matches.

Newport were now back to their old habit of winning their home games and losing their away fixtures. A 3-1 victory over Chesterfield was Billy Herrity's last game before National Service. The team was trailing 1-3 to Port Vale, with 20 minutes left, but hit back through two McPherson goals and one from Meyer, when goalkeeper Hancock dropped the ball.

A 4-2 F.A. Cup win over Hereford preceded a 5-1 League defeat of Halifax. McSeveney scored four, and Halifax centre-forward Whitelaw was sent off on his debut. After a 1-0 Cup defeat of Salisbury, came a visit from top side Southampton, before the season's biggest gate of 9,980. With County in front - through a McPherson header - ever unpopular referee Mann of Worcester abandoned the match. The crowd was still waiting three-quarters of an hour later!

By a fortunate coincidence, County were again drawn against Tottenham Hotspur in the Cup, then at their height with the highest priced team in the League. The pitch did not do justice to the match with the First Division leaders. Because of the weather, tons of sand were strewn across it, making it resemble Barry Island. Indeed, most of the profits had to be ploughed back (literally!) into the pitch. The gates were opened hours before kick-off, to admit the 24,000 ticket holders.

The match, in which Bryn Jones opposed his more famous brother, was an anti-climax, County losing 0–4.

County displayed erratic form, their defeats including a 2–6 thrashing at Bradford City and a 0–3 Welsh Cup defeat by Wrexham. In February, Percy Jones denied rumours in a Sunday newspaper, that County were to fold. Some supporters wrote to the press, suggesting a move to the newly constructed Glebelands athletic ground, taking with them the Somerton Park floodlights. Athletics and show–jumping meetings could be held, and British Rail could build a halt there!

County were always a better side under floodlights, and top side Southampton were walloped 5–1, with McPherson netting a brilliant

Bryn Jones (brother of the famous Cliff) tries a header against Grimsby.

hat–trick. A fortnight later, the consistent McSeveney played his 139th consecutive match, though he was stopped by injury a few games later.

With the pitch deteriorating, home form suffered, and Newport lost 1–3 to strugglers Accrington, but the side still managed to finish in a respectable position. Cardiff were promoted, and the County "Old Boy" Hudson laying on the goal which defeated Aston Villa.

During the close season, there were extensive ground improvements, running to £12,000. A new drainage system and pitch were constructed. There was additional covered accommodation and an extension to the Grandstand; new gates and turnstiles were put in at the Somerton Road end. Although Bryn Jones had been sold in February, there were no further sales during the close season. Morgan departed, and Hollyman and Wilcox retired. The famous Trevor Ford was signed, but this turned out to be a damp squib. Of more long-term importance was the signing of Granville Smith, destined to be a cornerstone of the side for seasons, and who was to eventually settle in the town.

Ford, back from exile in Holland, pulled an achilles tendon in pre–season training and his debut was long delayed. Nevertheless the season started with a bang, as Reading were beaten 5–2, with "Jim" Singer netting a hat–trick. Two days later an unchanged side was walloped 1–5 at Hull. On the second Saturday the team lost 1–4 at Coventry, and after eight matches County were 9th. After the following game with Notts County, however, Birmingham – who had offered £3,000 for Singer – now upped their bid to £4,500, plus £1,000 after 12 appearances. Singer, who had scored nine goals in nine games, was on his way.

In the newly inaugurated Football League Cup, Newport enjoyed a series of epic encounters with Southampton. Drawn at home, County were one up at half–time, but went 1–2 down in the second half. With the crowds drifting away, McPherson scored with a glorious header from a Fry corner. The replay at the Dell ended 2–2 after extra time, and the Saints' Chairman won the toss for venue. In the second replay young Burton became a makeshift inside-right. He scored a hat–trick, and Newport were 3–1 up, with half an hour left. After 78 minutes it was 3–3, however, late goals from Paine and O'Brien sealed the result. County made a more ignominious exit from the F.A. Cup, losing 1–4 at Shrewsbury.

Ford made his long awaited debut against Brentford, and scored his first goal in a 5–1 slamming of bottom club Chesterfield. He was to make only nine first team appearances however, and was unhappy at continuing in the reserves.

A national players' strike was averted in January, whilst County's form continued to be up an down – a mixture of heavy defeats, including a 0–6 hammering at Notts County, and decent wins. In the Welsh Cup, the side lost 1–2 at Cardiff despite an excellent display. It was the first time that winning the trophy meant entry into Europe.

In a moderate League position and out of all Cup competitions, the crunch was coming. The Board announced that the club could not manage on its gates of 4,000 – which were not helped by fixture clashes with the rugby club and bad traffic jams in the town – and Burton was sold to Norwich for £12,000. On the same day the dissatisfied Ford departed for Romford.

The final run in was disastrous, with one win and eight defeats in 13 matches. One of the few bright moments came with a McPherson hat-trick in a 5-1 tanning of Watford, but by now the gates had dipped below 3,000. At least there were more youngsters emerging with the likes of Sanders, Rathbone, David Williams and Albert Derrick, the latter the son of the pre-war player. At neighbouring Lovells, old County player Roy McDonald left after 23 years as Manager.

In the close season, Lucas — part of the furniture at Somerton Park — departed. Going for a big name, the Directors appointed Bobby Evans as player-manager. The popular player had been signed by Chelsea for a considerable fee, but was freed to pursue a managerial career. There were drastic changes to staff, too drastic, with hindsight. Sherwood may have been ready for retirement, but players such as McPherson, McSeveney, Riggs, Meyer and Dixon had been ultra consistent members of the team. In came an influx of Scottish players, Finlay, Robertson, Buchanan and Bowman, later being joined by others. The Englishman George Harris also arrived, and the new players had to prove that they could gel with the remnants of the "Old Guard". At this time the old maximum wage rule was rescinded, and Bowman was reputedly on a high wage.

11,027 saw County take the field, in an unfamiliar all amber strip against Grimsby, interest having been greatly increased by the capture of Evans. In a gloomy start, Weare injured a hand, and was replaced in goal by Evans. Grimsby won with two goals from Scottish international Mickey Cullen. After three games, County had neither a point nor a goal. Bowman at last broke County's duck, securing a point at Barnsley. In midweek, fellow strugglers Brentford were entertained, with a crowd of only half that of the opening fixture.

Three Newport goals had gone in by half-time, tne final result being 6-1. Buchanan had obtained a hat-trick, and Bowman had despatched a 40 yard left foot rocket into the goal at the Railway end. Surely, the corner had been turned? Three days later, the side won 2-1 at Ashton Gate, Bowman scoring the winner with a long range drive.

Of the next eleven games, including two League Cup encounters with Shrewsbury, not one match was won. A 2-2 draw with Portsmouth was in fact County's best display of the season, for Pompey were an outstanding side. But at their traditional graveyard, Meadow Lane, the side was slaughtered 1-8. Nevertheless, many older supporters still maintain that under Evans they saw some of their best football at Somerton Park, though the forwards could not convert their chances. Probably, the Scottish style of play was not suited to the rough and tumble of Third Division football. Yet another Scot, Moffat, now joined.

By the year's end, the side won only three League games and one F.A. Cup match. After an 87th minute Cup defeat at non-League Weymouth, Walsh was bought for £3,000. This was negated, when Finlay broke a leg at Grimsby.

A New Year A.G.M. gave Evans a vote of confidence, but by mid- February, the team had lost nine successive matches and failed to win any of the last 14. Wilcox was sacked as Trainer, and in mid March Evans followed suit. Percy Jones resigned as Chairman, being replaced by John Bailey. Lucas, still at the "Black Horse", took over as Manager. From January until the end of season, the side won only four games, and over the whole season 31 matches were lost. The side scored 44 goals (Smith being top with 9) and conceded 102. County, were cast into the outer darkness of the Fourth, from a relatively comfortable niche in the Third Division.

At Loftus Road - Sherwood tackles Bedford of Q.P.R., and Weare is ready to take the ball.

# CHAPTER 6

## Seventeen Years Hard Labour

In and Out. (Left) Evergreen manager Billy Lucas, with his well-loved bow tie and pipe takes over again. (Right) Mr. and Mrs. Bobby Evans' arrival at Newport Station, but they soon departed.

The following season (1962–63) was to be County's Golden Jubilee, and at least it could be no worse than the one just gone. The end of the season had seen Pring, Sheffield and Rathbone blooded, and after that most of the Scots had departed, along with George Harris. Lucas, assisted again by Ray Wilcox, made a number of signings, including Derek Sullivan and Colin Hudson. The two who made the most impact were Joe Bonson and Ralph Hunt, who both threatened to rewrite Newport's goalscoring record book. The Ground received something of a facelift in the close season. The Grandstand was painted, and there were other improvements.

With a tremendous fightback, the team was triumphant in the opening match at Hartlepool, winning 3–2. Incredibly, 10,500 turned up to see an unchanged side entertain Oldham, the result being a disappointing 0–0 draw. There were almost 3,000 less for the following match with Darlington. The visiting Manager, Eddie Carr, received a tremendous ovation, and the game was drawn 2–2, with Hunt scoring twice.

County secured a point a game for the first dozen matches, but a good attack and bad defence made results unpredictable. A four game spell included a 3–6 defeat at Lincoln, a 6–0 victory over Barrow (with Hunt scoring three) and a 1–5 reverse at Oxford, where Jones scored four. By early October, County had the top two scorers in Division Four, and Sheffield had netted a dozen for the reserves.

For the one and only time, the club had a reasonable League Cup run. Gillingham were beaten 2–1 and Aldershot 3–0 away, thanks to a Bonson hat-trick.

The result was a home tie with Manchester City, and just under 10,000 saw a fighting performance, as Newport went down 1–2.

County could put out a settled side, many of whom were locals. In the F.A. Cup, versus Q.P.R., a disputed goal at the White City put County out. Results were reasonable up to Christmas, but this was the year of the Big Freeze, and earlier form was to count for nothing. Incredibly, after December the 22nd, the next team Newport played was Torquay on February the 27th! Of County's first five matches, four were lost, although during this spell, Rowland, an admirably consistent and gifted player, broke McSeveney's record of consecutive matches. Another player in the same mould, Len Hill, now had a brief run in the side.

After 27 games, County had slipped to 21st, with Bonson and Hunt losing their scoring touch. Newport had netted in every match until March the 4th. In mid-March, Frowen and Welsh international Webster were signed to bolster the side. In the Welsh Cup, County obtained away wins over Merthyr (4–0), Holywell (6–2, with Hunt scoring a hat-trick) and Swansea (1–0). Although the League season had not ended in glory, at least Ralph Hunt had scored 27 goals and beaten the post-war record of Parker and Johnston. Now the side had only to beat Borough United and County would be in Europe! Few fans even knew the whereabouts of Borough, which had been formed by the amalgamation of Conway Borough and Llandudno Junction in 1954. The home and away legs were to be played on a points system, so scores would be irrelevant.

On the evening of April 27th, County played at Nant-y-Coed. Hunt and Bebb scored, as did Russell, with a penalty – County had lost 1-2! At least a win at Somerton would keep County alive, but the ball would not go in, and little Borough United were in Europe. They went one better later, by beating Sliema Wanderers, but some years afterwards were wound up.

Off the field, there were some close season improvements, and it was intended to construct a new flight of steps up to Somerton Bridge, the old steps – with the antiquated gate – only taking one person at a time. On the playing side County now seemed even more understaffed. Many first teamers such as Peake, Bowman, Hudson and Walsh moved on, and the only incoming players were the amateur Graham Reynolds and promising Gil Reece. To make matters worse, Webster was to miss the season's start, due to a hernia operation.

A point was secured from the first match at windy Doncaster. Two days later County hammered Bradford Park Avenue 5-2, Sheffield heading three second half goals. In late August the Arms Park Company announced that greyhound racing would cease at Somerton Park, the last meeting in fact taking place on Tuesday October the 29th. The County Board, who were renting the Ground for £1,250 per annum, had the option of buying it. The Football Club Directors reportedly offered £20,000, but nothing was agreed. Eventually, they were to cajole the Borough Council into buying the Ground for £30,000 in October. The Council agreed to lease it to County for a minimum of 21 years.

In their first home game of the season, County defeated Brighton 2-0, and despite a narrow League Cup defeat by Millwall, and a 0-3 loss at rain-soaked Chester, the side was doing well. After eight games, Newport were in second place, behind Gillingham. On September the 14th, George Walters was bought for £2,000 to strengthen the defence.

After an excellent start the rot set in. In a run of five matches – four of which were at home – only one victory was achieved. The return of Webster made little impression, and after 15 games, County were 14th, and heading downwards. Not that their matches lacked entertainment. Newport were trailing 1-2 at Torquay with 29 minutes left, when eight goals were scored in a 17 minute spell. Stubbs scored five times, with County eventually losing the match 3-8!

With things going badly, Sheffield, Rathbone and Williams all sought transfers. On a more encouraging note, promising winger Mike Kear had broken into the first team. With little to play for in the League, the team now set off on a long overdue F.A. Cup run. It did not get off to the most encouraging start. Hunt opened the scoring at non-League Hereford, but Bonson missed a penalty on the sticky pitch, and Dixon equalised. The replay took place two days later, after incessant rain, and this time County triumphed 4-0, Hunt notching a hat-trick. Soon after, Rowland suffered the rare indignity of being dropped. Young Hill took his place at left-half and established himself there for the rest of the season, Rowland soon reappearing at right-half.

(Left) Leading goalscorer Ralph Hunt, tragically killed after his transfer to Chesterfield.
(Above) Laurie Sheffield - ace goalscorer during the 60's.

After two intervening League defeats, County met Watford in the Second Round of the Cup. After 50 seconds Smith collected a bad clearance and scored. Before half-time he added a second, and that was enough. Struggling County suffered another blow, when Kear, who had made a significant impact in his half dozen League games, was sold to Nottingham Forest for £7,000, in order to reduce the club's debts.

In the Cup's Third Round, Fourth Division County were drawn at home against Sheffield Wednesday, sixth in Division One. Less than 10,000 turned up, and in the first half international Holliday scored, following a Weare blunder. Three minutes after the break, Bonson headed the equaliser and was mobbed by fans. Hearts sank when Finney put Wednesday in front with a brilliant oblique shot, but after 67 minutes Bonson collected a faulty clearance by McLaren and drove in from 12 yards. Four minutes later the unthinkable happened; Hunt helped in a Smith shot, and County were leading. A third of the crowd invaded the pitch bringing fears of abandonment. The fans sang "Cwm Rhondda" with all the fervour of a rugby crowd. Several minutes of injury time were played, nerves were jangling, then Weare made an acrobatic last minute save. The referee blew, and County were through!

League games were an anticlimax, and Newport lost 0-1 to Chester and 0-3 to York. At least County had the advantage that they were putting out an unchanged side for match after match. Several thousand fans travelled to Burnley for the Fourth Round of the F.A. Cup. Willie Morgan opened the scoring after a Weare error, and County were fighting for all they were worth. Sheffield equalised, but a 55th minute Connelly header was enough to curtail Newport's interest in the Cup.

Bonson followed a Welsh Cup hat-trick against Haverfordwest with two League goals versus Barrow. Then he scored with a header which knocked Swansea out of the Welsh Cup. Around this time the Council completed the purchase of Somerton Park, County obtained a licence for a new club in the old greyhound clubhouse, also announcing that the sport of speedway would be coming to Newport.

In the Welsh Cup, Newport fought back to achieve a commendable draw with Cardiff, with Hill injured. On a snow cleared pitch the side lost the replay to a 55th minute goal from Mel Charles.

April the 17th saw the birth of Newport speedway, with a match versus Cradley Heath. It was to enjoy years of success at one time attracting bigger gates than County. For the football team, it was a case of playing out the season. At least Bonson regained his shooting boots, obtaining a hat-trick versus Southport. He scored his 100th League goal in the Lincoln game, which marked Reece's debut. In 42 matches Bonson netted 25 goals, and then joined Brentford for £6,000. Hunt and Webster were also allowed to depart.

For the new season Ken Morgan, ex-Ironside Jim Singer, Jack Swindells and reserve goalkeeper Keith Beswick were signed; Walters was elected Captain. The season started well, a Sheffield goal defeating Darlington. Four days later the side was beating Crewe, but had to settle for a draw. Unfortunately, the shared points sequence extended to County's home games, the first three being score draws, before Southport were hammered 5-0. A week later Newport were beating leaders Bradford City, until the latter saved their unbeaten record two minutes from time. Unhappily, Singer who had been knocking in a few goals had injured a knee at Brighton in the previous away game. This was ultimately to terminate his career, and had a detrimental effect on the team.

Laurie Sheffield was still scoring goals. Notts County had knocked Newport out of the League Cup, but in the League match at Somerton, Sheffield scored a great hat-trick taking Newport to 5th. Many scouts had turned up to watch Jeff Astle, but he was well subdued by the lanky Rathbone. A couple of narrow away defeats were followed by a 4-1 win at Barrow. Morgan scored two fine goals, and after a shaky start, settled down to become an influential player.

In mid-October, Pring was sold to Rotherham for £7,000. At least this time County had a ready made replacement in Gil Reece. In his first match of the season ten man Newport beat Hartlepools 2-0, even with Bird missing a second half penalty! Experienced John McCole was signed on extended loan as injury cover. In the home match with Lincoln the "Imps" were thrashed 7-0. Morgan was, at first, credited with four goals, but later given a doubtful Bracewell own goal. Rowland and Hill (who scored a 25 yarder), prompted their forwards outstandingly.

Newport Wasps had made an impressive start to their speedway career, and before County's home game with Millwall, the Provincial Speedway Knock-out Cup was presented to them. County's own thoughts now turned to the F.A. Cup, and Midland League Spalding were beaten 5-3. Newport were in the top half of the table, still in the Cup, and their new Social Club and Buffet Bar had just been opened, at a cost of over £8,000. Over a 14 year period County had received £65,000 from the Supporters' Club.

Two tragic accidents occurred in late 1964. After the Stockport match, 22-year-old John Nibloe drove into a stone wall on his return journey and was killed. Less than a month afterwards, the news filtered through that Ralph Hunt had died at Grantham, also following a match. He was buried in Norwich just before Christmas. On a happier note, Mansfield were beaten in the F.A. Cup - County scored three second half goals, and only Welsh-born goalie Treharne prevented a rout.

Injuries began taking their toll on the small squad, and despite Sheffield's prodigious goal scoring, the team was gradually sliding down the table.

Over 2,000 travelled to Elm Park in the F.A. Cup and saw County fight a fine rearguard action, after Rowland had become a passenger. It looked all over for County until Reece equalised with an 88th minute header. Two days later 13,000 turned up for the replay – 4,000 more than for the Sheffield Wednesday game! Newport could not match their earlier performance however, and lost to an 84th minute goal from Peter Shreeves. After a 2–3 defeat at Swansea, in the Welsh Cup, County were facing their annual struggle to survive the second half of the season.

After 30 matches, Sheffield had scored 20 times, but the defence was letting in goals just as quickly. Five were conceded at Southport, and in the next home League game, versus Bradford P.A., the side was 1–3 down, but hit back to win 4–3. Inquiries for Ivor Allchurch, valued by Cardiff at £6,000, seemed mainly designed for publicity. Although Singer was regularly reported to be "back in training", he never reappeared in the first team.

Newport had an eight match spell, in which they never conceded less than two goals. Gates dropped and McCole was released. 18-year-old David Pugh came into the side after a reserve team hat-trick at Pembroke. Everything seemed to be going wrong. At York, County were drawing 1–1, when referee Bullough halted the match for a snowstorm. When play resumed, County lost 1–5. At Millwall they were drawing 0–0 at half-time, but proceeded to lose 0–4.

Despite the small staff Swindells was allowed to leave with his father desperately ill and his mother bed-ridden; he scored many goals in non-League football. County were just playing out the remainder of the season, although Sheffield, who scored a hat-trick against Torquay, went on to notch a post-war record 27 League goals. For Newport fans there was one further blow when Reece, who had shown exceptional form, was sold to Sheffield United, on April the 17th, for £10,000. In two seasons the club had sold three wingers, but it did, at least, give 18-year-old Ken Wookey, son of the pre-war player, the chance to play at Chesterfield. Without three regulars County recorded a sparkling 4–1 win.

During the close season Sheffield was sold to Doncaster, thus over a couple of seasons County had lost not only three wingers, but Bonson, Hunt and Sheffield. On a more encouraging note Newport received not only £5,000, but also the fair haired Irish forward, Alfie Hale, who was to soon become a Somerton favourite. Also signed were Welsh international Derek Tapscott, Malcolm Cook and David Jones. Early incidents did not augur well, for by early August four players were out injured. Smith, just recovering from a broken leg, fractured it again in a friendly with Swansea. Singer, once again "raring to go", broke down in training and his unhappy return to Somerton Park was over.

County, captained by Rathbone now that Walters was part-time, again started with an encouraging away win, with

Stopper centre-half Graham Rathbone, played over 200 games for County's first team.

Morgan scoring twice at Chesterfield. Promotion was needed at all costs, for a preponderance of mediocre Northern sides in the Division did little to stimulate interest. Indeed, by the season's end, gates would dip below 2,000. Significantly, amateur Graham Reynolds was now leading the forward line, in place of Sheffield or Bonson. League form was erratic, with good wins mixed with bad defeats, such as 2–5 at Hartlepools, and 1–6 at Chester. County made their traditional First Round exit in the League Cup, this time losing to Southend, and in the F.A. Cup there was a humiliating farewell at non-League Bath.

To make matters worse, Reynolds, registered as an amateur, was suspended for three months by the Welsh F.A. for accepting money. Fortunately Hale was ready to make a belated debut, after which he did not miss a match. Tapscott however, played only a dozen times. After 29 games County had 18 points and were 16th. A Welsh Cup defeat by Chester made matters worse, and no gate reached 3,000 in the second half of the season.

There were some bright spots. Hale accumulated 21 goals in 34 appearances. Reynolds returned, and, against Bradford P.A., Thomas became the club's youngest ever debutant at 16. The reserves came second in the Welsh League, the Championship being won by Lovells, with a clear nine points lead.

Another blow was encountered, when for domestic reasons, Hale decided to return to Ireland. He signed for Waterford for £3,000, and the fee was received in postal orders, coins and stamps! Tapscott, Cook and Walters also departed, and there was no major signing.

General football Interest in the new season was heightened by England's World Cup victory, and County began with a reasonable draw at Lincoln, Jones netting twice. In a home League Cup encounter with Swansea, a poor first half performance meant a 1-2 defeat. Despite some poor results, attendances showed an increase, possibly because the side contained numerous locals, such as Rowland, Bird, Hill, Williams and Thomas.

Three successive wins were followed by five games without a success. Frazer made little impact at centre-forward, so Jones was tried there, and against Chesterfield he obtained a hat-trick. Another quick F.A. Cup exit was a bitter blow, when Brighton won 2-1 at Somerton.

Llanelli were beaten 6-2 in the Welsh Cup, with Jones again scoring three, however, with more Fourth Division mediocrity in store gates took another nosedive. At least travelling had now been made easier with the opening of the Severn Bridge on September the 9th.

In February, Lucas, who had been running the club, off and on, for a decade, left for Swansea. Because of constant enforced sales he had been unable to get Newport out of the Fourth Division. Les Graham, who had been looking after the youth side, took his place.

In November, with Rathbone sold to Grimsby, County secured the transfer of talented Alan Williams, who became the only Englishman in the side. Another local youngster, Alan Smith, made the side at left-half. At the end of February, a strange and fearsome Northener, Melling, was signed to beef up the forward line.

By the time Bradford City were beaten, 2-1 away, County had gone 19 League matches without a win, and for the home match with Bradford City no more than 1,222 had turned up. In March, Trevor Morris joined Graham in running the club, and under the pair a re-election application was avoided, but these were grim times. At least there was an abundance of local talent, and both David Pugh and Jeff Thomas were under-23 internationals.

There were various close season staff changes. With Beswick having been ousted by Weare, during the second

(Top) Determined winger Granville Smith of the 1960's played in the final match at Somerton! (Below) Polished John Rowland, would have been 'capped' with any higher Division club.

half of the season, Timson was now taken on as a second goalkeeper.

Bird and Morgan departed, the latter having a successful spell as Cwmbran player-manager. Other signings included craggy full-back Joe Wilson, the somewhat erratic winger Gerald King, and the much travelled and disappointing forward Billy Stark.

The opening match of the 1967-68 season was an unsatisfactory 1-1 home draw with Rochdale, but at least the crowd was just under 5,000. The second game was away to Swindon in the League Cup, a competition which was now growing in stature. County secured a 1-1 result, thanks to a Nurse own goal, and a week later Swindon were beaten 2-0 at Somerton.

After three unbeaten League games County took on Blackpool in the Second Round. The crowd was a healthy 13,157. It was a great game with Hill starring for Newport. Milne scored the only goal with a superb 15 yard shot, which Timson almost saved.

County were normally able to put out an unchanged side. After eleven games they had secured 14 points and were 5th, two points behind the leaders. Melling scored a hat-trick against Wrexham, but the bubble soon burst, for the goals dried up, with none at all scored in four consecutive matches. There was no money to enter the transfer market, the only signing being Harry Robinson, who came on a free transfer. In November, Melling and Jones were sold to Mansfield.

Newport had secured one point from five matches when the F.A. Cup arrived, and amazingly Third Division Gillingham were thrashed 3-0 at Somerton Park. Around this time, Cyril Adams, Harry Morgan and Cyril Rogers joined the Board, whilst the singer Tom Jones was made honorary President.

There was little money available, but Tony Buck and Tony Jones were bought from Oxford, which gave the club a rare boost. Timson made only one first team appearance after December and gave up professional football, disillusioned with his progress. County fell back on their old reliable Len Weare.

The County on an away day during the late 1960's.

Guildford were beaten 1–0, in the Second Round of the Cup, and in the Third, County had the plum draw of First Division Southampton. Unfortunately Tony Jones was ineligible, and throughout their Cup run, County had to call on the less effective Stark. There were 5,000 Newportonians among the crowd of over 20,000 at the match. Chivers had just left for Spurs, and Saul was making his debut, and it was he that gave Alan Williams the slip during the match, and scored. Hill was later fouled, and the Newport fans held their breath as King ran up to take the penalty. He crashed the ball into the net, with his boot flying off in the opposite direction!

Three days later 17,600 saw the replay. Saints went two up, in 28 minutes, through Saul and Sydenham, but ten minutes into the second half Alan Williams pulled one back with a great header. Two minutes later the sides were level thanks to a Hill special, and this led to hundreds of small boys running on to the pitch. Hill was later brought down but no penalty was awarded, then Gabriel was injured. Young Mick Channon came on, and within two minutes, he scored with a rocket shot at the Railway end. Newport were pressing hard for the equaliser when the referee blew up – a few minutes early.

There was now a buoyancy around Somerton Park, and five consecutive games were won, including two Welsh Cup matches, but in the semi-final, County unexpectedly lost to non-League Hereford, the winner coming from ex-Ironside, Albert Derrick. The club was forever suffering from its small playing staff, and, against Aldershot was forced to play half-back Wood in goal. The only benefit of the situation was that promising youngsters Cooper and Young were given runs in the first team. But the hopeful signs were undermined by poor support, and for the final two home matches attendances again dipped below 2,000.

There were no exciting close season signings, though Mike McLaughlin – a late entry into League football – was to give the club good service as full-back. Ian Hamilton, who had been a useful player with Bristol Rovers, was already badly crocked, and proved to be more of a liability than anything else.

Times were changing, for as another Fourth Division season commenced (1968–69), it was an age of fighting on the terraces and over publicised hooliganism came upon the scene. Even at humble Somerton Park individuals would be escorted around the perimeter of the pitch, with their arms behind their backs. Great would be the ironic cheering as the numbskulls were taken away by the police.

The side for the opening match, at Grimsby, had an unfamiliar look, and there were soon other changes which boded ill. Goalkeeper David Jones had been signed on trial when Weare and Timson had been injured, and he played in the 0–3 defeat at Grimsby, but was soon on his way. Captain Alan Williams had for some time been unhappy, and walked off the pitch in one reserve match. He departed after just one game, as did Joe Wilson who played in the following League Cup match at Bristol City. McLaughlin was ineligible for the game, because the club had forgotten to post his registration forms! Normally a happy club, County was experiencing a bad patch, and it showed on the pitch. They became one of the last teams in the country to score, following their first five matches without a goal.

Suddenly the team began a good run, which included an excellent victory over Southend, who were beaten 4–1 at Somerton, with Buck scoring twice. Four out of five matches were won, and County shot up from 23rd to 9th. Lucas' Swansea team were beaten 2–1, before a 5,000 crowd, and Buck turned himself into a folk hero by scoring all five in a 5–1 victory at Bradford P.A.

The good patch ended as quickly as it had begun, and from October the 5th until the end of the year the side failed to score more than once in a game. At least the defence was playing quite well, with the likes of Weare, Rowland and Wood, giving good accounts. The team strip and programme cover were changed to tangerine and white, as the club sought a change of image and luck.

In the F.A. Cup, an away draw, at Exeter, gave cause for hope, but a crowd of over 6,000 saw the side go to pieces in the replay, scoring two own goals, in a 1-3 defeat. In late December, local motor dealer, Cyril Rogers became Chairman. The Mayor launched an appeal for funds, but the public, which had heard the story once too often, was apathetic.

After 21, games, County were 17th. A 4-2 win over Peterborough, in January, proved a flash in the pan, the next result being a 0-5 rout, at Port Vale. The side lost to Swansea in the Welsh Cup, after extra time, in a replay. A match was held with Portsmouth, for Rowland's testimonial. The visitors won 8-3, Hiron seeming to score every time he touched the ball. David Williams was now in a plaster cast, and the club suffered another blow, when star forward Buck was sold to Rochdale, for a moderate fee. Things looked black, and, on March 10th, a Special General Meeting of the Supporters' Social Club was held, to arrange a programme of fund raising events. Crowds were plummeting. In February, 1,504 arrived to watch Scunthorpe, and, in April, 1,192 for Bradford P.A.

Locals sometimes filled nine places in the Newport side. On April 21st, a benevolent Headmaster permitted schoolboy Steve Aizlewood to have the day off, and play at Chesterfield. With the side deep in the re-election mire, Graham was sacked before the final match, at Workington. This was not the only black news. On May 7th, Lovells Athletic, 4th in the Welsh League, sent in a letter of resignation. Gates had dropped from under three figures to 20 or so, and, with changes in the Company, it was considered undesirable to continue. It was a great blow, especially for Manager Selwyn Kemp, with the club for 17 years. Lovells had provided many players for Newport County, such as Rowland and Hill.

For County there was a reprieve, though with re-election came a warning regarding future applications, especially from clubs with poor Ground facilities. In early July, the Geordie, Bobby Ferguson was appointed player-manager. Some players, such as McLelland, Jones and Towland left and, despite the difficult situation, some able players were signed. Lovells' demise meant the acquisition of Roddy Jones, soon an institution at the club. Ron Radford arrived, a player whose powerful shot later became "Goal of the Season" on BBC TV. Also arriving were the sprightly Bristol Rovers' veteran, Ray Mabbutt, promising Andy White and Old Boy, Albert Derrick.

A mascot, Tangerine Tommy, was designed to try to "sell" the club, but cracks on the playing side could not be papered over. The opening game, home to York, was lost 1-2. The amateur centre-forward, Delaney, was substituted, and soon left the club. For young Saunders, it was also his only first team appearance of the season. Sprague was also missing for the next match, 1 2-3 League Cup defeat by Swansea. Following a 0-3 defeat at Oldham, the home crowd had dropped from 4,206 versus York to 2,525 against Exeter. The match was won 2-0, but now Supporters' Club membership was only half what it had been a few years before. Despite some bad reverses, games were won in the Autumn, and, after 14 games, the side had scrambled briefly to tenth.

There was the odd bright spot. Weare made his 500th appearance, against Darlington, McLoughlin and Hill were playing consistently and young Aizlewood was a regular, but, when injury dogged Derrick stopped scoring goals, there was no consistent goal scorer left in the side. In the F.A. Cup, Colchester were beaten 2-1, as were Hereford in the Second Round. Hereford complained noisily, after Wood had climbed on Ken Brown's back for his match-winning header. After this came one point from four League matches, a 0-1 Third Round defeat at Gillingham, two more League reverses and a Welsh Cup replay defeat at Hereford. This was followed by one League victory in seven matches!

Gates continued to fall, and Wilcox was sacked, after 31 years with the club. President Tom Jones gave a concert in Cardiff's "Capitol", though, according to some accounts, the club was worse off, after the deduction of expenses! In March, County made their first purchase since Buck and Jones, when Coldrick was bought for £4,000. Although he was a whole-hearted player, one signing could not stem the tide. Although eight of their final twelve matches were at home, and they had four games in hand over Workington, re-election was looming. Despite winning two of their final three games, 1-0 at Halifax being their first away win since November 4th, 1968, Newport were doomed, when Workington unexpectedly won 3-0 at Notts County. For the last game, only 1,009 watched the side beat Grimsby 1-0.

Despite earlier warnings, the club obtained re-election, with over 30 votes. On the terraces, concrete replaced sleepers, and a Social Club was opened, where the greyhound clubhouse had been. The programme featured Tangerine Tommy on a tangerine cover, and Radio Tangerine blared out the club's theme song - "Tangerine, Tangerine." It may have given older supporters the pip, but, at least, the club was making the effort. Along with Derrick and the retiring Weare, out went the consistent Hill and McLoughlin and the promising Cooper, the latter enjoying a long career in lower Division football. Ron Stitfall joined the staff, and in came two players destined to make their mark. Willie Brown was signed for a small fee scraped up by supporters. John Macey was the first goalkeeper truly to replace Weare.

At the A.G.M., the club had to appeal for tracksuits and for volunteers to paint dressing rooms. The first game, home to Northampton, at least saw a gate of 4,515, but was lost to an 84th minute header. The next game was, in retrospect, to prove a red letter day – Reading were beaten 2-1, in the League Cup. The first away game pointed to the future. County's defence disintegrated, and Redrobe scored three, in a 6-1 Southport victory. Three more League defeats were followed by a 1-4 League Cup loss and a further five League reverses. After ten matches, Newport had no points. On October 3rd, fans heard, via the media, the fantastic news that the team had failed to lose, drawing 2-2 at distant Hartlepool.

Two loan signings were made, Darrell and ex-Ironside, Harry Harris, who had long given up his goalscoring role. Three more games were lost, then County entertained Workington, for whom Wilson and Wookey now played. With County 0-2 down, Harris rolled up his sleeves, and went forward, to convert a Darrell corner. Brown dribbled round Burridge, to make it 2-2. Then came another four defeats.

The blackest day came on November 21st. In the F.A. Cup, County were hammered 1-6 at non-League Barnet, which equalled Derby's record defeat by a non-League side. This was the nail in the coffin for Ferguson as Manager, though he continued as a player. Inevitably, he was replaced by Lucas, who stated: *"If we are to die as a Football League club, let us die honourably and with dignity"*.

Between the Barnet debacle and the year's end, only one more point was secured, at Southport. To the end of December, all the team had achieved was three 2-2 draws. With the club unable to buy players, the only hope for salvation lay in Lucas' skills as a Manager. The club's appalling record was attracting publicity. Could it continue? Would it break records, such as Bolton's 22 games without a victory in 1902-03, or Crewe's 30 in 1956-57? It was something of a two-edged sword. On one side were the mockers, who would ridicule the side, and, on the other, those who, with the British love of the underdog, wanted the club to succeed.

1971 began more hopefully, with Roddy Jones securing a point at Exeter. Six days later, the unbelievable happened, as County entertained Southend, on a wet pitch. After 38 minutes, Jones tapped home from a Redford corner. Later, White jinked past three defenders, to fire a fierce left foot shot past Lloyd. At the end, the players received a great ovation. It was Lucas' birthday, and a finer present could not have been found! Before their win, County had secured 4 points from 25 games. They were 4 points behind Barrow, 13 behind Hartlepools. Hereford and Wigan had strong claims to League membership. After a 1-1 draw with Cardiff, in the Welsh Cup, County went out 0-4 in the replay, but the League was the only important thing. Barrow were beaten 3-2 and Stockport 3-1. The latter game was the start of a good run, with five games out of seven won. Gates, which had dipped below 1,500, began to exceed 3,000.

Barrow were left bottom. Notts County, ten points clear at the top, came to Somerton and were beaten 2-1 and newcomers Cambridge lost 2-0, as Saunders blotted out Hateley and Hollett. On March 20th, the side visited Brentford, who had won their previous eleven home matches. In the mud, County secured their first away win – 3-0. It was the greatest comeback since Lazarus!

After 39 games, Newport were on 21 points, two behind Hartlepools. By the season's end, after a Brown hat-trick against Darlington, County were 22nd. They had no right to expect re-election, but, after their great fightback, and some pleading from Lucas, they achieved it. It was their third successive re-election plea, and Lucas vowed he would not be involved in another.

For the forthcoming season, the pitch, regarded as the worst in the League, was improved. It was suffering because of speedway, the corners being returfed every game, and grit being sprayed all over it. There were some Ground improvements and the establishment of a Vice-Presidents' Club. There was one major move on the staff side, with the signing of well-known Brian Harris as player-coach. There was a minor sensation, when Revie signed the improving Saunders for Leeds. While the fee was peanuts for Leeds, it was a godsend for Newport. Ferguson, unexpectedly to achieve honours with Ipswich, naturally left, as did Radford.

Although County won none of their first four League or League Cup games, they began with 4,000 gates, because of the earlier fightback. There was still a largely local side, with Macey, Brown and Harris the only "foreigners." Ominously, a 2-1 defeat of Colchester was County's only success in their first nine League matches, and the side was struggling in 23rd place. Then, County's fortunes looked up for a change, with four of the next five games being won. The run included away wins at Hartlepools, where White scored a brilliant individual goal, and Gillingham.

In the F.A. Cup, Newport were drawn away to dreaded Notts County. Before an 11,976 crowd, only Lynch saved the side from a fate worse than 0-6. After this, County won only one of their next seven matches, and Coldrick's departure for a cartilage operation did nothing to improve matters. There was still enough confidence about the club, however, to begin improving the floodlights and make a few signings. Ex-Ironsides Dai Jones and Len Hill came back, along with useful young defender, Peter Passey. Encouragingly, the Boxing Day match with Chester was viewed by 7,664 – the largest home gate since 1962.

Hopes of a good Welsh Cup run, brought on by wins over Ebbw Vale and Bangor, were dashed at Wrexham, on March 22nd. Even in the gloomiest times, there was never a shortage of humour. Against Brentford, on February 26th, the side ran out wearing unfamiliar kit, which a firm had asked them to try out. Instead of the usual one stripe on each side of the shorts, there were stripes all round, making the players look like Elizabethan dandies. The sight brought raucous wolf whistles, and the kit had mysteriously disappeared by the next game!

The season's end was remarkable. Darlington were beaten 4-0, with White scoring direct from a corner. A point versus Exeter was followed by two against Stockport, thanks to a superb White goal. Workington became the only side to defeat County in their final ten games. Crewe and Reading were beaten, as were Colchester, 2-0 up in the second half. At Stockport, there was a remarkable 4-4 draw. For the first time in four years, County would not have to apply for re-election! The players were up all night, and Newport was not reached until 7a.m. the next morning! Eleven points were gained from the final six games – promotion form.

Ironically, the highly promising Aizlewood had missed the successful run, but he had enjoyed a good season and represented the Welsh under-23 side versus England, marking Malcolm McDonald.

Late in the season, the dissatisfied Harris had held a long conversation with Lucas and Cyril Rogers, and, at the end of it, had been appointed Assistant Manager.

In the close season, locals Alan Smith and George Young departed, as did Passey, though the loan signing was later to return on a full-time basis. It did not help matters, when young Swain broke his leg in a pre-season fame. There were three incoming transfers of note. Under-23 international Dennis Hawkins started with a bang, but quickly fizzled out and left. Bob Summerhayes was a developing player, with a deft touch, and full-back Willie Screen soon became a firm favourite, with his whole-hearted defending.

After ten inglorious years, fans were hoping that County could escape from the Fourth Division. After six games, the side was unbeaten. In late August, came some notable games. In the hame game with Chester, the visitors opened the scoring – for County – as young John Relish, playing his third game, stuck a 14th minute White centre past Eadie. He later scored at the right end, but Willie Brown, in his 100th League appearance, netted twice.

Hill missed a twice taken penalty. In a League Cup replay with Swansea, Brown scored three, all with his head. In the next match, at Colchester, Harris was due for his 500th appearance. A derailment at Southall delayed the team for 90 minutes. The players arrived 15 minutes before the start, rushing from taxis to the dressing rooms. It did them no harm, for they won 3-1.

The team now suffered a seven match spell without a win. A 0-3 League Cup defeat by Ipswich was expected, but there was an unfortunate 0-5 League defeat at Reading, with both Thomas and Wood stretchered off. Just as suddenly, the team recaptured the form of the previous season. A 1-0 win at Northampton, via a Roddy Jones goal, heralded a run of six wins in seven matches. Hill and Williams both made their 300th appearance, and Brown and Jones began to forge an effective partnership up front.

By early November, County were fourth, but a run of four defeats in five matches knocked them back down. In the F.A. Cup, amateurs Alton Town were beaten 5-1. Harris scored twice, but refused the chance of a penalty kick, which could have given him a hat-trick. Torquay were beaten in the next round, but, of more long-term significance was the home League match with newcomers Hereford. Harris was brought down in the game, but no penalty was given. Ten minutes later, Hereford were given a penalty for a blatant dive, and Redrobe netted. Six were booked by Mr. Yates, along with goalkeeper Macey, for comments on the way off. The attendance was 8,776.

An unlucky 2-3 loss at Workington, before Christmas, pushed Newport down to 11th, but, from Boxing Day, the side won five successive matches. In the F.A. Cup, County were holding Millwall, until White lost the ball on the halfway line, after which it was one-way traffic. In a Welsh Cup replay, Brown scored another hat-trick against Swansea.

After a 5-1 League hammering of Gillingham, 11,350 turned up for a Welsh Cup match with Cardiff. A 1-3 loss was soon forgotten, as County won their next three League games.

Rod Jones heads a goal against Bury (28th of April 1973)

Then came a crucial loss of form, with County failing to score in six matches out of eight. On April 7th, many Newportonians were among the 14,849, who saw County lose 0-2 at Hereford, Owen and Jenkins scoring in the second half. Bookings included County's trainer and both goalies!

When County travelled to Doncaster, supporters were amazed to hear the result – Newport had triumphed 5-1. The season's last week saw three matches. On the Monday night, came a 0-1 defeat at Stockport, Hart scoring. The next day, Workington were beaten 2-0. All depended on the home match with Bury, a game that will long be remembered by the 7,390 who saw it. With County's traditional 3.15 kick-off, other results would be known before the end. Coldrick converted a 22nd minute penalty. A Warburton header equalised matters in the 55th minute, but, in the 67th, Aizlewood netted. A Roddy Jones deflection put Newport 3-1 up. Towards the finish, a roar went up. Those fans with transistors had heard that Crewe had beaten Hereford 1-0. Players and fans jumped for joy. The finale was filled with unbearable tension. Tierney scored with 6 minutes left. Dai Jones made it 4-2, in the 86th minute, Holt 4-3, in the 88th. At last, County were up! Alas, it was not to be. Some idiot at the BBC had reversed the scores. Hereford had won. With County's fixtures completed, promotion depended on Aldershot's game with Stockport.

Some Newport fans travelled North, and saw a 1-1 draw. Promotion had been lost by a fractional goal average difference of 0.12. It was one of the cruellest blows in County's existence.

Despite this major disappointment, it was Newport's best season for years, and for their part, the youth side had won the inaugural S.A. Brain Trophy and the Gwent Premier League. Ironically, it was one of Newport rugby's worst ever campaigns.

Record signing Brian Godfrey

Buoyed up by the near miss, the Board took the unheard of step of signing a player for £10,000, the vastly experienced Brian Godfrey. Was he the missing link, that would get the club out of the Fourth Division? Bristol Rovers veteran Harold Jarman also arrived, along with new reserve goalkeeper Don Payne. Unfortunately, David Williams and Jeff Thomas departed through injury. Sprague, who had intended to retire, was persuaded to re-sign in September.

The expectant fan was now due for a piece of typical Newport disappointment. Three draws, in the opening three matches, were followed by four consecutive defeats. Dumped out of the League Cup by Swindon, County were struggling at the foot of the table. Things improved, when – amid the wind and rain – Crewe were beaten 4-2, with two goals apiece from Jarman and Aizlewood. The next game, with Rotherham, was won by a Roddy Jones goal.

From November the 9th, the side won five League matches in a row. In the middle of this run, however, came another ignominious F.A.Cup defeat. At sloping Loakes Park, Isthmian League Wycombe Wanderers beat County 3-1, scoring all three goals in an 8 minute spell. But in the League, Newport had climbed to 7th, and young centre-half Steve Aizlewood was proving a real asset, scoring goals as well as stopping them.

County's League position began to deteriorate from late December, the side having a four match spell of conceding three goals a time. The surroundings did not always help, and at Workington, Newport were watched by a "crowd" of 749. The home Welsh Cup-tie with Merthyr was noteworthy for a couple of reasons. With a national power crisis in progress, matches were being switched to Sundays, with entry to this game being via a 50p programme. The other interest lay in the winning goal, for Jarman's penalty shot hit the bar, and he proceeded to head the rebound into the net. The sharp-eyed referee must have spotted that goalie Dilwyn John had touched the ball on to the bar, for, if Jarman had touched it twice, the goal would have been disallowed. County's luck did not extend to the next round, for 1,232 turned up to see a match as interesting as watching paint dry, as Shrewsbury went through 1-0.

In January, Harris was made Manager, with Lucas moving to General Manager, however, a series of low scoring games failed to enthuse the fans. After the previous season, it was all an anti-climax, and by March, gates had dipped below 2,000.

With little to play for, the run-in held only two matches of note. Against Workington, Captain Brian Godfrey scored a hat-trick, and Brian Harris was granted a testimonial game versus Everton, the match being kicked off by the legendry "Dixie" Dean.

A 0-5 defeat by Bury meant a far different end of season from the previous year, when the same side had been beaten 4-3. Things had begun to go wrong with the breaking up of the Brown-Jones partnership. Brown was loaned to

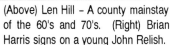
(Above) Len Hill - A county mainstay of the 60's and 70's. (Right) Brian Harris signs on a young John Relish.

Hereford, with Jenkins making the opposite journey. While Jenkins did little, Brown scored five goals in nine games for Hereford.

For the new season, Harris decided to quit playing and concentrate on management. A few players left, notably Len Hill, and John Relish arrived, along with the experienced Cardiff pair of Bobby Woodruff and Gary Bell. Bristol City striker Eddie Woods soon came on loan, and Andy White, about to play for a local rugby side, finally re-signed.

The season got off to a decent start, for after an initial defeat at Hartlepool, a fine Woodruff shot beat Torquay in the League Cup. This continued with a 2-1 win over Darlington and two Roddy Jones goals finished off Doncaster. A Woods debut goal helped to defeat Swansea 3-0.

High winds on the Severn Bridge prevented Woods and Godfrey from arriving and playing in the next match, the side losing 2-4 to Shrewsbury. The team suffered the same scoreline in the League Cup-tie, away to Chelsea. After an unhappy game at Reading, with a controversial penalty – and Aizlewood sent off for handling – the team bounced back with three successive wins. Around this time, County were above midway in the table.

A 1-2 defeat at Barnsley proved to be Brown's last first team outing, for with White back, and Woods a regular, he could not find a place. Despite the reasonable League form, gates were moderate, and the hoped for Cup boost did not materialise. A good F.A.Cup victory at Exeter was followed by a 1-3 home defeat by Walsall. In the Welsh Cup, the side managed a 2-2 draw at Stourbridge, with substitute Graham Rogers heading a goal on his debut.

In the final match of 1974, County lost 0-3 at League leaders Mansfield. Aizlewood was injured early on and was out of the team for months.

Of the first five games of 1975, four were won. Typically, a 1-4 defeat came against bottom club Scunthorpe. Stourbridge were thrashed 5-1 in the Welsh Cup, and League Cup semi-finalists Chester were beaten 3-0. Against Stockport, with Woods off injured, County drew 1-1. They were now third, but badly missing Aizlewood, Newport soon went into a steep slump, going eight games without a win – promotion disappearing in a puff of smoke. Rylands and Parsons were signed, but too late to make any impact.

A Welsh Cup replay victory over Swansea was followed by a 0-1 home defeat by Cardiff, despite County gaining seventeen corners to Cardiff's two. Even for this match, the crowd was under 4,000, and for the next match, with Barnsley, it was 1,773. The disillusioned Harris resigned, claiming that the people of Newport were interested only in *"Betting, Booze and Bingo."* Since he was leaving to take over a pub in Chepstow, he seemed to be jumping on the bandwagon!

County now reverted to the inevitable Lucas, and the only remaining memory from the end of season is Wynne Hooper's unexpected hat-trick against Rochdale. After initial success under Lucas, the team gathered only two points for the last six matches. At least there had been some pluses over the season, for Woods had hit 21 League goals, and the reserves had won the Welsh League, for the first time in twenty years.

Although Lucas remained as General Manager, the experienced defender Dave Elliott was brought in as player-manager, and Alastair Love from came with him from Southend. That was the only signing, while departures included Coldrick, Payne and Summerhayes. There was nothing to inspire the fans' confidence, and matters were not helped when Godfrey missed the first few matches. He was late returning from playing with Portland Timbers, in America.

County made an incredible start, beating Lincoln 3-1 and Workington 2-1. To the uninitiated, this might not appear incredible, but County had not won their opening two League matches since 1934! The First Round of the League Cup was now played on a home and away basis, and County could win neither match against Exeter.

A 2-0 victory over Southport saw Newport joint top, with Reading. After a 0-2 reverse at Bournemouth, the side travelled to Swansea, where Aizlewood put the team two up in 15 minutes, but the match was finally drawn. The next three games were won, and County were back in fourth place. On October the 18th, Newport visited Huddersfield, and the game was watched by Harold Wilson, who had never seen his side lose since entering No.10 Downing Street. County lost the eventful match 1-2, having had a goal disallowed, while one of Huddersfield's was clearly offside. Huddersfield's Bobby Campbell broke his leg in the match.

County enjoyed a five match unbeaten spell, but suddenly everything went wrong at Doncaster, where the side conceded five goals in six minutes, to lose 1-5. In the F.A.Cup, County were two up against Swindon, but eventually only drew, and the replay was lost 0-3. At Hartlepool, County gave their worst performance so far, losing 1-4. The last three matches of 1975 produced one point, against 10 man Crewe, and versus Northampton Relish broke his leg just before half-time. A bright start had turned into a dismal downward spiral, not helped by the usual financial constraints.

As the year turned, County were at least unbeaten at home, but this did not last long. In the first match of 1976, Newport lost 1-5, Tranmere's Ronnie Moore scoring four – the heaviest home defeat since 1953. The money was scraped up to sign Woods full-time, and after the home game debacle, Norwich goalkeeper Mervyn Cawston was signed on loan. He showed impressive form, saving a penalty versus Stockport, but County could not afford to buy him, and at this time, eight Newport players were out injured. County lost to Hereford in the Welsh Cup, with Aizlewood scoring for both sides. The team now took one point from seven League matches and was plunging headlong down the table.

In February, with the crisis worsening, Elliott was removed as Manager. The matter was not handled in a tactful way, and he was later ordered to keep away from Somerton Park. In came Jimmy Scoular, who after a wonderful spell at Ninian Park had been out of football for two years. It could not be said that Scoular waved a magic wand, for of

his first ten matches, nine were lost! Cyril Rogers, stung by adverse publicity, claimed that the Board had been unable to allow time for Elliott to gain experience, though there had been no noticeable improvement since. Comedian Frank Carson was now an Executive Director, and at times there appeared to be eleven jokers on the pitch.

As soon as Elliott left, Aizlewood was sold to Swindon, for a record fee. Scoular could only sign the likes of Pimblett, on loan, and Peter Morgan who had been driving a forklift since his last League club. The most noteworthy debutant at this time was Mark Aizlewood, if anything a more precocious talent than his brother.

Things had turned sour for supporters and, after a 1-0 success against Brentford, there were six successive defeats. With many fans disenchanted by Elliott's treatment and appalling form under Scoular, gates hit rock bottom; the attendances for the Brentford and Watford matches were 1,150 and 1,092.

One point was secured from the final five matches, and another re-election request was inevitable. Fortunately, Scoular was a well respected figure and the League status was preserved. The only bright spot lay with the youth team. By achieving results such as 14-0 versus Chepstow, the side had accumulated 100 goals by Christmas, and now Mark Aizlewood was on the verge of becoming a regular in the first team.

There were major close season changes. With County not far from bankrupt, Scoular was forced to take up the hammer and paintbrush himself, to improve his surroundings, just as he had the task of cutting sandwiches for the away trips! A Frank Carson cabaret raised £700, and new medical and changing facilities were somehow provided. Apart from Elliott and Love, departures included Godfrey, Macey, Passey, Preece and Hancock. Woodruff was forced to retire because of back problems, and Screen decided to leave. With his useful contacts, Scoular was able to recruit ace goalscorer Brian Clark, talented midfielder John Emanuel, internationals Villars and Derrett, goalkeeper Gary Plumley and others.

Apart from these alterations to playing staff, and the arrival of Ronnie Bird as trainer-coach, there were other changes which transformed the club's image. The strip was changed to blue and white stripes, with blue shorts, the programme was given a blue cover, and even the kick-off for matches was changed from 3.15 to 3.00 p.m. While many of the alterations were laudable, the overall impact was so overpowering, that it felt like watching Cardiff City reserves! For the opening fixture, a League Cup encounter with Swansea, six County players had been associated with the Bluebirds, along with the Manager and Trainer, and they were even wearing Cardiff colours!

The Swansea game was lost 1-4, but at least the home leg was won, by a Bell penalty. That, alas, was the end of the good news, for in the first five matches just one goal and one point were obtained, which left the side languishing in 24th spot. The team was only going down to narrow defeats, but second placed Aldershot were beaten 2-1, thanks to two fine second half goals from Clark. With Mark Williams securing the points at Southport, the corner seemed to have been turned. Of the next eight League matches, five were drawn, but of greater consequence was the off the field situation. In October, it was apparent that the club was in a financial crisis. At least on this occasion the more pleasant side of soccer could be seen, for an appeal raised £3,500, and supporters of Bradford City and Southend (to which three fans made a 180 mile sponsored walk) made collections. Dave Mackay and Des Anderson donated their fees from newspaper articles, and on November the 30th, Gordon Milne brought his Coventry side to Somerton, where, on a soaking night, County suffered an embarrassing 1-7 defeat. On December the 8th, a South Wales XI played Manchester United at Ninian Park. Disappointingly few Newport players were in the side, but 13,000 spectators and £8,000 takings allowed County to continue.

The crisis brought the old chestnut of a proposed move, this time to Cwmbran Stadium, but as ever, County stayed put. With a slight financial easing, Scoular was able to sign his old stalwart Don Murray from Hearts. A good Cup run would have been ideal, and County were drawn away to Bournemouth. The side had played there in a League encounter 18 days earlier, and in a less than dirty game, Murray and Bell had been sent off and three booked, including Clark, for the first time in his career. On this second occasion, Newport drew 0-0, and won the replay 3-0 at Somerton, with Parsons scoring twice. But a seven match losing run began, the run including a 1-4 home League Cup defeat by Swansea. One of the few brighter moments came with Relish's return, after a year out with a broken leg, but this reappearance came in a 0-5 reverse at Colchester.

In the first six League games of 1977, one goal was scored, and for the home game with Darlington the gate was 1,428. Something had to give, and Scoular resigned after the Darlington match, and left after a Welsh Cup defeat by Swansea. His place was taken by Colin Addison, who had come to prominence as the Hereford Manager. He stated that he looked on the job as a personal challenge, and who could disagree? County were losing every match, and would almost certainly be voted out of the League in June. At least the club now had, under Ron Warry, a new Board, with more businesslike aims.

For the Stockport match, Bird picked the side which unluckily lost 1-2. A 0-0 draw with Scunthorpe, in bad conditions, suggested an upturn, but the next four games were lost. Under Scoular, who had been in charge for almost a year, the team had only twice scored more than one goal in a League match. Not unnaturally the pattern continued, but Addison, who had been an attacker, began to place more emphasis on the forwards. There was a chink of light when Southport were beaten 3-1, with Parsons

scoring twice. Dave Bruton was signed on loan, and now Brian Preece and Tony Byrne came from Hereford. All three would play their part in the efforts to ward off extinction.

The away form was bad, but home results improved noticeably, and gates crept back over the 2,000 mark. Brentford and Bradford City were beaten, then League leaders, Cambridge arrived and were hammered 4-2. Clark scored a hat-trick and was presented with the ball. In a hard battle with Bournemouth, Preece scored the only goal after 80 minutes, then, at long last, an away win was secured, thanks to Woods, at Hartlepool. County had moved up to 22nd. A woods hat-trick against Rochdale kept up the momentum, but fans were brought back to earth, when Exeter won 3-0 at Somerton. April ended with a dour 0-0 draw at Halifax.

County faced a daunting task, placed 22nd and with only five matches left to play, but at least four were at home. On May the 3rd, Watford were convincingly beaten 3-0, and four days later, Newport conceded a bad goal against Crewe, but Woods eventually obtained a close range winner. Against Southend, a Relish goal, just after half-time, and two from Preece in the last two minutes, gave the team a 3-0 win.

The two games left were against struggling Workington. On May the 14th, 1,285 saw a hard earned County win, thanks to an early Preece goal and a good Plumley save. The final match was at home, giving Newport a psychological advantage, and such was the confidence, that the programme bore "The Great Escape" on its cover. 8,313 turned up, and it was a fight to the death, for whoever lost would almost certainly go out of the League. So much was at stake, that it was never going to be a great game. The elegant Woods struck the winner, and at the end of the match there were unforgettable scenes, as the players threw their shirts into the crowd. County had played five games in May and won them all. Their re-election brochure, already prepared, could now be ripped up, but there was every sympathy for Workington, who were about to be voted out of the League. The dynamic Addison, normally dressed in his flamboyant red shirt, was well aware of the value of publicity, and did everything he could to give the club a modern image, and to communicate with fans. There was a link with the past however, when Lucas was brought back as youth advisor.

The new season was just like old times. County were to revert to black and amber, and the programme was relaunched as the "Amber Note"; the kick-off even went back to 3.15. There was a resurgence of enthusiasm and season ticket sales were up. Volunteers were painting away, and Chairman Ron Warry erected an enormous nameboard at the back of the stand. County even had ex-rugby player George Newey circulating around John Frost Square, as a sandwich board man. There was a new emphasis on the commercial side, with Ground advertising and a subscription draw – dreamt up by David Hando.

Andy White, the speedy County left-winger.
He played in the final match at Somerton.

On the playing side, White, Parsons and Morgan departed, as did Villars and Murray early in the season. Preece was signed full-time and local Shane Walker arrived. The most significant signing, however, proved to be Howard Goddard, a striker of rare potential.

An opening 1–3 League Cup defeat at Portsmouth could not be retrieved, despite a decent 3–2 win in the home leg. In the opening League match, Newport were two up midway through the second half, but let the game slip to a 2–2 draw. Huddersfield were beaten 2–0, with Walker scoring a rocket free kick. Against Rochdale, Plumley salvaged a win by sprinting back and scooping the ball off the line. Goddard scored an excellent goal against Swansea, which secured the points. Fortunately the club now had a settled side, and after 15 League games only 14 players had made a full appearance in the side. County were now confident enough to turn down a five figure offer for Woods.

October was a sad month, for things had not been going well for Newport speedway. Because of the franchise system, the Gulf Oil League side had recently been transferred to Bristol, with the lesser National League coming to Somerton. Gloomy prophecies were fulfilled, for on October 7th, the last meeting of Newport Wasps took place. No longer would the sound of the bikes roar across Newport on a Friday night. Fans would have to travel more than 70 miles to Swindon to see a meeting.

In the same month, County held an Open Day as part of its initiative to "sell" the club and communicate with the local community.

Fans could see around the dressing rooms, officials' rooms and the like, and for a number of years it became a popular event.

After a dozen games the County had 15 points and were sixth. With the club's rapid improvement other teams were bound to take notice, and around this time Addison was being linked with the Sheffield United job. Eventually, so many clubs were after Addison's obvious talents that it began to have an unsettling effect on the County.

Up front there were Woods, who scored a hat–trick against Scunthorpe, and the developing Goddard. Behind them were the subtle skills of Emanuel. The precocious Aizlewood soon established himself as a first–teamer, and the gates mirrored the improvement, since even for teams such as Stockport, Torquay and Halifax, 4,000 were turning up.

After an unbeaten run of four League games, came the F.A.Cup, and at Somerton, Exeter were lucky to survive. Key was brilliant in goal, and on one occasion Goddard hit one post then the other. In Devon, Plumley saved Bowker's penalty shot, but the side went down 2–4. Just before the Cup games, County had suffered a great blow, when Woods, his goal tally already in double figures, injured a leg. He was out until April and played only one more match all season. Fortunately, County had Goddard and the veteran Clark to fall back on.

In the Autumn, Warry was out as Chairman, his place being taken by Richard Ford. Addison turned down the chance of managing Swansea, having changed his mind after the Directors had revealed their plans to him at a Board meeting. A later offer from W.B.A. was also declined.

As December came County were fourth. At Southend they were 2–0 up with 15 minutes left, but slithered to a 2–4 defeat. For the Boxing Day match, and also the first game of 1978, crowds of over 7,000 turned up. County scored three times in the first game and five times in the second. Their play was attracting the fans, and nine successive home games were won. Things were further boosted by the introduction on January 1st of a lottery, giving a first prize of £1,000.

Reasonable form was maintained until February, when three matches were lost, including a home defeat by Bangor in the Welsh Cup, and a 0–4 hammering at Swansea. This bad spell was quickly redressed for the next three matches, all at home, were won. That was the end of the good spell however, for the rest of the season was abysmal.

The absence of Woods and other injuries, took their toll. Addison made his first purchase but Sinclair scored only one goal in 15 matches. In a patchwork side numerous players were tried, including unknown locals, McLaughlin – who had been playing rugby – and Cup Final goalie Ian Turner, on loan.

Long-term prospects were bright though, with Aizlewood, Lowndes and Vaughan destined to play for Wales. In the short-term, things were disastrous, with not one of the final 12 games won. With 10 games left, County were 4th, yet at the end of the season they finished 17th. Eleven successive away matches were lost, but for the fans worse was to follow. Although bids for Aizlewood had been turned down, the club announced that with the side now out of the promotion hunt, he was being sold to Luton, for a record £50,000 fee.

In May, Addison departed, becoming Asst. Manager at West Brom. In his place the Board appointed Len Ashurst, an experienced player, but an unknown quantity in management. County also lost their Commercial Manager Mike Lewis, who joined Spurs.

It was a blow, when Emanuel decided to leave, with Preece and Walker also going. Ashurst began to bring in the first members of a side which will never be forgotten by Newport fans. One or two, such as Armstrong and Warriner, never established themselves, but most became regulars. Newcomers included the cool defender Richard Walden, whose Manager – Jack Charlton – was less than happy with the Tribunal valuation of £3,500, and Trevor Thompson, whose fee was reduced as part of the Addison deal. Free transfer Grant Davies soon proved a workmanlike defender, and Neil Bailey impressed in midfield. County soon splashed out £15,000 of the Aizlewood fee on Keith Oakes, who was to prove the cornerstone of Ashurst's defence, and a bargain at the price.

Somerton Park received a close season facelift. The speedway track was gone and the pitch improved. Concrete had been laid in place of sleepers on the terraces, and a new £3,000 multi-gym constructed.

Things were changing at County, a club with the unenviable record of being the only side never promoted from the Fourth Division. Such was the optimism that 2,000 turned up for the Open Day on September 3rd.

The opening home League Cup-tie with Swansea was watched by 5,572 and brought a 2-1 victory, thanks to great goals from Woods and Mark Williams, but the away leg was a disaster – a 0-5 defeat. The start of the League season did little to encourage fans, for the opening seven matches saw six defeats, and a narrow 3-2 win at newcomers Wigan. After six matches, Ron Walker was dropped – never to return – and Mark Williams soon left the first team, whereas young Vaughan and Lowndes were now regulars. The forecasters of doom were proved wrong, as the influence of Ashurst began to transform the side and County began an eight game unbeaten run.

Supporters were surprised when the club again splashed out money to sign Dave Bruton, who had been earlier on loan. In the first seven League matches, no side scored less than two goals against the defence, yet from mid-September until the New Year, only Scunthorpe and Northampton scored more than one! Even a fractured arm for Oakes could not upset the rhythm of the team.

Many fans travelled to Hereford, where County won a dour cup-tie through an 85th minute Goddard penalty. Another struggle followed, against Worcester, who had been beaten only once in 26 matches. 7,196 turned up at Somerton Park to see a 0-0 draw. The crowd exceeded 10,000 for the replay, which County won, and so for the first time in six years the side was through to the Third Round.

There was great anticipation when Newport were drawn home to West Ham. The game was made all-ticket, and a temporary stand was erected at the Railway end. There was confidence in the Newport camp, with the side having shot up from near the bottom of the table to eighth. On the night, fans saw a Goddard goal, a superb "Pop" Robson equaliser and a never to be forgotten Woods winner. It was the club's greatest moment since Sheffield Wednesday had been humbled, more than a decade before. County were in the Fourth Round.

January saw plenty of activity, with Clark retiring through injury, Jimmy Goodfellow arriving – as reserve team coach – and Lowndes making the Welsh Under-21 squad. After the West Ham game, County, with the aid of special boots, beat Reading 3-2 on an icy pitch. The conquerors of the mighty Hammers were themselves now humbled 0-2, by Ton Pentre in the Welsh Cup. Newport were disappointed to draw Colchester in the Fourth Round of the F.A.Cup. So much ice lay on the ground that supporters risked life and limb in going to Somerton Park, where the game finished 0-0, and the replay was lost 0-1. County experienced something of a hang-over in the next match, at Portsmouth, with Vaughan sent off and four players booked.

Despite the Cup setback, County's bandwagon rolled on. Two more stars of the Ashurst side were signed – the skilful Moore and fiery Tynan. County's transfer record was broken three times during the season. On February the 27th, new floodlights were used, but, on a muddy pitch the side was overcome 2-4 by Bradford City. From mid-March, five successive games were won, giving hope for the coming season. Under Ashurst, the team had won a record nine away matches, and of the side which had opened the season, only five were left at the end Now established as regulars were Vaughan, Lowndes, Oakes, Tynan, Moore, Bruton and Bailey.

# CHAPTER 7

## From Rags to Riches

In June 1979, Ashurst boosted confidence by turning down the chance of managing his native Sunderland F.C.. The improved pitch was enlarged by 4 yards, while the Ground had been painted, and the terracing renewed. For the first time since 1963, there was no new face in the opening line-up. County made an unlucky start, in the League Cup, after the home leg was won by a Tynan goal. 0-2 down at Plymouth, County were awarded a last minute penalty, and Goalkeeper Hards saved the shot, with Goddard netting the rebound. Referee Lester Shapter ruled the game was over after the first kick, and Newport were out.

Colin Addison raises a well deserved Bell's Whisky Award

It was eventually bought from Newport Corporation in the Spring.

Two Vaughan goals ensured victory at Tranmere, and started off Newport's best ever League run. Narrow wins over Doncaster and Wigan were followed by a 5-2 thrashing of Halifax, and an excellent 3-0 win at Crewe. A 3-1 victory over Stockport equalled County's record of six successive League wins, and 6,513 saw County create a new record, with a 3-0 win over Torquay.

Even more saw a 1-0 win at Hereford, when Moore was sent off, in a physical game. Vaughan picked up a loose back pass, to ensure a 1-0 success at Peterborough, by which time County were fourth, with Portsmouth a point behind. A crowd of 8,113 saw a somewhat mediocre match against bottom placed Rochdale, but Moore scored off the inside of a post. The County's run, now in double figures, ended at distant Darlington. With the side 1-0 up, through Moore, Oakes attempted to clear, and sliced the ball over Plumley's head. The marvellous run extended to Welsh Cup wins over Wrexham and Merthyr.

County's 13 game unbeaten record ended at Bradford City, the 3-0 defeat including two 25 yard goals. A superb Aldridge header beat Hartlepool, and promotion was expected to be confirmed at struggling Rochdale. With much media interest, it turned out to be the worst day of the season with Rochdale winning 2-0.

The first two League matches, versus Port Vale and Aldershot, were won. Goals were somewhat hard to come by, but centre-back Oakes scored in three consecutive matches. The home match with Lincoln saw a significant change. At half-time, John Aldridge - signed in April - replaced Goddard. Already the leading Welsh League scorer, he went on to become one of the best known players developed by Newport.

The home game with Aldershot began a significant run. Shocked by a 15 second goal, County hit back to win 4-2, with Aldridge scoring twice. The next four games were won, but the success at Portsmouth was bitter-sweet. A 2-0 victory, before 20,755, was soured when Goddard's right leg was broken by Davey's tackle. Out for the season, his career never really recovered. Over 7,000 turned up to see the home match with Portsmouth, when the visitors hit back three times, but Tynan headed a spectacular winner from a Relish free kick. Ten days later, County equalled their record best away result, when Aldridge scored his first hat-trick, in a 5-0 win, at Stockport. Newport had a tough F.A.Cup draw, and went down 0-1, at Fratton Park.

After a 4-0 win over Darlington, the remainder of the year was mediocre, despite the record £40,000 signing of Gwyther, who did not establish himself in the side until February. Although this poor spell lasted until mid-February, Cardiff were beaten 2-0 in the Welsh Cup, with Oakes showing outstanding form. Off the field, plans to develop the Railway end were shelved, as the Board began in December to negotiate for the purchase of Somerton Park.

Tommy Tynan scores the final goal at Walsall, to make the score 4-2, and clinch promotion.

For the final match, at Walsall, there were 4,000 Newportonians among the 9,251 crowd. Mid-way through the first half, Aldridge scored twice in 60 seconds. A Buckley penalty pulled one back, but before the interval, Gwyther made it 3-1. With 26 minutes left, Penn scored easily, then ten minutes from time Tynan headed the goal which put County into Division Three. The team finished in third place, setting various new County records. The reserves won the Welsh League and the youth team, the Gwent League.

On May the 6th, almost 10,000 turned up to watch the first leg of the Welsh Cup Final. The semi-final between Swansea and Shrewsbury had gone to penalties, and when Waddle had kicked Swansea's last effort over the bar, it had meant that County would be playing in Europe, as they would be the only Welsh side in the Final.

(Above) Tynan, Bailey and Oakes drink a toast.
(Below) County's celebration after promotion.

On the night, Tynan was the hero scoring both goals in a 2-1 win. At the finish, thousands of fans congregated on the pitch, and six days later, the side enjoyed a 3-0 success, through Lowndes, Tynan and Gwyther. County had won all four games against Second Division opposition. County Captain, Keith Oakes, collected the Welsh Cup from Ivor Pursey.

On Wednesday, May the 21st, an open top bus took the team and staff from Somerton Park to the Civic Centre, when thousands of cheering fans, festooned in Newport colours, lined the route. On August the 21st, a promotion Dinner was held, and a special menu card, similar to the one of 1939, was produced.

There was now a different atmosphere. Third Division football, for the first time since 1962, and Europe lay ahead. The only significant signing was Elsey, but off the pitch there was considerably more activity.

£20,000 was spent on the playing surface, more comfortable seating was installed, and David Williams returned as Asst. Trainer.

A 0-1 League Cup defeat at Hereford was followed by a thumping 5-0 win in the return. County secured an admirable 1-1 League draw at Burnley, but the first home match was lost 1-2, to Charlton. Four days later, a Tynan penalty brought a 2-1 win over Millwall. After the League Cup defeat by Notts County, interest was centred on the Cup Winners' Cup, where County were paired with Crusaders of Ireland. 6,285 turned up, for the historic event, when four players scored, in a rousing 4-0 win. After two disappointing League defeats, the side drew 0-0, in Ireland, and they were through to the next round.

A Lowndes goal beat Brentford away, but after nine matches, County were 22nd. At least, the side now had a major new signing, as Kendall was bought from Spurs for £45,000, but he was unfortunately signed too late to play in any of the European games. A failure to score in three of the next four League matches did not bode well for the next European encounter, but County were drawn against little known Norwegians, Haugar. A 0-0 draw in Norway was the forerunner of better things, for Newport won four consecutive League matches and hammered Haugar 6-0, in the return.

In the F.A.Cup Newport lost 0-2 to Plymouth, but in the Welsh Cup gained a replay win over Worcester. League-wise, County's form slumped dramatically from mid-November, and of the nine matches played up to the end of the year, not one was won. The defence was solid, but only once did the attack score more than one goal. Ashurst plunged into the transfer market, pressurising the Board into paying £80,000 for his "missing link", the strapping striker Alan Waddle. Newport's highest ever fee would ultimately lead the club into a downward spiral.

County attack before a packed 18,000 crowd
in the European Cup-Winners Cup.

With something of a recession, the lottery income was down, wages were 21 per cent up due to promotion, the Ground was being bought, and money was being spent which the club did not have. At least, Waddle's debut saw a 4-0 thrashing of Sheffield United, followed by a 3-0 Welsh Cup win over Ton Pentre. The following month, Bangor were beaten 3-1.

On February 28th, Lowndes equalled County's record of 152 consecutive appearances and scored in a 5-1 hammering of Chesterfield. 200 fans made the journey to the next match, away to the East Germans, Karl Zeiss Jena. The opposition included seven full internationals, and fans at home could scarcely believe the result. County had drawn 2-2, with both goals coming from livewire Tommy Tynan. The television cameras came to Somerton Park, where the humble occupants were now creating European interest, and an all-ticket crowd of 18,000 arrived for the return leg. No-one present will ever forget the night, the sickening sight of the ball going past Plumley into the net, the torrent of County shots and headers, stopped only by bad luck or the brilliance of the German keeper, the ball that appeared to go over the line. However undeserved the defeat, the side was now out of Europe. County soon had the chance to return, but a 1-2 defeat at Hereford, followed by a 1-1 home draw meant that the opportunity was spurned.

In early April, Lowndes was omitted after 160 consecutive games. With six matches left, County were 20th in the table, but fortunately three of those were won.

On May the 12th, an unusual friendly took place, arranged so that the club could view Mustapha Hukic, a Yugoslav international. Although he performed quite well against Birmingham, he was not signed.

In June, came the death of County stalwart, J.R. Wardell, at 95. He had been involved in the club's formation in 1912, and had been a Director for two long spells, between 1919 and 1953.

During the close season, Plumley and Dave Bruton departed. Young Paul Bodin and experienced Terry Lees were signed, and on July the 30th, Jeff Johnson was bought for £60,000. Aldridge would not re-sign or train, and only changed his mind in late August.

It was a sign of County's changed circumstances that the side undertook a six day trip to Eire, playing games against Cork and Limerick. But unfortunately, various pre-season injuries accrued.

At a late stage, Newport were invited to participate in the new Group Cup, and were unbeaten in three matches. In the League, wins were now worth three points, and 5,000 saw the game with Chesterfield, in which Johnson scored the only goal. A 3-2 League Cup win at Torquay was followed by a 4-0 victory at Southend. With County 0-2 down against Oxford, Waddle came on as substitute, and in pouring rain netted twice in a 3-2 win. County had won their first three matches of a season for the first time in 47 years. Former star Goddard was allowed to join Blackpool on loan, and scored twice in a 5–0 hammering of Crewe.

The slump many had feared, soon arrived, for of the dozen League and League Cup matches following the Oxford Game, only one was won, and the attack only once scored more than one goal. Ashurst announced that he had too many forwards and was making them available for transfer. Against Millwall, Goddard played his first League match for two years, but on December the 14th he was freed to join Bournemouth. After a 2–0 win over Carlisle, four matches were lost, including a First Round F.A.Cup match at Colchester. After starting unbeaten in its first three matches, the side had slipped to 16th, after 15 games.

In late November the Board announced that trainer–coach Goodfellow and others would have to leave, a move which upset Ashurst, but the recession had cut gates by 25 per cent. A 5–0 Welsh Cup win over Taff's Well was followed by a 3–2 victory over Wimbledon, the only League win in a two month spell.

The year ended with a 1–1 draw at Gillingham in icy conditions, and the new one began with an entertaining 3–1 defeat of Reading – in pouring rain. On January the 30th, bankrupt Bristol City arrived. The club was only saved when eight of their players agreed to terminate their contracts, and a new Company was set up. By the time County were in this position, the loophole had been closed!

On February the 8th, Ashurst was sacked. It was not unexpected, for the manager had spent £300,000, the side was struggling and gates were dwindling. The post was not advertised however, for it was simply announced that Addison – sacked two weeks earlier by Derby – was returning. Ashurst, despite his enforced departure, was accorded a testimonial game with Manchester City on March 2nd.

Addison had no magic wand to wave. There was only one success in the 14 matches following the Reading victory, and the side was knocked out of all cup competitions. Eventually however, his influence began to work through, and only two of the final eleven games were lost. The side ended as it had begun, with three straight wins, and safety was assured. Waddle, Ashurst's great white hope, was given a free transfer in April, and Bodin – a future international – was also released. Walden, the popular veteran, decided to quit League football, his place being taken by the competent Vaughan Jones. In mid–August 1981, talented Kenny Stroud arrived, and the unimpressive Lees had the remainder of his contract bought out. It was a small squad left, and it was a great blow, when Oakes fractured his right foot.

Off the pitch, Bobby Smith became Assistant Manager, and the club attempted a new share issue. The reserves, who had been taken out of the Welsh League, were prevented at a late stage from joining the Western League. On a national level, three sides were now to be promoted from Division Three, a four step rule was introduced for goal-keepers, and deliberate handball became a sending off offence.

Early League Trophy games included a 5–1 hammering of Exeter, and a 4–1 win at Ashton Gate – where the Rolling Stones had recently played before somewhat larger crowds. A satisfactory start would have been better, if Kendall had not fallen foul of the new goalkeeping rules. Because he held on to the ball for longer than six seconds, the referee awarded a free kick, and Plymouth equalised. In the League Cup, Exeter were annihilated 6–0, and five out of six League games were won, with Orient being beaten 5–1 away. Johnson, the £60,000 signing, did not play a League game for the club, and after a loan spell he was allowed to join Gillingham for £10,000. Ashurst's two biggest signings had been disastrous for the club.

Five forwards of County's great days of the early 80's - (from left) Tynan, Lowndes, Aldridge, Moore and Gwyther.

Richard Ford and his fellow directors receive the deeds to Somerton Park.

At Preston, Tynan missed a penalty, and by the season's end, the club and supporters would rue such easy points dropped. In the League Cup, Everton won 2–0 at Somerton Park, but in Liverpool County were unlucky not to win. In November, Goff Prosser and John Adams strengthened the Board, and highly talented defender Terry Boyle was signed. Newport were hovering around 4th in the table at this time, with Cardiff just above them, and Aldridge scored a first half hat–trick versus Bournemouth.

With Gwyther and Relish as makeshift centre–backs, the side could only draw 0–0 at Enfield in the F.A.Cup, although a Tynan hat–trick led to a 4–2 replay win. In the Welsh Cup, Ashurst's Cardiff went out to a 20 yard Vaughan shot, and the crowd was a healthy 7,800. A League win over Gillingham was followed by a 1–0 F.A.Cup victory over Orient, Tynan netting a penalty after 84 minutes. A disappointing spell then developed with one victory in nine matches. The run included a last minute defeat at Cardiff, and the first home League reverse since March, by Oxford.

County made a good start to the New Year with an injury time win over Exeter, and in the F.A.Cup, Gwyther put the side in front against Everton, but sadly, Kendall misjudged a ball minutes from the end. A tremendous battle developed in the replay, but despite an excellent Aldridge goal, County went down 1–2. Possibly because of their exertions, County went down by the same score against Doncaster, and had now drifted to 7th. Things were made worse when the side was thrashed 1–4, at Wrexham. All cup involvement ended with defeat in the strange League Trophy. After the opening games, in August, the semi-final was held at the end of January! County drew 0–0 at Chester, but overall lost 4–5 on penalties.

Off the field, there were already danger signs, for in early February, County, needing £100,000 to help balance their books, were refused help by the F.A. of Wales.

The club was £300,000 in the red, and losing £500 every week. At the end of the month the Council agreed to a commercial loan of £120,000.

County had a settled side, indeed by the season's end nine players had made over 40 League appearances, ane over 40 Leagueling that of the promotion season, the side won ten games out of eleven. The sequence began with a 3–0 home win over Preston, before only 2,317. After a 3–1 win at Bristol Rovers, Lowndes scored a hat–trick against Orient, who were 0–4 down at half–time. After a 0–2 reverse at Sheffield United, came three more wins then three away victories. Then came a real "event". The Ninian Park derby had attracted a vast crowd by Third Division standards. But the queue for the Easter Monday game blocked Somerton Lane, as 16,052 arrived – the largest League gate since August 1950! The match itself was an anti–climax, but at least County had all the luck. Two Cardiff "goals" were ruled offside, and the inevitable Aldridge netted the winner. With the side now top of the League, the "Argus" spoke of *"County's New Promotion"*.

Things were as bad off the pitch as they were good on it, for only the immediate forwarding of £81,000 by the Council saved the club from a Court appearance. County's team was now so good that both Lowndes and Vaughan were selected for the Welsh squad versus Bulgaria. But high expectations were soon dispelled, for after an away defeat at Gillingham, a crowd of over 10,000 saw County crash to three second half Portsmouth goals; County were down to 3rd. After a 1–2 defeat at Walsall, rumours abounded that the club did not want promotion because of the crippling costs of new safety regulations in Division Two. However dubious the rumours, fans voted with their feet, and only 4,344 saw the Wrexham match. Tynan bagged a hat–trick, and goalkeeper Niedzwicki was sent off. County, requiring three wins from their final seven matches, had obtained one, with three games left. A 0–3 defeat at Millwall was followed by the long trek to Huddersfield, where a battling performance could not avert a 0–1 loss. The promotion dream was over, and a final 1–1 draw with Exeter was irrelevant. The fact that Jarvis, Lilygreen and Woodruff had scored over 20 goals for the youth team suggested long-term hope for the club, but things were overshadowed by the parlous financial situation, and too many near misses when success seemed assured.

The prospect for the 1983–84 season seemed less than encouraging. A major blow was the new ruling that clubs would keep the money from home League gates, a move designed to favour the better supported clubs. The failure to obtain promotion meant drastic cutbacks, and out went stalwarts Davies, Gwyther, Moore and Plumley. On August the 5th came a hammer blow, when Tynan, as popular in his own way as Eddie Carr – and the scorer of 25 League goals – was sold to Plymouth for £55,000. A 5 per cent rise was offered to players, and Lowndes took advantage of the new freedom of contract law to join Millwall for £55,000.

The team to face Bristol Rovers contained only two debutants. These were significant however, for Tynan and Lowndes had been replaced by the mediocre Martinez and Woodruff, a youth player; Woodruff was substituted by Ceri Williams, a Youth Opportunities apprentice. County won 2–1, but the only other joy before the end of September was a 4–3 victory over Bradford City. In the League Cup, County were beaten twice by lowly Torquay, one goal coming when goalie Kendall, the Clown Prince of Newport soccer, headed the ball to a Torquay player! A trip to recent League entrants Wimbledon ended 0–6, and for the second home game, the opening attendance had been halved.

After six matches the side was 15th in the table, but in early October came a move which greatly boosted matters. Vaughan and Elsey left for Cardiff, with Lewis, Micallef and Linden Jones moving to Newport, and five of the next six games were won. After 14 games, the side had shot up to 6th, just two points behind the 2nd club. More players were signed. Roy Carter was bought for £10,000, Trevor Matthewson came from Stockport and loan signing Neville Chamberlain became the first coloured player to appear in the County first team. The defence and midfield were playing well, but Aldridge was now ploughing a lone furrow up front.

In Cup competitions, County were drawn against non-League opposition. In the F.A.Cup, Newport beat Poole Town, after a replay, and then Harrow Borough. In the Welsh Cup, Bridgend were beaten 5–1. Old warhorse Roddy Jones scored against Bridgend, in a rare appearance, and Woodruff – father and son – opposed each other in the game. At this time, the side lost Oakes, with a fractured cheek, and Lindon Jones, with facial injuries.

1984 began with a major disappointment. Many fans travelled to Plymouth for the F.A.Cup, and were less than happy with the refereeing. Five minutes into injury time, Carter gave away a penalty, and who should step up to give Plymouth an unexpected reprieve, but old hero Tommy Tynan! Boyle was sent off after the final whistle. In the replay, played in atrocious weather, Rogers knocked out County six minutes from the end. In the Welsh Cup, a 6–0 win over amateurs Lex XI was followed by a home defeat by Wrexham. In the League, four goals were conceded, in quick succession, to Bristol Rovers, Rotherham and Port Vale.

David Pearce displays his Lonsdale belt.

The only local success in September came when David Pearce, who lived adjacent to the Ground, beat Neville Meade for the British Heavyweight Boxing Championship!

John Aldridge in action,
as Nigel Vaughan looks on.

The side just played out the rest of the season, and the fact that 29 players appeared in the first team spoke for itself. Crowds, recently 5,000 or more, were now down to 2,000. The club was in the first stage of a lingering road to collapse. The first major blow came on March 20th, when Aldridge informed the club that he would not be with them for the forthcoming season, and there was little option but to sell him to Oxford, for £70,000. Unfortunately, the Directors did not have the foresight to include a clause regarding any future resales, and he was later sold for over £1,000,000.

There were now undesirable rows on the Board. Joe Ford had already left, and Thorneycroft resigned in early May over the decision to retain Smith and to boost Addison's salary. On August the 7th, Richard Ford, whose integrity was questioned by Thorneycroft, resigned through ill-health, though he was hoping to be employed later as Chief Executive. On August the 11th, retired businessman Archie Menzies took over as Chairman, but made it clear that it was a reluctant move and that a younger man should have the post.

The near-promotion team of a year earlier had been well and truly dismantled. The dissatisfied Oakes was allowed to join Gillingham, along with newcomer Micallef, and many fans were upset when the consistent Vaughan Jones was given a free transfer. He joined Cardiff and was still playing League football many years later.

Even for a small squad numerous signings needed to be made. Chamberlain came on a full-time basis, young Kent came from West Brom., and walking mountain Saxby from Luton. Local man Tony Pulis arrived via Bristol Rovers for £10,000, and soon proved his worth with his strong tackling. Cooper and international David Giles soon became first team regulars, and the latter – who scored on his debut – had by then played for all four Welsh Football League sides. The opening match saw Plumley returning on loan to replace the injured Kendall.

None of the first seven League or Cup matches were won, and the first victory, 3–2 against Millwall, marked the final appearance of Saxby, Green and Ceri Williams. Off the pitch the situation was even worse, for without any advanced publicity, it was revealed that the Ground had been sold back to the Borough Council. The club was left with no collateral, and was soon struggling to find even the rent for Somerton Park

The side was not helping itself. Against Aldershot, in the F.A.Cup, Matthewson gave away a penalty, and in the replay Carter gave away a penalty and Matthewson scored an own goal, as County crashed 0–4. For Brentford's visit, the attendance was 1,591. Addison now became sick, with a viral illness brought on by overwork. Smith took his place, on a temporary basis, at which time he had 12 fit players available. The final six games of 1984 produced just one win – when Tynan was sent off for Plymouth, at Somerton Park!

Surprisingly, January brought three big wins. In the Welsh Cup, Cardiff Corries were beaten 4–0, in the Freight Rover Trophy, Exeter were overcome 3–0, and County achieved a 5–2 League win over Brentford. Fans at home were shocked to hear that young Cooper had scored four times, for despite Cooper's goals, and Chamberlain's earlier three at Derby, County had lacked an experienced striker all season. Because of injury problems, County were forced to utilise non-contract Kellow and veteran Gwyther, on loan from Port Talbot.

County were enjoying more success in cup competitions than in the League. In the Freight Rover Trophy, they earned a reprieve, for although they lost 3–4 to Swansea on penalties, they discovered that they had gone through to the next round as one of the two highest scoring losers. In the Welsh Cup, the side lost the first leg of the semi-final 0–1 away to Bangor, and when Shrewsbury beat Swansea, it meant that the winners of the Newport tie would automatically qualify for Europe. County gave a dreadful performance, and drew the uninspiring second leg 0–0.

On April the 9th at Swansea airport, Vice-President David Hando parachuted from a Cessna 207, at 2,200 feet. Fortunately, the parachute opened, or there might never have been a Newport A.F.C. to take over from County! The death defying stunt raised over £800 in sponsorship, and at around the same time Newport signed a £15,000 sponsorship deal with the "Argus".

Of the final ten League games, none was won, but in the Freight Rover Trophy, Bristol City were beaten, as were Orient, on penalties, with the decisive one being taken by goalkeeper Kendall. Brentford were the opposition for the Southern Final, the winners of which would take on the Northern victors, at Wembley. Despite Kendall's penalty save, the side was thrashed 0–6, the final whistle coming as a relief to the Newport fans. 39,897 were to witness the Final.

On May the 23rd, Addison, who had 12 months of his contract to go, agreed to leave in order to save the club. Five days later, Smith was appointed Manager, with Richard Ford returning, as "honorary" General Manager. Secretary Phil Dauncey was made redundant, though his position was soon filled by Keith Saunders on a part-time basis. Figures released on May the 31st showed that on a greatly reduced turnover of £255,125, County had made a loss of £168,436. In July, the promising Cooper left for Plymouth, but the deal of £15,000 plus Staniforth did little to offset the massive debt accruing. There were great changes on the playing front, and departures included Reid, Kent, Matthewson and Emmanuel. At the season's start, the club had 12 professionals and three non-contract players.

This was a time of great problems for football, which was involved in a running battle with the Government. Addison's benefit match with Manchester United even had to be staged in Hereford, because United could not travel abroad!

Terry Boyle in action against Swansea City in August 1985.

Seven players made their debuts in the opening League game, with Doncaster. These included the illustrious Leighton James, now player-coach. County were having to put out a different eleven for every match early on, which did nothing to help. In the League Cup, the side made its traditional First Round exit, this time to Bristol Rovers. In the League, two excellent wins were achieved at Wolves and Bournemouth. Against the former, Andy Miles scored twice, but he was surprisingly sent packing after a few more games. In between these two matches came a 1–2 home defeat by Cardiff, in which Linden Jones was accidentally kicked by his colleague Dowman, and subsequently forced to endure a long spell in the Royal Gwent Hospital!

In September, Reck and McManus came on loan, while Peacock was becoming a promising defender. Following a 3–0 victory over Bristol Rovers, the picture became one of unmitigated gloom. Fifteen League games went by without a win, and only eight goals were scored. Nine of the matches were drawn, but that counted for little, with three points awarded for a victory. Gates were regularly under 2,000, but on one occasion the side attracted a gate of 6,449 and national attention. Reading were going for Spurs' 25 year old record of 11 consecutive start of season victories; they duly obtained it by winning 2–0. Times were hard for County, and for the away match at Brentford, six fans completed a 135 mile sponsored walk.

From late November, things improved. Steve Berry, who had played for Sunderland in the League Cup Final was bought fro £5,000, and in the Welsh Cup, Ton Pentre were beaten 4–2. After Southend had been overcome 1–0 in the F.A.Cup, Torquay were beaten in a replay, after extra time.

Six League matches passed without defeat. In the New Year, however, things again began to deteriorate. A 0–2 F.A.Cup defeat at Sunderland was expected, but Welsh Cup hopes were ended by Kidderminster, and the League results went downhill. Off the field, came a momentous event with the setting up of the Lifeline Society. A well publicised meeting to establish the Society was held at the new Leisure Centre. The scheme was based on one in operation at Bolton, and Nat Lofthouse attended the meeting. The Board members present announced that it was now the only way to save the club, and within six weeks, the Society had 1,000 members and over the first season it was o raise £40,000 for the club.

Defeat on February 22nd, ironically against Bolton, began a run of eight straight losses. 0–4 at Bolton, 1–5 at home to Walsall, 1–3 at Bristol City... the goals started to rain in.

Eventually, Bobby Smith had had enough, and stepped down to let someone else have a go, and on the March 10th, John Relish was appointed on a temporary basis. He became the player-manager who never kicked a ball, for he was injured for the rest of the season. A well respected figure, who had battled to overcome broken legs. Relish now inspired the side to fight hard against relegation. Also of help was the veteran international Bob Latchford, who agreed to assist the side until the end of the season, and his size and experience were of benefit up front.

The revival started at Derby, when 11,251 saw Newport fight back from a one goal deficit, and equalise through Carter. A last minute Staniforth penalty beat Bury, but defeat came at York. Six matches were left.

Against Chesterfield, Brown shot wide for the visitors in the last minute in a 3–3 draw, and the side was now 21st, but Cardiff and Swansea were even lower. At Notts County, Mardenborough's dismissal and three bookings could not prevent Newport winning 2–1. Boyle secured another point from Derby, and Darlington lost 3–0. At Gillingham, a 20 yard injury time strike from Linden Jones brought three points. It was the first time the Gills had failed to score at home since March 1984. A final 0–0 draw at Blackpool meant County were safe.

It was supremely ironic that, with the club's terminal decline now underway, County were for the only time, the premier side in Wales, with Cardiff and Swansea being relegated. With the side in a precarious situation, Relish declined the permanent managerial position, preferring the security of a post with the P.F.A.

he had been born in Newport, Washington, and followed County's results as a Sports Broadcaster in Canada. He had seen a few County games, contacted County fan Maurice Salway, then been introduced to the Board by George Thorneycroft.

On the pitch, Exeter were beaten over two legs, in the League Cup, and after two 1–2 defeats plus a 2–2 draw, the team won three successive League games. In the League Cup, Newport gained a plum draw with Everton, and a 0–4 reverse at Goodison was not unexpected, but four goals were also conceded at Bury, with Greenwood scoring a hat-trick. A Sugrue knee injury put him out for the season. A 0–2 loss at Brentford was followed by the Everton return leg. Many Newport fans missed Carter's early goal, but it was Everton who ran out 5–1 winners, with Wilkinson scoring a hat-trick and Mullen contributing an own goal.

July 1986. Mullen leads the County lads in training.

During the close season, Boyle, the linchpin of the County defence, decided to drop down a Division and join Cardiff. Eventually, a fee of £22,500 was decided by a Tribunal. The Board decided to appoint Jimmy Mullen, the Cardiff central defender, as player–manager, whereupon Leighton James, who was upset at what he saw as a snub, left the club.

For the forthcoming season, the experienced Gibbins and Vinter were the main signings. Pulis was freed, to join Bournemouth, and the long–term hope of the club lay in the reserves, where players such as Freestone and Peacock had First Division potential.

In August, speculation began about a possible takeover. A few weeks later, Robert Phillips revealed on the front of the "Football Argus", that mystery Canadian businessman Jerry Sherman was to make an offer of £750,000 for the club. His interest in the club reportedly sprang from the fact that

O'Shea came on loan from Spurs, but things did not improve, and the Carlisle home game proved disastrous, with 18–year–old Peacock breaking a leg and Linden Jones suffering another injury.

By October the 6th, the "Argus", which had earlier spoken of a "fairytale takeover", was now reporting "takeover doubts". Sherman – whose offer had been accepted by the Board – began to stall, saying he wanted the Directors to resign before he would pay them a few days later. By mid November, it was a "fading takeover bid", with even Thorneycroft having to admit that he had not heard from Sherman for weeks. On November the 17th, Menzies stepped down as Chairman, being replaced by Estate Agent, Alan Darlow, with Ford rejoining as Managing Director.

By early November, the team had gone ten matches without winning. After one match, Mullen criticised his team's fans in the press. During the month, things improved, with three consecutive wins, the team beating Bolton in the League,

Swansea in the Welsh Cup (with four teenagers) and Bromsgrove in the F.A.Cup. Middlesbrough ended the run with a last minute goal at Somerton Park, and no more games were won in 1986. The side lost to Fulham in the F.A.Cup, and Hereford in the Freight Rover, with Stant scoring a hat-trick.

In mid December, Darlow set up an executive Board of local businessmen, to study County's financial problems. On a positive note there was an attempt to sort out the deep lying financial problems. On the negative side, the Board that developed under Darlow consisted of non-football men, and Directors rarely travelled to away matches.

Bad news published in the press was confirmed in the Bournemouth programme: *"Following an application to the High Court on 16th February 1987, Robert Ellis and Stuart Lindsay of Chartered Accountants, Touche Ross & Co., have been appointed Joint Administrators of Newport County A.F.C. Ltd."* The article went on to state that the club's collapse had been prevented only by the sale of Somerton Park, and that there was an estimated deficiency of £459,000. Mullen had just left the club, having joined his friend, Ian Porterfield, at Aberdeen. The senior professional, John Lewis, was appointed player-manager for the rest of the season, with David Wiliams to assist him. It was reported, on March the 4th, that Sherman was contacting the Administrators and making a new bid.

After 28 games, the team was in 22nd position, having managed to win one home and four away games. The club began to use a great number of players, including many youngsters or short-term loan signings, the total eventually mounting to 33. The signing of Taylor and Thackeray could do nothing to halt the slide. Berry and Mardenborough departed, along with two goalkeepers. At the turn of the year, Kendall had joined Wolves for £25,000, and on March the 9th, Freestone, a strapping 18-year-old joined Chelsea for a record fee. The latter transfer involved £90,000 down, and a possible eventual total of £160,000. Freestone was supposed to stay at Newport on loan until the end of the season, but this was soon overruled, and the club had to rely on the inexperienced Dillon.

Somehow, the team that was crashing to relegation was heading for the Welsh Cup Final. Shrewsbury ended up with 10 men, and their centre-half in goal. County equalised against Aberystwyth in the final minute. In the first leg of the semi-final, goalie Salmon kicked the ball to Taylor, who lobbed home from 30 yards.

In the return, Gibbins equalised three minutes from time, and County were in the Final. County continued to show dreadful League form, losing their penultimate match 1-6 to Port Vale, with Andy Jones scoring five. They were next to face non-League Merthyr in the Welsh Cup Final, and the sides drew 2-2 after extra time. County's two came from newcomer Thackeray, and Merthyr's first from ex-Ironside Bob Latchford. Thackeray was unfit for the replay, due to a hamstring injury, and after three minutes the Martyrs were in front, through a Chris Baird penalty. Merthyr then attempted to kick County off the pitch. Referee Ffrancon Roberts, it was generally agreed, had an awful match, and when Steve Williams performed a dreadful tackle on Sherlock (which saw him carried off), the perpetrator was not even booked. County lost 0-1, and so the last ray of hope at the end of a terrible season had disappeared.

The day after the replay, nine players, including four who had appeared in the Final, were cleared out. Lewis had been offered a two year deal a month before, and there had been an application, at the start of May for an extension of the Administration. The close season of 1987 was one of deep crisis. On June 16th, the *"Argus"* reported, *"It's the end of the road"*, stating that £400,000 was needed for survival, and the Court having given 14 days for new proposals. Newport Council offered £90,000, which unnamed officials dismissed as a *"joke"* and an *"insult"*. On June the 22nd, it was reported that £160,000 was required by the following Monday, and meanwhile the Football League was also pressing for an undertaking that the club would fulfil the forthcoming season's fixtures. On a brighter note, there was a sponsorship deal with Nissan, plus Lee and Turner, which would bring in at least £25,000 over three months. On June the 29th, the popular Linden Jones was sold to Reading, with a Tribunal eventually deciding on a £33,000 fee. On August the 7th, it was announced that creditors had accepted a rescue package; Chelsea paid £30,000, to complete the Freestone deal, the P.F.A. loaned £50,000, and astonishingly it was announced that Wimbledon had agreed to pay £85,000 for 18-year-old Richard Jones. Darlow stated: *"We are not fair weather friends. In 8 months, we have put right the mistakes of the last fifteen years."* The package soon began to unravel, as Wimbledon pulled out of the proposed Jones deal. For legal reasons he was prevented from playing, but eventually the case was dropped and he resumed performing for County. An Action Fund was set up, as supporters did what they could, and 21 undertook a sponsored walk to Bristol. In the face of massive debts, however, there was little the individual fan could do.

# CHAPTER 8

## Death and The Phoenix

August 1987. Robbie Taylor tries a shot against Burnley.

The team, with many new faces, approached a season in the Fourth Division, and supporters could take little comfort from the fact that the club would never appear on the football coupons all season, because of its critical position. The side began with a welcome League point at Hartlepool, but because of the situation that was then current in football, County were forced to play both legs of the League Cup-tie with Cardiff at Ninian Park. The Railway end at Somerton needed to be developed in a secure fashion, to hold visiting fans, and this White Elephant was eventually completed for around £70,000 with the help of the Football Trust. Surprisingly, newcomer Paul Evans scored two good goals in the first cup-tie, and a second leg draw meant that County were through.

In a 0–1 home defeat by Burnley, Brignull – who promised to be a useful general – was sent off. He was injured in the following match and was subsequently forced to give up League football. After five matches, Newport had one point, and this run was followed with a 3–1 home win over Torquay that was watched by 1,368. In the next eight matches, County could manage only one draw. Both legs of the League Cup encounter with Crystal Palace were lost, and the League match draw came from a dismal Sunday 0–0 result with Hereford, which was followed by a some barracking. The Board, with gates down to 1,200, decided to sack Lewis as Manager.

Lewis, who had not been allowed to buy one player, was naturally disgruntled and quickly joined Swansea, as a player.

Who would be the new Manager? Bobby Moore? Lawrie McMenemy? Press speculation proved way off target, as the Board selected the unknown Brian Eastick. His early comments, that he would be employing the "offside" game, did little to swell the small band of supporters, and for the Freight Rover match with Port Vale, only 569 were present. Five days after Eastick's appointment, the Administration was dropped, with Touche Ross being left purely as advisors.

Eastick's arrival was followed by the coming of a host of loan players. Whatever their abilities, the duration of their stays was so short that any stability in the side was an impossibility. By the end of the year, over 30 players had appeared in the first team! There was an attempt to make the club more professional, with the appointment of Keith Mincher as physio-coach, but the club was by then beginning its death throes.

Tranmere, in administration at the same time, soon overcame their difficulties and were able to afford £75,000 for Steel and Harvey. For Newport County it was ever downward.

After Eastick's appointment, the side achieved a few decent results, but then the team began to make schoolboy errors. One calamity followed another, including the injury to talented goalkeeper Bradshaw, which put him out for months; reserve goalkeeper Dillon was meanwhile hurt in a reserve match. Tim Carter was signed on loan, which meant that the useful Downes could not remain. After one game, Bristol transferred Carter, and so County were back to square one! The side lost ten of its last eleven matches of 1987.

On January the 4th, local builder Brian Stent – who had walked out on the club five months before after being accused of making unauthorised press statements – returned as Chairman. He announced that he would be making £40,000 available for players. Gary Brook cost £6,500, and then Paul Bodin – who was previously with County – was bought for £15,000 and Darren Carr (earlier on loan) for £3,000. For a short time, the side gave improved perform-ances.

On February the 9th, Darlow and his friends on the Board, who had earlier failed to appear at a crisis meeting held by the club's supporters, turned up by taxi for a Board meeting, handed over their resignations and left. Stent, who had been in charge for a matter of weeks then resigned himself, claiming he had not known the true financial situation when he had taken over. Only the two Worthy brothers, who had been on the Board for just a few weeks, were left. When it was revealed that Tony Worthy was receiving treatment for the stress, under which he was operating, it gave little confidence to the club's remaining fans. Salway, of the Supporters' Club, became a Director, but it was Tony Worthy who was subsidising the County, and on March the 5th, he instructed Eastick to sell as many players as he could.

In a very short time, eight first–teamers were to leave the club, with Bodin, later a regular for Wales, going for £30,000, and the others departing for smaller fees or on free transfers. On March the 11th, Eastick himself was sacked, a move opposed by Alan Worthy. Eastick agreed to leave for a smaller fee than he was entitled to, and offered to stay on to negotiate transfers, but his offer was ignored. The consistent Hodson, who walked straight into W.B.A.'s Second Division side, was sold for £5,000. On March the 22nd, unhappy Newport Council announced that they were withholding the £60,000 they had promised.

By February, 20 different players had scored for the side, the leading marksman having accumulated two! The side now contained many locals, who were little more than amateurs. After his meeting with the local Council, Tony Worthy announced: *"We are about to go to the wall. It looks like the end. It is unlikely that Newport County will ever play again".*

Understandably, the makeshift side under caretaker Manager David Williams could do little on the pitch, and nine consecutive matches were lost. In a five game spell one

goal was scored and 24 conceded! Torquay and Bolton netted six each. That the club should carry on to the end of the season seemed a miracle, but it did. Against Peterborough, the club experienced its lowest ever home League gate of 988, but by then the side was simply going through the motions. Supporters were amazed when they heard that the final away game, at Darlington, had been won. On May the 7th, 2,560 assembled to watch the club's final League match. A special souvenir programme was issued, to "celebrate" the event. 16–year–old Dean Boughen became the 41st player to be used, as the side containing eight teenagers lost to Rochdale. Robbie Taylor was left as leading scorer for the season, with four goals!

County run out for their last ever Football League match. Darren Peacock (left), went on to find fame in the Premier League, but for 16 year old Dean Boughen it was his only appearance in the League.

Around the time of the last match there was much off the field activity. Williams resigned as Manager, reverting to Trainer. The Worthys stood down, and Salway announced that a London consortium would be running the club. The unknown Bruce Henderson, Tim Woods and James Dickie became Directors. In July, Eddie May, who had been managing abroad, became County Manager with John Mahoney as his Assistant.

Glynne Millett in action during the last match versus Rochdale.

The Barnet game was not a howling success, particularly for Bird, in goal, with the final result being a record 1–7 home defeat.

The side had a few good players – such as the fast-raiding winger, Sanderson and the young defender, Peacock – but after a 17 months lay off with a broken leg, the latter proceeded to break his fingers, by jamming them in a car door. His presence was sorely missed, with the side doing badly, but remarkably gates rarely dipped below the 1,000 mark.

Things slightly improved, and in the Clubcall Cup, County won 5–4 at Yeovil, after extra time. Yeovil had three men sent off, and missed a penalty! International Chris Marustik signed, and scored after three minutes of his debut.

The Council, which was owed £23,000, obtained a Court Order and evicted the club from Somerton Park. In August, May resigned as Manager, less than a month after his appointment, and Mahoney took over. County, who had only a handful of players left, were banned from using YTS players, whilst those that remained refused to play pre-season friendlies, because their last two pay cheques had bounced. On August the 8th, the club without a Ground and with few staff was on the verge of being kicked out of the Vauxhall Conference.

Only 24 hours before the season's opening was a start assured, when on the morning of August the 18th, a sum of money exceeding the rent outstanding was handed to the Council. After a successful application, the keys were handed over at 4.45 p.m. on Friday. Tremendous efforts were needed to prepare the Ground for a match the following Tuesday. Club members had been meeting at John and Anne Pring's house and in the "Cross Hands", while the lottery had continued in near impossible conditions.

Mahoney likewise did the seemingly impossible. Players were signed from any source, and an unfamiliar team took the field on August the 20th, losing 0–3 at Stafford Rangers. On Tuesday, Somerton Park was indeed opened, and 1,871 incredulous fans turned up to see the side go down to a narrow 1–2 defeat. After four games, the team was bottom, with no points, and by their 7th match, 23 players had been used.

In the 4th qualifying Round of the F.A.Cup, Weymouth were beaten 2–1. Despite the critical financial situation, the club appointed Les Chappell as Assistant Manager, and announced that it wanted 17 or 18 full-time professionals.

On October the 31st, a petition was made in Court for the winding up of Newport County. On April the 14th, Sherman had signed an agreement on behalf of his company, JLA Atlantic Capital, and on August the 16th, he had agreed to pay £10,000 down, with £122,000 to follow over two months. Only the downpayment had been paid, and Sherman, who had already suffered much adverse publicity because of alleged fraud, now received more bad press. Only four days after the winding up order, the players and officials stayed at the four star "Cavendish" Hotel, in London, and ate at top restaurants. On November the 12th, the club programme confirmed what had previously only been a rumour, that Sherman was indeed the new Chairman of Newport County; the Directors were listed as Sherman, Henderson and Salway. This did much to shake confidence in the continuance of the Club, although a sponsorship deal of £30,000 with JLA Atlantic was announced, with this company's logo appearing on the player's shirts.

The playing side improved. Weymouth were beaten 4–0, and Bridgend 6–0 in the Welsh Cup, with Sugrue scoring a hat-trick. However, in December 4 games out of 5 were lost, although County did obtain one piece of rare good publicity, when entry to one holiday match was made possible by the donation of canned goods and the like; Age Concern received 3,308 cans, 138 turkeys, and 552 match tickets.

Things were ominous, as 1989 began. However, on the pitch Sugrue scored another Welsh Cup hat–trick, this time against Caernarfon. Because of injuries, Chappell played, and became the oldest player to represent County. On January the 31st, Sherman told the *"Argus"* that he had placed a six figure sum in his solicitors' bank account. On February the 6th, came another High Court appearance. The winding up order was adjourned and the club was given another two weeks, which allowed them to play the Welsh Cup match with Hereford. 1,666 turned up, but Peacock gave the ball away to McLoughlin five minutes from the end, and the game was lost. On February the 17th, Sherman announced that he had given the order to clear all County's debts. Meanwhile the club was still signing players, and coloured Derek Dawkins was bought for £8,000. Sherman also stated that he had just received authority for a scheme which would guarantee Newport County £40,000 a week. Five days later, the *"Argus"* revealed that bailiffs had gone into Somerton Park, and taken away the multi–gym, treatment table, weighing scales and furniture. When questioned by the newspaper, Director Salway replied: *"Mind your own business"*. Two days later, the club signed Kenny Allen, plus Gavin Mahoney, on trial, and goalkeeper Allen was persuaded to give up his job as a postman; he never had time to play for County.

On February the 27th, County was wound up. Sherman wanted a two day delay, stating that a *"banking slip–up had prevented the transfer of money"*.

The match with Altrincham, on the 20th of February was postponed because of torrential rain, and three days later County's final game was witnessed by 895 hardy souls. It was a Clubcall Cup encounter with Kidderminster. The game, which went to extra time, ended in a remarkable 5–6 defeat.

The winding up order of February the 27th provoked, not unnaturally, an emergency meeting of the Vauxhall Conference, and on March the 1st, the club was ordered in Court to pay up, or it would be the end. The following day, Newport County was fully wound up, though it was not quite as definite as it seemed at the time, and an immediate takeover would have been possible. The next day, with the club in the process of being wound up, saw the A.G.M. of the Lifeline Society. The meeting, attended by 300, voted to continue Lifeline, which had already donated £100,000 to Newport County. The meeting voted to give a £50 donation to every member of the County staff, for they were now unemployed.

On March the 10th came a symbolic act, when Somerton Park, which had so recently seen an 18,000 crowd for European football, was closed, and the Ground was pad-locked. A week later, came an 8 hour emergency meeting of the Vauxhall Conference, for three fixtures had already been postponed. The next day, County were due to play Enfield, and the events which now ensued were farcical. Enfield were forced to travel to Newport, for a match which would not take place. The team arrived, to find padlocked gates, and no club officials to meet them. at 3.01 p.m., referee Martin Sims called the game off, and Enfield went to train at Llanwern's ground.

# County farce as Enfield set off

## ☐ By Nick Gray

IN a farcical situation as the final sad steps were being taken in the Newport County saga, Enfield were travelling down to Somerton Park today with no real prospect of play-ing County.

They were accompanied by Conference secretary Peter Hunter.

He said this morning: "We have got to follow the rules to the nth degree.

"If Enfield didn't turn up and Newport managed to get the game on, we would look a right bunch of fools.

"Newport are squirming and squirming. They now realise this isn't just finance they are losing, but a football team."

Hunter added if the game was not played today, County would be expelled tonight but their record would not be expunged until any appeal had been considered, or the two-week time limit for an appeal had elapsed.

Enfield secretary Keith Wortley said this morning: "We have visions of being scared into climbing over the wall to get the game played. But there is no way we will do that.

"Officially we are travelling down expecting to play. But the players don't really feel that. We are a pawn in this."

Newport borough council chief executive Chris Tapp said this morning that he had received no official request from any person connected with County to stage the game.

A County Supporters' Club official had rung up, but no-body else.

Told that Enfield would be travelling to Somerton Park County chairman Jerry Sherman said this morning: "It is a little bit ridiculous that they are doing that.

"We informed the league on Thursday that there would be no sense going. But if they want a day out in Newport, then good luck to them."

Sherman, who accused the Conference of acting ir-responsibly, said he had "other business" and would not be at the ground today.

Sherman confirmed he would be appealing against the Conference's decision to expel County.

A letter of expulsion was sent the next day, giving County until 5 p.m. on March 30th to appeal. True to form, Sherman appealed, with five minutes to spare, and the revised League table was retracted.

On the more than appropriate April Fools' Day came an event that more than any other brought home to County's faithful fans that the end had arrived. At Abbey Auctions, on East Dock Road, all of County's goods were auctioned off. Six hundred lots were made up, containing items that varied from the sublime to the ridiculous. Along with European mementoes, went the club's stretcher, the sign to the Manager's Office and a box of black arm bands. The sale realised £12,000.

The following week the F.A. Registrations Panel disallowed County's appeal, and on April the 4th, a revised table was issued, with County's record expunged. On May the 11th, the dependable Sherman assured the Vauxhall Conference that all debts would be paid off, and asked them to reverse the expulsion, but it was ruled that the club was outside the Pyramid, because of its mid–season expulsion.

Earlier, on the 14th of April, there had been a Special General Meeting of the Lifeline Society, attended by over 400, at which it was decided to investigate the possibility of setting up a new club. On May the 23rd, an application for a lease on Somerton Park was, not unnaturally, turned down.

# Final chapter as County go under

**NEWPORT County's 77-year history finally came to an end today. Liquidators Touche Ross wound the club up fully, giving players redundancy terms.**

The news came through at lunch time after desperate talks to come up with a salvage package failed yesterday.

Chairman Jerry Sherman had continually promised to pay off the club's £126,145 debts. But he did not meet Touche Ross' "final" deadline" of 3.30pm and Touche Ross' patience finally came to an end.

County captain Phil Brignull said at lunchtime today: "The club has folded. The players have been served with their redundancy notices.

"Touche Ross came to the club today and told the players the situation. It is obviously a very sad day for all concerned.

"A lot of the lads are upset about it. There is still talk about Mr Sherman buying the club back but that is a complicated procedure.

"The future is not so bad for me as I have a job (insurance representative). But I feel most

☐ **By Nick Gray**

sorry for the lads at the club who have now got to start looking elsewhere.

"There are some good players at the club and some not so good ones.

"I can't be too critical of Mr Sherman because no one knows exactly what is going on.

"But this thing has gone on and on."

There are twenty players on contracts with County, 14 of hom are full-timers. There are also four apprentices at the club, plus office staff.

County's scheduled home game with Stafford Rangers this Saturday is now off.

Two Gwent businessmen are prepared to step in to save the club but a spokesman said they had been put off from doing so quickly because Touche Ross demanded a definite decision by 10am today.

Conference secretary

Peter Hunter said the league would have to stage an emergency committee meeting to discuss these plans if they came to fruition.

"We had a similar precedent in Kettering Town," said Mr Hunter.

"They were not in liquidation, but were on the verge of folding, and we nursed them through. We obviously want to see Newport continue."

County chairman Sherman and locally-based director Maurice

Salway were unavailable for comment.

Other director Bruce Henderson said he had not been involved in yesterday's talks and did not know the outcome.

County secretary Keith Saunders said he understood Sherman wanted to form a new company and hoped Saturday's game would go ahead.

Manager John Mahoney was taking the players for training this morning.

On June the 6th, the new Club – to be known as Newport A.F.C. – was refused the backing of the F.A. of Wales for an application to the Hellenic League, and on the next day

came another blow. The Council had finally come up with the tentative offer of the Glebelands Athletics Stadium, which provoked complaints from local sides. The Council then announced that the club could only use the stadium if it played in the Gwent County League, since membership of the Hellenic League would entail £60,000 improvements to the venue. Since the aim of the club's formation was to ultimately return to the Football League, the offer was turned down. There were frantic calls to arrange groundsharing, the only suitable agreement proving to be with Moreton Town, 75 miles away from Newport. All the efforts proved worthwhile, when the fledgling club was accepted into the Gloucestershire F.A. and the Premier Division of the Hellenic League.

On June the 10th, a 9 a.m. Press Conference, at Lysaght's Institute, was attended by not only pressmen, but 200 fans. Confusion reigned three days later, when the unbelievable news came out that Newport County had been accepted into the former Vauxhall–Opel League, although there appeared little prospect of Sherman paying off the massive debts. Over 400 were present, on the sweltering evening of June 16th, when the new club was formally launched, also at Lysaght's Institute. After the humiliations of the recent past, new hope was born, and the new slogan adopted was *"Football with a future."* Chairman David Hando spoke with great eloquence. Great were the cheers when the popular John Relish was revealed as the new Manager, and when the officials of Moreton Town were introduced.

Unlike County, the new club was to be run and controlled by the fans, with more than a dozen supporters making up the committee. £15,000 was collected in share capital.

Barry Town had an easier route into English football than Newport A.F.C., for when the Beazer League's Coventry Sporting went bankrupt, Barry took over their fixtures. On August the 7th, 200 fans saw A.F.C. play their first match, a friendly with Kidlington.

In 85 degree heat, Lilygreen scored the first of the club's four goals. The next day, ghostly Newport County, still managed by Mahoney, staged their first training session at Tredegar Park. On August the 14th, County were expelled from their League, with Sherman as usual asking for another two days!

594 fans were present for A.F.C.'s first match at London Road, Moreton, and a 58th minute Parselle goal beat Pegasus Juniors. Considering the distance from Newport that the Ground was situated, the level of support the new club received was tremendous, even though many were unable to make the journey. To maintain one source of revenue, and retain contact with those unable to travel, a shop was leased in the Kingsway Centre "In Shops", to sell programmes and other souvenirs.

The Council, having mellowed somewhat, offered to allow the club to build a stadium at Coronation Park. A.F.C. eventually persuaded the Council to offer instead a place a Spytty Park, where a multi-sport stadium was being planned.

In late September, the new club spent £8,000 it could ill afford, to buy the rights to the old club's name. Because of the outstanding debts, the club could not call itself *"County"*, but Sherman was still around and was adversely affecting such things as sponsorship. The move at least prevented him from terming himself "Chairman of Newport County" any longer, and he soon disappeared from the scene.

On October the 26th, more Newportonians than normal had the chance to see the side, when A.F.C. travelled to play Cardiff City, in the Welsh Cup. A thousand fans travelled to Ninian Park, and the players excelled themselves in going down to a narrow 0–1 defeat. Two days earlier, the County Supporters' Club had changed its name to the A.F.C. Supporters Club.

In January, the Council turned down another request to use Somerton Park, and in a well supported *"Argus"* poll, 3,420 voted for A.F.C. to be allowed into the Ground, and 305 against. Nevertheless, in January the club's future began to brighten, for after a mediocre start, playing matters started to improve, with Lilygreen and Jarvis knocking in the goals. Ruislip Park were beaten 8–0, in which match ex-County player Brian Preece scored the best goal of the season. Sadly, he was to die in a road accident two years later.

Eventually, A.F.C. finished as Champions, with 23 wins and 75 points from 34 matches. Cup matters were more complicated, after the side drew 1–1 in early May with Abingdon, after extra time.

Newport AFC chairman David Hando (left), and manager John Relish proudly display the Federated Homes Premier Division Trophy.

After much wrangling, the replay did not take place until early in the following season. A Painter goal, one minute from time, meant that A.F.C. had achieved the "double" in their first season.

In the close season of 1990, with the agreement of the Council and the F.A.of Wales, the club was allowed into Somerton Park. It was like a wilderness, overgrown and vandalised. Much of the repair work was done for nothing by individuals and firms, and Lifeline donated £10,000 to the total costs of £21,000.

The team was exempted until Round Two of the Welsh Cup, but prevented by the F.A.of Wales from playing in the F.A.Cup. Spytty Park was the next item on the agenda, with £300,000 needed to build a new clubhouse within the £3,000,000 development. The season began with 3-0 wins over Rushden and Alvechurch. Lilygreen scored a hat-trick, in a 5-0 victory at Redditch, and after five games, A.F.C. were top on goal difference; but storm clouds now began to blow in. At first, it had been suggested that membership of the new League of Wales would be voluntary.

Two young ladies help AFC move back to Somerton Park.

As a special gesture, the first match was a friendly against A.F.C.'s former landlords Moreton Town. Although not much of a match, 2,534 were present to celebrate the return. On August the 18th, the side won its first Beazer Homes League match, but from then on League form was poor. There was so much pressure at Somerton Park, that the side did better in their away fixtures. In the Welsh Cup, the team had a record 9-0 victory over Pontlottyn, then Pembroke and Cardiff Corries were both beaten 3-0. In the League, however, A.F.C. were 20th after 13 games, and two matches later they were bottom. In December, there was talk of the proposed League of Wales and the fact that clubs not joining could, even if qualifying through winning the Welsh Cup, be banned from Europe.

In January, the club received a welcome £10,000 from the Gwent County Council for advertising. The team lost 0-1 to Colwyn Bay, in the Welsh Cup, but League form improved especially after A.F.C.'s first purchase, ex-County forward Phil Green. The side embarked on a good winning run, and eventually ended in a creditable 7th position. Supporters were looking forward with some optimism to the new season.

Now the F.A.of Wales, in typical autocratic fashion, began to coerce clubs, many of whom had no desire to leave their present Leagues. For A.F.C., formed to try and regain Football League membership, there was no attraction for there would be no entry into the English football Pyramid.

A.F.C.'s results began to suffer as off the field matters began to dominate. All Welsh teams, apart from the three Football League clubs, would be forced into the new League of Wales.

Those three were exempted, because a legal battle could have bankrupted the F.A.of Wales. Eight of the senior non-League sides acted together to fight the ban on English football, becoming known as the *"Irate Eight"*. After 19 games, A.F.C. has slipped down to 13th.

The saga of the League of Wales continued to run and run, collecting much newspaper space. It was not until September the 23rd, that the possibility of clubs being forced out of their current Leagues was first mentioned. On the 30th of November, members of the F.A. of Wales, voted by a 2-1 majority to impose the ban. When the clubs appealed, a three-man Tribunal was set up.

The hearing was first arranged for January, and was ultimately deferred for a fortnight. When the outcome was finally revealed, it transpired that Merthyr's appeal was allowed, since the Vauxhall Conference was virtually the "Fifth Division" of the Football League, but all the other appeals were turned down.

Although A.F.C. had slipped down the table, some good Cup performances were given, for in the F.A. Trophy, Bideford, Saltash and Stroud were beaten. In the Welsh Cup the side beat Bridgend 3-0, before losing by the same score at Cardiff City, where pouring rain and a completely waterlogged pitch made play farcical.

# NEWPORT AFC TO COME HOME IN £1.8m PLAN

**A PLAN for a massive £1.85m sports complex for Newport – including a new home for "exiled" Newport AFC – was unvelled today.**

## New sports centre development at Spytty Playing Fields

The ambitious scheme centres on the Homes League on a shared pitch at Moreton-

Will a return to Newport ever become a reality?

What on earth did 1992 hold in store for Newport A.F.C.? On February the 13th, the *"Western Mail"* revealed that the rebels were pondering exile. The same night, a crisis meeting of supporters was held at the Pill Labour Hall, James St. By this time, it had become clear that no accommodation with the F.A.of Wales was possible. That day in fact, Alun Evans – the secretary of the F.A. of Wales – had walked out of a meeting with the rebel clubs, in Shrewsbury. There was one ray of hope, for Evans had indicated that he would not impede any of the clubs from moving to Grounds in England. At the Supporters' meeting, various alternatives were put to those present.

The unanimous decision was to return to exile, whilst maintaining a presence in Newport. A.F.C. would groundshare with Gloucester City, while a new club, 'A.F.C. 'Newport', would be set up, to bring on local talent, and to also avoid a situation where the senior club would lose its base in the town.

Would Newport A.F.C. eventually be able to move into the new stadium, or would some local club get there first? It was underlined to those present that exile would involve extra expenditure of £50,000, but the meeting reached the view that there was no alternative.

Over its first few years of existence, A.F.C. had convinced the Council of its viability, and the club was given per-mission to continue using the offices and bars at Somerton Park on a temporary basis, which helped to mitigate the difficulties of exile. The proposal to form the new club was not so fortunate however.

A.F.C. Newport was set up under a Board led by Eddie Wulff, but the F.A.of Wales took so long to investigate any possible links with Newport A.F.C., that the project was eventually scrapped.

In the programme for the match versus Stroud on February the 18th, David Hando gave voice to the frustration of the Board and fans: *"After all the time and effort and money that we have all put into the club, it has come to this. The supporters, players, management, staff and Directors of Newport A.F.C. created a club from nothing, sustained it in exile for a season, returned to Newport in triumph as League Champions and Cup winners, rescued Somerton Park from dereliction, ran three successful teams, retained gates remarkable for our present level of football, and in difficult economic circumstances ensured that we owe no-one a penny.... All this progress had been brought to a shuddering halt, not by the economic situation or financial disaster or falling gates or poor play or bad management, but by the body charged with the responsibility of improving standards of football in Wales".*

In the early months of 1992, results improved, and after 27 games the side was back in 7th place. The team's status was safe, and people's minds were more concerned with the season to come. However, on one Tuesday evening in March, A.F.C. did make the headlines. A match with Redditch was heading for a 0–1 defeat, when referee Baker decided to blow for time as the ball was on its way into the visitors' net. The fact that he had already played nine minutes of injury time did not help matters.

Uproar ensued, and half a dozen supporters attempted to climb over the fence and approach the official. In late May, the club was fined £500 by the F.A.of Wales, and ordered to play the first two matches of the following season behind closed doors. After appeal, only the fine was imposed.

This was not the only occasion when A.F.C. made the headlines, when, earlier in the year there had been a small fire in the old Greyhound Stand at Somerton Park. On Tuesday the 14th of April, those returning from an away game found the Social Club ablaze. Much of it had to be demolished so that the final home game with Barry could take place six days later. The controls of the floodlights were also destroyed. It was a nostalgic occasion when the side played its last competitive game at the old Ground, the more so since many old County players had been invited to the match.

On a warm sunny morning, a crowd of 1,051 saw Prew score a 22nd minute goal, as A.F.C. won their final game at the Ground. Like Newport County, Aldershot had also played their last match and gone into liquidation. Some of their supporters turned up at Somerton Park, to see the match and to seek information on how to set up a new club.

Of the rebel non−League clubs, who fought the F.A. of Wales' ruling, A.F.C., Caernarfon, Colwyn Bay and Barri (who changed their name from Barry Town, to emphasise their true Welsh origins) took the actual step of going into exile. The F.A. of Wales also found an excuse for banning Newport and Colwyn Bay from the Welsh Cup, though, for Newport there was the compensation that they were now entitled to play in the F.A.Cup. The actions of the rebel clubs in taking their rebellion to the limit did not endear them to the top brass of the Welsh authorities, and in late July, the then President of the body − Tommy Forse − made these now infamous comments: *"They are no more Welsh than Gateshead. They will not survive and perhaps some decent clubs will come up in those areas to replace those who have gone to England".* Secretary Evans made the dire prophecy that the five non−League clubs (including Rhyl who also turned down the new League) would go bust within two years, and that the three Football League clubs would go part−time within four.

Thus, Newport A.F.C. set its collective mind on its second adventure beyond the frontier, in far England. The economic situation in a way did the club a favour, for it was able to recruit useful players who were unable to find new Football League clubs. These included old Newport County favourites Mark Kendall, Linden Jones and Steve Lowndes. Also signed were the capable local footballers, Kyle Charles and George Brown, plus ex−Hereford Shane Jones, the squad being a strong one, for the standard of football.

And so we return, at long last, to the vehicles which began this book. The side began by attracting gates of around 500. Many travelled down by car, while others made the journey by coach. As Winter approached and crowds dropped, there were various permutations of coach travel. Fans began travelling with the team, while the Supporters' Club's vintage vehicle did not always manage the return journey from Gloucester! No doubt generations to come will be entertained with stories of Newportonians' travels. Some of the tales will need little embellishment.

A.F.C. began with a bang, winning their first four League matches, ultimately however, the team was to become a victim of its own success. Engaged in four Cup competitions, the side did remarkably well, often beating teams from a higher division. Over the early months of the season two thirds of the matches played were Cup games. A backlog of League matches accrued, and a large injury list built up. A.F.C. gave some fine performances with Linden Jones giving some sterling display in defence, Lilygreen slotting in the goals and others playing admirably. The side came within one match of appearing in the first round proper of the F.A.Cup, but unfortunately was outplayed for the first time all season, as Sutton United won 4−1, before a crowd of over 800. Doughty Cup fighters Sutton also knocked A.F.C. out of the F.A.Trophy.

Things sagged in mid−season. Injuries meant that the side could not always provide two proper substitutes, and there were further blows when two of the regulars − Towler and Kendall − both left to join the Police Force. In February, the team went four matches without a win, and Manager John Relish resigned. Nothing can take away from his achievements in the club's first three and a half years. There was little upheaval following the resignation however, as his deputy, Graham Rogers stepped up. The side began a much better run but unfortunately had lost too much ground earlier on. However, the side − bolstered by the signing of ex−Newport County international Nigel Vaughan − proved itself one of the best in the Midland Division of the Beazer League, finishing frustratingly close to the top of the table.

What of the future? The traditional home of Newport soccer, Somerton Park, is set to become a building site. Will there be an Aldridge Avenue, a Tynan Terrace, a Wilcox Way? Who knows, but it will be an historic, if very sad, occasion when the old ground is demolished. Fortunately there is the new Spytty Stadium to cater for the needs of football. And what of the future course of Newport soccer? No−one who has studied the past will be rash enough to make any predictions. However, Newport football has survived two World Wars, a war with the F.A.of Wales, liquidations, expulsions from the Football League and Vauxhall Conference, and two periods of exile. In one form or another, it will continue to survive.

# CHAPTER 9

## The End of an Era

Shortly after the announcement of Somerton Park's imminent demolition, a friendly match was arranged by John Payne of Pill A.F.C. to mark the passing of the old ground. Many of the past County and present Newport A.F.C. players agreed to turn out, and some – such as Keith Oakes and Richard Walden – travelled considerable distances just to take part. It was a bright evening on Tuesday June the 22nd, and conditions were ideal for football. The scene was reminiscent of the old days, as waiting supporters queued back to Somerton Lane. To give a blow by blow account of what happened is pointless, for what mattered was not the football, but the meeting together, on one final occasion, of old friends on and off the pitch. It was intended to follow a five a side match with a full game between Newport Past and Newport Present. In the event rules were not strictly adhered to, for 'Newport Past' ended up with thirteen players – and nobody who wanted to play was refused a game!

For those who stood on the terraces, chatting to old companions, there was a mixture of thoughts and emotions. There was the shock of seeing familiar faces, decades older; memories of long past games, still vividly remembered; thoughts on how the old Club, after almost eighty years of existence had been allowed to drift into oblivion. Some of the veterans, seeing boys scattered around the terraces, wondered how the youngsters could recapture the dreams of their own long gone youth, when there was no longer any Senior team in the town.

The main match, which included many respected players from the past, ended four–all, and because of the previously vandalised controls it was impossible to use the old floodlights. When the game finished and hundreds of supporters ran on to the pitch, for one last time, the Summer sky was starting to darken. Twilight began to settle on Somerton Park, on Newport County and on history. The last few remaining assets of County may have been auctioned off, but the memories will never be for sale......

## Stars return for Somerton Park farewell

FORMER Newport County favourites return to the scene of their triumphs tomorrow night for the Past v Present match to mark the end of soccer at Somerton Park before the old stadium is pulled down (writes John Francis).

Most of the players from County's golden spell in the early 80s, when they won the Fourth Division and Welsh Cup double and reached the European Cupwinners' Cup quarter-finals, will parade their skills again, among them Keith Oakes and Kevin Moore, who travel from Peterborough and Blackpool respectively for the game, sponsored by the South Wales Argus.

Goalscoring duo John Aldridge and Tommy Tynan will be out of the country, but Dave Gwyther, who scored County's first goal in Europe, will play alongside Eddie Woods, who scored the goal which knocked West Ham out of the FA Cup.

Past squad: Gary Plumley, Richard Walden, Darren Peacock, Grant Davies, John Relish, Vaughan Jones, Ken Stroud, Tony Pulis, Karl Elsey, Eddie Woods, Dave Gwyther, Keith Oakes, Kevin Moore.

Present squad: Mark Kendall, John Macey, Peter Mason, George Brown, Phil Coyne, Mike Pratt, Graham Rogers, John Lewis, Dave Jarvis, Mark Price, Norman Parselle, Ray Pulis, Chris Lilygreen, Phil Green, Darren Porretta. Kick-off 7pm.

■Before the main match a five-a-side game will be staged. Among those taking part: Steve Aizlewood, Granville Smith, George Young, David Williams, Andy White, Jeff Thomas, John Macey, Terry Lynch, Len Hill, Allan Wood, David Jones, Mike Hancock, Paul Preece, Alex Beattie. Kick-off 6.30pm.

At half time during the main match other County personalities will be introduced, including Fred Stansfield, Ken Hollyman, Arthur 'Buller' Lever, Don Murray, Bob Smith, Bill and Alan Herritty, Jimmy Singer, Derek Tapscott, Ron Bird, Danny Newall, Ray Wilcox, Albert Derrick and John Rowland.

"The response has been superb," said John Payne, of Pill AFC, who are organising the occasion. "We are honoured to get this match off the ground and we ask as many people as possible to turn up and make it a really good send-off for Somerton Park."

Admission is £2 (£1 children and senior citizens). All proceeds go to the Brian Preece Fund.

# APPENDIX: Statistical Section

## Notes

Since the publication of the book: *'The Ironsides – A Lifetime in The League'* † , the County's statistics have been completely rechecked, and there are slight differences between figures quoted in the two books. The figures for early seasons are on occasions unreliable, as are wartime seasons, and substitute appearances present something of a nightmare for statisticians.

The presentation of the seasonal figures is straightforward and generally self–explanatory. The following points are given, to avoid confusion:–

The total appearances and goals given in each seasonal table include those for other Cup matches (as detailed on pages 169 to 174). Substitute appearances are shown as plus (+) figures, i.e. 16+3 = 16 starting appearances plus three as substitute.

'Home' matches are shown in upper case, 'away' games in lower case.

Cup matches: Preliminary and Qualifying rounds are suffixed 'P' and 'Q' (e.g. 3Q = 3rd qualifying round), replays are suffixed 'R', and two–legged ties are suffixed 'L' (e.g. 1/2L = first round, second leg). Q/F = Quarter–final, etc.

(† Copies of this book are available from 'Yore Publications', see page 176)

## SEASON 1912-13 Southern League Div 2

| | Date | Opposition | Res. | Att. | Goalscorers |
|---|---|---|---|---|---|
| 1 | 7 Sep | MID-RHONDDA | 3-0 | 5000 | McDougall, G.Fyfe, Vowles |
| 2 | 14 | Cardiff City | 0-2 | 8000 | |
| 3 | 21 | SWANSEA TOWN | 0-1 | 5000 | |
| 4 | 28 | Llanelly | 1-2 | 4000 | Hall |
| 5 | 12 Oct | TREHARRIS | 2-1 | 6000 | G.Fyfe, Holt |
| 6 | 23 Nov | ABERDARE | 2-2 | | Lean, G.Fyfe |
| 7 | 30 | Mardy | 0-5 | | |
| 8 | 7 Dec | Ton Pentre | 1-1 | | Lean |
| 9 | 25 | Southend United | 0-1 | 11000 | |
| 10 | 28 | LLANELLY | 3-1 | | W.A.Fyfe(2), Holt |
| 11 | 16 Jan | MARDY | 1-2 | | W.A.Fyfe |
| 12 | 18 | LUTON TOWN | 5-1 | | W.A.Fyfe(2), G.Fyfe, Holt(2) |
| 13 | 1 Feb | TON PENTRE | 4-1 | | W.A.Fyfe, Bowdler, Hall(2) |
| 14 | 8 | CARDIFF CITY | 1-3 | 8000 | Holt |
| 15 | 22 | Mid-Rhondda | 1-0 | | Holt |
| 16 | 1 Mar | Swansea Town | 1-2 | 10200 | Hall |
| 17 | 8 | Croydon Common | 0-1 | | |
| 18 | 15 | CROYDON COMMON | 1-2 | | Bowdler |
| 19 | 31 | Pontypridd | 0-0 | | |
| 20 | 3 Apr | Treharris | 0-0 | | |
| 21 | 5 | Luton Town | 0-5 | | |
| 22 | 7 | SOUTHEND UNITED | 0-2 | | |
| 23 | 12 | PONTYPRIDD | 3-1 | | Groves, W.A.Fyfe, Hall |
| 24 | 19 | Abedare | 0-0 | | |

| Player | League | | F.A.Cup | | Total | |
|---|---|---|---|---|---|---|
| | App | Gls. | App | Gls. | App | Gls. |
| Bowdler W.A. | 19 | 2 | | | 23 | 3 |
| Cox A. | 4 | 0 | | | 8 | 0 |
| Davies W. | 1 | 0 | | | 1 | 0 |
| Ewing D. | 5 | 0 | | | 10 | 0 |
| Fletcher W. | 2 | 0 | | | 2 | 0 |
| Fullerton W. | 2 | 0 | | | 2 | 0 |
| Fyfe G. | 12 | 4 | | | 17 | 5 |
| Fyfe W.A. | 15 | 7 | | | 15 | 7 |
| Groves G. | 4 | 1 | | | 4 | 1 |
| Hall P. | 24 | 5 | | | 29 | 5 |
| Hammett E.D.G. | 6 | 0 | | | 6 | 0 |
| Hollinshead W. | 2 | 0 | | | 2 | 0 |
| Holt A. | 16 | 6 | | | 21 | 7 |
| Husbands E. | 22 | 0 | | | 27 | 0 |
| Jones E. | 4 | 0 | | | 4 | 0 |
| Lean L. | 22 | 2 | | | 26 | 3 |
| McDougall D. | 22 | 1 | | | 26 | 1 |
| Perry J. | 21 | 0 | | | 26 | 0 |
| Taylor W. | 21 | 0 | | | 22 | 0 |
| Thornton T. | 17 | 0 | | | 18 | 0 |
| Vowles R. | 8 | 1 | | | 11 | 1 |
| Westwood E. | 15 | 0 | | | 19 | 0 |

(Not entered for F.A.Cup)

The above figures are approximate,
due to limited Press coverage of matches.

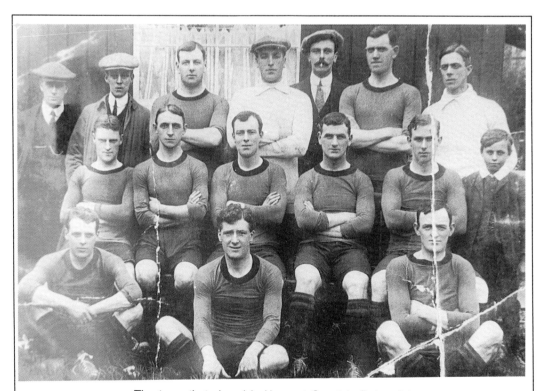

**The team that played in Newport County's first match**
(Staff only) (Back) Lean, Husbands, Taylor, Good (Trainer)
(Middle) Holt, Hall, Vowles, G.Fyfe, Westwood.   (Front) Cox, Thornton, McDougall (Player/Manager)

# SEASON 1913-14  Southern League Division 2

|  | Date | Opposition | Res. | Att. | Goalscorers |
|---|---|---|---|---|---|
| 1 | 6 Sep | PONTYPRIDD | 2-1 | 5000 | Tomlinson(2) |
| 2 | 13 | Pontypridd | 0-0 | 7000 | |
| 3 | 20 | CROYDON COMMON | 0-1 | 5000 | |
| 4 | 4 Oct | Mardy | 1-1 | | Enright |
| 5 | 18 | CAERPHILLY | 2-2 | 6000 | Flanders, Butler |
| 6 | 25 | Swansea Town | 0-3 | 8500 | |
| 7 | 22 Nov | SWANSEA TOWN | 0-3 | 3914 | |
| 8 | 29 | Caerphilly | 1-0 | 700 | Green |
| 9 | 6 Dec | STOKE | 3-2 | 3500 | Matthews, Enright(2) |
| 10 | 13 | Mid-Rhondda | 1-3 | 3000 | Lindley |
| 11 | 20 | MARDY | 4-0 | 5000 | Flanders, Edwards, E.Hammett, Matthews |
| 12 | 25 | LUTON TOWN | 2-0 | 10000 | Matthews, E.Hammett |
| 13 | 26 | Luton Town | 0-1 | 8000 | |
| 14 | 27 | Brentford | 0-3 | 6000 | |
| 15 | 1 Jan | Aberdare | 0-0 | | |
| 16 | 10 | Ton Pentre | 2-1 | | Matthews, E.Hammett |
| 17 | 17 | ABERDARE | 4-0 | 3000 | Preece, Butler, E.Hammett(2) |
| 18 | 24 | MID-RHONDDA | 2-0 | | Matthews, Enright |
| 19 | 31 | ABERTILLERY | 2-1 | 3000 | Matthews, E.Hammett |
| 20 | 7 Feb | TON PENTRE | 4-1 | | Flanders, Edwards, Matthews, Enright |
| 21 | 9 | Abertillery | 1-1 | | Lindley |
| 22 | 14 | Barry | 2-6 | | Lindley, Tomlinson |
| 23 | 21 | Croydon Common | 0-0 | | |
| 24 | 28 | Treharris | 2-0 | | Edwards, Lindley |
| 25 | 28 Mar | Stoke | 0-2 | | |
| 26 | 4 Apr | BRENTFORD | 3-2 | 3500 | Butler, E.Hammett, Tomlinson |
| 27 | 11 | TREHARRIS | 6-0 | 2000 | Matthews(2), E.Hammett(4) |
| 28 | 18 | BARRY | 2-2 | 4000 | E.Hammett, Tomlinson |
| 29 | 28 | Llanelly | 2-2 | | Edwards, Matthews |
| 30 | 30 | LLANELLY | 1-0 | 1500 | Preece |

| Player | League | | F.A.Cup | | Total | |
|---|---|---|---|---|---|---|
| | App | Gls | App | Gls | App | Gls |
| Bullock P. | 5 | 0 | – | – | 5 | 0 |
| Butler J. | 23 | 3 | 3 | 1 | 32 | 7 |
| Davies M. | 1 | 0 | – | – | 1 | 0 |
| Edwards A. | 26 | 4 | 2 | 0 | 35 | 6 |
| Ellis | 1 | 0 | – | – | 1 | 0 |
| Enright J. | 23 | 5 | 3 | 1 | 32 | 9 |
| Flanders F. | 30 | 3 | 4 | 0 | 41 | 3 |
| Green H. | 27 | 1 | 4 | 2 | 37 | 4 |
| Griffiths S. | 1 | 0 | – | – | 1 | 0 |
| Hammett E.D.G. | 13 | 12 | 2 | 0 | 16 | 14 |
| Hammett R.H. | 1 | 0 | – | – | 1 | 0 |
| Harding F. | 3 | 0 | 3 | 0 | 8 | 0 |
| Husbands E. | 4 | 0 | – | – | 4 | 0 |
| Lindley F. | 25 | 4 | 4 | 1 | 35 | 6 |
| Matthews W. | 28 | 10 | 4 | 6 | 39 | 20 |
| McLeod R. | 26 | 0 | 4 | 0 | 37 | 0 |
| Newman | 1 | 0 | – | – | 1 | 0 |
| Payne A. | 2 | 0 | – | – | 2 | 0 |
| Preece A. | 20 | 2 | 1 | 0 | 26 | 3 |
| Smart J. | 20 | 0 | 4 | 1 | 31 | 1 |
| Spittle T. | 27 | 0 | 4 | 0 | 38 | 1 |
| Tait J.R. | 1 | 0 | – | – | 1 | 0 |
| Tomlinson T. | 20 | 5 | 2 | 1 | 25 | 6 |
| Wilkinson F. | 1 | 0 | – | – | 1 | 0 |
| Winter | 1 | 0 | – | – | 1 | 0 |

Trainer Fred Good has been credited
with two appearances, but it has
not been possible to confirm this.

## F.A.Cup

| 1Q | 27 Sep | MOND NICKEL WORKS | 6-1 | 4000 | Green, Lindley, Tomlinson, Matthews(3) |
|---|---|---|---|---|---|
| 2Q | 11 Oct | CARDIFF CORRIES | 6-1 | 4000 | Green, Matthews(3), Butler, Enright |
| 3Q | 1 Nov | ABERDARE | 1-1 | 7000 | Smart |
| 3Q | 10 | Aberdare | 0-1 | 1600 | |

(Back) Green, Edwards, McLeod, Flanders, Good (Trainer).(Middle) Lindley, Matthews, Butler, E.Hammett, Tomlinson.(Front) Spittle, Preece

# SEASON 1914-15 *Southern League Division 2*

| | Date | Opposition | Res. | Att. | Goalscorers |
|---|---|---|---|---|---|
| 1 | 5 Sep | STALYBRIDGE CELTIC | 0-1 | 2000 | |
| 2 | 19 | MERTHYR TOWN | 1-0 | | Hammett |
| 3 | 22 | Ebbw Vale | 2-3 | | Flanders(2) |
| 4 | 3 Oct | LLANELLY | 2-0 | | Jarvis, Hammett |
| 5 | 17 | Mid-Rhondda | 0-0 | | |
| 6 | 31 | Pontypridd | 1-1 | | Evans |
| 7 | 14 Nov | Brentford | 0-1 | 3000 | |
| 8 | 28 | Coventry City | 1-10 | 4000 | Evans |
| 9 | 5 Dec | STOKE | 0-1 | | |
| 10 | 19 | TON PENTRE | 1-2 | | Spittle |
| 11 | 2 Jan | Stalybridge Celtic | 0-1 | | |
| 12 | 9 | Stoke | 1-3 | | Flanders |
| 13 | 16 | SWANSEA TOWN | 1-0 | | Groves |
| 14 | 23 | Merthyr Town | 1-2 | | Messer |
| 15 | 30 | EBBW VALE | 3-0 | | Hammett(2), Jarvis |
| 16 | 6 Feb | Llanelly | 1-3 | | Preece |
| 17 | 13 | Barry | 1-3 | | Hammett |
| 18 | 20 | MID-RHONDDA | 3-1 | | Spittle(2), Hammett |
| 19 | 6 Mar | PONTYPRIDD | 1-1 | | Hammett |
| 20 | 13 | Swansea Town | 0-2 | 4000 | |
| 21 | 20 | BRENTFORD | 5-0 | | Williams(3), Howells, Jarvis |
| 22 | 3 Apr | COVENTRY CITY | 0-1 | | |
| 23 | 5 | BARRY | 2-0 | | Groves, Williams |
| 24 | 24 | Ton Pentre | 0-6 | | |

## F.A.Cup

| | Date | Opposition | Res. | Att. | Goalscorers |
|---|---|---|---|---|---|
| P | 26 Sep | RHIWDERRIN | 8-0 | | Unrecorded |
| 1Q | 10 Oct | MILFORD | 6-0 | | Hammett(3), Evans(2), Edwards |
| 2Q | 24 | RHYMNEY | 3-1 | | Evans(2), Groves |
| 3Q | 7 Nov | BARRY | 4-2 | | Hammett(2), Evans, Groves |
| 4Q | 21 | Swansea Town | 0-1 | 5000 | |

| Player | League | | F.A.Cup | | Total | |
|---|---|---|---|---|---|---|
| | App | Gls. | App | Gls. | App | Gls. |
| Adams | 6 | 0 | | | | |
| Bulpitt W. | 4 | 0 | | | | |
| Cleverly A. | 18 | 0 | | | | |
| Dunbarton | 1 | 0 | | | | |
| Edwards A. | 24 | 0 | | | | |
| Evans C. | 4 | 2 | | | | |
| Flanders F. | 20 | 3 | | | | |
| Good F. | 2 | 0 | | | | |
| Groves G. | 20 | 2 | | | | |
| Hammett E.D.G. | 17 | 7 | | | | |
| Harper | 1 | 0 | | | | |
| Houldin | 2 | 0 | | | | |
| Howells | 2 | 1 | | | | |
| Jagger | 3 | 0 | | | | |
| Jarvis J. | 23 | 3 | | | | |
| Jones E.A. | 12 | 0 | | | | |
| Jones J. | 2 | 0 | | | | |
| Lewis | 1 | 0 | | | | |
| Messer W. | 17 | 1 | | | | |
| Preece A. | 20 | 1 | | | | |
| Sedgeley H. | 24 | 0 | | | | |
| Spittle T. | 20 | 3 | | | | |
| Tomlinson T. | 7 | 0 | | | | |
| Wells | 1 | 0 | | | | |
| Williams I. | 13 | 4 | | | | |

League appearances are approximate
due to limited Press coverage.
Cup appearances have proved impossible
to confirm, and therefore all have been omitted.

(No known team group for 1914/15 season. This group was playing in War-time regional football – April 1916)
(Back) Preece, ? , ? , Royster(Director), Jones, Moss(Chairman), Thorneycroft & Williams (Directors), ? ,Carwardine (Director)
? , Hollis (Sec/Manager), ? , ? , Cox (Director)  (Front) ? , ? , ? , Husbands, Davies, ? , ? .

# SEASON 1919-20 *Southern League Division 1*

| | Date | Opposition | Res. | Att. | Goalscorers |
|---|---|---|---|---|---|
| 1 | 30 Aug | Norwich City | 1–4 | 5000 | Jones |
| 2 | 1 Sep | Southend United | 0–3 | 2500 | |
| 3 | 6 | BRENTFORD | 2–4 | 5500 | Harris, Dobson |
| 4 | 8 | SOUTHEND UNITED | 0–0 | 4000 | |
| 5 | 11 | WATFORD | 0–1 | 4000 | |
| 6 | 13 | Merthyr Town | 0–3 | 8000 | |
| 7 | 20 | PLYMOUTH ARGYLE | 2–1 | 7000 | Lockley, Richards |
| 8 | 27 | Bristol Rovers | 1–2 | 10000 | Savage |
| 9 | 4 Oct | READING | 0–0 | 6040 | |
| 10 | 6 | Millwall | 1–5 | 6000 | Savage |
| 11 | 11 | Southampton | 0–2 | 6000 | |
| 12 | 16 | Q.P.Rangers | 0–1 | 6000 | |
| 13 | 18 | LUTON TOWN | 0–0 | 6414 | |
| 14 | 25 | Gillingham | 3–1 | 6000 | Savage(3) |
| 15 | 1 Nov | SWANSEA TOWN | 0–3 | 6137 | |
| 16 | 8 | Exeter City | 2–1 | 4000 | Collins(2) |
| 17 | 15 | CARDIFF CITY | 1–3 | 8410 | Richards |
| 18 | 29 | SWINDON TOWN | 2–0 | 3957 | Dobson, Gaughan |
| 19 | 13 Dec | BRIGHTON & H.A. | 1–0 | 4608 | Mann |
| 20 | 25 | NORTHAMPTON TOWN | 3–0 | 5671 | Mann(2), Gaughan |
| 21 | 26 | Northampton Town | 1–5 | 8000 | Devlin |
| 22 | 27 | Portsmouth | 1–3 | 13800 | Gaughan |
| 23 | 3 Jan | NORWICH CITY | 5–2 | 5807 | Dobson(2), Mann(2), Devlin |
| 24 | 17 | Brentford | 1–2 | 7000 | Devlin |
| 25 | 24 | MERTHYR TOWN | 2–0 | 4554 | Mann, Gaughan |
| 26 | 7 Feb | BRISTOL ROVERS | 0–2 | 6419 | |
| 27 | 14 | Reading | 0–2 | | |
| 28 | 21 | SOUTHAMPTON | 1–1 | 6362 | Mann |
| 29 | 28 | Luton Town | 0–4 | 8000 | |
| 30 | 6 Mar | GILLINGHAM | 4–0 | 4050 | Devlin(2), Dobson, Gaughan |
| 31 | 13 | Swansea Town | 1–2 | 15000 | Dobson |
| 32 | 20 | EXETER CITY | 4–1 | 6004 | Dobson(2), Savage(2) |
| 33 | 24 | Watford | 0–0 | 4000 | |
| 34 | 27 | Cardiff City | 0–0 | 18000 | |
| 35 | 2 Apr | CRYSTAL PALACE | 1–0 | 10084 | Dobson |
| 36 | 3 | Q.P.RANGERS | 3–0 | 7990 | Richards(2), Dobson |
| 37 | 5 | Crystal Palace | 0–3 | 14800 | |
| 38 | 10 | Swindon Town | 0–3 | 9000 | |
| 39 | 14 | Plymouth Argyle | 0–3 | 4000 | |
| 40 | 17 | MILLWALL | 0–0 | 6485 | |
| 41 | 24 | Brighton & H.A. | 1–3 | 10000 | Lockley |
| 42 | 1 May | PORTSMOUTH | 1–0 | 10371 | Gaughan |

| Player | League | | F.A.Cup | | Total | |
|---|---|---|---|---|---|---|
| | App | Gls. | App | Gls. | App | Gls. |
| Barnacle R. | 1 | 0 | – | – | 1 | 0 |
| Brooks A.W. | 4 | 0 | 1 | 0 | 5 | 0 |
| Collins E. | 40 | 2 | 4 | 0 | 47 | 2 |
| Cooper J. | 39 | 0 | 5 | 0 | 45 | 0 |
| Devlin W. | 19 | 5 | 4 | 1 | 25 | 6 |
| Dobson H. | 38 | 10 | 4 | 0 | 43 | 10 |
| Dyson H. | 3 | 0 | – | – | 3 | 0 |
| Edwards E.A. | 24 | 0 | 5 | 0 | 29 | 0 |
| Evans B. | 2 | 0 | – | – | 4 | 0 |
| Gaughan W.B. | 38 | 6 | 5 | 0 | 46 | 6 |
| Gittins J. | 2 | 0 | – | – | 2 | 0 |
| Good F. | 1 | 0 | – | – | 1 | 0 |
| Griffin J.H. | 36 | 0 | 5 | 0 | 43 | 0 |
| Groves G. | 40 | 0 | 5 | 0 | 48 | 0 |
| Harris H. | 9 | 1 | – | – | 9 | 1 |
| Hindmarsh J. | 9 | 0 | 1 | 0 | 13 | 0 |
| Hodges A.E. | – | – | – | – | 3 | 2 |
| Jones E. | 12 | 1 | – | – | 13 | 1 |
| Kelson H.J. | 33 | 0 | 4 | 0 | 40 | 0 |
| Lockley W. | 21 | 2 | 1 | 1 | 24 | 3 |
| Mann J.F. | 33 | 7 | 5 | 2 | 38 | 9 |
| Mayo W.H. | 4 | 0 | – | – | 4 | 0 |
| Parkes H.A. | 1 | 0 | – | – | 2 | 0 |
| Peet A. | 2 | 0 | – | – | 2 | 0 |
| Perry T. | 1 | 0 | – | – | 1 | 0 |
| Richards W. | 11 | 4 | 1 | 2 | 13 | 6 |
| Rowlands H.L. | 1 | 0 | – | – | 1 | 0 |
| Rushton J. | 1 | 0 | – | – | 1 | 0 |
| Savage G. | 35 | 7 | 5 | 1 | 42 | 8 |
| Worden F.W. | 1 | 0 | – | – | 1 | 0 |
| Young W. | 1 | 0 | – | – | 1 | 0 |
| Own Goals | | | | | | 1 |

The 'Argus' credited Johnson and Rogers with one appearance each, but this has not been verified.

| | | | | | | | |
|---|---|---|---|---|---|---|---|
| 9 | Swansea Town | 42 | 16 | 11 | 15 | 53 | 45 | 43 |
| 10 | Exeter City | 42 | 17 | 9 | 16 | 57 | 51 | 43 |
| 11 | Southend United | 42 | 13 | 17 | 12 | 46 | 48 | 43 |
| 12 | Norwich City | 42 | 15 | 11 | 16 | 64 | 57 | 41 |
| 13 | Swindon Town | 42 | 17 | 7 | 18 | 65 | 68 | 41 |
| 14 | Millwall | 42 | 14 | 12 | 16 | 52 | 55 | 40 |
| 15 | Brentford | 42 | 15 | 10 | 17 | 52 | 59 | 40 |
| 16 | Brighton & Hove A | 42 | 14 | 8 | 20 | 60 | 72 | 36 |
| 17 | Bristol Rovers | 42 | 11 | 13 | 18 | 61 | 78 | 35 |
| 18 | Newport County | 42 | 13 | 7 | 22 | 45 | 70 | 33 |
| 19 | Northampton Tow | 42 | 12 | 9 | 21 | 64 | 103 | 33 |
| 20 | Luton Town | 42 | 10 | 10 | 22 | 51 | 76 | 30 |
| 21 | Merthyr Town | 42 | 9 | 11 | 22 | 47 | 78 | 29 |
| 22 | Gillingham | 42 | 10 | 7 | 25 | 34 | 74 | 27 |

Bottom positions only

## F.A.Cup

| | | | | | |
|---|---|---|---|---|---|
| 4Q | 22 Nov | BATH CITY | 5–2 | 2575 | Richards(2), Lockley, Mann, Savage |
| 5Q | 6 Dec | MERTHYR TOWN | 1–0 | 4606 | Mann |
| 6Q | 20 | EXETER CITY | 1–0 | 7764 | Devlin |
| 1 | 10 Jan | LEICESTER CITY | 0–0 | 7523 | |
| 1/R | 15 | Leicester City | 0–2 | 21000 | |

(Back) Good (Trainer), Groves, Harris, Cooper, Griffin, Kelson
(Front) Mayo, Dobson, Gaughan, Collins, Mann, Savage

# SEASON 1920-21    Division 3

| | Date | Opposition | Res. | Att. | Goalscorers |
|---|---|---|---|---|---|
| 1 | 28 Aug | READING | 0-1 | 14500 | |
| 2 | 1 Sep | Bristol Rovers | 2-3 | 10000 | Walker, Wolstenholme |
| 3 | 4 | Reading | 0-4 | 10000 | |
| 4 | 9 | BRISTOL ROVERS | 0-2 | 8000 | |
| 5 | 11 | Plymouth Argyle | 1-5 | 12000 | Wolstenholme |
| 6 | 18 | PLYMOUTH ARGYLE | 0-0 | 8000 | |
| 7 | 25 | Exeter City | 1-0 | 8000 | Wolstenholme |
| 8 | 2 Oct | EXETER CITY | 2-0 | 8000 | Wolstenholme(2) |
| 9 | 9 | MILLWALL | 3-1 | 14000 | Devlin(2), Walker |
| 10 | 16 | Millwall | 0-1 | 20000 | |
| 11 | 21 | SWINDON TOWN | 0-1 | 10000 | |
| 12 | 23 | PORTSMOUTH | 1-0 | 9000 | Devlin |
| 13 | 30 | Portsmouth | 2-0 | 13679 | Devlin, Dobson |
| 14 | 6 Nov | GILLINGHAM | 1-0 | 7000 | Wolstenholme |
| 15 | 13 | Gillingham | 4-1 | 8000 | Dobson, Wolstenholme, Blott, Devlin |
| 16 | 27 | Swindon Town | 0-5 | 7000 | |
| 17 | 4 Dec | WATFORD | 0-2 | 6000 | |
| 18 | 11 | Watford | 1-5 | 7000 | Wright |
| 19 | 18 | Brentford | 2-2 | 6000 | Wright, Thompson |
| 20 | 25 | SOUTHEND UNITED | 1-1 | 9000 | Dobson |
| 21 | 27 | Southend United | 1-2 | 10000 | Walker |
| 22 | 1 Jan | BRENTFORD | 3-1 | 7500 | Dobson, Walker, Cox |
| 23 | 13 | NORWICH CITY | 2-0 | 4000 | Wright, Cox |
| 24 | 22 | Norwich City | 0-3 | 5000 | |
| 25 | 29 | NORTHAMPTON TOWN | 1-1 | 8000 | Dobson |
| 26 | 5 Feb | Northampton Town | 2-0 | 8000 | Groves, Wright |
| 27 | 12 | CRYSTAL PALACE | 0-1 | 12000 | |
| 28 | 19 | Crystal Palace | 0-2 | 7000 | |
| 29 | 26 | BRIGHTON & H.A. | 0-4 | 8000 | |
| 30 | 5 Mar | Brighton & H.A. | 0-1 | 8000 | |
| 31 | 12 | GRIMSBY TOWN | 2-1 | 8000 | Devlin, Kelson |
| 32 | 19 | Grimsby Town | 1-1 | 9000 | Devlin |
| 33 | 25 | MERTHYR TOWN | 0-3 | 12600 | |
| 34 | 26 | Q.P.Rangers | 0-2 | 10000 | |
| 35 | 28 | Merthyr Town | 2-1 | 6000 | Gaughan, Devlin |
| 36 | 2 Apr | Q.P.RANGERS | 1-3 | 7500 | Devlin |
| 37 | 9 | SWANSEA TOWN | 1-1 | 6000 | Walker |
| 38 | 16 | Swansea Town | 2-1 | 14000 | Dobson, Wolstenholme |
| 39 | 23 | Luton Town | 2-2 | 9000 | Walker, Devlin |
| 40 | 30 | LUTON TOWN | 2-0 | 5000 | Devlin(2) |
| 41 | 2 May | Southampton | 0-0 | 6000 | |
| 42 | 7 | SOUTHAMPTON | 0-0 | 8000 | |

## F.A.Cup

| | | | | | |
|---|---|---|---|---|---|
| 4Q | 20 Nov | MERTHYR TOWN | 0-0 | 15000 | |
| 4Q/R | 25 | Merthyr Town | 0-4 | 15000 | |

| Player | League | | F.A.Cup | | Total | |
|---|---|---|---|---|---|---|
| | App | Gls. | App | Gls. | App | Gls. |
| Blott S.P. | 15 | 1 | 1 | 0 | 17 | 1 |
| Cooper J. | 41 | 0 | 2 | 0 | 45 | 0 |
| Cox W. | 6 | 2 | – | – | 6 | 2 |
| Davis S.G. | 13 | 0 | 2 | 0 | 15 | 0 |
| Devlin W. | 26 | 12 | 2 | 0 | 28 | 12 |
| Dobson H. | 39 | 6 | 2 | 0 | 43 | 8 |
| Edwards E.A. | 35 | 0 | 2 | 0 | 39 | 0 |
| Edwards W.F. | 29 | 0 | 1 | 0 | 31 | 0 |
| Gaughan W.B. | 34 | 1 | 2 | 0 | 37 | 1 |
| Gittins J. | 1 | 0 | – | – | 1 | 0 |
| Griffin J.H. | 21 | 0 | – | – | 23 | 0 |
| Groves G. | 20 | 1 | – | – | 22 | 1 |
| Hillman A.G. | 16 | 0 | 2 | 0 | 19 | 0 |
| Jones E. | 8 | 0 | 1 | 0 | 10 | 0 |
| Kelson H.J. | 11 | 1 | – | – | 11 | 1 |
| McMillan J. | 21 | 0 | – | – | 22 | 0 |
| Pullen H. | 21 | 0 | – | – | 22 | 0 |
| Thompson W. | 17 | 1 | – | – | 19 | 1 |
| Toone P. | 1 | 0 | – | – | 1 | 0 |
| Walker A.M. | 40 | 6 | 2 | 0 | 44 | 7 |
| Wolstenholme A. | 29 | 8 | 2 | 0 | 31 | 8 |
| Woodall H. | 1 | 0 | – | – | 2 | 0 |
| Wright H.F. | 17 | 4 | – | – | 18 | 5 |

| | | P | W | D | L | F | A | Pts |
|---|---|---|---|---|---|---|---|---|
| 1 | Crystal Palace | 42 | 24 | 11 | 7 | 70 | 34 | 59 |
| 2 | Southampton | 42 | 19 | 16 | 7 | 64 | 28 | 54 |
| 3 | QPR | 42 | 22 | 9 | 11 | 61 | 32 | 53 |
| 4 | Swindon | 42 | 21 | 10 | 11 | 73 | 49 | 52 |
| 5 | Swansea | 42 | 18 | 15 | 9 | 56 | 45 | 51 |
| 6 | Watford | 42 | 20 | 8 | 14 | 59 | 44 | 48 |
| 7 | Millwall Ath | 42 | 18 | 11 | 13 | 42 | 30 | 47 |
| 8 | Merthyr Town | 42 | 15 | 15 | 12 | 60 | 49 | 45 |
| 9 | Luton | 42 | 16 | 12 | 14 | 61 | 56 | 44 |
| 10 | Bristol Rovers | 42 | 18 | 7 | 17 | 68 | 57 | 43 |
| 11 | Plymouth | 42 | 11 | 21 | 10 | 35 | 34 | 43 |
| 12 | Portsmouth | 42 | 12 | 15 | 15 | 46 | 48 | 39 |
| 13 | Grimsby | 42 | 15 | 9 | 18 | 49 | 59 | 39 |
| 14 | Northampton | 42 | 15 | 8 | 19 | 59 | 75 | 38 |
| 15 | Newport | 42 | 14 | 9 | 19 | 43 | 64 | 37 |
| 16 | Norwich | 42 | 10 | 16 | 16 | 44 | 53 | 36 |
| 17 | Southend | 42 | 14 | 8 | 20 | 44 | 61 | 36 |
| 18 | Brighton | 42 | 14 | 8 | 20 | 42 | 61 | 36 |
| 19 | Exeter | 42 | 10 | 15 | 17 | 39 | 54 | 35 |
| 20 | Reading | 42 | 12 | 7 | 23 | 42 | 59 | 31 |
| 21 | Brentford | 42 | 9 | 12 | 21 | 42 | 67 | 30 |
| 22 | Gillingham | 42 | 8 | 12 | 22 | 34 | 74 | 28 |

(Back) Perry, Hodges, W.Edwards, Williams, Walker, Vickers, Young, Gittins.
(Middle) Hindmarsh (Player/Caoch), Thompson, Chivers, Davis, Cooper, Pullen, Wright, Devlin, Jones,
Parkes(Sec./Manager). (Front) Griffin, Kelson, Groves, Wostenholme, Dobson, Gaughan, E.Edwards, Blott, Hillman.

# SEASON 1921-22     Division 3(South)

| | Date | Opposition | Res. | Att. | Goalscorers |
|---|---|---|---|---|---|
| 1 | 27 Aug | Reading | 0-1 | 11000 | |
| 2 | 29 | Q.P.RANGERS | 0-1 | 8000 | |
| 3 | 3 Sep | READING | 1-0 | 7000 | Devlin |
| 4 | 5 | Q.P.Rangers | 1-2 | 7000 | Devlin |
| 5 | 10 | Luton Town | 0-4 | 10000 | |
| 6 | 12 | SOUTHEND UNITED | 2-1 | 6000 | Walker, W.Edwards |
| 7 | 17 | LUTON TOWN | 2-2 | 8000 | Devlin, Lythgoe |
| 8 | 24 | Norwich City | 2-2 | 8000 | Walker, W.Edwards |
| 9 | 1 Oct | NORWICH CITY | 1-0 | 8000 | Dobson |
| 10 | 8 | Swindon Town | 2-3 | 9000 | W.Edwards(2) |
| 11 | 15 | SWINDON TOWN | 4-0 | 8000 | Gaughan(2), Devlin, Lythgoe |
| 12 | 22 | PLYMOUTH ARGYLE | 0-0 | 8000 | |
| 13 | 29 | Plymouth Argyle | 0-1 | 14000 | |
| 14 | 5 Nov | MERTHYR TOWN | 0-2 | 10000 | |
| 15 | 12 | Merthyr Town | 1-2 | 10000 | W.Edwards |
| 16 | 19 | Portsmouth | 3-4 | 13000 | W.Edwards(2), Devlin |
| 17 | 26 | PORTSMOUTH | 0-0 | 8000 | |
| 18 | 10 Dec | Southend United | 1-0 | 12000 | Price |
| 19 | 24 | Swansea Town | 2-2 | 10000 | Lythgoe, Gaughan |
| 20 | 26 | Millwall | 1-1 | 17000 | Walker |
| 21 | 27 | MILLWALL | 1-0 | 10000 | W.Edwards |
| 22 | 31 | Exeter City | 2-2 | 5000 | Groves, W.Edwards |
| 23 | 2 Jan | SWANSEA TOWN | 2-3 | 9000 | Devlin(2) |
| 24 | 14 | EXETER CITY | 1-1 | 9000 | Walker |
| 25 | 21 | Bristol Rovers | 4-3 | 8000 | Lythgoe(2), Brittan(2) |
| 26 | 28 | BRISTOL ROVERS | 0-1 | 6000 | |
| 27 | 4 Feb | Brentford | 0-1 | 8000 | |
| 28 | 11 | BRENTFORD | 2-1 | 6500 | Walker, Devlin |
| 29 | 18 | Aberdare Athletic | 0-3 | 7000 | |
| 30 | 25 | ABERDARE ATHLETIC | 1-0 | 9000 | Devlin |
| 31 | 4 Mar | Brighton & H.A. | 0-3 | 8000 | |
| 32 | 11 | BRIGHTON & H.A. | 0-1 | 9000 | |
| 33 | 18 | WATFORD | 0-0 | 7000 | |
| 34 | 25 | Watford | 0-1 | 5000 | |
| 35 | 8 Apr | Charlton Athletic | 1-1 | 6000 | Gaughan |
| 36 | 14 | Gillingham | 2-0 | 10000 | Groves, Walker |
| 37 | 15 | NORTHAMPTON TOWN | 2-2 | 8000 | W.Edwards, Gittins |
| 38 | 17 | GILLINGHAM | 1-1 | 9000 | Walker |
| 39 | 22 | Northampton Town | 0-2 | 3000 | |
| 40 | 27 | CHARLTON ATHLETIC | 2-1 | 6000 | Walker, Shelton |
| 41 | 29 | SOUTHAMPTON | 0-1 | 8000 | |
| 42 | 6 May | Southampton | 0-5 | 9000 | |

## F.A.Cup

| | | | | | |
|---|---|---|---|---|---|
| 5Q | 3 Dec | BATH CITY | 2-0 | 6000 | Devlin, Walker |
| 6Q | 17 | Wrexham | 0-0 | 8000 | |
| 6Q/R | 21 | WREXHAM | 3-0 | 5000 | Devlin(3) |
| 1 | 7 Jan | Newcastle United | 0-6 | 28507 | |

| Player | League | | F.A.Cup | | Total | |
|---|---|---|---|---|---|---|
| | App | Gls. | App | Gls. | App | Gls. |
| Arch W.H. | 29 | 0 | 2 | 0 | 32 | 0 |
| Blott S.P. | 1 | 0 | – | – | 1 | 0 |
| Brittan C.H. | 7 | 2 | – | – | 8 | 2 |
| Cooper J. | 40 | 0 | 4 | 0 | 45 | 0 |
| Devlin W. | 31 | 9 | 4 | 4 | 35 | 13 |
| Dobson H. | 27 | 1 | 4 | 0 | 32 | 1 |
| Edwards E.A. | 42 | 0 | 4 | 0 | 46 | 0 |
| Edwards W.F. | 40 | 10 | 4 | 0 | 45 | 10 |
| Flanders F. | 15 | 0 | 3 | 0 | 18 | 0 |
| Gaughan W.B. | 35 | 4 | 4 | 0 | 40 | 5 |
| Gittins J. | 16 | 1 | – | – | 16 | 1 |
| Graham H. | 1 | 0 | – | – | 1 | 0 |
| Griffin J.H. | 36 | 0 | 3 | 0 | 40 | 0 |
| Groves G. | 36 | 2 | 4 | 0 | 41 | 2 |
| Lowe E. | 2 | 0 | – | – | 2 | 0 |
| Lythgoe J. | 35 | 5 | 1 | 0 | 37 | 5 |
| McMillan J. | 4 | 0 | – | – | 4 | 0 |
| Price F. | 27 | 1 | 3 | 0 | 31 | 1 |
| Shelton J. | 3 | 1 | – | – | 3 | 1 |
| Walker A.M. | 35 | 8 | 4 | 1 | 40 | 9 |

| | | P | W | D | L | F | A | Pts |
|---|---|---|---|---|---|---|---|---|
| 1 | Southampton | 42 | 23 | 15 | 4 | 68 | 21 | 61 |
| 2 | Plymouth | 42 | 25 | 11 | 6 | 63 | 24 | 61 |
| 3 | Portsmouth | 42 | 18 | 17 | 7 | 62 | 39 | 53 |
| 4 | Luton | 42 | 22 | 8 | 12 | 64 | 35 | 52 |
| 5 | QPR | 42 | 18 | 13 | 11 | 53 | 44 | 49 |
| 6 | Swindon | 42 | 16 | 13 | 13 | 72 | 60 | 45 |
| 7 | Watford | 42 | 13 | 18 | 11 | 54 | 48 | 44 |
| 8 | Aberdare Ath | 42 | 17 | 10 | 15 | 57 | 51 | 44 |
| 9 | Brentford | 42 | 16 | 11 | 15 | 52 | 43 | 43 |
| 10 | Swansea | 42 | 13 | 15 | 14 | 50 | 47 | 41 |
| 11 | Merthyr Town | 42 | 17 | 6 | 19 | 45 | 56 | 40 |
| 12 | Millwall Ath | 42 | 10 | 18 | 14 | 38 | 42 | 38 |
| 13 | Reading | 42 | 14 | 18 | 10 | 40 | 47 | 38 |
| 14 | Bristol Rovers | 42 | 14 | 10 | 18 | 52 | 67 | 38 |
| 15 | Norwich | 42 | 12 | 13 | 17 | 50 | 62 | 37 |
| 16 | Charlton | 42 | 13 | 11 | 18 | 43 | 56 | 37 |
| 17 | Northampton | 42 | 13 | 11 | 18 | 47 | 71 | 37 |
| 18 | Gillingham | 42 | 14 | 8 | 20 | 47 | 60 | 36 |
| 19 | Brighton | 42 | 13 | 9 | 20 | 45 | 51 | 35 |
| 20 | Newport | 42 | 11 | 12 | 19 | 44 | 61 | 34 |
| 21 | Exeter | 42 | 11 | 12 | 19 | 38 | 59 | 34 |
| 22 | Southend | 42 | 8 | 11 | 23 | 34 | 74 | 27 |

NEWPORT COUNTY. 1921-22.

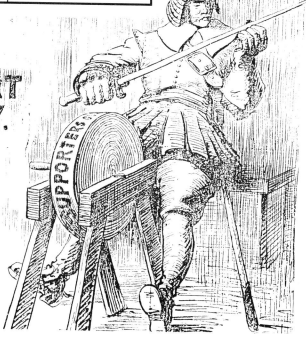

# SEASON 1922-23 Division 3(South)

| | Date | Opposition | Res. | Att. | Goalscorers |
|---|---|---|---|---|---|
| 1 | 26 Aug | SOUTHEND UNITED | 0-2 | 11500 | |
| 2 | 28 | Bristol Rovers | 1-3 | 12000 | Whitton |
| 3 | 2 Sep | Southend United | 1-3 | 9000 | W.Edwards |
| 4 | 7 | BRISTOL ROVERS | 4-1 | 7000 | W.Edwards, Patterson, Fletcher, Brittan |
| 5 | 9 | Bristol City | 0-2 | 10000 | |
| 6 | 16 | BRISTOL CITY | 0-1 | 9500 | |
| 7 | 23 | Portsmouth | 0-2 | 14294 | |
| 8 | 30 | PORTSMOUTH | 0-0 | 9000 | |
| 9 | 7 Oct | Millwall | 0-0 | 18000 | |
| 10 | 14 | MILLWALL | 0-0 | 12000 | |
| 11 | 21 | MERTHYR TOWN | 1-1 | 8000 | Morgan(og) |
| 12 | 28 | Merthyr Town | 0-1 | 5000 | |
| 13 | 4 Nov | LUTON TOWN | 0-3 | 5000 | |
| 14 | 11 | Luton Town | 0-1 | 8500 | |
| 15 | 18 | Q.P.RANGERS | 1-0 | 7000 | Wood |
| 16 | 25 | Q.P.Rangers | 1-1 | 5000 | Gittins |
| 17 | 9 Dec | GILLINGHAM | 2-1 | 8000 | Whitton, Graham |
| 18 | 16 | BRIGHTON & H.A. | 1-0 | 8000 | Conner |
| 19 | 23 | Brighton & H.A. | 1-2 | 7000 | Wood |
| 20 | 26 | Swansea Town | 1-5 | 16000 | Conner |
| 21 | 27 | SWANSEA TOWN | 1-2 | 6000 | Conner |
| 22 | 30 | Swindon Town | 2-2 | 4000 | McDonald, Conner |
| 23 | 6 Jan | SWINDON TOWN | 2-2 | 10000 | Hampton(2) |
| 24 | 13 | Gillingham | 0-3 | 6000 | |
| 25 | 20 | ABERDARE ATHLETIC | 0-0 | 7000 | |
| 26 | 27 | Aberdare Athletic | 2-6 | 7000 | Whitton(2) |
| 27 | 3 Feb | EXETER CITY | 6-2 | 8000 | Lowes(2), Conner(2), Gaughan, Wood |
| 28 | 10 | Exeter City | 0-4 | 5000 | |
| 29 | 17 | Northampton Town | 1-2 | 10000 | Lowes |
| 30 | 24 | NORTHAMPTON TOWN | 1-1 | 6000 | Charlton |
| 31 | 3 Mar | Norwich City | 1-1 | 4563 | Lowes |
| 32 | 10 | NORWICH CITY | 1-3 | 7000 | Groves |
| 33 | 17 | Brentford | 0-0 | 5000 | |
| 34 | 24 | BRENTFORD | 0-1 | 4000 | |
| 35 | 30 | Reading | 0-2 | 10000 | |
| 36 | 31 | Watford | 1-2 | 6000 | Lowes |
| 37 | 2 Apr | READING | 3-0 | 7000 | Lowes(2), Charlton |
| 38 | 7 | WATFORD | 0-1 | 7000 | |
| 39 | 14 | Charlton Athletic | 0-6 | 5000 | |
| 40 | 21 | CHARLTON ATHLETIC | 4-0 | 4000 | Gittins, Whitton, Lowes, Gaughan |
| 41 | 28 | Plymouth Argyle | 0-1 | 8000 | |
| 42 | 5 May | PLYMOUTH ARGYLE | 1-0 | 7000 | Conner |

## F.A.Cup

| | Date | Opposition | Res. | Att. | Goalscorers |
|---|---|---|---|---|---|
| 5Q | 2 Dec | Aberdare Athletic | 1-1 | 8000 | Conner |
| 5Q | 7 | ABERDARE ATHLETIC | 1-1 | 10000 | Gittins |
| 5Q | 11 | Aberdare Athletic | 1-2 | 6500 | Groves (At Cardiff) |

| Player | League | | F.A.Cup | | Total | |
|---|---|---|---|---|---|---|
| | App | Gls. | App | Gls. | App | Gls. |
| Beddow H. | 1 | 0 | – | – | 1 | 0 |
| Beer W.J. | 1 | 0 | – | – | 1 | 0 |
| Brittan C.H. | 16 | 1 | 1 | 0 | 18 | 1 |
| Carr A.G. | 39 | 0 | 3 | 0 | 44 | 0 |
| Charlton W.G. | 19 | 2 | – | – | 20 | 3 |
| Conner J. | 27 | 7 | 3 | 2 | 32 | 9 |
| Dimmick E. | 23 | 0 | 1 | 0 | 24 | 0 |
| Edwards E.A. | 36 | 0 | 3 | 0 | 40 | 0 |
| Edwards W.F. | 10 | 2 | – | – | 10 | 2 |
| Evans J.H. | 4 | 0 | – | – | 5 | 0 |
| Fletcher H.W. | 1 | 1 | – | – | 1 | 1 |
| Gaughan W.B. | 22 | 2 | 2 | 0 | 26 | 2 |
| Gittins J. | 10 | 2 | 3 | 0 | 13 | 3 |
| Graham H. | 5 | 1 | – | – | 5 | 1 |
| Griffin J.H. | 19 | 0 | 3 | 0 | 23 | 0 |
| Groves G. | 39 | 1 | 3 | 1 | 44 | 3 |
| Hampton J.H. | 14 | 2 | 1 | 0 | 16 | 4 |
| Lee J.A. | 4 | 0 | – | – | 4 | 0 |
| Lewis J. | 6 | 0 | – | – | 6 | 0 |
| Lowe E. | 3 | 0 | – | – | 3 | 0 |
| Lowes T. | 35 | 8 | 2 | 0 | 39 | 8 |
| McDonald R.W. | 8 | 1 | – | – | 8 | 1 |
| Nairn W.J. | 29 | 0 | 2 | 0 | 33 | 0 |
| Ogley W. | 16 | 0 | – | – | 17 | 0 |
| Patterson D. | 12 | 1 | – | – | 13 | 2 |
| Venables A. | 1 | 0 | – | – | 1 | 0 |
| White T. | 20 | 0 | 3 | 0 | 25 | 0 |
| Whitton P.A. | 29 | 5 | 2 | 0 | 31 | 5 |
| Wood A.B. | 13 | 3 | 1 | 0 | 14 | 3 |
| Own Goals. | | 1 | | | | 1 |

### Bottom positions only

| | | P | W | D | L | F | A | Pts |
|---|---|---|---|---|---|---|---|---|
| 12 | Charlton | 42 | 14 | 14 | 14 | 55 | 51 | 42 |
| 13 | Bristol Rovers | 42 | 13 | 16 | 13 | 35 | 36 | 42 |
| 14 | Brentford | 42 | 13 | 12 | 17 | 41 | 51 | 38 |
| 15 | Southend | 42 | 12 | 13 | 17 | 49 | 54 | 37 |
| 16 | Gillingham | 42 | 15 | 7 | 20 | 51 | 59 | 37 |
| 17 | Merthyr Town | 42 | 11 | 14 | 17 | 39 | 48 | 36 |
| 18 | Norwich | 42 | 13 | 10 | 19 | 51 | 71 | 36 |
| 19 | Reading | 42 | 10 | 14 | 18 | 36 | 55 | 34 |
| 20 | Exeter | 42 | 13 | 7 | 22 | 47 | 84 | 33 |
| 21 | Aberdare Ath | 42 | 9 | 11 | 22 | 42 | 70 | 29 |
| 22 | Newport | 42 | 8 | 11 | 23 | 40 | 70 | 27 |

(Reserve team line-up) (Back) Evans, Lewis, Bray, White, Lee, Thomas (Asst.Trainer).
(Front) Brittan, Nairn, Gittins, Patterson, Wood, Gaughan (All 1st team players except Bray).

# SEASON 1923-24    Division 3(South)

| | Date | Opposition | Res. | Att. | Goalscorers |
|---|---|---|---|---|---|
| 1 | 25 Aug | EXETER CITY | 2-0 | 10000 | Lowes, Cook |
| 2 | 29 | Portsmouth | 0-5 | 7353 | |
| 3 | 1 Sep | Exeter City | 0-5 | 8000 | |
| 4 | 6 | PORTSMOUTH | 2-1 | 8000 | Lowes, Cook |
| 5 | 8 | SOUTHEND UNITED | 5-0 | 9000 | Conner(2), Bell(2), Lowe |
| 6 | 12 | Q.P.Rangers | 3-0 | 10000 | Lowes(2), Bell |
| 7 | 15 | Southend United | 0-2 | 10000 | |
| 8 | 22 | NORTHAMPTON TOWN | 1-1 | 9500 | Bell |
| 9 | 29 | Northampton Town | 0-0 | 10000 | |
| 10 | 6 Oct | Charlton Athletic | 1-2 | 5000 | Bell |
| 11 | 13 | CHARLTON ATHLETIC | 0-1 | 9000 | |
| 12 | 20 | Gillingham | 1-2 | 7000 | Bell |
| 13 | 27 | GILLINGHAM | 2-1 | 8000 | Bell(2) |
| 14 | 3 Nov | NORWICH CITY | 1-0 | 7800 | Charlton |
| 15 | 10 | Norwich City | 1-3 | 7000 | Conner |
| 16 | 1 Dec | SWINDON TOWN | 3-0 | 8000 | Charlton, Bell, Lowes |
| 17 | 8 | Swindon Town | 0-3 | 4626 | |
| 18 | 15 | PLYMOUTH ARGYLE | 1-2 | 8000 | Lowes |
| 19 | 22 | Plymouth Argyle | 2-3 | 9000 | Nicholls(2) |
| 20 | 25 | Merthyr Town | 3-3 | 6000 | Conner(3) |
| 21 | 26 | MERTHYR TOWN | 4-4 | 8000 | Lowes(2), Carney, Nicholls |
| 22 | 29 | WATFORD | 1-0 | 8000 | Cook |
| 23 | 1 Jan | Q.P.RANGERS | 2-1 | 8000 | Lowes(2) |
| 24 | 5 | Watford | 2-8 | | Conner(2) |
| 25 | 26 | Brentford | 0-0 | 5000 | |
| 26 | 2 Feb | BRISTOL ROVERS | 1-0 | 7000 | Conner |
| 27 | 9 | Bristol Rovers | 0-0 | 8000 | |
| 28 | 16 | BRIGHTON & H.A. | 0-0 | 7000 | |
| 29 | 1 Mar | LUTON TOWN | 1-0 | 9000 | Charlton |
| 30 | 8 | Luton Town | 0-2 | 5000 | |
| 31 | 15 | Reading | 1-1 | 8000 | Conner |
| 32 | 22 | READING | 2-0 | 6000 | Conner, Lowes |
| 33 | 26 | Brighton & H.A. | 0-4 | 3000 | |
| 34 | 29 | BOURNEMOUTH & B.A. | 2-0 | 8000 | Conner, Lowes |
| 35 | 5 Apr | Bournemouth & B.A. | 1-0 | 4000 | Conner |
| 36 | 12 | Millwall | 1-2 | 15000 | Cook |
| 37 | 18 | Swansea Town | 1-2 | 16000 | Nicholls |
| 38 | 19 | MILLWALL | 2-1 | 10000 | Ogley, Conner |
| 39 | 21 | SWANSEA TOWN | 4-1 | 12000 | Conner, Lowes, Gittins, Ogley |
| 40 | 22 | BRENTFORD | 3-2 | 6000 | Conner, Lowes, Gittins |
| 41 | 26 | Aberdare Athletic | 0-2 | 4000 | |
| 42 | 3 May | ABERDARE ATHLETIC | 0-0 | 8000 | |

### F.A.Cup

| | | | | | |
|---|---|---|---|---|---|
| 4Q | 17 Nov | Exeter City | 0-2 | 10000 | |

| Player | League | | F.A.Cup | | Total | |
|---|---|---|---|---|---|---|
| | App | Gls. | App | Gls. | App | Gls. |
| Bell J.J. | 21 | 9 | 1 | 0 | 22 | 9 |
| Brittan C.H. | – | – | 1 | 0 | 2 | 0 |
| Carney J.M. | 31 | 1 | – | – | 36 | 2 |
| Carr A.G. | 41 | 0 | 1 | 0 | 48 | 0 |
| Charlton W.G. | 38 | 3 | – | – | 43 | 5 |
| Conner J. | 42 | 16 | 1 | 0 | 49 | 18 |
| Cook F. | 42 | 4 | 1 | 0 | 49 | 4 |
| Dimmick J. | 30 | 0 | 1 | 0 | 37 | 0 |
| Gaughan W.B. | 3 | 0 | – | – | 3 | 0 |
| Gittins J. | 13 | 2 | – | – | 18 | 2 |
| Groves G. | 5 | 0 | – | – | 5 | 0 |
| Knowles F. | 16 | 0 | 1 | 0 | 17 | 0 |
| Lewis J. | 20 | 0 | 1 | 0 | 21 | 0 |
| Lowes T. | 38 | 15 | 1 | 0 | 43 | 18 |
| Nairn W.J. | 29 | 0 | 1 | 0 | 31 | 0 |
| Nicholls J.B.L. | 11 | 4 | – | – | 13 | 5 |
| Ogley W. | 23 | 2 | – | – | 28 | 2 |
| Round F. | 1 | 0 | – | – | 1 | 0 |
| Sanderson F.C. | 1 | 0 | – | – | 2 | 0 |
| Taylor F.E. | 2 | 0 | – | – | 3 | 0 |
| White T. | 17 | 0 | – | – | 23 | 0 |
| Whitton P.A. | 38 | 0 | 1 | 0 | 45 | 0 |

| | | P | W | D | L | F | A | Pts |
|---|---|---|---|---|---|---|---|---|
| 1 | Portsmouth | 42 | 24 | 11 | 7 | 87 | 30 | 59 |
| 2 | Plymouth | 42 | 23 | 9 | 10 | 70 | 34 | 55 |
| 3 | Millwall Ath | 42 | 22 | 10 | 10 | 64 | 38 | 54 |
| 4 | Swansea | 42 | 22 | 8 | 12 | 60 | 48 | 52 |
| 5 | Brighton | 42 | 21 | 9 | 12 | 68 | 37 | 51 |
| 6 | Swindon | 42 | 17 | 13 | 12 | 58 | 44 | 47 |
| 7 | Luton | 42 | 16 | 14 | 12 | 50 | 44 | 46 |
| 8 | Northampton | 42 | 17 | 11 | 14 | 64 | 47 | 45 |
| 9 | Bristol Rovers | 42 | 15 | 13 | 14 | 52 | 46 | 43 |
| 10 | Newport | 42 | 17 | 9 | 16 | 56 | 64 | 43 |
| 11 | Norwich | 42 | 16 | 8 | 18 | 60 | 59 | 40 |
| 12 | Aberdare Ath | 42 | 12 | 14 | 16 | 45 | 58 | 38 |
| 13 | Merthyr Town | 42 | 11 | 16 | 15 | 45 | 65 | 38 |
| 14 | Charlton | 42 | 11 | 15 | 16 | 38 | 45 | 37 |
| 15 | Gillingham | 42 | 12 | 13 | 17 | 43 | 58 | 37 |
| 16 | Exeter | 42 | 15 | 7 | 20 | 37 | 52 | 37 |
| 17 | Brentford | 42 | 14 | 8 | 20 | 54 | 71 | 36 |
| 18 | Reading | 42 | 13 | 9 | 20 | 51 | 57 | 35 |
| 19 | Southend | 42 | 12 | 10 | 20 | 53 | 84 | 34 |
| 20 | Watford | 42 | 9 | 15 | 18 | 45 | 54 | 33 |
| 21 | Bournemouth | 42 | 11 | 11 | 20 | 40 | 65 | 33 |
| 22 | QPR | 42 | 11 | 9 | 22 | 37 | 77 | 31 |

(Back) White, Charlton, Ogley, Nairn, Carr, Knowles, Dougall, Whitton, Groves.
(Middle) Thorneycroft (Dir.), Hindmarsh (Sec./Man.), Cook, Dimmock, Conner, Bell, Lowes, Lewis, Chatt (Trainer).
(Front) Patterson, Sanderson, Carney, Taylor.

# SEASON 1924-25    Division 3(South)

| | Date | Opposition | Res. | Att. | Goalscorers |
|---|---|---|---|---|---|
| 1 | 30 Aug | Q.P.RANGERS | 0-0 | 10000 | |
| 2 | 3 Sep | Reading | 1-0 | 8270 | Turnbull |
| 3 | 6 | Charlton Athletic | 0-1 | 8000 | |
| 4 | 11 | READING | 1-1 | 6000 | Charlton |
| 5 | 13 | NORTHAMPTON TOWN | 1-0 | 6000 | Gittins |
| 6 | 15 | Brentford | 0-2 | 4000 | |
| 7 | 20 | Watford | 5-0 | | Charlton(4), Conner |
| 8 | 27 | SOUTHEND UNITED | 1-1 | 9000 | Jenkins |
| 9 | 29 | Merthyr Town | 0-1 | 4000 | |
| 10 | 4 Oct | Brighton & H.A. | 1-4 | 12000 | Cook |
| 11 | 11 | Bristol Rovers | 1-0 | 10000 | Charlton |
| 12 | 18 | EXETER CITY | 2-1 | 7000 | Gittins, Lowes |
| 13 | 25 | PLYMOUTH ARGYLE | 0-0 | 12000 | |
| 14 | 1 Nov | Bristol City | 0-2 | 8000 | |
| 15 | 8 | SWINDON TOWN | 3-1 | 10000 | Carney, Charlton, Conner |
| 16 | 22 | NORWICH CITY | 3-0 | 6000 | Nairn, Lowes, Forward |
| 17 | 6 Dec | MILLWALL | 2-3 | 7000 | Charlton, Lowes |
| 18 | 13 | Luton Town | 2-2 | | Nairn, Conner |
| 19 | 20 | GILLINGHAM | 2-0 | 8000 | Lowes(2) |
| 20 | 25 | Bournemouth & B.A. | 0-0 | 6000 | |
| 21 | 26 | BOURNEMOUTH & B.A. | 2-0 | 8000 | Charlton, Gittins |
| 22 | 27 | Q.P.Rangers | 3-4 | 3000 | Taylor(2), H.White |
| 23 | 10 Jan | Aberdare Athletic | 3-1 | 5000 | Forward, Taylor, Wetherby |
| 24 | 17 | Northampton Town | 2-0 | 6000 | Nairn, Taylor |
| 25 | 24 | WATFORD | 3-0 | 8000 | Nairn, Charlton, Taylor |
| 26 | 31 | Southend United | 1-0 | 8000 | Taylor |
| 27 | 7 Feb | BRIGHTON & H.A. | 0-0 | 12000 | |
| 28 | 14 | BRISTOL ROVERS | 4-1 | 12000 | Whitton, Charlton, Turnbull, Hiles |
| 29 | 21 | Exeter City | 3-4 | 7000 | Turnbull, Forward, Taylor |
| 30 | 28 | Plymouth Argyle | 2-0 | | Taylor(2) |
| 31 | 7 Mar | BRISTOL CITY | 0-2 | 11800 | |
| 32 | 14 | Swindon Town | 2-2 | 8028 | Fred McKenzie, Taylor |
| 33 | 21 | ABERDARE ATHLETIC | 1-0 | 7000 | Turnbull |
| 34 | 28 | Norwich City | 1-2 | 5000 | Wetherby |
| 35 | 4 Apr | BRENTFORD | 1-0 | 5000 | Taylor |
| 36 | 10 | SWANSEA TOWN | 3-0 | 15000 | Charlton(2), Lowes |
| 37 | 11 | Millwall | 0-3 | 12000 | |
| 38 | 13 | Swansea Town | 0-1 | 22000 | |
| 39 | 14 | CHARLTON ATHLETIC | 2-1 | 6000 | Charlton, Wetherby |
| 40 | 18 | LUTON TOWN | 1-1 | 7000 | Nairn |
| 41 | 25 | Gillingham | 0-1 | 5000 | |
| 42 | 2 May | MERTHYR TOWN | 3-0 | 7000 | Lowes(2), Forward |

| Player | League | | F.A.Cup | | Total | |
|---|---|---|---|---|---|---|
| | App | Gls. | App | Gls. | App | Gls. |
| Black J. | 3 | 0 | – | – | 4 | 0 |
| Carney J.M. | 38 | 1 | 5 | 1 | 44 | 2 |
| Charlton W.G. | 31 | 14 | 2 | 0 | 35 | 14 |
| Conner J. | 15 | 3 | 4 | 0 | 19 | 3 |
| Cook F. | 40 | 1 | 5 | 0 | 46 | 1 |
| Dimmick E. | 22 | 0 | 5 | 0 | 28 | 0 |
| Elwell T.D.O. | – | – | – | – | 1 | 0 |
| Forward F.J. | 39 | 4 | 5 | 1 | 45 | 5 |
| Gittins J. | 26 | 3 | 3 | 1 | 29 | 4 |
| Hayward W.A. | – | – | – | – | 1 | 0 |
| Hiles W.R. | 4 | 1 | 1 | 0 | 6 | 1 |
| Jenkins H. | 3 | 1 | – | – | 3 | 1 |
| Lowes T. | 22 | 8 | 5 | 3 | 28 | 11 |
| McKenzie Frank. | 28 | 0 | 4 | 0 | 33 | 0 |
| McKenzie Fred.T. | 37 | 1 | 5 | 0 | 42 | 1 |
| Maidment J.H.C. | 42 | 0 | 5 | 0 | 49 | 0 |
| Nairn W.J. | 34 | 5 | 5 | 1 | 40 | 6 |
| Sanderson F.C | 2 | 0 | – | – | 4 | 0 |
| Taylor F.E. | 19 | 11 | – | – | 21 | 12 |
| Turnbull W. | 6 | 4 | – | – | 6 | 4 |
| Wetherby T. | 26 | 3 | 1 | 0 | 29 | 3 |
| White H. | 1 | 1 | – | – | 1 | 1 |
| White T. | 11 | 0 | – | – | 11 | 0 |
| Whitton P.A. | 12 | 1 | – | – | 14 | 2 |

|  | | P | W | D | L | F | A | Pts |
|---|---|---|---|---|---|---|---|---|
| 1 | Swansea | 42 | 23 | 11 | 8 | 68 | 35 | 57 |
| 2 | Plymouth | 42 | 23 | 10 | 9 | 77 | 38 | 56 |
| 3 | Bristol City | 42 | 22 | 9 | 11 | 60 | 41 | 53 |
| 4 | Swindon | 42 | 20 | 11 | 11 | 66 | 38 | 51 |
| 5 | Millwall Ath | 42 | 18 | 13 | 11 | 58 | 38 | 49 |
| 6 | Newport | 42 | 20 | 9 | 13 | 62 | 42 | 49 |
| 7 | Exeter | 42 | 19 | 9 | 14 | 59 | 48 | 47 |
| 8 | Brighton | 42 | 19 | 8 | 15 | 59 | 45 | 46 |
| 9 | Northampton | 42 | 20 | 6 | 16 | 51 | 44 | 46 |
| 10 | Southend | 42 | 19 | 5 | 18 | 51 | 61 | 43 |
| 11 | Watford | 42 | 17 | 9 | 16 | 38 | 47 | 43 |
| 12 | Norwich | 42 | 14 | 13 | 15 | 53 | 51 | 41 |
| 13 | Gillingham | 42 | 13 | 14 | 15 | 35 | 44 | 40 |
| 14 | Reading | 42 | 14 | 10 | 18 | 37 | 38 | 38 |
| 15 | Charlton | 42 | 13 | 12 | 17 | 46 | 48 | 38 |
| 16 | Luton | 42 | 10 | 17 | 15 | 49 | 57 | 37 |
| 17 | Bristol Rovers | 42 | 12 | 13 | 17 | 42 | 49 | 37 |
| 18 | Aberdare Ath | 42 | 14 | 9 | 19 | 54 | 67 | 37 |
| 19 | QPR | 42 | 14 | 8 | 20 | 42 | 63 | 36 |
| 20 | Bournemouth | 42 | 13 | 8 | 21 | 40 | 58 | 34 |
| 21 | Brentford | 42 | 9 | 7 | 26 | 38 | 91 | 25 |
| 22 | Merthyr Town | 42 | 8 | 5 | 29 | 35 | 77 | 21 |

## F.A.Cup

| 4Q | 15 Nov | Aberdare Athletic | 0-0 | 10000 | |
|---|---|---|---|---|---|
| 4QR | 20 | ABERDARE ATHLETIC | 3-0 | 6000 | Carney, Lowes, Forward |
| 5Q | 29 | Exeter City | 1-1 | 11000 | Gittins |
| 5QR | 4 Dec | EXETER CITY | 3-3 | 4600 | Lowes(2), Nairn |
| 5Q2R | 8 | Exeter City * | 0-1 | 5000 | * Played at Ashton Gate |

(Back) J.R.Williams (Dir.), Fred McKenzie, Wetherby, Maidment, Nairn, Charlton, Chatt(Trainer).
(Middle) Cook, Carney, Hindmarsh (Manager), Forward, Gittins.   (Front) Taylor, Frank McKenzie.

# SEASON 1925-26     *Division 3(South)*

| | Date | Opposition | Res. | Att. | Goalscorers |
|---|---|---|---|---|---|
| 1 | 29 Aug | BRIGHTON & H.A. | 4-3 | 11232 | Davis(3), Taylor |
| 2 | 3 Sep | Charlton Athletic | 0-0 | 4968 | |
| 3 | 5 | Luton Town | 2-4 | 6816 | Davis(2) |
| 4 | 12 | Q.P.RANGERS | 4-1 | 8834 | Davis(3), Lowes |
| 5 | 17 | CHARLTON ATHLETIC | 0-0 | 6152 | |
| 6 | 19 | Bristol Rovers | 2-2 | 4096 | Davis(2) |
| 7 | 23 | Bournemouth & B.A. | 2-0 | 4137 | Lowes, Armstrong(og) |
| 8 | 26 | SWINDON TOWN | 0-4 | 8144 | |
| 9 | 1 Oct | BOURNEMOUTH & B.A. | 1-2 | 5092 | Davis |
| 10 | 3 | Exeter City | 1-2 | 8206 | Gittins |
| 11 | 10 | READING | 1-1 | 7053 | Nairn |
| 12 | 17 | ABERDARE ATHLETIC | 0-0 | 8083 | |
| 13 | 24 | Northampton Town | 0-2 | 7987 | |
| 14 | 31 | BRENTFORD | 2-3 | 4933 | Taylor, Cook |
| 15 | 7 Nov | Watford | 1-5 | 5393 | Coates |
| 16 | 14 | SOUTHEND UNITED | 1-0 | 4503 | Davis |
| 17 | 21 | Plymouth Argyle | 0-3 | 12495 | |
| 18 | 19 Dec | Norwich City | 0-0 | 4660 | |
| 19 | 25 | Merthyr Town | 1-4 | 5716 | Drinnan |
| 20 | 26 | MERTHYR TOWN | 3-1 | 7882 | Carney(3) |
| 21 | 28 | BRISTOL CITY | 1-0 | 4593 | Carney |
| 22 | 2 Jan | Brighton & H.A. | 1-2 | 7398 | Carney |
| 23 | 16 | LUTON TOWN | 2-1 | 4498 | Coates, Drinnan |
| 24 | 23 | Q.P.Rangers | 2-0 | 6385 | Carney, Cook |
| 25 | 30 | BRISTOL ROVERS | 3-1 | 3472 | Carney, Cook, Coates |
| 26 | 6 Feb | Swindon Town | 1-2 | 5687 | Carney |
| 27 | 10 | Crystal Palace | 2-4 | 4228 | Forward(2) |
| 28 | 13 | EXETER CITY | 3-0 | 5437 | Davis(2), Drinnan |
| 29 | 20 | Reading | 1-2 | 11705 | Davis |
| 30 | 25 | MILLWALL | 1-0 | 4425 | Forward |
| 31 | 27 | Aberdare Athleic | 0-2 | 4346 | |
| 32 | 6 Mar | NORTHAMPTON TOWN | 3-0 | 5293 | Coates, Smith, Drinnan |
| 33 | 13 | Brentford | 3-3 | 9643 | Davis(2), Coates |
| 34 | 20 | WATFORD | 3-3 | 5282 | Carney(2), Drinnan |
| 35 | 27 | Southend United | 1-4 | 6124 | Drinnan |
| 36 | 2 Apr | Gillingham | 0-2 | 7138 | |
| 37 | 3 | PLYMOUTH ARGYLE | 0-3 | 7343 | |
| 38 | 5 | GILLINGHAM | 4-0 | 5500 | Drinnan(2), Gittins, Davis |
| 39 | 10 | Bristol City | 2-1 | 9802 | Carney, Davis |
| 40 | 17 | CRYSTAL PALACE | 2-3 | 4477 | Smith, Drinnan |
| 41 | 24 | Millwall | 3-3 | 12884 | Davis, Lowes, Drinnan |
| 42 | 1 May | NORWICH CITY | 1-1 | 3284 | Dennington(og) |

### F.A.Cup

| | Date | Opposition | Res. | Att. | Goalscorers |
|---|---|---|---|---|---|
| 5Q | 28 Nov | Weymouth | 1-0 | 3465 | Taylor |
| 6Q | 12 Dec | NORTHAMPTON TOWN | 1-3 | 10266 | Drinnan |

| Player | League | | F.A.Cup | | Total | |
|---|---|---|---|---|---|---|
| | App | Gls. | App | Gls. | App | Gls. |
| Bowsher S.J. | 28 | 0 | 2 | 0 | 35 | 0 |
| Carney J.M. | 33 | 11 | – | – | 37 | 14 |
| Coates W.A. | 26 | 5 | – | – | 29 | 7 |
| Cook F. | 37 | 3 | 2 | 0 | 44 | 3 |
| Cunningham J. | 2 | 0 | – | – | 2 | 0 |
| Davis J.A.R. | 34 | 20 | 2 | 0 | 39 | 21 |
| Dimmick E. | 9 | 0 | – | – | 9 | 0 |
| Drinnan J.M. | 21 | 10 | 1 | 1 | 26 | 12 |
| Elwell T.D.O. | 1 | 0 | – | – | 2 | 0 |
| Forward F.J. | 36 | 3 | 2 | 0 | 42 | 3 |
| Gittins J. | 7 | 2 | – | – | 10 | 2 |
| Gwyther B.P. | 1 | 0 | – | – | 1 | 0 |
| Hayward W.A. | 4 | 0 | – | – | 4 | 0 |
| Hiles W.R. | 6 | 0 | – | – | 6 | 0 |
| James W.H. | 2 | 0 | – | – | 2 | 0 |
| Lowes T. | 14 | 3 | 1 | 0 | 15 | 3 |
| McKenzie Frank. | 37 | 0 | 2 | 0 | 42 | 0 |
| McKenzie Fred.T. | 29 | 0 | 2 | 0 | 31 | 0 |
| Maidment J.H.C. | 40 | 0 | 2 | 0 | 47 | 0 |
| Nairn W.J | 34 | 1 | 2 | 0 | 39 | 1 |
| Sanderson F.C. | 10 | 0 | – | – | 14 | 0 |
| Smith E. | 28 | 2 | 2 | 0 | 35 | 2 |
| Taylor F.E. | 13 | 2 | 2 | 1 | 16 | 3 |
| Wetherby T. | 10 | 0 | – | – | 12 | 0 |
| Own Goals | | 2 | | | | 2 |

### Bottom positions only

| | P | W | D | L | F | A | Pts |
|---|---|---|---|---|---|---|---|
| 6 Swindon | 42 | 20 | 6 | 16 | 69 | 64 | 46 |
| 7 Luton | 42 | 18 | 7 | 17 | 80 | 75 | 43 |
| 8 Bournemouth | 42 | 17 | 9 | 16 | 75 | 91 | 43 |
| 9 Aberdare | 42 | 17 | 8 | 17 | 74 | 66 | 42 |
| 10 Gillingham | 42 | 17 | 8 | 17 | 53 | 49 | 42 |
| 11 Southend | 42 | 19 | 4 | 19 | 78 | 73 | 42 |
| 12 Northampton | 42 | 17 | 7 | 18 | 82 | 80 | 41 |
| 13 Crystal Palace | 42 | 19 | 3 | 20 | 75 | 79 | 41 |
| 14 Merthyr Town | 42 | 14 | 11 | 17 | 69 | 75 | 39 |
| 15 Watford | 42 | 15 | 9 | 18 | 73 | 89 | 39 |
| 16 Norwich | 42 | 15 | 9 | 18 | 58 | 73 | 39 |
| 17 Newport | 42 | 14 | 10 | 18 | 64 | 74 | 38 |
| 18 Brentford | 42 | 16 | 6 | 20 | 69 | 94 | 38 |
| 19 Bristol Rovers | 42 | 15 | 6 | 21 | 66 | 69 | 36 |
| 20 Exeter | 42 | 15 | 5 | 22 | 72 | 70 | 35 |
| 21 Charlton | 42 | 11 | 13 | 18 | 48 | 68 | 35 |
| 22 QPR | 42 | 6 | 9 | 27 | 37 | 84 | 21 |

(Back) Chatt (Trainer), Forward, Cook, Maidment, Sanderson, Cunningham, Lowes, Smith, Bowsher, Elwell.
(Middle) Drinnan, Wardell, Nairn, Carney, Frank McKenzie, Fred McKenzie, Davis, Hiles.
(Front) Coates, Hayward, White, Dimmick, Taylor, Jones (Groundsman), Thomas (Asst.Trainer)

# SEASON 1926/27 Division 3 (South)

| | Date | Opposition | Res. | Att. | Goalscorers |
|---|---|---|---|---|---|
| 1 | 28 Aug | PLYMOUTH ARGYLE | 2-1 | 9262 | Nairn, Holland |
| 2 | 1 Sep | Bristol City | 1-4 | 13478 | Carney |
| 3 | 4 | Merthyr Town | 2-1 | 5259 | Forward, Clarke(og) |
| 4 | 9 | BRISTOL CITY | 0-0 | 7888 | |
| 5 | 11 | Aberdare Athletic | 1-0 | 2741 | Johnson |
| 6 | 18 | GILLINGHAM | 1-0 | 7141 | Price |
| 7 | 25 | Watford | 0-0 | 7720 | |
| 8 | 30 | CHARLTON ATHLETIC | 2-1 | 4687 | Nairn, Price |
| 9 | 2 Oct | CRYSTAL PALACE | 2-1 | 6985 | Price, Gittins |
| 10 | 9 | Coventry City | 1-3 | 7931 | James |
| 11 | 16 | LUTON TOWN | 3-2 | 6821 | Johnson, James, Gittins |
| 12 | 23 | Southend United | 0-5 | 6481 | |
| 13 | 30 | EXETER CITY | 2-0 | 6454 | James, Gittins |
| 14 | 6 Nov | Swindon Town | 1-3 | 4870 | Gittins |
| 15 | 13 | BRISTOL ROVERS | 1-0 | 3927 | Nairn |
| 16 | 20 | Millwall | 1-4 | 7004 | Holland |
| 17 | 4 Dec | Northampton Town | 2-1 | 5508 | Price(2) |
| 18 | 11 | MILLWALL | 1-1 | 5345 | Nairn |
| 19 | 18 | Norwich City | 0-1 | 6667 | |
| 20 | 25 | BOURNEMOUTH & B.A. | 2-1 | 6359 | Nairn, Forward |
| 21 | 27 | Bournemouth & B.A. | 1-2 | 8916 | Nairn |
| 22 | 1 Jan | NORTHAMPTON TOWN | 1-0 | 5006 | Johnson |
| 23 | 8 | Gillingham | 1-0 | 4611 | Price |
| 24 | 15 | Plymouth Argyle | 1-4 | 8943 | Price |
| 25 | 22 | MERTHYR TOWN | 4-3 | 5083 | Johnson, Price, Nairn, Forward |
| 26 | 29 | ABERDARE ATHLETIC | 5-2 | 3436 | Johnson(2), Drinnan, Forward, Gittins |
| 27 | 12 Feb | WATFORD | 2-1 | 4291 | Gittins, Hiles |
| 28 | 19 | Crystal Palace | 2-6 | 10328 | Johnson, Weaver |
| 29 | 26 | COVENTRY CITY | 4-1 | 3856 | James(2), Bowsher, Gittins |
| 30 | 5 Mar | Luton Town | 1-4 | 5240 | Johnson |
| 31 | 12 | SOUTHEND UNITED | 3-0 | 4725 | Gittins, Hiles, Weaver |
| 32 | 19 | Exeter City | 1-2 | 6509 | James |
| 33 | 26 | SWINDON TOWN | 5-3 | 4751 | James(2), Weaver(2), Hiles |
| 34 | 31 | BRIGHTON & H.A. | 0-1 | 2956 | |
| 35 | 2 Apr | Bristol Rovers | 0-4 | 5544 | |
| 36 | 15 | Q.P. RANGERS | 0-2 | 5938 | |
| 37 | 16 | Brentford | 1-1 | 7801 | Walker |
| 38 | 18 | Q.P. Rangers | 0-2 | 9057 | |
| 39 | 25 | BRENTFORD | 0-0 | 1721 | |
| 40 | 28 | Charlton Athletic | 0-3 | 4010 | |
| 41 | 30 | Brighton & H.A. | 0-1 | 6045 | |
| 42 | 7 May | NORWICH CITY | 0-0 | 2425 | |

## F.A.Cup

| | | | | | |
|---|---|---|---|---|---|
| 1 | 27 Nov | Poole Athletic | 0-1 | 2666 | |

| Player | League | | F.A.Cup | | Total | |
|---|---|---|---|---|---|---|
| | App | Gls | App | Gls | App | Gls |
| Anderson R. | 28 | 0 | – | – | 29 | 0 |
| Bowsher S.J. | 40 | 1 | 1 | 0 | 42 | 1 |
| Carney J.M. | 16 | 1 | – | – | 16 | 1 |
| Connor J.C.T. | 13 | 0 | 1 | 0 | 15 | 0 |
| Drinnan J.M. | 21 | 1 | 1 | 0 | 23 | 1 |
| Elwell T.D.O. | 3 | 0 | – | – | 3 | 0 |
| Forward F.J. | 26 | 4 | 1 | 0 | 27 | 4 |
| Gittins J. | 31 | 8 | 1 | 0 | 33 | 8 |
| Hiles W.R. | 18 | 3 | – | – | 19 | 3 |
| Hinton I.F. | 31 | 0 | 1 | 0 | 33 | 0 |
| Holland J. | 10 | 2 | – | – | 10 | 2 |
| James W.H. | 18 | 9 | 1 | 0 | 20 | 9 |
| Johnson G.H. | 38 | 8 | 1 | 0 | 40 | 8 |
| Maidment J.H.C. | 42 | 0 | 1 | 0 | 44 | 0 |
| Nairn W.J. | 36 | 7 | 1 | 0 | 37 | 7 |
| Price D.W. | 24 | 8 | – | – | 24 | 8 |
| Pritchard T.F. | 17 | 0 | – | – | 17 | 0 |
| Pugh R.A.L. | 2 | 0 | – | – | 2 | 0 |
| Smith E. | 25 | 0 | 1 | 0 | 26 | 0 |
| Walker F. | 3 | 1 | – | – | 3 | 1 |
| Wardell A. | 4 | 0 | – | – | 4 | 0 |
| Weaver R.W. | 11 | 4 | – | – | 11 | 4 |
| Wetherby T. | 3 | 0 | – | – | 3 | 0 |
| Wilson C.W. | 2 | 0 | – | – | 3 | 0 |

### Top positions only

| | | P | W | D | L | F | A | Pts |
|---|---|---|---|---|---|---|---|---|
| 1 | Bristol City | 42 | 27 | 8 | 7 | 104 | 54 | 62 |
| 2 | Plymouth | 42 | 25 | 10 | 7 | 95 | 61 | 60 |
| 3 | Millwall | 42 | 23 | 10 | 9 | 89 | 51 | 56 |
| 4 | Brighton | 42 | 21 | 11 | 10 | 79 | 50 | 53 |
| 5 | Swindon | 42 | 21 | 9 | 12 | 100 | 85 | 51 |
| 6 | Crystal Palace | 42 | 18 | 9 | 15 | 84 | 81 | 45 |
| 7 | Bournemouth | 42 | 18 | 8 | 16 | 78 | 66 | 44 |
| 8 | Luton | 42 | 15 | 14 | 13 | 68 | 66 | 44 |
| 9 | Newport | 42 | 19 | 6 | 17 | 57 | 71 | 44 |
| 10 | Bristol Rovers | 42 | 16 | 9 | 17 | 78 | 80 | 41 |
| 11 | Brentford | 42 | 13 | 14 | 15 | 70 | 61 | 40 |
| 12 | Exeter | 42 | 15 | 10 | 17 | 76 | 73 | 40 |
| 13 | Charlton | 42 | 16 | 8 | 18 | 60 | 61 | 40 |
| 14 | QPR | 42 | 15 | 9 | 18 | 65 | 71 | 39 |
| 15 | Coventry | 42 | 15 | 7 | 20 | 71 | 86 | 37 |
| 16 | Norwich | 42 | 12 | 11 | 19 | 59 | 71 | 35 |
| 17 | Merthyr Town | 42 | 13 | 9 | 20 | 63 | 80 | 35 |
| 18 | Northampton | 42 | 15 | 5 | 22 | 59 | 83 | 35 |

(Back) Chatt (Trainer), James, Drinnan, Pugh, Pearson, Maidment, Elwell, Connor, Hinton, Jones (Groundsman)
(Middle) Hindmarsh (Manager), Bowsher, Smith, Forward, Nairn, Johnson, Carney, Holland, Wilson
(Front) Price, Pritchard, Wetherby, Wardell, Anderson, Hiles

## SEASON 1927/28 Division 3 (South)

| | Date | Opposition | Res. | Att. | Goalscorers |
|---|---|---|---|---|---|
| 1 | 27 Aug | Q.P.Rangers | 2-4 | 15489 | Gittins, Barratt |
| 2 | 1 Sept | BRIGHTON & H.A. | 3-1 | 6146 | Weaver(2), Waterston |
| 3 | 3 | WATFORD | 3-2 | 7362 | Gittins(2), Waterston |
| 4 | 10 | Charlton Athletic | 2-3 | 7946 | Pritchard, Weaver |
| 5 | 14 | Brighton & H.A. | 4-1 | 3700 | Weaver(3), Pick |
| 6 | 17 | BRISTOL ROVERS | 3-1 | 7862 | Gittins, Brittan, Weaver |
| 7 | 24 | Plymouth Argyle | 0-2 | 10011 | |
| 8 | 1 Oct | MERTHYR TOWN | 1-1 | 3147 | Brittan |
| 9 | 8 | Walsall | 3-0 | 11738 | Pick(2), Weaver |
| 10 | 15 | GILLINGHAM | 1-1 | 6589 | Barratt |
| 11 | 22 | Luton Town | 1-1 | 5192 | Maidment |
| 12 | 29 | BRENTFORD | 3-0 | 5790 | Maidment, Barratt, Weaver |
| 13 | 5 Nov | Bournemouth & B.A. | 0-0 | 5324 | |
| 14 | 12 | MILLWALL | 1-3 | 5727 | Waterston |
| 15 | 19 | Crystal Palace | 0-2 | 8683 | |
| 16 | 3 Dec | Torquay United | 1-1 | 3489 | Waterston |
| 17 | 17 | Northampton Town | 2-1 | 8945 | Gittins, Waterston |
| 18 | 24 | SOUTHEND UNITED | 3-2 | 3837 | Gittins(2), Waterston |
| 19 | 26 | SWINDON TOWN | 1-3 | 3610 | Young |
| 20 | 27 | Swindon Town | 1-4 | 9715 | Waterston |
| 21 | 7 Jan | Watford | 3-2 | 5972 | Harper, Waterston, Young |
| 22 | 14 | NORWICH CITY | 2-2 | 2875 | Waterston(2) |
| 23 | 21 | CHARLTON ATHLETIC | 4-3 | 3737 | Waterston(4) |
| 24 | 28 | Bristol Rovers | 1-2 | 4265 | Gittins |
| 25 | 4 Feb | PLYMOUTH ARGYLE | 1-1 | 3502 | Harper |
| 26 | 11 | Merthyr Town | 2-0 | 2229 | Gittins(2) |
| 27 | 18 | WALSALL | 4-1 | 5561 | Brittan(3), Gittins |
| 28 | 25 | Gillingham | 0-4 | 5932 | |
| 29 | 3 Mar | LUTON TOWN | 7-2 | 3995 | Waterston(3), Gittins(2), Harper, Pick |
| 30 | 10 | Brentford | 1-3 | 5759 | Waterston |
| 31 | 17 | BOURNEMOUTH & B.A. | 4-3 | 3754 | Gittins(2), Waterston, Brittan |
| 32 | 22 | EXETER CITY | 1-0 | 2108 | Gittins |
| 33 | 24 | Millwall | 1-5 | 15558 | Richardson |
| 34 | 6 Apr | Q.P. RANGERS | 1-6 | 5918 | Thomas |
| 35 | 7 | Norwich City | 1-1 | 7641 | Thomas |
| 36 | 9 | COVENTRY CITY | 3-0 | 5170 | Waterston(3) |
| 37 | 10 | Coventry City | 2-0 | 10295 | Waterston, Young |
| 38 | 14 | TORQUAY UNITED | 2-2 | 3199 | Waterston, Barratt |
| 39 | 21 | Exeter City | 1-5 | 4912 | Gittins |
| 40 | 26 | CRYSTAL PALACE | 0-3 | 2554 | |
| 41 | 28 | NORTHAMPTON TOWN | 4-1 | 2753 | Waterston(2), Harper, Gittins |
| 42 | 5 May | Southend United | 1-5 | 4796 | Waterston |

### F.A.Cup

| | | | | | |
|---|---|---|---|---|---|
| 1 | 26 Nov | SWINDON TOWN | 0-1 | 9600 | |

| Player | League | | F.A.Cup | | Total | |
|---|---|---|---|---|---|---|
| | App | Gls. | App | Gls. | App | Gls. |
| Anderson R. | 42 | 0 | 1 | 0 | 44 | 0 |
| Barratt P. | 18 | 4 | 1 | 0 | 20 | 5 |
| Blakemore L. | 4 | 0 | – | – | 4 | 0 |
| Bowsher S.J. | 33 | 0 | 1 | 0 | 35 | 0 |
| Brittan C.H. | 19 | 6 | 1 | 0 | 20 | 6 |
| Clifford J.C.T. | 2 | 0 | – | – | 2 | 0 |
| Gittins J. | 34 | 18 | 1 | 0 | 35 | 18 |
| Harper T. | 18 | 4 | – | – | 19 | 4 |
| Hinton I.F. | 42 | 0 | 1 | 0 | 44 | 0 |
| Maidment J.H.C. | 38 | 2 | 1 | 0 | 40 | 2 |
| Nairn W.J. | 3 | 0 | – | – | 3 | 0 |
| Pick W.E. | 16 | 4 | – | – | 16 | 4 |
| Pritchard T.F. | 6 | 1 | – | – | 6 | 1 |
| Pugh R.A.L. | 28 | 0 | 1 | 0 | 30 | 0 |
| Richardson S. | 41 | 1 | 1 | 0 | 43 | 1 |
| Sims S. | 4 | 0 | – | – | 4 | 0 |
| Taylor D. | 4 | 0 | – | – | 4 | 0 |
| Thomas W.R. | 20 | 2 | – | – | 21 | 2 |
| Walker F | 3 | 0 | – | – | 3 | 0 |
| Wardell A. | 3 | 0 | – | – | 3 | 0 |
| Waterston A.R. | 30 | 27 | 1 | 0 | 32 | 27 |
| Weaver R.W. | 12 | 9 | – | – | 12 | 9 |
| Wetherby T. | 1 | 0 | – | – | 1 | 0 |
| Williams W. | 6 | 0 | – | – | 6 | 0 |
| Young H. | 35 | 3 | 1 | 0 | 37 | 3 |

### Top positions only

| | | P | W | D | L | F | A | Pts |
|---|---|---|---|---|---|---|---|---|
| 5 | Crystal Palace | 42 | 18 | 12 | 12 | 79 | 72 | 48 |
| 6 | Swindon | 42 | 19 | 9 | 14 | 90 | 69 | 47 |
| 7 | Exeter | 42 | 17 | 12 | 13 | 70 | 60 | 46 |
| 8 | Southend | 42 | 20 | 6 | 16 | 80 | 64 | 46 |
| 9 | Newport | 42 | 18 | 9 | 15 | 81 | 84 | 45 |
| 10 | QPR | 42 | 17 | 9 | 16 | 72 | 71 | 43 |
| 11 | Charlton | 42 | 15 | 13 | 14 | 60 | 70 | 43 |
| 12 | Brentford | 42 | 16 | 8 | 18 | 76 | 74 | 40 |
| 13 | Luton | 42 | 16 | 7 | 19 | 94 | 87 | 39 |
| 14 | Bournemouth | 42 | 13 | 12 | 17 | 72 | 79 | 38 |
| 15 | Watford | 42 | 14 | 10 | 18 | 68 | 78 | 38 |
| 16 | Gillingham | 42 | 13 | 11 | 18 | 62 | 81 | 37 |
| 17 | Norwich | 42 | 10 | 16 | 16 | 66 | 70 | 36 |
| 18 | Walsall | 42 | 12 | 9 | 21 | 75 | 101 | 33 |
| 19 | Bristol Rovers | 42 | 14 | 4 | 24 | 67 | 93 | 32 |
| 20 | Coventry | 42 | 11 | 9 | 22 | 67 | 96 | 31 |
| 21 | Merthyr Town | 42 | 9 | 13 | 20 | 53 | 91 | 31 |
| 22 | Torquay | 42 | 8 | 14 | 20 | 53 | 103 | 30 |

(Back) Harper, Bowsher, Maidment, Pritchard, Hinton, Anderson.
(Front) Barrett, Gittins, Nairn, Waterson, Young.

# SEASON 1928-29 Division 3 (South)

| | Date | Opposition | Res. | Att. | Goalscorers |
|---|---|---|---|---|---|
| 1 | 25 Aug | WALSALL | 3–1 | 6035 | Harper, Gittins, Waterston |
| 2 | 30 | Q.P Rangers | 0–0 | 9920 | |
| 3 | 1 Sep | Charlton Athletic | 2–2 | 10718 | Bowsher, Waterston |
| 4 | 6 | Q.P.RANGERS | 0–0 | 5293 | |
| 5 | 8 | Crystal Palace | 1–1 | 14796 | Gittins |
| 6 | 15 | SWINDON TOWN | 0–1 | 7737 | |
| 7 | 22 | Torquay United | 1–4 | 5908 | Wardell |
| 8 | 29 | GILLINGHAM | 5–0 | 4354 | Waterston(3), Bowsher, Thomas |
| 9 | 6 Oct | Plymouth Argyle | 2–5 | 11597 | Thomas, Wardell |
| 10 | 13 | FULHAM | 3–3 | 6994 | Waterston(2), Watts |
| 11 | 20 | NORTHAMPTON TOWN | 0–3 | 4405 | |
| 12 | 27 | Coventry City | 1–3 | 10876 | Gittins |
| 13 | 3 Nov | LUTON TOWN | 1–2 | 4177 | Waterston |
| 14 | 10 | Brentford | 3–1 | 5395 | Gittins, Waterston, Wardell |
| 15 | 17 | BOURNEMOUTH & B.A. | 0–2 | 3309 | |
| 16 | 1 Dec | SOUTHEND UNITED | 2–2 | 3725 | Reid, Ward |
| 17 | 15 | BRIGHTON & H.A. | 1–2 | 2174 | Gittins |
| 18 | 22 | Norwich City | 1–3 | 4824 | Wardell |
| 19 | 25 | WATFORD | 0–2 | 3351 | |
| 20 | 26 | Watford | 0–3 | 9463 | |
| 21 | 29 | Walsall | 1–3 | 5940 | Thomas |
| 22 | 5 Jan | CHARLTON ATHLETIC | 2–0 | 2401 | Gittins, Young |
| 23 | 12 | Merthyr Town | 1–2 | 2603 | Thomas |
| 24 | 19 | CRYSTAL PALACE | 1–3 | 3399 | Wardell |
| 25 | 2 Feb | TORQUAY UNITED | 4–1 | 1835 | Maidment, Pugh, G Richardson, Wardell |
| 26 | 9 | Gillingham | 4–0 | 3223 | Pugh(2), G Richardson(2) |
| 27 | 23 | Fulham | 3–2 | 15361 | Pugh, Wardell, G Richardson |
| 28 | 2 Mar | Northampton Town | 0–7 | 8864 | |
| 29 | 9 | COVENTRY CITY | 2–1 | 4398 | Pugh, G Richardson |
| 30 | 16 | Luton Town | 2–5 | 8782 | Gittins, Buckler |
| 31 | 20 | Exeter City | 1–6 | 2255 | G Richardson |
| 32 | 23 | BRENTFORD | 1–1 | 3090 | Pugh |
| 33 | 29 | Bristol Rovers | 3–0 | 10375 | G Richardson(2), Young |
| 34 | 30 | Bournemouth & B.A. | 1–0 | 5190 | G Richardson |
| 35 | 1 Apr | BRISTOL ROVERS | 2–0 | 5659 | Pugh, Gittins |
| 36 | 6 | MERTHYR TOWN | 6–1 | 3599 | Pugh(3), Thomas(2), Young |
| 37 | 13 | Southend United | 2–4 | 4820 | Pugh, Thomas |
| 38 | 18 | PLYMOUTH ARGYLE | 1–0 | 3499 | Pugh |
| 39 | 20 | EXETER CITY | 1–1 | 3058 | Thomas |
| 40 | 27 | Brighton & H.A. | 1–2 | 4759 | Thomas |
| 41 | 1 May | Swindon Town | 2–5 | 1542 | G Richardson(2) |
| 42 | 4 | NORWICH CITY | 2–2 | 2117 | Wardell(2) |

## F.A.Cup

| | Date | Opposition | Res. | Att. | Goalscorers |
|---|---|---|---|---|---|
| 1 | 24 Nov | WOKING TOWN | 7–0 | 3800 | Young(3), Pugh(2), Gittins, Reid |
| 2 | 8 Dec | Norwich City | 0–6 | 9072 | |

| Player | League | | F.A.Cup | | Total | |
|---|---|---|---|---|---|---|
| | App | Gls. | App | Gls. | App | Gls. |
| Anderson R. | 42 | 0 | 2 | 0 | 46 | 0 |
| Blakemore L. | 7 | 0 | 2 | 0 | 9 | 0 |
| Bowsher S.J. | 18 | 2 | 2 | 0 | 20 | 2 |
| Buckler T.C. | 1 | 1 | – | – | 1 | 1 |
| Clifford J.C.T. | 5 | 0 | – | – | 5 | 0 |
| Gittins J. | 36 | 8 | 2 | 1 | 39 | 9 |
| Harper T. | 5 | 1 | 1 | 0 | 7 | 1 |
| Hill J.T. | 2 | 0 | – | – | 2 | 0 |
| Hinton I.F. | 11 | 0 | – | – | 11 | 0 |
| Maidment J.H.C. | 36 | 1 | – | – | 38 | 2 |
| Nairn W.J. | 20 | 0 | 1 | 0 | 22 | 0 |
| Pick W.E. | 4 | 0 | – | – | 4 | 0 |
| Pugh R.A.L. | 36 | 12 | 1 | 2 | 39 | 14 |
| Reid J.E. | 29 | 1 | 2 | 1 | 33 | 2 |
| Richardson G.W | 18 | 11 | 2 | 0 | 22 | 15 |
| Richardson S. | 39 | 0 | 1 | 0 | 42 | 0 |
| Riley V. | 16 | 0 | – | – | 18 | 0 |
| Taylor D. | 4 | 0 | – | – | 4 | 0 |
| Thomas W.R. | 36 | 9 | 2 | 0 | 40 | 9 |
| Ward D. | 6 | 1 | – | – | 7 | 1 |
| Wardell A. | 34 | 9 | 1 | 0 | 36 | 9 |
| Waterston A.R. | 13 | 9 | – | – | 13 | 9 |
| Watts F. | 6 | 1 | 1 | 0 | 8 | 1 |
| Wheeler G.H. | 6 | 0 | – | – | 6 | 0 |
| Witton J. | 3 | 0 | – | – | 3 | 0 |
| Young H. | 29 | 3 | 2 | 3 | 31 | 6 |

### Bottom positions only

| | P | W | D | L | F | A | Pts |
|---|---|---|---|---|---|---|---|
| 5 Fulham | 42 | 21 | 10 | 11 | 101 | 71 | 52 |
| 6 QPR | 42 | 19 | 14 | 9 | 82 | 61 | 52 |
| 7 Luton | 42 | 19 | 11 | 12 | 89 | 73 | 49 |
| 8 Watford | 42 | 19 | 10 | 13 | 79 | 74 | 48 |
| 9 Bournemouth | 42 | 19 | 9 | 14 | 84 | 77 | 47 |
| 10 Swindon | 42 | 15 | 13 | 14 | 75 | 72 | 43 |
| 11 Coventry | 42 | 14 | 14 | 14 | 62 | 57 | 42 |
| 12 Southend | 42 | 15 | 11 | 16 | 80 | 75 | 41 |
| 13 Brentford | 42 | 14 | 10 | 18 | 56 | 60 | 38 |
| 14 Walsall | 42 | 13 | 12 | 17 | 73 | 79 | 38 |
| 15 Brighton | 42 | 16 | 6 | 20 | 58 | 76 | 38 |
| 16 Newport | 42 | 13 | 9 | 20 | 69 | 86 | 35 |
| 17 Norwich | 42 | 14 | 6 | 22 | 69 | 81 | 34 |
| 18 Torquay | 42 | 14 | 6 | 22 | 66 | 84 | 34 |
| 19 Bristol Rovers | 42 | 13 | 7 | 22 | 60 | 79 | 33 |
| 20 Merthyr Town | 42 | 11 | 8 | 23 | 55 | 103 | 30 |
| 21 Exeter | 42 | 9 | 11 | 22 | 67 | 88 | 29 |
| 22 Gillingham | 42 | 10 | 9 | 23 | 43 | 83 | 29 |

(Back) S.Richardson, Anderson, Blakemore, Reid, Bowsher
(Front) Wardell, Witton, Ward, Pugh, Thomas, Clifford

# SEASON 1929-30 Division 3 (South)

| | Date | Opposition | Res. | Att. | Goalscorers |
|---|---|---|---|---|---|
| 1 | 31 Aug | Southend United | 1-2 | 8186 | Morris |
| 2 | 5 Sep | SWINDON TOWN | 2-1 | 4860 | G Richardson, Thomas |
| 3 | 7 | WATFORD | 1-0 | 4887 | G Richardson |
| 4 | 9 | Swindon Town | 1-5 | 4952 | Gittins |
| 5 | 14 | Coventry City | 0-2 | 15456 | |
| 6 | 21 | CLAPTON ORIENT | 0-0 | 4877 | |
| 7 | 25 | Crystal Palace | 0-1 | 9445 | |
| 8 | 28 | Brentford | 0-1 | 11073 | |
| 9 | 5 Oct | BRISTOL ROVERS | 2-2 | 2471 | Gittins, Richards |
| 10 | 12 | Brighton & H.A. | 2-3 | 7877 | Riley, Morris |
| 11 | 19 | Luton Town | 2-4 | 8825 | G Richardson, Thomas |
| 12 | 26 | BOURNEMOUTH & B.A. | 1-1 | 3640 | Witton |
| 13 | 2 Nov | Walsall | 1-2 | 5424 | Morris |
| 14 | 9 | Q.P.RANGERS | 4-5 | 3527 | Martin(3), Morris |
| 15 | 16 | Fulham | 1-2 | 28211 | Martin |
| 16 | 23 | NORWICH CITY | 4-4 | 2541 | Martin(2), Gittins, Thomas |
| 17 | 7 Dec | GILLINGHAM | 5-1 | 1991 | Martin(3), G Richardson, Seymour |
| 18 | 21 | EXETER CITY | 4-1 | 2606 | Martin(2), Seymour, Alderson(og) |
| 19 | 25 | TORQUAY UNITED | 2-1 | 3337 | Morris, Thomas |
| 20 | 26 | Torquay United | 2-3 | 5928 | Martin, Seymour |
| 21 | 31 | Northampton Town | 0-2 | 5797 | |
| 22 | 4 Jan | Watford | 3-2 | 5851 | Martin(2), McKenna |
| 23 | 18 | COVENTRY CITY | 4-2 | 3963 | Martin(3), McKenna |
| 24 | 25 | SOUTHEND UNITED | 0-0 | 4945 | |
| 25 | 1 Feb | BRENTFORD | 1-3 | 3827 | Gittins |
| 26 | 8 | Bristol Rovers | 3-2 | 5469 | Martin(2), McKenna |
| 27 | 22 | LUTON TOWN | 0-0 | 3879 | |
| 28 | 1 Mar | Bournemouth & B.A. | 1-1 | 5509 | Riley |
| 29 | 3 | BRIGHTON & H.A. | 2-2 | 2670 | Martin(2) |
| 30 | 8 | WALSALL | 3-2 | 4260 | Gittins, Seymour, Martin |
| 31 | 15 | Q.P.Rangers | 1-4 | 7926 | Martin |
| 32 | 22 | FULHAM | 1-1 | 4626 | Martin |
| 33 | 29 | Norwich City | 1-4 | 8473 | Thomas |
| 34 | 31 | Clapton Orient | 1-3 | 2362 | Riley |
| 35 | 5 Apr | CRYSTAL PALACE | 0-0 | 3324 | |
| 36 | 10 | MERTHYR TOWN | 10-0 | 1997 | Martin(5), Gittins(2), Thomas, Bagley, Lawson |
| 37 | 12 | Gillingham | 0-5 | 2743 | |
| 38 | 18 | Plymouth Argyle | 1-3 | 26409 | Thomas |
| 39 | 19 | NORTHAMPTON TOWN | 2-1 | 3282 | Martin(2) |
| 40 | 21 | PLYMOUTH ARGYLE | 0-2 | 10766 | |
| 41 | 26 | Exeter City | 4-0 | 3723 | Martin(3), Seymour |
| 42 | 3 May | Merthyr Town | 1-5 | 1189 | McKenna |

## F.A.Cup

| | | | | | |
|---|---|---|---|---|---|
| 1 | 30 Nov | KETTERING TOWN | 3-2 | 3721 | Morris, Thomas, Martin |
| 2 | 14 Dec | WALSALL | 2-3 | 4121 | Morris, Martin |

| Player | League | | F.A.Cup | | Total | |
|---|---|---|---|---|---|---|
| | App | Gls. | App | Gls. | App | Gls. |
| Anderson R. | 25 | 0 | 2 | 0 | 28 | 0 |
| Bagley W. | 9 | 1 | – | – | 10 | 1 |
| Blakemore L. | 21 | 0 | – | – | 23 | 0 |
| Chapman W. | – | – | – | – | 1 | 0 |
| Clarke W.V. | – | – | – | – | 1 | 0 |
| Clifford J.C.T. | 5 | 0 | – | – | 7 | 0 |
| Gittins J. | 31 | 7 | – | – | 32 | 8 |
| Hugh A.R. | 11 | 0 | – | – | 12 | 0 |
| Jones W. | – | – | – | – | 1 | 0 |
| Kitson G. | – | – | – | – | 1 | 0 |
| Lawson H.S.R. | 28 | 1 | 2 | 0 | 31 | 1 |
| Maidment J.H.C. | 21 | 0 | 2 | 0 | 23 | 0 |
| Martin T.J. | 29 | 34 | 2 | 2 | 32 | 37 |
| McKenna F.C. | 24 | 4 | – | – | 25 | 4 |
| Morris H. | 22 | 5 | 2 | 2 | 24 | 7 |
| Nairn W.J. | 33 | 0 | 1 | 0 | 34 | 0 |
| Reid J.E. | 33 | 0 | 1 | 0 | 34 | 0 |
| Richards P. | 4 | 1 | – | – | 4 | 1 |
| Richardson G.W. | 12 | 4 | 2 | 0 | 14 | 4 |
| Richardson S. | 32 | 0 | 2 | 0 | 34 | 0 |
| Riley V. | 31 | 3 | 1 | 0 | 33 | 3 |
| Rutherford G. | 4 | 0 | – | – | 5 | 0 |
| Seymour C. | 24 | 5 | 2 | 0 | 28 | 6 |
| Thomas W.R. | 40 | 7 | 2 | 1 | 42 | 8 |
| Wardell A. | – | – | – | – | 1 | 0 |
| Wheeler G.H. | 14 | 0 | 1 | 0 | 16 | 0 |
| Witton J. | 6 | 1 | – | – | 7 | 1 |
| Worthy R.F. | 3 | 0 | – | – | 3 | 0 |
| Own Goals. | | 1 | | | | 1 |

### Bottom positions only

| | P | W | D | L | F | A | Pts |
|---|---|---|---|---|---|---|---|
| 8 Norwich | 42 | 18 | 10 | 14 | 88 | 77 | 46 |
| 9 Crystal Palace | 42 | 17 | 12 | 13 | 81 | 74 | 46 |
| 10 Bournemouth | 42 | 15 | 13 | 14 | 72 | 61 | 43 |
| 11 Southend | 42 | 15 | 13 | 14 | 69 | 59 | 43 |
| 12 Clapton Orient | 42 | 14 | 13 | 15 | 55 | 62 | 41 |
| 13 Luton | 42 | 14 | 12 | 16 | 64 | 78 | 40 |
| 14 Swindon | 42 | 13 | 12 | 17 | 73 | 83 | 38 |
| 15 Watford | 42 | 15 | 8 | 19 | 60 | 73 | 38 |
| 16 Exeter | 42 | 12 | 11 | 19 | 67 | 73 | 35 |
| 17 Walsall | 42 | 13 | 8 | 21 | 71 | 78 | 34 |
| 18 Newport | 42 | 12 | 10 | 20 | 74 | 85 | 34 |
| 19 Torquay | 42 | 10 | 11 | 21 | 64 | 94 | 31 |
| 20 Bristol Rovers | 42 | 11 | 8 | 23 | 67 | 93 | 30 |
| 21 Gillingham | 42 | 11 | 8 | 23 | 51 | 80 | 30 |
| 22 Merthyr Town | 42 | 6 | 9 | 27 | 60 | 135 | 21 |

(Back)  Chatt (Trainer), Lawson, Anderson, Maidment, Reid, Riley
(Front)  Morris, Gittins, Martin, Witton, Thomas, Worthy

# SEASON 1930–31 Division 3 (South)

| | Date | Opposition | Res. | Att. | Goalscorers |
|---|---|---|---|---|---|
| 1 | 30 Aug | TORQUAY UNITED | 2–1 | 3905 | Riley, Matson |
| 2 | 4 Sep | Clapton Orient | 1–3 | 5505 | Welsh |
| 3 | 6 | Northampton Town | 0–1 | 13239 | |
| 4 | 10 | Gillingham | 1–4 | 3181 | Thomas |
| 5 | 13 | BRENTFORD | 0–2 | 2758 | |
| 6 | 15 | GILLINGHAM | 1–3 | 3181 | Wheeler |
| 7 | 20 | Crystal Palace | 1–7 | 12625 | Davies |
| 8 | 27 | SOUTHEND UNITED | 3–1 | 2711 | Davies(2), Thomas |
| 9 | 4 Oct | Luton Town | 1–3 | 8097 | Gittins |
| 10 | 11 | BRISTOL ROVERS | 1–1 | 3951 | Seymour |
| 11 | 18 | NOTTS COUNTY | 2–3 | 5245 | Seymour(2) |
| 12 | 25 | Watford | 2–6 | 6214 | Pearce(2) |
| 13 | 1 Nov | BOURNEMOUTH & B.A. | 7–3 | 2827 | Seymour(3), Pearce(3), Davies |
| 14 | 8 | Swindon Town | 4–4 | 4808 | Pearce(2), Hickie, Davies |
| 15 | 15 | FULHAM | 1–3 | 4082 | Pearce |
| 16 | 22 | Coventry City | 4–6 | 8276 | Pearce(2), Hickie, Gittins |
| 17 | 6 Dec | Q.P.Rangers | 1–7 | 6566 | Davies |
| 18 | 18 | NORWICH CITY | 3–0 | 1116 | Pearce(2), Gittins |
| 19 | 20 | Thames | 1–3 | 816 | Pearce |
| 20 | 25 | EXETER CITY | 4–0 | 3264 | Pearce(2), Gittins, Davies |
| 21 | 26 | Exeter City | 0–3 | 9548 | |
| 22 | 27 | Torquay United | 0–3 | 4561 | |
| 23 | 3 Jan | NORTHAMPTON TOWN | 5–2 | 2977 | Pearce(2), Gittins, Brown, Bagley |
| 24 | 17 | Brentford | 2–3 | 7170 | Brown, Thomas |
| 25 | 22 | WALSALL | 1–1 | 2125 | Witton |
| 26 | 26 | CRYSTAL PALACE | 2–1 | 1967 | Gittins(2) |
| 27 | 31 | Southend United | 2–6 | 5506 | Witton(2) |
| 28 | 7 Feb | LUTON TOWN | 3–1 | 2868 | Glidden(2), Witton |
| 29 | 14 | Bristol Rovers | 0–2 | 8160 | |
| 30 | 21 | Notts County | 0–5 | 11913 | |
| 31 | 28 | WATFORD | 0–2 | 2310 | |
| 32 | 7 Mar | Bournemouth & B.A. | 2–4 | 3091 | Seymour, Brown |
| 33 | 14 | SWINDON TOWN | 3–1 | 2872 | Gittins(2), Pearce |
| 34 | 21 | Fulham | 1–0 | 10124 | Gittins |
| 35 | 28 | COVENTRY CITY | 1–1 | 2950 | Gittins |
| 36 | 3 Apr | Brighton & H.A. | 0–5 | 5992 | |
| 37 | 4 | Walsall | 0–1 | 3321 | |
| 38 | 6 | BRIGHTON & H.A. | 2–0 | 3346 | Gittins, Thomas |
| 39 | 11 | Q.P.RANGERS | 2–3 | 2899 | Pearce(2) |
| 40 | 18 | Norwich City | 1–4 | 4563 | Pearce |
| 41 | 25 | THAMES | 1–1 | 1309 | Bagley |
| 42 | 2 May | CLAPTON ORIENT | 1–1 | 1873 | Gittins |

## F.A.Cup

| | Date | Opposition | Res. | Att. | Goalscorers |
|---|---|---|---|---|---|
| 1 | 29 Nov | Dulwich Hamlet | 2–2 | 7500 | Pearce(2), |
| 1R | 4 Dec | DULWICH HAMLET | 4–1 | 4500 | Davies, Pearce, Brown, Bagley |
| 2 | 13 | Walsall | 0–4 | 7676 | |

| Player | League | | F.A.Cup | | Total | |
|---|---|---|---|---|---|---|
| | App | Gls. | App | Gls. | App | Gls. |
| Apsey T.L. | 2 | 0 | – | – | 2 | 0 |
| Bagley W. | 25 | 2 | 2 | 1 | 28 | 3 |
| Blakemore L. | 41 | 0 | 3 | 0 | 45 | 0 |
| Boots G.H. | 1 | 0 | – | – | 1 | 0 |
| Brown H. | 34 | 3 | 3 | 1 | 38 | 4 |
| Clarke W.V. | 5 | 0 | – | – | 6 | 0 |
| Clifford J.C.T. | 31 | 0 | 1 | 0 | 33 | 0 |
| Davies V. | 22 | 7 | 2 | 1 | 24 | 8 |
| Fox W.V. | 37 | 0 | 3 | 0 | 41 | 0 |
| Gittins J. | 33 | 13 | 3 | 0 | 36 | 13 |
| Glidden S. | 4 | 2 | 1 | 0 | 6 | 2 |
| Hickie W. | 24 | 2 | 3 | 0 | 27 | 2 |
| Hugh A.R. | 2 | 0 | – | – | 3 | 0 |
| Jones W. | 4 | 0 | – | – | 4 | 0 |
| Lawson H.S.R. | 27 | 0 | 3 | 0 | 30 | 0 |
| Matson F.R. | 1 | 1 | – | – | 1 | 1 |
| Nairn W.J. | 8 | 0 | – | – | 8 | 0 |
| Pearce C. | 26 | 21 | 3 | 3 | 30 | 26 |
| Richardson S. | 14 | 0 | 2 | 0 | 16 | 0 |
| Riley V. | 34 | 1 | 3 | 0 | 37 | 1 |
| Seymour C. | 14 | 7 | – | – | 14 | 7 |
| Thomas W.R. | 34 | 4 | 1 | 0 | 36 | 4 |
| Wardell A. | 2 | 0 | – | – | 2 | 0 |
| Way | – | – | – | – | 1 | 0 |
| Welsh W. | 6 | 1 | – | – | 6 | 1 |
| Wheeler G.H. | 26 | 1 | – | – | 26 | 1 |
| Witton J. | 5 | 4 | – | – | 5 | 4 |

### Bottom positions only

| | | P | W | D | L | F | A | Pts |
|---|---|---|---|---|---|---|---|---|
| 8 | QPR | 42 | 20 | 3 | 19 | 82 | 75 | 43 |
| 9 | Fulham | 42 | 18 | 7 | 17 | 77 | 75 | 43 |
| 10 | Bournemouth | 42 | 15 | 13 | 14 | 72 | 73 | 43 |
| 11 | Torquay | 42 | 17 | 9 | 16 | 80 | 84 | 43 |
| 12 | Swindon | 42 | 18 | 6 | 18 | 89 | 94 | 42 |
| 13 | Exeter | 42 | 17 | 8 | 17 | 84 | 90 | 42 |
| 14 | Coventry | 42 | 16 | 9 | 17 | 75 | 65 | 41 |
| 15 | Bristol Rovers | 42 | 16 | 8 | 18 | 75 | 92 | 40 |
| 16 | Gillingham | 42 | 14 | 10 | 18 | 61 | 76 | 38 |
| 17 | Walsall | 42 | 14 | 9 | 19 | 78 | 95 | 37 |
| 18 | Watford | 42 | 14 | 7 | 21 | 72 | 75 | 35 |
| 19 | Clapton Orient | 42 | 14 | 7 | 21 | 63 | 91 | 35 |
| 20 | Thames | 42 | 13 | 8 | 21 | 54 | 93 | 34 |
| 21 | Norwich | 42 | 10 | 8 | 24 | 47 | 76 | 28 |
| 22 | Newport | 42 | 11 | 6 | 25 | 69 | 111 | 28 |

(Back) Clifford, Fox, Blakemore, Wheeler, Riley
(Front) Brown, Gittins, Pearce, Bagley, Thomas, Lawson

| | Date | Opposition | Res. | Att. | Goalscorers |
|---|---|---|---|---|---|
| 1 | 29 Aug | MERTHYR TOWN | 4-2 | | Peed(2), Thomas, Bagley |
| 2 | 7 Sep | YEOVIL & PETTERS | 1-1 | | Gittins |
| 3 | 17 | Bath City | 3-3 | | Peed(2), Brittan |
| 4 | 21 | Llanelly | 2-2 | 4000 | Peed, Brittan |
| 5 | 26 | BATH CITY | 2-2 | | Thomas, Brittan |
| 6 | 10 Oct | EXETER CITY RES. | 1-1 | | Peed |
| 7 | 17 | Bristol Rovers Res. | 1-0 | 3000 | Gittins |
| 8 | 24 | LLANELLY | 1-2 | | Peed |
| 9 | 31 | Taunton Town | 1-2 | | Peed |
| 10 | 7 Nov | EBBW VALE | 7-2 | | Gittins(3), Peed(3), Bagley |
| 11 | 21 | BRISTOL ROVERS RES. | 6-2 | | Gittins(2), Thomas(2), Peed, W.Clarke |
| 12 | 5 Dec | SWINDON TOWN RES. | 6-1 | | S.Jones(2), Gittins, Thomas, Brittan, Bagley |
| 13 | 25 | Barry | 2-4 | | Bagley, Brittan |
| 14 | 26 | BARRY | 11-1 | | Gittins(4), Peed(3), Thomas(2), Bagley, |
| 15 | 2 Jan | Merthyr Town | 3-3 | | S.Jones |
| 16 | 16 | TAUNTON TOWN | 10-2 | | Bagley, S.Jones, Gittins |
| 17 | 20 Feb | Exeter City Res. | 1-3 | 3000 | |
| 18 | 27 | TORQUAY UNITED RES. | 3-0 | | |
| 19 | 5 Mar | Torquay United Res. | 0-6 | | |
| 20 | 19 | Swindon Town Res. | 0-5 | | A.Clarke, Brittan(2) |
| 21 | 25 | Plymouth Argyle Res. | 0-0 | | Peed, Brittan |
| 22 | 26 | Ebbw Vale | 3-2 | | |
| 23 | 28 | PLYMOUTH ARGYLE | 2-3 | | |
| 24 | 29 | Yeovil & Petters | 0-3 | 300 | |

| Player | League | | F.A.Cup | | Total | |
|---|---|---|---|---|---|---|
| | App | Gls. | App | Gls. | App | Gls. |
| Bagley W. | 24 | 7 | | | 27 | 8 |
| Blakemore L. | 24 | 0 | | | 27 | 0 |
| Brittan C.H. | 17 | 12 | | | 19 | 12 |
| Clarke A.W. | 1 | 1 | | | 1 | 1 |
| Clarke W.V. | 23 | 1 | | | 26 | 1 |
| Clifford J.C.T. | 15 | 0 | | | 16 | 0 |
| Davies V. | 6 | 0 | | | 6 | 0 |
| Dowd | 5 | 0 | | | 5 | 0 |
| Ford | 1 | 0 | | | 1 | 0 |
| Gittins J. | 22 | 13 | | | 24 | 14 |
| Hugh A.R. | 12 | 0 | | | 14 | 0 |
| Jones S.E. | 7 | 4 | | | 9 | 4 |
| Jones T. | 4 | 0 | | | 5 | 0 |
| Jones W. | 16 | 0 | | | 19 | 0 |
| Kitson G. | 15 | 0 | | | 17 | 0 |
| Madley.L. | 2 | 0 | | | 2 | 0 |
| Peed F.E. | 22 | 24 | | | 25 | 24 |
| Skuse | 2 | 0 | | | 2 | 0 |
| Thomas W. | 23 | 8 | | | 26 | 8 |
| Wheeler G.H | 21 | 0 | | | 24 | 0 |
| Worthy R.F. | 2 | 0 | | | 2 | 0 |

## F.A.Cup
FA Cup not entered, banned.

| | | P | W | D | L | F | A | Pts |
|---|---|---|---|---|---|---|---|---|
| 1 | Yeovil & Petters United | 24 | 16 | 4 | 4 | 65 | 31 | 36 |
| 2 | Plymouth Argyle (Res.) | 24 | 15 | 5 | 4 | 81 | 31 | 35 |
| 3 | Bath City | 24 | 12 | 7 | 5 | 50 | 33 | 31 |
| 4 | Llanelly | 24 | 12 | 4 | 8 | 65 | 46 | 28 |
| 5 | Taunton Town | 24 | 13 | 2 | 9 | 53 | 58 | 28 |
| 6 | Newport County | 24 | 10 | 6 | 8 | 70 | 51 | 26 |
| 7 | Exeter City (Res.) | 24 | 9 | 7 | 8 | 59 | 43 | 25 |
| 8 | Merthyr Town | 24 | 9 | 4 | 11 | 66 | 73 | 22 |
| 9 | Bristol Rovers (Res.) | 24 | 8 | 4 | 12 | 54 | 47 | 20 |
| 10 | Swindon Town (Res.) | 24 | 8 | 4 | 12 | 54 | 95 | 20 |
| 11 | Barry | 24 | 7 | 3 | 14 | 58 | 76 | 17 |
| 12 | Torquay United (Res.) | 24 | 5 | 6 | 13 | 43 | 66 | 16 |
| 13 | Ebbw Vale | 24 | 3 | 2 | 19 | 34 | 102 | 8 |

# EBBW VALE CAUGHT IN A FLOOD.

## OUT GENERALED BY THE COUNTY.

### BY " OGWEN."

Things went badly with Ebbw Vale's team of amateurs in a Southern League game with Newport County at Somerton Park this afternoon.

Although the County took things very easily, the quality of the opposition can be realised by the fact that Newport led 5—1 at the interval.

Again to-day the defence was Ebbw Vale's biggest handicap. The tackling and goal-keeping was even worse than what I saw on the Sports Ground last week. The forwards are in a different category, but without good quality half-backs it was quite plain that they can make little impression in any game.

Of the County, it need only be said that they were faster all round, cleverer in every sense, and far ahead of the amateurs in their ideas of linking play between half-back and forwards. Gittins scored three times in the first half, and Bagley and Peed got the other goals for the County. S. Jones scored a brilliant goal for Ebbw Vale.

**Newport County:** Blakemore; Kitson, Wheeler; Clifford, Clark, W. Jones; Brittan, Gittins, Peed, Bagley, Thomas.

**Ebbw Vale:** Roch; J. H. Blackham, P. Morris; L. Jones, T. Edmunds, C. Johnson; T. Organ, M. Allan, Jarrett Davies, J. Cope, Stan Jones.

Referee: Captain A. Evans, Cardiff.

Newport County fielded the team which defeated Swansea Town on Thursday, while Ebbw Vale put T. Organ at outside right which enabled C. Johnson to fall back to the half-backline.

Straight from the kick-off Brittan cork-screwed his way past Johnson, Edmunds, and Morris. He crossed the ball before the goal-mouth, and Peed missed it.

On the other wing, however, Thomas was more sure, and he ran the ball to the goal-mouth. Here, Roch jumped up and caught the ball in the aid. He was immediately pushed over the line by Peed.

Ball and player seemed to me to go over the line, but the referee shook his head and gestured the play to proceed after Roch had kicked away. Three times the County forwards got clean through in quick time. They found very little obstacle in the Ebbw Vale half-back line, and the Blues' goal was saved by the County's poor shooting more than any-thing else. Peed tore away furiously from Edmunds when Morris and Blackham threatened to sandwich him he shot at goal for Roch to gather the ball quite safely. Ebbw Vale were by no means cowed, for in a flash T. Organ, in whom they appeared to pin great faith twice shook himself free of Jones and Wheeler. On the first occasion he drove over the bar, and the second time he slipped

# SEASON 1932–33 Division 3(South)

| | Date | Opposition | Res. | Att. | Goalscorers |
|---|---|---|---|---|---|
| 1 | 27 Aug | CLAPTON ORIENT | 0–2 | 7805 | |
| 2 | 31 | Swindon Town | 0–2 | 5074 | |
| 3 | 3 Sep | Northampton Town | 0–8 | 8920 | |
| 4 | 5 | SWINDON TOWN | 1–2 | 3674 | Weale |
| 5 | 10 | BRISTOL CITY | 1–1 | 6025 | Gitlins |
| 6 | 14 | Southend United | 0–3 | 5687 | |
| 7 | 17 | Coventry City | 1–3 | 12766 | Green |
| 8 | 24 | BRENTFORD | 1–6 | 7343 | Weale |
| 9 | 1 Oct | Torquay United | 0–4 | 3960 | |
| 10 | 8 | EXETER CITY | 1–1 | 5268 | Lumley |
| 11 | 15 | Luton Town | 2–2 | 6504 | Rogers, Bagley |
| 12 | 22 | Cardiff City | 3–1 | 10163 | Bagley, Thomas, Peed |
| 13 | 29 | READING | 3–3 | 5375 | Thomas, Weale, Peed |
| 14 | 5 Nov | Norwich City | 1–3 | 9913 | Thomas |
| 15 | 17 | BRIGHTON & H.A. | 5–2 | 3750 | Weale(2), Bagley, Green, Peed |
| 16 | 19 | Bristol Rovers | 2–2 | 8910 | Weale, Peed |
| 17 | 3 Dec | Q.P.Rangers | 1–6 | 6514 | Green |
| 18 | 17 | Crystal Palace | 0–0 | 8644 | |
| 19 | 24 | GILLINGHAM | 0–2 | 4113 | |
| 20 | 26 | WATFORD | 2–0 | 5044 | Weale, Green |
| 21 | 27 | Watford | 2–3 | 9131 | Green, Armand |
| 22 | 31 | Clapton Orient | 1–3 | 4278 | Thomas |
| 23 | 7 Jan | NORTHAMPTON TOWN | 0–3 | 4217 | |
| 24 | 14 | BOURNEMOUTH & B.A. | 1–1 | 2237 | Bagley |
| 25 | 19 | ALDERSHOT | 2–1 | 1902 | Rogers(2) |
| 26 | 21 | Bristol City | 2–3 | 4800 | Bagley, Weale |
| 27 | 28 | COVENTRY CITY | 2–1 | 3150 | Bagley(2) |
| 28 | 4 Feb | Brentford | 0–6 | 10060 | |
| 29 | 9 | SOUTHEND UNITED | 1–3 | 1769 | Thomas |
| 30 | 11 | TORQUAY UNITED | 3–1 | 3098 | Gardner(2), Thomas |
| 31 | 18 | Exeter City | 0–4 | 6598 | |
| 32 | 4 Mar | CARDIFF CITY | 4–2 | 7933 | Gardner(2), Bagley, Green |
| 33 | 11 | Reading | 1–4 | 7742 | Green |
| 34 | 18 | NORWICH CITY | 3–4 | 4490 | Gardner(2) Thomas |
| 35 | 25 | Brighton & H.A. | 0–1 | 5045 | |
| 36 | 1 Apr | BRISTOL ROVERS | 3–1 | 3588 | Gardner(2), Thomas |
| 37 | 6 | LUTON TOWN | 3–2 | 2344 | Thomas(2), Gardner |
| 38 | 8 | Aldershot | 1–2 | 3340 | Gardner |
| 39 | 15 | Q.P.RANGERS | 5–1 | 4120 | Thomas(2), Green(2), Gardner |
| 40 | 17 | Bournemouth & B.A. | 2–1 | 5540 | Collins, Lumley |
| 41 | 29 | CRYSTAL PALACE | 1–3 | 5168 | Gardner |
| 42 | 6 May | Gillingham | 0–2 | 5737 | |

## F.A.Cup

| | Date | | Res. | | Goalscorers |
|---|---|---|---|---|---|
| 1 | 25 Nov | ILFORD | 4–2 | | Green(3), Weale |
| 2 | 10 Dec | Folkestone | 1–2 | | Weale |

| Player | League | | F.A.Cup | | Total | |
|---|---|---|---|---|---|---|
| | App | Gls. | App | Gls. | App | Gls. |
| Armand J.E. | 3 | 1 | 1 | 0 | 4 | 1 |
| Bagley W. | 37 | 8 | 2 | 0 | 42 | 8 |
| Charlton S. | 32 | 0 | 2 | 0 | 36 | 0 |
| Clarke W.V. | 13 | 0 | – | – | 15 | 0 |
| Collins W.E. | 6 | 1 | – | – | 6 | 1 |
| Cunningham B.J. | 3 | 0 | – | – | 3 | 0 |
| Dreyer F. | 1 | 0 | – | – | 2 | 0 |
| Gardner J. | 13 | 12 | – | – | 13 | 12 |
| Gardner J.R. | 3 | 0 | – | – | 3 | 0 |
| Gittins J. | 18 | 1 | – | – | 20 | 1 |
| Green T.F. | 22 | 9 | 2 | 3 | 26 | 13 |
| Hackett E. | 4 | 0 | – | – | 4 | 0 |
| Hugh A.R. | 30 | 0 | 2 | 0 | 34 | 0 |
| John E.J. | 37 | 0 | 2 | 0 | 41 | 0 |
| Jones S.E. | 2 | 0 | – | – | 2 | 0 |
| Jones W. | 2 | 0 | – | – | 2 | 0 |
| Lennox W. | 22 | 0 | 2 | 0 | 24 | 0 |
| Lumley S. | 14 | 2 | – | – | 16 | 5 |
| Peed F.E. | 13 | 4 | 1 | 0 | 15 | 4 |
| Rogers W. | 22 | 3 | 1 | 0 | 25 | 3 |
| Solly A.W. | 38 | 0 | 2 | 0 | 43 | 0 |
| Solly C.B. | 1 | 0 | – | – | 1 | 0 |
| Summers W. | 36 | 0 | 2 | 0 | 40 | 0 |
| Talbot R.C. | 10 | 0 | – | – | 11 | 0 |
| Thomas W.R. | 40 | 12 | 1 | 0 | 44 | 12 |
| Weale R.H. | 26 | 8 | 2 | 2 | 30 | 10 |
| Wheeler G.H. | 14 | 0 | – | – | 15 | 0 |

### Bottom positions only given

| | | P | W | D | L | F | A | Pts |
|---|---|---|---|---|---|---|---|---|
| 8 | Northampton | 42 | 18 | 8 | 16 | 76 | 66 | 44 |
| 9 | Bristol Rovers | 42 | 15 | 14 | 13 | 61 | 56 | 44 |
| 10 | Torquay | 42 | 16 | 12 | 14 | 72 | 67 | 44 |
| 11 | Watford | 42 | 16 | 12 | 14 | 66 | 63 | 44 |
| 12 | Brighton | 42 | 17 | 8 | 17 | 66 | 65 | 42 |
| 13 | Southend | 42 | 15 | 11 | 16 | 65 | 82 | 41 |
| 14 | Luton | 42 | 13 | 13 | 16 | 78 | 78 | 39 |
| 15 | Bristol City | 42 | 12 | 13 | 17 | 83 | 90 | 37 |
| 16 | QPR | 42 | 13 | 11 | 18 | 72 | 87 | 37 |
| 17 | Aldershot | 42 | 13 | 10 | 19 | 61 | 72 | 36 |
| 18 | Bournemouth | 42 | 12 | 12 | 18 | 60 | 81 | 36 |
| 19 | Cardiff | 42 | 12 | 7 | 23 | 69 | 99 | 31 |
| 20 | Clapton Orient | 42 | 8 | 13 | 21 | 59 | 93 | 29 |
| 21 | Newport | 42 | 11 | 7 | 24 | 61 | 105 | 29 |
| 22 | Swindon | 42 | 9 | 11 | 22 | 60 | 105 | 29 |

(Back) J.R.Gardner, Talbot, Hugh, A.W.Solly, Wheeler, Gibbon (Trainer) John. (Front) Collins, Gittins, Lennox, Green, Thomas, Summers

# SEASON 1933–34 Division 3(South)

| # | Date | Opposition | Res. | Att. | Goalscorers |
|---|---|---|---|---|---|
| 1 | 26 Aug | SWINDON TOWN | 1-2 | 8871 | Burgess |
| 2 | 28 | Clapton Orient | 0-3 | 6675 | |
| 3 | 2 Sep | Brighton & H.A. | 1-1 | 6878 | Smith |
| 4 | 4 | CLAPTON ORIENT | 1-1 | 5894 | Millar |
| 5 | 9 | ALDERSHOT | 1-2 | 6760 | Barklam |
| 6 | 16 | Luton Town | 1-1 | 10072 | Higgins |
| 7 | 23 | NORTHAMPTON TOWN | 2-0 | 4842 | Higgins, Taylor |
| 8 | 30 | Torquay United | 2-1 | 3729 | Higgins, Taylor |
| 9 | 7 Oct | Q.P.RANGERS | 1-2 | 7463 | Taylor |
| 10 | 14 | Gillingham | 0-1 | 4630 | |
| 11 | 21 | EXETER CITY | 1-0 | 7562 | Taylor |
| 12 | 28 | Cardiff City | 1-1 | 16175 | John |
| 13 | 4 Nov | BOURNEMOUTH & B.A. | 1-1 | 7079 | Reynolds |
| 14 | 11 | Charlton Athletic | 1-6 | 9771 | Taylor |
| 15 | 18 | WATFORD | 0-3 | 5301 | |
| 16 | 2 Dec | COVENTRY CITY | 0-0 | 3672 | |
| 17 | 16 | BRISTOL ROVERS | 1-0 | 3522 | Reynolds |
| 18 | 23 | Crystal Palace | 1-1 | 10755 | Higgins |
| 19 | 25 | BRISTOL CITY | 2-2 | 8039 | Higgins(2) |
| 20 | 26 | Bristol City | 1-1 | 16836 | Riley(og) |
| 21 | 30 | Swindon Town | 1-1 | 7809 | Burgess |
| 22 | 6 Jan | BRIGHTON & H.A. | 2-2 | 4694 | Higgins, Jones |
| 23 | 13 | Reading | 0-4 | 4608 | |
| 24 | 20 | Aldershot | 2-3 | 4253 | Higgins(2) |
| 25 | 27 | LUTON TOWN | 1-2 | 5524 | Haycox |
| 26 | 3 Feb | Northampton Town | 3-5 | 5048 | Thomas(2), Reynolds |
| 27 | 10 | TORQUAY UNITED | 0-0 | 4680 | |
| 28 | 17 | Q.P.Rangers | 1-2 | 7278 | Reed |
| 29 | 24 | GILLINGHAM | 3-1 | 3589 | Reed(2), Burgess |
| 30 | 3 Mar | Exeter City | 1-1 | 4903 | Reed |
| 31 | 10 | CARDIFF CITY | 2-2 | 10438 | Reynolds, Burgess |
| 32 | 14 | Southend United | 5-3 | 2580 | Reed(4), Worthy(og) |
| 33 | 17 | Bournemouth & B.A. | 0-0 | 3402 | |
| 34 | 24 | CHARLTON ATHLETIC | 1-1 | 5909 | W.Clarke |
| 35 | 30 | NORWICH CITY | 0-0 | 8965 | |
| 36 | 31 | Watford | 0-3 | 5675 | |
| 37 | 2 Apr | Norwich City | 1-2 | 22433 | Reed |
| 38 | 7 | READING | 1-2 | 5924 | Taylor |
| 39 | 14 | Coventry City | 2-5 | 10424 | Burgess, Higgins |
| 40 | 21 | SOUTHEND UNITED | 3-0 | 4728 | Green(2), Reed |
| 41 | 28 | Bristol Rovers | 0-2 | 4749 | |
| 42 | 5 May | CRYSTAL PALACE | 1-0 | 3930 | Green |

| Player | League | | F.A.Cup | | Total | |
|---|---|---|---|---|---|---|
| | App | Gls. | App | Gls. | App | Gls. |
| Barklam H. | 3 | 1 | – | – | 3 | 1 |
| Boots G.H. | 2 | 0 | – | – | 2 | 0 |
| Bowsher S.J. | 5 | 0 | – | – | 8 | 1 |
| Burgess J.W. | 29 | 5 | 3 | 3 | 33 | 8 |
| Clarke A.W. | – | – | – | – | 4 | 1 |
| Clarke W.V. | 28 | 1 | 3 | 0 | 34 | 1 |
| Clifford J.C.T. | 2 | 0 | – | – | 5 | 0 |
| Emery H.J. | 40 | 0 | 3 | 0 | 49 | 0 |
| Green T.F. | 15 | 3 | – | – | 18 | 6 |
| Griffiths A.A. | 1 | 0 | – | – | 3 | 1 |
| Haycox J.H. | 2 | 1 | – | – | 8 | 6 |
| Higgins A.K. | 34 | 10 | 3 | 1 | 42 | 12 |
| Hugh A.R. | 14 | 0 | 2 | 0 | 20 | 0 |
| John E.J. | 18 | 1 | – | – | 25 | 1 |
| Jones. V.W. | 33 | 1 | 3 | 0 | 36 | 1 |
| Jordan G. | 32 | 0 | 3 | 0 | 37 | 0 |
| Kitson G. | – | – | – | – | 2 | 0 |
| McLaughlan H.M. | 26 | 0 | – | – | 28 | 0 |
| Millar W. | 7 | 1 | – | – | 10 | 1 |
| Perkins T. | – | – | – | – | 1 | 0 |
| Reed G. | 16 | 10 | – | – | 17 | 10 |
| Reynolds W. | 41 | 4 | 3 | 1 | 47 | 8 |
| Robinson R. | 41 | 0 | 3 | 0 | 45 | 0 |
| Smith G. | 4 | 1 | 1 | 0 | 8 | 1 |
| Taylor G. | 11 | 6 | 3 | 2 | 15 | 8 |
| Thomas W.R. | 35 | 2 | 3 | 2 | 41 | 8 |
| Whitehouse C.H. | 8 | 0 | – | – | 12 | 0 |
| Woolliscroft A. | 15 | 0 | – | – | 19 | 1 |
| Own Goals | | 2 | | | | 2 |

## F.A.Cup

| # | Date | Opposition | Res. | Att. | Goalscorers |
|---|---|---|---|---|---|
| 1 | 25 Nov | Dulwich Hamlet | 2-2 | 11500 | Burgess, Higgins |
| 1/R | 30 | DULWICH HAMLET | 6-2 | 4500 | Burgess(2), Taylor(2), Reynolds, Thomas |
| 2 | 9 Dec | Workington | 1-3 | 8000 | Thomas |

Bottom positions only given

| | P | W | D | L | F | A | Pts |
|---|---|---|---|---|---|---|---|
| 9 Exeter | 42 | 16 | 11 | 15 | 68 | 57 | 43 |
| 10 Brighton | 42 | 15 | 13 | 14 | 68 | 60 | 43 |
| 11 Clapton Orient | 42 | 16 | 10 | 16 | 75 | 69 | 42 |
| 12 Crystal Palace | 42 | 16 | 9 | 17 | 71 | 67 | 41 |
| 13 Northampton | 42 | 14 | 12 | 16 | 71 | 78 | 40 |
| 14 Aldershot | 42 | 13 | 12 | 17 | 52 | 71 | 38 |
| 15 Watford | 42 | 15 | 7 | 20 | 71 | 63 | 37 |
| 16 Southend | 42 | 12 | 10 | 20 | 51 | 74 | 34 |
| 17 Gillingham | 42 | 11 | 11 | 20 | 75 | 96 | 33 |
| 18 Newport | 42 | 8 | 17 | 17 | 49 | 70 | 33 |
| 19 Bristol City | 42 | 10 | 13 | 19 | 58 | 85 | 33 |
| 20 Torquay | 42 | 13 | 7 | 22 | 53 | 93 | 33 |
| 21 Bournemouth | 42 | 9 | 9 | 24 | 60 | 102 | 27 |
| 22 Cardiff | 42 | 9 | 6 | 27 | 57 | 105 | 24 |

(Back) Clarke, Robinson, Emery, Gibbon (Trainer), McLaughlan, Whitehouse.
(Front) Reynolds, Higgins, Reed, Burgess, Jones, Jordan

# SEASON 1934-35 Division 3(South)

| | Date | Opposition | Res. | Att. | Goalscorers |
|---|---|---|---|---|---|
| 1 | 25 Aug | Exeter City | 1-0 | 8295 | Bird |
| 2 | 27 | BOURNEMOUTH & B.A. | 6-1 | 7651 | Bird(2), Burgess(2), Higgins, Green |
| 3 | 1 Sep | BRISTOL CITY | 2-0 | 10978 | Higgins, Bird |
| 4 | 6 | Bournemouth & B.A. | 1-3 | 5722 | Bird |
| 5 | 8 | Millwall | 0-2 | 16142 | |
| 6 | 15 | COVENTRY CITY | 2-1 | 10580 | Bird, Weaver |
| 7 | 22 | Clapton Orient | 0-4 | 4715 | |
| 8 | 29 | GILLINGHAM | 2-2 | 5460 | Bird(2) |
| 9 | 6 Oct | Reading | 1-3 | 8074 | Bird |
| 10 | 13 | NORTHAMPTON TOWN | 1-3 | 6365 | Bird |
| 11 | 20 | BRIGHTON & H.A. | 1-0 | 3696 | King(og) |
| 12 | 27 | Cardiff City | 4-3 | 16131 | Whitehouse, Green, Burgess, Weaver |
| 13 | 3 Nov | BRISTOL ROVERS | 1-1 | 7146 | Bird |
| 14 | 10 | Southend United | 1-0 | 5498 | Bird |
| 15 | 17 | TORQUAY UNITED | 1-4 | 6185 | Bird |
| 16 | 1 Dec | CRYSTAL PALACE | 2-3 | 4317 | Thomas, Cook |
| 17 | 8 | Charlton Athletic | 0-6 | 10186 | |
| 18 | 15 | ALDERSHOT | 2-0 | 3155 | Bird, White |
| 19 | 22 | Swindon Town | 0-0 | 6121 | |
| 20 | 25 | WATFORD | 0-1 | 7290 | |
| 21 | 26 | Watford | 0-7 | 11695 | |
| 22 | 29 | EXETER CITY | 1-3 | 4174 | Bird |
| 23 | 5 Jan | Bristol City | 1-2 | 8968 | Thomas |
| 24 | 12 | Q.P.Rangers | 1-4 | 4511 | Burgess |
| 25 | 19 | MILLWALL | 1-2 | 2948 | White |
| 26 | 26 | Coventry City | 0-5 | 11525 | |
| 27 | 2 Feb | CLAPTON ORIENT | 3-3 | 2738 | Clarke(2), Bird |
| 28 | 9 | Gillingham | 0-5 | 3689 | |
| 29 | 23 | Northampton Town | 0-2 | 2925 | |
| 30 | 28 | READING | 2-2 | 2399 | Weaver(2) |
| 31 | 2 Mar | Brighton & H.A. | 1-3 | 5687 | Reynolds |
| 32 | 9 | CARDIFF CITY | 4-0 | 8461 | Weaver(2), Clarke(2) |
| 33 | 16 | Bristol Rovers | 3-5 | 6306 | Burgess, Perks, Clarke |
| 34 | 23 | SOUTHEND UNITED | 0-5 | 3005 | |
| 35 | 30 | Torquay United | 1-2 | 2941 | White |
| 36 | 6 Apr | Q.P.RANGERS | 2-1 | 2912 | Weaver, Haycox |
| 37 | 13 | Crystal Palace | 0-6 | 8323 | |
| 38 | 19 | LUTON TOWN | 2-4 | 4052 | Haycox(2) |
| 39 | 20 | CHARLTON ATHLETIC | 0-2 | 3287 | |
| 40 | 22 | Luton Town | 1-4 | 8759 | Weaver |
| 41 | 27 | Aldershot | 2-3 | 2810 | Thomas(2) |
| 42 | 4 May | SWINDON TOWN | 1-2 | 2110 | Thomas |

## F.A.Cup

| | | | | | |
|---|---|---|---|---|---|
| 1 | 24 Nov | Swindon Town | 0-4 | 12776 | |

| Player | League | | F.A.Cup | | Total | |
|---|---|---|---|---|---|---|
| | App | Gls. | App | Gls. | App | Gls. |
| Bird A. | 29 | 16 | 1 | 0 | 31 | 17 |
| Burgess J.W. | 39 | 5 | 1 | 0 | 41 | 5 |
| Clarke A.W. | 15 | 5 | – | – | 15 | 5 |
| Cook E.J. | 4 | 1 | – | – | 5 | 1 |
| Davies J.H. | 17 | 0 | – | – | 18 | 0 |
| Emery. H.J. | 37 | 0 | 1 | 0 | 40 | 0 |
| Green T.F. | 13 | 2 | – | – | 14 | 2 |
| Haycox J.H. | 11 | 3 | – | – | 11 | 3 |
| Higgins A.K. | 6 | 2 | – | – | 6 | 2 |
| Kitson G. | 6 | 0 | 1 | 0 | 7 | 0 |
| Lawson T. | 11 | 0 | – | – | 11 | 0 |
| Litherland E.H. | 1 | 0 | – | – | 1 | 0 |
| McKenzie Fred.T | 22 | 0 | 1 | 0 | 23 | 0 |
| McLaughlan H.M. | 27 | 0 | 1 | 0 | 30 | 0 |
| Morgan H.H. | 4 | 0 | – | – | 4 | 0 |
| Odell G.W. | 24 | 0 | 1 | 0 | 25 | 0 |
| Paget W.S.T. | 6 | 0 | – | – | 8 | 0 |
| Parsons J.W. | 4 | 0 | – | – | 4 | 0 |
| Perks H. | 8 | 1 | – | – | 9 | 1 |
| Reynolds W. | 18 | 1 | 1 | 0 | 20 | 2 |
| Robinson R. | 30 | 0 | 1 | 0 | 33 | 0 |
| Russell G.H. | 16 | 0 | – | – | 17 | 0 |
| Simmonds | – | – | – | – | 1 | 0 |
| Thomas W.R. | 36 | 5 | 1 | 0 | 38 | 5 |
| Weaver R.W. | 29 | 8 | – | – | 31 | 8 |
| White W.W. | | | | | | |
| Whitehouse C.H. | 25 | 1 | – | – | 26 | 1 |
| Williamson D.L. | 5 | 0 | – | – | 5 | 0 |
| Own Goals | | | | | | |

### Bottom positions only given

| | | P | W | D | L | F | A | Pts |
|---|---|---|---|---|---|---|---|---|
| 7 | Northampton | 42 | 19 | 8 | 15 | 65 | 67 | 46 |
| 8 | Bristol Rovers | 42 | 17 | 10 | 15 | 73 | 77 | 44 |
| 9 | Brighton | 42 | 17 | 9 | 16 | 69 | 62 | 43 |
| 10 | Torquay | 42 | 18 | 6 | 18 | 81 | 75 | 42 |
| 11 | Exeter | 42 | 16 | 9 | 17 | 70 | 75 | 41 |
| 12 | Millwall | 42 | 17 | 7 | 18 | 57 | 62 | 41 |
| 13 | QPR | 42 | 16 | 9 | 17 | 63 | 72 | 41 |
| 14 | Clapton Orient | 42 | 15 | 10 | 17 | 65 | 65 | 40 |
| 15 | Bristol City | 42 | 15 | 9 | 18 | 52 | 68 | 39 |
| 16 | Swindon | 42 | 13 | 12 | 17 | 67 | 78 | 38 |
| 17 | Bournemouth | 42 | 15 | 7 | 20 | 54 | 71 | 37 |
| 18 | Aldershot | 42 | 13 | 10 | 19 | 50 | 75 | 36 |
| 19 | Cardiff | 42 | 13 | 9 | 20 | 62 | 82 | 35 |
| 20 | Gillingham | 42 | 11 | 13 | 18 | 55 | 75 | 35 |
| 21 | Southend | 42 | 11 | 9 | 22 | 65 | 78 | 31 |
| 22 | Newport | 42 | 10 | 5 | 27 | 54 | 112 | 25 |

(Back) McKenzie, Parsons, McLaughlan, Emery, Cook, Bird, Robinson
(Front) Haycox, Davies, White, Reynolds, Burgess, Litherland, Kitson

# SEASON 1935-36 Division 3(South)

| | Date | Opposition | Res. | Att. | Goalscorers |
|---|---|---|---|---|---|
| 1 | 31 Aug | SWINDON TOWN | 2-2 | 11408 | Green, Smith |
| 2 | 4 Sep | Bristol City | 2-1 | 14933 | Green, McKay |
| 3 | 7 | Coventry City | 1-7 | 17138 | Thomas |
| 4 | 9 | BRISTOL CITY | 2-0 | 7885 | McKay, White |
| 5 | 14 | CARDIFF CITY | 0-0 | 15858 | |
| 6 | 16 | Millwall | 2-2 | 3751 | Smith(2) |
| 7 | 21 | EXETER CITY | 2-1 | 8232 | Smith, Thomas |
| 8 | 28 | Brighton & H.A. | 1-7 | 7246 | Green |
| 9 | 5 Oct | Q.P.RANGERS | 3-4 | 6033 | Burgess(2), Parle |
| 10 | 12 | Watford | 5-2 | 8110 | Smith(3), Parle(2) |
| 11 | 19 | Gillingham | 0-3 | 5025 | |
| 12 | 26 | BOURNEMOUTH & B.A. | 0-0 | 6320 | |
| 13 | 2 Nov | Luton Town | 0-7 | 10085 | |
| 14 | 9 | READING | 1-5 | 6471 | McKay |
| 15 | 16 | Bristol Rovers | 0-3 | 7698 | |
| 16 | 23 | CLAPTON ORIENT | 2-3 | 4724 | Thomas, Derrick |
| 17 | 7 Dec | NORTHAMPTON TOWN | 5-1 | 3780 | Derrick(3), Burgess(2) |
| 18 | 18 | Crystal Palace | 0-6 | 2165 | |
| 19 | 25 | TORQUAY UNITED | 1-6 | 5459 | Burgess |
| 20 | 26 | Torquay United | 2-3 | 5233 | Parle(2) |
| 21 | 28 | Swindon Town | 1-1 | 5629 | D.Jones |
| 22 | 4 Jan | COVENTRY CITY | 2-1 | 5166 | Derrick, Parle |
| 23 | 18 | Cardiff City | 0-2 | 10981 | |
| 24 | 22 | Southend United | 2-1 | 3328 | Smith, Appleby |
| 25 | 25 | Exeter City | 3-3 | 3688 | Derrick(2), Appleby |
| 26 | 1 Feb | BRIGHTON & H.A. | 0-2 | 4751 | |
| 27 | 8 | Q.P.Rangers | 1-1 | 10419 | Derrick |
| 28 | 15 | WATFORD | 0-5 | 5405 | |
| 29 | 27 | NOTTS COUNTY | 1-2 | 2818 | Thomas |
| 30 | 29 | Reading | 1-2 | 5607 | Appleby |
| 31 | 7 Mar | CRYSTAL PALACE | 2-5 | 3232 | Thomas, Derrick |
| 32 | 14 | Bournemouth & B.A. | 0-2 | 5396 | |
| 33 | 19 | GILLINGHAM | 4-2 | 2515 | Parle(2), Smith, Thomas |
| 34 | 21 | BRISTOL ROVERS | 1-0 | 5890 | Smith |
| 35 | 28 | Clapton Orient | 0-4 | 7449 | |
| 36 | 4 Apr | SOUTHEND UNITED | 3-1 | 3445 | Clarke(2), Thomas |
| 37 | 10 | Aldershot | 1-1 | 6239 | Derrick |
| 38 | 11 | Northampton Town | 0-3 | 5219 | |
| 39 | 13 | ALDERSHOT | 1-1 | 5368 | Derrick |
| 40 | 18 | LUTON TOWN | 0-2 | 6356 | |
| 41 | 25 | Notts County | 2-6 | 2180 | Derrick(2), |
| 42 | 2 May | MILLWALL | 4-1 | 2617 | Derrick(2), Appleby, Thomas |

## F.A.Cup

| | Date | Opposition | Res. | Att. | Goalscorers |
|---|---|---|---|---|---|
| 1 | 30 Nov | SOUTHEND UNITED | 0-1 | 4000 | |

| Player | League | | F.A.Cup | | Total | |
|---|---|---|---|---|---|---|
| | App | Gls. | App | Gls. | App | Gls. |
| Appleby T.A. | 12 | 4 | – | – | 14 | 4 |
| Briggs A.L. | 40 | 0 | – | – | 42 | 0 |
| Burgess J.W. | 35 | 5 | 1 | 0 | 38 | 5 |
| Calder R. | 14 | 0 | 1 | 0 | 16 | 0 |
| Clarke A.W. | 11 | 2 | – | – | 11 | 2 |
| Craven J.G. | 28 | 0 | – | – | 29 | 0 |
| Davies J.H. | 19 | 0 | 1 | 0 | 21 | 0 |
| Derrick A.E. | 26 | 15 | 1 | 0 | 28 | 15 |
| Green T.F | 6 | 3 | 1 | 0 | 7 | 3 |
| Helsby T | 10 | 0 | – | – | 11 | 0 |
| Jenkins E.J. | 34 | 0 | 1 | 0 | 37 | 0 |
| Jones D.G. | 15 | 1 | – | – | 15 | 1 |
| Jones T.R.B. | 11 | 0 | – | – | 11 | 0 |
| Kelso J. | 42 | 0 | 1 | 0 | 45 | 0 |
| Lewis D.R. | 10 | 0 | – | – | 10 | 0 |
| McKay R. | 16 | 3 | 1 | 0 | 18 | 3 |
| O'Mahoney M.T. | 8 | 0 | – | – | 8 | 0 |
| Parle J.J. | 35 | 8 | 1 | 0 | 37 | 8 |
| Pritchard A. | 2 | 0 | – | – | 2 | 0 |
| Rennie A. | 3 | 0 | – | – | 3 | 0 |
| Sadler J. | 2 | 0 | – | – | 2 | 0 |
| Smith J. | 26 | 10 | – | – | 28 | 10 |
| Thomas W.R. | 29 | 8 | 1 | 0 | 31 | 8 |
| White F. | 17 | 1 | – | – | 18 | 1 |
| Whitehouse C.H. | 9 | 0 | – | – | 10 | 0 |
| Williamson D.L. | 2 | 0 | 1 | 0 | 3 | 0 |

Bottom positions only given

| | | P | W | D | L | F | A | Pts |
|---|---|---|---|---|---|---|---|---|
| 8 | Bournemouth | 42 | 16 | 11 | 15 | 60 | 56 | 43 |
| 9 | Notts County | 42 | 15 | 12 | 15 | 60 | 57 | 42 |
| 10 | Torquay | 42 | 16 | 9 | 17 | 62 | 62 | 41 |
| 11 | Aldershot | 42 | 14 | 12 | 16 | 53 | 61 | 40 |
| 12 | Millwall | 42 | 14 | 12 | 16 | 58 | 71 | 40 |
| 13 | Bristol City | 42 | 15 | 10 | 17 | 48 | 59 | 40 |
| 14 | Clapton Orient | 42 | 16 | 6 | 20 | 55 | 61 | 38 |
| 15 | Northampton | 42 | 15 | 8 | 19 | 62 | 90 | 38 |
| 16 | Gillingham | 42 | 14 | 9 | 19 | 66 | 77 | 37 |
| 17 | Bristol Rovers | 42 | 14 | 9 | 19 | 69 | 95 | 37 |
| 18 | Southend | 42 | 13 | 10 | 19 | 61 | 62 | 36 |
| 19 | Swindon | 42 | 14 | 8 | 20 | 64 | 73 | 36 |
| 20 | Cardiff | 42 | 13 | 10 | 19 | 60 | 73 | 36 |
| 21 | Newport | 42 | 11 | 9 | 22 | 60 | 111 | 31 |
| 22 | Exeter | 42 | 8 | 11 | 23 | 59 | 93 | 27 |

(Back) Whitehouse, Martin (Trainer), Calder, Briggs, Kelso, Helsby, Page (Manager)
(Front) Derrick, Pritchard, Smith, Parle, Thomas, Davies.

# SEASON 1936-37 Division 3(South)

| | Date | Opposition | Res. | Att. | Goalscorers |
|---|------|-----------|------|------|-------------|
| 1 | 29 Aug | WATFORD | 1-3 | 10267 | Hickman |
| 2 | 2 Sep | Brighton & H.A. | 0-2 | 7738 | |
| 3 | 5 | Southend United | 2-9 | 7346 | Lowry, Hickman |
| 4 | 10 | BRIGHTON & H.A. | 1-4 | 7005 | Thomas |
| 5 | 12 | CARDIFF CITY | 2-3 | 16732 | W.M.Owen(2) |
| 6 | 16 | Bristol Rovers | 1-1 | 10524 | Crisp |
| 7 | 19 | GILLINGHAM | 0-0 | 8436 | |
| 8 | 26 | Aldershot | 0-2 | 3947 | |
| 9 | 3 Oct | SWINDON TOWN | 1-1 | 6084 | Edwards |
| 10 | 10 | Millwall | 2-7 | 21333 | Hickman(2) |
| 11 | 17 | Crystal Palace | 1-6 | 14882 | Chadwick |
| 12 | 24 | EXETER CITY | 2-0 | 10428 | Carr, Sullivan |
| 13 | 31 | Reading | 4-4 | 4880 | Chadwick(2), Lowry, Carr |
| 14 | 7 Nov | Q.P.RANGERS | 1-2 | 10267 | Chadwick |
| 15 | 14 | Bristol City | 1-3 | 14467 | Carr |
| 16 | 21 | TORQUAY UNITED | 1-1 | 8650 | Derrick |
| 17 | 5 Dec | CLAPTON ORIENT | 1-1 | 8667 | Chadwick |
| 18 | 19 | LUTON TOWN | 2-1 | 7654 | Wood, Duggan |
| 19 | 25 | Northampton Town | 2-3 | 12371 | Chadwick, Duggan |
| 20 | 26 | Watford | 0-3 | 8140 | |
| 21 | 28 | NORTHAMPTON TOWN | 1-3 | 8756 | Wood |
| 22 | 2 Jan | SOUTHEND UNITED | 6-2 | 4754 | Chadwick(3), Wood(2), Duggan |
| 23 | 9 | Cardiff City | 1-0 | 24681 | Duggan |
| 24 | 16 | Notts County | 1-3 | 10914 | Sullivan |
| 25 | 23 | Gillingham | 4-4 | 6125 | Derrick(3), Kelso |
| 26 | 30 | ALDERSHOT | 4-0 | 4292 | Derrick(2), Carr, Sullivan |
| 27 | 6 Feb | Swindon Town | 2-1 | 7872 | Sullivan, Wood |
| 28 | 13 | MILLWALL | 1-2 | 9369 | Sullivan |
| 29 | 20 | CRYSTAL PALACE | 1-1 | 8319 | Carr |
| 30 | 27 | Exeter City | 1-3 | 4117 | Derrick |
| 31 | 6 Mar | READING | 3-0 | 8449 | Chadwick(3) |
| 32 | 13 | Q.P.Rangers | 2-6 | 11738 | Duggan, Derrick |
| 33 | 20 | BRISTOL CITY | 0-0 | 8749 | |
| 34 | 26 | BOURNEMOUTH & B.A. | 4-0 | 10007 | Derrick(2) Duggan, Wood |
| 35 | 27 | Torquay United | 2-1 | 4212 | Chadwick(2) |
| 36 | 29 | Bournemouth & B.A. | 0-5 | 9373 | |
| 37 | 3 Apr | NOTTS COUNTY | 2-0 | 12324 | Wood, Derrick |
| 38 | 10 | Clapton Orient | 2-1 | 6054 | Thomas, Wood |
| 39 | 17 | WALSALL | 1-2 | 9238 | Thomas |
| 40 | 24 | Luton Town | 0-5 | 14469 | |
| 41 | 26 | Walsall | 2-1 | 2760 | Webb, Wood |
| 42 | 1 May | BRISTOL ROVERS | 2-2 | 6143 | Derrick, Sullivan |

| Player | League | | F.A.Cup | | Total | |
|--------|--------|------|---------|------|-------|------|
| | App | Gls. | App | Gls. | App | Gls. |
| Appleby T.A. | 2 | 0 | – | – | 2 | 0 |
| Bowles J.C. | 4 | 0 | – | – | 6 | 0 |
| Carr L.L. | 25 | 5 | 2 | 0 | 29 | 6 |
| Chadwick F.W. | 22 | 14 | 2 | 1 | 27 | 17 |
| Clarke A.W. | 3 | 0 | – | – | 3 | 0 |
| Crisp G.H. | 10 | 1 | – | – | 12 | 3 |
| Derrick A.E. | 23 | 12 | 2 | 0 | 29 | 19 |
| Duggan H.A. | 32 | 6 | 2 | 3 | 36 | 9 |
| Edwards L. | 40 | 1 | 1 | 0 | 43 | 1 |
| Ellis B.R. | 1 | 0 | – | – | 1 | 0 |
| Hall G.W.E. | 28 | 0 | – | – | 31 | 0 |
| Hickman J.E.A.W. | 6 | 4 | – | – | 7 | 4 |
| Hillier E.J.G. | 22 | 0 | 2 | 0 | 24 | 0 |
| John W.R. | 10 | 0 | – | – | 11 | 0 |
| Kelso J. | 37 | 1 | 2 | 0 | 42 | 1 |
| Lawrance R.S. | 5 | 0 | – | – | 6 | 0 |
| Low N.H. | 28 | 0 | 2 | 0 | 33 | 0 |
| Lowry S.H. | 14 | 2 | – | – | 15 | 2 |
| Marsh F.J. | 6 | 0 | – | – | 7 | 0 |
| Owen W.(M) | 15 | 2 | – | – | 17 | 2 |
| Pritchard A. | 2 | 0 | – | – | 2 | 0 |
| Richards D. | 1 | 0 | – | – | 1 | 0 |
| Sullivan M.J. | 23 | 6 | 2 | 1 | 26 | 7 |
| Thomas W.R. | 10 | 3 | – | – | 11 | 3 |
| Vickers J. | 19 | 0 | 2 | 0 | 22 | 0 |
| Webb H. | 32 | 1 | 2 | 0 | 38 | 2 |
| Williams B.D. | 18 | 0 | – | – | 20 | 0 |
| Wood T. | 24 | 9 | 1 | 0 | 27 | 11 |

## F.A.Cup

| | Date | Opposition | Res. | Att. | Goalscorers |
|---|------|-----------|------|------|-------------|
| 1 | 28 Nov | BRISTOL CITY | 3-0 | 11165 | Chadwick, Duggan, Sullivan |
| 2 | 12 Dec | Reading | 2-7 | 10790 | Duggan(2) |

Bottom positions only given

| | | P | W | D | L | F | A | Pts |
|---|---|---|---|---|---|---|---|-----|
| 8 | Millwall | 42 | 18 | 10 | 14 | 64 | 54 | 46 |
| 9 | QPR | 42 | 18 | 9 | 15 | 73 | 52 | 45 |
| 10 | Southend | 42 | 17 | 11 | 14 | 78 | 67 | 45 |
| 11 | Gillingham | 42 | 18 | 8 | 16 | 52 | 66 | 44 |
| 12 | Clapton Orient | 42 | 14 | 15 | 13 | 52 | 52 | 43 |
| 13 | Swindon | 42 | 14 | 11 | 17 | 75 | 73 | 39 |
| 14 | Crystal Palace | 42 | 13 | 12 | 17 | 62 | 61 | 38 |
| 15 | Bristol Rovers | 42 | 16 | 4 | 22 | 71 | 80 | 36 |
| 16 | Bristol City | 42 | 15 | 6 | 21 | 58 | 70 | 36 |
| 17 | Walsall | 42 | 13 | 10 | 19 | 62 | 84 | 36 |
| 18 | Cardiff | 42 | 14 | 7 | 21 | 54 | 87 | 35 |
| 19 | Newport | 42 | 12 | 10 | 20 | 67 | 98 | 34 |
| 20 | Torquay | 42 | 11 | 10 | 21 | 57 | 80 | 32 |
| 21 | Exeter | 42 | 10 | 12 | 20 | 59 | 88 | 32 |
| 22 | Aldershot | 42 | 7 | 9 | 26 | 50 | 89 | 23 |

Ben Williams and the lads in 'civvies' at Somerton Park.
At the time hands in trouser pockets were compulsory!

## SEASON 1937-38 Division 3(South)

| | Date | Opposition | Res. | Att. | Goalscorers |
|---|---|---|---|---|---|
| 1 | 28 Aug | EXETER CITY | 2-2 | 13597 | Wood, Hickman |
| 2 | 1 Sep | Gillingham | 0-1 | 6295 | |
| 3 | 4 | Swindon Town | 2-3 | 10958 | Derrick, Wood |
| 4 | 9 | GILLINGHAM | 2-0 | 5662 | H.Webb, Sullivan |
| 5 | 11 | ALDERSHOT | 4-0 | 10546 | Derrick(2), Duggan, H.Webb |
| 6 | 13 | Walsall | 1-3 | 3621 | Duggan |
| 7 | 18 | Millwall | 0-4 | 23061 | |
| 8 | 25 | READING | 2-2 | 11510 | Derrick, Wood |
| 9 | 2 Oct | Crystal Palace | 0-3 | 15362 | |
| 10 | 9 | NOTTS COUNTY | 3-0 | 11574 | Wood(2), Derrick |
| 11 | 16 | CARDIFF CITY | 1-1 | 24268 | Derrick |
| 12 | 23 | Bournemouth & B.A. | 1-1 | 4741 | Hickman |
| 13 | 30 | BRIGHTON & H.A. | 1-0 | 7999 | Derrick |
| 14 | 6 Nov | Q.P.Rangers | 0-0 | 11558 | |
| 15 | 13 | SOUTHEND UNITED | 2-0 | 9295 | Hickman(2) |
| 16 | 20 | Clapton Orient | 2-0 | 6702 | Duggan, Hickman |
| 17 | 4 Dec | Mansfield Town | 1-1 | 2946 | W.M.Owen |
| 18 | 18 | Northampton Town | 0-2 | 4989 | |
| 19 | 25 | Watford | 0-3 | 7473 | |
| 20 | 27 | WATFORD | 0-0 | 13820 | |
| 21 | 1 Jan | Exeter City | 0-2 | 5655 | |
| 22 | 13 | TORQUAY UNITED | 0-2 | 3713 | |
| 23 | 15 | SWINDON TOWN | 2-0 | 4340 | Wood(2) |
| 24 | 22 | Aldershot | 0-5 | 4032 | |
| 25 | 29 | MILLWALL | 3-1 | 7406 | Hickman, Derrick, W.E.Owen |
| 26 | 3 Feb | Reading | 1-2 | 9136 | Chadwick |
| 27 | 12 | CRYSTAL PALACE | 0-0 | 7933 | |
| 28 | 19 | Notts County | 1-1 | 12843 | Chadwick |
| 29 | 26 | Cardiff City | 1-3 | 25608 | Wood |
| 30 | 5 Mar | BOURNEMOUTH & B.A. | 1-1 | 8285 | Hickman |
| 31 | 12 | Brighton & H.A. | 0-1 | 9345 | |
| 32 | 19 | Q.P.RANGERS | 1-1 | 10225 | James(og) |
| 33 | 26 | Southend United | 2-0 | 5570 | Chadwick(2) |
| 34 | 2 Apr | CLAPTON ORIENT | 3-1 | 7085 | Wood, W.E.Owen, Chadwick |
| 35 | 9 | Torquay United | 0-0 | 3994 | |
| 36 | 15 | Bristol City | 0-0 | 26907 | |
| 37 | 16 | MANSFIELD TOWN | 1-0 | 8087 | Hickman |
| 38 | 18 | BRISTOL CITY | 0-0 | 17008 | |
| 39 | 23 | Bristol Rovers | 0-2 | 6492 | |
| 40 | 30 | NORTHAMPTON TOWN | 0-0 | 4436 | |
| 41 | 5 May | BRISTOL ROVERS | 2-2 | 3671 | W.M.owen, Sullivan |
| 42 | 7 | WALSALL | 1-2 | 3766 | Hickman |

### F.A.Cup

| | Date | Opposition | Res. | Att. | Goalscorers |
|---|---|---|---|---|---|
| 1 | 27 Nov | Kidderminster H. | 2-2 | 6353 | H.Webb, Derrick |
| 1R | 3 Dec | KIDDERMINSTER H. | 4-1 | 7300 | J.Brinton(3), Duggan |
| 2 | 11 | BOURNEMOUTH & B.A. | 2-1 | 10500 | Duggan, Derrick |
| 3 | 8 Jan | Bradford Park Avenue | 4-7 | 11000 | Duggan, Hickman, W.M.Owen, Derrick |

| Player | League | | F.A.Cup | | Total | |
|---|---|---|---|---|---|---|
| | App | Gls | App | Gls | App | Gls |
| Brinton E.J. | 36 | 0 | 2 | 0 | 41 | 0 |
| Brinton J.V. | 6 | 0 | 2 | 3 | 9 | 3 |
| Brown | – | – | – | – | 1 | 0 |
| Chadwick F.W. | 18 | 5 | 2 | 0 | 24 | 6 |
| Derrick A.E. | 37 | 8 | 4 | 3 | 45 | 11 |
| Duggan H.A. | 26 | 3 | 4 | 3 | 32 | 7 |
| Edwards D.S. | 2 | 0 | – | – | 2 | 0 |
| Edwards L. | 1 | 0 | – | – | 2 | 0 |
| Ellis B.R. | 1 | 0 | – | – | 1 | 0 |
| Foote E. | 1 | 0 | – | – | 1 | 0 |
| Hickman J.E.A.W. | 29 | 9 | 2 | 1 | 35 | 12 |
| Kelso J. | 40 | 0 | 4 | 0 | 46 | 0 |
| Lawrance R.S. | 26 | 0 | 3 | 0 | 31 | 0 |
| Low N.H. | 38 | 0 | 4 | 0 | 47 | 0 |
| Mogford R.W.G. | – | – | – | – | 2 | 0 |
| Owen W.(E) | 34 | 2 | 2 | 0 | 39 | 4 |
| Owen W.(M) | 22 | 2 | 3 | 1 | 29 | 5 |
| Parkin R. | – | – | – | – | 1 | 0 |
| Pearson H. | 42 | 0 | 4 | 0 | 50 | 0 |
| Sullivan M.J. | 15 | 2 | – | – | 16 | 2 |
| Webb H. | 22 | 2 | 4 | 1 | 28 | 3 |
| Webb J.A. | 20 | 0 | – | – | 23 | 0 |
| Wheeler J.A. | 7 | 0 | – | – | 9 | 0 |
| Wood T. | 39 | 9 | 4 | 0 | 47 | 12 |
| Own Goals | | 1 | | | | 1 |

Bottom positions only given

| | | P | W | D | L | F | A | Pts |
|---|---|---|---|---|---|---|---|---|
| 8 | Swindon | 42 | 17 | 10 | 15 | 49 | 49 | 44 |
| 9 | Northampton | 42 | 17 | 9 | 16 | 51 | 57 | 43 |
| 10 | Cardiff | 42 | 15 | 12 | 15 | 67 | 54 | 42 |
| 11 | Notts County | 42 | 16 | 9 | 17 | 50 | 50 | 41 |
| 12 | Southend | 42 | 15 | 10 | 17 | 70 | 68 | 40 |
| 13 | Bournemouth | 42 | 14 | 12 | 16 | 56 | 57 | 40 |
| 14 | Mansfield | 42 | 15 | 9 | 18 | 62 | 67 | 39 |
| 15 | Bristol Rovers | 42 | 13 | 13 | 16 | 46 | 61 | 39 |
| 16 | Newport | 42 | 11 | 16 | 15 | 43 | 52 | 38 |
| 17 | Exeter | 42 | 13 | 12 | 17 | 57 | 70 | 38 |
| 18 | Aldershot | 42 | 15 | 5 | 22 | 39 | 59 | 35 |
| 19 | Clapton Orient | 42 | 13 | 7 | 22 | 42 | 61 | 33 |
| 20 | Torquay | 42 | 9 | 12 | 21 | 38 | 73 | 30 |
| 21 | Walsall | 42 | 11 | 7 | 24 | 52 | 88 | 29 |
| 22 | Gillingham | 42 | 10 | 6 | 26 | 36 | 77 | 26 |

(Back) Bowsher (Trainer), H.Webb, Wheeler, Pearson, B.Williams, Kelso, E.Brinton, Low
(Front) Duggan, Wood, Derrick, Wright (Chairman), Sullivan, J.Brinton, Lawrance.

# SEASON 1938-39 Division 3(South)

| | Date | Opposition | Res. | Att. | Goalscorers |
|---|---|---|---|---|---|
| 1 | 27 Aug | Clapton Orient | 3-1 | 10596 | Carr, Duggan, Hearty (o.g.) |
| 2 | 29 | Port Vale | 1-2 | 6240 | Hickman |
| 3 | 3 Sep | CARDIFF CITY | 3-0 | 18387 | Hydes(2), Carr |
| 4 | 8 | WATFORD | 1-0 | 8500 | Derrick |
| 5 | 10 | NORTHAMPTON TOWN | 1-1 | 11534 | Hickman |
| 6 | 14 | Watford | 1-1 | 5310 | Derrick |
| 7 | 17 | Notts County | 0-2 | 10834 | |
| 8 | 24 | ALDERSHOT | 1-0 | 9652 | Duggan |
| 9 | 1 Oct | Bristol City | 2-0 | 14497 | Hickman, Duggan |
| 10 | 8 | CRYSTAL PALACE | 2-0 | 10631 | Wood, Derrick |
| 11 | 15 | Ipswich Town | 4-1 | 13843 | Wood(2), Hickman, Derrick |
| 12 | 22 | EXETER CITY | 0-0 | 11423 | |
| 13 | 29 | Bristol Rovers | 0-0 | 12546 | |
| 14 | 5 Nov | BRIGHTON & H.A. | 2-0 | 11290 | Duggan, Derrick |
| 15 | 12 | Bournemouth & B.A. | 1-0 | 7857 | Derrick |
| 16 | 19 | WALSALL | 2-1 | 9870 | Wood(2) |
| 17 | 3 Dec | Q.P.RANGERS | 2-0 | 12338 | Carr, Hydes |
| 18 | 17 | READING | 2-0 | 9870 | Derrick, Hydes |
| 19 | 24 | CLAPTON ORIENT | 2-1 | 9323 | Hydes(2) |
| 20 | 26 | Swindon Town | 0-8 | 9023 | |
| 21 | 27 | SWINDON TOWN | 6-4 | 20586 | Carr(3), Hickman, Hydes, Parkhouse (o.g.) |
| 22 | 31 | Cardiff City | 2-1 | 40187 | Hydes, Carr |
| 23 | 12 Jan | Mansfield Town | 2-0 | 1419 | Hydes, Hickman |
| 24 | 14 | Northampton Town | 0-1 | 9025 | |
| 25 | 22 | Reading | 1-0 | 11292 | Hydes |
| 26 | 28 | Aldershot | 0-1 | 7999 | |
| 27 | 1 Feb | NOTTS COUNTY | 2-1 | 7010 | Brinton, Carr |
| 28 | 4 | BRISTOL CITY | 0-2 | 12436 | |
| 29 | 11 | Crystal Palace | 1-1 | 29155 | Derrick |
| 30 | 18 | IPSWICH TOWN | 3-2 | 12257 | Hydes(2), Wood |
| 31 | 25 | Exeter City | 1-3 | 9370 | Brinton |
| 32 | 4 Mar | BRISTOL ROVERS | 2-0 | 9722 | W.M.Owen, Warren (o.g.) |
| 33 | 11 | Brighton & H.A. | 0-0 | 15157 | |
| 34 | 18 | BOURNEMOUTH & B.A. | 2-2 | 11637 | Carr, Hickman |
| 35 | 25 | Walsall | 1-1 | 7500 | Hydes |
| 36 | 1 Apr | MANSFIELD TOWN | 0-0 | 10600 | |
| 37 | 7 | TORQUAY UNITED | 1-0 | 14677 | Brinton |
| 38 | 8 | Q.P.Rangers | 0-0 | 14864 | |
| 39 | 10 | Torquay United | 1-1 | 6863 | Derrick |
| 40 | 15 | SOUTHEND UNITED | 3-0 | 11397 | Derrick, Hickman, Wood |
| 41 | 29 | PORT VALE | 0-2 | 7260 | |
| 42 | 2 May | Southend United | 0-5 | 2815 | |

## F.A.Cup

| | | | | | |
|---|---|---|---|---|---|
| 1 | 26 Nov | Reading | 3-3 | 19106 | Hydes(2), Derrick |
| 1R | 5 Dec | READING | 3-1 | 10760 | Wood(2), Hydes |
| 2 | 10 | Horden Colliery | 3-2 | 7180 | Wood(2), Hickman |
| 3 | 7 Jan | WALSALL | 0-2 | 9645 | |

| Player | League | | F.A.Cup | | Total | |
|---|---|---|---|---|---|---|
| | App | Gls. | App | Gls. | App | Gls. |
| Brinton E.J. | 39 | 3 | 3 | 0 | 46 | 4 |
| Carr L.L. | 39 | 9 | 4 | 0 | 45 | 9 |
| Derrick A.E. | 39 | 10 | 4 | 1 | 46 | 11 |
| Duggan H.A. | 30 | 4 | 1 | 0 | 34 | 5 |
| Ferguson A. | 41 | 0 | 4 | 0 | 49 | 0 |
| Harvey J.H. | 2 | 0 | – | – | 2 | 0 |
| Hickman J.E.A.W. | 36 | 8 | 4 | 1 | 43 | 9 |
| Higgins A.K. | 2 | 0 | – | – | 3 | 1 |
| Hydes A.J.E. | 27 | 13 | 4 | 3 | 32 | 16 |
| Lawrance R.S. | 7 | 0 | – | – | 9 | 0 |
| Low N.H. | 42 | 0 | 4 | 0 | 48 | 0 |
| Mogford R.W.G. | 1 | 0 | – | – | 3 | 0 |
| Newall D.J. | 1 | 0 | – | – | 1 | 0 |
| Owen W.(E) | 2 | 0 | – | – | 4 | 0 |
| Owen W.(M) | 28 | 1 | 4 | 0 | 36 | 1 |
| Richards L.G. | 30 | 0 | 1 | 0 | 33 | 0 |
| Roberts W.S. | 41 | 0 | 3 | 0 | 45 | 0 |
| Turner C.J. | 1 | 0 | – | – | 1 | 0 |
| Webb J.A. | 13 | 0 | 3 | 0 | 20 | 0 |
| Wheeler J.A. | – | – | 1 | 0 | 2 | 0 |
| Williams D. | – | – | – | – | 2 | 0 |
| Wood T. | 41 | 7 | 4 | 4 | 45 | 11 |
| Wookey K.W. | – | – | – | – | 1 | 0 |
| Own Goals | | 3 | | | | 3 |

| | | P | W | D | L | F | A | Pts |
|---|---|---|---|---|---|---|---|---|
| 1 | Newport | 42 | 22 | 11 | 9 | 58 | 45 | 55 |
| 2 | Crystal Palace | 42 | 20 | 12 | 10 | 71 | 52 | 52 |
| 3 | Brighton | 42 | 19 | 11 | 12 | 68 | 49 | 49 |
| 4 | Watford | 42 | 17 | 12 | 13 | 62 | 51 | 46 |
| 5 | Reading | 42 | 16 | 14 | 12 | 69 | 59 | 46 |
| 6 | QPR | 42 | 15 | 14 | 13 | 68 | 49 | 44 |
| 7 | Ipswich | 42 | 16 | 12 | 14 | 62 | 52 | 44 |
| 8 | Bristol City | 42 | 16 | 12 | 14 | 61 | 63 | 44 |
| 9 | Swindon | 42 | 18 | 8 | 16 | 72 | 77 | 44 |
| 10 | Aldershot | 42 | 16 | 12 | 14 | 53 | 66 | 44 |
| 11 | Notts County | 42 | 17 | 9 | 16 | 59 | 54 | 43 |
| 12 | Southend | 42 | 16 | 9 | 17 | 61 | 64 | 41 |
| 13 | Cardiff | 42 | 15 | 11 | 16 | 61 | 65 | 41 |
| 14 | Exeter | 42 | 13 | 14 | 15 | 65 | 82 | 40 |
| 15 | Bournemouth | 42 | 13 | 13 | 16 | 52 | 58 | 39 |
| 16 | Mansfield | 42 | 12 | 15 | 15 | 44 | 62 | 39 |
| 17 | Northampton | 42 | 15 | 8 | 19 | 51 | 58 | 38 |
| 18 | Port Vale | 42 | 14 | 9 | 19 | 52 | 58 | 37 |
| 19 | Torquay | 42 | 14 | 9 | 19 | 54 | 70 | 37 |
| 20 | Clapton Orient | 42 | 11 | 13 | 18 | 53 | 55 | 35 |
| 21 | Walsall | 42 | 11 | 11 | 20 | 68 | 69 | 33 |
| 22 | Bristol Rovers | 42 | 10 | 13 | 19 | 55 | 61 | 33 |

(Back) Morris, Webb, Hydes, Roberts, Hares.  (Standing) Poyntz (Trainer), Thomas (Res.Trainer), W.M.Owen, Hickman, Lawrence, Ferguson, Reid, Low, Mead, Richards, Thomas (Asst.Sec.), McCandless (Sec./Man.)
(Seated) Dr.Wade (Dir.), Derrick, Wood (Dir.), Duggan, Petty (Chair.), Carr, Wardell (Dir.), Wood, Nixon (Dir.)
(Front) R.Wilcox, Mogford, Harvey, Brinton, Williams, W.E.Owen, Hogg, Cureton, Sockett (Office)

## SEASON 1939/40 Division 2

| | Date | Opposition | Res. | Att. | Goalscorers |
|---|---|---|---|---|---|
| 1 | 26 Aug | SOUTHAMPTON | 3-1 | 13810 | Hydes(2), Hickman |
| 2 | 31 | TOTTENHAM H. | 1-1 | 19700 | Hickman |
| 3 | 1 Sep | Nottingham F. | 1-2 | 9,521 | Hydes |
| | | Football League programme abandoned | | | |

## War League (South-West)

| | Date | Opposition | Res. | Att. | Goalscorers |
|---|---|---|---|---|---|
| 1 | 21 Oct | SWINDON TOWN | 0-2 | 1824 | |
| 2 | 28 | Bristol Rovers | 3-2 | 1186 | Carr (2), Robbins |
| 3 | 4 Nov | Swansea Town | 2-1 | 3000 | Carr, Robbins |
| 4 | 11 | TORQUAY UNITED | 1-0 | 802 | Robbins |
| 5 | 25 | CARDIFF CITY | 3-1 | 2228 | Robbins (3) |
| 6 | 2 Dec | Plymouth A. | 0-2 | 3500 | |
| 7 | 9 | Swindon Town | 1-2 | 3145 | Robbins |
| 8 | 16 | BRISTOL ROVERS | 0-1 | 1752 | |
| 9 | 23 | SWANSEA TOWN | 2-2 | 1000 | Brinton, Hydes |
| 10 | 25 | BRISTOL CITY | 1-1 | 2100 | Robbins |
| 11 | 26 | Bristol City | 3-1 | 2763 | Robbins (2), Carr |
| 12 | 30 | Torquay United | 2-6 | 1000 | Wookey, Carr |
| 13 | 13 Jan | Cardiff City | 0-1 | 4000 | |
| 14 | 10 Feb | Swansea Town | 2-2 | 3000 | Robbins, Higgins |
| 15 | 24 | Bristol City | 2-6 | 1799 | Morgan (o.g.), Roberts (o.g.) |
| 16 | 9 Mar | Plymouth A. | 0-3 | 3800 | |
| 17 | 16 | Swindon Town | 3-3 | 3182 | Wookey, Robbnis, Appleby |
| 18 | 22 | Bristol Rovers | 5-3 | 3240 | Wookey (2), Carr, Robbins, Appleby |
| 19 | 25 | BRISTOL ROVERS | 0-2 | 4179 | |
| 20 | 30 | SWANSEA TOWN | 1-5 | 1200 | Brinton |
| 21 | 6 Apr | Torquay United | 3-4 | 1515 | Brinton, Robbins, Appleby |
| 22 | 4 May | BRISTOL CITY | 4-1 | 2000 | Brinton, Mogford, Robbins, Appleby |
| 23 | 13 | Cardiff City | 1-4 | 2000 | Robbins |
| 24 | 18 | SWINDON TOWN | 5-2 | 600 | Wookey (2), W.M.Owen, W.E.Owen, Appleby |
| 25 | 25 | CARDIFF CITY | 4-1 | 600 | Appleby (2), Wookey, Ballsom (o.g.) |
| 26 | 1 Jun | TORQUAY UNITED | 11-0 | 500 | Appleby(4),W.E.Owen(4),Wookey,Newall,Lawrance |
| 27 | 7 | PLYMOUTH A. | 6-3 | | Appl'y(2),W.M.Owen,Lawrance,Wookey,Anthony(O.G) |
| 28 | 8 | PLYMOUTH A. | 5-2 | | Appleby (3), Webb, Newall |

| Player | F. League | | War Lge. | | Total | |
|---|---|---|---|---|---|---|
| | App | Gls. | App | Gls. | App | Gls. |
| Appleby T.A. | – | – | 13 | 16 | 17 | 17 |
| Ballsom G. | – | – | 1 | 0 | 1 | 0 |
| Brinton E.J. | 3 | 0 | 19 | 4 | 27 | 6 |
| Carr L.L. | – | – | 16 | 6 | 18 | 6 |
| Clarke A.W. | – | – | 4 | 0 | 4 | 0 |
| Duggan H.A. | 3 | 0 | 6 | 0 | 10 | 0 |
| Egan H. | – | – | – | – | 2 | 1 |
| Ferguson A. | 3 | 0 | 28 | 0 | 39 | 0 |
| Ford L. | – | – | 1 | 0 | 1 | 0 |
| Granville A. | – | – | 1 | 0 | 1 | 0 |
| Hares W. | – | – | 5 | 0 | 6 | 0 |
| Hickman J.E.A.W. | 3 | 2 | 8 | 0 | 12 | 2 |
| Higgins A.K. | – | – | 4 | 1 | 6 | 2 |
| Hydes A.J.E. | 3 | 3 | 6 | 1 | 10 | 5 |
| Jewell W. | – | – | 1 | 0 | 1 | 0 |
| Lawrance R.S. | – | – | 5 | 2 | 8 | 2 |
| Low N.H. | 3 | 0 | 24 | 0 | 33 | 0 |
| Mead T. | – | – | 3 | 0 | 3 | 0 |
| Mogford R.W.G. | – | – | 2 | 1 | 2 | 1 |
| Newall D.J. | – | – | 14 | 2 | 20 | 3 |
| O'Reilly T. | – | – | 2 | 0 | 2 | 0 |
| Owen W. (E.) | 3 | 0 | 26 | 5 | 37 | 5 |
| Owen W. (M.) | 3 | 0 | 26 | 2 | 37 | 3 |
| Richards L.G. | 3 | 0 | 19 | 0 | 28 | 0 |
| Robbins W. | – | – | 22 | 16 | 30 | 22 |
| Webb J.A. | 3 | 0 | 27 | 1 | 38 | 1 |
| Wilcox R. | – | – | 9 | 0 | 11 | 0 |
| Williams D. | – | – | 1 | 0 | 1 | 0 |
| Wood T. | 3 | 0 | – | – | 3 | 0 |
| Wookey K.W. | – | – | 15 | 9 | 21 | 11 |
| Own Goals | | | | 4 | | 4 |

N.B. The War League figures are approximate,
due to limited press coverage.

(Back) Menzies (Secretary), Richards, Low, Ferguson, Webb, Robbins, Bowsher (Trainer)
(Front) W.M.Owen, Appleby, Egan, Wookey, Brinton, W.E.Owen.

# SEASON 1945-46 Football League(South)

| | Date | Opposition | Res. | Att. | Goalscorers |
|---|---|---|---|---|---|
| 1 | 25 Aug | Brentford | 1-2 | 12079 | Derrick |
| 2 | 30 | FULHAM | 1-5 | 7538 | Wilkins |
| 3 | 1 Sep | BRENTFORD | 0-5 | 8769 | |
| 4 | 8 | CHELSEA | 1-3 | 11677 | Derrick |
| 5 | 13 | CHARLTON ATHLETIC | 2-1 | 6958 | Derrick, Wilkins |
| 6 | 15 | Chelsea | 0-2 | 20685 | |
| 7 | 22 | Millwall | 0-4 | 16159 | |
| 8 | 29 | MILLWALL | 3-1 | 12735 | Derrick(2), Wilkins |
| 9 | 6 Oct | Southampton | 2-6 | 14483 | Derrick, E Brinton |
| 10 | 13 | SOUTHAMPTON | 0-0 | 14089 | |
| 11 | 20 | Derby County | 1-4 | 16688 | E.Brinton |
| 12 | 27 | DERBY COUNTY | 1-4 | 13118 | W.M.Owen |
| 13 | 3 Nov | LEICESTER CITY | 2-0 | 10045 | Derrick(2) |
| 14 | 10 | Leicester City | 0-2 | 11659 | |
| 15 | 15 | Coventry City | 1-7 | 3146 | Newcombe |
| 16 | 22 | COVENTRY CITY | 1-3 | 4449 | Derrick |
| 17 | 1 Dec | LUTON TOWN | 4-0 | 6553 | Derrick(3), Wookey |
| 18 | 19 | Aston Villa | 2-5 | 12844 | Carr(2) |
| 19 | 22 | ASTON VILLA | 0-4 | 15119 | |
| 20 | 25 | ARSENAL | 1-2 | 13003 | Avery |
| 21 | 26 | Arsenal | 0-7 | 16536 | |
| 22 | 29 | Charlton Athletic | 0-2 | 17173 | |
| 23 | 12 Jan | Plymouth Argyle | 3-0 | 18060 | Carr, Granville, Leamon |
| 24 | 19 | PLYMOUTH ARGYLE | 2-1 | 8179 | Batty, Leamon |
| 25 | 26 | PORTSMOUTH | 4-2 | 8632 | Leamon(2), Wookey, Batty |
| 26 | 2 Feb | Portsmouth | 3-2 | 10261 | Leamon(2), Batty |
| 27 | 16 | NOTTINGHAM FOREST | 2-4 | 11678 | Leamon, Carr |
| 28 | 23 | SWANSEA TOWN | 3-1 | 13415 | Leamon(2), Carr |
| 29 | 2 Mar | Swansea Town | 0-3 | 19485 | |
| 30 | 9 | WOLVERHAMPTON W. | 1-3 | 15339 | Batty |
| 31 | 16 | Wolverhampton W. | 2-5 | 26233 | Granville, Leamon |
| 32 | 23 | West Ham United | 1-4 | 12000 | Granville |
| 33 | 30 | WEST HAM UNITED | 2-2 | 13000 | Leamon(2) |
| 34 | 6 Apr | W.B.ALBION | 0-3 | 14014 | |
| 35 | 13 | W.B.Albion | 0-6 | 18690 | |
| 36 | 19 | Birmingham City | 2-3 | 14220 | Mogford, Carr |
| 37 | 20 | TOTTENHAM HOTSPUR | 1-4 | 13766 | Granville |
| 38 | 22 | BIRMINGHAM CITY | 0-1 | 13410 | |
| 39 | 23 | Nottingham Forest | 2-7 | 7726 | Lucas(2) |
| 40 | 27 | Tottenham Hotspur | 0-1 | 15223 | |
| 41 | 1 May | Luton Town | 0-1 | 9000 | |
| 42 | 4 | Fulham | 1-3 | 15000 | Rawcliffe |

## F.A.Cup

| | Date | Opposition | Res. | Att. | Goalscorers |
|---|---|---|---|---|---|
| 1/1L | 17 Nov | Torquay United | 1-0 | 4000 | Derrick |
| 1/2L | 24 | TORQUAY UNITED | 1-1 | 7178 | Derrick |
| 2/1L | 8 Dec | EXETER CITY | 5-1 | 5606 | Derrick(2), E Brinton, Carr, Wookey |
| 2/2L | 15 | Exeter City | 3-1 | 9000 | Hydes(2), Wilkins |
| 3/1L | 5 Jan | Southampton | 3-4 | 22000 | Derrick, Wookey, Granville |
| 3/2L | 10 | SOUTHAMPTON | 1-2 | 8509 | W.M.Owen |

| Player | League | | F.A.Cup | | Total | |
|---|---|---|---|---|---|---|
| | App | Gls. | App | Gls. | App | Gls. |
| Appleby T.A. | 5 | 0 | – | – | 5 | 0 |
| Avery R. | 15 | 1 | 4 | 0 | 19 | 1 |
| Batty S.G. | 21 | 4 | 2 | 0 | 23 | 4 |
| Boatwright E. | 5 | 0 | 1 | 0 | 6 | 0 |
| Brinton E.J. | 28 | 2 | 5 | 1 | 33 | 3 |
| Brinton J.V. | 3 | 0 | – | – | 3 | 0 |
| Cabrje J. | 2 | 0 | – | – | 2 | 0 |
| Carr L.L. | 30 | 6 | 6 | 1 | 36 | 7 |
| Clarke W.V. | 3 | 0 | 2 | 0 | 5 | 0 |
| Clifford J. | 1 | 0 | – | – | 1 | 0 |
| Dearnley B. | 1 | 0 | – | – | 1 | 0 |
| Derrick A.E. | 20 | 12 | 6 | 5 | 26 | 17 |
| Edwards T. | 1 | 0 | – | – | 1 | 0 |
| Ferguson A. | 35 | 0 | 6 | 0 | 41 | 0 |
| Goldstraw A. | 9 | 0 | – | – | 9 | 0 |
| Granville N.T. | 19 | 4 | 2 | 1 | 21 | 5 |
| Hares W. | 1 | 0 | – | – | 1 | 0 |
| Harris W. | 2 | 0 | – | – | 2 | 0 |
| Howarth S. | 1 | 0 | – | – | 1 | 0 |
| Hydes A.J.E. | 2 | 0 | 1 | 2 | 3 | 2 |
| Jones J. | 1 | 0 | – | – | 1 | 0 |
| Kinnell R. | 1 | 0 | – | – | 1 | 0 |
| Lawrance R.S. | 1 | 0 | – | – | 1 | 0 |
| Leamon F.W. | 16 | 12 | – | – | 16 | 12 |
| Low N.H. | 42 | 0 | 5 | 0 | 47 | 0 |
| Lucas W.H | 3 | 2 | – | – | 3 | 2 |
| McNab A. | 7 | 0 | – | – | 7 | 0 |
| Mead T. | 1 | 0 | 1 | 0 | 2 | 0 |
| Mogford R.W.G. | 7 | 1 | – | – | 7 | 1 |
| Newcombe G. | 9 | 1 | – | – | 9 | 1 |
| Owen W (E) | 3 | 0 | – | – | 3 | 0 |
| Owen W (M) | 41 | 1 | 6 | 1 | 47 | 2 |
| Peacock G. | 3 | 0 | – | – | 3 | 0 |
| Pollard J. | 2 | 0 | – | – | 2 | 0 |
| Rawcliffe F | 1 | 1 | – | – | 1 | 1 |
| Roberts W.S. | 20 | 0 | 2 | 0 | 22 | 0 |
| Shergold E. | 2 | 0 | – | – | 2 | 0 |
| Southam J.H. | 3 | 0 | – | – | 3 | 0 |
| Thomas W. | 11 | 0 | 5 | 0 | 16 | 0 |
| Turner C.J. | 5 | 0 | – | – | 5 | 0 |
| Warhurst F. | 12 | 0 | – | – | 12 | 0 |
| Wayte R. | 2 | 0 | – | – | 2 | 0 |
| Webb J.A. | 8 | 0 | 2 | 0 | 10 | 0 |
| Wilkins R. | 15 | 3 | 4 | 1 | 19 | 4 |
| Williams R. | 3 | 0 | – | – | 3 | 0 |
| Witcomb D.F. | 1 | 0 | – | – | 1 | 0 |
| Wood T. | 3 | 0 | – | – | 3 | 0 |
| Wookey K.W. | 35 | 2 | 6 | 2 | 41 | 4 |

(Back) McCandless (Sec./Manager), Ald. J.R.Wardell (Dir.), W.M.Owen, Roberts, Ferguson, Low, Warhurst, Bowsher (Trainer). (Middle) Wilkins, Derrick, Lt.Col. W.Harold John (Chair.), Brinton, Boatwright. (Front) Wookey, Newcombe.

# SEASON 1946-47    *Division 2*

| | Date | Opposition | Res. | Att. | Goalscorers |
|---|---|---|---|---|---|
| 1 | 7 Sep | Nottingham Forest | 1-6 | 24417 | Leamon |
| 2 | 9 | Burnley | 2-3 | 18008 | Rawcliffe, Keenan |
| 3 | 14 | COVENTRY CITY | 4-2 | 14104 | Wookey(2), Bowen, Leamon |
| 4 | 19 | TOTTENHAM HOTSPUR | 2-4 | 18169 | Bowen, Mogford |
| 5 | 21 | Birmingham City | 1-1 | 28832 | Mogford |
| 6 | 28 | W.B.ALBION | 2-7 | 17614 | Mogford, Davis |
| 7 | 5 Oct | Newcastle United | 0-13 | 52137 | |
| 8 | 7 | Tottenham Hotspur | 1-3 | 14540 | Tickridge (og) |
| 9 | 12 | SWANSEA TOWN | 2-4 | 18715 | Leamon, Carr |
| 10 | 19 | Bury | 1-0 | 13214 | Batty |
| 11 | 24 | SOUTHAMPTON | 1-2 | 11149 | Carr |
| 12 | 26 | LUTON TOWN | 1-3 | 11480 | Carr |
| 13 | 2 Nov | Plymouth Argyle | 1-4 | 23175 | Mogford |
| 14 | 9 | LEICESTER CITY | 2-3 | 12350 | Rawcliffe(2) |
| 15 | 16 | Chesterfield | 0-2 | 12030 | |
| 16 | 23 | MILLWALL | 3-1 | 9742 | Rawcliffe(2), Carr |
| 17 | 30 | Bradford Park Ave | 1-2 | 12555 | Carr |
| 18 | 7 Dec | MANCHESTER CITY | 0-3 | 13641 | |
| 19 | 21 | SHEFFIELD WEDNESDAY | 4-3 | 10680 | Carr(3), Lewis |
| 20 | 25 | FULHAM | 4-2 | 13862 | Rawcliffe(2), Carr, Watson(og) |
| 21 | 26 | Fulham | 1-4 | 20098 | Carr |
| 22 | 28 | Southampton | 1-5 | 17778 | Rawcliffe |
| 23 | 4 Jan | NOTTINGHAM FOREST | 2-5 | 13150 | Carr, Lewis |
| 24 | 18 | Coventry City | 0-6 | 18762 | |
| 25 | 1 Feb | W.B.Albion | 2-2 | 15089 | Carr(2) |
| 26 | 8 | West Ham United | 0-3 | 12447 | |
| 27 | 15 | Swansea Town | 1-5 | 19655 | Williams |
| 28 | 15 Mar | Leicester City | 0-3 | 20455 | |
| 29 | 22 | CHESTERFIELD | 3-0 | 10358 | Rawcliffe, Newall, Carr |
| 30 | 29 | Millwall | 1-3 | 18154 | Carr |
| 31 | 4 Apr | Barnsley | 1-3 | 14999 | Batty |
| 32 | 7 | BARNSLEY | 2-1 | 11013 | Rawcliffe(2) |
| 33 | 19 | WEST HAM UNITED | 1-1 | 12793 | Rawcliffe |
| 34 | 26 | Sheffield Wednesday | 1-2 | 21555 | Carr |
| 35 | 3 May | BURNLEY | 0-3 | 14751 | |
| 36 | 10 | PLYMOUTH ARGYLE | 1-0 | 9181 | Roffi |
| 37 | 17 | BRADFORD PARK AVE | 1-3 | 10159 | Lewis |
| 38 | 24 | BURY | 2-0 | 8875 | Lewis, Roffi |
| 39 | 26 | BIRMINGHAM CITY | 0-3 | 12028 | |
| 40 | 31 | Luton Town | 3-6 | 7814 | Rawcliffe, Carr, Harper |
| 41 | 7 Jun | NEWCASTLE UNITED | 4-2 | 8798 | Carr(2), Rawcliffe, Haddon |
| 42 | 14 | Manchester City | 1-5 | 25431 | Roffi |

## F.A.Cup

| | Date | Opposition | Res. | Att. | Goalscorers |
|---|---|---|---|---|---|
| 3 | 11 Jan | Coventry City | 2-5 | 21457 | Batty, Hayward |

| Player | League | | F.A.Cup | | Total | |
|---|---|---|---|---|---|---|
| | App | Gls. | App | Gls. | App | Gls. |
| Ainge R.P | 5 | 0 | – | – | 5 | 0 |
| Bakewell H. | 8 | 0 | – | – | 8 | 0 |
| Batty S.G. | 26 | 2 | 1 | 1 | 31 | 4 |
| Bowen T.H. | 13 | 2 | – | – | 15 | 2 |
| Boyd J.R. | – | – | – | – | 1 | 0 |
| Brookin W.J. | 2 | 0 | – | – | 4 | 0 |
| Cabrie D. | 9 | 0 | – | – | 11 | 0 |
| Carr E.M. | 33 | 19 | 1 | 0 | 36 | 19 |
| Craddock L.M. | 7 | 0 | – | – | 7 | 0 |
| Davis E. | 3 | 1 | – | – | 3 | 1 |
| Emmanuel D.L. | 6 | 0 | – | – | 6 | 0 |
| Granville N.T. | 1 | 0 | – | – | 1 | 0 |
| Haddon H.L. | 4 | 1 | – | – | 4 | 1 |
| Hammill J. | 5 | 0 | – | – | 5 | 0 |
| Harper R | 19 | 1 | 1 | 0 | 21 | 1 |
| Hayward D.S. | 2 | 0 | 1 | 1 | 4 | 1 |
| Hodge J.O. | 1 | 0 | – | – | 1 | 0 |
| Hogg G.S. | – | – | – | – | 1 | 1 |
| Johnston J. | – | – | – | – | 2 | 0 |
| Jones R. | 17 | 0 | – | – | 18 | 0 |
| Keenan W.G. | 4 | 1 | – | – | 4 | 1 |
| Leamon F.W. | 4 | 3 | – | – | 4 | 3 |
| Lewis I.S. | 23 | 4 | 1 | 0 | 25 | 4 |
| Low N.H | 4 | 0 | – | – | 4 | 0 |
| McBlain A. | 5 | 0 | – | – | 8 | 0 |
| McNab A. | 3 | 0 | – | – | 3 | 0 |
| Mogford R.W.G. | 7 | 4 | – | – | 9 | 7 |
| Newall D.J. | 16 | 1 | 1 | 0 | 20 | 2 |
| Newbold A. | 22 | 0 | 1 | 0 | 23 | 0 |
| Oldham G. | 39 | 0 | – | – | 42 | 0 |
| Owen W.(M) | 4 | 0 | – | – | 4 | 0 |
| Pollard J. | – | – | – | – | 2 | 0 |
| Prangley S. | 7 | 0 | – | – | 7 | 0 |
| Rawcliffe F. | 37 | 14 | – | – | 41 | 17 |
| Roffi G.T. | 7 | 3 | – | – | 8 | 3 |
| Saunders D.F. | 7 | 0 | 1 | 0 | 8 | 0 |
| Smith A.O.S. | 4 | 0 | – | – | 4 | 0 |
| Smith W.V. | 6 | 0 | – | – | 10 | 0 |
| Sneddon W.C. | 18 | 0 | – | – | 20 | 0 |
| Southam J.H. | 8 | 0 | – | – | 8 | 0 |
| Thomas M. | – | – | – | – | 1 | 0 |
| Turner C.J. | 28 | 0 | 1 | 0 | 32 | 0 |
| Wilcox R. | 22 | 0 | 1 | 0 | 26 | 0 |
| Wilkins R. | 1 | 0 | – | – | 1 | 0 |
| Williams H. | 11 | 1 | 1 | 0 | 16 | 1 |
| Wookey K.W. | 14 | 2 | – | – | 14 | 2 |
| Own Goals | | 2 | | | | 3 |

Bottom positions only

| | P | W | D | L | F | A | Pts |
|---|---|---|---|---|---|---|---|
| 19 Plymouth | 42 | 14 | 5 | 23 | 79 | 96 | 33 |
| 20 Sheff Wed | 42 | 12 | 8 | 22 | 67 | 88 | 32 |
| 21 Swansea | 42 | 11 | 7 | 24 | 55 | 83 | 29 |
| 22 Newport | 42 | 10 | 3 | 29 | 61 | 133 | 23 |

(Back)  Newbold, Saunders, Jones, Turner, Oldham, Hayward
(Front) Lewis, Carr, Sneddon, Rawcliffe, Harper

# SEASON 1947-48 Division 3(South)

| | Date | Opposition | Res. | Att. | Goalscorers |
|---|---|---|---|---|---|
| 1 | 23 Aug | Reading | 0-0 | 13890 | |
| 2 | 28 | BRISTOL CITY | 1-0 | 16565 | Batty |
| 3 | 30 | WALSALL | 4-2 | 13591 | Carr(3), Roffi |
| 4 | 3 Sep | Bristol City | 0-1 | 25706 | |
| 5 | 6 | Leyton Orient | 2-2 | 14407 | Williams, Mogford |
| 6 | 11 | BOURNEMOUTH & B.A. | 2-2 | 13977 | Williams, Mogford |
| 7 | 13 | EXETER CITY | 3-0 | 13185 | Williams(2), Harper |
| 8 | 17 | Bournemouth & B.A. | 0-5 | 17391 | |
| 9 | 20 | Swindon Town | 2-1 | 18642 | Shergold, Mogford |
| 10 | 27 | Southend United | 0-1 | 11447 | |
| 11 | 4 Oct | NOTTS COUNTY | 3-1 | 14015 | Williams, Mogford, Emmanuel |
| 12 | 11 | TORQUAY UNITED | 0-1 | 11933 | |
| 13 | 18 | Crystal Palace | 1-2 | 16353 | Williams |
| 14 | 25 | ALDERSHOT | 2-2 | 11506 | Mogford, Emmanuel |
| 15 | 1 Nov | Northampton Town | 1-1 | 9289 | Allen |
| 16 | 8 | BRISTOL ROVERS | 2-2 | 12877 | Emmanuel(2) |
| 17 | 15 | Norwich City | 2-1 | 16072 | Roffi, Allen |
| 18 | 22 | BRIGHTON & H.A. | 1-1 | 5817 | McBlain |
| 19 | 6 Dec | Q.P.RANGERS | 0-0 | 13230 | |
| 20 | 20 | READING | 2-0 | 10161 | Carr, Emmanuel |
| 21 | 25 | IPSWICH TOWN | 3-1 | 12308 | Carr(2), W.Lewis |
| 22 | 27 | Ipswich Town | 0-3 | 11880 | |
| 23 | 3 Jan | Walsall | 1-1 | 16847 | Carr |
| 24 | 10 | Watford | 2-1 | 7427 | Allen, Harper |
| 25 | 17 | LEYTON ORIENT | 3-2 | 10255 | Carr(2), Allen |
| 26 | 24 | Port Vale | 1-4 | 10816 | Roffi |
| 27 | 31 | Exeter City | 4-4 | 9711 | W.Lewis(2), Williams, Johnson(og) |
| 28 | 14 Feb | SOUTHEND UNITED | 1-5 | 10640 | Carr |
| 29 | 21 | Notts County | 1-4 | 17762 | Hayward |
| 30 | 28 | Torquay United | 1-4 | 6235 | Hayward |
| 31 | 6 Mar | CRYSTAL PALACE | 3-1 | 8732 | W.Lewis(2), Allen |
| 32 | 13 | Aldershot | 2-1 | 5792 | Roffi, Shergold |
| 33 | 20 | NORTHAMPTON TOWN | 1-2 | 8567 | Allen |
| 34 | 26 | Swansea Town | 0-3 | 21861 | |
| 35 | 27 | Bristol Rovers | 3-2 | 13607 | Allen(2), Emmanuel |
| 36 | 29 | SWANSEA TOWN | 1-1 | 15134 | W.Lewis |
| 37 | 3 Apr | NORWICH CITY | 1-1 | 8929 | Williams |
| 38 | 8 | SWINDON TOWN | 2-0 | 7421 | Williams, Emmanuel |
| 39 | 10 | Brighton & H.A. | 0-3 | 14247 | |
| 40 | 17 | WATFORD | 3-4 | 8878 | Williams, Roffi, Shergold |
| 41 | 24 | Q.P.Rangers | 0-1 | 20905 | |
| 42 | 1 May | PORT VALE | 0-0 | 8309 | |

## F.A.Cup

| | Date | Opposition | Res. | Att. | Goalscorers |
|---|---|---|---|---|---|
| 1 | 29 Nov | SOUTHEND UNITED | 3-2 | 11050 | Roffi, Lewis, Allen |
| 2 | 13 Dec | Reading | 0-3 | 16000 | |

| Player | League | | F.A.Cup | | Total | |
|---|---|---|---|---|---|---|
| | App | Gls. | App | Gls. | App | Gls. |
| Allen B.W. | 26 | 8 | 2 | 1 | 29 | 9 |
| Aston A.J. | 1 | 0 | – | – | 1 | 0 |
| Batty S.G. | 34 | 1 | 2 | 0 | 37 | 1 |
| Boyd J.R. | 1 | 0 | – | – | 1 | 0 |
| Carr E.M. | 23 | 10 | – | – | 24 | 11 |
| Emmanuel D.L. | 27 | 7 | 2 | 0 | 30 | 7 |
| Haddon H.L. | 3 | 0 | – | – | 3 | 0 |
| Hammill J. | 7 | 0 | – | – | 7 | 0 |
| Harper R. | 28 | 2 | – | – | 29 | 2 |
| Hayward D.S. | 9 | 2 | – | – | 10 | 2 |
| Hodge J.O. | – | – | – | – | 1 | 0 |
| Jones R. | 2 | 0 | – | – | 2 | 0 |
| Joy H.C. | 2 | 0 | – | – | 2 | 0 |
| Lewis I.S. | 4 | 0 | – | – | 4 | 0 |
| Lewis W. | 25 | 6 | 2 | 1 | 28 | 7 |
| Loveman R.K. | 11 | 0 | – | – | 11 | 0 |
| McBlain A. | 29 | 1 | 2 | 0 | 31 | 1 |
| Mogford R.W.G. | 12 | 5 | – | – | 12 | 5 |
| Newall D.J. | 5 | 0 | – | – | 5 | 0 |
| Oldham G. | 24 | 0 | – | – | 24 | 0 |
| Pincott F.C. | 14 | 0 | – | – | 14 | 0 |
| Roffi G.T. | 20 | 5 | 2 | 1 | 22 | 6 |
| Sage F.R. | 1 | 0 | – | – | 1 | 0 |
| Shergold W.R. | 26 | 3 | 2 | 0 | 29 | 3 |
| Smith A.O.S. | 23 | 0 | 2 | 0 | 25 | 0 |
| Smith W.V. | 3 | 0 | – | – | 3 | 0 |
| Sutherland J.C. | 26 | 0 | 2 | 0 | 28 | 0 |
| Turner C.J. | 8 | 0 | | | 9 | 0 |
| Wilcox R. | 40 | 0 | 2 | 0 | 43 | 0 |
| Williams H. | 28 | 10 | 2 | 0 | 30 | 10 |
| Own Goals. | | 1 | | | | 1 |

### Top positions only

| | | P | W | D | L | F | A | Pts |
|---|---|---|---|---|---|---|---|---|
| 1 | QPR | 42 | 26 | 9 | 7 | 74 | 37 | 61 |
| 2 | Bournemouth | 42 | 24 | 9 | 9 | 76 | 35 | 57 |
| 3 | Walsall | 42 | 21 | 9 | 12 | 70 | 40 | 51 |
| 4 | Ipswich | 42 | 23 | 3 | 16 | 67 | 61 | 49 |
| 5 | Swansea | 42 | 18 | 12 | 12 | 70 | 52 | 48 |
| 6 | Notts County | 42 | 19 | 8 | 15 | 68 | 59 | 46 |
| 7 | Bristol City | 42 | 18 | 7 | 17 | 77 | 65 | 43 |
| 8 | Port Vale | 42 | 16 | 11 | 15 | 63 | 54 | 43 |
| 9 | Southend | 42 | 15 | 13 | 14 | 51 | 58 | 43 |
| 10 | Reading | 42 | 15 | 11 | 16 | 56 | 58 | 41 |
| 11 | Exeter | 42 | 15 | 11 | 16 | 55 | 63 | 41 |
| 12 | Newport | 42 | 14 | 13 | 15 | 61 | 73 | 41 |
| 13 | Crystal Palace | 42 | 13 | 13 | 16 | 49 | 49 | 39 |
| 14 | Northampton | 42 | 14 | 11 | 17 | 58 | 72 | 39 |
| 15 | Watford | 42 | 14 | 10 | 18 | 57 | 79 | 38 |
| 16 | Swindon | 42 | 10 | 16 | 16 | 41 | 46 | 36 |
| 17 | Leyton Orient | 42 | 13 | 10 | 19 | 51 | 73 | 36 |

(Back) Joy, Sutherland, Bowen, Smith, Hayward, Emmanuel
(Front) Williams, W.Lewis, Wilcox, Allen, Harper

## SEASON 1948–49 Division 3(South)

| | Date | Opposition | Res. | Att. | Goalscorers |
|---|---|---|---|---|---|
| 1 | 21 Aug | BOURNEMOUTH & B.A. | 1-2 | 11015 | Parker |
| 2 | 25 | Watford | 2-2 | 10568 | Carr, Harper |
| 3 | 28 | Ipswich Town | 1-5 | 17990 | Harper |
| 4 | 2 Sep | WATFORD | 1-1 | 4552 | Parker |
| 5 | 4 | NOTTS COUNTY | 3-3 | 16776 | Lewis, Parker, Harper |
| 6 | 8 | Reading | 1-4 | 12076 | Lewis |
| 7 | 11 | Walsall | 1-3 | 12711 | Parker |
| 8 | 16 | READING | 1-1 | 9863 | Parker |
| 9 | 18 | TORQUAY UNITED | 1-2 | 10664 | Parker |
| 10 | 25 | Bristol Rovers | 1-3 | 22277 | H.Williams |
| 11 | 2 Oct | SWINDON TOWN | 4-1 | 11657 | Lewis(2), H.Williams, Newall |
| 12 | 9 | Leyton Orient | 2-5 | 14692 | Parker, H.J.Williams |
| 13 | 16 | PORT VALE | 2-2 | 10037 | H.Williams, Parker |
| 14 | 23 | Northampton Town | 1-2 | 8178 | Parker |
| 15 | 30 | NORWICH CITY | 4-3 | 11068 | Carr(3), Comley |
| 16 | 6 Nov | Brighton & H.A. | 2-3 | 17011 | Parker(2) |
| 17 | 13 | SOUTHEND UNITED | 4-2 | 12262 | H Williams, Carr, Comley, Parker |
| 18 | 20 | Millwall | 1-3 | 25441 | Parker |
| 19 | 4 Dec | Swindon Town | 2-5 | 14893 | Parker, Carr |
| 20 | 18 | Bournemouth & B.A. | 2-1 | 13188 | Roffi, Comley |
| 21 | 25 | CRYSTAL PALACE | 5-0 | 15115 | Carr(2), Comley(2), Harper |
| 22 | 27 | Crystal Palace | 1-0 | 10951 | Parker |
| 23 | 1 Jan | IPSWICH TOWN | 3-0 | 9465 | Carr(2), Comley |
| 24 | 15 | Notts County | 1-11 | 26843 | Carr |
| 25 | 22 | WALSALL | 1-1 | 14536 | Roffi |
| 26 | 19 Feb | BRISTOL ROVERS | 2-1 | 20502 | Roffi, Parker |
| 27 | 5 Mar | LEYTON ORIENT | 3-2 | 6701 | Comley(2), Parker |
| 28 | 12 | Port Vale | 2-1 | 9487 | Carr(2) |
| 29 | 19 | NORTHAMPTON TOWN | 2-0 | 14869 | Carr(2) |
| 30 | 23 | Torquay United | 0-4 | 6538 | |
| 31 | 26 | Norwich City | 0-0 | 23214 | |
| 32 | 2 Apr | BRIGHTON & H.A. | 1-1 | 11779 | Carr |
| 33 | 7 | BRISTOL CITY | 0-2 | 10278 | |
| 34 | 9 | Southend United | 1-0 | 7865 | Lewis |
| 35 | 15 | SWANSEA TOWN | 2-5 | 21167 | Parker, Carr |
| 36 | 16 | MILLWALL | 1-2 | 11067 | Parker |
| 37 | 18 | Swansea Town | 1-2 | 28623 | Parker |
| 38 | 23 | Aldershot | 2-1 | 7288 | H.Williams(2) |
| 39 | 28 | ALDERSHOT | 0-2 | 8096 | |
| 40 | 30 | EXETER CITY | 0-2 | 7964 | |
| 41 | 4 May | Exeter City | 2-1 | 6593 | Hayward(2) |
| 42 | 7 | Bristol City | 1-1 | 13188 | Roffi |

### F.A.Cup

| | Date | Opposition | Res. | Att. | Goalscorers |
|---|---|---|---|---|---|
| 1 | 27 Nov | BRIGHTON & H.A. | 3-1 | 14000 | Comley(2), Parker |
| 2 | 11 Dec | Leytonstone | 4-3 | 10000 | Carr(2), Harper, Comley |
| 3 | 8 Jan | Leeds United | 3-1 | 31500 | Roffi, Carr, Comley |
| 4 | 29 | HUDDERSFIELD TOWN | 3-3 | 22500 | H.Williams, Carr, Comley |
| 4R | 5 Feb | Huddersfield Town | 3-1 | 34183 | Parker(2), Carr |
| 5 | 12 | Portsmouth | 2-3 | 45581 | Carr, Harper |

| Player | League | | F.A.Cup | | Total | |
|---|---|---|---|---|---|---|
| | App | Gls. | App | Gls. | App | Gls. |
| Bowen T.H. | 2 | 0 | – | – | 2 | 0 |
| Bradford L. | 24 | 0 | 6 | 0 | 31 | 0 |
| Carr E.M. | 30 | 17 | 6 | 6 | 37 | 23 |
| Comley L.G. | 27 | 8 | 6 | 5 | 33 | 13 |
| Grant A.F. | 20 | 0 | 5 | 0 | 25 | 0 |
| Haddon H.L. | 3 | 0 | – | – | 3 | 0 |
| Harper R. | 30 | 4 | 6 | 2 | 37 | 6 |
| Hayward D.S. | 39 | 2 | 4 | 0 | 44 | 2 |
| Lewis W. | 18 | 5 | – | – | 18 | 5 |
| Loveman R.K. | 9 | 0 | 1 | 0 | 10 | 0 |
| Matthews D.I. | 6 | 0 | – | – | 7 | 0 |
| McBlain A. | 2 | 0 | – | – | 2 | 0 |
| McCrindle W. | 2 | 0 | – | – | 2 | 0 |
| Morrall A.D. | 28 | 0 | 3 | 0 | 32 | 0 |
| Newall D.J. | 26 | 1 | 6 | 0 | 33 | 1 |
| O'Neill T.H. | 9 | 0 | – | – | 10 | 0 |
| Orphan L.J. | 1 | 0 | – | – | 1 | 0 |
| Parker R.E. | 38 | 20 | 5 | 3 | 43 | 23 |
| Roberts O.J. | 7 | 0 | – | – | 7 | 0 |
| Roffi G.T. | 42 | 4 | 6 | 1 | 49 | 5 |
| Sage F.R. | 2 | 0 | – | – | 2 | 0 |
| Shergold W.R. | 14 | 0 | – | – | 15 | 0 |
| Sutherland J.C. | 6 | 0 | – | – | 6 | 0 |
| Wilcox R. | 39 | 0 | 6 | 0 | 45 | 0 |
| Williams H. | 36 | 6 | 6 | 1 | 43 | 7 |
| Williams H.J. | 2 | 1 | – | – | 2 | |

| | | P | W | D | L | F | A | Pts |
|---|---|---|---|---|---|---|---|---|
| 1 | Swansea | 42 | 27 | 8 | 7 | 87 | 34 | 62 |
| 2 | Reading | 42 | 25 | 5 | 12 | 77 | 50 | 55 |
| 3 | Bournemouth | 42 | 22 | 8 | 12 | 69 | 48 | 52 |
| 4 | Swindon | 42 | 18 | 15 | 9 | 64 | 56 | 51 |
| 5 | Bristol Rovers | 42 | 19 | 10 | 13 | 61 | 51 | 48 |
| 6 | Brighton | 42 | 15 | 18 | 9 | 55 | 55 | 48 |
| 7 | Ipswich | 42 | 18 | 9 | 15 | 78 | 77 | 45 |
| 8 | Millwall | 42 | 17 | 11 | 14 | 63 | 64 | 45 |
| 9 | Torquay | 42 | 17 | 11 | 14 | 65 | 70 | 45 |
| 10 | Norwich | 42 | 16 | 12 | 14 | 67 | 49 | 44 |
| 11 | Notts County | 42 | 19 | 5 | 18 | 102 | 68 | 43 |
| 12 | Exeter | 42 | 15 | 10 | 17 | 63 | 76 | 40 |
| 13 | Port Vale | 42 | 14 | 11 | 17 | 51 | 54 | 39 |
| 14 | Walsall | 42 | 15 | 8 | 19 | 56 | 64 | 38 |
| 15 | Newport | 42 | 14 | 9 | 19 | 68 | 92 | 37 |
| 16 | Bristol City | 42 | 11 | 14 | 17 | 44 | 62 | 36 |
| 17 | Watford | 42 | 10 | 15 | 17 | 41 | 54 | 35 |
| 18 | Southend | 42 | 9 | 16 | 17 | 41 | 46 | 34 |
| 19 | Leyton Orient | 42 | 11 | 12 | 19 | 58 | 80 | 34 |
| 20 | Northampton | 42 | 12 | 9 | 21 | 51 | 62 | 33 |
| 21 | Aldershot | 42 | 11 | 11 | 20 | 48 | 59 | 33 |
| 22 | Crystal Palace | 42 | 8 | 11 | 23 | 38 | 76 | 27 |

(Back) Newall, Hayward, Roffi, Grant, Bradford, Parker, Morrall
(Front) Harper, Carr, Wilcox, Comley, Williams

# SEASON 1949-50 Division 3(South)

| | Date | Opposition | Res. | Att. | Goalscorers |
|---|---|---|---|---|---|
| 1 | 20 Aug | NORWICH CITY | 3-2 | 16238 | Hayward, Comley, Parker |
| 2 | 25 | Northampton Town | 3-4 | 12718 | Parker(2), Comley |
| 3 | 27 | Southend United | 0-6 | 11577 | |
| 4 | 1 Sep | NORTHAMPTON TOWN | 1-4 | 12536 | Carr |
| 5 | 3 | Bristol City | 0-6 | 20007 | |
| 6 | 7 | Torquay United | 3-5 | 9414 | Comley, Parker, Carr |
| 7 | 10 | BRIGHTON & H.A. | 0-1 | 11157 | |
| 8 | 15 | TORQUAY UNITED | 1-0 | 10462 | Harper |
| 9 | 17 | Walsall | 0-2 | 10846 | |
| 10 | 24 | MILLWALL | 4-3 | 12773 | Parker(2), Gardner(2) |
| 11 | 1 Oct | Swindon Town | 1-1 | 15284 | Roffi |
| 12 | 8 | NOTTS COUNTY | 1-1 | 21543 | Newall |
| 13 | 15 | Port Vale | 0-1 | 12599 | |
| 14 | 22 | IPSWICH TOWN | 1-0 | 11419 | Comley |
| 15 | 29 | Exeter City | 3-3 | 8095 | Comley, Parker, Griffiths |
| 16 | 5 Nov | LEYTON ORIENT | 3-2 | 11792 | Roffi(2), Griffiths |
| 17 | 12 | Reading | 1-4 | 15300 | Payne |
| 18 | 19 | WATFORD | 3-3 | 11884 | Comley(2), Harper |
| 19 | 3 Dec | BOURNEMOUTH & B.A. | 5-0 | 10560 | Comley(2), Parker, Harper, Roffi |
| 20 | 17 | Norwich City | 0-4 | 17895 | |
| 21 | 26 | ALDERSHOT | 6-0 | 13860 | Harper(2), Griffiths(2), Comley, Parker |
| 22 | 27 | Aldershot | 1-4 | 7318 | Griffiths |
| 23 | 31 | BRISTOL CITY | 6-4 | 13208 | Bowen(3), Parker(2), Comley |
| 24 | 14 Jan | Brighton & H.A. | 0-5 | 11502 | |
| 25 | 21 | WALSALL | 2-1 | 8840 | Comley(2) |
| 26 | 28 | Crystal Palace | 0-1 | 9895 | |
| 27 | 18 Feb | SWINDON TOWN | 1-2 | 10622 | Roffi |
| 28 | 25 | Notts County | 0-7 | 28427 | |
| 29 | 4 Mar | PORT VALE | 1-1 | 8762 | Griffiths |
| 30 | 11 | Ipswich Town | 0-1 | 12678 | |
| 31 | 18 | EXETER CITY | 1-2 | 6414 | Comley |
| 32 | 25 | Leyton Orient | 1-2 | 8819 | Parker |
| 33 | 30 | SOUTHEND UNITED | 2-1 | 7297 | Comley, Parker |
| 34 | 1 Apr | READING | 1-1 | 9923 | Roffi |
| 35 | 7 | NOTTINGHAM FOREST | 4-1 | 13337 | Roffi(2), Comley, Parker |
| 36 | 8 | Watford | 1-0 | 11729 | Roffi |
| 37 | 10 | Nottingham Forest | 0-3 | 15799 | |
| 38 | 15 | CRYSTAL PALACE | 2-2 | 11459 | Comley, Parker |
| 39 | 22 | Bournemouth & B.A. | 1-1 | 10842 | Comley |
| 40 | 24 | Bristol Rovers | 0-3 | 10657 | |
| 41 | 29 | BRISTOL ROVERS | 2-3 | 8173 | Comley, Roffi |
| 42 | 1 May | Millwall | 2-1 | 15472 | Hayward, Bowen |

## F.A.Cup

| | | | | | |
|---|---|---|---|---|---|
| 1 | 26 Nov | Crystal Palace | 3-0 | 12719 | Comley, Payne, Griffiths |
| 2 | 10 Dec | GATESHEAD | 1-1 | 15184 | Harper |
| 2R | 14 | Gateshead | 2-1 | 14000 | Parker, Harper |
| 3 | 7 Jan | PORT VALE | 1-2 | 17781 | Comley |

| Player | League | | F.A.Cup | | Total | |
|---|---|---|---|---|---|---|
| | App | Gls. | App | Gls. | App | Gls. |
| Amphlett R.H. | 13 | 0 | – | – | 13 | 0 |
| Ashton R.W. | 10 | 0 | – | – | 10 | 0 |
| Bowen T.H. | 22 | 4 | 1 | 0 | 24 | 4 |
| Carr E.M. | 12 | 2 | – | – | 12 | 2 |
| Comley L.G. | 41 | 19 | 4 | 2 | 46 | 21 |
| Depear E.R. | 16 | 0 | – | – | 17 | 0 |
| Fearnley H.L. | 25 | 0 | 2 | 0 | 28 | 0 |
| Gardner F.C. | 4 | 2 | – | – | 4 | 2 |
| Griffiths K.G. | 14 | 6 | 4 | 1 | 19 | 7 |
| Harper R. | 37 | 5 | 4 | 2 | 42 | 7 |
| Hayward D.S | 29 | 2 | 4 | 0 | 33 | 2 |
| Hodge E. | 7 | 0 | 2 | 0 | 9 | 0 |
| Lewis W. | 6 | 0 | – | – | 6 | 0 |
| McCrindle W. | 3 | 0 | 3 | 0 | 6 | 0 |
| Newall D.J. | 41 | 1 | 4 | 0 | 45 | 1 |
| Parker R.E. | 38 | 15 | 4 | 1 | 42 | 16 |
| Payne E.E.H. | 12 | 1 | 3 | 1 | 16 | 2 |
| Reid W.D. | 9 | 0 | 1 | 0 | 11 | 0 |
| Roffi G.T. | 34 | 10 | 3 | 0 | 37 | 10 |
| Shergold W.R. | 12 | 0 | – | – | 12 | 0 |
| Stansfield F. | 21 | 0 | 4 | 0 | 26 | 0 |
| Staples L.E. | 8 | 0 | – | – | 9 | 0 |
| Wilcox R. | 24 | 0 | – | – | 24 | 0 |
| Williams G.R. | 5 | 0 | – | – | 5 | 0 |
| Williams M. | 19 | 0 | 1 | 0 | 21 | 0 |

| | | P | W | D | L | F | A | Pts |
|---|---|---|---|---|---|---|---|---|
| 1 | Notts County | 42 | 25 | 8 | 9 | 95 | 50 | 58 |
| 2 | Northampton | 42 | 20 | 11 | 11 | 72 | 50 | 51 |
| 3 | Southend | 42 | 19 | 13 | 10 | 66 | 48 | 51 |
| 4 | Nottm Forest | 42 | 20 | 9 | 13 | 67 | 39 | 49 |
| 5 | Torquay | 42 | 19 | 10 | 13 | 66 | 63 | 48 |
| 6 | Watford | 42 | 16 | 13 | 13 | 45 | 35 | 45 |
| 7 | Crystal Palace | 42 | 15 | 14 | 13 | 55 | 54 | 44 |
| 8 | Brighton | 42 | 16 | 12 | 14 | 57 | 69 | 44 |
| 9 | Bristol Rovers | 42 | 19 | 5 | 18 | 51 | 51 | 43 |
| 10 | Reading | 42 | 17 | 8 | 17 | 70 | 64 | 42 |
| 11 | Norwich | 42 | 16 | 10 | 16 | 65 | 63 | 42 |
| 12 | Bournemouth | 42 | 16 | 10 | 16 | 57 | 56 | 42 |
| 13 | Port Vale | 42 | 15 | 11 | 16 | 47 | 42 | 41 |
| 14 | Swindon | 42 | 15 | 11 | 16 | 59 | 62 | 41 |
| 15 | Bristol City | 42 | 15 | 10 | 17 | 60 | 61 | 40 |
| 16 | Exeter | 42 | 14 | 11 | 17 | 63 | 75 | 39 |
| 17 | Ipswich | 42 | 12 | 11 | 19 | 57 | 86 | 35 |
| 18 | Leyton Orient | 42 | 12 | 11 | 19 | 53 | 85 | 35 |
| 19 | Walsall | 42 | 9 | 16 | 17 | 61 | 62 | 34 |
| 20 | Aldershot | 42 | 13 | 8 | 21 | 48 | 60 | 34 |
| 21 | Newport | 42 | 13 | 8 | 21 | 67 | 98 | 34 |
| 22 | Millwall | 42 | 14 | 4 | 24 | 55 | 63 | 32 |

(Back) Hayward, (? Amateur), Fearnley, Travis, G. Williams, Reid, Depear, Pritchard, M.Williams.
(Middle) Lewis, Bowen, Wilcox, Shergold, Carr, Comley, H.Williams.
(Front) Newall, Parker, Harper, Orphan, (? Amateur), Onions.

# SEASON 1950-51 Division 3(South)

| | Date | Opposition | Res. | Att. | Goalscorers |
|---|---|---|---|---|---|
| 1 | 19 Aug | NOTTINGHAM FOREST | 0-2 | 16595 | |
| 2 | 24 | Port Vale | 0-1 | 30196 | |
| 3 | 26 | Torquay United | 4-3 | 10276 | Cowley, Parker, Roffi, Shergold |
| 4 | 31 | PORT VALE | 2-1 | 13537 | Parker, Moore |
| 5 | 2 Sep | ALDERSHOT | 7-0 | 13696 | Roffi(4), Parker(2), M.Haines |
| 6 | 7 | Watford | 2-0 | 9451 | Parker, Moore |
| 7 | 9 | Swindon Town | 0-2 | 14021 | |
| 8 | 14 | WATFORD | 2-2 | 12116 | Newall, M.Haines |
| 9 | 16 | COLCHESTER UNITED | 2-0 | 16021 | Parker(2) |
| 10 | 21 | NORTHAMPTON TOWN | 2-2 | 13845 | Parker, Moore |
| 11 | 23 | Bristol Rovers | 0-1 | 19816 | |
| 12 | 30 | CRYSTAL PALACE | 2-4 | 10114 | Cowley, Moore |
| 13 | 7 Oct | MILLWALL | 2-3 | 13129 | Moore, Beattie |
| 14 | 14 | Bristol City | 1-2 | 22930 | Parker |
| 15 | 21 | GILLINGHAM | 1-0 | 9828 | Shergold |
| 16 | 28 | Bournemouth & B.A. | 0-2 | 13466 | |
| 17 | 4 Nov | EXETER CITY | 0-3 | 10653 | |
| 18 | 11 | Southend United | 0-3 | 9882 | |
| 19 | 18 | READING | 5-0 | 8529 | Birch(2), Parker, Shergold, Aston |
| 20 | 2 Dec | IPSWICH TOWN | 1-2 | 11496 | Hayward |
| 21 | 23 | TORQUAY UNITED | 2-1 | 8369 | Parker, Shergold |
| 22 | 25 | Walsall | 0-0 | 7832 | |
| 23 | 26 | WALSALL | 3-0 | 13160 | Parker, Moore, Birch |
| 24 | 30 | Aldershot | 1-3 | 6291 | Moore |
| 25 | 13 Jan | SWINDON TOWN | 2-1 | 12485 | Shergold, Birch |
| 26 | 20 | Colchester United | 1-1 | 8230 | Birch |
| 27 | 3 Feb | BRISTOL ROVERS | 2-1 | 11802 | Birch(2) |
| 28 | 10 | Plymouth Argyle | 1-1 | 13408 | Parker |
| 29 | 17 | Crystal Palace | 1-1 | 9990 | Shergold |
| 30 | 24 | Millwall | 4-2 | 15788 | Parker, Moore, Shergold, Beattie |
| 31 | 3 Mar | BRISTOL CITY | 0-1 | 11494 | |
| 32 | 10 | Gillingham | 1-0 | 9040 | Birch |
| 33 | 24 | Exeter City | 2-2 | 7565 | Parker, Beattie |
| 34 | 26 | Norwich City | 1-2 | 35267 | Birch |
| 35 | 31 | SOUTHEND UNITED | 6-1 | 9544 | Moore(2), Shergold(2), Parker, Birch |
| 36 | 5 Apr | Northampton Town | 4-1 | 6425 | Moore(2), Hayward, Parker |
| 37 | 7 | Reading | 0-5 | 12939 | |
| 38 | 12 | Leyotn Orient | 3-0 | 8270 | Parker, Moore, Shergold |
| 39 | 14 | PLYMOUTH ARGYLE | 2-0 | 11962 | Parker, Moore |
| 40 | 18 | Brighton & H.A. | 1-9 | 12114 | Parker |
| 41 | 21 | Ipswich Town | 1-2 | 10294 | Moore |
| 42 | 25 | NORWICH CITY | 1-1 | 13862 | moore |
| 43 | 28 | LEYTON ORIENT | 0-0 | 7564 | |
| 44 | 30 | BOURNEMOUTH & B.A. | 1-0 | 5563 | Shergold |
| 45 | 2 May | Nottingham Forest | 1-2 | 21468 | Parker |
| 46 | 5 | BRIGHTON & H.A. | 3-0 | 9274 | Parker, Moore, Birch |

## F.A.Cup

| | | | | | |
|---|---|---|---|---|---|
| 1 | 25 Nov | WALSALL | 4-2 | 13891 | Parker(2), Hayward, Shergold |
| 2 | 9 Dec | Hereford United | 3-0 | 15526 | Parker, Moore, Shergold |
| 3 | 6 Jan | READING | 3-2 | 12086 | Parker, Birch, Shergold |
| 4 | 27 | NORWICH CITY | 0-2 | 20293 | |

| Player | League | | F.A.Cup | | Total | |
|---|---|---|---|---|---|---|
| | App | Gls. | App | Gls. | App | Gls. |
| Ashton R.W. | 1 | 0 | – | – | 1 | 0 |
| Aston A.J. | 5 | 1 | 1 | 0 | 6 | 1 |
| Bartholemew H. | 3 | 0 | – | – | 3 | 0 |
| Beattie G. | 35 | 3 | 4 | 0 | 43 | 3 |
| Birch C. | 28 | 11 | 4 | 1 | 35 | 12 |
| Comley L.G. | 8 | 2 | – | – | 8 | 2 |
| Davies A.L. | 1 | 0 | – | – | 2 | 0 |
| Evans H.W.R. | 2 | 0 | – | – | 2 | 0 |
| Fearnley H.L. | 24 | 0 | 3 | 0 | 27 | 0 |
| Haines D.N. | 1 | 0 | – | – | 1 | 0 |
| Haines M.J. | 14 | 2 | – | – | 14 | 2 |
| Hayward D.S. | 45 | 2 | 4 | 1 | 53 | 4 |
| James W.G. | 6 | 0 | – | – | 7 | 1 |
| Lester L.J. | 2 | 0 | – | – | 2 | 0 |
| Lunn W.J. | 2 | 0 | – | – | 4 | 0 |
| Molloy W.G. | 3 | 0 | – | – | 4 | 0 |
| Moore J.F.B. | 43 | 17 | 3 | 1 | 50 | 20 |
| Newall D.J. | 44 | 1 | 4 | 0 | 50 | 2 |
| Parker R.E. | 46 | 22 | 4 | 4 | 53 | 27 |
| Pope T.J. | 21 | 0 | 1 | 0 | 26 | 0 |
| Poyner R.C. | 1 | 0 | – | – | 1 | 0 |
| Roffi G.T. | 9 | 5 | – | – | 9 | 5 |
| Shegold W.R. | 36 | 11 | 4 | 3 | 43 | 14 |
| Staples L.E. | 42 | 0 | 4 | 0 | 50 | 0 |
| Stroud W.J.A. | 31 | 0 | 4 | 0 | 37 | 1 |
| Wilcox R. | 45 | 0 | 4 | 0 | 53 | 0 |
| Williams M. | 8 | 0 | – | – | 8 | 0 |

| | | P | W | D | L | F | A | Pts |
|---|---|---|---|---|---|---|---|---|
| 1 | Nottm Forest | 46 | 30 | 10 | 6 | 110 | 40 | 70 |
| 2 | Norwich | 46 | 25 | 14 | 7 | 82 | 45 | 64 |
| 3 | Reading | 46 | 21 | 15 | 10 | 88 | 53 | 57 |
| 4 | Plymouth | 46 | 24 | 9 | 13 | 85 | 55 | 57 |
| 5 | Millwall | 46 | 23 | 10 | 13 | 80 | 57 | 56 |
| 6 | Bristol Rovers | 46 | 20 | 15 | 11 | 64 | 42 | 55 |
| 7 | Southend | 46 | 21 | 10 | 15 | 92 | 69 | 52 |
| 8 | Ipswich | 46 | 23 | 6 | 17 | 69 | 58 | 52 |
| 9 | Bournemouth | 46 | 22 | 7 | 17 | 65 | 57 | 51 |
| 10 | Bristol City | 46 | 20 | 11 | 15 | 64 | 59 | 51 |
| 11 | Newport | 46 | 19 | 9 | 18 | 77 | 70 | 47 |
| 12 | Port Vale | 46 | 16 | 13 | 17 | 60 | 65 | 45 |
| 13 | Brighton | 46 | 13 | 17 | 16 | 71 | 79 | 43 |
| 14 | Exeter | 46 | 18 | 6 | 22 | 62 | 85 | 42 |
| 15 | Walsall | 46 | 15 | 10 | 21 | 52 | 62 | 40 |
| 16 | Colchester | 46 | 14 | 12 | 20 | 63 | 76 | 40 |
| 17 | Swindon | 46 | 18 | 4 | 24 | 55 | 67 | 40 |
| 18 | Aldershot | 46 | 15 | 10 | 21 | 56 | 88 | 40 |
| 19 | Leyton Orient | 46 | 15 | 8 | 23 | 53 | 75 | 38 |
| 20 | Torquay | 46 | 14 | 9 | 23 | 64 | 81 | 37 |
| 21 | Northampton | 46 | 10 | 16 | 20 | 55 | 67 | 36 |
| 22 | Gillingham | 46 | 13 | 9 | 24 | 69 | 101 | 35 |
| 23 | Watford | 46 | 9 | 11 | 26 | 54 | 88 | 29 |
| 24 | Crystal Palace | 46 | 8 | 11 | 27 | 33 | 84 | 27 |

(Back) Lawrence (Train./Coach), Hayward, James, Roffi, Bartholomew, Fearnley, Pope, Wilcox, Nelson, Lunn, Kitson (Asst./Train.) (Middle) Moore, Williams, Comley, Aston, Parker, Newall, Staples. (Front) Stroud, Haines, Poyner, Morgan, Shergold, Slatter.

# SEASON 1951–52 Division 3(South)

| | Date | Opposition | Res. | Att. | Goalscorers |
|---|---|---|---|---|---|
| 1 | 18 Aug | Bristol City | 1–3 | 30048 | Parker |
| 2 | 20 | NORTHAMPTON TOWN | 2–2 | 16802 | Birch, Moore |
| 3 | 25 | IPSWICH TOWN | 2–1 | 13062 | Parker, Moore |
| 4 | 1 Sep | Torquay United | 2–1 | 6411 | Birch, Shergold |
| 5 | 6 | Northampton Town | 0–5 | 10203 | |
| 6 | 8 | GILLINGHAM | 1–1 | 10725 | Birch |
| 7 | 12 | Reading | 2–1 | 16050 | James(2) |
| 8 | 15 | Brighton & H.A. | 2–1 | 10949 | Birch, James |
| 9 | 17 | READING | 3–1 | 11879 | Parker(2), James |
| 10 | 22 | MILLWALL | 2–1 | 12797 | Birch, Evans |
| 11 | 29 | Bournemouth & B.A. | 1–5 | 12494 | James |
| 12 | 6 Oct | Aldershot | 0–4 | 8801 | |
| 13 | 13 | WATFORD | 2–5 | 9636 | Parker, Donaldson |
| 14 | 20 | Bristol Rovers | 1–1 | 17396 | Beattie |
| 15 | 27 | PLYMOUTH ARGYLE | 3–3 | 10065 | Birch, Beattie, Moore |
| 16 | 3 Nov | Norwich City | 2–1 | 25828 | Beattie, Shergold |
| 17 | 10 | EXETER CITY | 4–0 | 10920 | Parker(2), Shergold(2) |
| 18 | 17 | Colchester United | 1–2 | 7729 | Birch |
| 19 | 1 Dec | Swindon Town | 1–1 | 12007 | Shergold |
| 20 | 22 | Ipswich Town | 1–3 | 9609 | Beattie |
| 21 | 25 | SHREWSBURY TOWN | 3–1 | 9982 | Moore(2), Parker |
| 22 | 26 | Shrewsbury Town | 3–1 | 9982 | Beattie(2), Birch, Parker |
| 23 | 29 | TORQUAY UNITED | 1–2 | 11650 | Parker |
| 24 | 5 Jan | Gillingham | 3–2 | 10410 | Parker, Moore, Nelson |
| 25 | 17 | SOUTHEND UNITED | 3–0 | 4897 | Birch, Beattie, Moore |
| 26 | 19 | BRIGHTON & H.A. | 1–1 | 10333 | Beattie |
| 27 | 26 | Millwall | 0–2 | 17761 | |
| 28 | 9 Feb | BOURNEMOUTH & B.A. | 2–0 | 11148 | Parker, Shergold |
| 29 | 16 | ALDERSHOT | 4–2 | 9792 | Parker(3), Shergold |
| 30 | 23 | PORT VALE | 1–1 | 11593 | Moore |
| 31 | 1 Mar | Watford | 1–1 | 9270 | Parker |
| 32 | 8 | BRISTOL ROVERS | 2–2 | 13113 | Parker, Moore |
| 33 | 15 | Plymouth Argyle | 0–5 | 17939 | |
| 34 | 22 | NORWICH CITY | 2–2 | 10350 | Beattie, Parker |
| 35 | 24 | Port Vale | 2–4 | 5908 | Shergold, Potts(og) |
| 36 | 29 | Exeter City | 4–3 | 4076 | Birch, Parker, Shergold, Moore |
| 37 | 3 Apr | LEYTON ORIENT | 1–0 | 7137 | Moore |
| 38 | 5 | COLCHESTER UNITED | 0–1 | 6821 | |
| 39 | 11 | WALSALL | 4–2 | 9385 | Moore(3), Beattie |
| 40 | 12 | Crystal Palace | 1–1 | 14904 | Lunn |
| 41 | 14 | Walsall | 1–0 | 7700 | Shergold |
| 42 | 19 | SWINDON TOWN | 0–0 | 9217 | |
| 43 | 24 | CRYSTAL PALACE | 1–0 | 6942 | Moore |
| 44 | 26 | Leyton Orient | 1–1 | 6579 | Banner(og) |
| 45 | 28 | BRISTOL CITY | 1–0 | 7714 | Nelson |
| 46 | 3 May | Southend United | 1–2 | 6438 | Moore |

### F.A.Cup

| | Date | Opposition | Res. | Att. | Goalscorers |
|---|---|---|---|---|---|
| 1 | 24 Nov | BARRY TOWN | 4–0 | 11844 | Moore(3), Beattie |
| 2 | 15 Dec | Leytonstone | 2–2 | 10500 | Birch, Beattie |
| 2R | 20 | LEYTONSTONE | 3–0 | 10737 | Moore(2), Beattie |
| 3 | 12 Jan | Sheffield United | 0–2 | 34486 | |

| Player | League | | F.A.Cup | | Total | |
|---|---|---|---|---|---|---|
| | App | Gls. | App | Gls. | App | Gls. |
| Beattie G. | 38 | 10 | 4 | 3 | 43 | 13 |
| Birch C. | 44 | 10 | 4 | 1 | 48 | 11 |
| Donaldson J.D. | 28 | 1 | 4 | 0 | 34 | 2 |
| Evans H.W.R. | 12 | 1 | – | – | 13 | 1 |
| Fearnley H.L. | 19 | 0 | 3 | 0 | 23 | 0 |
| Griffiths W.R. | 3 | 0 | – | – | 3 | 0 |
| Haines D.N. | 18 | 0 | 4 | 0 | 24 | 0 |
| Hayward D.S. | 28 | 0 | – | – | 30 | 0 |
| James W.G. | 7 | 5 | – | – | 8 | 7 |
| Lunn W.J. | 4 | 1 | – | – | 6 | 2 |
| Mitchell J. | – | – | – | – | 1 | 0 |
| Molloy W.G. | – | – | – | – | 1 | 1 |
| Moore J.F.B. | 46 | 16 | 4 | 5 | 52 | 24 |
| Nelson J.A. | 10 | 2 | – | – | 11 | 4 |
| Newall D.J. | 42 | 0 | 4 | 0 | 47 | 0 |
| Parker R.E. | 35 | 19 | 4 | 0 | 39 | 19 |
| Pope T.J. | 24 | 0 | 1 | 0 | 25 | 0 |
| Poyner R.C. | 1 | 0 | – | – | 1 | 0 |
| Shergold W.R. | 43 | 10 | 4 | 0 | 47 | 10 |
| Staples L.E. | 45 | 0 | 4 | 0 | 50 | 0 |
| Stroud W.J.A. | 18 | 0 | – | – | 19 | 0 |
| Waite T.J.A. | 3 | 0 | – | – | 1 | 0 |
| Wilcox R. | 37 | 0 | 4 | 0 | 42 | 0 |
| Williams M. | 1 | 0 | – | 0 | 1 | 0 |
| Own Goals | | 2 | | | | 2 |

| | | P | W | D | L | F | A | Pts |
|---|---|---|---|---|---|---|---|---|
| 1 | Plymouth | 46 | 29 | 8 | 9 | 107 | 53 | 66 |
| 2 | Reading | 46 | 29 | 3 | 14 | 112 | 60 | 61 |
| 3 | Norwich | 46 | 26 | 9 | 11 | 89 | 50 | 61 |
| 4 | Millwall | 46 | 23 | 12 | 11 | 74 | 53 | 58 |
| 5 | Brighton | 46 | 24 | 10 | 12 | 87 | 63 | 58 |
| 6 | Newport | 46 | 21 | 12 | 13 | 77 | 76 | 54 |
| 7 | Bristol Rovers | 46 | 20 | 12 | 14 | 89 | 53 | 52 |
| 8 | Northampton | 46 | 22 | 5 | 19 | 93 | 74 | 49 |
| 9 | Southend | 46 | 19 | 10 | 17 | 75 | 66 | 48 |
| 10 | Colchester | 46 | 17 | 12 | 17 | 56 | 77 | 46 |
| 11 | Torquay | 46 | 17 | 10 | 19 | 86 | 98 | 44 |
| 12 | Aldershot | 46 | 18 | 8 | 20 | 78 | 89 | 44 |
| 13 | Port Vale | 46 | 14 | 15 | 17 | 50 | 66 | 43 |
| 14 | Bournemouth | 46 | 16 | 10 | 20 | 69 | 75 | 42 |
| 15 | Bristol City | 46 | 15 | 12 | 19 | 58 | 69 | 42 |
| 16 | Swindon | 46 | 14 | 14 | 18 | 51 | 68 | 42 |
| 17 | Ipswich | 46 | 16 | 9 | 21 | 63 | 74 | 41 |
| 18 | Leyton Orient | 46 | 16 | 9 | 21 | 55 | 68 | 41 |
| 19 | Crystal Palace | 46 | 15 | 9 | 22 | 61 | 80 | 39 |
| 20 | Shrewsbury | 46 | 13 | 10 | 23 | 62 | 86 | 36 |
| 21 | Watford | 46 | 13 | 10 | 23 | 57 | 81 | 36 |
| 22 | Gillingham | 46 | 11 | 13 | 22 | 71 | 81 | 35 |
| 23 | Exeter | 46 | 13 | 9 | 24 | 65 | 86 | 35 |
| 24 | Walsall | 46 | 13 | 5 | 28 | 55 | 94 | 31 |

(Back) Staples, Stroud, Hayward, Pope, Wilcox, Birch, Lawrance (Trainer/Coach).
(Front) Beattie, Parker, Newall, Shergold, Moore.

## SEASON 1952-53 Division 3(South)

| | Date | Opposition | Res. | Att. | Goalscorers |
|---|---|---|---|---|---|
| 1 | 23 Aug | GILLINGHAM | 1-2 | 11111 | Moore |
| 2 | 28 | Walsall | 3-1 | 10062 | Parker(2), Birch |
| 3 | 30 | Crystal Palace | 1-2 | 14394 | Parker |
| 4 | 4 Sep | WALSALL | 3-2 | 8231 | Shergold, Moore, Nelson |
| 5 | 6 | BRISTOL CITY | 4-3 | 9573 | Shergold, Moore, Nelson, Roberts(og) |
| 6 | 11 | BOURNEMOUTH & B.A. | 2-1 | 9127 | Shergold, Moore, |
| 7 | 13 | Torquay United | 3-3 | 7084 | Parker(3) |
| 8 | 17 | Bournemouth & B.A. | 2-1 | 10187 | Parker, Nelson |
| 9 | 20 | NORTHAMPTON TOWN | 4-1 | 10481 | Parker(2), Moore(2) |
| 10 | 25 | COVENTRY CITY | 4-4 | 10935 | Staples(2), Birch, Parker |
| 11 | 27 | Leyton Orient | 1-2 | 11744 | Shergold |
| 12 | 1 Oct | Reading | 1-2 | 6739 | Moore |
| 13 | 4 | IPSWICH TOWN | 1-3 | 9645 | Moore |
| 14 | 11 | SHREWSBURY TOWN | 4-2 | 9322 | Beattie, Parker, Shergold, Moore |
| 15 | 18 | Q.P.Rangers | 2-4 | 14800 | Beattie, Parker |
| 16 | 25 | SWINDON TOWN | 3-0 | 7971 | Parker(2), Moore |
| 17 | 1 Nov | Aldershot | 2-2 | 6100 | Parker(2) |
| 18 | 8 | COLCHESTER UNITED | 0-1 | 8989 | |
| 19 | 15 | Norwich City | 0-2 | 23899 | |
| 20 | 29 | Exeter City | 2-3 | 6848 | Beattie, Moore |
| 21 | 13 Dec | Millwall | 0-3 | 12622 | |
| 22 | 20 | Gillingham | 1-1 | 7179 | Moore |
| 23 | 25 | BRIGHTON & H.A. | 0-3 | 10627 | |
| 24 | 27 | Brighton & H.A. | 2-2 | 15309 | Birch, Shergold |
| 25 | 3 Jan | CRYSTAL PALACE | 3-2 | 8062 | Beattie, Shergold, Briggs(og) |
| 26 | 15 | SOUTHEND UNITED | 0-1 | 3100 | |
| 27 | 17 | Bristol City | 0-2 | 20572 | |
| 28 | 24 | TORQUAY UNITED | 3-0 | 8038 | Evans(3) |
| 29 | 31 | Southend United | 0-1 | 5690 | |
| 30 | 7 Feb | Northampton town | 0-5 | 13250 | |
| 31 | 14 | LEYTON ORIENT | 0-1 | 5182 | |
| 32 | 21 | Ipswich Town | 0-3 | 10019 | |
| 33 | 28 | Shrewsbury Town | 1-1 | 8528 | Beattie |
| 34 | 7 Mar | Q.P.RANGERS | 2-0 | 7971 | Beattie, Graham |
| 35 | 14 | Swindon Town | 0-2 | 7445 | |
| 36 | 21 | ALDERSHOT | 2-1 | 7929 | Beattie, Graham |
| 37 | 28 | Colchester United | 3-3 | 6200 | Graham(2), Beattie |
| 38 | 3 Apr | WATFORD | 1-1 | 9319 | Beattie |
| 39 | 4 | NORWICH CITY | 1-1 | 8375 | Graham |
| 40 | 6 | Watford | 1-0 | 11455 | Beattie |
| 41 | 11 | Coventry City | 1-0 | 11204 | Graham |
| 42 | 13 | BRISTOL ROVERS | 2-2 | 16007 | Stroud, Graham |
| 43 | 18 | EXETER CITY | 1-0 | 8220 | Evans |
| 44 | 23 | READING | 1-0 | 8405 | Hayward |
| 45 | 25 | Bristol Rovers | 1-3 | 29451 | Beattie |
| 46 | 30 | MILLWALL | 1-3 | 6728 | Graham |

### F.A.Cup

| | Date | Opposition | Res. | Att. | Goalscorers |
|---|---|---|---|---|---|
| 1 | 22 Nov | WALSALL | 2-1 | 10000 | Beattie, Moore |
| 2 | 6 Dec | GAINSBOROUGH TRIN. | 2-1 | 9911 | Beattie, Parker |
| 3 | 10 Jan | SHEFFIELD UNITED | 1-4 | 22000 | Moore |

| Player | League | | F.A.Cup | | Total | |
|---|---|---|---|---|---|---|
| | App | Gls. | App | Gls. | App | Gls. |
| Barton D.J. | 7 | 0 | – | – | 7 | 0 |
| Beattie G. | 40 | 11 | 3 | 2 | 44 | 16 |
| Birch C. | 38 | 3 | 2 | 0 | 42 | 3 |
| Donaldson J.D. | 8 | 0 | 1 | 0 | 11 | 0 |
| Evans E.B. | 18 | 4 | – | – | 19 | 6 |
| Fearnley H.L. | 35 | 0 | 2 | 0 | 38 | 0 |
| Graham L. | 14 | 8 | – | – | 14 | 8 |
| Haines D.N. | 31 | 0 | – | – | 33 | 0 |
| Hayward D.S. | 26 | 1 | 3 | 0 | 29 | 1 |
| Kemp S. | – | – | – | – | 1 | 0 |
| Moore J.F.B. | 32 | 12 | 3 | 2 | 35 | 14 |
| Morrey B.J. | 7 | 0 | – | – | 9 | 3 |
| Nelson J.A. | 6 | 3 | 1 | 0 | 7 | 3 |
| Newall D.J. | 37 | 0 | 3 | 0 | 41 | 0 |
| Parker R.E. | 28 | 16 | 3 | 1 | 31 | 17 |
| Pemberton S.R. | 1 | 0 | – | – | 1 | 0 |
| Pope T.J. | 10 | 0 | 1 | 0 | 12 | 0 |
| Pugsley D.G. | 1 | 0 | – | – | 1 | 0 |
| Rees J.F. | 2 | 0 | – | – | 3 | 1 |
| Shergold W.R. | 31 | 7 | 2 | 0 | 34 | 8 |
| Staples L.E. | 17 | 2 | – | – | 17 | 2 |
| Stroud W.J.A. | 13 | 1 | – | – | 14 | 1 |
| Waite T.J.A. | 36 | 0 | 3 | 0 | 41 | 0 |
| Wharton J.E. | 12 | 0 | – | – | 12 | 0 |
| Wilcox C. | 13 | 0 | 3 | 0 | 18 | 0 |
| Wilcox R. | 43 | 0 | 3 | 0 | 47 | 0 |
| Own Goals | | 2 | | | | 2 |

| | | P | W | D | L | F | A | Pts |
|---|---|---|---|---|---|---|---|---|
| 1 | Bristol Rovers | 46 | 26 | 12 | 8 | 92 | 46 | 64 |
| 2 | Millwall | 46 | 24 | 14 | 8 | 82 | 44 | 62 |
| 3 | Northampton | 46 | 26 | 10 | 10 | 109 | 70 | 62 |
| 4 | Norwich | 26 | 25 | 10 | 11 | 99 | 55 | 60 |
| 5 | Bristol City | 46 | 22 | 15 | 9 | 95 | 61 | 59 |
| 6 | Coventry | 46 | 19 | 12 | 15 | 77 | 62 | 50 |
| 7 | Brighton | 46 | 19 | 12 | 15 | 81 | 75 | 50 |
| 8 | Southend | 46 | 18 | 13 | 15 | 69 | 74 | 49 |
| 9 | Bournemouth | 46 | 19 | 9 | 18 | 74 | 69 | 47 |
| 10 | Watford | 46 | 15 | 17 | 14 | 62 | 63 | 47 |
| 11 | Reading | 46 | 19 | 8 | 19 | 69 | 64 | 46 |
| 12 | Torquay | 46 | 18 | 9 | 19 | 87 | 88 | 45 |
| 13 | Crystal Palace | 46 | 15 | 13 | 18 | 66 | 82 | 43 |
| 14 | Leyton Orient | 46 | 16 | 10 | 20 | 68 | 73 | 42 |
| 15 | Newport | 46 | 16 | 10 | 20 | 70 | 82 | 42 |
| 16 | Ipswich | 46 | 13 | 15 | 18 | 60 | 69 | 41 |
| 17 | Exeter | 46 | 13 | 14 | 19 | 61 | 71 | 40 |
| 18 | Swindon | 46 | 14 | 12 | 20 | 64 | 79 | 40 |
| 19 | Aldershot | 46 | 12 | 15 | 19 | 61 | 77 | 39 |
| 20 | Gillingham | 46 | 12 | 15 | 19 | 55 | 74 | 39 |
| 21 | QPR | 46 | 12 | 15 | 19 | 61 | 82 | 39 |
| 22 | Colchester | 46 | 12 | 14 | 20 | 59 | 76 | 38 |
| 23 | Shrewsbury | 46 | 12 | 12 | 22 | 68 | 91 | 36 |
| 24 | Walsall | 46 | 7 | 10 | 29 | 56 | 118 | 24 |

(Back) Newall, Staples, Pope, Haines, Stroud.
(Front) Birch, Beattie, Parker, Shergold, Moore, R.Wilcox.

# SEASON 1953-54 Division 3(South)

| | Date | Opposition | Res. | Att. | Goalscorers |
|---|---|---|---|---|---|
| 1 | 20 Aug | READING | 4-1 | 10332 | Parker(2), Graham, Nelson |
| 2 | 22 | Swindon Town | 1-7 | 13444 | Parker |
| 3 | 24 | SOUTHAMPTON | 0-4 | 8571 | |
| 4 | 29 | WALSALL | 4-2 | 3770 | Parker(2), Morrey, Graham |
| 5 | 2 Sep | Southampton | 0-4 | 14454 | |
| 6 | 5 | Shrewsbury Town | 1-2 | 11540 | Graham |
| 7 | 7 | CRYSTAL PALACE | 1-3 | 6913 | Shergold |
| 8 | 12 | EXETER CITY | 0-3 | 6949 | |
| 9 | 16 | Crystal Palace | 0-3 | 8177 | |
| 10 | 19 | Northampton Town | 0-1 | 13100 | |
| 11 | 21 | ALDERSHOT | 2-2 | 2836 | Parker, Wharton |
| 12 | 26 | Norwich City | 0-2 | 23856 | |
| 13 | 30 | Aldershot | 0-2 | 4412 | |
| 14 | 3 Oct | Q.P.Rangers | 2-1 | 6817 | Graham, Parker |
| 15 | 10 | WATFORD | 0-1 | 5959 | |
| 16 | 17 | Brighton & H.A. | 2-4 | 15909 | Graham(2) |
| 17 | 24 | SOUTHEND UNITED | 3-2 | 6958 | Birch, Graham, Morrey |
| 18 | 31 | Reading | 1-4 | 8051 | Hayward |
| 19 | 7 Nov | LEYTON ORIENT | 1-1 | 7740 | Hayward |
| 20 | 14 | Millwall | 1-3 | 14314 | Birch |
| 21 | 28 | Bournemouth & B.A. | 1-1 | 9190 | Wharton |
| 22 | 5 Dec | COVENTRY CITY | 2-1 | 10572 | Waite, Shergold |
| 23 | 12 | Gillingham | 1-0 | 10004 | Graham |
| 24 | 19 | SWINDON TOWN | 2-0 | 9276 | Graham, Shergold |
| 25 | 25 | BRISTOL CITY | 3-2 | 14800 | Birch, Graham, Wharton |
| 26 | 26 | Bristol City | 0-3 | 24375 | |
| 27 | 2 Jan | Walsall | 1-0 | 6187 | Graham |
| 28 | 9 | Colchester United | 2-2 | 6434 | Graham, Haines |
| 29 | 16 | SHREWSBURY TOWN | 2-1 | 10005 | Birch, Graham |
| 30 | 23 | Exeter City | 0-1 | 8038 | |
| 31 | 6 Feb | NORTHAMPTON TOWN | 2-0 | 10191 | Graham, Saward |
| 32 | 13 | NORWICH CITY | 4-1 | 11968 | Graham(3), Lucas |
| 33 | 20 | Q.P.Rangers | 1-5 | 9315 | Graham |
| 34 | 27 | Watford | 0-1 | 12738 | |
| 35 | 6 Mar | BRIGHTON & H.A. | 1-0 | 11417 | Graham |
| 36 | 13 | Ipswich Town | 2-1 | 12531 | Graham, Hollyman |
| 37 | 20 | BOURNEMOUTH & B.A. | 4-0 | 10421 | Graham, Wharton, Shergold, Saward |
| 38 | 27 | Leyton Oient | 0-3 | 9683 | |
| 39 | 3 Apr | MILLWALL | 0-0 | 9049 | |
| 40 | 10 | Coventry City | 2-1 | 7940 | Graham, Shergold |
| 41 | 16 | TORQUAY UNITED | 2-0 | 12450 | Graham, Wharton |
| 42 | 17 | GILLINGHAM | 1-0 | 9409 | Saward |
| 43 | 19 | Torquay United | 2-3 | 6501 | Wharton(2) |
| 44 | 22 | COLCHESTER UNITED | 1-1 | 7596 | Graham |
| 45 | 24 | Southend United | 1-0 | 5993 | Graham |
| 46 | 26 | IPSWICH TOWN | 1-2 | 11258 | Saward |

| Player | League | | F.A.Cup | | Total | |
|---|---|---|---|---|---|---|
| | App | Gls. | App | Gls. | App | Gls. |
| Barton D.J. | 16 | 0 | – | – | 17 | 0 |
| Birch C. | 33 | 4 | 2 | 1 | 38 | 5 |
| Graham L. | 42 | 24 | 2 | 0 | 48 | 28 |
| Haines D.N. | 28 | 1 | – | – | 32 | 1 |
| Hayward D.S. | 35 | 2 | 2 | 0 | 40 | 2 |
| Hollyman K.C. | 18 | 1 | – | – | 21 | 1 |
| Hudson C.A.R. | 1 | 0 | – | – | 1 | 0 |
| Hughes I. | 40 | 0 | 1 | 0 | 42 | 0 |
| Lucas W.H. | 21 | 1 | – | – | 25 | 5 |
| Morrey B.J. | 17 | 2 | – | – | 17 | 2 |
| Nelson J.A. | 3 | 1 | – | – | 3 | 1 |
| Newall D.J. | 16 | 0 | 2 | 0 | 18 | 0 |
| Parker R.E. | 16 | 7 | 2 | 1 | 18 | 8 |
| Pope T.J. | 6 | 0 | 1 | 0 | 10 | 0 |
| Reed T.R. | 1 | 0 | – | – | 1 | 0 |
| Saward L.R. | 16 | 4 | – | – | 18 | 6 |
| Shergold W.R. | 31 | 6 | 2 | 0 | 37 | 6 |
| Staples L.E. | 25 | 0 | 2 | 0 | 27 | 0 |
| Thomas G.V. | 8 | 0 | – | – | 9 | 0 |
| Thomas K. | – | – | 2 | 1 | 2 | 1 |
| Waite T.J.A. | 18 | 1 | 1 | 0 | 19 | 1 |
| Wharton J.E. | 33 | 7 | – | – | 36 | 10 |
| Wilcox C. | 18 | 0 | 1 | 0 | 19 | 0 |
| Wilcox R. | 39 | 0 | 2 | 0 | 45 | 0 |
| Whitcomb D.F. | 25 | 0 | – | – | 29 | 0 |

## F.A.Cup

| | Date | | Res. | Att. | Goalscorers |
|---|---|---|---|---|---|
| 1 | 21 Nov | Cambridge United | 2-2 | 7500 | Birch, K.Thomas |
| 1r | 26 | CAMBRIDGE UNITED | 1-2 | 7434 | Parker |

| | | P | W | D | L | F | A | Pts |
|---|---|---|---|---|---|---|---|---|
| 1 | Ipswich | 46 | 27 | 10 | 9 | 82 | 51 | 61 |
| 2 | Brighton | 46 | 26 | 9 | 11 | 86 | 61 | 61 |
| 3 | Bristol City | 46 | 25 | 6 | 15 | 88 | 66 | 56 |
| 4 | Watford | 46 | 21 | 10 | 15 | 85 | 69 | 52 |
| 5 | Northampton | 46 | 20 | 11 | 15 | 82 | 55 | 51 |
| 6 | Southampton | 46 | 22 | 7 | 17 | 76 | 63 | 51 |
| 7 | Norwich | 46 | 20 | 11 | 15 | 73 | 66 | 51 |
| 8 | Reading | 46 | 20 | 9 | 17 | 86 | 73 | 49 |
| 9 | Exeter | 46 | 20 | 8 | 18 | 68 | 58 | 48 |
| 10 | Gillingham | 46 | 19 | 10 | 17 | 61 | 66 | 48 |
| 11 | Leyton Orient | 46 | 18 | 11 | 17 | 79 | 73 | 47 |
| 12 | Millwall | 46 | 19 | 9 | 18 | 74 | 77 | 47 |
| 13 | Torquay | 46 | 17 | 12 | 17 | 81 | 88 | 46 |
| 14 | Coventry | 46 | 18 | 9 | 19 | 61 | 56 | 45 |
| 15 | Newport | 46 | 19 | 6 | 21 | 61 | 81 | 44 |
| 16 | Southend | 46 | 18 | 7 | 21 | 69 | 71 | 43 |
| 17 | Aldershot | 46 | 17 | 9 | 20 | 74 | 86 | 43 |
| 18 | QPR | 46 | 16 | 10 | 20 | 60 | 68 | 42 |
| 19 | Bournemouth | 46 | 16 | 8 | 22 | 67 | 70 | 40 |
| 20 | Swindon | 46 | 15 | 10 | 21 | 67 | 70 | 40 |
| 21 | Shrewsbury | 46 | 14 | 12 | 20 | 65 | 76 | 40 |
| 22 | Crystal Palace | 46 | 14 | 12 | 20 | 60 | 86 | 40 |
| 23 | Colchester | 46 | 10 | 10 | 26 | 50 | 78 | 30 |
| 24 | Walsall | 46 | 9 | 8 | 29 | 40 | 87 | 26 |

(Back) Birch, Thomas, Whitcomb, Hughes, Hayward, Wilcox, Haines.
(Front) Hollyman, Lucas (Player/Man.), Wilcox, Graham, Shergold.

# SEASON 1954–55  Division 3(South)

| | Date | Opposition | Res. | Att. | Goalscorers |
|---|---|---|---|---|---|
| 1 | 21 Aug | NORTHAMPTON TOWN | 0-1 | 12710 | |
| 2 | 26 | NORWICH CITY | 1-1 | 13318 | Shergold |
| 3 | 28 | Watford | 2-3 | 14957 | Graham, Cooke(og) |
| 4 | 1 Sep | Norwich City | 0-2 | 16382 | |
| 5 | 4 | BOURNEMOUTH & B.A. | 1-1 | 9589 | Shergold |
| 6 | 7 | Southend United | 1-1 | 8025 | Wharton |
| 7 | 11 | Q.P.Rangers | 0-2 | 13115 | |
| 8 | 16 | SOUTHEND UNITED | 3-2 | 8050 | McGhee, Graham, Harris |
| 9 | 18 | Brighton & H.A. | 1-4 | 13419 | Shergold |
| 10 | 22 | Aldershot | 0-0 | 4863 | |
| 11 | 25 | EXETER CITY | 2-1 | 9166 | Lucas Wharton |
| 12 | 30 | ALDERSHOT | 2-1 | 6027 | Graham, Hudson |
| 13 | 2 Oct | Colchester United | 0-1 | 8691 | |
| 14 | 9 | COVENTRY CITY | 1-1 | 10327 | Graham |
| 15 | 16 | Southampton | 0-2 | 13880 | |
| 16 | 23 | MILLWALL | 2-1 | 9126 | Graham, Wharton |
| 17 | 30 | Torquay United | 3-2 | 7300 | Johnston(2), Graham |
| 18 | 6 Nov | GILLINGHAM | 1-3 | 9164 | Lucas |
| 19 | 13 | Reading | 1-2 | 9334 | Johnston |
| 20 | 27 | Walsall | 3-3 | 12059 | Johnston(2), Graham |
| 21 | 4 Dec | BRISTOL CITY | 2-2 | 10886 | Johnston(2) |
| 22 | 18 | Northampton Town | 2-2 | 6947 | Lucas, Harris |
| 23 | 25 | Crystal Palace | 1-2 | 8934 | Johnston |
| 24 | 27 | CRYSTAL PALACE | 0-1 | 13025 | |
| 25 | 1 Jan | WATFORD | 0-2 | 7132 | |
| 26 | 15 | Bournemouth & B.A. | 3-3 | 5830 | Shergold, Harris, Johnston |
| 27 | 22 | Q.P.RANGERS | 4-0 | 5457 | Harris(2), Johnston(2) |
| 28 | 5 Feb | BRIGHTON & H.A. | 1-3 | 7025 | Gilberg(og) |
| 29 | 12 | Exeter City | 1-1 | 6545 | Johnston |
| 30 | 19 | COLCHESTER UNITED | 0-0 | 5612 | |
| 31 | 5 Mar | SOUTHAMPTON | 0-1 | 7512 | |
| 32 | 12 | Millwall | 1-1 | 9086 | Johnston |
| 33 | 17 | Leyton Orient | 2-1 | 10600 | Graham, Johnston |
| 34 | 19 | TORQUAY UNITED | 1-1 | 6936 | Johnston |
| 35 | 26 | Gillingham | 2-4 | 7784 | Johnston(2) |
| 36 | 2 Apr | READING | 3-1 | 5066 | Johnston(2), Shergold |
| 37 | 4 | Coventry City | 2-3 | 3936 | Harris, Johnston |
| 38 | 8 | SWINDON TOWN | 2-2 | 8595 | Johnston, Hudson(og) |
| 39 | 9 | Shrewsbury Town | 0-3 | 8652 | |
| 40 | 11 | Swindon Town | 3-1 | 7957 | Lucas, Harris, Johnston |
| 41 | 16 | WALSALL | 1-0 | 7914 | Hudson |
| 42 | 21 | BRENTFORD | 3-1 | 7926 | Johnston(2), Harris |
| 43 | 23 | Bristol City | 0-0 | 27499 | |
| 44 | 28 | SHREWSBURY TOWN | 1-1 | 6762 | Johnston |
| 45 | 30 | LEYTON ORIENT | 1-2 | 5894 | Johnston |
| 46 | 2 May | Brentford | 0-1 | 5812 | |

## F.A.Cup

| | | | | | |
|---|---|---|---|---|---|
| 1 | 20 Nov | Gillingham | 0-2 | 10237 | |

| Player | League | | F.A.Cup | | Total | |
|---|---|---|---|---|---|---|
| | App | Gls. | App | Gls. | App | Gls. |
| Graham L. | 39 | 8 | 1 | 0 | 41 | 8 |
| Harris D.H. | 25 | 8 | – | – | 27 | 9 |
| Hayward D.S. | 37 | 0 | 1 | 0 | 40 | 0 |
| Hollyman K.C. | 36 | 0 | 1 | 0 | 39 | 0 |
| Hudson C.A.R. | 16 | 2 | – | – | 16 | 2 |
| Hughes I. | 24 | 0 | – | – | 26 | 0 |
| Johnston T.B. | 32 | 26 | 1 | 0 | 35 | 29 |
| Lever A.R. | 22 | 0 | – | – | 24 | 0 |
| Lewis N. | 15 | 0 | – | – | 15 | 0 |
| Lucas W.H. | 39 | 4 | 1 | 0 | 42 | 4 |
| McGhee J.W. | 10 | 1 | – | – | 11 | 3 |
| Newall D.J. | 5 | 0 | – | – | 5 | 0 |
| Pope T.J. | 22 | 0 | 1 | 0 | 23 | 0 |
| Prangley S. | – | – | – | – | 1 | 0 |
| Reed T.R. | 1 | 0 | – | – | 1 | 0 |
| Saward L.R. | 9 | 0 | – | – | 9 | 0 |
| Shergold W.R. | 41 | 5 | 1 | 0 | 44 | 6 |
| Staples L.E. | 20 | 0 | 1 | 0 | 21 | 0 |
| Stroud W.J.A. | 1 | 0 | – | – | 1 | 0 |
| Thomas G.V. | 37 | 0 | 1 | 0 | 40 | 0 |
| Wharton J.E. | 29 | 3 | 1 | 0 | 30 | 3 |
| Wilcox R. | 46 | 0 | 1 | 0 | 48 | 0 |
| Own Goal | | 3 | | | | 3 |

| | | P | W | D | L | F | A | Pts |
|---|---|---|---|---|---|---|---|---|
| 1 | Bristol City | 46 | 30 | 10 | 6 | 101 | 47 | 70 |
| 2 | Leyton Orient | 46 | 26 | 9 | 11 | 89 | 47 | 61 |
| 3 | Southampton | 46 | 24 | 11 | 11 | 75 | 51 | 59 |
| 4 | Gillingham | 46 | 20 | 15 | 11 | 77 | 66 | 55 |
| 5 | Millwall | 46 | 20 | 11 | 15 | 72 | 68 | 51 |
| 6 | Brighton | 46 | 20 | 10 | 16 | 76 | 63 | 50 |
| 7 | Watford | 46 | 18 | 14 | 14 | 71 | 62 | 50 |
| 8 | Torquay | 46 | 18 | 12 | 16 | 82 | 82 | 48 |
| 9 | Coventry | 46 | 18 | 11 | 17 | 67 | 59 | 47 |
| 10 | Southend | 46 | 17 | 12 | 17 | 83 | 80 | 46 |
| 11 | Brentford | 46 | 16 | 14 | 16 | 82 | 82 | 46 |
| 12 | Norwich | 46 | 18 | 10 | 18 | 60 | 60 | 46 |
| 13 | Northampton | 46 | 19 | 8 | 19 | 73 | 81 | 46 |
| 14 | Aldershot | 46 | 16 | 13 | 17 | 75 | 71 | 45 |
| 15 | QPR | 46 | 15 | 14 | 17 | 69 | 75 | 44 |
| 16 | Shrewsbury | 46 | 16 | 10 | 20 | 70 | 78 | 42 |
| 17 | Bournemouth | 46 | 12 | 18 | 16 | 57 | 65 | 42 |
| 18 | Reading | 46 | 13 | 15 | 18 | 65 | 73 | 41 |
| 19 | Newport | 46 | 11 | 16 | 19 | 60 | 73 | 38 |
| 20 | Crystal Palace | 46 | 11 | 16 | 19 | 52 | 80 | 38 |
| 21 | Swindon | 46 | 11 | 15 | 20 | 46 | 64 | 37 |
| 22 | Exeter | 46 | 11 | 15 | 20 | 47 | 73 | 37 |
| 23 | Walsall | 46 | 10 | 14 | 22 | 75 | 86 | 34 |
| 24 | Colchester | 46 | 9 | 13 | 24 | 53 | 91 | 31 |

(Back) Saward, Hayward, Hughes, Lever, Newall, Pope, Staples, Lewis
(Front) Lucas (P/Manager), Hollyman, McGhee, Wilcox, Shergold, Graham, Wharton

## SEASON 1955-56 Division 3(South)

| | Date | Opposition | Res. | Att. | Goalscorers |
|---|---|---|---|---|---|
| 1 | 20 Aug | Shrewsbury Town | 0-5 | 9987 | |
| 2 | 24 | Aldershot | 0-1 | 6212 | |
| 3 | 27 | IPSWICH TOWN | 2-1 | 8595 | Shergold(2) |
| 4 | 1 Sep | ALDERSHOT | 0-1 | 7906 | |
| 5 | 3 | Walsall | 3-3 | 14443 | Johnston(2), Beech |
| 6 | 8 | SOUTHAMPTON | 1-0 | 7048 | Harris |
| 7 | 10 | TORQUAY UNITED | 2-1 | 9012 | Beech, Brown |
| 8 | 14 | Southampton | 3-3 | 7779 | Shergold, Johnston, Harris |
| 9 | 17 | Southend United | 1-4 | 11243 | Johnston |
| 10 | 22 | CRYSTAL PALACE | 0-1 | 6601 | |
| 11 | 24 | Swindon Town | 2-1 | 7870 | Johnston, Harris |
| 12 | 29 | NORTHAMPTON TOWN | 0-1 | 8076 | |
| 13 | 1 Oct | Q.P.RANGERS | 2-1 | 7375 | Harris(2) |
| 14 | 8 | LEYTON ORIENT | 3-0 | 8904 | Johnston(3) |
| 15 | 15 | Colchester United | 1-2 | 8225 | Johnston |
| 16 | 22 | NORWICH CITY | 2-2 | 5977 | Johnston, Beech |
| 17 | 29 | Bournemouth & B.A. | 0-0 | 7459 | |
| 18 | 5 Nov | GILLINGHAM | 3-2 | 6745 | Johnston(2), Beech |
| 19 | 12 | Millwall | 4-2 | 9174 | Harris(3), Johnston |
| 20 | 26 | Watford | 1-1 | 7180 | Johnston |
| 21 | 3 Dec | BRENTFORD | 1-2 | 8035 | Hudson |
| 22 | 10 | Coventry City | 0-3 | 17325 | |
| 23 | 17 | SHREWSBURY TOWN | 1-2 | 5287 | Beech |
| 24 | 24 | Ipswich Town | 2-3 | 11631 | Johnston(2) |
| 25 | 26 | Brighton & H.A. | 1-4 | 13494 | Johnston |
| 26 | 27 | BRIGHTON & H.A. | 1-0 | 5907 | Johnston |
| 27 | 31 | WALSALL | 2-0 | 8008 | Harris(2) |
| 28 | 7 Jan | READING | 2-3 | 7605 | Harris, Beech |
| 29 | 14 | Torquay United | 1-1 | 6346 | Johnston |
| 30 | 11 Feb | Q.P.Rangers | 0-0 | 3781 | |
| 31 | 18 | Leyton Orient | 1-3 | 11154 | Johnston |
| 32 | 25 | COLCHESTER UNITED | 0-0 | 5588 | |
| 33 | 3 Mar | Norwich City | 3-2 | 14145 | Shergold, Harris, Brown |
| 34 | 10 | BOURNEMOUTH & B.A. | 1-0 | 6668 | Burgess |
| 35 | 17 | Gillingham | 2-3 | 6203 | Burgess, Harris |
| 36 | 24 | MILLWALL | 1-4 | 4567 | Hudson |
| 37 | 30 | EXETER CITY | 1-2 | 5976 | Harris |
| 38 | 31 | Reading | 0-3 | 7664 | |
| 39 | 2 Apr | Exeter City | 0-2 | 7363 | |
| 40 | 7 | WATFORD | 0-1 | 3993 | |
| 41 | 12 | SWINDON TOWN | 1-0 | 2346 | Hudson |
| 42 | 14 | Brentford | 1-1 | 5291 | Shergold |
| 43 | 19 | SOUTHEND UNITED | 2-0 | 4286 | Shergold, Burgess |
| 44 | 21 | COVENTRY CITY | 4-2 | 6100 | Burgess, Brown, Hudson, Tennant |
| 45 | 26 | Northampton Town | 0-5 | 3436 | |
| 46 | 28 | Crystal Palace | 0-1 | 7635 | |

| Player | League | | F.A.Cup | | Total | |
|---|---|---|---|---|---|---|
| | App | Gls. | App | Gls. | App | Gls. |
| Beech C. | 28 | 6 | 1 | 0 | 30 | 7 |
| Brown G. | 38 | 3 | 1 | 0 | 42 | 3 |
| Burgess M.R. | 13 | 4 | – | – | 14 | 4 |
| Capel J.E. | 3 | 0 | – | – | 3 | 0 |
| Dewsbury J. | 2 | 0 | – | – | 2 | 0 |
| Docherty T. | 40 | 0 | 1 | 0 | 44 | 1 |
| Harris D.H. | 45 | 14 | 1 | 0 | 49 | 19 |
| Hayward D.S. | 9 | 0 | – | – | 9 | 0 |
| Hollyman K.C. | 40 | 0 | 1 | 0 | 44 | 0 |
| Hudson C.A.R. | 21 | 4 | – | – | 23 | 7 |
| Hughes G. | 4 | 0 | – | – | 4 | 0 |
| Hughes I. | 13 | 0 | 1 | 0 | 14 | 0 |
| Johnston T.B. | 31 | 20 | 1 | 1 | 33 | 24 |
| Lever A.R. | 43 | 0 | 1 | 0 | 47 | 1 |
| Lucas W.H. | 13 | 0 | – | – | 13 | 0 |
| Montgomery S.W.J | 9 | 0 | – | – | 10 | 0 |
| Shergold W.R. | 40 | 6 | 1 | 0 | 44 | 7 |
| Staples L.E. | 3 | 0 | – | – | 3 | 0 |
| Tennant S.D.K. | 17 | 1 | – | – | 20 | 1 |
| Thomas G.V. | 24 | 0 | 1 | 0 | 26 | 0 |
| Weare L. | 33 | 0 | – | – | 36 | 0 |
| Wilcox R. | 37 | 0 | 1 | 0 | 40 | 0 |

| | | P | W | D | L | F | A | Pts |
|---|---|---|---|---|---|---|---|---|
| 1 | Leyton Orient | 46 | 29 | 8 | 9 | 106 | 49 | 66 |
| 2 | Brighton | 46 | 29 | 7 | 10 | 112 | 50 | 65 |
| 3 | Ipswich | 46 | 25 | 14 | 7 | 106 | 60 | 64 |
| 4 | Southend | 46 | 21 | 11 | 14 | 88 | 80 | 53 |
| 5 | Torquay | 46 | 20 | 12 | 14 | 86 | 63 | 52 |
| 6 | Brentford | 46 | 19 | 14 | 13 | 69 | 66 | 52 |
| 7 | Norwich | 46 | 19 | 13 | 14 | 86 | 82 | 51 |
| 8 | Coventry | 46 | 20 | 9 | 17 | 73 | 60 | 49 |
| 9 | Bournemouth | 46 | 19 | 10 | 17 | 63 | 51 | 48 |
| 10 | Gillingham | 46 | 19 | 10 | 17 | 69 | 71 | 48 |
| 11 | Northampton | 46 | 20 | 7 | 19 | 67 | 71 | 47 |
| 12 | Colchester | 46 | 18 | 11 | 17 | 76 | 81 | 47 |
| 13 | Shrewsbury | 46 | 17 | 12 | 17 | 69 | 66 | 46 |
| 14 | Southampton | 46 | 18 | 8 | 20 | 91 | 81 | 44 |
| 15 | Aldershot | 46 | 12 | 16 | 18 | 70 | 90 | 40 |
| 16 | Exeter | 46 | 15 | 10 | 21 | 58 | 77 | 40 |
| 17 | Reading | 46 | 15 | 9 | 22 | 70 | 79 | 39 |
| 18 | QPR | 46 | 14 | 11 | 21 | 64 | 86 | 39 |
| 19 | Newport | 46 | 15 | 9 | 22 | 58 | 79 | 39 |
| 20 | Walsall | 46 | 15 | 8 | 23 | 68 | 84 | 38 |
| 21 | Watford | 46 | 13 | 11 | 22 | 52 | 85 | 37 |
| 22 | Millwall | 46 | 15 | 6 | 25 | 83 | 100 | 36 |
| 23 | Crystal Palace | 46 | 12 | 10 | 24 | 54 | 83 | 34 |
| 24 | Swindon | 46 | 8 | 14 | 24 | 34 | 78 | 30 |

### F.A.Cup

| | | | | | | |
|---|---|---|---|---|---|---|
| 1 | 19 Nov | Brighton & H.A. | 1 8 | 19010 | Johnston | |

(Back) Beech, Lever, Thomas, Weare, Johnston, Docherty
(Front) Hollyman, Brown, Wilcox, Hudson, Shergold

# SEASON 1956-57 Division 3(South)

| | Date | Opposition | Res. | Att. | Goalscorers |
|---|---|---|---|---|---|
| 1 | 18 Aug | NORTHAMPTON TOWN | 3-0 | 11371 | Terry(2), Harris |
| 2 | 22 | Southend United | 3-3 | 10934 | Brown(2), Terry |
| 3 | 25 | Q.P.Rangers | 1-1 | 7844 | Harris |
| 4 | 30 | SOUTHEND UNITED | 2-1 | 12224 | Hudson, Brown |
| 5 | 1 Sep | PLYMOUTH ARGYLE | 4-1 | 12089 | Harris(2), Hudson, Terry |
| 6 | 5 | Exeter City | 0-2 | 5174 | |
| 7 | 8 | Reading | 0-0 | 11598 | |
| 8 | 13 | EXETER CITY | 1-1 | 10592 | Terry |
| 9 | 15 | WATFORD | 3-0 | 11547 | Terry, Burgess, Beech |
| 10 | 19 | Crystal Palace | 1-2 | 14132 | Terry |
| 11 | 22 | COLCHESTER UNITED | 1-0 | 12426 | Sheppeard |
| 12 | 27 | CRYSTAL PALACE | 2-2 | 8008 | Sherwood, Beech |
| 13 | 29 | Norwich City | 1-1 | 16920 | Terry |
| 14 | 6 Oct | Walsall | 0-0 | 10894 | |
| 15 | 13 | IPSWICH TOWN | 1-0 | 12673 | Terry |
| 16 | 20 | Bournemouth & B.A. | 1-2 | 10337 | Reynolds |
| 17 | 27 | TORQUAY UNITED | 3-0 | 12008 | Harris(2), Terry |
| 18 | 3 Nov | Millwall | 0-1 | 13127 | |
| 19 | 10 | BRIGHTON & H.A. | 0-0 | 9082 | |
| 20 | 24 | SWINDON TOWN | 2-1 | 9570 | Harris(2) |
| 21 | 1 Dec | Brentford | 0-0 | 11120 | |
| 22 | 15 | Northampton Town | 3-0 | 6289 | Hudson, Harris, Brown |
| 23 | 22 | Q.P.RANGERS | 1-1 | 7638 | Sherwood |
| 24 | 12 Jan | READING | 1-2 | 13840 | Hollyman |
| 25 | 19 | Watford | 0-5 | 7683 | |
| 26 | 2 Feb | Colchester United | 0-1 | 9705 | |
| 27 | 9 | NORWICH CITY | 3-1 | 7088 | Hudson, Harris, Burgess |
| 28 | 16 | WALSALL | 2-2 | 9115 | Sherwood, Sheppeard |
| 29 | 23 | Ipswich Town | 0-5 | 13346 | |
| 30 | 7 Mar | BOURNEMOUTH & B.A. | 5-3 | 8047 | Hudson(4), Lucas |
| 31 | 9 | Aldershot | 1-3 | 5123 | Hudson |
| 32 | 16 | MILLWALL | 0-0 | 7002 | |
| 33 | 21 | COVENTRY CITY | 3-0 | 6332 | Hudson, Terry, Harris |
| 34 | 23 | Brighton & H.A. | 0-2 | 12503 | |
| 35 | 30 | GILLINGHAM | 4-0 | 7017 | Hudson(2), Sheppeard, Harris |
| 36 | 4 Apr | SOUTHAMPTON | 2-3 | 6982 | Docherty, Harris |
| 37 | 6 | Swindon Town | 0-1 | 7889 | |
| 38 | 8 | Coventry City | 0-2 | 5569 | |
| 39 | 10 | Plymouth Argyle | 2-3 | 10148 | Hudson, Sheppeard |
| 40 | 13 | BRENTFORD | 3-0 | 5497 | Terry(2), Hudson |
| 41 | 19 | SHREWSBURY TOWN | 2-0 | 7783 | Terry, Harris |
| 42 | 20 | Torquay United | 0-4 | 8727 | |
| 43 | 22 | Shrewsbury Town | 0-2 | 7580 | |
| 44 | 27 | Gillingham | 1-1 | 4237 | Burgess |
| 45 | 2 May | ALDERSHOT | 3-0 | 4578 | Hudson, Terry, Harris |
| 46 | 4 | Southampton | 0-3 | 5721 | |

| Player | League | | F.A.Cup | | Total | |
|---|---|---|---|---|---|---|
| | App | Gls. | App | Gls. | App | Gls. |
| Beech C. | 11 | 2 | – | – | 13 | 2 |
| Brown G. | 27 | 4 | 4 | 1 | 32 | 5 |
| Burgess M.R. | 10 | 3 | – | – | 12 | 5 |
| Docherty T. | 35 | 1 | 4 | 0 | 43 | 1 |
| Harris D.H. | 44 | 15 | 5 | 3 | 53 | 20 |
| Herrity W.R. | 4 | 0 | – | – | 4 | 0 |
| Hollyman K.C. | 36 | 1 | 3 | 0 | 41 | 1 |
| Hudson C.A.R. | 44 | 15 | 5 | 1 | 53 | 17 |
| Lever A.R. | 7 | 0 | 1 | 0 | 10 | 0 |
| Lucas W.H. | 11 | 1 | 4 | 0 | 17 | 2 |
| Reynolds G.E.A. | 4 | 1 | – | – | 4 | 1 |
| Rodger J.M. | 1 | 0 | – | – | 1 | 0 |
| Sherwood A.T. | 42 | 3 | 5 | 0 | 50 | 3 |
| Sheppeard H.T. | 29 | 4 | 2 | 0 | 33 | 4 |
| Staples L.E. | 4 | 0 | 1 | 0 | 5 | 0 |
| Tennant S.D.K. | 17 | 0 | 1 | 0 | 19 | 0 |
| Terry P.A. | 33 | 15 | 5 | 2 | 39 | 18 |
| Thomas G.V. | 43 | 0 | 5 | 0 | 52 | 0 |
| Thomas P.J. | 2 | 0 | – | – | 2 | 0 |
| Weare L. | 46 | 0 | 5 | 0 | 55 | 0 |
| Wilcox R. | 46 | 0 | 5 | 0 | 55 | 0 |
| Williams H. | 10 | 0 | – | – | 12 | 0 |

| | | P | W | D | L | F | A | Pts |
|---|---|---|---|---|---|---|---|---|
| 1 | Ipswich | 46 | 25 | 9 | 12 | 101 | 54 | 59 |
| 2 | Torquay | 46 | 24 | 11 | 11 | 89 | 64 | 59 |
| 3 | Colchester | 46 | 22 | 14 | 10 | 84 | 56 | 58 |
| 4 | Southampton | 46 | 22 | 10 | 14 | 76 | 52 | 54 |
| 5 | Bournemouth | 46 | 19 | 14 | 13 | 88 | 62 | 52 |
| 6 | Brighton | 46 | 19 | 14 | 13 | 86 | 65 | 52 |
| 7 | Southend | 46 | 18 | 12 | 16 | 73 | 65 | 48 |
| 8 | Brentford | 46 | 16 | 16 | 14 | 78 | 76 | 48 |
| 9 | Shrewsbury | 46 | 15 | 18 | 13 | 72 | 79 | 48 |
| 10 | QPR | 46 | 18 | 11 | 17 | 61 | 60 | 47 |
| 11 | Watford | 46 | 18 | 10 | 18 | 72 | 75 | 46 |
| 12 | Newport | 46 | 16 | 13 | 17 | 65 | 62 | 45 |
| 13 | Reading | 46 | 18 | 9 | 19 | 80 | 81 | 45 |
| 14 | Northampton | 46 | 18 | 9 | 19 | 66 | 73 | 45 |
| 15 | Walsall | 46 | 16 | 12 | 18 | 80 | 74 | 44 |
| 16 | Coventry | 46 | 16 | 12 | 18 | 74 | 84 | 44 |
| 17 | Millwall | 46 | 16 | 12 | 18 | 64 | 84 | 44 |
| 18 | Plymouth | 46 | 16 | 11 | 19 | 68 | 73 | 43 |
| 19 | Aldershot | 46 | 15 | 12 | 19 | 79 | 92 | 42 |
| 20 | Crystal Palace | 46 | 11 | 18 | 17 | 62 | 75 | 40 |
| 21 | Exeter | 46 | 12 | 13 | 21 | 61 | 79 | 37 |
| 22 | Gillingham | 46 | 12 | 13 | 21 | 54 | 85 | 37 |
| 23 | Swindon | 46 | 15 | 6 | 25 | 66 | 96 | 36 |
| 24 | Norwich | 46 | 8 | 15 | 23 | 61 | 94 | 31 |

## F.A.Cup

| | Date | Opposition | Res. | Att. | Goalscorers |
|---|---|---|---|---|---|
| 1 | 17 Nov | Walsall | 1-0 | 12085 | Terry |
| 2 | 8 Dec | Gillingham | 2-1 | 8700 | Terry, Brown |
| 3 | 5 Jan | SOUTHAMPTON | 3-3 | 18562 | Harris(2), Hudson |
| 3R | 9 | Southampton | 1-0 | 22372 | Harris |
| 4 | 26 | ARSENAL | 0-2 | 22450 | |

(Back) Wilcox, Terry, Weare, Sheppeard, Harris, Docherty
(Front) Hudson, Hollyman, Sherwood, G.Thomas, Brown

# SEASON 1957-58 Division 3(South)

| | Date | Opposition | Res. | Att. | Goalscorers |
|---|---|---|---|---|---|
| 1 | 24 Aug | Swindon Town | 0-4 | 14396 | |
| 2 | 29 | COVENTRY CITY | 2-2 | 10654 | Harris, Brown |
| 3 | 31 | MILLWALL | 1-2 | 9320 | McSeveney |
| 4 | 2 Sep | Coventry City | 2-1 | 14759 | O'Halloran, P.Thomas |
| 5 | 7 | Gllingham | 1-0 | 8709 | Sherwood |
| 6 | 12 | WALSALL | 2-0 | 7700 | Sheppeard(2) |
| 7 | 14 | EXETER CITY | 0-0 | 9213 | |
| 8 | 19 | Walsall | 0-3 | 7688 | |
| 9 | 21 | Q.P.Rangers | 1-1 | 9065 | Harris |
| 10 | 28 | SOUTHEND UNITED | 1-0 | 8203 | Harris |
| 11 | 30 | Port Vale | 2-2 | 8659 | Terry, Harris |
| 12 | 5 Oct | Brighton & H.A. | 3-5 | 14560 | Terry, Harris, Graham |
| 13 | 12 | Shrewsbury Town | 1-1 | 6408 | Harris |
| 14 | 26 | Northampton Town | 3-0 | 7953 | O'Halloran, Harris, McSeveney |
| 15 | 28 | READING | 0-0 | 5048 | |
| 16 | 2 Nov | WATFORD | 2-1 | 8212 | Sherwood, McSeveney |
| 17 | 9 | Crystal Palace | 2-2 | 11082 | Terry, McSeveney |
| 18 | 11 | PORT VALE | 2-1 | 8480 | McSeveney, Rodger |
| 19 | 23 | Brentford | 1-2 | 13600 | Brown |
| 20 | 30 | COLCHESTER UNITED | 2-2 | 8866 | Harris, Dixon |
| 21 | 14 Dec | BOURNEMOUTH & B.A. | 3-1 | 5469 | Terry(2), Brown |
| 22 | 21 | SWINDON TOWN | 4-1 | 7815 | Terry(2), Sherwood, Harris |
| 23 | 25 | PLYMOUTH ARGYLE | 0-2 | 10680 | |
| 24 | 26 | Plymouth Argyle | 0-1 | 25936 | |
| 25 | 28 | Millwall | 2-1 | 9894 | Terry(2) |
| 26 | 4 Jan | SOUTHAMPTON | 1-1 | 5117 | Brown |
| 27 | 11 | GILLINGHAM | 5-0 | 6206 | Terry(2), McSeveney, Brown, Harris |
| 28 | 18 | Exeter City | 2-0 | 7471 | Dixon, Harris |
| 29 | 1 Feb | Q.P.RANGERS | 4-2 | 7543 | Terry(2), Harris, Brown |
| 30 | 8 | Southend United | 1-1 | 10093 | Terry |
| 31 | 15 | BRIGHTON & H.A. | 1-2 | 9424 | Terry |
| 32 | 22 | SHREWSBURY TOWN | 2-0 | 6268 | Dixon, Graham |
| 33 | 1 Mar | Reading | 0-1 | 15798 | |
| 34 | 6 | TORQUAY UNITED | 3-2 | 3200 | McSeveney(2), Harris |
| 35 | 8 | NORTHAMPTON TOWN | 0-1 | 6800 | |
| 36 | 15 | Watford | 2-2 | 7029 | Dixon, McSeveney |
| 37 | 22 | BRENTFORD | 1-2 | 5621 | Dixon |
| 38 | 29 | Bournemouth & B.A. | 3-4 | 11496 | Harris, McSeveney, Shergold |
| 39 | 4 Apr | Aldershot | 1-2 | 4665 | Singer |
| 40 | 5 | CRYSTAL PALACE | 0-0 | 4118 | |
| 41 | 7 | ALDERSHOT | 3-2 | 5555 | Singer(2), McSeveney |
| 42 | 12 | Colchester United | 1-1 | 7472 | Harris |
| 43 | 16 | Norwich City | 2-5 | 19486 | Harris, McSeveney |
| 44 | 19 | NORWICH CITY | 1-0 | 6081 | McSeveney |
| 45 | 23 | Southampton | 1-2 | 12925 | Harris |
| 46 | 26 | Torquay United | 2-2 | 5685 | Harris, McSeveney |

## F.A.Cup

| | | | | | |
|---|---|---|---|---|---|
| 1 | 16 Nov | Northampton Town | 0-3 | 9345 | |

| Player | League | | F.A.Cup | | Total | |
|---|---|---|---|---|---|---|
| | App | Gls. | App | Gls. | App | Gls. |
| Bird J.F. | 2 | 0 | – | – | 3 | 0 |
| Brown G. | 44 | 6 | 1 | 0 | 46 | 6 |
| Dixon C.H. | 31 | 5 | 1 | 0 | 33 | 5 |
| Docherty T. | 32 | 0 | 1 | 0 | 34 | 0 |
| Duncan T.M. | 1 | 0 | – | – | 1 | 0 |
| Graham L. | 36 | 2 | 1 | 0 | 37 | 2 |
| Harris D.H. | 43 | 18 | – | – | 44 | 18 |
| Hollyman K.C. | 45 | 0 | 1 | 0 | 47 | 0 |
| Hughes I. | 29 | 0 | 1 | 0 | 31 | 0 |
| Lucas W.H. | 10 | 0 | – | – | 10 | 0 |
| McSeveney J.H. | 46 | 14 | 1 | 0 | 48 | 15 |
| O'Halloran N. | 14 | 2 | – | – | 14 | 2 |
| Rodger J.M. | 4 | 1 | 1 | 0 | 5 | 1 |
| Sheppeard H.T. | 2 | 2 | – | – | 2 | 2 |
| Sherwood A.T. | 45 | 4 | 1 | 0 | 46 | 4 |
| Singer D.J. | 6 | 3 | – | – | 6 | 3 |
| Tennant S.D.K. | 6 | 0 | – | – | 7 | 0 |
| Terry P.A. | 22 | 15 | 1 | 0 | 24 | 16 |
| Thomas G.V. | 24 | 0 | – | – | 25 | 0 |
| Thomas P.J. | 4 | 1 | – | – | 4 | 1 |
| Weare L. | 17 | 0 | – | – | 17 | 0 |
| Wilcox R. | 43 | 0 | 1 | 0 | 44 | 0 |

| | | P | W | D | L | F | A | Pts |
|---|---|---|---|---|---|---|---|---|
| 1 | Brighton | 46 | 24 | 12 | 10 | 88 | 64 | 60 |
| 2 | Brentford | 46 | 24 | 10 | 12 | 82 | 56 | 58 |
| 3 | Plymouth | 46 | 25 | 8 | 13 | 67 | 48 | 58 |
| 4 | Swindon | 46 | 21 | 15 | 10 | 79 | 50 | 57 |
| 5 | Reading | 46 | 21 | 13 | 12 | 79 | 51 | 55 |
| 6 | Southampton | 46 | 22 | 10 | 14 | 112 | 72 | 54 |
| 7 | Southend | 46 | 21 | 12 | 13 | 90 | 58 | 54 |
| 8 | Norwich | 46 | 19 | 15 | 12 | 75 | 70 | 53 |
| 9 | Bournemouth | 46 | 21 | 9 | 16 | 81 | 74 | 51 |
| 10 | QPR | 46 | 18 | 14 | 14 | 64 | 65 | 50 |
| 11 | Newport | 46 | 17 | 14 | 15 | 73 | 67 | 48 |
| 12 | Colchester | 46 | 17 | 13 | 16 | 77 | 79 | 47 |
| 13 | Northampton | 46 | 19 | 6 | 21 | 87 | 79 | 44 |
| 14 | Crystal Palace | 46 | 15 | 13 | 18 | 70 | 72 | 43 |
| 15 | Port Vale | 46 | 16 | 10 | 20 | 67 | 58 | 42 |
| 16 | Watford | 46 | 13 | 16 | 17 | 59 | 77 | 42 |
| 17 | Shrewsbury | 46 | 15 | 10 | 21 | 49 | 71 | 40 |
| 18 | Aldershot | 46 | 12 | 16 | 18 | 59 | 89 | 40 |
| 19 | Coventry | 46 | 13 | 13 | 20 | 61 | 81 | 39 |
| 20 | Walsall | 46 | 14 | 9 | 23 | 61 | 75 | 37 |
| 21 | Torquay | 46 | 11 | 13 | 22 | 49 | 74 | 35 |
| 22 | Gillingham | 46 | 13 | 9 | 24 | 52 | 81 | 35 |
| 23 | Millwall | 46 | 11 | 9 | 26 | 63 | 91 | 31 |
| 24 | Exeter | 46 | 11 | 9 | 26 | 57 | 99 | 31 |

O'Halloran, Wilcox, Hughes, Lucas, Docherty
McSeveney, Graham, Sherwood, Hollyman, Harris, Brown

# SEASON 1958-59     *Division 3*

| | Date | Opposition | Res. | Att. | Goalscorers |
|---|---|---|---|---|---|
| 1 | 23 Aug | Norwich City | 0–3 | 25873 | |
| 2 | 27 | Accrington Stanley | 2–2 | 10284 | McPherson, Singer |
| 3 | 30 | CHESTERFIELD | 0–1 | 10968 | |
| 4 | 4 Sep | ACCRINGTON STANLEY | 2–1 | 8891 | McPherson, Singer |
| 5 | 6 | Notts County | 1–1 | 12249 | Singer |
| 6 | 10 | Wrexham | 0–0 | 13113 | |
| 7 | 13 | MANSFIELD TOWN | 1–0 | 8492 | Singer |
| 8 | 18 | WREXHAM | 2–1 | 8113 | Singer, Herrity |
| 9 | 20 | Swindon Town | 1–2 | 12522 | Singer |
| 10 | 22 | Halifax Town | 1–3 | 5150 | McSeveney |
| 11 | 27 | BRENTFORD | 0–1 | 8220 | |
| 12 | 2 Oct | HALIFAX TOWN | 0–2 | 6939 | |
| 13 | 4 | Hull City | 3–2 | 14753 | Jones, McPherson, Singer |
| 14 | 9 | BRADFORD CITY | 3–2 | 7317 | Graham, Singer, Rowland |
| 15 | 11 | Bury | 0–0 | 9412 | |
| 16 | 20 | Q.P.RANGERS | 3–1 | 8400 | McSeveney, McPherson, Graham |
| 17 | 25 | Rochdale | 1–1 | 4998 | McPherson |
| 18 | 1 Nov | DONCASTER ROVERS | 3–1 | 7316 | McPherson(2), Graham |
| 19 | 8 | Plymouth Argyle | 2–3 | 23482 | Singer, Hollyman |
| 20 | 22 | Colchester United | 2–3 | 7271 | McPherson, Graham |
| 21 | 29 | READING | 2–1 | 6184 | Graham, Sherwood |
| 22 | 13 Dec | BOURNEMOUTH & B.A. | 4–1 | 5392 | Jones, Dixon, McSeveney, McPherson |
| 23 | 20 | NORWICH CITY | 2–2 | 4538 | McSeveney, Jones |
| 24 | 25 | SOUTHAMPTON | 4–2 | 9034 | McPherson(2), McSeveney, Graham |
| 25 | 27 | Southampton | 3–3 | 21495 | Sherwood, McSeveney, McPherson |
| 26 | 3 Jan | Chesterfield | 1–3 | 9225 | McSeveney |
| 27 | 31 | Mansfield Town | 1–2 | 8347 | McSeveney |
| 28 | 7 Feb | SWINDON TOWN | 3–0 | 4346 | Jones, McPherson, Graham |
| 29 | 14 | Brentford | 0–3 | 10380 | |
| 30 | 21 | HULL CITY | 1–3 | 6988 | Sherwood |
| 31 | 28 | BURY | 1–1 | 5214 | Dixon |
| 32 | 2 Mar | Stockport County | 1–2 | 8079 | Graham |
| 33 | 7 | Q.P.Rangers | 2–4 | 5607 | Graham, Meyer |
| 34 | 9 | TRANMERE ROVERS | 3–0 | 4933 | Jones, Meyer, Rowland |
| 35 | 14 | ROCHDALE | 1–0 | 4469 | McPherson |
| 36 | 16 | NOTTS COUNTY | 3–1 | 5869 | McSeveney, Meyer, Brown |
| 37 | 21 | Doncaster Rovers | 0–1 | 3907 | |
| 38 | 28 | PLYMOUTH ARGYLE | 0–1 | 8108 | |
| 39 | 30 | Southend United | 0–1 | 9672 | |
| 40 | 4 Apr | Tranmere Rovers | 1–2 | 9301 | Meyer |
| 41 | 13 | SOUTHEND UNITED | 3–1 | 5070 | Graham(2), McSeveney |
| 42 | 18 | Reading | 3–1 | 7484 | McSeveney, McPherson, Meyer |
| 43 | 22 | Bradford City | 0–1 | 8926 | |
| 44 | 25 | STOCKPORT COUNTY | 2–0 | 2447 | Graham, Meyer |
| 45 | 29 | Bournemouth & B.A. | 1–1 | 7384 | Graham |
| 46 | 4 May | COLCHESTER UNITED | 0–1 | 4702 | |

## F.A.Cup

| | Date | Opposition | Res. | Att. | Goalscorers |
|---|---|---|---|---|---|
| 1 | 15 Nov | Wisbech Town | 2–2 | 5500 | McPherson, Graham |
| 1R | 17 | WISBECH TOWN | 4–1 | 4848 | McSeveney(2), McPherson, Graham |
| 2 | 6 Dec | Hereford United | 2–0 | 12012 | McPherson, Graham |
| 3 | 1 Jan | TORQUAY UNITED | 0–0 | 10600 | |
| 3R | 14 | Torquay United | 1–0 | 6567 | McPherson |
| 4 | 21 | Tottenham Hotspur | 1–4 | 50561 | Hollyman |

| Player | League | | F.A.Cup | | Total | |
|---|---|---|---|---|---|---|
| | App | Gls. | App | Gls. | App | Gls. |
| Bird J.F. | 6 | 0 | – | – | 6 | 0 |
| Brown G. | 28 | 1 | – | – | 29 | 1 |
| Burton A.D. | 1 | 0 | – | – | 1 | 0 |
| Dixon C.H. | 31 | 2 | 6 | 0 | 37 | 2 |
| Fry K.F. | 5 | 0 | – | – | 5 | 0 |
| Graham L. | 29 | 13 | 6 | 3 | 36 | 16 |
| Herrity W.R. | 4 | 1 | – | – | 4 | 1 |
| Hollyman K.C. | 39 | 1 | 6 | 1 | 46 | 2 |
| Jones B.R. | 40 | 5 | 6 | 0 | 47 | 5 |
| McPherson K. | 40 | 15 | 6 | 4 | 47 | 19 |
| McSeveney J.H. | 46 | 11 | 6 | 2 | 53 | 14 |
| Meyer B.J. | 14 | 6 | – | – | 14 | 6 |
| Peake D.J. | 32 | 0 | – | – | 33 | 0 |
| Riggs L.J. | 35 | 0 | 6 | 0 | 42 | 0 |
| Rowland J.O. | 32 | 2 | 6 | 0 | 39 | 2 |
| Sherwood A.T. | 44 | 3 | 6 | 0 | 51 | 3 |
| Singer D.J. | 19 | 9 | – | – | 19 | 9 |
| Thomas G.V. | 1 | 0 | – | – | 1 | 0 |
| Weare L. | 46 | 0 | 6 | 0 | 53 | 0 |
| Wilcox R. | 14 | 0 | 6 | 0 | 20 | 0 |

| | | P | W | D | L | F | A | Pts |
|---|---|---|---|---|---|---|---|---|
| 1 | Plymouth | 46 | 23 | 16 | 7 | 89 | 59 | 62 |
| 2 | Hull | 46 | 26 | 9 | 11 | 90 | 55 | 61 |
| 3 | Brentford | 46 | 21 | 15 | 10 | 76 | 49 | 57 |
| 4 | Norwich | 46 | 22 | 13 | 11 | 89 | 62 | 57 |
| 5 | Colchester | 46 | 21 | 10 | 15 | 71 | 67 | 52 |
| 6 | Reading | 46 | 21 | 8 | 17 | 78 | 63 | 50 |
| 7 | Tranmere | 46 | 21 | 8 | 17 | 82 | 67 | 50 |
| 8 | Southend | 46 | 21 | 8 | 17 | 85 | 80 | 50 |
| 9 | Halifax | 46 | 21 | 8 | 17 | 80 | 77 | 50 |
| 10 | Bury | 46 | 17 | 14 | 15 | 69 | 58 | 48 |
| 11 | Bradford City | 46 | 18 | 11 | 17 | 84 | 76 | 47 |
| 12 | Bournemouth | 46 | 17 | 12 | 17 | 69 | 69 | 46 |
| 13 | QPR | 46 | 19 | 8 | 19 | 74 | 77 | 46 |
| 14 | Southampton | 46 | 17 | 11 | 18 | 88 | 80 | 45 |
| 15 | Swindon | 46 | 16 | 13 | 17 | 59 | 57 | 45 |
| 16 | Chesterfield | 46 | 17 | 10 | 19 | 67 | 64 | 44 |
| 17 | Newport | 46 | 17 | 9 | 20 | 69 | 68 | 43 |
| 18 | Wrexham | 46 | 14 | 14 | 18 | 63 | 77 | 42 |
| 19 | Accrington | 46 | 15 | 12 | 19 | 71 | 87 | 42 |
| 20 | Mansfield | 46 | 14 | 13 | 19 | 73 | 98 | 41 |
| 21 | Stockport | 46 | 13 | 10 | 23 | 65 | 78 | 36 |
| 22 | Doncaster | 46 | 14 | 5 | 27 | 50 | 90 | 33 |
| 23 | Notts County | 46 | 8 | 13 | 25 | 55 | 96 | 29 |
| 24 | Rochdale | 46 | 8 | 12 | 26 | 37 | 79 | 28 |

County train for their cup-tie with Torquay - Trainer George Kitson looks on.

# SEASON 1959-60    Division 3

| | Date | Opposition | Res. | Att. | Goalscorers |
|---|---|---|---|---|---|
| 1 | 22 Aug | Wrexham | 0-0 | 13251 | |
| 2 | 24 | READING | 3-2 | 8005 | Jones(3) |
| 3 | 29 | GRIMSBY TOWN | 0-2 | 8965 | |
| 4 | 2 Sep | Reading | 1-0 | 14332 | Jones |
| 5 | 5 | Q.P.Rangers | 0-3 | 10700 | |
| 6 | 7 | TRANMERE ROVERS | 2-1 | 7826 | Jones, McPherson |
| 7 | 12 | BRADFORD CITY | 2-0 | 7634 | Riggs, McSeveney |
| 8 | 14 | Tranmere Rovers | 2-2 | 13924 | Sherwood, Jones |
| 9 | 19 | Coventry City | 1-1 | 18251 | McSeveney |
| 10 | 23 | Bournemouth & B.A. | 1-4 | 9322 | W.Herrity |
| 11 | 26 | YORK CITY | 3-2 | 8067 | McSeveney, Meyer, Sherwood |
| 12 | 28 | BOURNEMOUTH & B.A. | 5-2 | 9623 | Sherwood, Riggs, Jones, McPherson, Herrity |
| 13 | 3 Oct | Swindon Town | 0-1 | 14685 | |
| 14 | 10 | Shrewsbury Town | 2-6 | 9062 | W.Herrity, Meyer |
| 15 | 12 | CHESTERFIELD | 3-1 | 8217 | W.Herrity,(2), McPherson |
| 16 | 19 | PORT VALE | 4-3 | 8996 | McPherson(2), Meyer, McSeveney |
| 17 | 24 | Norwich City | 0-1 | 24140 | |
| 18 | 31 | BARNSLEY | 4-0 | 8430 | McSeveney(2), Morgan(2) |
| 19 | 7 Nov | Colchester United | 1-2 | 6620 | McSeveney |
| 20 | 21 | Mansfield Town | 1-3 | 6996 | Sherwood |
| 21 | 28 | HALIFAX TOWN | 5-1 | 7558 | McSeveney(4), Meyer |
| 22 | 12 Dec | BRENTFORD | 4-2 | 8401 | Meyer(2), Dixon, McSeveney |
| 23 | 26 | Southampton | 0-2 | 19167 | |
| 24 | 1 Jan | Chesterfield | 0-2 | 5900 | |
| 25 | 2 | Grimsby Town | 1-0 | 9188 | McSeveney |
| 26 | 16 | Q.P.RANGERS | 2-3 | 5180 | Dixon, McSeveney |
| 27 | 23 | Bradford City | 2-6 | 10838 | Singer(2), |
| 28 | 30 | Bury | 1-0 | 6545 | Singer |
| 29 | 12 Feb | York City | 0-2 | 7758 | |
| 30 | 15 | COVENTRY CITY | 2-0 | 4764 | Dixon, McPherson |
| 31 | 20 | SWINDON TOWN | 1-3 | 4979 | Hollyman |
| 32 | 27 | SHREWSBURY TOWN | 1-3 | 4738 | Sherwood |
| 33 | 29 | WREXHAM | 4-1 | 4206 | McPherson(2), Sherwood, McSeveney |
| 34 | 5 Mar | Port Vale | 1-2 | 9073 | McSeveney |
| 35 | 7 | SOUTHAMPTON | 5-1 | 6429 | McPherson(3), Morgan, Meyer |
| 36 | 12 | NORWICH CITY | 1-1 | 6106 | McPherson |
| 37 | 19 | Halifax Town | 1-2 | 4409 | McSeveney |
| 38 | 21 | SOUTHEND UNITED | 1-1 | 5652 | Singer |
| 39 | 26 | COLCHESTER UNITED | 3-2 | 4322 | McPherson(2), Singer |
| 40 | 2 Apr | Southend United | 2-3 | 8513 | McPherson, Sherwood |
| 41 | 9 | MANSFIELD TOWN | 0-1 | 4473 | |
| 42 | 15 | ACCRINGTON STANLEY | 1-3 | 3314 | McPherson |
| 43 | 16 | Barnsley | 2-0 | 5597 | Dixon, Meyer |
| 44 | 18 | Accrington Stanley | 0-0 | 2202 | |
| 45 | 23 | BURY | 3-1 | 4264 | Dixon, Singer, Meyer |
| 46 | 30 | Brentford | 2-1 | 7900 | Dixon, Burton |

## F.A.Cup

| | Date | | Res. | Att. | Goalscorers |
|---|---|---|---|---|---|
| 1 | 14 Nov | HEREFORD UNITED | 4-2 | 10391 | Dixon, McPherson, McSeveney, Meyer |
| 2 | 5 Dec | Salisbury Town | 1-0 | 6600 | Meyer |
| 3 | 9 Jan | TOTTENHAM HOTSPUR | 0-4 | 24000 | |

| Player | League | | F.A.Cup | | Total | |
|---|---|---|---|---|---|---|
| | App | Gls. | App | Gls. | App | Gls. |
| Bird J.F. | 28 | 0 | 1 | 0 | 30 | 0 |
| Burton A.D. | 31 | 1 | 3 | 0 | 35 | 1 |
| Clarke W.J. | 2 | 0 | – | – | 3 | 0 |
| Dixon C.H. | 29 | 6 | 2 | 1 | 33 | 8 |
| Fry K.F. | 17 | 0 | 1 | 0 | 18 | 0 |
| Herrity A.M. | 1 | 0 | – | – | 1 | 0 |
| Herrity W.R. | 12 | 5 | – | – | 12 | 5 |
| Hollyman K.C. | 17 | 1 | 3 | 0 | 21 | 1 |
| Jones B.R. | 31 | 7 | 3 | 0 | 25 | 8 |
| McPherson K. | 44 | 16 | 3 | 1 | 49 | 17 |
| McSeveney J.H. | 42 | 17 | 3 | 1 | 47 | 21 |
| Meyer B.J. | 25 | 9 | 3 | 2 | 29 | 11 |
| Morgan W. | 26 | 3 | 3 | 0 | 29 | 3 |
| Peake D.J. | 17 | 0 | – | – | 18 | 0 |
| Riggs L.J. | 37 | 2 | 3 | 0 | 41 | 2 |
| Rowland J.O. | 35 | 0 | – | – | 37 | 0 |
| Sherwood A.T. | 37 | 7 | 2 | 0 | 41 | 7 |
| Singer D.J. | 18 | 6 | – | – | 20 | 6 |
| Weare L. | 44 | 0 | 3 | 0 | 48 | 0 |
| Wilcox R. | 13 | 0 | – | – | 14 | 0 |

| | | P | W | D | L | F | A | Pts |
|---|---|---|---|---|---|---|---|---|
| 1 | Southampton | 46 | 26 | 9 | 11 | 106 | 75 | 61 |
| 2 | Norwich | 46 | 24 | 11 | 11 | 82 | 54 | 59 |
| 3 | Shrewsbury | 46 | 18 | 16 | 12 | 97 | 75 | 52 |
| 4 | Coventry | 46 | 21 | 10 | 15 | 78 | 63 | 52 |
| 5 | Grimsby | 46 | 18 | 16 | 12 | 87 | 70 | 52 |
| 6 | Brentford | 46 | 21 | 9 | 16 | 78 | 61 | 51 |
| 7 | Bury | 46 | 21 | 9 | 16 | 64 | 51 | 51 |
| 8 | QPR | 46 | 18 | 13 | 15 | 73 | 54 | 49 |
| 9 | Colchester | 46 | 18 | 11 | 17 | 83 | 74 | 47 |
| 10 | Bournemouth | 46 | 17 | 13 | 16 | 72 | 72 | 47 |
| 11 | Reading | 46 | 18 | 10 | 18 | 84 | 77 | 46 |
| 12 | Southend | 46 | 19 | 8 | 19 | 76 | 74 | 46 |
| 13 | Newport | 46 | 20 | 6 | 20 | 80 | 79 | 46 |
| 14 | Port Vale | 46 | 19 | 8 | 19 | 80 | 79 | 46 |
| 15 | Halifax | 46 | 18 | 10 | 18 | 70 | 72 | 46 |
| 16 | Swindon | 46 | 19 | 8 | 19 | 69 | 78 | 46 |
| 17 | Barnsley | 46 | 15 | 14 | 17 | 65 | 66 | 44 |
| 18 | Chesterfield | 46 | 18 | 7 | 21 | 71 | 84 | 43 |
| 19 | Bradford City | 46 | 15 | 12 | 19 | 66 | 74 | 42 |
| 20 | Tranmere | 46 | 14 | 13 | 19 | 72 | 75 | 41 |
| 21 | York | 46 | 13 | 12 | 21 | 57 | 73 | 38 |
| 22 | Mansfield | 46 | 15 | 6 | 25 | 81 | 112 | 36 |
| 23 | Wrexham | 46 | 14 | 8 | 24 | 68 | 101 | 36 |
| 24 | Accrington | 46 | 11 | 5 | 30 | 57 | 123 | 27 |

(Back) Fry, Meyer, Rowland, McPherson, Weare, Burton, Riggs, Morgan
(Front) Dixon, McSeveney, Sherwood, Hollyman, Jones

# SEASON 1960-61    Division 3

| | Date | Opposition | Res. | Att. | Goalscorers |
|---|---|---|---|---|---|
| 1 | 20 Aug | READING | 5-2 | 8586 | Singer(3), Dixon, McPherson |
| 2 | 22 | Hull City | 1-5 | 9811 | Burton |
| 3 | 27 | Coventry City | 1-4 | 11819 | McPherson |
| 4 | 29 | HULL CITY | 3-1 | 7306 | Singer(2), Riggs |
| 5 | 3 Sep | BRISTOL CITY | 4-1 | 8538 | McPherson(3), Fry |
| 6 | 6 | Walsall | 2-2 | 6700 | Singer, Rawlings(og) |
| 7 | 10 | Q.P.Rangers | 0-2 | 7301 | |
| 8 | 15 | WALSALL | 4-2 | 5585 | McSeveney(2), Singer(2) |
| 9 | 17 | NOTTS COUNTY | 2-2 | 7779 | McSeveney, Singer |
| 10 | 20 | Grimsby Town | 1-2 | 12288 | Welbourne(og) |
| 11 | 24 | Bournemouth & B.A. | 2-2 | 8507 | Meyer(2) |
| 12 | 26 | GRIMSBY TOWN | 1-1 | 9232 | Dixon |
| 13 | 1 Oct | BRADFORD CITY | 1-0 | 4547 | Meyer |
| 14 | 8 | HALIFAX TOWN | 1-1 | 3698 | McPherson |
| 15 | 15 | Tranmere Rovers | 4-2 | 7827 | Meyer(2), Sherwood. McPherson |
| 16 | 29 | Brentford | 4-2 | 7600 | Burton(2), McSeveney, McPherson |
| 17 | 12 Nov | Torquay United | 0-0 | 6875 | |
| 18 | 5 Dec | CHESTERFIELD | 5-1 | 6713 | Burton Mcsevenley Ford Sears(og) Allison(og) |
| 19 | 10 | Bury | 1-4 | 7349 | Ford |
| 20 | 17 | Reading | 3-2 | 5780 | McPherson, Fry, Meyer |
| 21 | 22 | COLCHESTER UNITED | 3-2 | 6186 | Burton(2), Meyer |
| 22 | 26 | Colchester United | 1-1 | 6732 | McPherson |
| 23 | 7 Jan | Southend United | 2-4 | 6037 | Burton, McPherson |
| 24 | 14 | Bristol City | 0-3 | 11886 | |
| 25 | 23 | Q.P.RANGERS | 1-3 | 6610 | Ford |
| 26 | 28 | SWINDON TOWN | 2-0 | 3350 | McSeveney, McPherson |
| 27 | 4 Feb | Notts County | 0-6 | 10673 | |
| 28 | 11 | BOURNEMOUTH & B.A. | 2-0 | 3790 | McPherson, Meyer |
| 29 | 13 | PORT VALE | 2-1 | 5100 | McPherson, Smith |
| 30 | 18 | Bradford City | 2-1 | 8820 | Dixon, Meyer |
| 31 | 25 | Chesterfield | 0-1 | 3586 | |
| 32 | 4 Mar | TRANMERE ROVERS | 1-0 | 4608 | Meyer |
| 33 | 6 | WATFORD | 5-1 | 5208 | McPherson(3), Smith, Meyer |
| 34 | 11 | Watford | 1-4 | 9188 | Rowland |
| 35 | 13 | BARNSLEY | 2-3 | 6198 | McPherson(2) |
| 36 | 18 | BRENTFORD | 0-1 | 3756 | |
| 37 | 20 | COVENTRY CITY | 3-3 | 3660 | Meyer(2), Sherwood |
| 38 | 25 | Swindon Town | 0-2 | 7904 | |
| 39 | 1 Apr | TORQUAY UNITED | 2-2 | 3872 | Sherwood, McSeveney |
| 40 | 3 | SHREWSBURY TOWN | 1-1 | 2785 | McSevenly |
| 41 | 8 | Port Vale | 1-3 | 6302 | McSeveney |
| 42 | 15 | SOUTHEND UNITED | 1-2 | 2917 | Sherwood |
| 43 | 17 | Shrewsbury Town | 0-5 | 5877 | |
| 44 | 22 | Halifax Town | 1-2 | 3589 | McPherson |
| 45 | 24 | Barnsley | 3-1 | 4025 | McSeveney, Smith, Derrick |
| 46 | 29 | BURY | 0-0 | 3523 | |

| Player | League | | F.A.Cup | | Total | |
|---|---|---|---|---|---|---|
| | App | Gls. | App | Gls. | App | Gls. |
| Bird J.F. | 34 | 0 | 1 | 0 | 40 | 0 |
| Burton A.D. | 21 | 7 | 1 | 0 | 26 | 10 |
| Derrick E.A. | 3 | 1 | – | – | 3 | 1 |
| Dixon C.H. | 16 | 3 | – | – | 18 | 4 |
| Ford T. | 8 | 3 | 1 | 0 | 9 | 3 |
| Fry K.F. | 31 | 2 | 1 | 0 | 35 | 2 |
| Herrity A.M. | 11 | 0 | – | – | 12 | 0 |
| Herrity W.R. | 10 | 0 | – | – | 11 | 0 |
| McPherson K. | 44 | 20 | 1 | 0 | 50 | 22 |
| McSeveney J.H. | 38 | 10 | 1 | 1 | 44 | 13 |
| Meyer B.J. | 30 | 13 | – | – | 35 | 14 |
| Peake D.J. | 42 | 0 | 1 | 0 | 48 | 0 |
| Rathbone G.C. | 3 | 0 | – | – | 3 | 0 |
| Riggs L.J. | 38 | 1 | 1 | 0 | 43 | 1 |
| Rowland J.O. | 46 | 1 | 1 | 0 | 52 | 1 |
| Sanders P.C.W. | 3 | 0 | – | – | 3 | 0 |
| Sherwood A.T. | 37 | 4 | 1 | 0 | 40 | 4 |
| Singer D.J. | 9 | 9 | – | – | 9 | 9 |
| Smith G. | 31 | 3 | – | – | 34 | 5 |
| Weare L. | 46 | 0 | 1 | 0 | 52 | 0 |
| Williams D.S. | 5 | 0 | – | – | 5 | 0 |
| Own Goals | | 4 | | | | 4 |

| | | P | W | D | L | F | A | Pts |
|---|---|---|---|---|---|---|---|---|
| 1 | Bury | 46 | 30 | 8 | 8 | 108 | 45 | 68 |
| 2 | Walsall | 46 | 28 | 6 | 12 | 98 | 60 | 62 |
| 3 | QPR | 46 | 25 | 10 | 11 | 93 | 60 | 60 |
| 4 | Watford | 46 | 20 | 12 | 14 | 85 | 72 | 52 |
| 5 | Notts County | 46 | 21 | 9 | 16 | 82 | 77 | 51 |
| 6 | Grimsby | 46 | 20 | 10 | 16 | 77 | 69 | 50 |
| 7 | Port Vale | 46 | 17 | 15 | 14 | 96 | 79 | 49 |
| 8 | Barnsley | 46 | 21 | 7 | 18 | 83 | 80 | 49 |
| 9 | Halifax | 46 | 16 | 17 | 13 | 71 | 78 | 49 |
| 10 | Shrewsbury | 46 | 15 | 16 | 15 | 83 | 75 | 46 |
| 11 | Hull | 46 | 17 | 12 | 17 | 73 | 73 | 46 |
| 12 | Torquay | 46 | 14 | 17 | 15 | 75 | 83 | 45 |
| 13 | Newport | 46 | 17 | 11 | 18 | 81 | 90 | 45 |
| 14 | Bristol City | 46 | 17 | 10 | 19 | 70 | 68 | 44 |
| 15 | Coventry | 46 | 16 | 12 | 18 | 80 | 83 | 44 |
| 16 | Swindon | 46 | 14 | 15 | 17 | 62 | 55 | 43 |
| 17 | Brentford | 46 | 13 | 17 | 16 | 56 | 70 | 43 |
| 18 | Reading | 46 | 14 | 12 | 20 | 72 | 83 | 40 |
| 19 | Bournemouth | 46 | 15 | 10 | 21 | 58 | 76 | 40 |
| 20 | Southend | 46 | 14 | 11 | 21 | 60 | 76 | 39 |
| 21 | Tranmere | 46 | 15 | 8 | 23 | 79 | 115 | 38 |
| 22 | Bradford City | 46 | 11 | 14 | 21 | 65 | 87 | 36 |
| 23 | Colchester | 46 | 11 | 11 | 24 | 68 | 101 | 33 |
| 24 | Chesterfield | 46 | 10 | 12 | 24 | 67 | 87 | 32 |

## F.A.Cup

| | Date | Opposition | Res. | Att. | Goalscorers |
|---|---|---|---|---|---|
| 1 | 5 Nov | Shrewsbury Town | 1-4 | 11496 | McSeveney |

(Back) Bird, Burton, Rowland, Weare, Peake, Sherwood
(Front) Dixon, McSeveney, McPherson, Singer, Smith

# SEASON 1961–62    Division 3

| | Date | Opposition | Res. | Att. | Goalscorers |
|---|---|---|---|---|---|
| 1 | 19 Aug | GRIMSBY TOWN | 0-2 | 11027 | |
| 2 | 21 | BARNSLEY | 0-2 | 8727 | |
| 3 | 25 | Coventry City | 0-3 | 12675 | |
| 4 | 30 | Barnsley | 1-1 | 6901 | Bowman |
| 5 | 2 Sep | BRENTFORD | 6-1 | 5757 | Buchanan(3), Robertson(2), Bowman |
| 6 | 5 | Bristol City | 2-1 | 15588 | Bowman, Smith |
| 7 | 8 | Reading | 1-2 | 17441 | Robertson |
| 8 | 16 | Portsmouth | 2-2 | 14006 | Bowman, Buchanan |
| 9 | 18 | BRADFORD PARK AVE | 1-2 | 10458 | Robertson |
| 10 | 23 | SOUTHEND UNITED | 0-3 | 6407 | |
| 11 | 30 | Notts County | 1-8 | 6356 | Harris |
| 12 | 2 Oct | PETERBOROUGH UTD | 2-3 | 9027 | Smith, W Herrity |
| 13 | 7 | Q.P.RANGERS | 2-4 | 5440 | Bowman, Harris |
| 14 | 9 | Peterborough Utd | 1-2 | 13029 | Finlay |
| 15 | 14 | Halifax Town | 0-0 | 5161 | |
| 16 | 16 | BRISTOL CITY | 3-1 | 7006 | Harris(3) |
| 17 | 21 | BOURNEMOUTH & B.A. | 0-1 | 7392 | |
| 18 | 25 | Bradford Park Ave | 1-4 | 9370 | Smith |
| 19 | 28 | Crystal Palace | 0-2 | 17885 | |
| 20 | 11 Nov | Northampton Town | 0-5 | 7845 | |
| 21 | 18 | HULL CITY | 0-2 | 5089 | |
| 22 | 2 Dec | SWINDON TOWN | 2-2 | 4506 | Smith(2) |
| 23 | 9 | Torquay United | 2-3 | 4065 | Buchanan, Walsh |
| 24 | 16 | Grimsby Town | 0-1 | 4575 | |
| 25 | 23 | COVENTRY CITY | 1-2 | 3360 | Robertson |
| 26 | 26 | Port Vale | 0-3 | 12182 | |
| 27 | 13 Jan | Brentford | 1-3 | 7750 | Smith |
| 28 | 27 | Watford | 1-3 | 8167 | Smith |
| 29 | 5 Feb | PORTSMOUTH | 0-5 | 5655 | |
| 30 | 10 | Southend United | 0-1 | 6175 | |
| 31 | 17 | NOTTS COUNTY | 2-0 | 2597 | Harris, Moffat |
| 32 | 24 | Q.P.Rangers | 0-4 | 7697 | |
| 33 | 5 Mar | HALIFAX TOWN | 0-1 | 2956 | |
| 34 | 10 | Bournemouth & B.A. | 1-2 | 10610 | Bowman |
| 35 | 12 | PORT VALE | 1-1 | 2504 | Moffat |
| 36 | 17 | CRYSTAL PALACE | 2-1 | 2276 | Buchanan, Smith |
| 37 | 19 | READING | 0-0 | 2639 | |
| 38 | 23 | Lincoln City | 2-3 | 5359 | Walsh(2) |
| 39 | 26 | LINCOLN CITY | 4-0 | 3062 | Moffat(2), Buchanan, Harris |
| 40 | 31 | NORTHAMPTON TOWN | 0-0 | 2568 | |
| 41 | 7 Apr | Hull City | 0-4 | 3235 | |
| 42 | 14 | WATFORD | 0-0 | 2346 | |
| 43 | 16 | SHREWSBURY TOWN | 3-2 | 2003 | Smith, Harris, Moffat |
| 44 | 21 | Swindon Town | 0-3 | 7881 | |
| 45 | 23 | Shrewsbury Town | 1-4 | 6650 | W Herrity |
| 46 | 28 | TORQUAY UNITED | 0-3 | 2295 | |

## F.A.Cup

| | Date | | Res. | Att. | Goalscorers |
|---|---|---|---|---|---|
| 1 | 4 Nov | Reading | 1-1 | 10564 | W Herrity |
| 1R | 6 | READING | 1-0 | 8548 | W Herrity |
| 2 | 25 | Weymouth | 0-1 | 6500 | |

| Player | League | | F.A.Cup | | Total | |
|---|---|---|---|---|---|---|
| | App | Gls. | App | Gls. | App | Gls. |
| Bird J.F. | 24 | 0 | 3 | 0 | 30 | 0 |
| Bowman A. | 42 | 6 | 3 | 0 | 48 | 7 |
| Buchanan J. | 31 | 7 | 2 | 0 | 35 | 7 |
| Clarke W.J. | 10 | 0 | 3 | 0 | 13 | 0 |
| Edmunds R.E. | 4 | 0 | – | – | 4 | 0 |
| Evans R. | 31 | 0 | 3 | 0 | 36 | 0 |
| Finlay A.J. | 20 | 1 | 3 | 0 | 25 | 1 |
| Fry K.F. | 5 | 0 | – | – | 7 | 0 |
| Harris G.A. | 31 | 8 | 1 | 0 | 34 | 9 |
| Herrity A.M. | 16 | 0 | – | – | 19 | 0 |
| Herrity W.R. | 14 | 2 | 3 | 2 | 18 | 4 |
| Hinshelwood W.A.A. | 3 | 0 | – | – | 3 | 0 |
| Moffat A. | 17 | 5 | – | – | 17 | 5 |
| Peake D.J. | 28 | 0 | – | – | 29 | 0 |
| Pring K.D. | 5 | 0 | – | – | 5 | 0 |
| Rathbone G.C. | 1 | 0 | – | – | 1 | 0 |
| Robertson J. | 29 | 5 | 3 | 0 | 35 | 5 |
| Rowland J.O. | 46 | 0 | 3 | 0 | 52 | 0 |
| Scott R.J. | 15 | 0 | – | – | 15 | 0 |
| Sheffield L.J. | 1 | 0 | – | – | 1 | 0 |
| Smith G. | 40 | 9 | 3 | 0 | 45 | 9 |
| Thomas D.A. | 31 | 0 | 3 | 0 | 34 | 0 |
| Walsh J.B. | 20 | 3 | – | – | 21 | 3 |
| Weare L. | 36 | 0 | – | – | 39 | 0 |
| Williams D.S. | 6 | 0 | – | – | 6 | 0 |

| | | P | W | D | L | F | A | Pts |
|---|---|---|---|---|---|---|---|---|
| 1 | Portsmouth | 46 | 27 | 11 | 8 | 87 | 47 | 65 |
| 2 | Grimsby | 46 | 28 | 6 | 12 | 80 | 56 | 62 |
| 3 | Bournemouth | 46 | 21 | 17 | 8 | 69 | 45 | 59 |
| 4 | QPR | 46 | 24 | 11 | 11 | 111 | 73 | 59 |
| 5 | Peterborough | 46 | 26 | 6 | 14 | 107 | 82 | 58 |
| 6 | Bristol City | 46 | 23 | 8 | 15 | 94 | 72 | 54 |
| 7 | Reading | 46 | 22 | 9 | 15 | 77 | 66 | 53 |
| 8 | Northampton | 46 | 20 | 11 | 15 | 85 | 57 | 51 |
| 9 | Swindon | 46 | 17 | 15 | 14 | 78 | 71 | 49 |
| 10 | Hull | 46 | 20 | 8 | 18 | 67 | 54 | 48 |
| 11 | Bradford PA | 46 | 20 | 7 | 19 | 80 | 78 | 47 |
| 12 | Port Vale | 46 | 17 | 11 | 18 | 65 | 58 | 45 |
| 13 | Notts County | 46 | 17 | 9 | 20 | 67 | 74 | 43 |
| 14 | Coventry | 46 | 16 | 11 | 19 | 64 | 71 | 43 |
| 15 | Crystal Palace | 46 | 14 | 14 | 18 | 83 | 80 | 42 |
| 16 | Southend | 46 | 13 | 16 | 17 | 57 | 69 | 42 |
| 17 | Watford | 46 | 14 | 13 | 19 | 63 | 74 | 41 |
| 18 | Halifax | 46 | 15 | 10 | 21 | 62 | 84 | 40 |
| 19 | Shrewsbury | 46 | 13 | 12 | 21 | 73 | 84 | 38 |
| 20 | Barnsley | 46 | 13 | 12 | 21 | 71 | 95 | 38 |
| 21 | Torquay | 46 | 15 | 6 | 25 | 76 | 100 | 36 |
| 22 | Lincoln | 46 | 9 | 17 | 20 | 57 | 87 | 35 |
| 23 | Brentford | 46 | 13 | 8 | 25 | 53 | 93 | 34 |
| 24 | Newport | 46 | 7 | 8 | 31 | 46 | 102 | 22 |

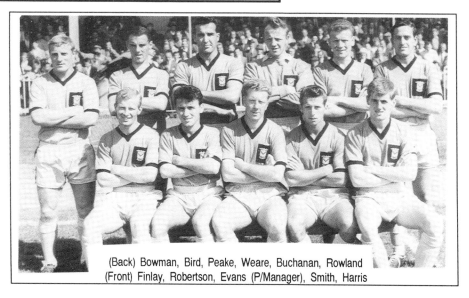

(Back) Bowman, Bird, Peake, Weare, Buchanan, Rowland
(Front) Finlay, Robertson, Evans (P/Manager), Smith, Harris

# SEASON 1962–63    Division 4

| | Date | Opposition | Res. | Att. | Goalscorers |
|---|---|---|---|---|---|
| 1 | 18 Aug | Hartlepools United | 3–2 | 5234 | Hunt(2), Herrity |
| 2 | 20 | OLDHAM ATHLETIC | 0–0 | 10488 | |
| 3 | 25 | DARLINGTON | 2–2 | 7786 | Hunt(2) |
| 4 | 29 | Oldham Athletic | 2–3 | 18082 | Hunt, Gordon |
| 5 | 1 Sep | Southport | 1–2 | 3885 | Bonson |
| 6 | 3 | LINCOLN CITY | 2–1 | 6864 | Hudson, Smith |
| 7 | 8 | ALDERSHOT | 2–2 | 6002 | Bonson, Sheffield |
| 8 | 12 | Lincoln City | 3–6 | 5006 | Hunt(2), Bonson |
| 9 | 17 | Stockport County | 1–1 | 3704 | Hunt |
| 10 | 15 | BARROW | 6–0 | 5733 | Hunt(3), Bonson(2), Thomas |
| 11 | 22 | Oxford United | 1–5 | 9131 | Bonson, |
| 12 | 29 | BRADFORD CITY | 2–0 | 4700 | Bonson, Flockett(o.g.) |
| 13 | 1 Oct | CHESTERFIELD | 2–3 | 6029 | Bonson, Hunt |
| 14 | 6 | CREWE ALEXANDRA | 5–1 | 4737 | Hunt(3), Herrity, Bird |
| 15 | 13 | Chester | 2–2 | 8034 | Herrity, Bonson |
| 16 | 18 | YORK CITY | 1–3 | 5406 | Hunt |
| 17 | 27 | Brentford | 1–3 | 11300 | Bonson |
| 18 | 10 Nov | Chesterfield | 2–1 | 6425 | Hunt(2) |
| 19 | 17 | EXETER CITY | 4–0 | 3221 | Bonson(3), Hunt |
| 20 | 1 Dec | MANSFIELD TOWN | 1–1 | 5399 | Bonson |
| 21 | 8 | Doncaster Rovers | 2–2 | 3875 | Herrity, Bonson |
| 22 | 10 | TRANMERE ROVERS | 1–2 | 4536 | Rowland |
| 23 | 15 | HARTLEPOOLS UNITED | 2–1 | 2830 | Bonson, Hunt |
| 24 | 22 | Darlington | 2–4 | 3701 | Bonson(2) |
| 25 | 27 Feb | Torquay United | 1–3 | 4027 | Smith |
| 26 | 4 Mar | CHESTER | 0–1 | 3721 | |
| 27 | 8 | York City | 0–2 | 4081 | |
| 28 | 11 | SOUTHPORT | 1–0 | 2522 | Hill |
| 29 | 13 | Crewe Alexandra | 1–4 | 6293 | Sheffield |
| 30 | 16 | BRENTFORD | 1–4 | 2891 | Smith |
| 31 | 18 | TORQUAY UNITED | 1–0 | 3654 | Hunt |
| 32 | 23 | Rochdale | 3–3 | 3029 | Hudson, Hunt, Smith |
| 33 | 1 Apr | WORKINGTON | 2–2 | 4065 | Bowman, Bonson |
| 34 | 6 | Exeter City | 0–1 | 5258 | |
| 35 | 12 | Tranmere Rovers | 0–0 | 10738 | |
| 36 | 13 | GILLINGHAM | 2–0 | 2821 | Hunt, Sheffield |
| 37 | 20 | Mansfield Town | 1–2 | 6038 | Rathbone |
| 38 | 24 | Gillingham | 1–3 | 5867 | Sheffield |
| 39 | 27 | DONCASTER ROVERS | 2–4 | 2242 | Hunt(2) |
| 40 | 1 May | Bradford City | 4–3 | 1983 | Bonson(2), Smith(2) |
| 41 | 4 | STOCKPORT COUNTY | 3–1 | 2573 | Rowland, Sheffield, Hunt |
| 42 | 11 | Workington | 0–4 | 3128 | |
| 43 | 13 | Barrow | 0–3 | 3640 | |
| 44 | 18 | Aldershot | 1–2 | 3003 | Smith |
| 45 | 20 | ROCHDALE | 1–1 | 2387 | Bonson |
| 46 | 23 | OXFORD UNITED | 1–0 | 3442 | Hunt |

## F.A.Cup

| | | | | | |
|---|---|---|---|---|---|
| 1 | 3 Nov | Q.P.Rangers | 2–3 | 12240 | Herrity, Bonson |

| Player | League | | F.A.Cup | | Total | |
|---|---|---|---|---|---|---|
| | App | Gls. | App | Gls. | App | Gls. |
| Bird J.F. | 35 | 1 | 1 | 0 | 43 | 1 |
| Bonson J. | 41 | 22 | 1 | 1 | 49 | 27 |
| Bowman A. | 27 | 1 | – | – | 31 | 1 |
| Collins R.L. | 1 | 0 | – | – | 1 | 0 |
| Frowen J. | 11 | 0 | – | – | 14 | 0 |
| Gordon P.J. | 8 | 1 | – | – | 9 | 1 |
| Herrity W.R. | 18 | 4 | 1 | 1 | 21 | 7 |
| Hill L.W. | 4 | 1 | – | – | 4 | 1 |
| Hudson C.A.R. | 30 | 2 | 1 | 0 | 36 | 4 |
| Hunt R.A.R. | 44 | 27 | 1 | 0 | 52 | 32 |
| Peake D.J. | 10 | 0 | – | – | 11 | 0 |
| Pring K.D. | 14 | 0 | – | – | 18 | 0 |
| Rathbone G.C. | 35 | 1 | 1 | 0 | 43 | 1 |
| Rees R.C. | 4 | 0 | – | – | 5 | 0 |
| Rowland J.O. | 41 | 2 | 1 | 0 | 50 | 2 |
| Scott R.J. | 3 | 0 | – | – | 3 | 0 |
| Sheffield L.J. | 17 | 7 | – | – | 23 | 10 |
| Smith G. | 36 | 5 | 1 | 0 | 43 | 5 |
| Sullivan D. | 23 | 0 | – | – | 27 | 0 |
| Thomas D.A. | 27 | 1 | 1 | 0 | 31 | 1 |
| Walsh J.B. | 7 | 0 | – | – | 7 | 0 |
| Weare L. | 41 | 0 | 1 | 0 | 49 | 0 |
| Webster C. | 8 | 0 | – | 0 | 9 | 1 |
| Williams D.S. | 21 | 0 | 1 | 0 | 26 | 0 |
| Own Goals | | 1 | | | | 2 |

| | | P | W | D | L | F | A | Pts |
|---|---|---|---|---|---|---|---|---|
| 1 | Brentford | 46 | 27 | 8 | 11 | 98 | 64 | 62 |
| 2 | Oldham | 46 | 24 | 11 | 11 | 95 | 60 | 59 |
| 3 | Crewe | 46 | 24 | 11 | 11 | 86 | 58 | 59 |
| 4 | Mansfield | 46 | 24 | 9 | 13 | 108 | 69 | 57 |
| 5 | Gillingham | 46 | 22 | 13 | 11 | 71 | 49 | 57 |
| 6 | Torquay | 46 | 20 | 16 | 10 | 75 | 56 | 56 |
| 7 | Rochdale | 46 | 20 | 11 | 15 | 67 | 59 | 51 |
| 8 | Tranmere | 46 | 20 | 10 | 16 | 81 | 67 | 50 |
| 9 | Barrow | 46 | 19 | 12 | 15 | 82 | 80 | 50 |
| 10 | Workington | 46 | 17 | 13 | 16 | 76 | 68 | 47 |
| 11 | Aldershot | 46 | 15 | 17 | 14 | 73 | 69 | 47 |
| 12 | Darlington | 46 | 19 | 6 | 21 | 72 | 87 | 44 |
| 13 | Southport | 46 | 15 | 14 | 17 | 72 | 106 | 44 |
| 14 | York | 46 | 16 | 11 | 19 | 67 | 62 | 43 |
| 15 | Chesterfield | 46 | 13 | 16 | 17 | 70 | 64 | 42 |
| 16 | Doncaster | 46 | 14 | 14 | 18 | 64 | 77 | 42 |
| 17 | Exeter | 46 | 16 | 10 | 20 | 57 | 77 | 42 |
| 18 | Oxford | 46 | 13 | 15 | 18 | 70 | 71 | 41 |
| 19 | Stockport | 46 | 15 | 11 | 20 | 56 | 70 | 41 |
| 20 | Newport | 46 | 14 | 11 | 21 | 76 | 90 | 39 |
| 21 | Chester | 46 | 15 | 9 | 22 | 51 | 66 | 39 |
| 22 | Lincoln | 46 | 13 | 9 | 24 | 68 | 89 | 35 |
| 23 | Bradford City | 46 | 11 | 10 | 25 | 64 | 93 | 32 |
| 24 | Hartlepools | 46 | 7 | 11 | 28 | 56 | 104 | 25 |

(Back)  Bird, Sullivan, Weare, Frowen, Hunt, Rathbone.
(Front)  Pring, Rowland, Bonson, Sheffield, Smith.

# SEASON 1963-64    Division 4

| | Date | Opposition | Res. | Att. | Goalscorers |
|---|---|---|---|---|---|
| 1 | 24 Aug | Doncaster Rovers | 1-1 | 6040 | Smith |
| 2 | 26 | Bradford Park Ave | 5-2 | 6312 | Sheffield(3), Bonson, Hunt |
| 3 | 31 | BRIGHTON & H.A. | 2-0 | 6200 | Smith, Pring |
| 4 | 7 Sep | Chester | 0-3 | 5372 | |
| 5 | 9 | BRADFORD PARK AVE | 4-0 | 4537 | Sheffield(2), Bonson, Pring |
| 6 | 14 | YORK CITY | 0-0 | 5200 | |
| 7 | 16 | Chesterfield | 1-0 | 7474 | Hunt |
| 8 | 21 | Barrow | 1-1 | 4137 | Pring |
| 9 | 28 | ROCHDALE | 1-1 | 4878 | Smith |
| 10 | 30 | CHESTERFIELD | 0-1 | 5866 | |
| 11 | 5 Oct | Oxford United | 1-2 | 6144 | Hunt |
| 12 | 7 | BRADFORD CITY | 3-1 | 4972 | Bonson(2), Hunt |
| 13 | 12 | CARLISLE UNITED | 1-4 | 5489 | Bonson |
| 14 | 16 | Bradford City | 1-2 | 3371 | Bonson |
| 15 | 19 | Torquay United | 3-8 | 4274 | Bonson(2), Hunt |
| 16 | 21 | WORKINGTON | 0-0 | 3381 | |
| 17 | 26 | HALIFAX TOWN | 4-2 | 3182 | Smith, Bonson, Hunt, Webster |
| 18 | 2 Nov | Tranmere Rovers | 3-2 | 5090 | Bonson, Hunt, Webster |
| 19 | 9 | DARLINGTON | 1-2 | 3388 | Bonson |
| 20 | 23 | EXETER CITY | 0-1 | 3339 | |
| 21 | 30 | Southport | 2-4 | 2830 | Bonson, Hunt |
| 22 | 14 Dec | DONCASTER ROVERS | 1-0 | 2344 | Sheffield |
| 23 | 21 | Brighton & H.A. | 2-1 | 7752 | Bonson(2) |
| 24 | 26 | Aldershot | 0-2 | 5763 | |
| 25 | 28 | ALDERSHOT | 2-1 | 3666 | Hunt, Webster |
| 26 | 11 Jan | CHESTER | 0-1 | 3983 | |
| 27 | 18 | York City | 0-3 | 2114 | |
| 28 | 3 Feb | BARROW | 3-0 | 3274 | Bonson(2), Smith |
| 29 | 8 | Rochdale | 1-0 | 2444 | Bonson |
| 30 | 22 | Carlisle United | 3-3 | 7528 | Sheffield(2), Bonson |
| 31 | 24 | Workington | 0-2 | 3800 | |
| 32 | 29 | TORQUAY UNITED | 0-3 | 4018 | |
| 33 | 2 Mar | OXFORD UNITED | 1-0 | 3142 | Sheffield |
| 34 | 7 | Halifax Town | 0-2 | 2790 | |
| 35 | 14 | TRANMERE ROVERS | 0-2 | 1800 | |
| 36 | 23 | Darlington | 1-3 | 2836 | Sheffield |
| 37 | 27 | Stockport County | 0-1 | 2890 | |
| 38 | 28 | LINCOLN CITY | 4-2 | 2300 | Rowland, Sheffield, Hunt, Hill |
| 39 | 30 | STOCKPORT COUNTY | 3-1 | 2966 | Reynolds(2), Smith |
| 40 | 4 Apr | Exeter City | 1-3 | 6077 | Reynolds |
| 41 | 6 | Harlepools United | 1-1 | 3844 | Bonson |
| 42 | 11 | SOUTHPORT | 3-0 | 2492 | Bonson(3) |
| 43 | 18 | Gillingham | 1-1 | 9854 | Sheffield |
| 44 | 22 | Lincoln City | 1-2 | 2803 | Bonson |
| 45 | 25 | HARTLEPOOLS UNITED | 2-1 | 2521 | Bonson(2) |
| 46 | 30 | GILLINGHAM | 0-1 | 3229 | |

| Player | League | | F.A.Cup | | Total | |
|---|---|---|---|---|---|---|
| | App | Gls. | App | Gls. | App | Gls. |
| Bird J.F. | 35 | 0 | 5 | 0 | 44 | 1 |
| Bonson J. | 42 | 25 | 5 | 2 | 52 | 32 |
| Frowen J. | 22 | 0 | – | – | 24 | 0 |
| Hill L.W. | 25 | 1 | 3 | 0 | 33 | 1 |
| Hunt R.A.R. | 39 | 10 | 5 | 5 | 48 | 16 |
| Kear M.P. | 6 | 0 | 3 | 0 | 9 | 0 |
| Pring K.D. | 27 | 3 | – | – | 30 | 3 |
| Rathbone G.C. | 45 | 0 | 5 | 0 | 55 | 0 |
| Reece G.I. | 3 | 0 | – | – | 3 | 0 |
| Reynolds G.E.A. | 11 | 3 | – | – | 11 | 3 |
| Rowland J.O. | 45 | 1 | 4 | 0 | 54 | 1 |
| Sheffield L.J. | 35 | 12 | 2 | 1 | 42 | 16 |
| Smith G. | 41 | 6 | 5 | 2 | 50 | 8 |
| Walters G. | 40 | 0 | 5 | 0 | 49 | 0 |
| Weare L. | 46 | 0 | 5 | 0 | 56 | 0 |
| Webster C. | 23 | 3 | 5 | 1 | 30 | 4 |
| Williams D.S. | 21 | 0 | 3 | 0 | 26 | 0 |
| Own Goals | | | | | | 1 |

| | | P | W | D | L | F | A | Pts |
|---|---|---|---|---|---|---|---|---|
| 1 | Gillingham | 46 | 23 | 14 | 9 | 59 | 30 | 60 |
| 2 | Carlisle | 46 | 25 | 10 | 11 | 113 | 58 | 60 |
| 3 | Workington | 46 | 24 | 11 | 11 | 76 | 52 | 59 |
| 4 | Exeter | 46 | 20 | 18 | 8 | 62 | 37 | 58 |
| 5 | Bradford City | 46 | 25 | 6 | 15 | 76 | 62 | 56 |
| 6 | Torquay | 46 | 20 | 11 | 15 | 80 | 54 | 51 |
| 7 | Tranmere | 46 | 20 | 11 | 15 | 85 | 73 | 51 |
| 8 | Brighton | 46 | 19 | 12 | 15 | 71 | 52 | 50 |
| 9 | Aldershot | 46 | 19 | 10 | 17 | 83 | 78 | 48 |
| 10 | Halifax | 46 | 17 | 14 | 15 | 77 | 77 | 48 |
| 11 | Lincoln | 46 | 19 | 9 | 18 | 67 | 75 | 47 |
| 12 | Chester | 46 | 19 | 8 | 19 | 65 | 60 | 46 |
| 13 | Bradford PA | 46 | 18 | 9 | 19 | 75 | 81 | 45 |
| 14 | Doncaster | 46 | 15 | 12 | 19 | 70 | 75 | 42 |
| 15 | Newport | 46 | 17 | 8 | 21 | 64 | 73 | 42 |
| 16 | Chesterfield | 46 | 15 | 12 | 19 | 57 | 71 | 42 |
| 17 | Stockport | 46 | 15 | 12 | 19 | 50 | 68 | 42 |
| 18 | Oxford | 46 | 14 | 13 | 19 | 59 | 63 | 41 |
| 19 | Darlington | 46 | 14 | 12 | 20 | 66 | 93 | 40 |
| 20 | Rochdale | 46 | 12 | 15 | 19 | 56 | 59 | 39 |
| 21 | Southport | 46 | 15 | 9 | 22 | 63 | 88 | 39 |
| 22 | York | 46 | 14 | 7 | 25 | 52 | 66 | 35 |
| 23 | Hartlepools | 46 | 12 | 9 | 25 | 54 | 93 | 33 |
| 24 | Barrow | 46 | 6 | 18 | 22 | 51 | 93 | 30 |

## F.A.Cup

| | Date | Opposition | Res. | Att. | Goalscorers |
|---|---|---|---|---|---|
| 1 | 16 Nov | Hereford United | 1-1 | 7000 | Hunt |
| 1R | 18 | HEREFORD UNITED | 4-0 | 3457 | Hunt(3), Webster |
| 2 | 7 Dec | WATFORD | 2-0 | 5353 | Smith |
| 3 | 4 Jan | SHEFFIELD WED | 3-2 | 8928 | Bonson(2), Hunt |
| 4 | 25 | Burnley | 1-2 | 23019 | Sheffield |

(Back) Bird, Rowland, Weare, Hunt, Rathbone, Sheffield, Screen
(Front) Smith, Bonson, Williams, Hill

| | Date | Opposition | Res. | Att. | Goalscorers |
|---|---|---|---|---|---|
| 1 | 22 Aug | Darlington | 1-0 | 4702 | Sheffield |
| 2 | 26 | Crewe Alexandra | 1-1 | 4830 | Singer |
| 3 | 29 | TRANMERE ROVERS | 1-1 | 5600 | Singer |
| 4 | 31 | CREWE ALEXANDRA | 2-2 | 5600 | Smith, Sheffield |
| 5 | 5 Sep | Wrexham | 2-4 | 6546 | Sheffield, Singer |
| 6 | 7 | BRIGHTON & H.A. | 1-1 | 6119 | Sheffield |
| 7 | 12 | SOUTHPORT | 5-0 | 4075 | Sheffield(2), Singer(2), Morgan |
| 8 | 15 | Brighton & H.A. | 0-1 | 13980 | |
| 9 | 19 | Bradford Park Ave. | 2-2 | 8003 | Smith, Sheffield |
| 10 | 26 | ALDERSHOT | 2-1 | 4242 | Morgan(2) |
| 11 | 28 | NOTTS COUNTY | 3-1 | 5802 | Sheffield(3) |
| 12 | 3 Oct | Doncaster Rovers | 0-1 | 14402 | |
| 13 | 8 | Notts County | 0-1 | 6137 | |
| 14 | 10 | Barrow | 4-1 | 2718 | Morgan(2), Sheffield, Swindells |
| 15 | 12 | HALIFAX TOWN | 0-2 | 5315 | |
| 16 | 17 | HARTLEPOOLS UNITED | 2-0 | 3582 | Morgan, Sheffield |
| 17 | 19 | Halifax Town | 0-2 | 3154 | |
| 18 | 24 | Rochdale | 0-2 | 4283 | |
| 19 | 26 | LINCOLN CITY | 7-0 | 4300 | Morgan(5), Smith, Hill |
| 20 | 31 | MILLWALL | 2-2 | 5392 | Swindells, Reece |
| 21 | 7 Nov | Bradford City | 0-1 | 3751 | |
| 22 | 21 | Torquay United | 2-2 | 4159 | Morgan, Sheffield |
| 23 | 28 | STOCKPORT COUNTY | 2-0 | 3815 | Sheffield(2) |
| 24 | 12 Dec | DARLINGTON | 2-1 | 3023 | Morgan, Swindells |
| 25 | 18 | Tranmere Rovers | 2-3 | 7080 | Rathbone, Sheffield |
| 26 | 26 | OXFORD UNITED | 0-3 | 6730 | |
| 27 | 2 Jan | WREXHAM | 2-0 | 3960 | Rathbone, Sheffield |
| 28 | 16 | Southport | 3-5 | 7685 | McCole(2), Reece |
| 29 | 23 | BRADFORD PARK AVE. | 4-3 | 3417 | Reece(2), Smith, Sheffield |
| 30 | 30 | CHESTER | 0-1 | 3219 | |
| 31 | 6 Feb | Aldershot | 1-2 | 4101 | Hill |
| 32 | 13 | DONCASTER ROVERS | 1-0 | 2605 | Morgan |
| 33 | 17 | Oxford United | 1-4 | 6775 | Sheffield |
| 34 | 20 | BARROW | 2-2 | 2057 | Rowland, Reece |
| 35 | 27 | Hartlepools United | 4-2 | 6357 | Morgan(2), Reece(2) |
| 36 | 1 Mar | York City | 1-5 | 5773 | Pugh |
| 37 | 13 | Millwall | 0-4 | 6705 | |
| 38 | 19 | BRADFORD CITY | 4-2 | 2421 | Hill, Morgan, Sheffield, Reece |
| 39 | 26 | Chester | 3-4 | 5843 | Sheffield(2), Hill |
| 40 | 29 | ROCHDALE | 2-3 | 2761 | Hill, Sheffield |
| 41 | 3 Apr | TORQUAY UNITED | 4-0 | 3020 | Sheffield(3), Smith |
| 42 | 10 | Stockport County | 0-2 | 4497 | |
| 43 | 16 | Chesterfield | 1-2 | 7390 | Hill |
| 44 | 17 | YORK CITY | 2-0 | 2329 | Reece, Sheffield |
| 45 | 19 | CHESTERFIELD | 4-1 | 2801 | Rathbone, Smith, Reynolds, Blakey(og) |
| 46 | 24 | Lincoln City | 3-4 | 2296 | Walters, Rowland, Reynolds |

| Player | League | | F.A.Cup | | Total | |
|---|---|---|---|---|---|---|
| | App | Gls. | App | Gls. | App | Gls. |
| Beswick K. | 3 | 0 | – | – | 3 | 0 |
| Bird J.F. | 35 | 0 | 3 | 0 | 39 | 0 |
| Davies P. | 1 | 0 | – | – | 1 | 0 |
| Frowen J | 29 | 0 | 4 | 1 | 34 | 1 |
| Hill L.W. | 45 | 6 | 4 | 0 | 51 | 6 |
| McCole J. | 6 | 2 | – | – | 7 | 3 |
| Morgan K.G. | 44 | 17 | 4 | 1 | 49 | 19 |
| Pring K.D. | 15 | 0 | – | – | 16 | 1 |
| Pugh D. | 7 | 1 | – | – | 7 | 1 |
| Rathbone G.C. | 46 | 3 | 4 | 0 | 52 | 3 |
| Reece G.I. | 29 | 9 | 4 | 2 | 34 | 11 |
| Reynolds G.E.A. | 8 | 2 | – | – | 8 | 2 |
| Rowland J.O. | 45 | 2 | 3 | 0 | 49 | 2 |
| Sheffield L.J. | 38 | 27 | 4 | 2 | 44 | 29 |
| Singer D.J. | 8 | 5 | – | – | 9 | 5 |
| Smith G. | 44 | 6 | 4 | 1 | 50 | 7 |
| Swindells J. | 23 | 3 | 4 | 3 | 28 | 6 |
| Walters G. | 28 | 1 | 1 | 0 | 31 | 1 |
| Weare L. | 43 | 0 | 4 | 0 | 49 | 0 |
| Williams D.S. | 8 | 0 | 1 | 0 | 10 | 0 |
| Wookey K.G. | 1 | 0 | – | – | 1 | 0 |
| Own Goals | | 1 | | | | 2 |

| | | P | W | D | L | F | A | Pts |
|---|---|---|---|---|---|---|---|---|
| 1 | Brighton | 46 | 26 | 11 | 9 | 102 | 57 | 63 |
| 2 | Millwall | 46 | 23 | 16 | 7 | 78 | 45 | 62 |
| 3 | York | 46 | 28 | 6 | 12 | 91 | 56 | 62 |
| 4 | Oxford | 46 | 23 | 15 | 8 | 87 | 44 | 61 |
| 5 | Tranmere | 46 | 27 | 6 | 13 | 99 | 56 | 60 |
| 6 | Rochdale | 46 | 22 | 14 | 10 | 74 | 53 | 58 |
| 7 | Bradford PA | 46 | 20 | 17 | 9 | 86 | 62 | 57 |
| 8 | Chester | 46 | 25 | 6 | 15 | 119 | 81 | 56 |
| 9 | Doncaster | 46 | 20 | 11 | 15 | 84 | 72 | 51 |
| 10 | Crewe | 46 | 18 | 13 | 15 | 90 | 81 | 49 |
| 11 | Torquay | 46 | 21 | 7 | 18 | 70 | 70 | 49 |
| 12 | Chesterfield | 46 | 20 | 8 | 18 | 58 | 70 | 48 |
| 13 | Notts County | 46 | 15 | 14 | 17 | 61 | 73 | 44 |
| 14 | Wrexham | 46 | 17 | 9 | 20 | 84 | 92 | 43 |
| 15 | Hartlepools | 46 | 15 | 13 | 18 | 61 | 85 | 43 |
| 16 | Newport | 46 | 17 | 8 | 21 | 85 | 81 | 42 |
| 17 | Darlington | 46 | 18 | 6 | 22 | 84 | 87 | 42 |
| 18 | Aldershot | 46 | 15 | 7 | 24 | 64 | 84 | 37 |
| 19 | Bradford City | 46 | 12 | 8 | 26 | 70 | 88 | 32 |
| 20 | Southport | 46 | 8 | 16 | 22 | 58 | 89 | 32 |
| 21 | Barrow | 46 | 12 | 6 | 28 | 59 | 105 | 30 |
| 22 | Lincoln | 46 | 11 | 6 | 29 | 58 | 99 | 28 |
| 23 | Halifax | 46 | 11 | 6 | 29 | 54 | 103 | 28 |
| 24 | Stockport | 46 | 10 | 7 | 29 | 44 | 87 | 27 |

## F.A.Cup

| | Date | Opposition | Res. | Att. | Goalscorers |
|---|---|---|---|---|---|
| 1 | 14 Nov | SPALDING UNITED | 5-3 | 4115 | Swindells(2), Morgan, Frowen, Reece |
| 2 | 5 Dec | MANSFIELD TOWN | 3-0 | 5304 | Sheffield(2), Smith |
| 3 | 9 Jan | Reading | 2-2 | 11998 | Swindells, Reece |
| 3R | 11 | READING | 0-1 | 13118 | |

(Back) Rathbone, Rowland, Weare, Morgan, Bird, Pring
(Front) Smith, Sheffield, Walters, Singer, Hill.

# SEASON 1965-66    Division 4

| | Date | Opposition | Res. | Att. | Goalscorers |
|---|---|---|---|---|---|
| 1 | 21 Aug | Chesterfield | 2-1 | 5958 | Morgan(2) |
| 2 | 25 | Torquay United | 0-1 | 7489 | |
| 3 | 28 | ROCHDALE | 1-1 | 3673 | Reynolds |
| 4 | 4 Sep | Luton Town | 1-2 | 4899 | Morgan |
| 5 | 11 | BARROW | 3-2 | 2741 | Morgan, Pugh, Reynolds |
| 6 | 13 | TORQUAY UNITED | 3-2 | 3814 | Morgan(2), Pugh |
| 7 | 18 | Hartlepools United | 2-5 | 4939 | Hill, Jones |
| 8 | 25 | DONCASTER ROVERS | 4-0 | 2970 | Pugh, Hill, Bird, Williams |
| 9 | 2 Oct | Southport | 0-2 | 3537 | |
| 10 | 6 | Aldershot | 1-2 | 5037 | Morgan |
| 11 | 9 | HALIFAX TOWN | 3-1 | 2800 | Morgan, Pugh, Jones |
| 12 | 16 | Chester | 1-6 | 8027 | Morgan |
| 13 | 25 | NOTTS COUNTY | 1-2 | 3985 | Hill |
| 14 | 30 | Lincoln City | 1-1 | 3590 | Jones |
| 15 | 8 Nov | DARLINGTON | 3-0 | 2911 | Rathbone, Pugh, Hale |
| 16 | 19 | TRANMERE ROVERS | 0-0 | 2516 | |
| 17 | 22 | ALDERSHOT | 3-1 | 2180 | Bird, Smith, Hale |
| 18 | 27 | Colchester United | 2-3 | 3593 | Jones, Hale |
| 19 | 11 Dec | Bradford City | 2-3 | 3717 | Hill, Hale |
| 20 | 31 | Halifax Town | 4-4 | 2570 | Walters, Smith, Wookey, Westlake(og) |
| 21 | 8 Jan | STOCKPORT COUNTY | 1-0 | 2760 | Wookey |
| 22 | 15 | Notts County | 1-1 | 4605 | Hall |
| 23 | 31 | CHESTERFIELD | 3-4 | 2866 | Reynolds(2), Hale |
| 24 | 5 Feb | Rochdale | 1-2 | 2167 | Smith |
| 25 | 12 | Bradford Park Ave | 1-6 | 4358 | Hale |
| 26 | 26 | Barrow | 2-2 | 3532 | Morgan, Smith |
| 27 | 2 Mar | Crewe Alexandra | 2-2 | 2751 | Hale(2) |
| 28 | 7 | BRADFORD PARK AVE | 3-1 | 2817 | Morgan(2), Tapscott |
| 29 | 12 | HARTLEPOOLS UNITED | 3-0 | 2250 | Morgan, Pugh, Hale |
| 30 | 19 | Doncaster Rovers | 0-1 | 12365 | |
| 31 | 24 | CREWE ALEXANDRA | 1-0 | 2502 | Hall |
| 32 | 25 | SOUTHPORT | 1-1 | 1997 | Morgan |
| 33 | 9 Apr | BARNSLEY | 1-0 | 2328 | Reynolds |
| 34 | 11 | PORT VALE | 0-1 | 2257 | |
| 35 | 12 | Port Vale | 0-3 | 4496 | |
| 36 | 15 | Tranmere Rovers | 1-0 | 3766 | Wookey |
| 37 | 25 | Wrexham | 1-0 | 3106 | Hall |
| 38 | 29 | Barnsley | 2-2 | 1697 | Jones, Hale |
| 39 | 2 May | LINCOLN CITY | 0-0 | 2176 | |
| 40 | 7 | BRADFORD CITY | 2-2 | 1855 | Morgan, Hale |
| 41 | 9 | Darlington | 1-0 | 10923 | Hale |
| 42 | 16 | WREXHAM | 2-2 | 1884 | Hale, Pugh |
| 43 | 20 | Stockport County | 1-2 | 3586 | Jones |
| 44 | 23 | CHESTER | 3-2 | 1700 | Hale(2), Morgan |
| 45 | 25 | LUTON TOWN | 3-1 | 2173 | Hale(2), Morgan |
| 46 | 28 | COLCHESTER UNITED | 2-1 | 2905 | Morgan, Hale |

| Player | League | | F.A.Cup | | Total | |
|---|---|---|---|---|---|---|
| | App | Gls. | App | Gls. | App | Gls. |
| Beswick K. | 22 | 0 | – | – | 24 | 0 |
| Bird J.F. | 45 | 2 | 1 | 0 | 51 | 3 |
| Cook M.I. | 30+2 | 0 | 1 | 0 | 36+2 | 0 |
| Frowen J. | 5+1 | 0 | – | – | 7+1 | 0 |
| Hale A. | 34 | 21 | 1 | 0 | 38 | 24 |
| Hill L.W. | 36 | 5 | 1 | 0 | 40 | 6 |
| Jones D.A.B. | 26 | 5 | 1 | 0 | 30 | 5 |
| Morgan K.G. | 42 | 18 | 1 | 0 | 47 | 19 |
| Pugh D. | 32+ | 7 | 1 | 0 | 36+1 | 7 |
| Rathbone G.C. | 45 | 1 | 1 | 0 | 51 | 1 |
| Reynolds G.E.A. | 20+1 | 5 | – | – | 23+1 | 6 |
| Rowlands J.O. | 44+1 | 0 | 1 | 0 | 50+1 | 0 |
| Smith G. | 21 | 4 | – | – | 23 | 4 |
| Tapscott D.J.R. | 12+1 | 1 | – | – | 14+1 | 1 |
| Thomas J. | 11 | 0 | – | – | 11 | 0 |
| Walters G. | 12 | 1 | 1 | 0 | 15 | 1 |
| Weare L. | 24 | 0 | 1 | 0 | 28 | 0 |
| Williams D.S. | 31 | 1 | – | – | 32 | 1 |
| Wood A.H. | 3 | 0 | – | – | 3 | 0 |
| Wookey K.G. | 11 | 3 | – | – | 13 | 3 |
| Own Goals | | 1 | | | | 1 |

| | P | W | D | L | F | A | Pts |
|---|---|---|---|---|---|---|---|
| 1 Doncaster | 46 | 24 | 11 | 11 | 85 | 54 | 59 |
| 2 Darlington | 46 | 25 | 9 | 12 | 72 | 53 | 59 |
| 3 Torquay | 46 | 24 | 10 | 12 | 72 | 49 | 58 |
| 4 Colchester | 46 | 23 | 10 | 13 | 70 | 47 | 56 |
| 5 Tranmere | 46 | 24 | 8 | 14 | 93 | 66 | 56 |
| 6 Luton | 46 | 24 | 8 | 14 | 90 | 70 | 56 |
| 7 Chester | 46 | 20 | 12 | 14 | 79 | 70 | 52 |
| 8 Notts County | 46 | 19 | 12 | 15 | 61 | 53 | 50 |
| 9 Newport | 46 | 18 | 12 | 16 | 75 | 75 | 48 |
| 10 Southport | 46 | 18 | 12 | 16 | 68 | 69 | 48 |
| 11 Bradford PA | 46 | 21 | 5 | 20 | 102 | 92 | 47 |
| 12 Barrow | 46 | 16 | 15 | 15 | 72 | 76 | 47 |
| 13 Stockport | 46 | 18 | 6 | 22 | 71 | 70 | 42 |
| 14 Crewe | 46 | 16 | 9 | 21 | 61 | 63 | 41 |
| 15 Halifax | 46 | 15 | 11 | 20 | 67 | 75 | 41 |
| 16 Barnsley | 46 | 15 | 10 | 21 | 74 | 78 | 40 |
| 17 Aldershot | 46 | 15 | 10 | 21 | 75 | 84 | 40 |
| 18 Hartlepools | 46 | 16 | 8 | 22 | 63 | 75 | 40 |
| 19 Port Vale | 46 | 15 | 9 | 22 | 48 | 59 | 39 |
| 20 Chesterfield | 46 | 13 | 13 | 20 | 62 | 78 | 39 |
| 21 Rochdale | 46 | 16 | 5 | 25 | 71 | 87 | 37 |
| 22 Lincoln | 46 | 13 | 11 | 22 | 57 | 82 | 37 |
| 23 Bradford City | 46 | 12 | 13 | 21 | 63 | 94 | 37 |
| 24 Wrexham | 46 | 13 | 9 | 24 | 72 | 104 | 35 |

## F.A.Cup

| | Date | Opposition | Res. | Att. | |
|---|---|---|---|---|---|
| 1 | 13 Nov | Bath City | 0-2 | 7330 | |

(Back) Saunders (Sec.), Rowland, Pugh, Beswick, Rathbone, Williams, Bird, Hill, Lucas (Manager)
(Front) Harris (Dir.), Thomas, Jones, Bailey (Chair.), Hale, Morgan, Jenkins (Dir.)

# SEASON 1966-67 Division 4

| | Date | Opposition | Res. | Att. | Goalscorers |
|---|---|---|---|---|---|
| 1 | 20 Aug | Lincoln City | 2-2 | 4037 | Jones(2) |
| 2 | 27 | BARNSLEY | 2-0 | 2939 | Winstanley(og), Parker(og) |
| 3 | 3 Sep | Luton Town | 1-3 | 5377 | Fraser |
| 4 | 5 | Chesterfield | 1-0 | 7027 | Thomas |
| 5 | 10 | ALDERSHOT | 1-2 | 2521 | Jones |
| 6 | 17 | Wrexham | 2-2 | 5935 | Pugh, Rathbone |
| 7 | 19 | Hartlepools United | 1-0 | 4096 | Jones |
| 8 | 24 | SOUTHEND UNITED | 3-0 | 2944 | Morgan(2), Hill |
| 9 | 26 | CHESTERFIELD | 4-1 | 5774 | Jones(3), Morgan |
| 10 | 30 | Tranmere Rovers | 1-2 | 5952 | Jones |
| 11 | 7 Oct | Stockport County | 0-0 | 12041 | |
| 12 | 15 | ROCHDALE | 2-2 | 4615 | Jones, Rathbone |
| 13 | 17 | HARTLEPOOLS UNITED | 0-2 | 5458 | |
| 14 | 22 | Southport | 0-1 | 6205 | |
| 15 | 24 | LUTON TOWN | 2-0 | 3451 | Fraser, Morgan |
| 16 | 29 | NOTTS COUNTY | 1-0 | 3670 | Gibson(og) |
| 17 | 5 Nov | Chester | 2-4 | 5257 | Hill, G.Smith |
| 18 | 12 | BRADFORD PARK AVE | 0-0 | 3139 | |
| 19 | 19 | Port Vale | 0-2 | 3883 | |
| 20 | 10 Dec | YORK CITY | 4-2 | 1872 | Morgan(2), Hill, Jackson(og) |
| 21 | 26 | Exeter City | 0-0 | 7044 | |
| 22 | 27 | EXETER CITY | 3-2 | 4082 | Jones(2), Morgan |
| 23 | 31 | Barnsley | 1-1 | 7610 | Morgan |
| 24 | 14 Jan | Aldershot | 0-5 | 4403 | |
| 25 | 21 | WREXHAM | 1-1 | 2882 | Wood |
| 26 | 4 Feb | Southend United | 0-1 | 7412 | |
| 27 | 13 | TRANMERE ROVERS | 1-2 | 2453 | Jones |
| 28 | 25 | STOCKPORT COUNTY | 1-1 | 2351 | Melling |
| 29 | 4 Mar | Rochdale | 0-2 | 2041 | |
| 30 | 6 | Barrow | 0-1 | 5186 | |
| 31 | 11 | Halifax Town | 2-2 | 3454 | G.Smith, Melling |
| 32 | 13 | LINCOLN CITY | 0-0 | 2245 | |
| 33 | 18 | SOUTHPORT | 0-0 | 2300 | |
| 34 | 25 | Crewe Alexandra | 2-3 | 4690 | G.Smith, Melling |
| 35 | 27 | Brentford | 1-1 | 9600 | Melling |
| 36 | 28 | BRENTFORD | 1-1 | 2546 | Bird |
| 37 | 3 Apr | CHESTER | 2-3 | 2591 | Jones, A.Williams |
| 38 | 8 | Bradford Park Ave | 1-3 | 2724 | Hill |
| 39 | 10 | BRADFORD CITY | 1-1 | 1222 | Reynolds |
| 40 | 17 | PORT VALE | 1-1 | 1912 | G.Smith |
| 41 | 22 | Notts County | 1-2 | 3455 | Melling |
| 42 | 26 | Bradford City | 2-1 | 3825 | Wood, Jones |
| 43 | 29 | BARROW | 0-1 | 2263 | |
| 44 | 1 May | HALIFAX TOWN | 3-0 | 1600 | Bird, Morgan, Melling |
| 45 | 5 | York City | 1-2 | 2605 | Melling |
| 46 | 13 | CREWE ALEXANDRA | 2-1 | 1539 | Jones, A.Williams |

| Player | League | | F.A.Cup | | Total | |
|---|---|---|---|---|---|---|
| | App | Gls | App | Gls | App | Gls |
| Beswick K. | 33 | 0 | 1 | 0 | 36 | 0 |
| Bird J.F. | 32 | 2 | – | – | 36 | 2 |
| Collins L. | 7 | 0 | – | – | 7 | 0 |
| Deacy M. | 1 | 0 | – | – | 1 | 0 |
| Fraser G. | 11+1 | 2 | 1 | 0 | 13+1 | 2 |
| Hill L.W. | 36 | 3 | 1 | 0 | 40 | 4 |
| Jones D.A.B. | 39 | 15 | 1 | 0 | 44 | 19 |
| Melling T. | 18 | 7 | – | – | 19 | 8 |
| Morgan K.G. | 39 | 9 | 1 | 0 | 45 | 9 |
| Pugh D. | 32+3 | 1 | 1 | 0 | 37+3 | 2 |
| Rathbone G.C. | 16 | 2 | – | – | 16 | 2 |
| Reynolds G.E.A. | 3 | 1 | – | – | 3 | 1 |
| Rowland J.O. | 43 | 0 | 1 | 0 | 48 | 0 |
| Smith A.F. | 11+1 | 0 | 0+1 | 0 | 13+2 | 0 |
| Smith G. | 27 | 5 | – | – | 31 | 5 |
| Thomas J. | 28+1 | 3 | 1 | 1 | 32+1 | 4 |
| Weare L. | 13 | 0 | – | – | 16 | 0 |
| Williams A. | 27 | 2 | 1 | 0 | 32 | 2 |
| Williams D.S. | 37 | 0 | 1 | 0 | 43 | 0 |
| Wood A.H. | 39 | 2 | 1 | 0 | 45 | 2 |
| Wookey K.G. | 14+1 | 0 | – | – | 15+1 | 0 |
| Own Goals | | 4 | | | | 4 |

| | | P | W | D | L | F | A | Pts |
|---|---|---|---|---|---|---|---|---|
| 1 | Stockport | 46 | 26 | 12 | 8 | 69 | 42 | 64 |
| 2 | Southport | 46 | 23 | 13 | 10 | 69 | 42 | 59 |
| 3 | Barrow | 46 | 24 | 11 | 11 | 76 | 54 | 59 |
| 4 | Tranmere | 46 | 22 | 14 | 10 | 66 | 43 | 58 |
| 5 | Crewe | 46 | 21 | 12 | 13 | 70 | 55 | 54 |
| 6 | Southend | 46 | 22 | 9 | 15 | 70 | 49 | 53 |
| 7 | Wrexham | 46 | 16 | 20 | 10 | 76 | 62 | 52 |
| 8 | Hartlepools | 46 | 22 | 7 | 17 | 66 | 64 | 51 |
| 9 | Brentford | 46 | 18 | 13 | 15 | 58 | 56 | 49 |
| 10 | Aldershot | 46 | 18 | 12 | 16 | 72 | 57 | 48 |
| 11 | Bradford City | 46 | 19 | 10 | 17 | 74 | 62 | 48 |
| 12 | Halifax | 46 | 15 | 14 | 17 | 59 | 68 | 44 |
| 13 | Port Vale | 46 | 14 | 15 | 17 | 55 | 58 | 43 |
| 14 | Exeter | 46 | 14 | 15 | 17 | 50 | 60 | 43 |
| 15 | Chesterfield | 46 | 17 | 8 | 21 | 60 | 63 | 42 |
| 16 | Barnsley | 46 | 13 | 15 | 18 | 60 | 64 | 41 |
| 17 | Luton | 46 | 16 | 9 | 21 | 59 | 73 | 41 |
| 18 | Newport | 46 | 12 | 16 | 18 | 56 | 63 | 40 |
| 19 | Chester | 46 | 15 | 10 | 21 | 54 | 78 | 40 |
| 20 | Notts County | 46 | 13 | 11 | 22 | 53 | 72 | 37 |
| 21 | Rochdale | 46 | 13 | 11 | 22 | 53 | 75 | 37 |
| 22 | York | 46 | 12 | 11 | 23 | 65 | 79 | 35 |
| 23 | Bradford PA | 46 | 11 | 13 | 22 | 52 | 79 | 35 |
| 24 | Lincoln | 46 | 9 | 13 | 24 | 58 | 82 | 31 |

## F.A.Cup

| | Date | Opposition | Res. | Att. | Goalscorers |
|---|---|---|---|---|---|
| 1 | 26 Nov | BRIGHTON & H.A. | 1-2 | 5000 | Thomas |

(Back) Jones, Bird, A.Williams, Wood, Beswick, Pugh, Reynolds.
(Front) Thomas, Hill, Rowland, Morgan, D.Williams.

# SEASON 1967-68   Division 4

| | Date | Opposition | Res. | Att. | Goalscorers |
|---|---|---|---|---|---|
| 1 | 19 Aug | ROCHDALE | 1-1 | 4848 | Melling |
| 2 | 26 | Brentford | 1-3 | 4511 | Wookey |
| 3 | 2 Sep | BRADFORD PARK AVE. | 4-0 | 3700 | D.Jones(2), Melling, Hill |
| 4 | 5 | YORK CITY | 2-1 | 4108 | D.Jones, King |
| 5 | 9 | Doncaster Rovers | 1-1 | 6207 | Hill |
| 6 | 16 | LUTON TOWN | 1-1 | 4635 | King |
| 7 | 22 | Southend United | 2-2 | 15389 | King(2) |
| 8 | 25 | York City | 1-0 | 3072 | King |
| 9 | 30 | WREXHAM | 3-2 | 5133 | Melling(3) |
| 10 | 3 Oct | HARTLEPOOLS UNITED | 2-0 | 2136 | Melling(2) |
| 11 | 7 | Lincoln City | 1-2 | 6689 | Stark |
| 12 | 14 | HALIFAX TOWN | 0-1 | 2657 | |
| 13 | 21 | Bradford City | 0-3 | 8123 | |
| 14 | 23 | Hartlepools United | 0-2 | 4942 | |
| 15 | 31 | CREWE ALEXANDRA | 0-0 | 3004 | |
| 16 | 4 Nov | Notts County | 1-3 | 4456 | D.Jones |
| 17 | 13 | Bradford Park Ave. | 2-0 | 2991 | Stark, Thomas |
| 18 | 18 | Chester | 1-2 | 3704 | Thomas |
| 19 | 21 | PORT VALE | 1-1 | 2434 | A.Smith |
| 20 | 25 | CHESTERFIELD | 0-3 | 2343 | |
| 21 | 2 Dec | Exeter City | 1-2 | 4208 | Hill |
| 22 | 16 | Rochdale | 3-4 | 1662 | Hill, Robinson, Buck |
| 23 | 23 | BRENTFORD | 2-2 | 2700 | Hill, King |
| 24 | 26 | Swansea Town | 2-4 | 12458 | Hill, A.Jones |
| 25 | 30 | SWANSEA TOWN | 3-0 | 6316 | A.Jones(2), Buck |
| 26 | 20 Jan | Luton Town | 1-1 | 10992 | Hill |
| 27 | 5 Feb | SOUTHEND UNITED | 2-0 | 2850 | Hill, Matthews(og) |
| 28 | 10 | Wrexham | 1-0 | 5544 | Hill |
| 29 | 17 | BARNSLEY | 3-0 | 4301 | Wookey, Buck, A.Jones |
| 30 | 24 | CHESTER | 1-1 | 4370 | A.Jones |
| 31 | 27 | DONCASTER ROVERS | 2-1 | 4642 | Hill, A.Jones |
| 32 | 2 Mar | Halifax Town | 1-4 | 4336 | King |
| 33 | 9 | Workington | 1-1 | 2838 | A.Jones |
| 34 | 16 | BRADFORD CITY | 0-3 | 3017 | |
| 35 | 23 | Crewe Alexandra | 1-1 | 4738 | A.Jones |
| 36 | 30 | NOTTS COUNTY | 1-0 | 2040 | Murphy(og) |
| 37 | 6 Apr | Port Vale | 1-0 | 3607 | Buck |
| 38 | 12 | Aldershot | 0-0 | 5411 | |
| 39 | 13 | LINCOLN CITY | 0-1 | 2542 | |
| 40 | 15 | ALDERSHOT | 0-2 | 2180 | |
| 41 | 20 | Chesterfield | 2-1 | 6200 | Hill, A.Williams |
| 42 | 23 | DARLINGTON | 1-0 | 2112 | Hill |
| 43 | 27 | EXETER CITY | 1-1 | 1605 | Hill |
| 44 | 29 | WORKINGTON | 2-1 | 1813 | King(2) |
| 45 | 4 May | Darlington | 0-1 | 3085 | |
| 46 | 11 | Barnsley | 2-4 | 12092 | A.Jones(2) |

## F.A.Cup

| | Date | | Res. | Att. | Goalscorers |
|---|---|---|---|---|---|
| 1 | 18 Dec | GILLINGHAM | 3-0 | 2452 | Hill, A.Williams, King |
| 2 | 6 Jan | Guildford City | 1-0 | 8774 | Buck |
| 3 | 27 | Southampton | 1-1 | 23789 | King |
| 3R | 30 | SOUTHAMPTON | 2-3 | 17600 | Hill, A.Williams |

| Player | League | | F.A.Cup | | Total | |
|---|---|---|---|---|---|---|
| | App | Gls. | App | Gls. | App | Gls. |
| Buck A.R. | 20 | 4 | 3 | 1 | 26 | 6 |
| Collins L. | 9 | 0 | – | – | 9 | 0 |
| Cooper T. | 11 | 0 | – | – | 11 | 0 |
| Deacy M. | 12 | 0 | – | – | 12 | 0 |
| Hill L.W. | 38+2 | 13 | 4 | 2 | 47+3 | 18 |
| Jones A.P. | 21 | 10 | – | – | 24 | 11 |
| Jones D.A.B. | 16 | 4 | – | – | 19 | 5 |
| Jones D.R. | 2 | 0 | – | – | 2 | 0 |
| King G.H. | 34 | 9 | 4 | 2 | 41 | 12 |
| Melling T. | 16 | 7 | – | – | 19 | 7 |
| Miles J.M | 3 | 0 | – | – | 3 | 0 |
| Pugh D. | 2+1 | 0 | – | – | 2+1 | 0 |
| Robinson H. | 20+1 | 1 | 4 | 0 | 27+1 | 1 |
| Rowland J.O. | 41 | 0 | 4 | 0 | 51 | 0 |
| Smith A.F. | 15+2 | 1 | – | – | 15+2 | 1 |
| Smith G. | 1 | 0 | – | – | 1 | 0 |
| Stark W.R. | 12 | 2 | 4 | 0 | 17 | 2 |
| Thomas J. | 32 | 2 | 1 | 0 | 38 | 4 |
| Timson D.Y. | 23 | 0 | 1 | 0 | 27 | 0 |
| Weare L | 17 | 0 | 3 | 0 | 23 | 0 |
| Williams A. | 36 | 1 | 4 | 2 | 46 | 3 |
| Williams D.S. | 30 | 0 | 4 | 0 | 40 | 0 |
| Wilson J. | 42+1 | 0 | 4 | 0 | 52+1 | 0 |
| Wood A.H. | 31+1 | 0 | 4 | 0 | 41+1 | 0 |
| Wookey K.G. | 13+4 | 2 | – | – | 14+4 | 2 |
| Young R.G. | 9 | 0 | – | – | 9 | 0 |
| Own Goals | | 2 | | | | 3 |

| | | P | W | D | L | F | A | Pts |
|---|---|---|---|---|---|---|---|---|
| 1 | Luton | 46 | 27 | 12 | 7 | 87 | 44 | 66 |
| 2 | Barnsley | 46 | 24 | 13 | 9 | 68 | 46 | 61 |
| 3 | Hartlepools | 46 | 25 | 10 | 11 | 60 | 46 | 60 |
| 4 | Crewe | 46 | 20 | 18 | 8 | 74 | 49 | 58 |
| 5 | Bradford City | 46 | 23 | 11 | 12 | 72 | 51 | 57 |
| 6 | Southend | 46 | 20 | 14 | 12 | 77 | 58 | 54 |
| 7 | Chesterfield | 46 | 21 | 11 | 14 | 71 | 50 | 53 |
| 8 | Wrexham | 46 | 20 | 13 | 13 | 72 | 53 | 53 |
| 9 | Aldershot | 46 | 18 | 17 | 11 | 70 | 55 | 53 |
| 10 | Doncaster | 46 | 18 | 15 | 13 | 66 | 56 | 51 |
| 11 | Halifax | 46 | 15 | 16 | 15 | 52 | 49 | 46 |
| 12 | Newport | 46 | 16 | 13 | 17 | 58 | 63 | 45 |
| 13 | Lincoln | 46 | 17 | 9 | 20 | 71 | 68 | 43 |
| 14 | Brentford | 46 | 18 | 7 | 21 | 61 | 64 | 43 |
| 15 | Swansea | 46 | 16 | 10 | 20 | 63 | 77 | 42 |
| 16 | Darlington | 46 | 12 | 17 | 17 | 47 | 53 | 41 |
| 17 | Notts County | 46 | 15 | 11 | 20 | 53 | 79 | 41 |
| 18 | Port Vale | 46 | 12 | 15 | 19 | 61 | 72 | 39 |
| 19 | Rochdale | 46 | 12 | 14 | 20 | 51 | 72 | 38 |
| 20 | Exeter | 46 | 11 | 16 | 19 | 45 | 65 | 38 |
| 21 | York | 46 | 11 | 14 | 21 | 65 | 68 | 36 |
| 22 | Chester | 46 | 9 | 14 | 23 | 57 | 78 | 32 |
| 23 | Workington | 46 | 10 | 11 | 25 | 54 | 87 | 31 |
| 24 | Bradford PA | 46 | 4 | 15 | 27 | 30 | 82 | 23 |

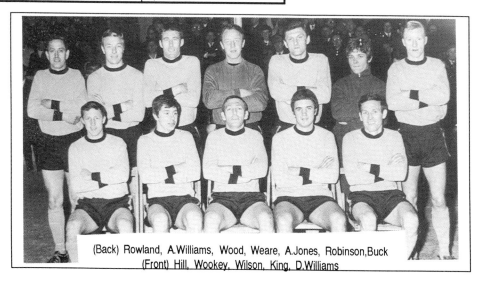

(Back) Rowland, A.Williams, Wood, Weare, A.Jones, Robinson, Buck
(Front) Hill, Wookey, Wilson, King, D.Williams

# SEASON 1968-69    Division 4

| | Date | Opposition | Res. | Att. | Goalscorers |
|---|---|---|---|---|---|
| 1 | 10 Aug | Grimsby Town | 0-3 | 4746 | |
| 2 | 17 | WORKINGTON | 0-0 | 3080 | |
| 3 | 24 | Lincoln City | 0-1 | 8038 | |
| 4 | 26 | DARLINGTON | 0-0 | 3164 | |
| 5 | 31 | SOUTHEND UNITED | 4-1 | 2925 | Buck(2), McLelland, Hill |
| 6 | 7 Sep | Notts County | 1-3 | 3579 | Hill |
| 7 | 14 | HALIFAX TOWN | 2-0 | 1564 | Hill, McLelland |
| 8 | 16 | SWANSEA TOWN | 2-1 | 5106 | McLelland, Robinson |
| 9 | 21 | Bradford Park Ave. | 5-1 | 3007 | Buck(5) |
| 10 | 28 | ALDERSHOT | 3-4 | 3919 | McLelland, Buck, Robinson |
| 11 | 5 Oct | Brentford | 1-1 | 7800 | Buck |
| 12 | 7 | Darlington | 0-1 | 8885 | |
| 13 | 12 | COLCHESTER UNITED | 1-0 | 3262 | McLelland |
| 14 | 18 | Scunthorpe United | 0-1 | 3238 | |
| 15 | 26 | YORK CITY | 1-1 | 2920 | Buck |
| 16 | 2 Nov | Peterborough Utd | 1-1 | 4792 | McLelland |
| 17 | 4 | Rochdale | 1-0 | 4223 | Hill |
| 18 | 8 | PORT VALE | 0-0 | 3137 | |
| 19 | 23 | CHESTERFIELD | 1-2 | 1766 | Buck |
| 20 | 30 | Bradford City | 1-1 | 5099 | Hill |
| 21 | 14 Dec | Colchester United | 1-2 | 3532 | Deacy |
| 22 | 26 | BRENTFORD | 1-1 | 3750 | McLaughlin |
| 23 | 28 | York City | 0-0 | 2787 | |
| 24 | 4 Jan | Aldershot | 0-4 | 6504 | |
| 25 | 11 | PETERBOROUGH UTD | 4-2 | 1649 | Buck, Hill, A.Jones, Deacy |
| 26 | 18 | Port Vale | 0-5 | 4040 | |
| 27 | 1 Feb | EXETER CITY | 2-1 | 1427 | Buck, Hill |
| 28 | 4 | Doncaster Rovers | 2-2 | 8321 | McLelland(2) |
| 29 | 10 | ROCHDALE | 1-1 | 2637 | Wood |
| 30 | 15 | BRADFORD CITY | 1-3 | 2104 | Thomas |
| 31 | 22 | Chester | 0-4 | 4519 | |
| 32 | 24 | SCUNTHORPE UNITED | 1-1 | 1504 | Hill |
| 33 | 28 | GRIMSBY TOWN | 2-0 | 1846 | Hill, Hamilton |
| 34 | 3 Mar | DONCASTER ROVERS | 0-0 | 2649 | |
| 35 | 12 | Exeter City | 0-2 | 3264 | |
| 36 | 15 | LINCOLN CITY | 2-1 | 1688 | McLaughlin, Brook(og) |
| 37 | 17 | CHESTER | 2-5 | 2100 | McLelland, Hooper |
| 38 | 29 | NOTTS COUNTY | 0-0 | 1749 | |
| 39 | 7 Apr | Swansea Town | 2-3 | 4753 | McLelland, Thomas |
| 40 | 8 | WREXHAM | 0-2 | 1848 | |
| 41 | 12 | BRADFORD PARK AVE. | 1-0 | 1192 | Hill |
| 42 | 14 | Wrexham | 0-4 | 3240 | |
| 43 | 19 | Halifax Town | 0-3 | 6445 | |
| 44 | 21 | Chesterfield | 1-2 | 2402 | Hill |
| 45 | 28 | Southend United | 0-1 | 11905 | |
| 46 | 8 May | Workington | 2-3 | 1225 | Rowland, Hamilton |

| Player | League | | F.A. Cup | | Total | |
|---|---|---|---|---|---|---|
| | App | Gls. | App | Gls. | App | Gls. |
| Aizlewood S. | 1 | 0 | – | – | 1 | 0 |
| Buck A.R. | 29 | 13 | 2 | 1 | 35 | 14 |
| Cooper T. | 35+1 | 0 | 2 | 0 | 40+1 | 1 |
| Deacy M. | 17+1 | 2 | – | – | 18+1 | 2 |
| Hamilton I. | 11+2 | 2 | – | – | 11+2 | 2 |
| Hill L.W. | 38 | 11 | 2 | 0 | 44 | 11 |
| Hooper W. | 6 | 1 | – | – | 6 | 1 |
| Jones A.P. | 32+1 | 1 | – | – | 34+2 | 1 |
| Jones B.H. | 13 | 0 | – | – | 13 | 0 |
| Jones D.R. | 1 | 0 | – | – | 1 | 0 |
| King G.H. | 15+3 | 0 | 2 | 0 | 17+4 | 0 |
| McLelland J. | 36 | 10 | 2 | 0 | 40 | 10 |
| McLaughlin M.A. | 46 | 2 | 2 | 0 | 51 | 2 |
| Miles J.M. | 1 | 0 | – | – | 1 | 0 |
| Robinson H. | 19 | 2 | – | – | 21 | 2 |
| Rowland J.O. | 44 | 1 | 2 | 0 | 50 | 1 |
| Smith A.F. | 8+2 | 0 | 0+1 | 0 | 8+3 | 0 |
| Thomas J. | 17 | 2 | – | – | 21 | 2 |
| Weare L. | 44 | 0 | 2 | 0 | 50 | 0 |
| Williams A. | 1 | 0 | – | – | 1 | 0 |
| Williams D.S. | 31 | 0 | 2 | 0 | 37 | 0 |
| Wilson J. | – | – | – | – | 1 | 0 |
| Wood A.H. | 27+1 | 1 | 2 | 0 | 32+1 | 1 |
| Wookey K.G. | 18+1 | 0 | 2 | 0 | 20+1 | 0 |
| Young R.G. | 16+3 | 0 | – | – | 19+3 | 0 |
| Own Goals | | 1 | | | | 1 |

| | | P | W | D | L | F | A | Pts |
|---|---|---|---|---|---|---|---|---|
| 1 | Doncaster | 46 | 21 | 17 | 8 | 65 | 38 | 59 |
| 2 | Halifax | 46 | 20 | 17 | 9 | 53 | 37 | 57 |
| 3 | Rochdale | 46 | 18 | 20 | 8 | 68 | 35 | 56 |
| 4 | Bradford City | 46 | 18 | 20 | 8 | 65 | 46 | 56 |
| 5 | Darlington | 46 | 17 | 18 | 11 | 62 | 45 | 52 |
| 6 | Colchester | 46 | 20 | 12 | 14 | 57 | 53 | 52 |
| 7 | Southend | 46 | 19 | 13 | 14 | 78 | 61 | 51 |
| 8 | Lincoln | 46 | 17 | 17 | 12 | 54 | 52 | 51 |
| 9 | Wrexham | 46 | 18 | 14 | 14 | 61 | 52 | 50 |
| 10 | Swansea | 46 | 19 | 11 | 16 | 58 | 54 | 49 |
| 11 | Brentford | 46 | 18 | 12 | 16 | 64 | 65 | 48 |
| 12 | Workington | 46 | 15 | 17 | 14 | 40 | 43 | 47 |
| 13 | Port Vale | 46 | 16 | 14 | 16 | 46 | 46 | 46 |
| 14 | Chester | 46 | 16 | 13 | 17 | 76 | 66 | 45 |
| 15 | Aldershot | 46 | 19 | 7 | 20 | 66 | 66 | 45 |
| 16 | Scunthorpe | 46 | 18 | 8 | 20 | 61 | 60 | 44 |
| 17 | Exeter | 46 | 16 | 11 | 19 | 66 | 65 | 43 |
| 18 | Peterborough | 46 | 13 | 16 | 17 | 60 | 57 | 42 |
| 19 | Notts County | 46 | 12 | 18 | 16 | 48 | 57 | 42 |
| 20 | Chesterfield | 46 | 13 | 15 | 18 | 43 | 50 | 41 |
| 21 | York | 46 | 14 | 11 | 21 | 53 | 75 | 39 |
| 22 | Newport | 46 | 11 | 14 | 21 | 49 | 74 | 36 |
| 23 | Grimsby | 46 | 9 | 15 | 22 | 47 | 69 | 33 |
| 24 | Bradford PA | 46 | 5 | 10 | 31 | 32 | 106 | 20 |

## F.A.Cup

| | Date | Opposition | Res. | Att. | Goalscorers |
|---|---|---|---|---|---|
| 1 | 16 Nov | Exeter City | 0-0 | 6045 | |
| 1R | 18 | EXETER CITY | 1-3 | 6065 | Buck |

(Back) Smith, Thomas, Buck, Weare, McLelland, Wood, A.Jones
(Front) Hamilton, D.Williams, Rowland, McLaughlin, Hill

# SEASON 1969-70     Division 4

| | Date | Opposition | Res. | Att. | Goalscorers |
|---|---|---|---|---|---|
| 1 | 9 Aug | YORK CITY | 1-2 | 4206 | Derrick |
| 2 | 16 | Oldham Athletic | 0-3 | 4585 | |
| 3 | 23 | EXETER CITY | 2-0 | 2525 | Hill, Derrick |
| 4 | 25 | Darlington | 0-0 | 3617 | |
| 5 | 30 | Aldershot | 1-1 | 5891 | Derrick |
| 6 | 6 Sep | BRENTFORD | 1-0 | 3203 | Derrick |
| 7 | 13 | Chesterfield | 0-4 | 4738 | |
| 8 | 15 | HARTLEPOOL | 1-1 | 2950 | Thomas |
| 9 | 20 | SOUTHEND UNITED | 4-0 | 2905 | Hill, Thomas, Young, Derrick |
| 10 | 27 | Northampton Town | 1-4 | 4665 | Cooper |
| 11 | 30 | Grimsby Town | 1-1 | 3359 | Derrick |
| 12 | 4 Oct | COLCHESTER UNITED | 4-1 | 2996 | Hill(2), Derrick, Raybould |
| 13 | 6 | OLDHAM ATHLETIC | 2-1 | 4229 | Derrick, Mabbutt |
| 14 | 11 | Peterborough Utd | 0-4 | 7002 | |
| 15 | 18 | Notts County | 1-4 | 4394 | Ferguson |
| 16 | 25 | CREWE ALEXANDRA | 0-0 | 2947 | |
| 17 | 1 Nov | Port Vale | 1-3 | 7477 | Smith |
| 18 | 8 | LINCOLN CITY | 3-1 | 2377 | Mabbutt(2), White |
| 19 | 22 | Wrexham | 0-3 | 8901 | |
| 20 | 25 | Swansea City | 1-1 | 8355 | Mabbutt |
| 21 | 29 | BRADFORD PARK AVE. | 5-1 | 2722 | Mabbutt(2), Radford(2), White |
| 22 | 13 Dec | CHESTERFIELD | 0-2 | 2381 | |
| 23 | 20 | Brentford | 0-1 | 4380 | |
| 24 | 26 | Exeter City | 1-1 | 6699 | Thomas |
| 25 | 27 | ALDERSHOT | 3-4 | 2200 | Smith, Mabbutt, White |
| 26 | 10 Jan | Southend United | 2-3 | 4147 | Mabbutt, Hill |
| 27 | 17 | NORTHAMPTON TOWN | 0-2 | 2277 | |
| 28 | 31 | Colchester United | 1-1 | 4679 | Wood(og) |
| 29 | 7 Feb | PETERBOROUGH UTD | 0-1 | 1590 | |
| 30 | 21 | Crewe Alexandra | 1-1 | 2815 | Mabbutt |
| 31 | 25 | Chester | 0-2 | 3664 | |
| 32 | 28 | NOTTS COUNTY | 1-0 | 1335 | Aizlewood |
| 33 | 4 Mar | Workington | 0-3 | 2000 | |
| 34 | 7 | WREXHAM | 1-2 | 2407 | Ferguson |
| 35 | 9 | SCUNTHORPE UNITED | 3-0 | 1917 | Hill, White, Mabbutt |
| 36 | 13 | Bradford Park Ave. | 1-1 | 1864 | Mabbutt |
| 37 | 16 | CHESTER | 3-1 | 2638 | Mabbutt, Jones, Hill |
| 38 | 21 | WORKINGTON | 0-1 | 2956 | |
| 39 | 27 | Lincoln City | 0-3 | 6394 | |
| 40 | 28 | Scunthorpe United | 0-4 | 3805 | |
| 41 | 30 | PORT VALE | 1-1 | 2218 | Wood |
| 42 | 4 Apr | DARLINGTON | 2-1 | 1607 | Mabbutt, Radford |
| 43 | 6 | SWANSEA CITY | 1-2 | 5537 | Hill |
| 44 | 13 | Hartlepool | 1-0 | 1473 | Coldrick |
| 45 | 21 | York City | 1-2 | 1888 | Hill |
| 46 | 25 | GRIMSBY TOWN | 1-0 | 1009 | Mabbutt |

| Player | League | | F.A.Cup | | Total | |
|---|---|---|---|---|---|---|
| | App | Gls. | App | Gls. | App | Gls. |
| Aizlewood S. | 16 | 1 | – | – | 16 | 1 |
| Brown R. | 8+1 | 0 | – | – | 8+1 | 0 |
| Coldrick G.G. | 9 | 1 | – | – | 9 | 1 |
| Cooper T. | 18+3 | 1 | – | – | 19+3 | 2 |
| Deacy M. | 16 | 0 | – | – | 18 | 0 |
| Delaney J.C. | 1 | 0 | – | – | 1 | 0 |
| Derrick E.A. | 25+1 | 8 | 2 | 0 | 30+1 | 8 |
| Ferguson R.B. | 30 | 2 | 3 | 0 | 36 | 2 |
| Hill L.W. | 45 | 9 | 3 | 0 | 51 | 10 |
| Hooper W. | 3+2 | 0 | – | – | 4+2 | 0 |
| Jones R. | 9 | 1 | – | – | 9 | 1 |
| Lynch T.J. | 17 | 0 | – | – | 17 | 0 |
| Mabbutt R.W. | 32+2 | 14 | 3 | 0 | 36+2 | 15 |
| McLaughlin M.A. | 44 | 0 | 3 | 0 | 50 | 0 |
| Radford R. | 34+1 | 3 | 3 | 0 | 40+1 | 4 |
| Raybould P.E. | 5+1 | 1 | – | – | 5+1 | 1 |
| Saunders J.T. | 1 | 0 | – | – | 1 | 0 |
| Smith A.F. | 20+3 | 2 | 1 | 0 | 22+4 | 2 |
| Sprague M.L. | 31+1 | 0 | – | – | 31+1 | 0 |
| Thomas J. | 16+2 | 3 | 3 | 2 | 22+2 | 6 |
| Weare L. | 29 | 0 | 3 | 0 | 35 | 0 |
| White A.C.J. | 26+4 | 4 | 3 | 1 | 30+5 | 5 |
| Williams D.S. | 38 | 0 | 3 | 0 | 44 | 0 |
| Wood A.H. | 18 | 1 | 3 | 1 | 22 | 2 |
| Young R.G. | 15+4 | 1 | – | – | 16+4 | 1 |
| Own Goals | | 1 | | | | 1 |

## F.A.Cup

| | Date | Opposition | Res. | Att. | Goalscorers |
|---|---|---|---|---|---|
| 1 | 15 Nov | COLCHESTER UNITED | 2-1 | 3800 | White, Thomas |
| 2 | 6 Dec | HEREFORD UNITED | 2-1 | 7810 | Wood, Thomas |
| 3 | 3 Jan | Gillingham | 0-1 | 9000 | |

| | | P | W | D | L | F | A | Pts |
|---|---|---|---|---|---|---|---|---|
| 1 | Chesterfield | 46 | 27 | 10 | 9 | 77 | 32 | 64 |
| 2 | Wrexham | 46 | 26 | 9 | 11 | 84 | 49 | 61 |
| 3 | Swansea | 46 | 21 | 18 | 7 | 66 | 45 | 60 |
| 4 | Port Vale | 46 | 20 | 19 | 7 | 61 | 33 | 59 |
| 5 | Brentford | 46 | 20 | 16 | 10 | 58 | 39 | 56 |
| 6 | Aldershot | 46 | 20 | 13 | 13 | 78 | 65 | 53 |
| 7 | Notts County | 46 | 22 | 8 | 16 | 73 | 62 | 52 |
| 8 | Lincoln | 46 | 17 | 16 | 13 | 66 | 52 | 50 |
| 9 | Peterborough | 46 | 17 | 14 | 15 | 77 | 69 | 48 |
| 10 | Colchester | 46 | 17 | 14 | 15 | 64 | 63 | 48 |
| 11 | Chester | 46 | 21 | 6 | 19 | 58 | 66 | 48 |
| 12 | Scunthorpe | 46 | 18 | 10 | 18 | 67 | 65 | 46 |
| 13 | York | 46 | 16 | 14 | 16 | 55 | 62 | 46 |
| 14 | Northampton | 46 | 16 | 12 | 18 | 64 | 55 | 44 |
| 15 | Crewe | 46 | 16 | 12 | 18 | 51 | 51 | 44 |
| 16 | Grimsby | 46 | 14 | 15 | 17 | 54 | 58 | 43 |
| 17 | Southend | 46 | 15 | 10 | 21 | 59 | 85 | 40 |
| 18 | Exeter | 46 | 14 | 11 | 21 | 57 | 59 | 39 |
| 19 | Oldham | 46 | 13 | 13 | 20 | 60 | 65 | 39 |
| 20 | Workington | 46 | 12 | 14 | 20 | 46 | 64 | 38 |
| 21 | Newport | 46 | 13 | 11 | 22 | 53 | 74 | 37 |
| 22 | Darlington | 46 | 13 | 10 | 23 | 53 | 73 | 36 |
| 23 | Hartlepool | 46 | 10 | 10 | 26 | 42 | 82 | 30 |
| 24 | Bradford P A | 46 | 6 | 11 | 29 | 41 | 96 | 23 |

(Back) Mabbutt, Raybould, Aizlewood, Weare, Ferguson, Young
(Front) Cooper, Hill, McLaughlin, Sprague, Williams, Derrick
(Martin Rogers-Mascot)

# SEASON 1970-71    Division 4

| | Date | Opposition | Res. | Att. | Goalscorers |
|---|---|---|---|---|---|
| 1 | 15 Aug | NORTHAMPTON TOWN | 0-1 | 4515 | |
| 2 | 21 | Southport | 1-6 | 2905 | Brown |
| 3 | 29 | BOURNEMOUTH & B.A. | 0-2 | 3079 | |
| 4 | 1 Sep | GRIMSBY TOWN | 0-1 | 2569 | |
| 5 | 5 | Peterborough Utd | 1-2 | 4647 | Jones |
| 6 | 12 | OLDHAM ATHLETIC | 1-4 | 1849 | Thomas |
| 7 | 19 | Darlington | 1-2 | 3309 | Jones |
| 8 | 23 | Notts County | 0-2 | 8445 | |
| 9 | 26 | CHESTER | 0-1 | 1827 | |
| 10 | 29 | EXETER CITY | 0-1 | 2169 | |
| 11 | 3 Oct | Hartlepool | 2-2 | 3238 | Hooper(2) |
| 12 | 10 | SCUNTHORPE UNITED | 2-3 | 3539 | Brown(2) |
| 13 | 17 | Northampton Town | 0-1 | 6171 | |
| 14 | 21 | Southend United | 0-3 | 4349 | |
| 15 | 24 | WORKINGTON | 2-2 | 2559 | D.H.Harris, Brown |
| 16 | 30 | York City | 0-1 | 3120 | |
| 17 | 7 Nov | BRENTFORD | 0-1 | 2407 | |
| 18 | 10 | COLCHESTER UNITED | 1-3 | 1973 | Jones |
| 19 | 14 | Cambridge United | 2-3 | 3608 | Jones, Radford |
| 20 | 27 | Stockport County | 2-3 | 3752 | Radford(2) |
| 21 | 5 Dec | ALDERSHOT | 1-2 | 2629 | Brown |
| 22 | 12 | Oldham Athletic | 0-4 | 7845 | |
| 23 | 19 | SOUTHPORT | 2-2 | 2805 | Hooper, D.H.Harris |
| 24 | 26 | Crewe Alexandra | 0-2 | 3058 | |
| 25 | 9 Jan | Exeter City | 1-1 | 4142 | Jones |
| 26 | 15 | SOUTHEND UNITED | 3-0 | 2308 | Jones, Brown, White |
| 27 | 23 | Barrow | 1-3 | 2075 | White |
| 28 | 6 Feb | Aldershot | 1-1 | 5686 | Wood |
| 29 | 12 | BARROW | 3-2 | 1542 | Jones, Coldrick, White |
| 30 | 20 | Colchester United | 2-4 | 6444 | Young, Brown |
| 31 | 26 | YORK CITY | 0-3 | 1753 | |
| 32 | 2 Mar | STOCKPORT COUNTY | 3-1 | 1479 | Jones(2), Thomas |
| 33 | 6 | Workington | 1-2 | 1748 | Thomas |
| 34 | 9 | NOTTS COUNTY | 2-1 | 2129 | Smith, Brown |
| 35 | 12 | CAMBRIDGE UNITED | 2-0 | 2587 | Smith(2) |
| 36 | 17 | Lincoln City | 1-1 | 4407 | Thomas |
| 37 | 20 | Brentford | 3-0 | 8402 | Thomas(2), Nelmes(og) |
| 38 | 27 | PETERBOROUGH UTD | 2-0 | 2588 | Hooper, Brown |
| 39 | 3 Apr | Bournemouth & B.A. | 2-2 | 8295 | Thomas, Hooper |
| 40 | 10 | CREWE ALEXANDRA | 1-3 | 3353 | Thomas |
| 41 | 13 | HARTLEPOOL | 2-0 | 3173 | Radford, Thomas |
| 42 | 17 | Scunthorpe United | 1-0 | 3075 | Brown |
| 43 | 20 | LINCOLN CITY | 2-2 | 3397 | Brown, Coldrick |
| 44 | 24 | DARLINGTON | 3-1 | 2756 | Brown(3) |
| 45 | 27 | Grimsby Town | 0-2 | 4710 | |
| 46 | 1 May | Chester | 1-2 | 2645 | Aizlewood |

| Player | League | | F.A.Cup | | Total | |
|---|---|---|---|---|---|---|
| | App | Gls. | App | Gls. | App | Gls. |
| Aizlewood S. | 14+6 | 1 | 1 | 0 | 16+6 | 1 |
| Brown W. | 42 | 14 | 1 | 0 | 47 | 16 |
| Coldrick G.G. | 42 | 2 | 1 | 0 | 47 | 2 |
| Darrell M.A. | 8 | 0 | – | – | 8 | 0 |
| Ferguson R.B. | 41 | 0 | 1 | 0 | 46 | 0 |
| Harris D.H. | 17 | 2 | – | – | 18 | 2 |
| Harris P. | 8+3 | 0 | 1 | 0 | 10+3 | 0 |
| Hooper W. | 22+2 | 5 | 0+1 | 0 | 23+4 | 5 |
| Jones R. | 26+3 | 9 | 1 | 1 | 30+3 | 10 |
| Lynch T.J. | 9 | 0 | – | – | 9 | 0 |
| Mabbutt R.W. | 7+4 | 0 | 1 | 0 | 9+4 | 0 |
| Macey J.R.T. | 37 | 0 | 1 | 0 | 42 | 0 |
| Radford R. | 29+2 | 4 | 1 | 0 | 32+2 | 4 |
| Saunders J.T. | 25+1 | 0 | – | – | 26+1 | 0 |
| Smith A.F. | 17+1 | 3 | – | – | 19+1 | 3 |
| Sprague M.L. | 8 | 0 | – | – | 9 | 0 |
| Thomas J. | 44 | 9 | 1 | 0 | 49 | 10 |
| White A.C.J. | 33+3 | 3 | – | – | 36+3 | 3 |
| Williams D.S. | 40 | 0 | 1 | 0 | 45 | 0 |
| Wood A.H. | 17 | 1 | – | – | 20 | 1 |
| Young R.G. | 20+2 | 1 | – | – | 20+3 | 2 |
| Own Goals | | 1 | | | | 1 |

| | | P | W | D | L | F | A | Pts |
|---|---|---|---|---|---|---|---|---|
| 1 | Notts County | 46 | 30 | 9 | 7 | 89 | 36 | 69 |
| 2 | Bournemouth | 46 | 24 | 12 | 10 | 81 | 46 | 60 |
| 3 | Oldham | 46 | 24 | 11 | 11 | 88 | 63 | 59 |
| 4 | York | 46 | 23 | 10 | 13 | 78 | 54 | 56 |
| 5 | Chester | 46 | 24 | 7 | 15 | 69 | 55 | 55 |
| 6 | Colchester | 46 | 21 | 12 | 13 | 70 | 54 | 54 |
| 7 | Northampton | 46 | 19 | 13 | 14 | 63 | 59 | 51 |
| 8 | Southport | 46 | 21 | 6 | 19 | 63 | 57 | 48 |
| 9 | Exeter | 46 | 17 | 14 | 15 | 67 | 68 | 48 |
| 10 | Workington | 46 | 18 | 12 | 16 | 48 | 49 | 48 |
| 11 | Stockport | 46 | 16 | 14 | 16 | 49 | 65 | 46 |
| 12 | Darlington | 46 | 17 | 11 | 18 | 58 | 57 | 45 |
| 13 | Aldershot | 46 | 14 | 17 | 15 | 66 | 71 | 45 |
| 14 | Brentford | 46 | 18 | 8 | 20 | 66 | 62 | 44 |
| 15 | Crewe | 46 | 18 | 8 | 20 | 75 | 76 | 44 |
| 16 | Peterborough | 46 | 18 | 7 | 21 | 70 | 71 | 43 |
| 17 | Scunthorpe | 46 | 15 | 13 | 18 | 56 | 61 | 43 |
| 18 | Southend | 46 | 14 | 15 | 17 | 53 | 66 | 43 |
| 19 | Grimsby | 46 | 18 | 7 | 21 | 57 | 71 | 43 |
| 20 | Cambridge | 46 | 15 | 13 | 18 | 51 | 66 | 43 |
| 21 | Lincoln | 46 | 13 | 13 | 20 | 70 | 71 | 39 |
| 22 | Newport | 46 | 10 | 8 | 28 | 55 | 85 | 28 |
| 23 | Hartlepool | 46 | 8 | 12 | 26 | 34 | 74 | 28 |
| 24 | Barrow | 46 | 7 | 8 | 31 | 51 | 90 | 22 |

## F.A.Cup

| 1 | 21 Nov | Barnet | 1-6 | 2994 | Jones |
|---|---|---|---|---|---|

(Back) Dr.Heffernan (Medical Off.), Thomas, Radford, Smith, Saunders, Aizlewood, Jones, Williams, Perkins, Stitfall (Trainer)  (Middle) Hooper, Young, White, Ferguson (P/Manager), P.Harris, Sprague, Coldrick  (Front) Macey, Lynch.

# SEASON 1971-72   Division 4

| | Date | Opposition | Res. | Att. | Goalscorers |
|---|---|---|---|---|---|
| 1 | 14 Aug | Doncaster Rovers | 2-4 | 4797 | Coldrick, Thomas |
| 2 | 21 | PETERBOROUGH UTD | 1-1 | 3963 | R.Jones |
| 3 | 28 | Lincoln City | 1-3 | 5265 | Brown |
| 4 | 31 | COLCHESTER UNITED | 2-1 | 4168 | Sprague, Brown |
| 5 | 4 Sep | NORTHAMPTON TOWN | 1-1 | 4300 | Thomas |
| 6 | 10 | Southport | 2-4 | 4206 | Young, Brown |
| 7 | 18 | ALDERSHOT | 2-3 | 3380 | White, Aizlewood |
| 8 | 25 | Darlington | 0-0 | 2254 | |
| 9 | 27 | Southend United | 1-3 | 7145 | White |
| 10 | 2 Oct | BURY | 2-1 | 2995 | Thomas, Young |
| 11 | 9 | Hartlepool | 1-0 | 2990 | White |
| 12 | 16 | DONCASTER ROVERS | 1-3 | 2770 | Brown |
| 13 | 23 | Gillingham | 2-1 | 5817 | Brown, Coldrick |
| 14 | 30 | CAMBRIDGE UNITED | 3-0 | 3824 | Thomas(2), Williams |
| 15 | 6 Nov | Brentford | 1-3 | 10480 | Thomas |
| 16 | 13 | BARROW | 2-1 | 3443 | Brown(2) |
| 17 | 27 | WORKINGTON | 0-1 | 2918 | |
| 18 | 4 Dec | Reading | 2-4 | 3680 | D.Jones, Young |
| 19 | 11 | LINCOLN CITY | 2-0 | 2987 | Brown(2) |
| 20 | 18 | Northampton Town | 1-1 | 4151 | Hooper |
| 21 | 27 | CHESTER | 1-0 | 7664 | Thomas |
| 22 | 1 Jan | Aldershot | 0-3 | 3120 | |
| 23 | 15 | Grimsby Town | 2-4 | 8112 | D.Jones(2) |
| 24 | 22 | SOUTHEND UNITED | 2-0 | 3535 | Hill, Thomas |
| 25 | 29 | Scunthorpe United | 0-1 | 4580 | |
| 26 | 5 Feb | Exeter City | 0-1 | 3732 | |
| 27 | 12 | GILLINGHAM | 1-2 | 3143 | D.Jones |
| 28 | 19 | Cambridge United | 1-0 | 4618 | D.Jones |
| 29 | 26 | BRENTFORD | 0-0 | 3271 | |
| 30 | 4 Mar | Barrow | 0-1 | 2196 | |
| 31 | 10 | HARTLEPOOL | 0-2 | 3170 | |
| 32 | 13 | GRIMSBY TOWN | 2-1 | 2870 | White, R.Jones |
| 33 | 18 | Peterborough Utd | 1-3 | 4028 | Hill |
| 34 | 24 | SOUTHPORT | 2-2 | 2699 | Brown, D.Jones |
| 35 | 31 | Bury | 0-3 | 5719 | |
| 36 | 1 Apr | Chester | 0-3 | 2563 | |
| 37 | 4 | DARLINGTON | 4-0 | 3196 | Thomas(2), White, Young |
| 38 | 8 | EXETER CITY | 0-0 | 2362 | |
| 39 | 11 | STOCKPORT COUNTY | 1-0 | 3359 | Hill |
| 40 | 15 | Workington | 0-3 | 1342 | |
| 41 | 18 | CREWE ALEXANDRA | 2-0 | 2958 | Thomas, White |
| 42 | 22 | READING | 2-1 | 3065 | R.Jones, Hill |
| 43 | 24 | Colchester United | 3-2 | 4311 | Brown, Hill, R.Jones |
| 44 | 28 | Stockport County | 4-4 | 1824 | D.Jones(2), R. Jones, Fogarty(og) |
| 45 | 1 May | SCUNTHORPE UNITED | 1-0 | 3686 | Hill |
| 46 | 3 | Crewe Alexandra | 2-1 | 1028 | R.Jones(2) |

| Player | League | | F.A. Cup | | Total | |
|---|---|---|---|---|---|---|
| | App | Gls. | App | Gls. | App | Gls. |
| Aizlewood S. | 35 | 1 | – | – | 38 | 1 |
| Brown W. | 40+1 | 11 | 1 | 0 | 45+1 | 13 |
| Coldrick G.G. | 21 | 2 | 1 | 0 | 24 | 2 |
| Green R. | 1 | 0 | – | – | 2 | 0 |
| Hancock M. | 1 | 0 | – | – | 1 | 0 |
| Harris B. | 38 | 0 | 1 | 0 | 43 | 0 |
| Harris P. | 12+7 | 0 | 1 | 0 | 15+7 | 0 |
| Hill L.W. | 21 | 6 | – | – | 23 | 6 |
| Hooper W. | 32 | 1 | 1 | 0 | 36 | 2 |
| Jones D.A.B. | 24+1 | 8 | – | – | 27+1 | 9 |
| Jones R. | 16+2 | 7 | – | – | 18+2 | 8 |
| Lynch T.J. | 30 | 0 | 1 | 0 | 34 | 0 |
| Macey J.R.T. | 16 | 0 | – | – | 17 | 0 |
| Passey P.T.J. | 20 | 0 | – | – | 20 | 0 |
| Smith A.F. | 16+4 | 0 | – | – | 19+4 | 0 |
| Sprague M.L. | 42 | 1 | 1 | 0 | 47 | 1 |
| Swain K.J. | 1 | 0 | – | – | 1 | 0 |
| Thomas J. | 44 | 11 | 1 | 0 | 49 | 12 |
| White A.C.J. | 27+4 | 6 | 1 | 0 | 29+5 | 6 |
| Williams D.S. | 26+2 | 1 | 1 | 0 | 27+3 | 1 |
| Wood A.H. | 13+3 | 0 | – | – | 13+4 | 0 |
| Young R.G. | 30+5 | 4 | 1 | 0 | 33+5 | 4 |
| Own goals | 1 | | | | | 1 |

| | | P | W | D | L | F | A | Pts |
|---|---|---|---|---|---|---|---|---|
| 1 | Grimsby | 46 | 28 | 7 | 11 | 88 | 56 | 63 |
| 2 | Southend | 46 | 24 | 12 | 10 | 81 | 55 | 60 |
| 3 | Brentford | 46 | 24 | 11 | 11 | 76 | 44 | 59 |
| 4 | Scunthorpe | 46 | 22 | 13 | 11 | 56 | 37 | 57 |
| 5 | Lincoln | 46 | 21 | 14 | 11 | 77 | 59 | 56 |
| 6 | Workington | 46 | 16 | 19 | 11 | 50 | 34 | 51 |
| 7 | Southport | 46 | 18 | 14 | 14 | 66 | 46 | 50 |
| 8 | Peterborough | 46 | 17 | 16 | 13 | 82 | 64 | 50 |
| 9 | Bury | 46 | 19 | 12 | 15 | 73 | 59 | 50 |
| 10 | Cambridge | 46 | 17 | 14 | 15 | 62 | 60 | 48 |
| 11 | Colchester | 46 | 19 | 10 | 17 | 70 | 69 | 48 |
| 12 | Doncaster | 46 | 16 | 14 | 16 | 56 | 63 | 46 |
| 13 | Gillingham | 46 | 16 | 13 | 17 | 61 | 67 | 45 |
| 14 | Newport | 46 | 18 | 8 | 20 | 60 | 72 | 44 |
| 15 | Exeter | 46 | 16 | 11 | 19 | 61 | 68 | 43 |
| 16 | Reading | 46 | 17 | 8 | 21 | 56 | 76 | 42 |
| 17 | Aldershot | 46 | 9 | 22 | 15 | 48 | 54 | 40 |
| 18 | Hartlepool | 46 | 17 | 6 | 23 | 58 | 69 | 40 |
| 19 | Darlington | 46 | 14 | 11 | 21 | 64 | 82 | 39 |
| 20 | Chester | 46 | 10 | 18 | 18 | 47 | 56 | 38 |
| 21 | Northampton | 46 | 12 | 13 | 21 | 66 | 79 | 37 |
| 22 | Barrow | 46 | 13 | 11 | 22 | 40 | 71 | 37 |
| 23 | Stockport | 46 | 9 | 14 | 23 | 55 | 87 | 32 |
| 24 | Crewe | 46 | 10 | 9 | 27 | 43 | 69 | 29 |

## F.A.Cup

| | | | | | |
|---|---|---|---|---|---|
| 1 | 20 Nov | Notts County | 0-6 | 11976 | |

(Back) Young, Aizlewood, Lynch, Macey, Brown, B.Harris
(Front) Swain, Williams, Coldrick, P.Harris, Saunders, White

# SEASON 1972–73    Division 4

| | Date | Opposition | Res. | Att. | Goalscorers |
|---|---|---|---|---|---|
| 1 | 12 Aug | Gillingham | 0–0 | 3719 | |
| 2 | 19 | CHESTER | 3–2 | 3342 | Relish(og), Brown(2) |
| 3 | 26 | Colchester United | 3–1 | 3639 | Coldrick, Hawkins, Thomas |
| 4 | 29 | Bury | 0–0 | 2834 | |
| 5 | 2 Sep | MANSFIELD TOWN | 0–1 | 4813 | |
| 6 | 9 | Torquay United | 2–2 | 3693 | Screen, Thomas |
| 7 | 16 | CAMBRIDGE UNITED | 0–2 | 3567 | |
| 8 | 19 | PETERBOROUGH UTD | 1–1 | 3013 | Thomas |
| 9 | 23 | Reading | 0–5 | 4107 | |
| 10 | 26 | Northampton Town | 1–0 | 4010 | R.Jones |
| 11 | 30 | STOCKPORT COUNTY | 1–0 | 3012 | Brown |
| 12 | 7 Oct | ALDERSHOT | 2–1 | 3504 | Dean(og), R.Jones |
| 13 | 11 | Bradford City | 1–2 | 1545 | Brown |
| 14 | 14 | Darlington | 3–2 | 1356 | Holbrook(og), Brown(2) |
| 15 | 21 | HARTLEPOOL | 5–1 | 3389 | R.Jones(2), Brown(2), Aizlewood |
| 16 | 24 | SOUTHPORT | 3–1 | 5615 | R.Jones(2), Hill |
| 17 | 28 | Exeter City | 0–0 | 4588 | |
| 18 | 4 Nov | NORTHAMPTON TOWN | 1–0 | 4825 | White |
| 19 | 11 | Peterborough Utd | 0–1 | 4480 | |
| 20 | 25 | Barnsley | 1–2 | 2063 | Brown |
| 21 | 28 | HEREFORD UNITED | 0–1 | 8776 | |
| 22 | 16 Dec | LINCOLN CITY | 2–2 | 2843 | Brown, Hooper |
| 23 | 23 | Workington | 2–3 | 1254 | Brown, P.Harris |
| 24 | 26 | READING | 1–0 | 5435 | Aizlewood |
| 25 | 30 | Chester | 2–0 | 2844 | Brown(2) |
| 26 | 6 Jan | COLCHESTER UNITED | 1–0 | 3465 | Screen |
| 27 | 23 | TORQUAY UNITED | 2–1 | 4395 | R.Jones(2) |
| 28 | 30 | Southport | 2–0 | 4451 | White, Summerhayes |
| 29 | 6 Feb | BRADFORD CITY | 0–0 | 5795 | |
| 30 | 10 | Cambridge United | 1–3 | 3496 | White |
| 31 | 17 | GILLINGHAM | 5–1 | 4235 | Lindsay(og), R.Jones(2), Hill, Coldrick |
| 32 | 24 | Lincoln City | 2–0 | 3023 | Screen, R.Jones |
| 33 | 2 Mar | Aldershot | 2–0 | 3951 | Screen, Summerhayes |
| 34 | 6 | DONCASTER ROVERS | 1–0 | 6674 | Brown |
| 35 | 9 | DARLINGTON | 0–0 | 7625 | |
| 36 | 16 | Hartlepool | 0–1 | 3649 | |
| 37 | 21 | Crewe Alexandra | 0–0 | 1991 | |
| 38 | 24 | EXETER CITY | 2–0 | 4817 | Brown, Passey |
| 39 | 26 | Mansfield Town | 0–0 | 6402 | |
| 40 | 31 | BARNSLEY | 1–1 | 4757 | R.Jones |
| 41 | 7 Apr | Hereford United | 0–2 | 14849 | |
| 42 | 14 | CREWE ALEXANDRA | 0–0 | 4090 | |
| 43 | 21 | Doncaster Rovers | 5–1 | 1942 | Screen, D.Jones, Coldrick, Hill, Brown |
| 44 | 23 | Stockport County | 0–1 | 2785 | |
| 45 | 24 | WORKINGTON | 2–0 | 5256 | D.Jones, Hill |
| 46 | 28 | BURY | 4–3 | 7390 | Coldrick, Aizlewood, R.Jones, D.Jones |

| Player | League | | F.A.Cup | | Total | |
|---|---|---|---|---|---|---|
| | App | Gls. | App | Gls. | App | Gls. |
| Aizlewood S. | 40 | 3 | 3 | 0 | 48 | 3 |
| Brown W. | 39 | 16 | 3 | 2 | 48 | 24 |
| Coldrick G.G. | 17+1 | 4 | – | – | 21+1 | 4 |
| Hancock M. | 2+1 | 0 | – | – | 2+1 | 0 |
| Harris B. | 37 | 0 | 2 | 2 | 42 | 2 |
| Harris P. | 0+1 | 1 | – | – | 0+1 | 1 |
| Hawkins D.R. | 9 | 1 | – | – | 12 | 1 |
| Hill L.W. | 45 | 4 | 3 | 0 | 53 | 5 |
| Hooper W. | 10+8 | 1 | 2+1 | 0 | 15+9 | 2 |
| Jones D.A.B. | 13+3 | 3 | 1+2 | 0 | 16+5 | 3 |
| Jones R. | 39 | 13 | 3 | 1 | 45 | 14 |
| Macey J.R.T. | 46 | 0 | 3 | 0 | 55 | 0 |
| Passey P.T.J. | 21 | 1 | 1 | 0 | 25 | 1 |
| Screen W.R. | 46 | 5 | 3 | 0 | 54 | 5 |
| Sprague M.L. | 42 | 0 | 3 | 0 | 51 | 0 |
| Summerhayes | 37 | 2 | 3 | 0 | 43 | 2 |
| Thomas J. | 14 | 3 | – | – | 17 | 3 |
| White A.C.J. | 40+3 | 3 | 3 | 1 | 48+3 | 4 |
| Williams D.S. | 8+2 | 0 | – | – | 9+2 | 0 |
| Wood A.H. | 1 | 0 | – | – | 1 | 0 |
| Own Goals | | 4 | | | | 4 |

| | | P | W | D | L | F | A | Pts |
|---|---|---|---|---|---|---|---|---|
| 1 | Southport | 46 | 36 | 10 | 10 | 71 | 48 | 62 |
| 2 | Hereford | 46 | 23 | 12 | 11 | 56 | 38 | 58 |
| 3 | Cambridge | 46 | 20 | 17 | 9 | 67 | 57 | 57 |
| 4 | Aldershot | 46 | 22 | 12 | 12 | 60 | 38 | 56 |
| 5 | Newport | 46 | 22 | 12 | 12 | 64 | 44 | 56 |
| 6 | Mansfield | 46 | 20 | 14 | 12 | 78 | 51 | 54 |
| 7 | Reading | 46 | 17 | 18 | 11 | 51 | 38 | 52 |
| 8 | Exeter | 46 | 18 | 14 | 14 | 57 | 51 | 50 |
| 9 | Gillingham | 46 | 19 | 11 | 16 | 63 | 58 | 49 |
| 10 | Lincoln | 46 | 16 | 16 | 14 | 64 | 57 | 48 |
| 11 | Stockport | 46 | 18 | 12 | 16 | 53 | 53 | 48 |
| 12 | Bury | 46 | 14 | 18 | 14 | 58 | 51 | 46 |
| 13 | Workington | 46 | 17 | 12 | 17 | 59 | 61 | 46 |
| 14 | Barnsley | 46 | 14 | 16 | 16 | 58 | 60 | 44 |
| 15 | Chester | 46 | 14 | 15 | 17 | 61 | 52 | 43 |
| 16 | Bradford | 46 | 16 | 11 | 19 | 61 | 65 | 43 |
| 17 | Doncaster | 46 | 15 | 12 | 19 | 49 | 58 | 42 |
| 18 | Torquay | 46 | 12 | 17 | 17 | 44 | 47 | 41 |
| 19 | Peterborough | 46 | 14 | 13 | 19 | 71 | 76 | 41 |
| 20 | Hartlepool | 46 | 12 | 17 | 17 | 34 | 49 | 41 |
| 21 | Crewe | 46 | 9 | 18 | 19 | 38 | 61 | 36 |
| 22 | Colchester | 46 | 10 | 11 | 25 | 48 | 76 | 31 |
| 23 | Northampton | 46 | 10 | 11 | 25 | 40 | 73 | 31 |
| 24 | Darlington | 46 | 7 | 15 | 24 | 42 | 85 | 29 |

## F.A.Cup

| | Date | Opposition | Res. | Att. | Goalscorers |
|---|---|---|---|---|---|
| 1 | 18 Nov | ALTON TOWN | 5–1 | 4692 | B.Harris(2), Brown, R.Jones, White |
| 2 | 9 Dec | Torquay United | 1–0 | 3724 | Brown |
| 3 | 13 Jan | Millwall | 0–3 | 10122 | |

(Back) Summerhayes, Coldrick, Macey, R.Jones, Aizlewood, White
(Front) Brown, Sprague, B.Harris, D.Jones, Hill, Screen

# SEASON 1973-74    Division 4

| | Date | Opposition | Res. | Att. | Goalscorers |
|---|---|---|---|---|---|
| 1 | 25 Aug | READING | 0-0 | 4843 | |
| 2 | 1 Sep | Gillingham | 1-1 | 3971 | Screen |
| 3 | 8 | CHESTER | 0-2 | 3660 | |
| 4 | 11 | Northampton Town | 0-1 | 4061 | |
| 5 | 15 | Colchester United | 1-4 | 3523 | Hill |
| 6 | 18 | CREWE ALEXANDRA | 4-2 | 2035 | Aizlewood(2), Jarman(2) |
| 7 | 22 | ROTHERHAM UNITED | 1-0 | 3138 | R.Jones |
| 8 | 28 | Stockport County | 1-1 | 2780 | Brown |
| 9 | 3 Oct | Crewe Alexandra | 1-4 | 1879 | Jarman |
| 10 | 9 | MANSFIELD TOWN | 2-0 | 3004 | Brown, R.Jones |
| 11 | 13 | Scunthorpe United | 0-0 | 2607 | |
| 12 | 20 | Barnsley | 1-1 | 2057 | Brown |
| 13 | 23 | NORTHAMPTON TOWN | 3-1 | 3592 | R.Jones, Aizlewood, Jarman |
| 14 | 27 | PETERBOROUGH UTD | 0-1 | 4327 | |
| 15 | 3 Nov | Lincoln City | 0-3 | 4389 | |
| 16 | 9 | DONCASTER ROVERS | 3-1 | 2852 | R.Jones, Godfrey, Summerhayes |
| 17 | 12 | Hartlepool | 1-0 | 1641 | Aizlewood |
| 18 | 17 | DARLINGTON | 2-0 | 2910 | Aizlewood, Godfrey |
| 19 | 1 Dec | BURY | 1-0 | 2346 | Hill |
| 20 | 8 | Exeter City | 1-0 | 3476 | Godfrey |
| 21 | 15 | Torquay United | 2-3 | 2505 | Aizlewood, Jarman |
| 22 | 22 | STOCKPORT COUNTY | 3-1 | 2546 | Hooper, R.Jones, Brown |
| 23 | 26 | Brentford | 1-1 | 5440 | Hill |
| 24 | 29 | Chester | 0-3 | 2661 | |
| 25 | 1 Jan | GILLINGHAM | 3-3 | 5888 | Brown, Hill, Summerhayes |
| 26 | 5 | Workington | 2-3 | 749 | Hooper, Brown |
| 27 | 12 | COLCHESTER UNITED | 1-3 | 3304 | Hooper |
| 28 | 19 | Reading | 1-1 | 4311 | R.Jones |
| 29 | 27 | EXETER CITY | 2-1 | 3812 | Screen, Brown |
| 30 | 3 Feb | TORQUAY UNITED | 2-2 | 3480 | Aizlewood, Godfrey |
| 31 | 10 | Rotherham United | 1-1 | 2933 | Leng(og) |
| 32 | 17 | SCUNTHORPE UNITED | 2-1 | 3051 | Hooper(2) |
| 33 | 24 | Mansfield Town | 1-2 | 3006 | Jarman |
| 34 | 2 Mar | BRENTFORD | 1-1 | 2167 | D.Jones |
| 35 | 9 | Peterborough Utd | 0-2 | 7354 | |
| 36 | 17 | BARNSLEY | 1-0 | 1808 | Jenkins |
| 37 | 22 | Doncaster Rovers | 0-2 | 1163 | |
| 38 | 25 | WORKINGTON | 4-0 | 1972 | Godfrey(3), Coldrick |
| 39 | 30 | LINCOLN CITY | 0-1 | 1908 | |
| 40 | 3 Apr | Bradford City | 0-3 | 2681 | |
| 41 | 6 | HARTLEPOOL | 0-0 | 1785 | |
| 42 | 13 | Darlington | 1-0 | 2322 | Hooper |
| 43 | 15 | Swansea City | 1-1 | 2303 | White |
| 44 | 16 | SWANSEA CITY | 2-1 | 3108 | Brown, Jarman |
| 45 | 22 | BRADFORD CITY | 2-2 | 1890 | Jarman, Brown |
| 46 | 27 | Bury | 0-5 | 6111 | |

| Player | League | | F.A.Cup | | Total | |
|---|---|---|---|---|---|---|
| | App | Gls. | App | Gls. | App | Gls. |
| Aizlewood S. | 31 | 7 | 1 | 0 | 35 | 7 |
| Brown W. | 37 | 9 | 1 | 0 | 42 | 10 |
| Coldrick G.G. | 34 | 1 | 1 | 0 | 36+1 | 1 |
| Copeland M. | 3+1 | 0 | – | – | 3+1 | 0 |
| Godfrey B.C. | 46 | 7 | 1 | 0 | 51 | 7 |
| Hancock M. | 13+1 | 0 | 1 | 0 | 15+1 | 0 |
| Harris B. | 10 | 0 | – | – | 12 | 0 |
| Hill L.W. | 27+4 | 4 | 1 | 0 | 29+4 | 4 |
| Hooper W. | 28 | 6 | 0+1 | 1 | 30+1 | 7 |
| Jarman H.J. | 34+6 | 8 | 1 | 0 | 39+6 | 11 |
| Jenkins D.J. | 6 | 1 | – | 6 | 1 | 1 |
| Johnston G. | 2+1 | 0 | – | – | 2+1 | 0 |
| Jones D.A.B. | 6 | 1 | – | – | 7 | 1 |
| Jones R. | 36+1 | 6 | 1 | 0 | 39+1 | 6 |
| Macey J.R.T. | 43 | 0 | 1 | 0 | 46 | 0 |
| Passey P.T.J. | 42 | 0 | – | – | 46 | 0 |
| Payne D. | 3 | 0 | – | – | 5 | 0 |
| Screen W.R. | 28+3 | 2 | 1 | 0 | 33+3 | 3 |
| Sprague M.L. | 32 | 0 | 1 | 0 | 34 | 0 |
| Summerhayes R.E. | 27+1 | 2 | – | – | 28+2 | 2 |
| Swain K.J. | 6+1 | 0 | – | – | 9+1 | 0 |
| White A.C.J. | 12+5 | 1 | – | – | 14+5 | 1 |
| Own Goals | | 1 | | | | 1 |

| | | P | W | D | L | F | A | Pts |
|---|---|---|---|---|---|---|---|---|
| 1 | Peterborough* | 46 | 27 | 11 | 8 | 75 | 38 | 65 |
| 2 | Gillingham* | 46 | 25 | 12 | 9 | 90 | 49 | 62 |
| 3 | Colchester* | 46 | 24 | 12 | 10 | 73 | 36 | 60 |
| 4 | Bury* | 46 | 24 | 11 | 11 | 81 | 49 | 59 |
| 5 | Northampton | 46 | 20 | 13 | 13 | 63 | 48 | 53 |
| 6 | Reading | 46 | 16 | 19 | 11 | 58 | 37 | 51 |
| 7 | Chester | 46 | 17 | 15 | 14 | 54 | 55 | 49 |
| 8 | Bradford | 46 | 17 | 14 | 15 | 58 | 52 | 48 |
| 9 | Newport† | 46 | 16 | 14 | 16 | 56 | 65 | 45 |
| 10 | Exeter† | 45 | 18 | 8 | 19 | 58 | 55 | 44 |
| 11 | Hartlepool | 46 | 16 | 12 | 18 | 48 | 47 | 44 |
| 12 | Lincoln | 46 | 16 | 12 | 18 | 63 | 67 | 44 |
| 13 | Barnsley | 46 | 17 | 10 | 19 | 58 | 64 | 44 |
| 14 | Swansea | 46 | 16 | 11 | 19 | 45 | 46 | 43 |
| 15 | Rotherham | 46 | 15 | 13 | 18 | 56 | 58 | 43 |
| 16 | Torquay | 46 | 13 | 17 | 16 | 52 | 57 | 43 |
| 17 | Mansfield | 46 | 13 | 17 | 16 | 62 | 69 | 43 |
| 18 | Scunthorpe† | 45 | 14 | 12 | 19 | 47 | 64 | 42 |
| 19 | Brentford | 46 | 12 | 16 | 18 | 48 | 50 | 40 |
| 20 | Darlington | 46 | 13 | 13 | 20 | 40 | 62 | 39 |
| 21 | Crewe | 46 | 14 | 10 | 22 | 43 | 71 | 38 |
| 22 | Doncaster | 46 | 12 | 11 | 23 | 47 | 80 | 35 |
| 23 | Workington | 46 | 11 | 13 | 22 | 43 | 74 | 35 |
| 24 | Stockport | 46 | 7 | 20 | 19 | 44 | 69 | 34 |

## F.A.Cup

| | Date | Opposition | Res. | Att. | Goalscorers |
|---|---|---|---|---|---|
| 1 | 24 Nov | Wycombe Wanderers | 1-3 | 6888 | Hooper |

(Back) Summerhayes, S.Aizlewood, Payne, Macey, R.Jones, Thomas, Copeland
(Middle) Jarman, Crosse, White, Swain, Guilfoyle, Rogers, Fisher, Godfrey
(Front) Screen, White, Passey, Brown, Harris, Coldrick, Hill, Hooper (Seated) Channing, M.Aizlewood

# SEASON 1974-75     *Division 4*

| | Date | Opposition | Res. | Att. | Goalscorers |
|---|---|---|---|---|---|
| 1 | 17 Aug | Hartlepool | 0-2 | 2559 | |
| 2 | 24 | DARLINGTON | 2-1 | 2707 | Godfrey, Hancock |
| 3 | 31 | Doncaster Rovers | 2-0 | 2156 | Jones(2) |
| 4 | 3 Sep | SWANSEA CITY | 3-0 | 3485 | Jones, Woods, Aizlewood |
| 5 | 7 | SHREWSBURY TOWN | 2-4 | 2754 | Jones, Hooper |
| 6 | 14 | Reading | 0-3 | 6360 | |
| 7 | 18 | Bradford City | 1-0 | 3829 | Jones |
| 8 | 21 | BRENTFORD | 1-0 | 3022 | Godfrey |
| 9 | 24 | WORKINGTON | 3-1 | 3250 | Jones, Bell, Woods |
| 10 | 28 | Barnsley | 1-2 | 4553 | Woods |
| 11 | 5 Oct | EXETER CITY | 1-2 | 3130 | Bell |
| 12 | 12 | Crewe Alexandra | 2-1 | 2861 | Jones, Woods |
| 13 | 15 | Swansea City | 0-2 | 3372 | |
| 14 | 18 | NORTHAMPTON TOWN | 2-1 | 2155 | Woods, Passey |
| 15 | 26 | Rochdale | 4-2 | 1208 | Jones(2), Godfrey, Woods |
| 16 | 2 Nov | Rotherham United | 1-1 | 4642 | Woods |
| 17 | 9 | STOCKPORT COUNTY | 3-3 | 2634 | Jones, Godfrey, Woods |
| 18 | 16 | Cambridge United | 1-1 | 2829 | Hooper |
| 19 | 30 | Southport | 3-1 | 1314 | Woods(2), Jones |
| 20 | 7 Dec | SCUNTHORPE UNITED | 2-0 | 3139 | Woodruff, Woods |
| 21 | 21 | TORQUAY UNITED | 1-0 | 2259 | White |
| 22 | 28 | Mansfield Town | 0-3 | 7920 | |
| 23 | 4 Jan | BRADFORD CITY | 2-1 | 3251 | Woods. Woodruff |
| 24 | 11 | Scunthorpe United | 1-4 | 1529 | Woods |
| 25 | 17 | SOUTHPORT | 1-0 | 2857 | Hooper |
| 26 | 25 | CHESTER | 3-0 | 4144 | Woods(2), Jones |
| 27 | 31 | Stockport County | 1-1 | 1975 | Jones |
| 28 | 8 Feb | ROTHERHAM UNITED | 1-1 | 4161 | Woods |
| 29 | 15 | Chester | 1-4 | 5427 | Jones |
| 30 | 22 | CAMBRIDGE UNITED | 1-2 | 3219 | Jones |
| 31 | 28 | DONCASTER ROVERS | 0-2 | 2252 | |
| 32 | 3 Mar | LINCOLN CITY | 1-1 | 2064 | Godfrey |
| 33 | 8 | Workington | 1-3 | 1248 | Woods |
| 34 | 15 | BARNSLEY | 3-4 | 1773 | Woods, Parsons, Pickering(og) |
| 35 | 17 | HARTLEPOOL | 2-0 | 1535 | Woods, Woodruff |
| 36 | 22 | Shrewsbury Town | 0-1 | 3465 | |
| 37 | 29 | Torquay United | 2-1 | 2139 | Woodruff, Parker(og) |
| 38 | 31 | MANSFIELD TOWN | 2-1 | 3663 | Woods, White |
| 39 | 1 Apr | Brentford | 0-0 | 5560 | |
| 40 | 5 | ROCHDALE | 3-2 | 1801 | Hooper(3) |
| 41 | 9 | Lincoln City | 2-5 | 5613 | Parsons(2) |
| 42 | 12 | Exeter City | 1-3 | 2755 | Woodruff |
| 43 | 15 | READING | 2-2 | 1536 | Woodruff, Parsons |
| 44 | 19 | CREWE ALEXANDRA | 1-1 | 1739 | Hancock |
| 45 | 21 | Darlington | 0-3 | 1959 | |
| 46 | 25 | Northampton Town | 2-3 | 2482 | Parsons, Woods |

## F.A.Cup

| | Date | Opposition | Res. | Att. | Goalscorers |
|---|---|---|---|---|---|
| 1 | 23 Nov | Exeter City | 2-1 | 4202 | Hooper, White |
| 2 | 14 Dec | WALSALL | 1-3 | 4765 | Jones |

| Player | League | | F.A.Cup | | Total | |
|---|---|---|---|---|---|---|
| | App | Gls. | App | Gls. | App | Gls. |
| Aizlewood S. | 24 | 1 | 2 | 0 | 28 | 1 |
| Bell G. | 34 | 2 | – | – | 39 | 2 |
| Brown W. | 8+1 | 0 | – | – | 9+2 | 1 |
| Coldrick G.G. | 33 | 0 | 2 | 0 | 41 | 0 |
| Godfrey B.C. | 36 | 5 | 2 | 0 | 44 | 6 |
| Hancock M. | 15+1 | 2 | – | – | 17+1 | 2 |
| Hooper W. | 44 | 6 | 2 | 1 | 53 | 9 |
| Jones R. | 44+1 | 15 | 2 | 1 | 52+1 | 18 |
| Macey J.R.T. | 17 | 0 | – | – | 20 | 0 |
| Parsons J.S. | 10+2 | 5 | – | – | 10+2 | 5 |
| Passey P.T.J. | 31 | 1 | 1 | 0 | 37 | 1 |
| Payne D. | 29 | 0 | 2 | 0 | 35 | 0 |
| Preece P.W. | 4+1 | 0 | – | – | 4+1 | 0 |
| Relish J.D. | 18+4 | 0 | 1 | 0 | 24+4 | 0 |
| Rogers G.R. | 0+4 | 0 | – | – | 1+5 | 1 |
| Rylands D.R. | 3 | 0 | – | – | 3 | 0 |
| Screen W.R. | 32+2 | 0 | 2 | 0 | 41+2 | 1 |
| Summerhayes R. | 10+5 | 0 | – | – | 10+7 | 0 |
| White A.C.J. | 32+3 | 2 | 2 | 1 | 39+3 | 3 |
| Woodruff R.W. | 41 | 6 | 2 | 0 | 49 | 10 |
| Woods E. | 41 | 21 | 2 | 0 | 49 | 21 |
| Own Goals | | 2 | | | | 3 |

| | | P | W | D | L | F | A | Pts |
|---|---|---|---|---|---|---|---|---|
| 1 | Mansfield | 46 | 28 | 12 | 6 | 90 | 40 | 68 |
| 2 | Shrewsbury | 46 | 26 | 10 | 10 | 80 | 43 | 62 |
| 3 | Rotherham | 46 | 22 | 15 | 9 | 71 | 41 | 59 |
| 4 | Chester | 46 | 23 | 11 | 12 | 64 | 38 | 57 |
| 5 | Lincoln | 46 | 21 | 15 | 10 | 79 | 48 | 57 |
| 6 | Cambridge | 46 | 20 | 14 | 12 | 62 | 44 | 54 |
| 7 | Reading | 46 | 21 | 10 | 15 | 63 | 47 | 52 |
| 8 | Brentford | 46 | 18 | 13 | 15 | 53 | 45 | 49 |
| 9 | Exeter | 46 | 19 | 11 | 16 | 60 | 63 | 49 |
| 10 | Bradford | 46 | 17 | 13 | 16 | 56 | 51 | 47 |
| 11 | Southport | 46 | 15 | 17 | 14 | 56 | 56 | 47 |
| 12 | Newport | 46 | 19 | 9 | 18 | 68 | 75 | 47 |
| 13 | Hartlepool | 46 | 16 | 11 | 19 | 52 | 62 | 43 |
| 14 | Torquay | 46 | 14 | 14 | 18 | 46 | 61 | 42 |
| 15 | Barnsley | 46 | 15 | 11 | 20 | 62 | 65 | 41 |
| 16 | Northampton | 46 | 15 | 11 | 20 | 67 | 73 | 41 |
| 17 | Doncaster | 46 | 14 | 12 | 20 | 65 | 79 | 40 |
| 18 | Crewe | 46 | 11 | 18 | 17 | 34 | 47 | 40 |
| 19 | Rochdale | 46 | 13 | 13 | 20 | 59 | 75 | 39 |
| 20 | Stockport | 46 | 12 | 14 | 20 | 43 | 70 | 38 |
| 21 | Darlington | 46 | 13 | 10 | 23 | 54 | 67 | 36 |
| 22 | Swansea | 46 | 15 | 6 | 25 | 26 | 73 | 36 |
| 23 | Workington | 46 | 10 | 11 | 25 | 46 | 66 | 31 |
| 24 | Scunthorpe | 46 | 7 | 15 | 24 | 41 | 78 | 29 |

(Back) Aizlewood, Jones, Summerhayes, Macey, Payne, Coldrick, Hancock, Screen.
(Front) Rogers, Hooper, Passey, Godfrey, White, Brown, Relish.

# SEASON 1975-76    Division 4

| | Date | Opposition | Res. | Att. | Goalscorers |
|---|---|---|---|---|---|
| 1 | 16 Aug | LINCOLN CITY | 3-1 | 2797 | Jones(2), Woods |
| 2 | 23 | Workington | 2-1 | 1425 | Woods, Jones |
| 3 | 30 | SCUNTHORPE UNITED | 0-0 | 2735 | |
| 4 | 6 Sep | Rochdale | 3-4 | 1119 | Woods(2), Jones |
| 5 | 13 | SOUTHPORT | 2-0 | 2342 | Godfrey, White |
| 6 | 20 | Bournemouth & B.A. | 0-2 | 3993 | |
| 7 | 23 | Swansea City | 2-2 | 4456 | S.Aizlewood(2) |
| 8 | 27 | CAMBRIDGE UNITED | 2-0 | 2244 | Parsons(2) |
| 9 | 4 Oct | Brentford | 3-1 | 5680 | Jones, Bell, Hooper |
| 10 | 11 | BARNSLEY | 1-0 | 3043 | Woods |
| 11 | 18 | Huddersfield Town | 1-2 | 5477 | Parsons |
| 12 | 20 | READING | 0-0 | 3955 | |
| 13 | 25 | EXETER CITY | 3-3 | 2871 | Parsons(2), Jones |
| 14 | 1 Nov | Torquay United | 1-1 | 2163 | Parsons |
| 15 | 3 | Stockport County | 1-0 | 2208 | Fogarty(og) |
| 16 | 8 | BRADFORD CITY | 3-1 | 2747 | Hooper, Love, White |
| 17 | 15 | Doncaster Rovers | 1-5 | 7793 | Parsons |
| 18 | 29 | Hartlepool | 1-4 | 2780 | Godfrey |
| 19 | 6 Dec | DARLINGTON | 4-1 | 1878 | Jones, Parsons, White, Craig(og) |
| 20 | 20 | Watford | 1-3 | 3261 | Parsons |
| 21 | 26 | CREWE ALEXANDRA | 2-2 | 3788 | Woodruff, Parsons |
| 22 | 27 | Northampton Town | 0-3 | 8448 | |
| 23 | 3 Jan | TRANMERE ROVERS | 1-5 | 2074 | Parsons |
| 24 | 10 | Scunthorpe United | 2-1 | 1879 | Woods(2) |
| 25 | 17 | BOURNEMOUTH & B.A. | 3-1 | 1496 | Parsons, White, Morgan(og) |
| 26 | 24 | Southport | 0-3 | 1268 | |
| 27 | 7 Feb | STOCKPORT COUNTY | 2-2 | 1652 | White, S.Aizlewood |
| 28 | 21 | DONCASTER ROVERS | 2-3 | 1543 | Parsons, Woods |
| 29 | 23 | SWANSEA CITY | 1-2 | 2040 | S.Aizlewood |
| 30 | 28 | Exeter City | 0-3 | 3447 | |
| 31 | 2 Mar | Reading | 0-1 | 6211 | |
| 32 | 5 | TORQUAY UNITED | 0-2 | 1588 | |
| 33 | 8 | BRENTFORD | 1-0 | 1150 | Parsons |
| 34 | 13 | Barnsley | 1-3 | 2587 | Woods |
| 35 | 15 | HUDDERSFIELD TOWN | 1-2 | 1374 | Parsons |
| 36 | 20 | HARTLEPOOL | 0-1 | 1230 | |
| 37 | 27 | Darlington | 0-4 | 1312 | |
| 38 | 31 | WATFORD | 0-2 | 1092 | |
| 39 | 3 Apr | Lincoln City | 1-4 | 8178 | M. Aizlewood |
| 40 | 7 | Cambridge United | 1-0 | 1361 | Love |
| 41 | 10 | ROCHDALE | 1-1 | 1331 | Jones |
| 42 | 14 | Tranmere Rovers | 1-3 | 2629 | Jones |
| 43 | 17 | Crewe Alexandra | 0-4 | 1971 | |
| 44 | 20 | NORTHAMPTON TOWN | 1-1 | 1728 | Jones |
| 45 | 24 | WORKINGTON | 2-3 | 1226 | Woods, Jones |
| 46 | 1 May | Bradford City | 0-3 | 1676 | |

## F.A.Cup

| | Date | Opposition | Res. | Att. | Goalscorers |
|---|---|---|---|---|---|
| 1 | 22 Nov | SWINDON TOWN | 2-2 | 5182 | Godfrey, Parsons |
| 1R | 25 | Swindon Town | 0-3 | 7574 | |

| Player | League | | F.A.Cup | | Total | |
|---|---|---|---|---|---|---|
| | App | Gls. | App | Gls. | App | Gls. |
| Aizlewood M. | 5+1 | 1 | – | – | 5+1 | 1 |
| Aizlewood S. | 30 | 4 | 2 | 0 | 35 | 5 |
| Bell G. | 35 | 1 | – | – | 38 | 1 |
| Cawston M.W. | 4 | 0 | – | – | 4 | 0 |
| Dowler M.J. | 7 | 0 | – | – | 7 | 0 |
| Elliott D. | 21 | 0 | 2 | 0 | 25 | 0 |
| Godfrey B.C. | 35+1 | 2 | 2 | 1 | 37+1 | 3 |
| Hancock M. | 20+6 | 0 | 2 | 0 | 23+6 | 0 |
| Hayes M. | 4+1 | 0 | – | – | 4+1 | 0 |
| Hooper W. | 17+1 | 2 | 2 | 0 | 21+1 | 2 |
| Jones R. | 35+1 | 11 | 2 | 0 | 39+1 | 11 |
| Love A. | 41+1 | 2 | 2 | 0 | 46+1 | 3 |
| Macey J.R.T. | 35 | 0 | 2 | 0 | 40 | 0 |
| Morgan P.T.J. | 9+1 | 0 | – | – | 9+1 | 0 |
| Parsons J.S. | 38 | 15 | 2 | 1 | 41 | 16 |
| Passey P.W. | 22 | 0 | – | – | 22 | 0 |
| Pimblett F.R. | 7 | 0 | – | – | 7 | 0 |
| Powell M.J. | 7 | 0 | – | – | 8 | 0 |
| Preece P.W. | 13+5 | 0 | – | – | 14+5 | 0 |
| Relish J.D. | 8 | 0 | 2 | 0 | 10 | 0 |
| Screen W.R. | 31 | 0 | 2 | 0 | 35 | 0 |
| White A.C.J. | 39+3 | 5 | 0+2 | 0 | 42+5 | 5 |
| Woodruff R.W. | 11 | 1 | – | – | 14 | 1 |
| Woods E. | 32 | 10 | – | – | 35 | 10 |
| Own Goals | | 3 | | | | 3 |

| | | P | W | D | L | F | A | Pts |
|---|---|---|---|---|---|---|---|---|
| 1 | Lincoln | 46 | 32 | 10 | 4 | 111 | 39 | 74 |
| 2 | Northampton | 46 | 29 | 10 | 7 | 87 | 40 | 68 |
| 3 | Reading | 46 | 24 | 12 | 10 | 70 | 51 | 60 |
| 4 | Tranmere | 46 | 24 | 10 | 12 | 89 | 55 | 58 |
| 5 | Huddersfield | 46 | 21 | 14 | 11 | 55 | 41 | 56 |
| 6 | Bournemouth | 46 | 20 | 12 | 14 | 57 | 48 | 52 |
| 7 | Exeter | 46 | 18 | 14 | 14 | 56 | 47 | 50 |
| 8 | Watford | 46 | 22 | 6 | 18 | 62 | 62 | 50 |
| 9 | Torquay | 46 | 18 | 14 | 14 | 55 | 63 | 50 |
| 10 | Doncaster | 46 | 19 | 11 | 16 | 75 | 69 | 49 |
| 11 | Swansea | 46 | 16 | 15 | 15 | 66 | 57 | 47 |
| 12 | Barnsley | 46 | 14 | 16 | 16 | 52 | 48 | 44 |
| 13 | Cambridge | 46 | 14 | 15 | 17 | 58 | 62 | 43 |
| 14 | Hartlepool | 46 | 16 | 10 | 20 | 62 | 78 | 42 |
| 15 | Rochdale | 46 | 12 | 18 | 16 | 40 | 54 | 42 |
| 16 | Crewe | 46 | 13 | 15 | 18 | 58 | 57 | 41 |
| 17 | Bradford | 46 | 12 | 17 | 17 | 63 | 65 | 41 |
| 18 | Brentford | 46 | 14 | 13 | 19 | 56 | 60 | 41 |
| 19 | Scunthorpe | 46 | 14 | 10 | 22 | 50 | 59 | 38 |
| 20 | Darlington | 46 | 14 | 10 | 22 | 48 | 57 | 38 |
| 21 | Stockport | 46 | 13 | 12 | 21 | 43 | 76 | 38 |
| 22 | Newport | 46 | 13 | 9 | 24 | 57 | 90 | 35 |
| 23 | Southport | 46 | 8 | 10 | 28 | 41 | 57 | 26 |
| 24 | Workington | 46 | 7 | 7 | 32 | 30 | 87 | 27 |

(Back) Passey, Woods, Hooper, Macey, S.Aizlewood, Hancock, Preece, Parsons.
(Front) Love, Woodruff, Jones, Bell, Elliot (P/Manager), White, Relish, Screen.

# SEASON 1976-77    Division 4

| # | Date | Opposition | Res. | Att. | Goalscorers |
|---|---|---|---|---|---|
| 1 | 21 Aug | STOCKPORT COUNTY | 0-1 | 2746 | |
| 2 | 23 | Darlington | 0-1 | 2684 | |
| 3 | 28 | Barnsley | 0-2 | 4166 | |
| 4 | 4 Sep | HUDDERSFIELD TOWN | 1-1 | 2284 | Bell |
| 5 | 10 | Doncaster Rovers | 0-1 | 3739 | |
| 6 | 18 | ALDERSHOT | 2-1 | 2490 | Clark(2) |
| 7 | 25 | Southport | 1-0 | 1313 | Williams |
| 8 | 2 Oct | TORQUAY UNITED | 0-0 | 2460 | |
| 9 | 9 | Brentford | 1-1 | 5890 | Woods |
| 10 | 16 | Bradford City | 1-3 | 5057 | Jones |
| 11 | 22 | SWANSEA CITY | 0-2 | 3416 | |
| 12 | 26 | HARTLEPOOL | 1-1 | 2330 | Woods |
| 13 | 29 | Southend United | 1-1 | 4821 | Villars |
| 14 | 2 Nov | Bournemouth & B.A. | 0-1 | 3570 | |
| 15 | 13 | Rochdale | 0-0 | 2482 | |
| 16 | 27 | HALIFAX TOWN | 1-1 | 2901 | Woods |
| 17 | 27 Dec | Cambridge United | 1-3 | 4865 | Woods |
| 18 | 1 Jan | Colchester United | 0-5 | 4614 | |
| 19 | 11 | Watford | 0-2 | 4600 | |
| 20 | 14 | DARLINGTON | 0-1 | 1428 | |
| 21 | 21 | Stockport County | 1-2 | 3450 | Bell |
| 22 | 28 | SCUNTHORPE UNITED | 0-0 | 1601 | |
| 23 | 12 Feb | Huddersfield Town | 0-3 | 5452 | |
| 24 | 22 | COLCHESTER UNITED | 1-2 | 1575 | Emanuel |
| 25 | 26 | Aldershot | 0-4 | 3285 | |
| 26 | 1 Mar | DONCASTER ROVERS | 1-2 | 1714 | Parsons |
| 27 | 4 | SOUTHPORT | 3-1 | 1569 | Parsons(2), Bruton |
| 28 | 12 | Torquay United | 0-1 | 3283 | |
| 29 | 18 | BRENTFORD | 3-1 | 1737 | Relish, Clark, White |
| 30 | 23 | Crewe Alexandra | 0-2 | 2110 | |
| 31 | 26 | BRADFORD CITY | 2-0 | 2096 | Clark, Woods |
| 32 | 28 | BARNSLEY | 1-1 | 2319 | Walker |
| 33 | 2 Apr | Swansea City | 1-3 | 3577 | Relish |
| 34 | 5 | CAMBRIDGE UNTED | 4-2 | 2306 | Clark(3), Relish |
| 35 | 9 | Exeter City | 0-1 | 5243 | |
| 36 | 12 | BOURNEMOUTH & B.A. | 1-0 | 2962 | Preece |
| 37 | 16 | Hartlepool | 1-0 | 1507 | Woods |
| 38 | 19 | Scunthorpe United | 0-1 | 1883 | |
| 39 | 23 | ROCHDALE | 3-0 | 2206 | Woods(3) |
| 40 | 26 | EXETER CITY | 0-3 | 3550 | |
| 41 | 30 | Halifax Town | 0-0 | 1299 | |
| 42 | 3 May | WATFORD | 3-0 | 2218 | Clark, Preece, Woods |
| 43 | 7 | CREWE ALEXANDRA | 2-1 | 2484 | Woods, Bevan(og) |
| 44 | 10 | SOUTHEND UNITED | 3-0 | 3356 | Preece(2), Relish |
| 45 | 14 | Workington | 1-0 | 1285 | Preece |
| 46 | 17 | WORKINGTON | 1-0 | 8313 | Woods |

| Player | League | | F.A. Cup | | Total | |
|---|---|---|---|---|---|---|
| | App | Gls. | App | Gls. | App | Gls. |
| Aizlewood M. | 4+1 | 0 | – | – | 4+1 | 0 |
| Bell G. | 45 | 2 | 2 | 0 | 50 | 3 |
| Bruton D.E. | 6 | 1 | – | – | 6 | 1 |
| Byrne A.B. | 16 | 0 | – | – | 16 | 0 |
| Clark B.D. | 39+2 | 8 | 3 | 0 | 44+3 | 8 |
| Derrett S.C. | 44 | 0 | 3 | 0 | 50 | 0 |
| Egan C.A. | 5+2 | 0 | – | – | 5+2 | 0 |
| Emanuel W.J. | 46 | 1 | 3 | 0 | 52 | 1 |
| Hooper W. | 3+1 | 0 | 1 | 0 | 5+1 | 0 |
| Jones R. | 28+6 | 1 | 1 | 0 | 31+6 | 1 |
| Morgan P.W. | 13+1 | 0 | – | – | 15+1 | 0 |
| Murray D.J. | 16+2 | 0 | 2 | 0 | 19+2 | 0 |
| Parsons J.S. | 9+1 | 3 | 3 | 2 | 14+2 | 6 |
| Plumley G.E. | 46 | 0 | 3 | 0 | 52 | 0 |
| Preece B.J. | 17+1 | 5 | – | – | 17+1 | 5 |
| Relish J.D. | 26 | 4 | – | – | 27 | 4 |
| Stokes C. | – | – | – | – | 1 | 0 |
| Vaughan N.M. | 1 | 0 | 1 | 0 | 2 | 0 |
| Villars A.K. | 23+6 | 1 | 3 | 0 | 28+6 | 1 |
| Walker R.L. | 39+1 | 1 | 3 | 0 | 45+1 | 1 |
| White A.C.J. | 16+3 | 1 | 2 | 0 | 19+3 | 1 |
| Williams M. | 23+5 | 1 | 2+1 | 0 | 25+6 | 1 |
| Woods E. | 41+2 | 12 | 1+1 | 1 | 45+3 | 14 |
| Own Goals | | 1 | | | | 1 |

| | | P | W | D | L | F | A | Pts |
|---|---|---|---|---|---|---|---|---|
| 1 | Cambridge | 46 | 26 | 13 | 7 | 87 | 40 | 65 |
| 2 | Exeter | 46 | 25 | 12 | 9 | 70 | 46 | 62 |
| 3 | Colchester | 46 | 25 | 9 | 12 | 77 | 43 | 59 |
| 4 | Bradford | 46 | 23 | 13 | 10 | 71 | 51 | 59 |
| 5 | Swansea | 46 | 25 | 8 | 13 | 82 | 68 | 58 |
| 6 | Barnsley | 46 | 23 | 9 | 14 | 62 | 39 | 55 |
| 7 | Watford | 46 | 18 | 15 | 13 | 67 | 55 | 51 |
| 8 | Doncaster | 46 | 21 | 9 | 16 | 61 | 65 | 51 |
| 9 | Huddersfield | 46 | 19 | 12 | 15 | 60 | 49 | 50 |
| 10 | Southend | 46 | 15 | 19 | 12 | 52 | 45 | 49 |
| 11 | Darlington | 46 | 18 | 13 | 15 | 59 | 64 | 49 |
| 12 | Crewe | 46 | 19 | 11 | 16 | 47 | 60 | 49 |
| 13 | Bournemouth | 46 | 15 | 18 | 13 | 55 | 44 | 48 |
| 14 | Stockport | 46 | 13 | 19 | 14 | 53 | 57 | 45 |
| 15 | Brentford | 46 | 18 | 7 | 21 | 77 | 76 | 43 |
| 16 | Torquay | 46 | 17 | 9 | 20 | 59 | 67 | 43 |
| 17 | Aldershot | 46 | 16 | 11 | 19 | 45 | 59 | 43 |
| 18 | Rochdale | 46 | 13 | 12 | 21 | 50 | 59 | 38 |
| 19 | Newport | 46 | 14 | 10 | 22 | 42 | 58 | 38 |
| 20 | Scunthorpe | 46 | 13 | 11 | 22 | 49 | 73 | 37 |
| 21 | Halifax | 46 | 11 | 14 | 21 | 47 | 58 | 36 |
| 22 | Hartlepool | 46 | 10 | 12 | 24 | 47 | 73 | 32 |
| 23 | Southport | 46 | 3 | 19 | 24 | 53 | 77 | 25 |
| 24 | Workington | 46 | 4 | 11 | 31 | 41 | 102 | 19 |

## F.A.Cup

| # | Date | Opposition | Res. | Att. | Goalscorers |
|---|---|---|---|---|---|
| 1 | 20 Nov | Bournemouth & B.A. | 0-0 | 4801 | |
| 1R | 23 | BOURNEMOUTH & B.A. | 3-0 | 3807 | Parsons(2), Woods |
| 2 | 11 Dec | Southend United | 0-3 | 5724 | |

(Back)  Bird (Train./Coach), Lowndes, Relish, Dowler, Walker, Clark, Plumley, Singer, Hodge, Villars.
(Front)  Emanuel, Derrett, Hooper, Bell, Scoular (Manager), Woods, White, Williams, Parsons.

# SEASON 1977-78    Division 4

| | Date | Opposition | Res. | Att. | Goalscorers |
|---|---|---|---|---|---|
| 1 | 20 Aug | Doncaster Rovers | 2-2 | 3041 | Preece, Clark |
| 2 | 27 | HUDDERSFIELD TOWN | 2-0 | 3367 | Woods, S.Walker |
| 3 | 3 Sep | Barnsley | 0-1 | 4009 | |
| 4 | 6 | YORK CITY | 2-1 | 2987 | Woods, Hope(og) |
| 5 | 10 | DARLINGTON | 1-1 | 2776 | Woods |
| 6 | 14 | Crewe Alexandra | 0-2 | 1812 | |
| 7 | 17 | Rochdale | 1-0 | 1116 | Woods |
| 8 | 24 | SWANSEA CITY | 1-0 | 5156 | Goddard |
| 9 | 27 | Wimbledon | 0-3 | 3941 | |
| 10 | 1 Oct | GRIMSBY TOWN | 3-0 | 2746 | Preece(2), Woods |
| 11 | 4 | SCUNTHORPE UNITED | 3-1 | 3191 | Woods(3) |
| 12 | 8 | Aldershot | 2-2 | 3452 | Preece, Woods |
| 13 | 15 | STOCKPORT COUNTY | 2-2 | 4083 | Preece, S.Walker |
| 14 | 22 | Watford | 0-2 | 10475 | |
| 15 | 29 | TORQUAY UNITED | 0-0 | 4137 | |
| 16 | 5 Nov | Northampton Town | 4-2 | 3568 | Goddard(2), Emanuel, R.Walker |
| 17 | 12 | HALIFAX TOWN | 2-0 | 3992 | Guscott, Woods |
| 18 | 19 | Southport | 3-3 | 1167 | Clark, Goddard, Williams |
| 19 | 3 Dec | HARTLEPOOL UNITED | 4-2 | 3233 | R.Walker, Goddard, Clark, Emanuel |
| 20 | 9 | Southend United | 2-4 | 5840 | Clark, Goddard |
| 21 | 26 | BOURNEMOUTH & B.A. | 3-2 | 7629 | Williams(2), Clark |
| 22 | 27 | Brentford | 3-3 | 8970 | Williams(2), Preece |
| 23 | 31 | Reading | 0-2 | 5808 | |
| 24 | 2 Jan | NORTHAMPTON TOWN | 5-3 | 7160 | Goddard(2), Clark(2), Jones |
| 25 | 7 | York City | 0-2 | 1971 | |
| 26 | 14 | DONCASTER ROVERS | 1-0 | 4029 | Williams |
| 27 | 21 | Huddersfield Town | 0-2 | 4894 | |
| 28 | 4 Feb | Darlington | 1-2 | 1744 | Clark |
| 29 | 11 | ROCHDALE | 3-0 | 4288 | Goddard(3) |
| 30 | 17 | Swansea City | 0-4 | 6056 | |
| 31 | 25 | Grimsby Town | 0-1 | 3937 | |
| 32 | 28 | BARNSLEY | 3-1 | 3523 | Goddard(2), R.Walker |
| 33 | 4 Mar | ALDERSHOT | 2-1 | 3737 | Aizlewood, Clark |
| 34 | 7 | CREWE ALEXANDRA | 1-0 | 4774 | Preece |
| 35 | 10 | Stockport County | 0-2 | 3863 | |
| 36 | 17 | WATFORD | 2-2 | 8409 | Goddard, R.Walker |
| 37 | 22 | Torquay United | 0-2 | 3055 | |
| 38 | 25 | BRENTFORD | 1-2 | 4953 | Goddard |
| 39 | 28 | Bournemouth & B.A. | 2-4 | 2479 | Williams, Jones |
| 40 | 1 Apr | READING | 0-0 | 2333 | |
| 41 | 4 | Scunthorpe United | 0-2 | 2457 | |
| 42 | 8 | Halifax Town | 1-3 | 1653 | Goddard |
| 43 | 15 | SOUTHPORT | 1-1 | 2440 | Sinclair |
| 44 | 22 | Hartlepool United | 1-1 | 1988 | Goddard |
| 45 | 25 | WIMBLEDON | 0-1 | 2112 | |
| 46 | 29 | SOUTHEND UNITED | 1-2 | 2364 | Emanuel |

## F.A.Cup

| | Date | Opposition | Res. | Att. | Goalscorers |
|---|---|---|---|---|---|
| 1 | 26 Nov | EXETER CITY | 1-1 | 6229 | Goddard |
| 1r | 30 | Exeter City | 2-4 | 5713 | Goddard, Clark |

| Player | League | | F.A.Cup | | Total | |
|---|---|---|---|---|---|---|
| | App | Gls. | App | Gls. | App | Gls. |
| Aizlewood M. | 26+1 | 1 | 2 | 0 | 31+1 | 1 |
| Bell G. | 12 | 0 | 2 | 0 | 16 | 0 |
| Byrne A.B. | 38 | 0 | 1 | 0 | 44 | 0 |
| Clark B.D. | 32+3 | 9 | 2 | 1 | 39+3 | 11 |
| Cosslett M.P. | 1 | 0 | – | – | 1 | 0 |
| Derrett S.C. | 17 | 0 | 2 | 0 | 21 | 0 |
| Dowler M.J. | 1 | 0 | – | – | 1 | 0 |
| Emanuel W.J. | 33 | 3 | 2 | 0 | 35 | 3 |
| Goddard H.J. | 37+4 | 17 | 2 | 2 | 42+4 | 19 |
| Guscott R.M. | 12+5 | 1 | 2 | 0 | 15+5 | 1 |
| Jones R. | 36+4 | 2 | – | – | 41+4 | 2 |
| Lowndes S.R. | 1+4 | 0 | – | – | 1+4 | 0 |
| McLaughlin M.A. | 7 | 0 | – | – | 7 | 0 |
| Plumley G.E. | 38 | 0 | 2 | 0 | 45 | 0 |
| Powell M. | 0+2 | 0 | – | – | 0+2 | 0 |
| Preece B.J. | 21+5 | 7 | – | – | 25+5 | 8 |
| Relish J.D. | 41 | 0 | – | – | 46 | 0 |
| Sinclair C.M. | 15 | 1 | – | – | 15 | 1 |
| Steel G. | 3 | 0 | – | – | 3 | 0 |
| Turner I. | 7 | 0 | – | – | 7 | 0 |
| Vaughan N.M. | 9+2 | 0 | 1+1 | 0 | 10+3 | 0 |
| Villars A.K. | – | – | 0+2 | 0 | 0+2 | 0 |
| Walker R.L. | 43 | 4 | 2 | 0 | 50 | 6 |
| Walker S. | 27+1 | 2 | – | – | 32+1 | 2 |
| Williams S.M. | 33+3 | 7 | 2 | 0 | 38+3 | 8 |
| Woods E. | 16 | 10 | – | – | 18 | 11 |
| Own Goals | | 1 | | | | 1 |

| | | P | W | D | L | F | A | Pts |
|---|---|---|---|---|---|---|---|---|
| 1 | Watford | 46 | 30 | 11 | 5 | 85 | 38 | 71 |
| 2 | Southend | 46 | 25 | 10 | 11 | 66 | 39 | 60 |
| 3 | Swansea | 46 | 23 | 10 | 13 | 87 | 47 | 56 |
| 4 | Brentford | 46 | 21 | 14 | 11 | 86 | 54 | 56 |
| 5 | Aldershot | 46 | 19 | 16 | 11 | 67 | 47 | 54 |
| 6 | Grimsby | 46 | 21 | 11 | 14 | 57 | 51 | 53 |
| 7 | Barnsley | 46 | 18 | 14 | 14 | 61 | 49 | 50 |
| 8 | Reading | 46 | 18 | 14 | 14 | 55 | 52 | 50 |
| 9 | Torquay | 46 | 16 | 15 | 15 | 57 | 56 | 47 |
| 10 | Northampton | 46 | 17 | 13 | 16 | 63 | 68 | 47 |
| 11 | Huddersfield | 46 | 15 | 15 | 16 | 63 | 55 | 45 |
| 12 | Doncaster | 46 | 14 | 17 | 15 | 52 | 65 | 45 |
| 13 | Wimbledon | 46 | 14 | 16 | 16 | 66 | 67 | 44 |
| 14 | Scunthorpe | 46 | 14 | 16 | 16 | 50 | 55 | 44 |
| 15 | Crewe | 46 | 15 | 14 | 17 | 50 | 69 | 44 |
| 16 | Newport | 46 | 16 | 11 | 19 | 65 | 73 | 43 |
| 17 | Bournemouth | 46 | 14 | 15 | 17 | 41 | 51 | 43 |
| 18 | Stockport | 46 | 16 | 10 | 20 | 56 | 56 | 42 |
| 19 | Darlington | 46 | 14 | 13 | 19 | 52 | 59 | 41 |
| 20 | Halifax | 46 | 10 | 21 | 15 | 52 | 62 | 41 |
| 21 | Hartlepool | 46 | 15 | 7 | 24 | 51 | 84 | 37 |
| 22 | York | 46 | 12 | 12 | 22 | 50 | 69 | 36 |
| 23 | Southport | 46 | 6 | 19 | 21 | 52 | 76 | 31 |
| 24 | Rochdale | 46 | 8 | 8 | 30 | 43 | 85 | 24 |

(Front) Bird(Train./Coach), Derrett, Murray, Woods, R.Walker, Plumley, Jones, Relish, Clark, Addison(Manager)
(Front) Byrne, Williams, Bell, Emanuel, Preece, Villars.

# SEASON 1978-79    Division 4

| | Date | Opposition | Res. | Att. | Goalscorers |
|---|---|---|---|---|---|
| 1 | 19 Aug | Bournemouth & B.A. | 1–3 | 3083 | Goddard |
| 2 | 22 | ALDERSHOT | 1–2 | 3374 | Williams |
| 3 | 26 | STOCKPORT COUNTY | 1–2 | 2659 | Goddard |
| 4 | 2 Sep | Wigan Athletic | 3–2 | 5319 | Sinclair, Goddard, Woods |
| 5 | 9 | Reading | 1–2 | 5089 | Vaughan |
| 6 | 12 | CREWE ALEXANDRA | 1–2 | 3176 | Woods |
| 7 | 16 | WIMBLEDON | 1–3 | 2903 | Clark |
| 8 | 23 | Bradford City | 3–1 | 4471 | Lowndes(2), Sinclair |
| 9 | 25 | Hartlepool United | 0–0 | 5491 | |
| 10 | 30 | YORK CITY | 1–1 | 3021 | Sinclair |
| 11 | 7 Oct | Scunthorpe United | 3–2 | 2453 | Bailey, Lowndes, Sinclair |
| 12 | 14 | HUDDERSFIELD TOWN | 2–1 | 3624 | Goddard(2) |
| 13 | 17 | ROCHDALE | 0–0 | 3472 | |
| 14 | 21 | Doncaster Rovers | 0–0 | 2008 | |
| 15 | 28 | BARNSLEY | 1–1 | 4570 | Lowndes |
| 16 | 4 Nov | Northampton Town | 1–3 | 3065 | Bruton |
| 17 | 10 | WIGAN ATHLETIC | 2–1 | 4142 | Goddard, Vaughan |
| 18 | 17 | Stockport County | 1–1 | 4009 | Warriner |
| 19 | 2 Dec | DARLINGTON | 2–1 | 3450 | Walden(2) |
| 20 | 9 | Grimsby Town | 0–1 | 3667 | |
| 21 | 22 | Hereford United | 3–0 | 2834 | Bruton, Goddard, Oakes |
| 22 | 26 | TORQUAY UNITED | 1–1 | 6930 | Wilson(og) |
| 23 | 30 | PORT VALE | 1–0 | 4104 | Goddard |
| 24 | 13 Jan | READING | 3–2 | 5968 | Goddard(2), Davies |
| 25 | 2 Feb | HARTLEPOOL UNITED | 3–2 | 3659 | Goddard(2), Lowndes |
| 26 | 20 | Portsmouth | 1–2 | 8206 | Moore |
| 27 | 24 | Huddersfield Town | 1–0 | 3361 | Bruton |
| 28 | 27 | BRADFORD CITY | 2–4 | 4225 | Oakes, Tynan |
| 29 | 3 Mar | DONCASTER ROVERS | 3–0 | 2550 | Moore, Tynan, Lowndes |
| 30 | 6 | Wimbledon | 0–0 | 2980 | |
| 31 | 10 | Barnsley | 0–1 | 9428 | |
| 32 | 13 | Crewe Alexandra | 1–0 | 1459 | Tynan |
| 33 | 16 | NORTHAMPTON TOWN | 2–1 | 3018 | Goddard, Bruton |
| 34 | 20 | York City | 2–1 | 2156 | Tynan, Goddard |
| 35 | 24 | Aldershot | 3–2 | 5243 | Tynan, Moore, Lowndes |
| 36 | 31 | HALIFAX TOWN | 2–0 | 3927 | Bruton, Vaughan |
| 37 | 7 Apr | Darlington | 0–1 | 1518 | |
| 38 | 11 | HEREFORD UNITED | 4–1 | 3771 | Goddard, Moore, Oakes, Lowndes |
| 39 | 14 | Torquay United | 0–2 | 3181 | |
| 40 | 16 | PORTSMOUTH | 1–2 | 5421 | Goddard |
| 41 | 18 | SCUNTHORPE UNITED | 2–0 | 2572 | Thompson, Oakes |
| 42 | 21 | Port Vale | 1–1 | 2444 | Tynan |
| 43 | 23 | Rochdale | 0–1 | 1457 | |
| 44 | 28 | GRIMSBY TOWN | 1–1 | 3049 | Oakes |
| 45 | 1 May | BOURNEMOUTH & B.A. | 2–0 | 2235 | Tynan, Vaughan |
| 46 | 5 | Halifax Town | 2–1 | 1007 | Goddard(2) |

| Player | League | | F.A.Cup | | Total | |
|---|---|---|---|---|---|---|
| | App | Gls. | App | Gls. | App | Gls. |
| Armstrong K.T. | 3+1 | 0 | – | – | 3+1 | 0 |
| Bailey N. | 20+1 | 1 | 1 | 0 | 22+1 | 1 |
| Brown J. | 2+1 | 0 | – | – | 2+1 | 0 |
| Bruton D.E. | 34 | 5 | 6 | 0 | 40 | 5 |
| Byrne A.B. | 26 | 0 | 6 | 0 | 35 | 0 |
| Clark B D. | 1+3 | 1 | 1 | 0 | 2+3 | 1 |
| Cosslett M.P. | 1 | 0 | – | – | 1 | 0 |
| Davies G. | 38 | 1 | 6 | 0 | 47 | 1 |
| Elliott D. | 0+2 | 0 | – | – | 0+2 | 0 |
| Goddard H.J. | 46 | 18 | 6 | 4 | 55 | 22 |
| Guscott R.M. | – | – | – | – | 0+1 | 0 |
| Jones R. | 2 | 0 | – | – | 2 | 0 |
| Lee T.W.G. | 1 | 0 | – | – | 2 | 0 |
| Lowndes S.R. | 43 | 8 | 6 | 0 | 50 | 8 |
| McGeady J.T. | 2 | 0 | – | – | 2 | 0 |
| Moore K.J. | 21 | 4 | – | – | 21 | 4 |
| Oakes K.B. | 34 | 5 | 4+1 | 0 | 39+1 | 5 |
| Plumley G.E. | 45 | 0 | 6 | 0 | 53 | 0 |
| Relish J.D. | 20+7 | 0 | 0+2 | 0 | 23+9 | 0 |
| Sinclair C.M. | 14+1 | 4 | 2+1 | 0 | 17+3 | 4 |
| Thompson J.T. | 26+2 | 1 | 5 | 0 | 34+2 | 1 |
| Tynan T.E. | 20 | 7 | – | – | 20 | 7 |
| Vaughan N.M. | 23+4 | 4 | 5 | 0 | 28+5 | 4 |
| Walden R.F. | 40 | 2 | 6 | 0 | 49 | 2 |
| Walker R.L. | 6 | 0 | – | – | 8 | 0 |
| Warriner S.W. | 16+4 | 1 | 2+1 | 0 | 20+5 | 1 |
| Williams M. | 3+1 | 1 | – | – | 5+1 | 2 |
| Woods E. | 19 | 2 | 4 | 1 | 25 | 4 |
| Own goals | | 1 | | | | 1 |

## F.A.Cup

| | Date | Opposition | Res. | Att. | Goalscorers |
|---|---|---|---|---|---|
| 1 | 25 Nov | Hereford United | 1–0 | 6939 | Goddard |
| 2 | 16 Dec | WORCESTER CITY | 0–0 | 7196 | |
| 2R | 18 | Worcester City | 2–1 | 10233 | Goddard(2) |
| 3 | 9 Jan | WEST HAM UNITED | 2–1 | 14124 | Woods, Goddard |
| 4 | 30 | COLCHESTER UNITED | 0–0 | 10329 | |
| 4R | 5 Feb | Colchester United | 0–1 | 7029 | |

| | | P | W | D | L | F | A | Pts |
|---|---|---|---|---|---|---|---|---|
| 1 | Reading | 46 | 26 | 13 | 7 | 76 | 35 | 65 |
| 2 | Grimsby | 46 | 26 | 9 | 11 | 82 | 49 | 61 |
| 3 | Wimbledon | 46 | 25 | 11 | 10 | 78 | 46 | 61 |
| 4 | Barnsley | 46 | 24 | 13 | 9 | 73 | 42 | 61 |
| 5 | Aldershot | 46 | 20 | 17 | 9 | 63 | 47 | 57 |
| 6 | Wigan | 46 | 21 | 13 | 12 | 63 | 48 | 55 |
| 7 | Portsmouth | 46 | 20 | 12 | 14 | 62 | 48 | 52 |
| 8 | Newport | 46 | 21 | 10 | 15 | 66 | 55 | 52 |
| 9 | Huddersfield | 46 | 18 | 11 | 17 | 57 | 53 | 47 |
| 10 | York | 46 | 18 | 11 | 17 | 51 | 55 | 47 |
| 11 | Torquay | 46 | 19 | 8 | 19 | 58 | 65 | 46 |
| 12 | Scunthorpe | 46 | 17 | 11 | 18 | 54 | 60 | 45 |
| 13 | Hartlepool | 46 | 13 | 18 | 15 | 57 | 66 | 44 |
| 14 | Hereford | 46 | 15 | 13 | 18 | 53 | 53 | 43 |
| 15 | Bradford C. | 46 | 17 | 9 | 20 | 62 | 68 | 43 |
| 16 | Port Vale | 46 | 14 | 14 | 18 | 57 | 70 | 42 |
| 17 | Stockport | 46 | 14 | 12 | 20 | 58 | 60 | 40 |
| 18 | Bournemouth | 46 | 14 | 11 | 21 | 47 | 48 | 39 |
| 19 | Northampton | 46 | 15 | 9 | 22 | 64 | 76 | 39 |
| 20 | Rochdale | 46 | 15 | 9 | 22 | 47 | 64 | 39 |
| 21 | Darlington | 46 | 11 | 15 | 20 | 49 | 66 | 37 |
| 22 | Doncaster | 46 | 13 | 11 | 22 | 50 | 73 | 37 |
| 23 | Halifax | 46 | 9 | 8 | 29 | 39 | 72 | 26 |
| 24 | Crewe | 46 | 6 | 14 | 26 | 43 | 90 | 26 |

(Back) Warriner, Thompson, Steel, Cosslett, Dowler, Fisher, Plumley, Walker, Woods, Jones, Davies
(Middle) Bird(Tainer/Coach), Sinclair, Relish, Lowndes, Goddard, Byrne M., Williams, Guscott, Vaughan, Brinkworth, Ashurst(Manager). (Front) Gillard, Smith, Brown, Evans, N.Williams, Taylor.

# SEASON 1979-80  Division 4

| | Date | Opposition | Res. | Att. | Goalscorers |
|---|---|---|---|---|---|
| 1 | 18 Aug | PORT VALE | 2-1 | 4008 | Vaughan, Goddard |
| 2 | 21 | Aldershot | 1-0 | 3537 | Moore |
| 3 | 25 | Bournemouth & B.A. | 2-3 | 5428 | Oakes, Goddard |
| 4 | 1 Sep | YORK CITY | 2-0 | 3818 | Oakes, Goddard |
| 5 | 8 | Huddersfield Town | 1-2 | 3134 | Oakes |
| 6 | 15 | BRADFORD CITY | 1-2 | 4089 | Vaughan |
| 7 | 18 | NORTHAMPTON TOWN | 2-1 | 3185 | Tynan, Goddard |
| 8 | 22 | Doncaster Rovers | 3-1 | 3338 | Thompson, Tynan, Goddard |
| 9 | 29 | LINCOLN CITY | 1-1 | 4035 | Guest(og) |
| 10 | 2 Oct | Northampton Town | 2-3 | 2346 | Bailey, Warriner |
| 11 | 6 | Halifax Town | 1-2 | 2530 | Goddard |
| 12 | 9 | ALDERSHOT | 4-2 | 3782 | Aldridge(2), Oakes, Jopling(og) |
| 13 | 13 | TRANMERE ROVERS | 2-0 | 4052 | Aldridge, Lowndes |
| 14 | 20 | Scunthorpe United | 3-1 | 1875 | Aldridge(2), Lowndes |
| 15 | 23 | Portsmouth | 2-0 | 20755 | Lowndes, Oakes |
| 16 | 27 | WIGAN ATHLETIC | 3-2 | 4910 | Tynan(2), Oakes |
| 17 | 3 Nov | Port Vale | 0-2 | 2980 | |
| 18 | 6 | PORTSMOUTH | 4-3 | 7115 | Tynan(2), Oakes, Aldridge |
| 19 | 10 | CREWE ALEXANDRA | 1-1 | 4718 | D.Bruton |
| 20 | 16 | Stockport County | 5-0 | 3407 | Aldridge(3), Oakes, D.Bruton |
| 21 | 1 Dec | DARLINGTON | 4-0 | 4127 | Lowndes(2), Oakes, Relish |
| 22 | 8 | Hartlepool United | 0-0 | 2587 | |
| 23 | 15 | SCUNTHORPE UNITED | 2-1 | 4158 | Walden, D.Bruton |
| 24 | 21 | PETERBOROUGH UTD | 1-1 | 4653 | Tynan |
| 25 | 26 | Torquay United | 0-2 | 5326 | |
| 26 | 29 | WALSALL | 0-1 | 7452 | |
| 27 | 1 Jan | HEREFORD UNITED | 1-0 | 7213 | Vaughan |
| 28 | 12 | York City | 1-2 | 2248 | Aldridge |
| 29 | 18 | HUDDERSFIELD TOWN | 2-2 | 4851 | Oakes, M.Bruton |
| 30 | 26 | BOURNEMOUTH & B.A. | 0-0 | 4833 | |
| 31 | 16 Feb | Lincoln City | 1-2 | 3346 | Lowndes |
| 32 | 22 | Tranmere Rovers | 2-0 | 2056 | Vaughan(2) |
| 33 | 26 | DONCASTER ROVERS | 2-1 | 4652 | Gwyther, Lowndes |
| 34 | 8 Mar | Wigan Athletic | 1-0 | 6128 | Oakes |
| 35 | 14 | HALIFAX TOWN | 5-2 | 4777 | Gwyther(2), Vaughan(2), Aldridge |
| 36 | 22 | Crewe Alexandra | 3-0 | 2592 | Vaughan, D.Bruton, Gwyther |
| 37 | 29 | STOCKPORT COUNTY | 3-1 | 4727 | Gwyther, Moore, Vaughan |
| 38 | 5 Apr | TORQUAY UNITED | 3-0 | 6513 | Moore, Gwyther, Vaughan |
| 39 | 7 | Hereford United | 2-0 | 7945 | Vaughan, Gwyther |
| 40 | 8 | Peterborough Utd | 1-0 | 5033 | Vaughan |
| 41 | 12 | ROCHDALE | 1-0 | 8113 | Moore |
| 42 | 19 | Darlington | 1-1 | 1906 | Moore |
| 43 | 22 | Bradford City | 0-3 | 8853 | |
| 44 | 26 | HARTLEPOOL UNITED | 1-0 | 8373 | Aldridge |
| 45 | 29 | Rochdale | 0-2 | 1616 | |
| 46 | 3 May | Walsall | 4-2 | 9251 | Aldridge(2), Gwyther, Tynan |

| Player | League | | F.A.Cup | | Total | |
|---|---|---|---|---|---|---|
| | App | Gls. | App | Gls. | App | Gls. |
| Aldridge J.W. | 35+3 | 14 | 1 | 0 | 41+3 | 16 |
| Bailey N. | 29 | 1 | 1 | 0 | 33 | 1 |
| Bruton D.E. | 28+3 | 4 | 1 | 0 | 34+3 | 4 |
| Bruton M. | 3+6 | 1 | – | – | 4+6 | 1 |
| Davies G. | 31+1 | 0 | – | – | 37+1 | 0 |
| Dowler M.J. | 7 | 0 | 1 | 0 | 8 | 0 |
| Goddard H.J. | 14 | 6 | – | – | 16 | 6 |
| Gwyther D. | 17+2 | 8 | – | – | 21+2 | 11 |
| Howey P. | – | – | 1 | 0 | 1 | 0 |
| Lowndes S.R. | 46 | 7 | 1 | 0 | 54 | 9 |
| Moore K.J. | 41 | 5 | – | – | 48 | 5 |
| Oakes K.B. | 45 | 11 | 1 | 0 | 53 | 11 |
| Plumley G.E. | 39 | 0 | – | – | 46 | 0 |
| Relish J.D. | 39 | 1 | 1 | 0 | 45 | 1 |
| Thompson J.T. | 6+1 | 1 | – | – | 6+3 | 1 |
| Tynan T.E. | 26+8 | 8 | 1 | 0 | 31+11 | 13 |
| Vaughan N.M. | 46 | 12 | 1 | 0 | 54 | 12 |
| Walden R.F. | 44 | 1 | 1 | 0 | 52 | 1 |
| Ward R. | 2 | 0 | – | – | 2 | 0 |
| Warriner S.W. | 8+2 | 1 | 0+1 | 0 | 8+3 | 1 |
| Own Goals | | 2 | | | | 2 |

| | | P | W | D | L | F | A | Pts |
|---|---|---|---|---|---|---|---|---|
| 1 | Huddersfield | 46 | 27 | 12 | 7 | 101 | 48 | 66 |
| 2 | Walsall | 46 | 23 | 18 | 5 | 75 | 47 | 64 |
| 3 | Newport | 46 | 27 | 7 | 12 | 83 | 50 | 61 |
| 4 | Portsmouth | 46 | 24 | 12 | 10 | 91 | 49 | 60 |
| 5 | Bradford | 46 | 24 | 12 | 10 | 77 | 50 | 60 |
| 6 | Wigan | 46 | 21 | 13 | 12 | 76 | 61 | 55 |
| 7 | Lincoln | 46 | 18 | 17 | 11 | 64 | 42 | 53 |
| 8 | Peterborough | 46 | 21 | 10 | 15 | 58 | 47 | 52 |
| 9 | Torquay | 46 | 15 | 17 | 14 | 70 | 69 | 47 |
| 10 | Aldershot | 46 | 16 | 13 | 17 | 62 | 53 | 45 |
| 11 | Bournemouth | 46 | 13 | 18 | 15 | 52 | 51 | 44 |
| 12 | Doncaster | 46 | 15 | 14 | 17 | 62 | 63 | 44 |
| 13 | Northampton | 46 | 16 | 12 | 18 | 51 | 66 | 44 |
| 14 | Scunthorpe | 46 | 14 | 15 | 17 | 58 | 75 | 43 |
| 15 | Tranmere | 46 | 14 | 13 | 19 | 50 | 56 | 41 |
| 16 | Stockport | 46 | 14 | 12 | 20 | 48 | 72 | 40 |
| 17 | York | 46 | 14 | 11 | 21 | 65 | 82 | 39 |
| 18 | Halifax | 46 | 13 | 13 | 20 | 46 | 72 | 39 |
| 19 | Hartlepool | 46 | 14 | 10 | 22 | 59 | 64 | 38 |
| 20 | Port Vale | 46 | 12 | 12 | 22 | 56 | 70 | 36 |
| 21 | Hereford | 46 | 11 | 14 | 21 | 38 | 52 | 36 |
| 22 | Darlington | 46 | 9 | 17 | 20 | 50 | 74 | 35 |
| 23 | Crewe | 46 | 11 | 13 | 22 | 35 | 68 | 35 |
| 24 | Rochdale | 46 | 7 | 13 | 26 | 33 | 79 | 27 |

## F.A.Cup

| | Date | Opposition | Res. | Att. | |
|---|---|---|---|---|---|
| 1 | 24 Nov | Portsmouth | 0-1 | 19459 | |

(Back) Walden, Oakes, Carey, Davies, M.Bruton, Thompson. (Middle) Goodfellow (Train./Coach), Walsh, Williams, Fyfe, Pearce, Plumley, Dowler, Johns, Relish, Brown, Ashurst (Manager). (Front) Aldridge, Vaughan, Warriner, Tynan, D.Bruton, Goddard, Lowndes, Moore, Bailey.

# SEASON 1980-81    Division 3

| | Date | Opposition | Res. | Att. | Goalscorers |
|---|---|---|---|---|---|
| 1 | 16 Aug | Burnley | 1-1 | 6715 | Aldridge |
| 2 | 19 | CHARLTON ATHLETIC | 1-2 | 8062 | Tynan |
| 3 | 23 | MILLWALL | 2-1 | 6620 | Tynan(2) |
| 4 | 30 | Carlisle United | 4-1 | 2859 | Aldridge, Elsey, Gwyther, Moore |
| 5 | 6 Sep | Gillingham | 2-3 | 4712 | Lowndes, Oakes |
| 6 | 13 | OXFORD UNITED | 0-1 | 5256 | |
| 7 | 20 | Chesterfield | 2-3 | 5277 | Gwyther, Tynan |
| 8 | 27 | PLYMOUTH ARGYLE | 0-2 | 6878 | |
| 9 | 4 Oct | Brentford | 1-0 | 6360 | Lowndes |
| 10 | 7 | READING | 0-0 | 5545 | |
| 11 | 11 | PORTSMOUTH | 2-1 | 7003 | Oakes(2) |
| 12 | 14 | Sheffield United | 0-2 | 9776 | |
| 13 | 18 | Walsall | 0-1 | 4335 | |
| 14 | 25 | HUDDERSFIELD TOWN | 3-2 | 6403 | Oakes, Lowndes, Gwyther |
| 15 | 28 | FULHAM | 2-1 | 6029 | Aldridge, Clement(og) |
| 16 | 1 Nov | Blackpool | 4-2 | 4556 | Oakes(2), Aldridge, Gwyther |
| 17 | 8 | HULL CITY | 4-0 | 5495 | Oakes, Gwyther, Bailey, Lowndes |
| 18 | 11 | Charlton Athletic | 0-3 | 6911 | |
| 19 | 15 | BURNLEY | 1-2 | 5370 | Tynan |
| 20 | 29 | Rotherham United | 0-1 | 5512 | |
| 21 | 3 Dec | Chester | 1-1 | 1640 | Lowndes |
| 22 | 6 | BARNSLEY | 0-1 | 5537 | |
| 23 | 13 | CHESTER | 1-1 | 4149 | Gwyther |
| 24 | 20 | Colchester United | 0-1 | 2160 | |
| 25 | 26 | SWINDON TOWN | 0-2 | 7086 | |
| 26 | 27 | Exeter City | 2-2 | 6295 | Tynan, Gwyther |
| 27 | 3 Jan | SHEFFIELD UNITED | 4-0 | 6630 | Gwyther, Lowndes, Moore, Tynan |
| 28 | 10 | Huddersfield Town | 1-4 | 9063 | Lowndes |
| 29 | 16 | ROTHERHAM UNITED | 0-1 | 4783 | |
| 30 | 31 | Millwall | 0-0 | 4913 | |
| 31 | 7 Feb | Oxford United | 1-0 | 4440 | Gwyther |
| 32 | 14 | GILLINGHAM | 1-1 | 5172 | Gwyther |
| 33 | 18 | Reading | 1-1 | 3876 | Lowndes |
| 34 | 21 | Plymouth Argyle | 2-3 | 4315 | Tynan, Gwyther |
| 35 | 28 | CHESTERFIELD | 5-1 | 5340 | Tynan(2), Gwyther, Oakes, Lowndes |
| 36 | 7 Mar | BRENTFORD | 1-1 | 5224 | Tynan |
| 37 | 14 | Portsmouth | 0-0 | 13208 | |
| 38 | 28 | Fulham | 1-2 | 4570 | Gwyther |
| 39 | 4 Apr | BLACKPOOL | 3-1 | 4514 | Aldridge(2), Waddle |
| 40 | 7 | WALSALL | 1-1 | 5446 | Moore |
| 41 | 18 | EXETER CITY | 2-1 | 5231 | Tynan, Waddle |
| 42 | 20 | Swindon Town | 1-1 | 8435 | Waddle |
| 43 | 25 | COLCHESTER UNITED | 1-0 | 4619 | Aldridge |
| 44 | 2 May | Barnsley | 1-4 | 15659 | Gwyther |
| 45 | 5 | CARLISLE UNITED | 4-0 | 3748 | Gwyther(2), Tynan, Vaughan |
| 46 | 7 | Hull City | 1-3 | 2059 | Elsey |

## F.A.Cup

| | | | | | |
|---|---|---|---|---|---|
| 1 | 22 Nov | Plymouth Argyle | 0-2 | 6719 | |

| Player | League | | F.A.Cup | | Total | |
|---|---|---|---|---|---|---|
| | App | Gls. | App | Gls. | App | Gls. |
| Aldridge J.W. | 23+4 | 7 | 0+1 | 0 | 32+6 | 12 |
| Bailey N. | 21 | 1 | 1 | 0 | 27+1 | 1 |
| Bishop R.J. | 3+4 | 0 | – | – | 3+4 | 0 |
| Bruton D.E. | 17 | 0 | – | – | 27 | 1 |
| Cunningham D. | – | – | – | – | 1 | 0 |
| Davies G. | 30 | 0 | 1 | 0 | 39+1 | 0 |
| Dowler M.J. | 4 | 0 | – | – | 5 | 0 |
| Elsey K.W. | 26+8 | 2 | 1 | 0 | 36+13 | 3 |
| Gwyther D. | 41 | 16 | 1 | 0 | 58 | 21 |
| Kendall M. | 28 | 0 | 1 | 0 | 34 | 0 |
| Lowndes S.R. | 39+1 | 9 | 1 | 0 | 56+1 | 12 |
| Moore K.J. | 43 | 3 | 1 | 0 | 58 | 8 |
| Oakes K.B. | 43 | 8 | 1 | 0 | 58 | 10 |
| Plumley G.E. | 14 | 0 | – | – | 24 | 0 |
| Relish J.D. | 32+1 | 0 | 1 | 0 | 46+1 | 0 |
| Tynan T.E. | 44+1 | 13 | 1 | 0 | 59+1 | 20 |
| Vaughan N.M. | 42+3 | 1 | – | – | 57+4 | 3 |
| Waddle A.R. | 8+1 | 3 | – | – | 8+1 | 3 |
| Walden R.F. | 44 | 0 | 1 | 0 | 61 | 0 |
| Ward R. | 0+1 | 0 | – | – | 0+1 | 0 |
| Warriner S.W. | 4+2 | 0 | – | – | 4+2 | 0 |
| Own Goals | | 1 | | | | 1 |

| | | P | W | D | L | F | A | Pts |
|---|---|---|---|---|---|---|---|---|
| 1 | Rotherham | 46 | 24 | 13 | 9 | 62 | 32 | 61 |
| 2 | Barnsley | 46 | 21 | 17 | 8 | 72 | 45 | 59 |
| 3 | Charlton | 46 | 25 | 9 | 12 | 63 | 44 | 59 |
| 4 | Huddersfield | 46 | 21 | 14 | 11 | 71 | 40 | 56 |
| 5 | Chesterfield | 46 | 23 | 10 | 13 | 72 | 48 | 56 |
| 6 | Portsmouth | 46 | 22 | 9 | 15 | 55 | 47 | 53 |
| 7 | Plymouth | 46 | 19 | 14 | 13 | 56 | 44 | 52 |
| 8 | Burnley | 46 | 18 | 14 | 14 | 60 | 48 | 50 |
| 9 | Brentford | 46 | 14 | 19 | 13 | 52 | 49 | 47 |
| 10 | Reading | 46 | 18 | 10 | 18 | 62 | 62 | 46 |
| 11 | Exeter | 46 | 16 | 13 | 17 | 62 | 66 | 45 |
| 12 | Newport | 46 | 15 | 13 | 18 | 64 | 61 | 43 |
| 13 | Fulham | 46 | 15 | 13 | 18 | 57 | 64 | 43 |
| 14 | Oxford | 46 | 13 | 17 | 16 | 39 | 47 | 43 |
| 15 | Gillingham | 46 | 12 | 18 | 16 | 48 | 58 | 42 |
| 16 | Millwall | 46 | 14 | 14 | 18 | 43 | 60 | 42 |
| 17 | Swindon | 46 | 13 | 15 | 18 | 51 | 56 | 41 |
| 18 | Chester | 46 | 15 | 11 | 20 | 41 | 48 | 41 |
| 19 | Carlisle | 46 | 14 | 13 | 19 | 57 | 70 | 41 |
| 20 | Walsall | 46 | 13 | 15 | 18 | 59 | 74 | 41 |
| 21 | Sheff United | 46 | 14 | 13 | 19 | 65 | 62 | 40 |
| 22 | Colchester | 46 | 14 | 11 | 21 | 45 | 65 | 39 |
| 23 | Blackpool | 46 | 9 | 14 | 23 | 45 | 75 | 32 |
| 24 | Hull | 46 | 8 | 16 | 22 | 40 | 71 | 32 |

(Back) Llewellyn, Elsey, Aldridge, Hamer, Gwyther, Stanton, Carey, Walden.
(Middle) Williams(Asst.Train./Coach), Lewis, Ward, Davies, Sherlock, Plumley, Dowler, Bruton, Relish, Bailey, Goodfellow(Train./Coach)
(Front) James, Warriner, Tynan, Oakes, Ashurst (Manager), Lowndes, Goddard, Moore, Vaughan.

# SEASON 1981-82     Division 3

| | Date | Opposition | Res. | Att. | Goalscorers |
|---|---|---|---|---|---|
| 1 | 29 Aug | CHESTERFIELD | 1-0 | 5079 | Johnson |
| 2 | 4 Sep | Southend United | 4-0 | 4620 | Aldridge, Gwyther, Tynan, Elsey |
| 3 | 12 | OXFORD UNITED | 3-2 | 5293 | Waddle(2), Aldridge |
| 4 | 19 | Bristol City | 1-2 | 7522 | Aldridge |
| 5 | 23 | Reading | 1-2 | 4542 | Aldridge |
| 6 | 26 | PRESTON NORTH END | 1-1 | 5064 | Anderson(og) |
| 7 | 29 | BRENTFORD | 0-1 | 4028 | |
| 8 | 3 Oct | Lincoln City | 2-2 | 3351 | Tynan(2) |
| 9 | 10 | DONCASTER ROVERS | 1-0 | 4579 | Gwyther |
| 10 | 17 | Fulham | 1-3 | 3988 | Tynan |
| 11 | 20 | MILLWALL | 1-1 | 4609 | Goddard |
| 12 | 24 | Portsmouth | 0-0 | 8787 | |
| 13 | 31 | CARLISLE UNITED | 2-0 | 3972 | Elsey(2) |
| 14 | 3 Nov | Bristol Rovers | 0-2 | 6464 | |
| 15 | 7 | Walsall | 1-3 | 4169 | Oakes |
| 16 | 14 | PLYMOUTH ARGYLE | 0-1 | 4428 | |
| 17 | 28 | EXETER CITY | 1-1 | 4149 | Waddle |
| 18 | 5 Dec | Wimbledon | 3-2 | 2056 | Tynan, Elsey, Waddle |
| 19 | 26 | CHESTER | 0-1 | 4901 | |
| 20 | 28 | Gillingham | 1-1 | 6055 | Moore |
| 21 | 2 Jan | READING | 3-1 | 2948 | Aldridge(2), Lowndes |
| 22 | 16 | Burnley | 1-2 | 4716 | Moore |
| 23 | 23 | Chesterfield | 0-1 | 4236 | |
| 24 | 30 | BRISTOL CITY | 1-1 | 5927 | Vaughan |
| 25 | 6 Feb | Oxford United | 1-1 | 5653 | Tynan |
| 26 | 13 | LINCOLN CITY | 0-0 | 3735 | |
| 27 | 20 | Brentford | 0-2 | 4297 | |
| 28 | 27 | Doncaster Rovers | 2-0 | 4190 | Bishop, Aldridge |
| 29 | 7 Mar | FULHAM | 1-3 | 5178 | Lowndes |
| 30 | 9 | Millwall | 0-1 | 3084 | |
| 31 | 13 | PORTSMOUTH | 1-1 | 4209 | Elsey |
| 32 | 16 | BRISTOL ROVERS | 1-1 | 5312 | Tynan |
| 33 | 20 | Carlisle United | 2-2 | 4042 | Aldridge, Tynan |
| 34 | 27 | WALSALL | 2-2 | 3484 | Serella(og), Tynan |
| 35 | 30 | Huddersfield Town | 0-2 | 4205 | |
| 36 | 2 Apr | Plymouth Argyle | 2-1 | 5148 | Elsey, Bishop |
| 37 | 10 | Chester | 2-0 | 1451 | Aldridge(2) |
| 38 | 12 | GILLINGHAM | 4-2 | 4353 | Tynan, Vaughan, Johnson, Gwyther |
| 39 | 17 | WIMBLEDON | 0-0 | 3900 | |
| 40 | 24 | Exeter City | 0-1 | 3168 | |
| 41 | 1 May | BURNLEY | 0-0 | 4024 | |
| 42 | 4 | Preston North End | 1-2 | 4972 | Vaughan |
| 43 | 8 | Swindon Town | 1-1 | 5676 | Aldridge |
| 44 | 11 | SOUTHEND UNITED | 3-2 | 3716 | Tynan(2), Elsey |
| 45 | 15 | HUDDERSFIELD TOWN | 1-0 | 4169 | Lowndes |
| 46 | 18 | SWINDON TOWN | 1-0 | 5906 | Tynan |

| Player | League | | F.A.Cup | | Total | |
|---|---|---|---|---|---|---|
| | App | Gls. | App | Gls. | App | Gls. |
| Aldridge J.W. | 32+4 | 11 | 1 | 0 | 35+4 | 12 |
| Bailey N. | 17+1 | 0 | 1 | 0 | 28+1 | 0 |
| Bishop R.J. | 5+6 | 2 | – | – | 6+8 | 3 |
| Davies G. | 41 | 0 | 1 | 0 | 51+1 | 0 |
| Elsey K.W. | 40 | 7 | 1 | 0 | 50+1 | 7 |
| Goddard H.J. | 4 | 1 | – | – | 8 | 1 |
| Gwyther D. | 20+6 | 3 | – | – | 27+8 | 4 |
| Johnson J.D. | 34 | 2 | – | – | 39 | 2 |
| Kendall M. | 46 | 0 | 1 | 0 | 57 | 0 |
| Lees T. | 25 | 0 | 1 | 0 | 30+1 | 1 |
| Lowndes S.R. | 28+3 | 3 | 1 | 0 | 33+4 | 3 |
| Moore K.J. | 28+1 | 2 | – | – | 33+1 | 3 |
| Oakes K.B. | 45 | 1 | 1 | 0 | 56 | 4 |
| Relish J.D. | 28 | 0 | 1 | 0 | 35 | 0 |
| Thomas R.J. | 3 | 0 | – | – | 3 | 0 |
| Tynan T.E. | 32+6 | 13 | 0+1 | 0 | 38+8 | 16 |
| Vaughan N.M. | 44 | 3 | 1 | 0 | 54+1 | 3 |
| Waddle A.R. | 11+7 | 4 | 1 | 0 | 16+8 | 4 |
| Walden R.F. | 23 | 0 | – | – | 28+1 | 0 |
| Own Goals | | 2 | | | | 2 |

| | | P | W | D | L | F | A | Pts |
|---|---|---|---|---|---|---|---|---|
| 1 | Burnley | 46 | 21 | 17 | 8 | 66 | 49 | 80 |
| 2 | Carlisle | 46 | 23 | 11 | 12 | 65 | 50 | 80 |
| 3 | Fulham | 46 | 21 | 15 | 10 | 77 | 51 | 78 |
| 4 | Lincoln | 46 | 21 | 14 | 11 | 66 | 40 | 77 |
| 5 | Oxford | 46 | 19 | 14 | 13 | 63 | 49 | 71 |
| 6 | Gillingham | 46 | 20 | 11 | 15 | 64 | 56 | 71 |
| 7 | Southend | 46 | 18 | 15 | 13 | 63 | 51 | 69 |
| 8 | Brentford | 46 | 19 | 11 | 16 | 56 | 47 | 68 |
| 9 | Millwall | 46 | 18 | 13 | 15 | 62 | 62 | 67 |
| 10 | Plymouth | 46 | 18 | 11 | 17 | 64 | 56 | 65 |
| 11 | Chesterfield | 46 | 18 | 10 | 18 | 67 | 58 | 64 |
| 12 | Reading | 46 | 17 | 11 | 18 | 67 | 75 | 62 |
| 13 | Portsmouth | 46 | 14 | 19 | 13 | 56 | 51 | 61 |
| 14 | Preston | 46 | 16 | 13 | 17 | 50 | 56 | 61 |
| 15 | Bristol Rovers* | 46 | 18 | 9 | 19 | 58 | 65 | 61 |
| 16 | Newport | 46 | 14 | 16 | 16 | 54 | 54 | 58 |
| 17 | Huddersfield | 46 | 15 | 12 | 19 | 64 | 59 | 57 |
| 18 | Exeter | 46 | 16 | 9 | 21 | 71 | 84 | 57 |
| 19 | Doncaster | 46 | 13 | 17 | 16 | 55 | 68 | 56 |
| 20 | Walsall | 46 | 13 | 14 | 19 | 51 | 55 | 53 |
| 21 | Wimbledon | 46 | 14 | 11 | 21 | 61 | 75 | 53 |
| 22 | Swindon | 46 | 13 | 13 | 20 | 55 | 71 | 52 |
| 23 | Bristol City | 46 | 11 | 13 | 22 | 40 | 65 | 46 |
| 24 | Chester | 46 | 7 | 11 | 28 | 36 | 78 | 32 |

## F.A.Cup

| | | | | | |
|---|---|---|---|---|---|
| 1 | 21 Nov | Colchester United | 0-2 | 3535 | |

(Back) Goodfellow (Asst.Man.), Gwyther, Tynan, Davies, Waddle, Kendall, Walden, Lees, Relish, Williams (Trainer).
(Front) Moore, Vaughan, Lowndes, Oakes, Ashurst (Manager), Bishop, Elsey, Bailey, Goddard.

# SEASON 1982-83    Division 3

| | Date | Opposition | Res. | Att. | Goalscorers |
|---|---|---|---|---|---|
| 1 | 28 Aug | Doncaster Rovers | 0-0 | 3471 | |
| 2 | 4 Sep | CHESTERFIELD | 1-0 | 3464 | Tynan |
| 3 | 7 | PLYMOUTH ARGYLE | 2-2 | 3741 | Tynan, Gwyther |
| 4 | 11 | Bradford City | 2-4 | 4793 | Aldridge, Tynan |
| 5 | 18 | HUDDERSFIELD TOWN | 2-1 | 3536 | Aldridge(2) |
| 6 | 25 | Portsmouth | 2-1 | 10833 | Vaughan, Aldridge |
| 7 | 28 | Brentford | 0-2 | 5706 | |
| 8 | 2 Oct | LINCOLN CITY | 1-0 | 3749 | Tynan |
| 9 | 9 | BRISTOL ROVERS | 2-0 | 5912 | Vaughan, Tynan |
| 10 | 16 | Orient | 5-1 | 2040 | Tynan(2), Elasey, Aldridge, Lowndes |
| 11 | 19 | Preston North End | 0-0 | 3747 | |
| 12 | 23 | SOUTHEND UNITED | 1-1 | 4338 | Oakes |
| 13 | 30 | Wigan Athletic | 1-0 | 4108 | Aldridge |
| 14 | 2 Nov | SHEFFIELD UNITED | 3-1 | 5017 | Aldridge, West(og), Tynan |
| 15 | 6 | Reading | 2-4 | 3058 | Bailey, Tynan |
| 16 | 13 | AFC BOURNEMOUTH | 5-1 | 4071 | Aldridge(3), Vaughan, Lowndes |
| 17 | 27 | Wrexham | 0-1 | 3246 | |
| 18 | 4 Dec | GILLINGHAM | 2-1 | 3727 | Elsey, Lowndes |
| 19 | 18 | WALSALL | 1-1 | 3572 | Vaughan |
| 20 | 27 | Cardiff City | 2-3 | 15972 | Bailey, Vaughan |
| 21 | 28 | OXFORD UNITED | 1-2 | 5836 | Tynan |
| 22 | 1 Jan | Exeetr City | 1-0 | 3505 | Elsey |
| 23 | 3 | MILLWALL | 2-2 | 4017 | Gwyther, Elsey |
| 24 | 15 | DONCASTER ROVERS | 1-2 | 3482 | Aldridge |
| 25 | 22 | Plymouth Argyle | 4-2 | 4287 | Tynan(2), Elsey, Lowndes |
| 26 | 29 | BRADFORD CITY | 1-1 | 3398 | Bailey |
| 27 | 1 Feb | Chesterfield | 1-3 | 1645 | Tynan |
| 28 | 6 | BRENTFORD | 0-0 | 3401 | |
| 29 | 15 | PRESTON NORTH END | 3-0 | 2317 | Tynan(2), Relish |
| 30 | 19 | Bristol Rovers | 3-1 | 6812 | Tynan(2), Aldridge |
| 31 | 26 | ORIENT | 4-1 | 3202 | Lowndes(3), Aldridge |
| 32 | 1 Mar | Sheffield United | 0-2 | 8704 | |
| 33 | 4 | Southend United | 4-1 | 2476 | Bailey, Vaughan, Lowndes, Aldridge |
| 34 | 12 | WIGAN ATHLETIC | 1-0 | 3647 | Aldridge |
| 35 | 19 | READING | 1-0 | 3588 | Tynan |
| 36 | 23 | Lincoln City | 4-1 | 4742 | Tynan(2), Lowndes(2) |
| 37 | 26 | AFC Bournemouth | 1-0 | 9121 | Vaughan |
| 38 | 2 Apr | Oxford United | 3-0 | 6640 | Tynan, Lowndes, Aldridge |
| 39 | 4 | CARDIFF CITY | 1-0 | 16052 | Relish |
| 40 | 9 | Gillingham | 0-2 | 4265 | |
| 41 | 16 | PORTSMOUTH | 0-3 | 10419 | |
| 42 | 23 | Walsall | 1-2 | 5141 | Tynan |
| 43 | 30 | WREXHAM | 4-0 | 4344 | Tynan(3), Lowndes |
| 44 | 2 May | Millwall | 0-3 | 5515 | |
| 45 | 7 | Huddersfield Town | 0-1 | 16509 | |
| 46 | 14 | EXETER CITY | 1-1 | 3520 | Williams |

| Player | League | | F.A.Cup | | Total | |
|---|---|---|---|---|---|---|
| | App | Gls. | App | Gls. | App | Gls. |
| Aldridge J.W. | 41 | 16 | 5 | 2 | 53+2 | 20 |
| Bailey N. | 37+3 | 4 | 5 | 0 | 51+3 | 7 |
| Boyle T.D.J. | 29+1 | 0 | 3 | 0 | 34+1 | 0 |
| Davies G. | 7+2 | 0 | 1+1 | 0 | 13+3 | 0 |
| Elsey K.W. | 41+1 | 5 | 5 | 0 | 54+1 | 7 |
| Flemming W. | – | – | – | – | 0+2 | 0 |
| Gwyther D. | 6+13 | 2 | 2+2 | 1 | 11+19 | 5 |
| Johnson J.D. | – | – | – | – | 1 | 0 |
| Jones V. | 43 | 0 | 5 | 0 | 56 | 0 |
| Kendall M. | 44 | 0 | 5 | 0 | 59 | 0 |
| Lowndes S.R. | 43 | 12 | 3 | 0 | 55 | 15 |
| Moore K.J. | 7+7 | 0 | 4+1 | 0 | 13+8 | 0 |
| Oakes K.B. | 28 | 1 | 1 | 0 | 33 | 2 |
| Plumley G.E. | 2 | 0 | – | – | 2 | 0 |
| Pulis R. | 0+1 | 0 | – | – | 1+1 | 0 |
| Reid A.J. | 2+2 | 0 | – | – | 2+2 | 0 |
| Relish J.D. | 43 | 2 | 3 | 0 | 54 | 2 |
| Stroud K.A. | 43 | 0 | 3 | 0 | 54 | 0 |
| Thorpe P. | – | – | – | – | 2+1 | 0 |
| Tynan T.E. | 46 | 25 | 5 | 4 | 61 | 33 |
| Vaughan N.M. | 43 | 7 | 5 | 0 | 58 | 10 |
| Williams C. | 1 | 1 | – | – | 4+1 | 2 |
| Own Goals | 1 | | | | | 1 |

| | | P | W | D | L | F | A | Pts |
|---|---|---|---|---|---|---|---|---|
| 1 | Portsmouth | 46 | 27 | 10 | 9 | 74 | 41 | 91 |
| 2 | Cardiff | 46 | 25 | 11 | 10 | 76 | 50 | 86 |
| 3 | Huddersfield | 46 | 23 | 13 | 10 | 84 | 49 | 82 |
| 4 | Newport | 46 | 23 | 9 | 14 | 76 | 54 | 78 |
| 5 | Oxford | 46 | 22 | 12 | 12 | 71 | 53 | 78 |
| 6 | Lincoln | 46 | 23 | 7 | 16 | 77 | 51 | 76 |
| 8 | Bristol Rovers | 46 | 22 | 9 | 15 | 84 | 57 | 75 |
| 8 | Plymouth | 46 | 19 | 8 | 19 | 61 | 66 | 65 |
| 9 | Brentford | 46 | 18 | 10 | 18 | 88 | 77 | 64 |
| 10 | Walsall | 46 | 17 | 13 | 16 | 64 | 63 | 64 |
| 11 | Sheff United | 46 | 19 | 7 | 20 | 62 | 64 | 64 |
| 12 | Bradford City | 46 | 16 | 13 | 17 | 68 | 69 | 61 |
| 13 | Gillingham | 46 | 16 | 13 | 17 | 58 | 59 | 61 |
| 14 | Bournemouth | 46 | 16 | 13 | 17 | 59 | 68 | 61 |
| 15 | Southend | 46 | 15 | 14 | 17 | 66 | 65 | 59 |
| 16 | Preston | 46 | 15 | 13 | 18 | 60 | 69 | 58 |
| 17 | Millwall | 46 | 14 | 13 | 19 | 64 | 78 | 55 |
| 18 | Wigan | 46 | 15 | 9 | 22 | 60 | 72 | 54 |
| 19 | Exeter | 46 | 14 | 12 | 20 | 81 | 104 | 54 |
| 20 | Orient | 46 | 15 | 9 | 22 | 64 | 88 | 54 |
| 21 | Reading | 46 | 12 | 17 | 17 | 63 | 80 | 53 |
| 22 | Wrexham | 46 | 12 | 15 | 19 | 57 | 76 | 51 |
| 23 | Doncaster | 46 | 9 | 11 | 26 | 57 | 97 | 38 |
| 24 | Chesterfield | 46 | 8 | 13 | 25 | 44 | 68 | 37 |

## F.A.Cup

| | | Date | Opposition | Res. | Att. | Goalscorers |
|---|---|---|---|---|---|---|
| 1 | | 20 Nov | Enfield | 0-0 | 2541 | |
| 1R | | 23 | ENFIELD | 4-2 | 4014 | Tynan(3), Aldridge |
| 2 | | 11 Dec | ORIENT | 1-0 | 4013 | Tynan |
| 3 | | 8 Jan | EVERTON | 1-1 | 9527 | Gwyther |
| 3R | | 11 | Everton | 1-2 | 18565 | Aldridge |

(Back) Jones, Kendall, Elsey. (Middle) Addison (Manager), Gwyther, Johnson, Aldridge, Bailey, Vaughan, Smith (Asst.Man.), Williams (Trainer). (Front) Bishop, Lowndes, Tynan, Oakes, Davies, Relish.

# SEASON 1983-84    Division 3

| | Date | Opposition | Res. | Att. | Goalscorers |
|---|---|---|---|---|---|
| 1 | 27 Aug | BRISTOL ROVERS | 2-1 | 5015 | Vaughan, Aldridge |
| 2 | 3 Sep | Wimbledon | 0-6 | 2007 | |
| 3 | 6 | Burnley | 0-2 | 6719 | |
| 4 | 10 | BRADFORD CITY | 4-3 | 2462 | Vaughan(2), Martinez, Aldridge |
| 5 | 17 | Walsall | 2-3 | 2818 | Vaughan, Elsey |
| 6 | 24 | SCUNTHORPE UNITED | 1-1 | 2679 | Vaughan |
| 7 | 27 | PRESTON NORTH END | 1-1 | 2542 | Aldridge |
| 8 | 1 Oct | Rotherham United | 1-0 | 4099 | Aldridge |
| 9 | 8 | ORIENT | 0-0 | 3213 | |
| 10 | 15 | Bolton Wanderers | 3-2 | 4928 | Farnworth(og), Reid, Carter |
| 11 | 18 | LINCOLN CITY | 1-0 | 3450 | Aldridge |
| 12 | 22 | Exeter City | 2-1 | 3970 | Aldridge(2) |
| 13 | 29 | PORT VALE | 2-1 | 3829 | Aldridge, Reid |
| 14 | 1 Nov | Millwall | 1-1 | 4352 | Aldirdge |
| 15 | 5 | SOUTHEND UNITED | 1-1 | 3769 | Aldridge |
| 16 | 12 | Hull City | 0-0 | 7853 | |
| 17 | 26 | Oxford United | 0-2 | 6330 | |
| 18 | 3 Dec | WIGAN ATHLETIC | 5-3 | 3196 | Aldridge(3), Reid, Lewis |
| 19 | 17 | SHEFFIELD UNITED | 0-2 | 4295 | |
| 20 | 26 | AFC Bournemouth | 1-1 | 7220 | Chamberlain |
| 21 | 27 | PLYMOUTH ARGYLE | 2-0 | 5154 | Aldridge(2) |
| 22 | 31 | Brentford | 0-2 | 4631 | |
| 23 | 14 Jan | Bristol Rovers | 0-4 | 6041 | |
| 24 | 22 | WALSALL | 3-1 | 4374 | Aldridge(2), Chamberlain |
| 25 | 4 Feb | ROTHERHAM UNITED | 1-4 | 2391 | Aldridge |
| 26 | 10 | Scunthorpe United | 3-3 | 2879 | Lilygreen, V.Jones, Williams |
| 27 | 14 | MILLWALL | 1-1 | 2070 | Aldridge |
| 28 | 18 | Port Vale | 2-4 | 3437 | V.Jones, Lilygreen |
| 29 | 25 | EXETER CITY | 1-0 | 2465 | Aldridge |
| 30 | 3 Mar | Lincoln City | 3-2 | 1780 | Reid(2), Oakes |
| 31 | 6 | WIMBLEDON | 1-1 | 2538 | Pratt |
| 32 | 10 | HULL CITY | 1-1 | 2813 | V.Jones |
| 33 | 17 | Orient | 2-2 | 2355 | Carter, Boyle |
| 34 | 24 | BOLTON WANDERERS | 2-3 | 2436 | Micallef, Lilygreen |
| 35 | 27 | GILLINGHAM | 1-0 | 1849 | Carter |
| 36 | 30 | Preston North End | 0-2 | 3534 | |
| 37 | 7 Apr | BURNLEY | 1-0 | 2306 | V.Jones |
| 38 | 14 | Wigan Athletic | 0-1 | 2903 | |
| 39 | 20 | Plymouth Argyle | 1-0 | 7654 | Green |
| 40 | 21 | AFC BOURNEMOUTH | 2-1 | 2356 | Reid, Green |
| 41 | 25 | Bradford City | 0-1 | 3347 | |
| 42 | 28 | OXFORD UNITED | 1-1 | 4562 | Carter |
| 43 | 30 | Southend United | 1-3 | 2108 | Pratt |
| 44 | 5 May | Gillingham | 1-4 | 3073 | Micallef |
| 45 | 7 | BRENTFORD | 1-1 | 2154 | Lilygreen |
| 46 | 12 | Sheffield United | 0-2 | 16700 | |

## F.A.Cup

| | Date | Opposition | Res. | Att. | Goalscorers |
|---|---|---|---|---|---|
| 1 | 20 Nov | Poole Town | 0-0 | 4521 | |
| 1R | 22 | POOLE TOWN | 3-1 | 3090 | Oakes, Aldridge, Lewis |
| 2 | 10 Dec | Harrow Borough | 3-1 | 2500 | Martinez(2), Chamberlain |
| 3 | 7 Jan | Plymouth Argyle | 2-2 | 6789 | Aldridge(2) |
| 3R | 10 | PLYMOUTH ARGYLE | 0-1 | 5459 | |

| Player | League | | F.A.Cup | | Total | |
|---|---|---|---|---|---|---|
| | App | Gls. | App | Gls. | App | Gls. |
| Aldridge J.W. | 28 | 20 | 5 | 3 | 37 | 27 |
| Bailey N. | 5 | 0 | – | – | 7 | 0 |
| Boyle T.D.J. | 45 | 1 | 5 | 0 | 56 | 3 |
| Carter R.W. | 37+2 | 4 | 5 | 0 | 46+2 | 5 |
| Chamberlain N.P. | 6 | 2 | 3 | 1 | 9 | 3 |
| Elsey K.W. | 7 | 1 | – | – | 9 | 1 |
| Green P. | 8+1 | 2 | – | – | 8+1 | 2 |
| Jones G.A. | 3 | 0 | – | – | 3 | 0 |
| Jones L. | 32 | 0 | 2 | 0 | 37 | 0 |
| Jones R. | – | – | – | – | 1 | 1 |
| Jones V. | 24+1 | 4 | 3 | 0 | 31+1 | 4 |
| Kendall M. | 43 | 0 | 5 | 0 | 54 | 0 |
| Layton J.H. | 1 | 0 | – | – | 1 | 0 |
| Lewis J. | 25 | 1 | 5 | 1 | 33 | 2 |
| Lilygreen C. | 15+7 | 4 | – | – | 18+7 | 5 |
| Martinez E. | 18+2 | 1 | 2+1 | 2 | 24+3 | 3 |
| Mather S. | 0+1 | 0 | – | – | 0+1 | 0 |
| Matthewson T. | 30+2 | 0 | 5 | 0 | 38+2 | 0 |
| Micallef C. | 22+2 | 2 | 4 | 0 | 27+3 | 2 |
| Morse R. | 0+1 | 0 | – | – | 0+1 | 0 |
| Oakes K.B. | 37 | 1 | 3 | 1 | 44 | 2 |
| Pratt M.W. | 3+3 | 2 | – | – | 4+3 | 2 |
| Randell C.W. | 15 | 0 | – | – | 15 | 0 |
| Reid A.J. | 37 | 6 | 5 | 0 | 47 | 7 |
| Relish J.D. | 30+4 | 0 | 3 | 0 | 36+5 | 2 |
| Stroud K.A. | 4+1 | 0 | – | – | 4+2 | 0 |
| Vaughan N.M. | 7 | 5 | – | – | 9 | 5 |
| Williams C. | 15+7 | 1 | – | – | 18+8 | 1 |
| Woodruff R.J. | 9+1 | 0 | | 0 | 11+3 | 1 |
| Own Goals | | 1 | | | | 1 |

| | | P | W | D | L | F | A | Pts |
|---|---|---|---|---|---|---|---|---|
| 1 | Oxford | 46 | 28 | 11 | 7 | 91 | 50 | 95 |
| 2 | Wimbledon | 46 | 26 | 9 | 11 | 97 | 76 | 87 |
| 3 | Sheff United | 46 | 24 | 11 | 11 | 86 | 53 | 83 |
| 4 | Hull | 46 | 23 | 14 | 9 | 71 | 38 | 83 |
| 5 | Bristol Rovers | 46 | 22 | 13 | 11 | 68 | 54 | 79 |
| 6 | Walsall | 46 | 22 | 9 | 15 | 68 | 61 | 75 |
| 7 | Bradford | 46 | 20 | 11 | 15 | 73 | 65 | 71 |
| 8 | Gillingham | 46 | 20 | 10 | 16 | 74 | 69 | 70 |
| 9 | Millwall | 46 | 18 | 13 | 15 | 71 | 65 | 67 |
| 10 | Bolton | 46 | 18 | 10 | 18 | 56 | 60 | 64 |
| 11 | Orient | 46 | 18 | 9 | 19 | 71 | 81 | 63 |
| 12 | Burnley | 46 | 16 | 14 | 16 | 76 | 61 | 62 |
| 13 | Newport | 46 | 16 | 14 | 16 | 58 | 75 | 62 |
| 14 | Lincoln | 46 | 17 | 10 | 19 | 59 | 62 | 61 |
| 15 | Wigan | 46 | 16 | 13 | 17 | 46 | 56 | 61 |
| 16 | Preston | 46 | 15 | 11 | 20 | 66 | 66 | 56 |
| 17 | Bournemouth | 46 | 16 | 7 | 23 | 63 | 73 | 55 |
| 18 | Rotherham | 46 | 15 | 9 | 22 | 57 | 64 | 54 |
| 19 | Plymouth | 46 | 13 | 12 | 21 | 56 | 62 | 51 |
| 20 | Brentford | 46 | 11 | 16 | 19 | 69 | 79 | 49 |
| 21 | Scunthorpe | 46 | 9 | 19 | 18 | 54 | 73 | 46 |
| 22 | Southend | 46 | 10 | 14 | 22 | 55 | 76 | 44 |
| 23 | Port Vale | 46 | 11 | 10 | 25 | 51 | 83 | 43 |
| 24 | Exeter | 46 | 6 | 15 | 25 | 50 | 84 | 33 |

(Back) Vaughan, Boyle, V.Jones, Relish, Stroud, Reid.
(Middle) Lilyman, Mather, Morse, Kendall, Welch, Pratt, C.Williams.
(Front) Aldridge, Pulis, Lowndes, Oakes, Woodruff, Elsey, Bailey.

# SEASON 1984-85    Division 3

| | Date | Opposition | Res. | Att. | Goalscorers |
|---|---|---|---|---|---|
| 1 | 25 Aug | Gillingham | 1-1 | 3422 | Reid |
| 2 | 1 Sep | BRISTOL CITY | 0-0 | 5079 | |
| 3 | 8 | York City | 0-2 | 4194 | |
| 4 | 18 | AFC BOURNEMOUTH | 1-1 | 2338 | L.Jones |
| 5 | 22 | Bradford City | 0-1 | 3514 | |
| 6 | 29 | MILLWALL | 3-2 | 2507 | Boyle, Carter, Kent |
| 7 | 2 Oct | Burnley | 0-2 | 3616 | |
| 8 | 6 | Wigan Athletic | 1-1 | 2601 | D.Giles |
| 9 | 13 | SWANSEA CITY | 2-0 | 5006 | Lewis, Reid |
| 10 | 20 | ORIENT | 2-0 | 2301 | L.Jones(2) |
| 11 | 23 | Rotherham United | 0-1 | 4297 | |
| 12 | 27 | Walsall | 1-1 | 4694 | Lewis |
| 13 | 3 Nov | CAMBRIDGE UNITED | 1-2 | 2161 | Carter |
| 14 | 7 | Lincoln City | 2-2 | 2331 | Boyle, Thompson(og) |
| 15 | 10 | BOLTON WANDERERS | 3-2 | 2073 | Boyle, Chamberlain, Cooper |
| 16 | 24 | Hull City | 0-2 | 6039 | |
| 17 | 27 | BRENTFORD | 2-0 | 1591 | Reid, Cooper |
| 18 | 1 Dec | DONCASTER ROVERS | 2-1 | 2016 | Carter, Kellow |
| 19 | 8 | ROTHERHAM UNITED | 0-2 | 2012 | |
| 20 | 15 | Bristol Rovers | 0-2 | 5405 | |
| 21 | 22 | Derby County | 3-3 | 11437 | Chamberlain(3) |
| 22 | 26 | READING | 1-2 | 3061 | Chamberlain |
| 23 | 29 | PLYMOUTH ARGYLE | 1-0 | 3003 | Chamberlain |
| 24 | 1 Jan | Preston North End | 1-1 | 3375 | Carter |
| 25 | 26 | Brentford | 5-2 | 3321 | Cooper(4), Kellow |
| 26 | 2 Feb | Millwall | 0-2 | 4009 | |
| 27 | 23 | Cambridge United | 2-1 | 1622 | Chamberlain(2) |
| 28 | 2 Mar | WALSALL | 1-2 | 2098 | Kellow |
| 29 | 9 | Orient | 1-1 | 2307 | Kellow |
| 30 | 12 | GILLINGHAM | 0-3 | 2129 | |
| 31 | 17 | Swansea City | 3-0 | 5160 | Chamberlain, Cooper, L.Jones |
| 32 | 20 | TORK CITY | 1-1 | 1535 | Kellow |
| 33 | 23 | WIGAN ATHLETIC | 1-1 | 1626 | Chamberlain |
| 34 | 30 | LINCOLN CITY | 2-1 | 1307 | Kellow, Reid |
| 35 | 2 Apr | BURNLEY | 2-1 | 1689 | Cooper(2) |
| 36 | 6 | Reading | 1-0 | 3591 | Chamberlain |
| 37 | 8 | PRESTON NORTH END | 3-3 | 2099 | Reid(2), Cooper |
| 38 | 13 | Bolton Wanderers | 1-3 | 4011 | Cooper |
| 39 | 16 | BRADFORD CITY | 0-1 | 2006 | |
| 40 | 20 | HULL CITY | 0-1 | 1885 | |
| 41 | 27 | Doncaster Rovers | 2-3 | 1883 | Chamberlain, L.Jones |
| 42 | 30 | Bristol City | 1-2 | 5952 | Chamberlain |
| 43 | 4 May | BRISTOL ROVERS | 1-1 | 2302 | Kellow |
| 44 | 6 | Plymouth Argyle | 0-1 | 5079 | |
| 45 | 11 | DERBY COUNTY | 1-3 | 4003 | Kellow |
| 46 | 13 | AFC Bournemouth | 0-3 | 2511 | |

## F.A.Cup

| | Date | | Res. | Att. | |
|---|---|---|---|---|---|
| 1 | 17 Nov | ALDERSHOT | 1-1 | 2452 | Pulis |
| 1R | 20 | Aldershot | 0-4 | 3807 | |

| Player | League | | F.A.Cup | | Total | |
|---|---|---|---|---|---|---|
| | App | Gls. | App | Gls. | App | Gls. |
| Boyle T.D.J. | 46 | 3 | 2 | 0 | 60 | 5 |
| Carter R.W. | 29 | 4 | 2 | 0 | 40 | 5 |
| Chamberlain N.P. | 39+2 | 13 | 2 | 0 | 52+2 | 17 |
| Cooper S.B. | 38 | 11 | 2 | 0 | 50 | 12 |
| Emmanuel J.G. | 12 | 0 | - | - | 16 | 0 |
| Giles D.C. | 28+4 | 1 | 2 | 0 | 38+5 | 1 |
| Giles P.A. | 0+1 | 0 | - | - | 1+1 | 0 |
| Giles P. | 3+4 | 0 | - | - | 4+5 | 0 |
| Gwyther D. | 1+1 | 0 | - | - | 1+1 | 0 |
| Jones G.A. | - | - | - | - | 1 | 0 |
| Jones L. | 44 | 5 | 2 | 0 | 58 | 9 |
| Kellow A. | 17+3 | 8 | 2 | 0 | 20+4 | 9 |
| Kendall M. | 44 | 0 | 2 | 0 | 58 | 0 |
| Kent K.J. | 23+10 | 1 | 0+1 | 0 | 29+14 | 2 |
| King S.A. | 1 | 0 | - | - | 1 | 0 |
| Lewis J. | 33 | 2 | 2 | 0 | 43 | 3 |
| Lilygreen C. | 3+6 | 0 | - | - | 4+10 | 0 |
| Matthewson T. | 43 | 0 | 2 | 0 | 57 | 1 |
| Plumley G.E. | 2 | 0 | - | - | 2 | 0 |
| Pratt M.W. | 1+2 | 0 | - | - | 2+5 | 0 |
| Pulis A.R. | 37 | 0 | 2 | 1 | 50 | 2 |
| Reid A.J. | 35 | 6 | 2 | 0 | 49 | 6 |
| Relish J.D. | 18 | 0 | - | - | 24+2 | 0 |
| Saxby M.W. | 6 | 0 | - | - | 8 | 0 |
| Tyler S. | 0+2 | 0 | - | - | 0+2 | 0 |
| Williams C. | 3+1 | 0 | - | - | | 0 |
| Own Goals | | 1 | | | | 1 |

| | | P | W | D | L | F | A | Pts |
|---|---|---|---|---|---|---|---|---|
| 1 | Bradford | 46 | 28 | 10 | 8 | 77 | 45 | 94 |
| 2 | Millwall | 46 | 26 | 12 | 8 | 83 | 42 | 90 |
| 3 | Hull City | 46 | 25 | 12 | 9 | 88 | 49 | 87 |
| 4 | Gillingham | 46 | 25 | 8 | 13 | 80 | 62 | 83 |
| 5 | Bristol City | 46 | 24 | 9 | 13 | 74 | 47 | 81 |
| 6 | Bristol Rovers | 46 | 21 | 12 | 13 | 66 | 48 | 75 |
| 7 | Derby | 46 | 19 | 13 | 14 | 65 | 54 | 70 |
| 8 | York | 46 | 20 | 9 | 17 | 70 | 57 | 69 |
| 9 | Reading | 46 | 19 | 12 | 15 | 68 | 62 | 69 |
| 10 | Bournemouth | 46 | 19 | 11 | 16 | 57 | 46 | 68 |
| 11 | Walsall | 46 | 18 | 13 | 15 | 58 | 52 | 67 |
| 12 | Rotherham | 46 | 18 | 11 | 17 | 55 | 55 | 65 |
| 13 | Brentford | 46 | 16 | 14 | 16 | 62 | 64 | 62 |
| 14 | Doncaster | 46 | 17 | 8 | 21 | 72 | 74 | 59 |
| 15 | Plymouth | 46 | 15 | 14 | 17 | 62 | 65 | 59 |
| 16 | Wigan | 46 | 15 | 14 | 17 | 60 | 64 | 59 |
| 17 | Bolton | 46 | 16 | 6 | 24 | 69 | 75 | 54 |
| 18 | Newport | 46 | 13 | 13 | 20 | 55 | 67 | 52 |
| 19 | Lincoln | 46 | 11 | 18 | 17 | 50 | 51 | 51 |
| 20 | Swansea | 46 | 12 | 11 | 23 | 53 | 80 | 47 |
| 21 | Burnley | 46 | 11 | 13 | 22 | 60 | 73 | 46 |
| 22 | Orient | 46 | 11 | 13 | 22 | 51 | 76 | 46 |
| 23 | Preston | 46 | 13 | 7 | 26 | 51 | 100 | 46 |
| 24 | Cambridge | 46 | 4 | 9 | 33 | 37 | 95 | 21 |

(Back) Smith (Asst.Man.), Emmanuel, Pulis, Lewis, Carter, Kendall, Matthewson, Saxby, Chamberlain, Green, Williams (Trainer/Coach)
(Front) Lilygreen, Pratt, Relish, Boyle, Addison (Manager), L.Jones, Kent, Williams, Reid.

# SEASON 1985-86     Division 3

| | Date | Opposition | Res. | Att. | Goalscorers |
|---|---|---|---|---|---|
| 1 | 17 Aug | DONCASTER ROVERS | 2-2 | 2375 | Boyle, Carter |
| 2 | 24 | Wolverhampton W. | 2-1 | 6073 | Miles(2) |
| 3 | 26 | CARDIFF CITY | 1-2 | 5027 | Carter |
| 4 | 31 | AFC Bournemouth | 1-0 | 3381 | Carter |
| 5 | 7 Sep | BRISTOL ROVERS | 3-0 | 2775 | James, Staniforth, Dowman |
| 6 | 14 | Plymouth Argyle | 0-2 | 3686 | |
| 7 | 17 | Swansea City | 1-1 | 5534 | Boyle |
| 8 | 21 | BOLTON WANDERERS | 0-1 | 2212 | |
| 9 | 28 | Walsall | 0-2 | 4586 | |
| 10 | 1 Oct | BRISTOL CITY | 1-1 | 3776 | Lewis |
| 11 | 5 | Lincoln City | 1-1 | 1989 | Staniforth |
| 12 | 12 | READING | 0-2 | 6449 | |
| 13 | 19 | Brentford | 0-0 | 3646 | |
| 14 | 22 | ROTHERHAM UNITED | 0-0 | 1817 | |
| 15 | 26 | Wigan Athletic | 0-0 | 3719 | |
| 16 | 2 Nov | GILLINGHAM | 1-1 | 1970 | P.Jones |
| 17 | 6 | YORK CITY | 1-1 | 1529 | Senior(og) |
| 18 | 9 | Chesterfield | 1-3 | 2420 | Gill |
| 19 | 23 | NOTTS COUNTY | 1-2 | 1946 | Carter |
| 20 | 14 Dec | BLACKPOOL | 1-1 | 1991 | Berry |
| 21 | 21 | WOLVERHAMPTON W. | 3-1 | 2222 | Mardenborough(2), Boyle |
| 22 | 26 | Bury | 1-1 | 3013 | Mardenborough |
| 23 | 28 | Cardiff City | 1-1 | 7450 | Staniforth |
| 24 | 11 Jan | AFC BOURNEMOUTH | 2-1 | 2333 | Boyle, Staniforth |
| 25 | 18 | Doncaster Rovers | 1-1 | 2336 | Relish |
| 26 | 25 | PLYMOUTH ARGYLE | 3-1 | 3007 | Staniforth, Berry, Hodges(og) |
| 27 | 1 Feb | Bristol Rovers | 0-2 | 3284 | |
| 28 | 4 | Rotherham United | 0-0 | 2975 | |
| 29 | 16 | SWANSEA CITY | 2-0 | 2805 | Relish, Mayes |
| 30 | 22 | Bolton Wanderers | 0-4 | 4063 | |
| 31 | 28 | WALSALL | 1-5 | 1530 | Boyle |
| 32 | 4 Mar | Bristol City | 1-3 | 4395 | Mardenborough |
| 33 | 8 | LINCOLN CITY | 1-2 | 1540 | James |
| 34 | 11 | BRENTFORD | 1-2 | 1508 | Berry |
| 35 | 15 | Reading | 0-2 | 4783 | |
| 36 | 18 | Darlington | 2-3 | 2508 | Carter, Latchford |
| 37 | 22 | WIGAN ATHLETIC | 3-4 | 1700 | Latchford(2), Mardenborough |
| 38 | 29 | Derby County | 1-1 | 11251 | Carter |
| 39 | 31 | BURY | 1-0 | 1983 | Staniforth |
| 40 | 5 Apr | York City | 1-3 | 3038 | Lewis |
| 41 | 12 | CHESTERFIELD | 3-3 | 1940 | Carter, Latchford, Staniforth |
| 42 | 19 | Notts County | 2-1 | 3279 | Staniforth, Mardenborough |
| 43 | 22 | DERBY COUNTY | 1-1 | 3049 | Boyle |
| 44 | 26 | DARLINGTON | 3-0 | 2848 | Mardenborough, Latchford, Staniforth |
| 45 | 29 | Gillingham | 1-0 | 2566 | L.Jones |
| 46 | 3 May | Blackpool | 0-0 | 3407 | |

## F.A.Cup

| | Date | Opposition | Res. | Att. | Goalscorers |
|---|---|---|---|---|---|
| 1 | 16 Nov | Southend United | 1-0 | 3343 | Mardenborough |
| 2 | 7 Dec | TORQUAY UNITED | 1-1 | 2386 | Berry |
| 2R | 10 | Torquay United | 3-2 | 1937 | P.Jones. Boyle, James |
| 3 | 4 Jan | Sunderland | 0-2 | 12352 | |

| Player | League | | F.A.Cup | | Total | |
|---|---|---|---|---|---|---|
| | App | Gls. | App | Gls. | App | Gls. |
| Berry S.A. | 26 | 3 | 3 | 1 | 33 | 5 |
| Boyle T.D.J. | 46 | 6 | 4 | 1 | 57 | 7 |
| Carter R.W. | 42 | 7 | 4 | 0 | 52+1 | 7 |
| Dowman S.J. | 9 | 1 | – | – | 11 | 1 |
| Giles D.C. | – | – | – | – | 1 | 0 |
| Gill K.J. | 13+6 | 1 | – | – | 17+7 | 1 |
| Hamer K. | 0+1 | 0 | – | – | 0+1 | 0 |
| James L. | 21+10 | 2 | 3+1 | 1 | 28+11 | 3 |
| Jones L. | 31 | 1 | 4 | 0 | 40 | 3 |
| Jones P. | 36 | 1 | 4 | 1 | 45 | 2 |
| Kendall M. | 46 | 0 | 4 | 0 | 56 | 0 |
| Latchford R.D. | 20 | 5 | – | – | 22 | 5 |
| Lewis J. | 44 | 2 | 4 | 0 | 54 | 2 |
| Mardenborough S.A. | 30+8 | 7 | 3+1 | 1 | 38+11 | 11 |
| Mayes A.K. | 3 | 1 | – | – | 3 | 1 |
| McManus S.J. | 4+1 | 0 | – | – | 4+1 | 0 |
| Miles A. | 3+1 | 2 | – | – | 4+2 | 2 |
| Moore J. | 2 | 0 | 2 | 0 | 4 | 0 |
| Peacock D. | 14+5 | 0 | 1 | 0 | 16+6 | 0 |
| Plumley G.E. | – | – | – | – | 1 | 0 |
| Pulis A.R. | 38+2 | 0 | 3 | 0 | 44+2 | 0 |
| Reck S.M. | 15 | 0 | 1 | 0 | 18 | 1 |
| Relish J. | 12+2 | 2 | 0+1 | 0 | 17+3 | 2 |
| Rogers G.R. | 6+1 | 0 | – | – | 7+1 | 0 |
| Staniforth G. | 45 | 9 | 4 | 0 | 55 | 9 |
| Tyler S. | 0+2 | 0 | – | – | | 0 |
| Own Goals | | 2 | | | | 3 |

```
                     P  W  D  L  F  A Pts
 1  Reading         46 29  7 10 67 50  94
 2  Plymouth        46 26  9 11 88 53  87
 3  Derby           46 23 15  8 80 41  84
 4  Wigan           46 23 14  9 82 48  83
 5  Gillingham      46 22 13 11 81 54  79
 6  Walsall         46 22  9 15 90 64  75
 7  York            46 20 11 15 77 58  71
 8  Notts County    46 19 14 13 71 60  71
 9  Bristol City    46 18 14 14 69 60  68
10  Brentford       46 18 12 16 58 61  66
11  Doncaster       46 16 16 14 45 52  64
12  Blackpool       46 17 12 17 66 55  63
13  Darlington      46 15 13 18 61 78  58
14  Rotherham       46 15 12 19 61 59  57
15  Bournemouth     46 15  9 22 65 72  54
16  Bristol Rovers  46 14 12 20 51 75  54
17  Chesterfield    46 13 14 19 61 64  53
18  Bolton          46 15  8 23 54 68  53
19  Newport         46 11 18 17 52 65  51
20  Bury            46 12 13 21 63 65  49
21  Lincoln         46 10 16 20 55 77  46
22  Cardiff         46 12  9 25 53 83  45
23  Wolves          46 11 10 25 57 98  43
24  Swansea         46 11 10 25 43 87  43
```

(Back) James, Rogers, Townsend, Dowman, Kendall, Matthewson, Carter, Pulis, Relish.
(Front) L.Jones, Lewis, Smith (Manager), Boyle, Williams (Director), Mardenborough, Staniforth.

# SEASON 1986-87     *Division 3*

| | Date | Opposition | Res. | Att. | Goalscorers |
|---|---|---|---|---|---|
| 1 | 23 Aug | GILLINGHAM | 1-2 | 2533 | Lewis |
| 2 | 30 | AFC Bournemouth | 1-2 | 2799 | Carter |
| 3 | 6 Sep | SWINDON TOWN | 2-2 | 3796 | Berry, Mardenborough |
| 4 | 13 | Wigan Athletic | 2-1 | 2004 | Lewis, Berry |
| 5 | 16 | Darlington | 3-1 | 1805 | Staniforth, Carter, Berry |
| 6 | 20 | DONCASTER ROVERS | 3-2 | 2382 | Carter, Lewis, Vinter |
| 7 | 27 | Bury | 3-4 | 2136 | Mardenborough, Carter, Vinter |
| 8 | 4 Oct | Brentford | 0-2 | 3231 | |
| 9 | 11 | CHESTER CITY | 2-2 | 2119 | Carter, Gibbins |
| 10 | 25 | Chesterfield | 2-3 | 1895 | Carter, Vinter |
| 11 | 28 | CARLISLE UNITED | 1-1 | 1540 | Gibbins |
| 12 | 1 Nov | NOTTS COUNTY | 1-1 | 1980 | Mardenborough |
| 13 | 4 | YORK CITY | 1-1 | 2079 | Vinter |
| 14 | 8 | Bolton Wanderers | 1-0 | 4530 | Millett |
| 15 | 22 | MIDDLESBROUGH | 0-1 | 2788 | |
| 16 | 25 | Mansfield Town | 0-1 | 2319 | |
| 17 | 29 | Blackpool | 1-1 | 3281 | Mardenborough |
| 18 | 2 Dec | BRISTOL CITY | 0-1 | 3205 | |
| 19 | 14 | Bristol Rovers | 2-2 | 2660 | Gibbins(2) |
| 20 | 20 | ROTHERHAM UNITED | 1-2 | 1760 | Dungworth(og) |
| 21 | 26 | Walsall | 0-2 | 6855 | |
| 22 | 27 | PORT VALE | 0-2 | 2103 | |
| 23 | 1 Jan | FULHAM | 0-0 | 2388 | |
| 24 | 3 | Middlesbrough | 0-2 | 9585 | |
| 25 | 25 | Swindon Town | 0-3 | 6620 | |
| 26 | 14 Feb | Doncaster Rovers | 1-0 | 1837 | Gibbins |
| 27 | 17 | Gillingham | 1-1 | 3542 | Gibbins |
| 28 | 21 | BURY | 2-2 | 1914 | Gibbins(2) |
| 29 | 24 | AFC BOURNEMOUTH | 0-1 | 2143 | |
| 30 | 28 | Carlisle United | 2-2 | 2192 | Gilligan, Vinter |
| 31 | 3 Mar | Notts County | 2-5 | 3814 | Staniforth, Vinter |
| 32 | 8 | CHESTERFIELD | 1-0 | 1567 | Carter |
| 33 | 14 | Bristol City | 0-4 | 9137 | |
| 34 | 17 | MANSFIELD TOWN | 0-3 | 1383 | |
| 35 | 21 | Chester City | 0-2 | 2561 | |
| 36 | 31 | WIGAN ATHLETIC | 1-2 | 1428 | Bailey |
| 37 | 4 Apr | BOLTON WANDERERS | 2-1 | 1193 | Taylor, Thackeray |
| 38 | 7 | BRENTFORD | 2-2 | 1596 | Giles, Staniforth |
| 39 | 11 | York City | 0-3 | 2202 | |
| 40 | 14 | DARLINGTON | 3-0 | 1315 | Lewis, Thackeray, Taylor |
| 41 | 18 | Fulham | 0-2 | 4234 | |
| 42 | 20 | WALSALL | 2-4 | 2003 | Taylor, Thackeray |
| 43 | 25 | Rotherham United | 1-3 | 2555 | Compton |
| 44 | 2 May | BLACKPOOL | 1-1 | 1247 | Staniforth |
| 45 | 4 | Port Vale | 1-6 | 2733 | Compton |
| 46 | 9 | BRISTOL ROVERS | 0-1 | 3165 | |

## F.A.Cup

| | Date | Opposition | Res. | Att. | Goalscorers |
|---|---|---|---|---|---|
| 1 | 15 Nov | Bromsgrove Rovers | 1-0 | 3440 | Vinter |
| 2 | 5 Dec | Fulham | 0-2 | 4052 | |

| Player | League | | | | F.A.Cup | | Total | |
|---|---|---|---|---|---|---|---|---|
| | App | Gls | App | Gls | App | Gls | App | Gls |
| Abbruzzese D.J. | 3 | 0 | – | – | | | 3 | 0 |
| Bailey N. | 7+1 | 1 | – | – | | | 8+1 | 1 |
| Berry S.A. | 34 | 3 | 2 | 0 | | | 45 | 3 |
| Blott J.P. | 1 | 0 | – | – | | | 1 | 0 |
| Bolton A.G. | 6+2 | 0 | – | – | | | 7+3 | 0 |
| Carter R.W. | 42 | 7 | 2 | 0 | | | 56 | 8 |
| Compton P.D. | 27 | 2 | – | – | | | 35 | 4 |
| Dillon A. | 10 | 0 | – | – | | | 15 | 0 |
| Freestone R. | 13 | 0 | – | – | | | 16 | 0 |
| Gibbins R.G. | 46 | 8 | 2 | 0 | | | 61 | 12 |
| Giles P.A. | 13 | 1 | – | – | | | 13 | 1 |
| Gilligan J.M. | 4+1 | 1 | – | – | | | 4+1 | 1 |
| Hamer K. | 3 | 0 | – | – | | | 4 | 0 |
| Jones L. | 34 | 0 | – | – | | | 47 | 0 |
| Jones P. | 18+1 | 0 | 2 | 0 | | | 25+1 | 1 |
| Jones R. | 3+7 | 0 | 0+1 | 0 | | | 8+8 | 0 |
| Kendall M. | 21 | 0 | 2 | 0 | | | 29 | 0 |
| Lewis J. | 43 | 4 | 2 | 0 | | | 59 | 4 |
| Mardenborough S.A. | 20+5 | 4 | 2 | 0 | | | 28+5 | 4 |
| Millett G. | 5+4 | 1 | – | – | | | 8+7 | 3 |
| Mills S.D. | 5+2 | 0 | – | – | | | 9+3 | 0 |
| Mullen J. | 19 | 0 | 2 | 0 | | | 27 | 0 |
| O'Shea T.J. | 10 | 0 | 2 | 0 | | | 13 | 0 |
| Peacock D. | 5 | 0 | – | – | | | 7 | 0 |
| Plumley G.E. | 1 | 0 | – | – | | | 1 | 0 |
| Relish J.D. | 3+1 | 0 | – | – | | | 5+1 | 0 |
| Sherlock S.G. | 16 | 0 | – | – | | | 21 | 0 |
| Staniforth G. | 40+3 | 4 | 2 | 0 | | | 54+4 | 4 |
| Sugrue P.A. | 1+1 | 0 | – | – | | | 1+1 | 0 |
| Taylor R. | 9 | 3 | – | – | | | 13 | 4 |
| Thackeray A.J. | 11 | 3 | – | – | | | 14 | 7 |
| Vinter M. | 30+2 | 6 | 2 | 1 | | | 42+2 | 11 |
| Withers D. | 3+1 | | – | | | | | |
| Own Goals | | 1 | | | | | | 2 |

### Bottom positions only

| | | | | | | | | |
|---|---|---|---|---|---|---|---|---|
| 7 | Notts County | 46 | 21 | 13 | 12 | 77 | 56 | 76 |
| 8 | Walsall | 46 | 22 | 9 | 15 | 80 | 67 | 75 |
| 9 | Blackpool | 46 | 16 | 16 | 14 | 74 | 59 | 64 |
| 10 | Mansfield | 46 | 15 | 16 | 15 | 52 | 55 | 61 |
| 11 | Brentford | 46 | 15 | 15 | 16 | 64 | 66 | 60 |
| 12 | Port Vale | 46 | 15 | 12 | 19 | 76 | 70 | 57 |
| 13 | Doncaster | 46 | 14 | 15 | 17 | 56 | 62 | 57 |
| 14 | Rotherham | 46 | 15 | 12 | 19 | 48 | 57 | 57 |
| 15 | Chester | 46 | 13 | 17 | 16 | 61 | 59 | 56 |
| 16 | Bury | 46 | 14 | 13 | 19 | 54 | 60 | 55 |
| 17 | Chesterfield | 46 | 13 | 15 | 18 | 56 | 69 | 54 |
| 18 | Fulham | 46 | 12 | 17 | 17 | 59 | 77 | 53 |
| 19 | Bristol Rovers | 46 | 13 | 12 | 21 | 49 | 75 | 51 |
| 20 | York | 46 | 12 | 13 | 21 | 55 | 79 | 49 |
| 21 | Bolton | 46 | 10 | 15 | 21 | 46 | 58 | 45 |
| 22 | Carlisle | 46 | 10 | 8 | 28 | 39 | 78 | 38 |
| 23 | Darlington | 46 | 7 | 16 | 23 | 45 | 77 | 37 |
| 24 | Newport | 46 | 8 | 13 | 25 | 49 | 86 | 37 |

(Back) Vinter, Berry, Mardenborough, Kendall, Freestone, Carter, Gibbins, L.Jones
(Front) Bolton, Peacock, Lewis, Mullen (Player/Man.), P.Jones, Mills, Staniforth.

# SEASON 1987-88    Division 4

| | Date | Opposition | Res. | Att. | Goalscorers |
|---|---|---|---|---|---|
| 1 | 15 Aug | Hartlepool United | 0-0 | 1926 | |
| 2 | 22 | BURNLEY | 0-1 | 2006 | |
| 3 | 29 | Exeter City | 0-3 | 2628 | |
| 4 | 31 | STOCKPORT COUNTY | 1-2 | 1626 | Giles |
| 5 | 5 Sep | Halifax Town | 1-3 | 1095 | Collins |
| 6 | 12 | TORQUAY UNITED | 3-1 | 1368 | Sherlock, Evans, Withers |
| 7 | 16 | Scarborough | 1-3 | 2345 | Evans |
| 8 | 19 | Scunthorpe United | 1-3 | 2004 | Tupling |
| 9 | 27 | HEREFORD UNITED | 0-0 | 1480 | |
| 10 | 29 | Leyton Orient | 1-4 | 3761 | Hodson |
| 11 | 3 Oct | COLCHESTER UNITED | 1-2 | 1200 | Thompson |
| 12 | 10 | Cambridge United | 0-4 | 1874 | |
| 13 | 17 | Swansea City | 2-1 | 3739 | Taylor(2) |
| 14 | 21 | Peterborough Utd | 0-3 | 3163 | |
| 15 | 24 | WREXHAM | 2-0 | 1470 | Thackeray, Preece |
| 16 | 31 | Wolverhampton W. | 1-2 | 6467 | Miller |
| 17 | 3 Nov | BOLTON WANDERERS | 0-1 | 1566 | |
| 18 | 7 | Carlisle United | 1-3 | 1766 | Preece |
| 19 | 21 | CARDIFF CITY | 1-2 | 4022 | Miller |
| 20 | 27 | Tranmere Rovers | 0-4 | 3252 | |
| 21 | 19 Dec | Rochdale | 0-3 | 1491 | |
| 22 | 26 | Hereford United | 2-4 | 3203 | Williams, Downes |
| 23 | 28 | CREWE ALEXANDRA | 1-2 | 1918 | Downes |
| 24 | 1 Jan | EXETER CITY | 1-1 | 1691 | Gibbins |
| 25 | 9 | Burnley | 0-2 | 5305 | |
| 26 | 12 | DARLINGTON | 2-1 | 1402 | Clement, Brook |
| 27 | 16 | SCUNTHORPE UNITED | 1-1 | 1760 | Sherlock |
| 28 | 29 | Stockport County | 1-5 | 2509 | Jones |
| 29 | 5 Feb | HALIFAX TOWN | 1-0 | 1509 | Mann |
| 30 | 13 | Crewe Alexandra | 1-2 | 2080 | Bodin |
| 31 | 19 | HARTLEPOOL UNITED | 2-3 | 1880 | Williams(2) |
| 32 | 26 | Colchester United | 0-0 | 1784 | |
| 33 | 1 Mar | LEYTON ORIENT | 0-0 | 1656 | |
| 34 | 5 | SWANSEA CITY | 1-2 | 2235 | Brook |
| 35 | 12 | CAMBRIDGE UNITED | 0-0 | 1208 | |
| 36 | 26 | Wrexham | 1-4 | 1627 | Millett |
| 37 | 2 Apr | CARLISLE UNITED | 1-2 | 1376 | Taylor |
| 38 | 4 | Cardiff City | 0-4 | 6536 | |
| 39 | 9 | PETERBOROUGH UTD | 0-4 | 988 | |
| 40 | 12 | SCARBOROUGH | 0-4 | 1025 | |
| 41 | 19 | Torquay United | 1-6 | 3416 | Hamer |
| 42 | 23 | Bolton Wanderers | 0-6 | 4357 | |
| 43 | 26 | WOLVERHAMPTON W. | 1-3 | 3409 | Tupling |
| 44 | 30 | TRANMERE ROVERS | 0-3 | 1110 | |
| 45 | 2 May | Darlington | 2-0 | 1675 | Thompson, Taylor |
| 46 | 7 | ROCHDALE | 0-1 | 2560 | |

## F.A.Cup

| | Date | Opposition | Res. | Att. | Goalscorers |
|---|---|---|---|---|---|
| 1 | 14 Nov | Northampton Town | 1-2 | 4581 | Holtham |

| Player | League | | F.A.Cup | | Total | |
|---|---|---|---|---|---|---|
| | App | Gls. | App | Gls. | App | Gls. |
| Abbruzzese D.J. | 21+1 | 0 | 1 | 0 | 23+1 | 0 |
| Bennett S. | 4+1 | 0 | – | – | 4+1 | 0 |
| Bodin P.J. | 6 | 1 | – | – | 6 | 1 |
| Boughen D. | 1 | 0 | – | – | 1 | 0 |
| Bradshaw P.W. | 23 | 0 | 1 | 0 | 27 | 0 |
| Brignull P.A. | 3 | 0 | – | – | 5 | 0 |
| Brook G | 14 | 2 | – | – | 14+1 | 2 |
| Carter T.D. | 1 | 0 | – | – | 1 | 0 |
| Carr D.J. | 9 | 0 | – | – | 10 | 1 |
| Clement A.D. | 5 | 1 | – | – | 6 | 1 |
| Coles D.A. | 14 | 0 | – | – | 14 | 0 |
| Collins R. | 4+2 | 1 | – | – | 4+2 | 1 |
| Davies R. | 0+2 | 0 | – | – | 0+2 | 0 |
| Dillon A. | 5 | 0 | – | – | 10 | 0 |
| Downes W.J. | 4 | 2 | – | – | 4 | 2 |
| Evans P. | 9+1 | 2 | – | – | 12+3 | 4 |
| Gibbins R.G. | 33 | 1 | 1 | 0 | 42 | 2 |
| Giles P.A. | 15+1 | 1 | 1 | 0 | 23+1 | 3 |
| Griffiths D. | 0+1 | 0 | – | – | 0+1 | 0 |
| Hamer K. | 12+1 | 1 | – | – | 12+1 | 1 |
| Hodson S.P. | 34 | 1 | 1 | 0 | 42 | 1 |
| Holtham D.M. | 4+2 | 0 | 0+1 | 1 | 5+4 | 1 |
| Hopkins A. | 2+4 | 0 | – | – | 2+4 | 0 |
| Jones R. | 28+3 | 1 | – | – | 31+3 | 1 |
| Lewis J. | 8 | 0 | – | – | 12 | 0 |
| Mann A.G. | 17 | 1 | – | – | 19 | 2 |
| Miller P.A. | 6 | 2 | – | – | 6 | 2 |
| Millett G. | 18+10 | 1 | – | – | 20+11 | 1 |
| O'Hagan P.J. | 3 | 0 | – | – | 3 | 0 |
| Osborne L. | 15 | 0 | 1 | 0 | 18 | 0 |
| Parselle N.J. | 4+6 | 0 | – | – | 5+7 | 0 |
| Peacock D. | 5 | 0 | – | – | 5 | 0 |
| Preece R. | 7+3 | 2 | 1 | 0 | 11+4 | 2 |
| Sherlock S.G. | 32+2 | 2 | 1 | 0 | 36+2 | 2 |
| Sugrue P.A. | – | – | – | – | 0+1 | 0 |
| Taylor R.S. | 28+6 | 4 | 1 | 0 | 34+6 | 5 |
| Thackeray A.J. | 42+1 | 1 | 1 | 0 | 49+3 | 2 |
| Thompson R.J. | 10+3 | 2 | 0+1 | 0 | 14+4 | 2 |
| Tupling S. | 30+3 | 2 | 1 | 0 | 39+3 | 4 |
| Williams P.A. | 26 | 3 | – | – | 30 | 3 |
| Withers D. | 4+3 | 1 | – | – | 6+3 | 1 |

### Bottom positions only

| | | | | | | | | | | | | |
|---|---|---|---|---|---|---|---|---|---|---|---|---|
| Crewe A | 46 | 7 | 11 | 5 | 25 | 19 | 6 | 8 | 9 | 32 | 34 | 58 |
| Halifax T† | 46 | 11 | 7 | 5 | 37 | 25 | 3 | 7 | 13 | 17 | 34 | 55 |
| Hereford U | 46 | 8 | 7 | 8 | 25 | 27 | 6 | 5 | 12 | 16 | 32 | 54 |
| Stockport Co | 46 | 7 | 7 | 9 | 26 | 26 | 5 | 8 | 10 | 18 | 32 | 51 |
| Rochdale | 46 | 5 | 9 | 9 | 28 | 34 | 6 | 6 | 11 | 19 | 42 | 48 |
| Exeter C | 46 | 8 | 6 | 9 | 33 | 29 | 3 | 7 | 13 | 20 | 39 | 46 |
| Carlisle U | 46 | 9 | 5 | 9 | 38 | 33 | 3 | 3 | 17 | 19 | 53 | 44 |
| Newport Co | 46 | 4 | 5 | 14 | 19 | 36 | 2 | 2 | 19 | 16 | 69 | 25 |

(Back) Lewis (Manager), Hodson, Gibbins (Player/Coach), Thompson, Dillon, P.Williams,
Collins, Tupling, Hamer, D.Williams (Trainer).
(Front) Giles, Withers, Millett, Brignull, Jones, Thackeray, Sherlock.

# SEASON 1988-89    GM Vauxhall Conference

|   | Date | Opposition | Res. | Att. | Goalscorers |
|---|------|------------|------|------|-------------|
| 1 | 20 Aug | Stafford Rangers | 0–3 | 1654 | |
| 2 | 23 | KETTERING TOWN | 1–2 | 1871 | Millett |
| 3 | 27 | Telford United | 1–3 | 1443 | Withers |
| 4 | 29 | Macclesfield Town | 0–3 | 1172 | |
| 5 | 3 Sep | AYLESBURY UNITED | 2–2 | 1175 | Ford, Withers |
| 6 | 5 | Fisher Athletic | 2–3 | 843 | Evans, Sanderson |
| 7 | 10 | BARNET | 1–7 | 1397 | Evans |
| 8 | 13 | YEOVIL TOWN | 1–1 | 1262 | Williams |
| 9 | 17 | WELLING UNITED | 0–1 | 1092 | |
| 10 | 24 | Kidderminster H. | 1–1 | 1419 | Sanderson |
| 11 | 27 | Wycombe Wanderers | 0–5 | 1672 | |
| 12 | 1 Oct | MAIDSTONE UNITED | 2–1 | 943 | Andrews, Williams |
| 13 | 8 | BOSTON UNITED | 1–1 | 1131 | Marustik |
| 14 | 15 | Altrincham | 0–1 | 1359 | |
| 15 | 22 | CHORLEY | 2–0 | 1149 | Brignull, Withers |
| 16 | 5 Nov | Enfield | 0–3 | 692 | |
| 17 | 8 | Sutton United | 1–1 | 924 | Sugrue |
| 18 | 12 | WEYMOUTH | 4–0 | 1238 | Withers, Sanderson, Foley, Ford |
| 19 | 26 | Runcorn | 0–0 | 821 | |
| 20 | 3 Dec | KIDDERMINSTER H | 1–2 | 1560 | Marustik |
| 21 | 10 | Chorley | 2–0 | 610 | Sanderson, Marustik |
| 22 | 17 | TELFORD UNITED | 0–3 | 1536 | |
| 23 | 26 | Cheltenham Town | 2–3 | 2288 | Banks, Sanderson |
| 24 | 31 | Northwich Victoria | 1–3 | 830 | Nuttell |
| 25 | 2 Jan | CHELTENHAM TOWN | 0–1 | 1686 | |
| 26 | 7 | Boston United | 1–1 | 1810 | Richards |
| 27 | 28 | WYCOMBE WANDERERS | 3–5 | 1382 | Sugrue, Giles(2) |
| 28 | 4 Feb | Barnet | 1–4 | 2526 | I.Thompson |
| 29 | 11 | Maidstone United | 1–2 | 857 | Richards |

LEAGUE FIXTURES NOT COMPLETED

## F.A.Cup

|   |   | Res. | Att. | Goalscorers |
|---|---|------|------|-------------|
| 4Q | WEYMOUTH | 2–1 | 1641 | Sanderson, Brignull |
| 1 | MAIDSTONE UNITED | 1–2 | 2148 | Sugrue |

| Player | League | | F.A.Cup | | Total | |
|--------|--------|------|---------|------|-------|------|
|  | App | Gls. | App | Gls. | App | Gls. |
| Abbruzzese D.J. | 8+3 | 0 | 1 | 0 | 10+4 | 1 |
| Ainley R. | – | – | – | – | 1+1 | 0 |
| Andrews K. | 17+2 | 1 | 1 | 0 | 21+2 | 1 |
| Banks C. | 15+5 | 1 | 1+1 | 0 | 22+6 | 3 |
| Bennett S. | 0+2 | 0 | – | – | 0+2 | 0 |
| Bickerton D. | 2+1 | 0 | – | – | 2+1 | 0 |
| Bird T. | 29 | 0 | 2 | 0 | 37 | 0 |
| Brignull P.A. | 13 | 1 | 1 | 1 | 16 | 2 |
| Chappell L. | – | – | – | – | 1 | 0 |
| Dawkins D. | – | – | – | – | 1 | 0 |
| Dillon A. | – | – | – | – | 1 | 0 |
| Evans R. | 11+2 | 2 | – | – | 12+5 | 2 |
| Foley W. | 7+3 | 1 | 1 | 0 | 10+5 | 2 |
| Ford F. | 16+1 | 2 | 1+1 | 0 | 21+3 | 2 |
| Gibbins R.G. | 2 | 0 | – | – | 3 | 0 |
| Giles D.C. | 3 | 2 | – | – | 3 | 2 |
| Gripton M. | 1+1 | 0 | – | – | 1+1 | 0 |
| Hamer K. | 1+1 | 0 | – | – | 1+1 | 0 |
| Jones G.A. | 2 | 0 | – | – | 2 | 0 |
| King A. | 1 | 0 | – | – | 1 | 0 |
| King J. | 2 | 0 | – | – | 2+1 | 0 |
| Marustik C. | 14 | 3 | 2 | 0 | 21 | 5 |
| McLaughlin J. | 2 | 0 | – | – | 2 | 0 |
| Millett G. | 12+2 | 1 | – | – | 13+2 | 1 |
| Mills S.D. | 0+1 | 0 | – | – | 0+1 | 0 |
| Morgan S. | 1+1 | 0 | – | – | 1+1 | 0 |
| Nuttell M. | 5 | 1 | – | – | 5 | 1 |
| Peacock D. | 14 | 0 | – | – | 16 | 0 |
| Preece R. | 0+2 | 0 | – | – | 0+2 | 0 |
| Richards G. | 14 | 2 | 1 | 0 | 21 | 3 |
| Rogers G.R. | 4+2 | 0 | – | – | 6+2 | 0 |
| Sanderson P. | 24+1 | 5 | 2 | 1 | 33+1 | 10 |
| Sherlock S.G. | 26 | 0 | 2 | 0 | 34 | 0 |
| Sugrue P.A. | 13+1 | 2 | 2 | 1 | 21+1 | 14 |
| Taylor R.S. | 1 | 0 | – | – | 1 | 0 |
| Thompson I. | 2+1 | 1 | – | – | 4+1 | 3 |
| Thompson M. | 15 | 0 | 1 | 0 | 18 | 0 |
| Walker S. | 2+1 | 0 | – | – | 2+1 | 0 |
| Williams P. | 22 | 2 | 2 | 0 | 28 | 2 |
| Withers D. | 18+2 | 4 | 2 | 0 | 24+2 | 4 |

(Back) Bennett, Banks, Sherlock, Peacock, Bird, Sanderson, Brignull, Abbruzzesse.   (Front) Williams, Andrews, Ford, Millett, Evans.

# NEWPORT A.F.C.

## SEASON 1989-90     *Federated Homes (Hellenic)League*

| | Date | Opposition | Res. | Att. | Goalscorers |
|---|---|---|---|---|---|
| 1 | 19 Aug | PEGASUS JUNIORS | 1-0 | 594 | Parselle |
| 2 | 30 | ALMONDSBURY P. | 1-0 | 285 | Rowberry |
| 3 | 6 Sep | SWINDON ATHLETIC | 1-3 | 244 | Richards |
| 4 | 9 | Wantage Town | 1-2 | 250 | Rowberry |
| 5 | 13 | Moreton Town | 3-0 | 382 | Lilygreen(2), Preece |
| 6 | 16 | Didcot Town | 2-1 | 265 | Lilygreen(2) |
| 7 | 23 | SUPERMARINE | 3-0 | 341 | Lilygreen(2), Preece |
| 8 | 30 | Fairford Town | 1-2 | 362 | Preece |
| 9 | 4 Nov | Bicester Town | 0-0 | 275 | |
| 10 | 18 | SHORTWOOD UNITED | 2-1 | 302 | Mallender, Evans |
| 11 | 25 | Kintbury Rangers | 0-3 | 353 | |
| 12 | 9 Dec | HEADINGTON AMAT. | 4-0 | 201 | Lilygreen(2), Jarvis(2) |
| 13 | 23 | MORETON TOWN | 2-1 | 504 | Preece, Lilygreen |
| 14 | 30 | Almondsbury P. | 1-1 | 498 | Jarvis |
| 15 | 13 Jan | SHARPNESS | 4-1 | 405 | Jarvis(2), Lilygreen(2) |
| 16 | 17 | BISHOPS CLEEVE | 3-0 | 251 | Jarvis(2), Herrity |
| 17 | 27 | Rayners Lane | 2-0 | 280 | Spink, Lilygreen |
| 18 | 10 Feb | Headington Amat. | 2-1 | 254 | Pratt, Lilygreen |
| 19 | 17 | RUISLIP PARK | 8-0 | 285 | Jarvis(3), Preece(2), Mallender, Herrity, Delicata(og) |
| 20 | 21 | DIDCOT TOWN | 1-0 | 412 | Lilygreen |
| 21 | 24 | Ruislip Park | 2-0 | 220 | Jarvis, Lilygreen |
| 22 | 3 Mar | KINTBURY RANGERS | 0-0 | 354 | |
| 23 | 7 | BICESTER TOWN | 3-0 | 405 | Spink(2), Lilygreen |
| 24 | 10 | Bishops Cleeve | 1-0 | 350 | Spink |
| 25 | 17 | Swindon Athletic | 0-0 | 257 | |
| 26 | 31 | Supermarine | 4-0 | 250 | Jarvis(2), Lilygreen, Painter |
| 27 | 4 Apr | Shortwood United | 2-5 | 517 | Rowberry, Pratt |
| 28 | 7 | WANTAGE TOWN | 2-1 | 337 | Jarvis(2) |
| 29 | 14 | Sharpness | 4-1 | 560 | Jarvis(2), Lilygreen(2) |
| 30 | 16 | ABINGDON UNITED | 1-1 | 411 | Jarvis |
| 31 | 21 | Pegasus Juniors | 1-1 | 560 | Jarvis |
| 32 | 28 | FAIRFORD TOWN | 4-2 | 471 | Lilygreen(2), Herrity, Jarvis |
| 33 | 2 May | Abingdon United | 3-1 | 450 | Lilygreen(2), Jarvis |
| 34 | 5 | RAYNERS LANE | 2-0 | 468 | Mallender, Herrity |

| Player | League | | F.A.Cup | | Total | |
|---|---|---|---|---|---|---|
| | App | Gls. | App | Gls. | App | Gls. |
| Beattie Alex | 0+1 | 0 | | | 0+3 | 0 |
| Bird T. | 32 | 0 | | | 42 | 0 |
| Evans R. | 8+2 | 1 | | | 10+4 | 2 |
| Herrity D. | 16 | 4 | | | 19 | 6 |
| Jarvis D. | 22 | 21 | | | 25 | 22 |
| King M. | 0+1 | 0 | | | 0+1 | 0 |
| Lilygreen C. | 31+1 | 23 | | | 40+1 | 28 |
| Mallender P. | 25 | 3 | | | 33 | 6 |
| Moore A. | 1+1 | 0 | | | 1+2 | 0 |
| Painter R. | 32 | 1 | | | 41 | 1 |
| Parselle N. | 21+3 | 1 | | | 27+3 | 3 |
| Pratt M. | 30 | 2 | | | 39 | 2 |
| Preece B. | 24+5 | 6 | | | 32+7 | 7 |
| Relish J.D. | 7+3 | 0 | | | 9+3 | 1 |
| Richards D. | 14+3 | 1 | | | 20+3 | 4 |
| Roberts K. | 2 | 0 | | | 2 | 0 |
| Rogers G. | 24 | 0 | | | 29 | 0 |
| Rowberry S. | 6+2 | 3 | | | 9+3 | 3 |
| Ryan D. | – | – | | | 1 | 0 |
| Smith R. | 3+4 | 0 | | | 3+5 | 0 |
| Spink G. | 31 | 4 | | | 40 | 4 |
| Stanton C. | 29 | 0 | | | 39 | 0 |
| Thomas A. | 0+2 | 0 | | | 1+2 | 0 |
| Travers J. | – | – | | | 0+1 | 0 |
| Vassallo B. | 7 | 0 | | | 8 | 0 |
| Willis R. | 9+4 | 0 | | | 14+4 | 0 |
| Own Goals | | 1 | | | | 1 |

### Top positions only

| | P | W | D | L | F | A | PTS |
|---|---|---|---|---|---|---|---|
| Newport AFC | 34 | 23 | 6 | 5 | 71 | 28 | 75 |
| Shortwood United | 34 | 20 | 7 | 7 | 81 | 39 | 67 |
| Abingdon United | 34 | 20 | 7 | 7 | 66 | 33 | 67 |
| Sharpness | 34 | 16 | 9 | 9 | 76 | 59 | 57 |
| Fairford Town | 34 | 17 | 6 | 11 | 59 | 42 | 57 |
| Bicester Town | 34 | 15 | 11 | 8 | 43 | 30 | 56 |

## F.A.Cup – Not entered

(Back) Mallender, Moore, Spink, Vassallo, Bird, Evans, Willis, Pratt.
(Front) Lilygreen, Painter, Parselle, Rowberry, Preece, Stanton.

# SEASON 1990-91     *Beazer Homes League (Midland Div)*

| | Date | Opposition | Res. | Att. | Goalscorers |
|---|---|---|---|---|---|
| 1 | 18 Aug | Leicester United | 2-0 | 548 | Doughty(2) |
| 2 | 22 | REDDITCH UNITED | 0-1 | 2271 | |
| 3 | 25 | KINGS LYNN | 1-3 | 1573 | Lilygreen |
| 4 | 27 | R.C.Warwick | 3-1 | 353 | Lilygreen(2), Doughty |
| 5 | 8 Sep | Spalding United | 0-0 | 343 | |
| 6 | 12 | STROUD | 0-1 | 1646 | |
| 7 | 15 | Dudley Town | 0-1 | 382 | |
| 8 | 29 | R.C.WARWICK | 1-2 | 745 | Jarvis |
| 9 | 13 Oct | Willenhall Town | 1-1 | 268 | Price |
| 10 | 27 | BILSTON TOWN | 1-0 | 706 | Doughty |
| 11 | 10 Nov | Nuneaton Borough | 1-2 | 958 | Lilygreen |
| 12 | 24 | HINCKLEY TOWN | 0-3 | 650 | |
| 13 | 1 Dec | Hednesford Town | 1-3 | 410 | Price |
| 14 | 4 | Redditch United | 0-1 | 312 | |
| 15 | 15 | ALVECHURCH | 1-1 | 502 | Price |
| 16 | 22 | Bedworth United | 2-4 | 302 | Jarvis, Parselle |
| 17 | 29 | DUDLEY TOWN | 0-1 | 608 | |
| 18 | 5 Jan | Grantham Town | 2-0 | 174 | Hawkins(2) |
| 19 | 12 | LEICESTER UNITED | 2-1 | 851 | Lilygreen, Hawkins |
| 20 | 26 | WILLENHALL TOWN | 3-2 | 607 | Lilygreen(2), Foley |
| 21 | 2 Feb | Alvechurch | 0-0 | 297 | |
| 22 | 16 | SUTTON COLDFIELD T. | 2-1 | 542 | Jarvis, Ellis |
| 23 | 20 | CORBY TOWN | 1-2 | 664 | Lilygreen |
| 24 | 23 | GRANTHAM TOWN | 1-3 | 736 | Lilygreen |
| 25 | 26 | Stroud | 1-0 | 240 | Foley |
| 26 | 2 Mar | NUNEATON BOROUGH | 4-1 | 619 | Prew, Foley, Jarvis, Lilygreen |
| 27 | 9 | TAMWORTH | 1-1 | 1045 | Lilygreen |
| 28 | 13 | BARRY TOWN | 1-0 | 1410 | Price |
| 29 | 16 | Hinckley Town | 1-0 | 220 | Jarvis |
| 30 | 23 | HEDNESFORD TOWN | 0-0 | 980 | |
| 31 | 26 | Stourbridge | 0-2 | 557 | |
| 32 | 30 | Barry Town | 0-1 | 933 | |
| 33 | 1 Apr | BRIDGNORTH TOWN | 4-1 | 705 | Green, Doughty, Price(2) |
| 34 | 6 | STOURBRIDGE | 1-0 | 710 | Green |
| 35 | 10 | SPALDING UNITED | 2-0 | 1024 | Price, Sherlock |
| 36 | 13 | Sutton Coldfield T. | 2-0 | 314 | Doughty, Lilygreen |
| 37 | 16 | Tamworth | 4-1 | 1079 | Lilygreen(2), Green, Price |
| 38 | 23 | Bilston Town | 2-1 | 207 | Prew, Green |
| 39 | 27 | Corby Town | 1-2 | 484 | Lilygreen |
| 40 | 28 | Kings Lynn | 1-2 | 399 | Doughty |
| 41 | 30 | Bridgnorth Town | 2-0 | 275 | Parselle, Green |
| 42 | 4 May | BEDWORTH UNITED | 2-0 | 1044 | Lilygreen, Green |

| Player | League | | F.A.Cup | | Total | |
|---|---|---|---|---|---|---|
| | App | Gls | App | Gls | App | Gls |
| Bird T. | 37 | 0 | | | 47 | 0 |
| Collicutt P. | 38 | 0 | | | 42+1 | 1 |
| Doughty S. | 12+8 | 7 | | | 14+10 | 8 |
| Ellis A. | 16+5 | 1 | | | 17+7 | 2 |
| Foley W. | 11+1 | 3 | | | 11+1 | 3 |
| Green P. | 9 | 6 | | | 9 | 6 |
| Griffiths A. | 25 | 0 | | | 26 | 0 |
| Harrison P. | 5+1 | 0 | | | 5+1 | 0 |
| Hawkins J. | 9+5 | 3 | | | 16+5 | 5 |
| Jarrett P. | 1 | 0 | | | 1 | 0 |
| Jarvis D. | 23+10 | 5 | | | 33+10 | 6 |
| Lilygreen C. | 39 | 16 | | | 49 | 22 |
| Mallender P. | 5+1 | 0 | | | 5+1 | 0 |
| O'Connell S. | – | – | | | 0+1 | 0 |
| Painter R. | 27 | 0 | | | 34+2 | 1 |
| Parselle N. | 39 | 2 | | | 49 | 3 |
| Porretta D. | 5+4 | 0 | | | 5+4 | 0 |
| Pratt M. | 10+4 | 0 | | | 19+4 | 0 |
| Preece B. | 2 | 0 | | | 4 | 1 |
| Prew J. | 31 | 2 | | | 34 | 2 |
| Price M. | 42 | 8 | | | 50 | 10 |
| Priday M. | 5 | 0 | | | 5 | 0 |
| Richards D. | 9+4 | 0 | | | 17+4 | 0 |
| Rogers G. | 13+1 | 0 | | | 14+1 | 0 |
| Rowberry S. | 4+8 | 0 | | | 4+11 | 1 |
| Sherlock S. | 15+1 | 1 | | | 15+1 | 1 |
| Smith R. | 4+3 | 0 | | | 11+4 | 1 |
| Stanton C. | 23+2 | 0 | | | 31+2 | 0 |
| Stroud K. | 2 | 0 | | | 3 | 2 |
| Vassallo B. | 0+2 | 0 | | | 0+3 | 0 |
| Wall J. | 0+2 | 0 | | | 0+2 | 0 |
| Waters R. | 1 | 0 | | | 1 | 0 |
| Willis R. | – | – | | | 1 | 0 |
| Own Goals | | | | | | 1 |

**F.A.Cup – Not entered**

| | | | | | | | |
|---|---|---|---|---|---|---|---|
| Stourbridge | 42 | 26 | 6 | 8 | 80 | 48 | 90 |
| Corby Town | 42 | 27 | 4 | 11 | 99 | 48 | 85 |
| Hednesford Town | 42 | 25 | 7 | 10 | 79 | 47 | 82 |
| Tamworth | 42 | 25 | 5 | 12 | 84 | 45 | 80 |
| Nuneaton Borough | 42 | 21 | 11 | 10 | 74 | 51 | *(4) 70 |
| Barry Town | 42 | 20 | 7 | 15 | 61 | 48 | 67 |
| Newport A.F.C. | 42 | 19 | 6 | 17 | 54 | 46 | 63 |
| King's Lynn | 42 | 17 | 9 | 16 | 53 | 62 | 60 |
| Grantham Town | 42 | 17 | 7 | 18 | 62 | 56 | 58 |
| Redditch United | 42 | 16 | 10 | 16 | 66 | 75 | 58 |
| Hinckley Town | 42 | 16 | 9 | 17 | 72 | 68 | 57 |
| Sutton Coldfield Town | 42 | 15 | 11 | 16 | 56 | 65 | 56 |
| Bedworth United | 42 | 15 | 9 | 18 | 57 | 73 | 54 |
| Bilston Town | 42 | 14 | 9 | 19 | 69 | 79 | 51 |
| Leicester United | 42 | 14 | 10 | 18 | 65 | 77 | *(1) 51 |
| Racing Club Warwick | 42 | 12 | 13 | 17 | 56 | 65 | 49 |
| Bridgnorth Town | 42 | 13 | 9 | 20 | 62 | 74 | 48 |
| Stroud | 42 | 11 | 14 | 17 | 51 | 64 | 47 |
| Dudley Town | 42 | 11 | 13 | 18 | 48 | 73 | 46 |
| Alvechurch | 42 | 10 | 8 | 22 | 58 | 69 | 38 |
| Willenhall Town | 42 | 10 | 10 | 22 | 58 | 69 | *(3) 37 |
| Spalding United | 42 | 8 | 9 | 25 | 35 | 70 | 33 |

(Back) Preece, Lilygreen, O'Connell, Pratt, Doughty, Hawkins, Bird, Willis, Collicutt, Rowberry, Mallender, Spink.
(Front) Richards, Stanton, Painter, Jarvis, Relish (Manager), Rogers (Asst.Manager), Parselle, Smith, Ellis, Price.

# SEASON 1991–92     Beazer Homes League (Midland Div)

| | Date | Opposition | Res. | Att. | Goalscorers |
|---|---|---|---|---|---|
| 1 | 17 Aug | Rushden Town | 3-0 | 397 | Foley(2), Timlin(og) |
| 2 | 20 | ALVECHURCH | 3-0 | 1027 | Green, Price, Foley |
| 3 | 24 | LEICESTER UNITED | 0-1 | 1071 | |
| 4 | 26 | Redditch United | 5-0 | 423 | Lilygreen(3), Bray, Ellis |
| 5 | 31 | Sutton Coldfield T. | 1-1 | 349 | Green |
| 6 | 3 Sep | BILSTON TOWN | 0-0 | 1076 | |
| 7 | 7 | Grantham Town | 3-3 | 962 | Green(2), Griffiths |
| 8 | 10 | Stroud | 3-2 | 703 | Green, Lilygreen, Sanderson |
| 9 | 28 | R.C.WARWICK | 5-0 | 708 | Green(2), Ellis, Price, Sanderson |
| 10 | 12 Oct | Hednesford Town | 1-2 | 793 | Green |
| 11 | 26 | Stourbridge | 3-2 | 337 | Sanderson(2), Green |
| 12 | 2 Nov | Nuneaton Borough | 0-2 | 583 | |
| 13 | 9 | GRANTHAM TOWN | 1-1 | 721 | Price |
| 14 | 16 | RUSHDEN TOWN | 1-3 | 612 | Bray |
| 15 | 23 | Bedworth United | 2-3 | 338 | Green(2) |
| 16 | 7 Dec | Solihull Borough | 1-3 | 314 | Price |
| 17 | 21 | HINCKLEY TOWN | 5-1 | 470 | Green(2), Price, Porretta, Hewitt |
| 18 | 26 | Barry Town | 2-2 | 924 | Price, Coyne |
| 19 | 28 | Dudley Town | 1-2 | 352 | Lilygreen |
| 20 | 1 Jan | YATE TOWN | 2-2 | 725 | Porretta, Lilygreen |
| 21 | 4 | SOLIHULL BOROUGH | 1-1 | 498 | Reynolds |
| 22 | 18 | KINGS LYNN | 3-1 | 471 | Lilygreen(3) |
| 23 | 25 | NUNEATON BOROUGH | 3-2 | 653 | Green(2), Coyne |
| 24 | 1 Feb | R.C.Warwick | 2-0 | 191 | Green, Porretta |
| 25 | 8 | BEDWORTH UNITED | 1-1 | 829 | Lilygreen |
| 26 | 15 | Bilston Town | 2-2 | 255 | Withers, Lilygreen |
| 27 | 18 | STROUD | 1-0 | 608 | Hewitt |
| 28 | 22 | SUTTON COLDFIELD T. | 2-2 | 697 | Price, Sanderson |
| 29 | 25 | STOURBRIDGE | 0-4 | 705 | |
| 30 | 29 | Leicester United | 0-0 | 228 | |
| 31 | 7 Mar | Bridgnorth Town | 1-1 | 271 | Green |
| 32 | 10 | TAMWORTH | 0-3 | 485 | |
| 33 | 17 | HEDNESFORD TOWN | 0-2 | 508 | |
| 34 | 21 | Tamworth | 0-1 | 746 | |
| 35 | 24 | REDDITCH UNITED | 0-1 | 511 | |
| 36 | 28 | DUDLEY TOWN | 3-1 | 504 | Price(2), Porretta |
| 37 | 11 Apr | BRIDGNORTH | 1-1 | 504 | Prew |
| 38 | 14 | Alvechurch | 0-2 | 185 | |
| 39 | 18 | Yate Town | 5-1 | 363 | Green(3), Draper, Lilygreen |
| 40 | 20 | BARRY TOWN | 1-0 | 1051 | Prew |
| 41 | 25 | Kings Lynn | 1-3 | 305 | Porretta |
| 42 | 3 May | Hinckley Town | 3-1 | 156 | Green(2), Porretta |

| Player | League | | F.A.Cup | | Total | |
|---|---|---|---|---|---|---|
| | App | Gls. | App | Gls. | App | Gls. |
| Bird T. | 8 | 0 | | | 8 | 0 |
| Bray M. | 13 | 2 | | | 18 | 3 |
| Collicutt P. | 26+2 | 0 | | | 32+2 | 0 |
| Coyne P. | 15 | 2 | | | 16 | 2 |
| Draper S. | 1+3 | 1 | | | 1+3 | 1 |
| Ellis A. | 10+2 | 2 | | | 13+2 | 2 |
| Foley W. | 2 | 3 | | | 2 | 3 |
| Green P. | 38 | 22 | | | 44 | 27 |
| Griffiths A. | 16 | 1 | | | 23 | 1 |
| Hewitt W. | 36+1 | 2 | | | 43+1 | 3 |
| Jarvis D. | 8+11 | 0 | | | 10+15 | 0 |
| John D. | 19 | 0 | | | 20 | 0 |
| Kilgour M. | 2 | 0 | | | 3 | 1 |
| Lewis A. | 6 | 0 | | | 6 | 0 |
| Lewis J. | 2 | 0 | | | 2 | 0 |
| Lilygreen C. | 25+8 | 12 | | | 28+11 | 13 |
| Mason P. | 34 | 0 | | | 42 | 0 |
| Morgan S. | 0+1 | 0 | | | 0+1 | 0 |
| Parselle N. | 2+1 | 0 | | | 4+1 | 0 |
| Porretta D. | 28+2 | 6 | | | 30+2 | 6 |
| Prew J. | 26+2 | 2 | | | 33+2 | 2 |
| Price M. | 37+1 | 9 | | | 45+1 | 12 |
| Reynolds E. | 4+7 | 1 | | | 4+7 | 1 |
| Rogers G | 2+1 | 0 | | | 3+1 | 0 |
| Sanderson C. | 31+1 | 5 | | | 39+1 | 9 |
| Sherlock S. | 0+1 | 0 | | | 0+1 | 0 |
| Stanton C. | 13+2 | 0 | | | 15+3 | 0 |
| Towler P. | 12 | 0 | | | 12 | 0 |
| Williams C. | 4 | 0 | | | 4+1 | 0 |
| Williams P. | 34+5 | 0 | | | 41+5 | 0 |
| Withers D. | 8+8 | | | | | 1 |
| Own Goals | | 1 | | | | 1 |

**F.A.Cup – Not entered**

| | P | W | D | L | F | A | Pts |
|---|---|---|---|---|---|---|---|
| Solihull Borough | 42 | 29 | 10 | 3 | 92 | 40 | 97 |
| Hednesford Town | 42 | 26 | 13 | 3 | 81 | 37 | 91 |
| Sutton Coldfield Town | 42 | 21 | 11 | 10 | 71 | 51 | 74 |
| Barry Town | 42 | 21 | 6 | 15 | 88 | 56 | 69 |
| Bedworth United | 42 | 16 | 15 | 11 | 67 | 63 | 63 |
| Nuneaton Borough | 42 | 17 | 11 | 14 | 68 | 53 | 62 |
| Tamworth | 42 | 16 | 12 | 14 | 66 | 52 | 60 |
| Rushden Town | 42 | 16 | 12 | 14 | 69 | 63 | 60 |
| Stourbridge | 42 | 17 | 8 | 17 | 85 | 62 | 59 |
| Newport A.F.C. | 42 | 15 | 13 | 14 | 72 | 60 | 58 |
| Yate Town | 42 | 14 | 15 | 13 | 65 | 64 | 57 |
| Bilston Town | 42 | 15 | 10 | 17 | 56 | 67 | 55 |
| Grantham Town | 42 | 11 | 17 | 14 | 59 | 55 | 50 |
| King's Lynn | 42 | 13 | 11 | 18 | 61 | 68 | 50 |
| Hinckley Town | 42 | 14 | 8 | 20 | 61 | 87 | 50 |
| Leicester United | 42 | 12 | 13 | 17 | 56 | 63 | 49 |
| Bridgnorth Town | 42 | 12 | 12 | 18 | 61 | 74 | 48 |
| Racing Club Warwick | 42 | 11 | 14 | 17 | 45 | 61 | 47 |
| Stroud | 42 | 14 | 4 | 24 | 66 | 88 | 46 |
| Redditch United | 42 | 12 | 8 | 22 | 52 | 92 | 44 |
| Alvechurch | 42 | 11 | 10 | 21 | 54 | 88 | 43 |
| Dudley Town | 42 | 8 | 9 | 25 | 41 | 92 | 33 |

(Back) Rogers (Asst.Man.), Stanton, Green, P.Williams, Bird, Hewitt, Lilygreen, Jarvis, Bray
(Front) Griffiths, Prew, Collicutt, Relish (Manager), Ellis, Price, Sherlock.

# SEASON 1992-93    Beazer Homes League (Midland Div)

| | Date | Opposition | Res. | Att. | Goalscorers |
|---|---|---|---|---|---|
| 1 | 22 Aug | Leicester United | 2-1 | 295 | Brown, M.Price |
| 2 | 26 | TAMWORTH | 3-2 | 506 | Lowndes, Lilygreen, Minton(og) |
| 3 | 31 | Forest Green Rovers | 2-1 | 633 | M.Price, Ford(og) |
| 4 | 5 Sep | GRANTHAM TOWN | 2-0 | 505 | Lowndes, M.Price |
| 5 | 9 | Evesham United | 2-2 | 779 | Lilygreen, Porretta |
| 6 | 3 Oct | NUNEATON BOROUGH | 0-3 | 668 | |
| 7 | 31 | Bedworth United | 1-0 | 347 | L.Jones |
| 8 | 7 Nov | WESTON SUPER MARE | 0-1 | 396 | |
| 9 | 14 | Gresley Rovers | 5-3 | 736 | Lilygreen(4), Jarvis |
| 10 | 21 | Tamworth | 3-4 | 595 | Charles, Jarvis, Pengelly |
| 11 | 5 Dec | KINGS LYNN | 4-1 | 302 | Williams, M.Price, Jarvis, Chiverton |
| 12 | 12 | Rushden & Diamonds | 0-1 | 352 | |
| 13 | 19 | HINCKLEY TOWN | 3-1 | 316 | Chiverton(2), Lilygreen |
| 14 | 28 | YATE TOWN | 3-1 | 407 | Lilygreen, Pengelly, Chiverton |
| 15 | 5 Jan | Bridgnorth Town | 1-0 | 232 | S.Jones |
| 16 | 9 | Sutton Coldfield T. | 4-2 | 352 | S.Jones, Lilygreen(2), Chiverton |
| 17 | 16 | Dudley Town | 1-0 | 338 | Chiverton |
| 18 | 20 | FOREST GREEN R. | 0-2 | 301 | |
| 19 | 27 | EVESHAM UNITED | 2-3 | 344 | Chiverton, Beattie |
| 20 | 6 Feb | Grantham Town | 0-1 | 321 | |
| 21 | 9 | Bilston Town | 1-1 | 165 | Lilygreen |
| 22 | 13 | STOURBRIDGE | 2-1 | 328 | Lilygreen, Coyne |
| 23 | 17 | LEICESTER UNITED | 1-1 | 254 | Pengelly |
| 24 | 20 | Nuneaton Borough | 1-1 | 1296 | Vaughan |
| 25 | 24 | RUSHDEN & DIAMONDS | 1-3 | 275 | Lilygreen |
| 26 | 27 | BEDWORTH UNITED | 1-3 | 290 | Lowndes |
| 27 | 10 Mar | R.C.WARWICK | 2-1 | 202 | Lewis, Chiverton |
| 28 | 13 | BRIDGNORTH TOWN | 2-0 | 242 | Lilygreen, M.Price |
| 29 | 14 | Kings Lynn | 1-1 | 271 | Lilygreen |
| 30 | 17 | Hinckley Town | 4-3 | 183 | Lilygreen, Chiverton, Campbell(og), Threlfall |
| 31 | 20 | Redditch United | 3-1 | 238 | Threlfall(2), Brown |
| 32 | 23 | Stourbridge | 3-1 | 321 | Brown, Lowndes, Vaughan |
| 33 | 27 | SUTTON COLDFIELD T. | 2-2 | 382 | Pulis, Chiverton |
| 34 | 31 | Barri | 1-4 | 271 | Chiverton |
| 35 | 3 Apr | BILSTON TOWN | 3-1 | 220 | Chiverton, M.Price, Lowndes |
| 36 | 10 | BARRI | 0-0 | 491 | |
| 37 | 12 | Yate Town | 2-0 | 516 | Pulis, Vaughan |
| 38 | 14 | GRESLEY ROVERS | 0-0 | 374 | |
| 39 | 17 | Weston Super mare | 0-3 | 475 | |
| 40 | 21 | REDDITCH UNITED | 2-1 | 178 | Threlfall, L.Jones |
| 41 | 24 | DUDLEY TOWN | 1-0 | 305 | Coyne |
| 42 | 1 May | R.C.Warwick | 2-1 | 193 | Lilygreen, Chiverton |

## F.A.Cup

| P | 29 Aug | Dawlish Town | 3-0 | 296 | Lilygreen(2), Charles |
|---|---|---|---|---|---|
| 1Q | 12 Sep | Forest Green Rovers | 2-1 | 419 | Jarvis(2) |
| 2Q | 26 | WORCESTER CITY | 3-0 | 685 | Towler, Lowndes, Lilygreen |
| 3Q | 10 Oct | CLEVEDON TOWN | 1-1 | 723 | Charles |
| 3QR | 14 | Clevedon Town | 1-1 | 940 | Lilygreen |
| 3Q2R | 19 | CLEVEDON TOWN | 4-2 | 599 | Charles(2), S.Jones, Pengelly |
| 4Q | 24 | SUTTON UNITED | 1-4 | 810 | Lilygreen |

| Player | League | | F.A.Cup | | Total | |
|---|---|---|---|---|---|---|
| | App | Gls. | App | Gls. | App | Gls. |
| Beattie Andy | 6 | 1 | – | – | 6 | 1 |
| Brown G. | 23+4 | 3 | 5 | 0 | 34+5 | 4 |
| Charles K. | 6+2 | 1 | 6 | 4 | 17+3 | 8 |
| Chiverton E. | 21+4 | 13 | 0+1 | 0 | 23+5 | 14 |
| Coyne P. | 28+2 | 2 | 1+1 | 0 | 34+3 | 3 |
| Foxwell D. | 0+1 | 0 | – | – | 0+1 | 0 |
| Green P. | 3+1 | 0 | 0+1 | 0 | 5+3 | 0 |
| Jarvis D. | 6+3 | 3 | 1+5 | 2 | 13+11 | 5 |
| Johansen T. | 3 | 0 | – | – | 3 | 0 |
| Jones L. | 38 | 2 | 7 | 0 | 53 | 2 |
| Jones S. | 14+5 | 2 | 6 | 1 | 24+7 | 4 |
| Kendall M. | 10 | 0 | 6 | 0 | 19 | 0 |
| Lewis J. | 28+1 | 1 | 7 | 0 | 41+1 | 1 |
| Lilygreen C. | 36 | 17 | 7 | 5 | 51+1 | 30 |
| Lowndes S. | 39+1 | 5 | 7 | 1 | 52+2 | 7 |
| Mason P. | 29 | 0 | 1 | 0 | 35 | 0 |
| Pengelly M. | 32+1 | 3 | 2+1 | 1 | 41+2 | 4 |
| Porretta D. | 6+7 | 1 | 2+1 | 0 | 11+9 | 1 |
| Price J. | 0+1 | 0 | – | – | 0+1 | 0 |
| Price M. | 38+1 | 6 | 6+1 | 0 | 50+3 | 7 |
| Pulis R. | 17+5 | 2 | – | – | 17+5 | 2 |
| Reynolds E. | – | – | 0+1 | 0 | 1+1 | 0 |
| Rogers G. | 3+4 | 0 | – | – | 3+4 | 0 |
| Threlfall D. | 11+8 | 4 | – | – | 11+8 | 4 |
| Towler P. | 14 | 0 | 7 | 1 | 29 | 1 |
| Vaughan N. | 23 | 3 | – | – | 23 | 3 |
| Weakley R. | – | – | – | – | 1 | 0 |
| Williams C. | 0+1 | 0 | – | – | 1+2 | 1 |
| Williams P. | 28+1 | 1 | 6 | 0 | 40+1 | 1 |
| Own Goals | | 3 | | | | 3 |

| | P | W | D | L | F | A | Pts |
|---|---|---|---|---|---|---|---|
| NUNEATON BORO' | 42 | 29 | 5 | 8 | 102 | 45 | 92 |
| GRESLEY ROVERS | 42 | 27 | 6 | 9 | 94 | 55 | 87 |
| RUSHDEN & DIA. | 42 | 25 | 10 | 7 | 85 | 41 | 85 |
| BARRI | 42 | 26 | 5 | 11 | 82 | 49 | 83 |
| NEWPORT A.F.C. | 42 | 23 | 8 | 11 | 73 | 58 | 77 |
| BEDWORTH UNITED | 42 | 22 | 8 | 12 | 72 | 55 | 74 |
| STOURBRIDGE | 42 | 17 | 9 | 16 | 93 | 79 | 60 |
| SUTTON COLDFIELD T. | 42 | 17 | 9 | 16 | 82 | 78 | 60 |
| REDDITCH UNITED | 42 | 18 | 6 | 18 | 75 | 79 | 60 |
| TAMWORTH | 42 | 18 | 6 | 18 | 75 | 79 | 60 |
| WESTON-S-MARE | 42 | 17 | 7 | 18 | 79 | 86 | 58 |
| LEICESTER UNITED | 42 | 16 | 9 | 17 | 67 | 67 | 57 |

Top positions only shown

(Back) Towler, Coyne, Green, Mason, Brown, Kendall, S.Jones, Lowndes.
(Front) Lewis, C.Williams, M.Price, Charles, L.Jones, Porretta.

# CUP COMPETITIONS (F.A.CUP SEE SEASONAL STATISTICS)

# NEWPORT COUNTY F.C.

## European Cup–Winners Cup

| Round | Date | Opposition | Result | Att. | Goalscorers |
|---|---|---|---|---|---|
| 1/1L | 16/9/80 | CRUSADERS | 4–0 | 6,285 | Bruton, Gwyther, Aldridge, Moore |
| 1/2L | 1/10/80 | Crusaders | 0–0 | 1,500 | |
| 2/1L | 22/10/80 | Haugar | 0–0 | 4,522 | |
| 2/2L | 4/11/80 | HAUGAR | 6–0 | 8,855 | Tynan(2),Lowndes,Gwyther,Aldridge,Moore |
| 3/1L | 4/3/81 | Carl Zeiss Jena | 2–2 | 16,000 | Tynan(2) |
| 3/2L | 18/3/81 | CARL ZEISS JENA | 0–1 | 18,000 | |

## Welsh Cup

| Round | Date | Opposition | Result | Att. | Goalscorers |
|---|---|---|---|---|---|
| 1P | 10/10/12 | MARDY | 1–0 | 2,000 | G.Fyfe |
| 2P * | 2/11/12 | Aberdare | 1–1 | 1,500 | Holt |
| 2P/R | 12/11/12 | Aberdare | 0–4 | | * After abandoned home game |
| | | | | | |
| 1 | 27/10/13 | Mid–Rhondda | 1–1 | 3,000 | Butler |
| 1/R | 3/11/13 | MID–RHONDDA | 6–0 | | Enright(3), E.Hammett(2), Matthews |
| 2 | 8/11/13 | CARDIFF CORRIES | 3–1 | | Edwards, Preece, Spittle |
| 3 | 8/12/13 | TROEDYRHIW | 1–1 | 2000 | Edwards |
| 3/R | 11/12/13 | Troedyrhiw | 1–3 | | Butler |
| | | | | | |
| 1 | 22/10/14 | ABERTILLERY | 3–0 | | Groves, Williams, Johnson |
| (Newport County believed to have scratched from competition) | | | | | |
| | | | | | |
| 3 | 15/1/21 | EBBW VALE | 4–0 | 5000 | Dobson(2), Walker, Wright |
| 4 | 31/1/21 | MERTHYR TOWN | 0–1 | 5000 | |
| | | | | | |
| 3 | 18/1/22 | Cardiff City | 1–7 | 6000 | Gaughan |
| | | | | | |
| 6 | 15/2/23 | PONTYPRIDD | 4–1 | | Hampton(2), Groves, Conner |
| 7 | 19/3/23 | Swansea Town | 2–4 | 8000 | Patterson, Charlton |
| | | | | | |
| 3 | 14/2/24 | LLANELLI | 5–2 | 2900 | Lowes(3), Conner(2) |
| 4 | 17/3/24 | CARDIFF CITY | 1–1 | 5500 | Charlton |
| 4/R | 24/3/24 | Cardiff City | 0–0 | 5000 | |
| 4/2R | 31/3/24 | CARDIFF CITY | 0–0 | 4000 | |
| 4/3R | 10/4/24 | Cardiff City | 3–0 | 2000 | Carney, Charlton, Nicholls |
| S/F | 16/4/24 | Wrexham | 0–1 | 7500 | |
| | | | | | |
| 5 | 5/3/25 | WELLINGTON | 2–0 | | Taylor, Whitton |
| 6 | 19/3/25 | WREXHAM | 0–1 | 3500 | |
| | | | | | |
| 5 | 18/3/26 | BARRY | 0–0 | | |
| 5/R | 24/3/26 | Barry | 3–2 | | Coates(2), Drinnan |
| 6 | 29/3/26 | Merthyr Town | 1–1 | | Carney |
| 6/R | 12/4/26 | MERTHYR TOWN | 2–0 | | Carney(2) |
| S/F | 21/4/26 | Ebbw Vale | 1–2 | | Davis |
| | | | | | |
| 6 | 10/3/27 | Lovells Athletic | 0–1 | | |
| | | | | | |
| 5 | 1/3/28 | HOLYWELL | Walkover | | |
| 6 | 29/3/28 | Rhyl | 1–3 | | Barratt |
| | | | | | |
| 5 | 28/2/29 | SWANSEA TOWN | 5–1 | | G.Richardson(4), Maidment |
| 6 | 25/3/29 | CARDIFF CITY | 0–1 | | |
| | | | | | |
| 5 | 20/3/30 | LOVELLS ATHLETIC | 3–2 | | Gittins, Seymour, Martin |
| 6 | 12/4/30 | Colwyn Bay | 0–4 | | |
| | | | | | |
| 5 | 26/2/31 | Shrewsbury Town | 2–5 | 3000 | Pearce(2) |
| | | | | | |
| 5 | 6/2/32 | CARDIFF CORRIES | 2–0 | | Gittins, Bagley |
| 6 | 17/3/32 | SWANSEA TOWN | 0–0 | | |
| 6/R | 4/4/32 | Swansea Town | 0–2 | | |
| | | | | | |
| 7 | 1/2/33 | Bristol City | 4–3 | 800 | Lumley(3), Green |
| 8 | 13/3/33 | SOUTHPORT | 0–0 | 2000 | |
| 8/R | 21/3/33 | Southport | 0–4 | | |

| | | | | | |
|---|---|---|---|---|---|
| 5 | 4/1/34 | Lovells Athletic | 3–1 | | Bowsher, Green, Haycox |
| 6 | 1/2/34 | CREWE ALEXANDRA | 2–2 | 2000 | Higgins, Green |
| 6/R | 7/2/34 | Crewe Alexandra | 5–4 | 2000 | Reynolds,Thomas,Green,Haycox, A.W.Clarke |
| 7 | 1/3/34 | TRANMERE ROVERS | 1–1 | 2000 | Haycox |
| 7/R | 8/3/34 | Tranmere Rovers | 2–5 | | Griffiths, Woolliscroft |
| | | | | | |
| 6 | 13/2/35 | Cardiff City | 2–3 | 2000 | Bird, Reynolds |
| | | | | | |
| 6 | 6/2/36 | Swansea Town | 0–1 | 1500 | |
| | | | | | |
| 6 | 22/2/37 | PORTH | 5–0 | | Derrick(3), Chadwick, Carr |
| 7 | 15/3/37 | SWANSEA TOWN | 7–0 | | Derrick(4), Crisp, Chadwick, Wood |
| S/F | 15/4/37 | Rhyl * | 2–3 | | Webb, Wood  (* At Shrewsbury Town) |
| | | | | | |
| 6 | 10/2/38 | BRISTOL CITY | 6–2 | 1095 | Hickman(2), W.E.Owen(2), Wood, Chadwick |
| 7 | 10/3/38 | CHELTENHAM TOWN | 1–0 | | Duggan |
| S/F | 26/4/38 | Shrewsbury Town | 2–3 | 8000 | W.M.Owen(2) |
| | | | | | |
| 6 | 8/3/39 | Cardiff City | 1–5 | | Higgins |
| | | | | | |
| 5 | 14/12/39 | LOVELLS ATHLETIC | 1–1 | | Higgins |
| 5/R | 4/1/40 | Lovells Athletic | 2–0 | | Robbins, Higgins |
| 6 | 3/2/40 | Barry Town | 3–2 | | Hydes(2), Brinton |
| 7 | 2/3/40 | Cardiff City | 1–1 | 3000 | Newall |
| 7/R | 18/3/40 | CARDIFF CITY | 5–0 | 800 | Robbins(2), W.M.Owen, Wookey, Appleby |
| S/F | 13/4/40 | Swansea Town | 0–1 | | |
| | | | | | |
| 5 | 15/1/47 | Barry Town | 3–3 | 1800 | Rawcliffe, Mogford, Hillman(O.G.) |
| 5/R | 22/1/47 | BARRY TOWN | 4–1 | 2000 | Mogford(2), Batty, Hogg |
| 6 | 24/4/47 | Shrewsbury Town | 0–0 | 5000 | |
| 6/R | 5/5/47 | Shrewsbury Town | 1–0 | | Newall |
| S/F | 14/5/47 | Chester | 2–3 | 7500 | Rawcliffe(2) |
| | | | | | |
| 5 | 15/1/48 | Merthyr Tydfil | 1–3 | 6000 | Carr |
| | | | | | |
| 5 | 12/1/49 | Milford Town | 0–2 | | |
| | | | | | |
| 5 | 12/1/50 | Merthyr Tydfil | 0–3 | | |
| | | | | | |
| 5 | 31/1/51 | Ebbw Vale | 2–1 | 3000 | James, Newall |
| 6 | 1/3/51 | SWANSEA TOWN | 2–1 | 7554 | Hayward, Parker |
| S/F | 23/4/51 | Merthyr Tydfil * | 1–1 | 23401 | Moore  (* At Cardiff City) |
| S/F/R | 26/4/51 | Merthyr Tydfil * | 1–4 | 12000 | Moore  (* At Cardiff City) |
| | | | | | |
| 5 | 3/1/52 | CONNAHS QUAY JUNIORS | 8–2 | 1878 | Moore(3), James(2), Nelson(2), Molloy |
| 6 | 28/1/52 | Rhyl | 2–3 | | Donaldson, Lunn |
| | | | | | |
| 5 | 1/1/53 | Haverfordwest | 8–1 | | Beattie(3), Evans(2), Morrey(2), Shergold |
| 6 | 29/1/53 | Swansea Town | 2–3 | 5500 | Rees, Morrey |
| | | | | | |
| 5 | 25/1/54 | SWANSEA TOWN | 6–2 | 3971 | Graham(2), Lucas(2), Saward(2) |
| 6 | 3/3/54 | Bangor City | 5–1 | 5000 | Wharton(2), Lucas(2), Graham |
| S/F | 17/3/54 | Chester * | 2–2 | 9800 | Graham, Wharton  (* At Cardiff City) |
| S/F/R | 5/4/54 | Chester * | 0–2 | 2927 | (* At Wrexham) |
| | | | | | |
| 5 | 13/1/55 | ABERGAVENNY THURSDAYS | 6–0 | 690 | McGhee(2), Johnston(2), Shergold, Harris |
| 6 | 17/2/55 | CARDIFF CITY | 1–3 | 10223 | Johnston |
| | | | | | |
| 5 | 28/1/56 | BARRY TOWN | 8–1 | 4033 | Johnston(3), Hudson(3), Harris(2) |
| 6 | 1/3/56 | LLANELLI | 5–1 | 1689 | Harris(2), Lever, Shergold, Docherty |
| S/F | 21/3/56 | Swansea Town * | 2–5 | 9655 | Harris, Beech  (* At Cardiff City) |
| | | | | | |
| 5 | 12/2/57 | MERTHYR TYDFIL | 3–1 | 1579 | Burgess(2), Harris |
| 6 | 21/2/57 | 55th T.R.TONFANAU | 3–1 | | Hudson, Terry, Harris |
| S/F | 28/3/57 | Swansea Town * | 1–1 | 12500 | Lucas  (* At cardiff City) |
| S/F/R | 1/4/57 | Swansea Town * | 0–3 | 7000 | (* At Cardiff City) |
| | | | | | |
| 5 | 30/1/58 | SWANSEA TOWN | 2–5 | 3500 | Terry, McSeveney |
| | | | | | |
| 5 | 29/1/59 | Swansea Town | 1–3 | 4200 | McSeveney |
| | | | | | |
| 5 | 3/2/60 | Caerau Athletic | 5–3 | | McSeveney(3), Dixon, Jones |
| 6 | 24/2/60 | Wrexham | 0–3 | | |

| | | | | | |
|---|---|---|---|---|---|
| 5 | 2/2/61 | Abergavenny Thursdays | 3–1 | | Dixon, McPherson, Smith |
| 6 | 16/2/61 | Cardiff City | 1–2 | 12192 | Meyer |
| 5 | 30/1/62 | Cardiff City | 1–4 | 5715 | Harris |
| 5 | 21/3/63 | Merthyr Tydfil | 4–0 | | Herrity, Bonson, Sheffield, Wood(O.G.) |
| 6 | 17/4/63 | Holywell | 6–2 | | Hunt(3), Hudson, Sheffield, Webster |
| S/F | 9/5/63 | Swansea Town | 1–0 | 5300 | Sheffield |
| Fin./1L | 27/5/63 | Borough United | 1–2 | 3000 | Hunt |
| Fin./2L | 30/5/63 | BOROUGH UNITED | 0–0 | 5605 | |
| 5 | 30/1/64 | HAVERFORDWEST | 5–2 | 1773 | Bonson(3), Bird, Sheffield |
| 6 | 20/2/64 | SWANSEA TOWN | 1–0 | 5950 | Sheffield |
| S/F | 11/3/64 | Cardiff City * | 2–2 | 5200 | Sheffield, Bonson  (* At Swansea) |
| S/F/R | 25/3/64 | Cardiff City * | 0–1 | 8400 | (* At Cardiff City) |
| 5 | 18/1/65 | SWANSEA TOWN | 2–3 | 5496 | Morgan, McCole |
| 5 | 5/1/66 | Hereford United | 2–1 | 6000 | Bird, Hale |
| 6 | 7/2/66 | CHESTER | 2–2 | 1776 | Hale(2) |
| 6/R | 16/2/66 | Chester | 0–2 | 5296 | |
| 5 | 7/1/67 | Llanelli | 6–2 | 2500 | Jones(3), Pugh, Thomas(2) |
| 6 | 16/2/67 | BANGOR CITY | 0–0 | 1479 | |
| 6/R | 22/2/67 | Bangor City | 1–0 | 1500 | Hill |
| S/F | 15/3/67 | CARDIFF CITY | 1–2 | 8500 | Melling |
| 5 | 3/2/68 | Welshpool | 4–0 | 2200 | Hill(2), Thomas, A.P.Jones |
| 6 | 19/2/68 | SWANSEA TOWN | 3–1 | 7833 | Thomas, Hill, Buck |
| S/F | 19/3/68 | HEREFORD UNITED | 0–1 | 5100 | |
| 5 | 14/1/69 | Swansea Town | 0–0 | 5173 | |
| 5/R | 21/1/69 | SWANSEA TOWN | 0–0 | 3872 | |
| 5/2R | 28/1/69 | Swansea Town | 1–2 | 6047 | Cooper |
| 5 | 20/1/70 | HEREFORD UNITED | 2–2 | 2584 | Radford, Mabbutt |
| 5/R | 28/1/70 | Hereford United | 1–2 | 5994 | Thomas |
| 5 | 2/3/71 | CARDIFF CITY | 1–1 | 6162 | Thomas |
| 5/R | 10/3/71 | Cardiff City | 0–4 | 10385 | |
| 5 | 8/1/72 | EBBW VALE | 3–1 | 1420 | Thomas, Brown, Hooper |
| 6 | 8/2/72 | Bangor City | 2–1 | 2609 | Brown, D.Jones |
| S/F | 22/3/72 | Wrexham | 0–2 | 3869 | |
| 4 | 9/1/73 | Swansea City | 0–0 | 2990 | |
| 4/R | 16/1/73 | SWANSEA CITY | 3–0 | 4042 | Brown(3) |
| 5 | 20/2/73 | CARDIFF CITY | 1–3 | 11350 | Hooper |
| 4 | 20/1/74 | MERTHYR TYDFIL | 1–0 | 2082 | Jarman |
| 5 | 26/2/74 | SHREWSBURY TOWN | 0–1 | 1232 | |
| 4 | 9/12/74 | Stourbridge | 2–2 | 1027 | Jones, Rogers |
| 4/R | 6/1/75 | STOURBRIDGE | 5–1 | 1666 | Woodruff(2), Hooper, Jones, Davies(O.G.) |
| 5 | 12/2/75 | SWANSEA CITY | 1–1 | 2368 | Hooper |
| 5/R | 17/2/75 | Swansea City | 2–1 | 2089 | Godfrey, Screen |
| S/F | 11/3/75 | CARDIFF CITY | 0–1 | 3808 | |
| 4 | 19/1/76 | HEREFORD UNITED | 1–2 | 2400 | S.Aizlewood |
| 4 | 18/1/77 | SWANSEA CITY | 1–4 | 3755 | Parsons |
| 4 | 17/1/78 | Swansea City | 0–0 | 7504 | |
| 4/R | 24/1/78 | SWANSEA CITY | 1–0 | 6098 | Williams |
| 5 | 14/2/78 | BANGOR CITY | 1–3 | 3604 | R.Walker |
| 4 | 15/1/79 | TON PENTRE | 0–2 | 1447 | |
| 4 | 22/1/80 | CARDIFF CITY | 2–0 | 7709 | Tynan, Aldridge |
| 5 | 4/3/80 | Wrexham | 1–0 | 4468 | Lowndes |
| S/F | 25/3/80 | MERTHYR TYDFIL | 3–1 | 6754 | Gwyther(2), Aldridge |
| Fin./1L | 6/5/80 | SHREWSBURY TOWN | 2–1 | 9950 | Tynan(2) |
| Fin./2L | 12/5/80 | Shrewsbury Town | 3–0 | 8993 | Lowndes, Tynan, Gwyther |

| | | | | | |
|---|---|---|---|---|---|
| 3 | 17/11/80 | WORCESTER CITY | 2–2 | 2937 | Moore, Elsey |
| 3/R | 24/11/80 | Worcester City | 3–2 | 3015 | Oakes, Lowndes, Aldridge |
| 4 | 6/1/81 | TON PENTRE | 3–0 | 2949 | Gwyther(2), Moore |
| 5 | 10/2/81 | BANGOR CITY | 3–1 | 3018 | Oakes, Vaughan, Tynan |
| S/F/1L | 25/3/81 | Hereford United | 1–2 | 5251 | Moore |
| S/F/2L | 31/3/81 | HEREFORD UNITED | 1–1 | 5994 | Lowndes |
| | | | | | |
| 3 | 1/12/81 | TAFF'S WELL | 5–0 | 1369 | Tynan(2), Oakes, Gwyther, Bishop |
| 4 | 15/12/81 | Cardiff City | 1–3 | 3916 | Oakes |
| | | | | | |
| 3 | 30/11/82 | CARDIFF CITY | 1–0 | 7800 | Vaughan |
| 4 | 19/1/83 | Wrexham | 1–4 | 1825 | Aldridge |
| | | | | | |
| 3 | 29/11/83 | BRIDGEND TOWN | 5–1 | 1494 | Relish, Boyle, Woodruff, Carter, R.Jones |
| 4 | 17/1/84 | LEX X1 | 6–0 | 1077 | Aldridge(3), Relish, Reid, Lilygreen |
| 5 | 7/2/84 | WREXHAM | 0–1 | 1812 | |
| | | | | | |
| 3 | 5/12/84 | Pembroke Borough | 2–0 | 1100 | L.Jones, Chamberlain |
| 4 | 5/1/85 | CARDIFF CORRIES | 4–0 | 1034 | Matthewson, Carter, Cooper, Boyle |
| 5 | 20/2/85 | WREXHAM | 3–2 | 1732 | L.Jones, Chamberlain, Pulis |
| S/F/1L | 10/4/85 | Bangor City | 0–1 | 1564 | |
| S/F/2L | 23/4/85 | BANGOR CITY | 0–0 | 2808 | |
| | | | | | |
| 3 | 26/11/86 | Ton Pentre | 4–2 | 1200 | Mardenborough (2), L.Jones, Mullen (O.G.) |
| 4 | 14/1/86 | KIDDERMINSTER HARRIERS | 3–3 | 1138 | Gill(2), L.Jones |
| 4/R | 3/2/86 | Kidderminster Harriers | 1–2 | 1008 | Gill |
| | | | | | |
| 3 | 11/11/86 | Swansea City | 3–1 | 4756 | P.Jones, Millett, Phelan(og) |
| 4 | 10/2/87 | Shrewsbury Town | 1–0 | 634 | Vinter |
| 5 | 11/3/87 | Aberystwyth Town | 3–3 | 3000 | Gibbins, Vinter, Millett |
| 5/R | 24/3/87 | ABERYSTWYTH TOWN | 3–0 | 1420 | Gibbins, Vinter, Compton |
| S/F/1L | 16/4/87 | WREXHAM | 2–1 | 2109 | Thackeray, Taylor |
| S/F/2L | 22/4/87 | Wrexham | 2–2 | 1989 | Thackeray, Gibbins |
| Fin. | 17/5/87 | Merthyr Tydfil * | 2–2 | 7150 | Thackeray(2)   (* At Cardiff City) |
| Fin./R | 21/5/87 | Merthyr Tydfil * | 0–1 | 6010 | (* At Cardiff City) |
| | | | | | |
| 3 | 30/11/87 | HAVERFORDWEST COUNTY | 2–4 | 521 | P.Giles, Carr |
| | | | | | |
| 3 | 15/11/88 | BRIDGEND TOWN | 6–0 | 817 | Sugrue(3), Foley, Marustik, Richards |
| 4 | 21/1/89 | CAERNARFON TOWN | 3–0 | 763 | Sugrue(3) |
| 5 | 7/2/89 | HEREFORD UNITED | 0–1 | 1666 | |

**Football League Cup (including subsequent sponsored titles)**

| | | | | | |
|---|---|---|---|---|---|
| 1 | 10/10/60 | SOUTHAMPTON | 2–2 | 7834 | McSeveney, McPherson |
| 1/R | 17/10/60 | Southampton | 2–2 | 8000 | McSeveney, Smith |
| 1/2R | 26/10/60 | Southampton | 3–5 | 8414 | Burton(3) |
| | | | | | |
| 1 | 11/9/61 | SHREWSBURY TOWN | 0–0 | 7500 | |
| 1/R | 28/9/61 | Shrewsbury Town | 1–3 | 8213 | Bowman |
| | | | | | |
| 1 | 5/9/62 | GILLINGHAM | 2–1 | 3864 | Hudson, Hunt |
| 2 | 26/9/62 | Aldershot | 3–0 | 5328 | Bonson(3) |
| 3 | 24/10/62 | MANCHESTER CITY | 1–2 | 9869 | Herrity |
| | | | | | |
| 1 | 4/9/63 | MILLWALL | 3–4 | 3168 | Bonson, Hunt, Williams(O.G.) |
| | | | | | |
| 1 | 2/9/64 | Notts County | 2–3 | 2881 | Pring, Edwards(O.G.) |
| | | | | | |
| 1 | 1/9/65 | SOUTHEND UNITED | 2–2 | 2925 | Morgan, Reynolds |
| 1/R | 6/9/65 | Southend United | 1–3 | 8644 | Hill |
| | | | | | |
| 1 | 24/8/66 | SWANSEA TOWN | 1–2 | 3816 | Jones |
| | | | | | |
| 1 | 22/8/67 | Swindon Town | 1–1 | 10870 | Nurse(O.G.) |
| 1/R | 29/8/67 | SWINDON TOWN | 2–0 | 6537 | D.Jones, King |
| 2 | 12/9/67 | BLACKPOOL | 0–1 | 13157 | |
| | | | | | |
| 1 | 13/8/68 | Bristol City | 0–2 | 9778 | |
| | | | | | |
| 1 | 12/8/69 | SWANSEA CITY | 2–3 | 3824 | Hill, Cooper |
| | | | | | |
| 1 | 18/8/70 | READING | 2–1 | 3624 | Brown, Young |
| 2 | 9/9/70 | Blackpool | 1–4 | 9828 | Brown |

| | | | | | |
|---|---|---|---|---|---|
| 1 | 17/8/71 | TORQUAY UNITED | 1–2 | 4316 | R.Jones |
| 1 | 15/8/72 | Swansea City | 1–1 | 3998 | Hill |
| 1/R | 22/8/72 | SWANSEA CITY | 3–0 | 5220 | Brown(3) |
| 2 | 5/9/72 | IPSWICH TOWN | 0–3 | 9516 | |
| 1 | 28/8/73 | Swindon Town | 3–3 | 6873 | Jarman, Screen, Brown |
| 1/R | 4/9/73 | SWINDON TOWN | 1–2 | 6007 | Jarman |
| 1 | 20/8/74 | TORQUAY UNITED | 1–0 | 3022 | Woodruff |
| 2 | 11/9/74 | Chelsea | 2–4 | 13322 | Woodruff, Brown |
| 1 | 19/8/75 | EXETER CITY | 1–1 | 2268 | Love |
| 1/R | 26/8/75 | Exeter City | 0–2 | | |
| 1/1L | 14/8/76 | Swansea City | 1–4 | 3281 | Woods |
| 1/2L | 17/8/76 | SWANSEA CITY | 1–0 | 2692 | Bell |
| 1/1L | 13/8/77 | Portsmouth | 1–3 | 7541 | Woods |
| 1/2L | 16/8/77 | PORTSMOUTH | 3–2 | 2895 | R.Walker, Preece, Clark |
| 1/1L | 12/8/78 | SWANSEA CITY | 2–1 | 5572 | Woods, M.Williams |
| 1/2L | 15/8/78 | Swansea City | 0–5 | 7834 | |
| 1/1L | 11/8/79 | PLYMOUTH ARGYLE | 1–0 | 4574 | Tynan |
| 1/2L | 14/8/79 | Plymouth Argyle | 0–2 | 4505 | |
| 1/1L | 9/8/80 | Hereford United | 0–1 | 7745 | |
| 1/2L | 12/8/80 | HEREFORD UNITED | 5–0 | 5683 | Tynan(2), Aldridge(2), Gwyther |
| 2/1L | 26/8/80 | NOTTS COUNTY | 1–1 | 6708 | Vaughan |
| 2/2L | 2/9/80 | Notts County | 0–2 | 4714 | |
| 1/1L | 2/9/81 | Torquay United | 3–2 | 2514 | Oakes, Moore, Aldridge |
| 1/2L | 15/9/81 | TORQUAY UNITED | 0–0 | 4203 | |
| 2/1l | 6/10/81 | Oldham Athletic | 0–1 | 5507 | |
| 2/2L | 27/10/81 | OLDHAM ATHLETIC | 0–0 | 4578 | |
| 1/1L | 1/9/82 | Exeter City | 2–1 | 2292 | Lowndes, Gwyther |
| 1/2L | 14/9/82 | EXETER CITY | 6–0 | 2684 | Vaughan(2), Lowndes, Aldridge, Tynan, Elsey |
| 2/1L | 5/10/82 | EVERTON | 0–2 | 8293 | |
| 2/2L | 27/10/82 | Everton | 2–2 | 8941 | Tynan, Oakes |
| 1/1L | 30/8/83 | TORQUAY UNITED | 2–3 | 2282 | Boyle, Aldridge |
| 1/2L | 14/9/83 | Torquay United | 0–1 | 2015 | |
| 1/1L | 28/8/84 | Bristol City | 1–2 | 5424 | Chamberlain |
| 1/2L | 4/9/84 | BRISTOL CITY | 0–3 | 3276 | |
| 1/1L | 20/8/85 | BRISTOL ROVERS | 0–2 | 2777 | |
| 1/2L | 3/9/85 | Bristol Rovers | 1–0 | 2012 | Reck |
| 1/1L | 27/8/86 | Exeter City | 0–0 | 1545 | |
| 1/2L | 2/9/86 | EXETER CITY | 1–0 | 1620 | Gibbins |
| 2/1L | 24/9/86 | Everton | 0–4 | 11959 | |
| 2/2L | 7/10/86 | EVERTON | 1–5 | 7172 | Carter |
| 1/1L | 18/8/87 | CARDIFF CITY * | 2–1 | 3383 | Evans(2)  (* Played at Cardiff City) |
| 1/2L | 25/8/87 | Cardiff City | 2–2 | 3550 | Taylor, Tupling |
| 2/1L | 22/9/87 | Crystal Palace | 0–4 | 6085 | |
| 2/2L | 6/10/87 | CRYSTAL PALACE | 0–2 | 1303 | |

## Division Three (South) Cup

| | | | | | |
|---|---|---|---|---|---|
| | 25/1/34 | SWINDON TOWN | 7–2 | 2292 | Thomas(3), Reynolds(2), Haycox(2) |
| | 22/2/34 | BRIGHTON & H.A. | 0–1 | 2000 | |
| | 22/10/34 | Northampton Town | 0–3 | 2500 | |
| | 2/10/35 | Southend United | 0–3 | 4000 | |
| | 1/10/36 | WATFORD | 1–4 | 2900 | Crisp |
| | 21/10/37 | WATFORD | 2–2 | 1000 | Woods(2) |
| | 27/10/37 | Watford | 0–4 | | |
| | 29/9/38 | BRISTOL ROVERS | 1–0 | 709 | Duggan |
| | 8/2/39 | Torquay United | 0–0 | | |
| | 22/2/39 | TORQUAY UNTITED | 1–3 | 618 | Brinton |

|  |  |  | South–West Cup |  |  |  |
|---|---|---|---|---|---|---|
|  | 20/4/40 | BIRMINGHAM CITY | 2–2 | 4500 | Robbins, Egan |
|  | 27/4/40 | Birmingham City | 2–5 | 6700 | Brinton, Wookey |

|  |  |  | Group Cup (League Trophy) |  |  |  |
|---|---|---|---|---|---|---|
| Prel. | 15/8/81 | TORQUAY UNITED | 0–0 | 2490 |  |
| Prel. | 18/8/81 | PLYMOUTH ARGYLE | 2–1 | 2316 | Tynan, Lees |
| Prel. | 22/8/81 | A.F.C Bournemouth | 0–0 | 2511 |  |
| 1 | 8/12/81 | GRIMSBY TOWN | 0–2 | 2206 |  |
| Prel. | 14/8/82 | TORQUAY UNITED | 0–1 | 1501 |  |
| Prel. | 18/8/82 | EXETER CITY | 5–1 | 1084 | Bailey(2), Tynan, Gwyther, Elsey |
| Prel. | 21/8/82 | Bristol City | 4–1 | 2226 | Lowndes, Bailey, Tynan, Williams |
| 1 | 26/1/83 | Chester | 0–0 * | 999 | (* Lost 4–5 on penalties) |

|  |  |  | Associate Members Cup |  |  |  |
|---|---|---|---|---|---|---|
| 1 | 28/2/84 | BRISTOL ROVERS | 0–1 | 2116 |  |

|  |  |  | Freight Rover Trophy |  |  |  |
|---|---|---|---|---|---|---|
| 1/1L | 22/1/85 | EXETER CITY | 3–0 | 1017 | L.Jones(2), Kellow |
| 1/2L | 6/2/85 | Exeter City | 1–1 | 1272 | Lewis |
| 2 | 4/4/85 | SWANSEA CITY | 0–0 | 2061 | Lost 3–4 on pens. Qual.–highest scoring losers |
| Q/F Sth. | 25/4/85 | Bristol City | 2–1 | 3167 | Chamberlain, Kent |
| S/F Sth. | 8/5/85 | Orient | 1–1 * | 1642 | Boyle  (* Won 4–2 on penalties) |
| Fin/Sth. | 17/5/85 | Brentford | 0–6 | 8214 |  |
| Prel. | 20/1/86 | Swansea City | 1–1 | 2863 | Berry |
| Prel. | 21/1/86 | CARDIFF CITY | 1–0 | 1863 | Mardenborough |
| Prel. | 10/12/86 | Hereford United | 0–4 | 1358 |  |
| Prel. | 6/1/87 | PORT VALE | 2–1 | 826 | Vinter, Compton |
| Prel. | 13/10/87 | PORT VALE | 2–0 | 569 | P.Giles, Gibbins |
| Prel. | 24/11/87 | Exeter City | 1–0 | 1006 | Thackeray |
| 1 | 19/1/88 | HEREFORD UNITED | 2–3 | 1232 | Tupling, Mann |

|  |  |  | Clubcall Cup |  |  |  |
|---|---|---|---|---|---|---|
| 1 | 5/10/88 | Yeovil Town | 5–4 | 1838 | Banks(2), Sanderson(2), Abbruzzese |
| 2 | 24/1/89 | Buxton | 4–3 | 429 | Sugrue(3), Sanderson |
| 3 | 21/2/89 | KIDDERMINSTER HARRIERS | 5–6 | 895 | Sugrue(2), Thompson(2), Sanderson |

|  |  |  | F.A.Trophy |  |  |  |
|---|---|---|---|---|---|---|
| 1 | 14/1/89 | Weymouth | 1–2 | 1119 | Marustik |

# NEWPORT A.F.C.

|  |  |  | Welsh Cup |  |  |  |
|---|---|---|---|---|---|---|
| 1 | 2/9/89 | STROUD | 3–1 | 369 | Parselle, Richards, Preece |
| 2 | 7/10/89 | BRECON CORRIES | 1–0 | 385 | Lilygreen |
| 3 | 25/10/89 | Cardiff City | 0–1 | 2929 |  |
| 1 | 1/9/90 | Pontlottyn | 9–0 | 420 | Lily'n(2),Hawkins(2),Doughty,Ellis,Rowberry,Smith,Preece |
| 2 | 6/10/90 | PEMBROKE BOROUGH | 3–0 | 514 | Stroud(2), Lilygreen |
| 3 | 6/11/90 | Cardiff Corries * | 3–0 | 701 | Price,Lilygreen,Hill(O.G.)  (* At Newport) |
| 4 | 19/1/91 | COLWYN BAY | 0–1 | 813 |  |
| 2 | 5/10/91 | BRIDGEND | 3–0 | 582 | Price(2), Sanderson |
| 3 | 29/10/91 | Cardiff city | 0–3 | 2423 |  |

1992/93 season – Banned

|  |  |  | Hellenic League Cup |  |  |  |
|---|---|---|---|---|---|---|
| 2 | 11/11/89 | Sharpness | 2–1 | 400 | Mallender, Evans |
| Q/Fin. | 20/1/90 | Wantage | 5–2 | 220 | Lilugreen(2), Herrity, Relish, Jarvis |
| S/Fin. | 24/3/90 | MORETON TOWN | 2–1 | 658 | Lilygreen, Richards |
| Final | 7/5/90 | Abingdon United * | 1–1 | 1780 | Herrity  (* At Almondsbury) |
| Fin./R | 30/8/90 | Abingdon United * | 1–0 | 521 | Painter  (* At Hounslow) |

|  |  |  | F.A.Trophy |  |  |  |
|---|---|---|---|---|---|---|
| 1Q | 22/9/90 | Weston–Super–Mare | 0–0 | 494 |  |
| 1Q/R | 26/9/90 | WESTON–SUPER–MARE | 3–1 | 1011 | Lilygreen(2), Jarvis |
| 2Q | 20/10/90 | STROUD | 0–3 | 886 |  |
| 1Q | 21/9/91 | Bideford | 1–0 | 350 | Green |
| 2Q | 19/10/91 | SALTASH | 5–4 | 521 | Green(3), Sanderson(2) |
| 3Q | 30/11/91 | Stroud | 3–1 | 463 | Green, Kilgour, Hewitt |
| 1 | 11/1/92 | Aylesbury United | 2–3 | 870 | Price, Sanderson |
| 1Q | 19/9/92 | Weymouth | 2–2 | 922 | Lilygreen, C.Williams |
| 1Q/R | 23/9/92 | WEYMOUTH | 2–1 | 397 | Charles, Lilygreen |
| 2Q | 17/10/92 | Trowbridge Town | 1–0 | 567 | Lilygreen |
| 3Q | 28/11/92 | SUTTON UNITED | 1–2 | 400 | Lilygreen |

**REJECTED F.C. VOLUME 1 (Reprint)** *(By Dave Twydell)* The 2nd Edition of this popular book – now in hardback – has minor additions, updates, corrections and has been re-typeset. This volume provides the comprehensive histories of: Aberdare Athletic, Ashington, Bootle, Bradford (Park Avenue), Burton (Swifts, Wanderers and United), Gateshead/South Shields, Glossop, Loughborough, Nelson, Stalybridge Celtic and Workington. The 288 well illustrated pages also contain the basic statistical details of each club. Price £12-95 plus £1-30 postage.

**REJECTED F.C. OF SCOTLAND – Vol. 1: Edinburgh and The South.** *(By Dave Twydell)* The first of three volumes on the written and basic statistical details of the Scottish ex-League Clubs (Edinburgh City, Leith Athletic, St.Bernards, Armadale, Broxburn United, Bathgate, Peebles Rovers, Mid-Annandale, Nithsdale Wanderers and Solway Star). Price £12-95 Plus £1-30 Postage. **(Volume 2 – Glasgow and District.** Same price with another 11 Clubs' histories, including Third Lanark).

**'GONE BUT NOT FORGOTTEN – PART 2'** *(By Dave Twydell)* The abbreviated histories of a variety of defunct non-League Clubs and Grounds; the old Hillingdon Borough, Wycombe's Loakes Park, Oswestry Town and Shirley Town are included in this edition (Part 1 is now sold out). A particular merit of these books is the high illustrative content, and with details for readers to track down the sites of the Grounds – 64 pages. Price £4-95 plus 45p postage

**PETERBOROUGH UNITED – The Official History of The Posh.** *(By Andy Groom and Mick Robinson)* 273 x 202 m.m. hardback (with full colour dust jacket) containing 240 (high quality paper) pages. An extensive and well illustrated text section details the club's history from the earliest days. The statistical section contains the complete match and team details from the Club's formation in 1934. (Reprint – The first print run sold out within five days). Price £14-95 plus £3-40 postage.

**CARDIFF CITY F.C. – The Official History of The Bluebirds:** *(By John Crooks).* Large format (273 x 202 m.m.), cased (hardback) with a full colour dust jacket and containing 320 pages, printed on high quality paper. Separate sections deal with the history of the Club in words and pictures, an abbreviated 'Who's Who' section (every League player recorded), a section on Ninian Park, and the full statistics (including line-ups) of every major competitive match from 1910-1991. *("In the Super League of Club Histories" – South Wales Echo)* Price £16-95 Plus £3-50 Postage.

**FOOTBALL LEAGUE – GROUNDS FOR A CHANGE** *(By Dave Twydell).* A 424 page, A5 sized, Hardback book. A comprehensive study of all the Grounds on which the current Football League Clubs previously played. Every Club that has moved Grounds is treated separately, with a 'Potted' history of each, plus 250 illustrations. As well as plenty of 'reading' material, this is likely to become a standard reference book. Price £13-95 Plus £1-70 Postage.

**THROUGH THE TURNSTILES** *(by Brian Tabner)* This incredible book which provides the average attendance of every Football League Club, for every season from 1888/89 to 1991/92. ('The best Football Book I have ever read' – was one reader's comment. " 'Yore Publications' best book to date – at the bottom end of the price range for a quality book. " – The Footballer Magazine) Well illustrated, and also relates the development of the game (angled towards attendances). Other sections give details of the best supported 'away' teams, season ticket sales over the years, etc. Large format (251x174 m.m.) hardback and 208 packed pages on high quality paper. An excellent read at £13-95 plus £1-70 Postage

**COVENTRY CITY FOOTBALLERS 1908 - 1993 (The Complete Who's Who)** By Martin & Paul O'Connor. One of the most detailed books of its type. Every Football (and Southern) League player has been included – around 700. Seasonal appearances of every player, brief personal details, 'pen pictures', together with very detailed information on the movements of the players to other clubs. In addition there are around 100 photo's of the Club's most memorable men, plus information on the principal players from the pre-Southern League days. A hardback book with 224 large pages. £13-95 plus £2-60 postage.

**HISTORY OF THE LANCASHIRE FOOTBALL ASSOCIATION 1878-1928.** A rare historical and fascinating hardback reprint (first published in 1928). Contains the history of the formative days of Lancashire football. Sections within the 288 pages include the early histories of about 20 Clubs (Manchester Utd., Wigan Borough, Rochdale, etc.), Lancashire Cup competitions, Biographies, etc. For those interested in the development of the game, this is a 'must', and you will definitely not be disappointed. Price £12-95 Plus £1-30 Postage.

**REJECTED F.C. - The Video** The video of the books (Rejected F.C. Volumes 1 and 2). Several hours of repeated entertainment. Includes extensive modern film shots, interviews with many personalities related to these teams, still shots to aid the telling of these Clubs' Histories... and an amazing collection of archive film (e.g. Ashington in 1924, pre-war New Brighton, Workington's last home League match, etc.). Every 'Rejected' club (from Accrington in 1888) is featured. Price £12-99 (incl. VAT), from major Video outlets.

### Of Particular interest to ex-County/AFC fans:

**THE IRONSIDES. A Lifetime in the League - Who's Who of Newport County** (By Tony Ambrosen) ("Providing a hugely enjoyable read and a valuable reference book" - South Wales Argus). Every player who appeared for the Club in the Football League is given a potted football and personal history, plus lengthy sections on the players during the Club's three periods in non-League football and details of all the Managers and Trainers. There are over 100 players' photographs within this A5 size 224 page book. A 'must' for statisticians and others interested in this former League club. Limited number of copies left. Price £8-95 Plus £1-00 Postage.

**MORE DEFUNCT F.C.** (By Dave Twydell). A follow up to the successful 'Defunct F.C.' book (Now out of print). Detailed and well illustrated histories of defunct Clubs - *Bedford Avenue, Lovell's Athletic, Romford, Rugby Town, Slough Centre and West Stanley* - including basic statistics, 230 pages. Price £6-75 Plus £1 postage.

**FOOTBALL PHOENIX** - The sequel to 'Rejected F.C. - The Video'. The stories on film of the five post-war League Clubs who became defunct and have successfully reformed (Gateshead, Accrington Stanley, Bradford P.A., Newport County and Aldershot). Film clips include all the goals from County's last game, and the Carl Zeiss match, plus Aldershot's last League game, and footage from 1970 of the new Stanley. 80 minutes of excellent entertainment at only £10-99.